#22
PALMS-RANCHO PAR
2920 OVERLAND AVE
LOS ANGELES, CA 90064
W9-BUP-807

ORSON WELLES

THE ROAD TO XANADU

by the same author

#22 PALMS RANCHO PARK
JUN 0 6 2016

To Gail Eichenthal

ORSON WELLES

THE ROAD TO XANADU

SIMON CALLOW

A most agreeable interview at CBS. Thanks

225408211
812.092 W449Ca

9 I 96

VIKING

VIKING
Published by the Penguin Group
Penguin Books USA Inc., 375 Hudson Street,
New York, New York 10014, U.S.A.
Penguin Books Ltd, 27 Wrights Lane,
London W8 5TZ, England
Penguin Books Australia Ltd, Ringwood,
Victoria, Australia
Penguin Books Canada Ltd, 10 Alcorn Avenue,
Toronto, Ontario, Canada M4V 3B2
Penguin Books (N.Z.) Ltd, 182–190 Wairau Road,
Auckland 10, New Zealand

Penguin Books Ltd, Registered Offices:
Harmondsworth, Middlesex, England

First American edition
Published in 1996 by Viking Penguin,
a division of Penguin Books USA Inc.

1 3 5 7 9 10 8 6 4 2

Copyright © Simon Callow, 1995
All rights reserved

Use of the works of and rights pertaining to Orson Welles have been granted through a special license from his daughter Beatrice Welles, c/o Thomas A. White, 8671 Wilshire Boulevard, Suite 718, Beverly Hills, CA 90211-2915; phone 310-657-9831; fax 310-657-6455. All rights reserved.

Page 618 constitutes an extension of this copyright page.

LIBRARY OF CONGRESS CATALOGING-IN-PUBLICATION DATA
Callow, Simon.
Orson Welles: the road to Xanadu / Simon Callow.
p. cm.
Originally published: London: J. Cape, 1995.
Filmography: p.
Includes bibliographical references and index.
ISBN 0-670-86722-5
1. Welles, Orson, 1915–1985. 2. Motion picture producers and directors—United States—Biography. 3. Actors—United States—Biography. I. Title.
PN1998.3.W45C36 1996
791.43′0233′092—dc20 95-37138

This book is printed on acid-free paper.
∞

Printed in the United States of America
Set in Bembo

Without limiting the rights under copyright reserved above, no part of this publication may be reproduced, stored in or introduced into a retrieval system, or transmitted, in any form or by any means (electronic, mechanical, photocopying, recording or otherwise), without the prior written permission of both the copyright owner and the above publisher of this book.

TO CHRISTOPHER

AND IN MEMORY OF
MICHEÁL MAC LIAMMÓIR
(1899–1978)
AND
JOHN HOUSEMAN
(1902–1988)

With apologies to John Livingston Lowes
(author of the original *Road to Xanadu*)
for cheek in borrowing the title
of his Coleridgean masterpiece.
Coleridge would perhaps have approved of
a little creative theft.

Contents

PART THREE

QUADRUPLE THREAT

PREFACE

Orson Welles and the Art of Biography

If you try to probe, I'll lie to you. Seventy-five percent of what I say in interviews is false. I'm like a hen protecting her eggs. I cannot talk. I must protect my work. Introspection is bad for me. I'm a medium, not an orator. Like certain oriental and Christian mystics, I think the 'self' is a kind of enemy. My work is what enables me to come out of myself. I like what I do, not what I am . . . Do you know the best service anyone could render to art? Destroy all biographies. Only art can explain the life of a man – and not the contrary.

Orson Welles to Jean Clay, 1962

OW: What's all that, for God's sake? You look like a one-man filing cabinet.
PB: Research.
OW: Throw it all away, Peter – it can only cripple the fine spirit of invention.

Peter Bogdanovich, *This is Orson Welles*, 1992

OW: I don't want *any* description of me to be accurate; I want it to be flattering. I don't think people who have to sing for their supper ever like to be described truthfully – not in print anyway. We need to sell tickets, so we need good reviews.
KT: How do you reconcile that with –
OW: For thirty years people have been asking me how I reconcile X with Y! The truthful answer is that I don't. Everything about me is a contradiction, and so is everything about everybody else. We are made out of oppositions; we live between two poles. There's a philistine and an aesthete in all of us, and a murderer and a saint. You don't reconcile the poles. You just recognise them.

Kenneth Tynan, *The World of Orson Welles*, 1967

A question mark hovers over practically every aspect of Welles's life and work. This is the more surprising since he is among the most fully documented artists of the twentieth century. The source of confusion is, almost without exception, Welles himself (an alternative title for the present volume might be, to adapt the title of the first full-length biography, *The Fabulist Orson Welles*); but he has been eagerly abetted in the construction of his personal myth by legions of interviewers, profile-writers and biographers, all, like him, unable to resist a good story. The result is that he now appears awesome but inexplicable, like an abandoned but world-famous monument in the middle of the jungle – the scale of it! the confidence of the people who built this! why was it abandoned? why was the right wing never completed? Welles himself, in his later interviews with Leslie Megahey for the BBC and Peter Bogdanovich for the book *This is Orson Welles*, assumed a charming tone of mellow bemusement at the events of his life, as if they were mysteriously beyond analysis, a sort of cosmic aberration.

The curious thing is that the real story, though sometimes less sensational, is so often more remarkable than the extrapolations. I have, I believe, been able to uncover quite a large number of missing details in Welles's life. My task in writing this study, however, has been as much to re-evaluate the known facts as to establish new ones. A great deal of the groundwork has been done by previous biographers, each with his or her own special area: Charles Higham, whose reconstruction of Welles's family tree is a virtuoso feat of research; Barbara Leaming, who got Welles's final version of his life from the horse's mouth; and Frank Brady, who spoke to many of Welles's associates now dead. Their work has been exhaustive; somehow the facts thus established fail to add up to a life-like image of the man – or of any man.

This is partly because they have focused exclusively on Welles himself. As an antidote to this, I have tried to put him back into the context from which he wrenched himself. There are a number of individual studies of specific areas of Welles's life (Robert Carringer's *The Making of Citizen Kane* is an excellent example) which have identified important collaborators hitherto hidden from history. This identification of the supporting cast has been my guiding principle at all times. Cleaning the canvas, as it were, I have aimed to reveal the surrounding figures and Welles's connection with them. Welles often declared himself opposed to the use of close-ups in cinematography; it was, he said, both undemocratic and unaesthetic to exclude the rest of the world to the advantage of a single figure in it. His biographers have been uninhibited by any such considerations, and have thus, whether they like Welles or not, sustained the myth he created of himself. The most important element of this myth was his originality. Welles was undoubtedly a most unusual individual, but he did not drop from Mars. His psychology, though complex, conformed to recognisable patterns; his career, while exceptional, was formed by the circumstances of his times and the conditions of his profession. I have tried at every turn to find out what else was going on while the famous events of his life were unfolding, what other people in the same sphere were up to, and what they thought of him – to restore, in short, a little of the texture of real life to the curious tissue of miraculous tales and genre scenes which pass for biography in Welles studies.

Many of the most often repeated incidents seem to be borrowed from children's Lives of Christ (a figure, incidentally, who held a life-long fascination for Welles). A version of Christ Among the Doctors can be found in the opening chapter of pretty well any Welles biography you care to open; as can the image of the master who sprang fully formed from his mother's womb, an essential element in any artist's biography, according to Kris and Kurz in *Legend, Myth and Magic in the Image of the Artist*, a book filled with resonance for the Welles scholar.

This approach is not designed to deny the charm or the creativity of the legends, simply to examine their origins and contrast and compare them with what actually happened, in an attempt to determine what Welles was like in the world, what impact he made on his associates and his times, and how – day by day – he went about the jobs of directing, writing and acting. Hitherto, the only credible representations of him have been those offered by John Houseman in *Run-through* and Micheál Mac Liammóir in *All about Hecuba* and *Put Money in thy Purse*. Both men engaged deeply with Welles and were beguiled and frustrated by him in equal measure. Their distinctly different views of him, though highly personal, are based on close observation and intense engagement, and written with precision and insight; both men were denounced by Welles, their witness called into question. I was lucky enough to know them personally and what they told me about Welles has been the starting point for my book, which is thus simultaneously a synthesis and a deconstruction.

It has been a question of asking, not simply is this true or false? (although sometimes that has been useful) but what does this mean? Even the recent past is another country, and the milieus in which Welles moved, social, theatrical, and political, should not be taken for granted. They did things differently there. I have looked at the often astonishing events of his life and tried to renew the surprise contained in them – the actual events rather than the ones he imagined. (Of course the reasons why he felt impelled to reinvent his life, and the specific details he chose to invent, are always revealing.) The hardest-bitten and least friendly of Welles's biographers have been mysteriously inclined to swallow his most improbable confections, and have failed to ask the most elementary questions. Somehow, like Hitler's captors in George Steiner's *The Portage to San Cristobal of A.H.*, they have been bewitched by their subject's silver tongue. One of the features of myth – one of its purposes, perhaps – is to discourage speculation: to create a framework in which everything is so extraordinary that nothing is questioned. Disbelief is automatically suspended.

I have challenged him and the record; I have questioned everything. I cannot pretend, of course, to have found all the answers, but I hope to have traced a credible path through his history, a path recorded not merely on his personal map, but on the larger one of his period and world. To this end, I have spoken to a large number of people who worked with him or knew him up to and including the making of *Kane*, which is as far as the present volume goes: schoolfriends, teachers, fellow actors, fellow directors, stage managers, assistants, secretaries, press agents. I have been in correspondence with yet more; as I have with some of the large army of Welles scholars, who have with astonishing generosity shared their researches in specific areas. I list all of them in the acknowledgements, but I must here name Andrea Nouryeh, whose as yet unpublished work on the Mercury Theatre is definitive, exhaustive and revelatory; Richard France, author of the only full-length study of Welles's work in the theatre, who supplied me with many of his original documents; and James Naremore, whose *The Magic World of Orson Welles* is the single indispensable volume on Welles. I have visited all the places in which Welles lived and the buildings in which he worked (when they still stand). Above all I have closely examined his own words, in letters, pronouncements, speeches, articles and, particularly revealing, in his unfilmed screenplay, *The Cradle Will Rock*, a dramatisation of the events surrounding one of his most famous productions. He was not – though he would have loved to have been, or to have been thought to have been – a natural writer, but he was a very characteristic one. The style was the man.

I have also closely studied the newspapers, because, paradoxically, that is where Welles's real life was. He was unable to resist a fix of publicity; merely to see a reporter's notebook was to unleash his powers of invention. He publicly constructed himself, from the earliest age – my first press clipping is headed ACTOR, POET, CARTOONIST – AND ONLY TEN – in a medium that he courted and denounced in equal measure; and the press returned the compliment. Together they concluded a sort of Faustian pact wherein Welles was meteorically advanced by sensation-hungry newspapers, to whom he pandered shamelessly, until at the height of his fame he fell foul of them; saddled with a preposterous reputation and a personality drawn by him and coloured by them, he found himself unemployable, his work overshadowed by his everexpanding Self. Even his body became legendary, out of control; whatever his soul consisted of protected from the world by wadding. Locked in a personal relationship as complex and curious as that of Lear and his fool, Welles and the newspapers needed and abominated each other in a co-dependency that only his death dissolved. It is no coincidence that his most famous work is the apotheosis of the newspaper film.

His death provoked an orgy of journalism. The main questions asked of him when he died were: what went wrong after *Citizen Kane*?; and why did he get so fat? This book, the first of two, tries to answer the question what went wrong before *Citizen Kane*? To the second question – by no means a foolish or shallow one – there is no simple answer, but I hope that by the end of this volume, enough of Welles's temperamental imperatives will have been revealed for his phenomenal physical expansion to seem, at the very least, unsurprising. The word phenomenal in this context is not used. loosely (by the end of his life his bulk warranted an entry in *The Guinness Book of Records*) and it is one that recurs at every stage of this study. He made himself into a phenomenon – courted phenomenality with brilliant determination – and it is as such that he must be considered. This is a terrible burden both for an artist and for a human being; neither the work nor the man can fully be separated from this alternative self. That, of course, was his purpose: to put himself and his work beyond criticism, so that both became merely manifestations of his legend.

This is an interesting but dangerous ploy, a life strategy (in the phrase of the pop psychologists) fraught with danger – principally the danger to the private self and its sources of nourishment for both work and life. Personality and art become a series of diversions, a continuous and costly firework display, momentarily dazzling but swiftly self-consuming – an auto-da-fé felo de se. In Welles's case, the fireworks were uniquely brilliant; the bonfire of his vanities made a gorgeous blaze, casting lively, lurid shadows in all directions. The cost to him, and the question of whether things could have been otherwise, are the real subjects of this book.

It is hard to resist comparison with that other O.W. whose famous phrase about putting his genius into his life, his talent into his work could equally be applied to Welles; as with Wilde, however, it was not so much that his life was a work of genius as that his life story has the quality of a work of fiction – as if he himself were the creation of a novelist of extravagant invention, his story deliberately shaped into an exemplary pattern – a warning to us all, perhaps. The similarity between Wilde and Welles is not merely accidental, a question of initials, a congruity of flamboyances, but chillingly precise in one particular: both men set out to conquer the world by seeking to master the instruments of publicity; both became its servants – perhaps, if it is not too melodramatic a phrase, its victims.

Part One

PRODIGY

CHAPTER ONE

Kenosha

THE ROAD to Xanadu begins in Kenosha, Wisconsin. The incongruity of his birthplace is commented on again and again in accounts of Welles. Every country has its joke towns, good for an easy laugh, and if Kenosha is not quite in the league of Oshkosh, Wisconsin, or Normal, Illinois, it is still sufficiently redolent of boondockery to seem to mock the very idea of aspiration in its sons and daughters. 'Orson is frightened to death of being thought ordinary in any way,' wrote Herbert Drake in an article entitled 'Orson Welles – Still a Four-Ply Genius' (he was thirty-two years old at the time). 'He is annoyed at his parents to this day because he sprang yelling into the world in prosaic Kenosha, Wisconsin.' To which Welles replies: 'I never blamed my folks for Kenosha – Kenosha has always blamed my folks for me.'

And it is true; Kenosha always felt slighted by Welles, but Welles expressed himself – not unaware of the incongruity – very warmly towards his origins. Wisconsin (along with Indiana and Illinois) embodies the very notion of the Mid-West, that decent, solid, flat heartland of America, from which everything of value in the national life has, according to some theories, sprung – created by men and women desperate to escape its cosy embrace. How could Orson Welles – immoderate and cosmopolitan, opposite qualities to those of the Mid-West – have anything to do with little old Kenosha, Wis? In fact Kenosha is neither little nor old, and though Welles was born there, of parents who were native Mid-Westerners, his stay was brief: before he was four he and his family had moved the barely sixty miles to Chicago, Illinois, still the Mid-West, in fact its capital city, but a planet apart. Kenosha, Wisconsin was none the less the scene of his earliest experience, and his family – mother and father, uncles, aunts, grandfather and grandmother – were prominent and engaged participants in its intense life. Welles's statement that he had never disowned Kenosha was true. He felt immense yearning for what he came to think of as its vanished charm, while ceasing himself to belong to it in any detectable form.

Like the vast majority of American settlements, it was of recent origin – the first settlers had arrived in 1835 – and when Welles was born, in 1915, there were still people alive who could remember those founding fathers and mothers who had named their little harbour town on the shore of Lake Michigan, Southport. Within fifteen years it had grown sufficiently – aided by the all-important railroad – to incorporate itself as a city, taking the old Indian name of Kenosha, meaning pike, after the fish that they so plentifully trawled out of the lake. From then on, its growth was prodigious. Almost overnight a society was constructed: schools, courts, streets, squares, hotels, factories. Like a thousand other towns across America, it created itself by willpower, inspired by twin visions of wealth and civic pride. From the beginning, there were parallel resolves to provide for the mind and the soul as well as for the body: in addition to assembly lines, furnaces and forges, there would be libraries, and concert-halls, and parks – especially parks, to the extent that Kenosha was familiarly known as Park City. None of this, material or spiritual, commercial or artistic, was achieved without a struggle. As it happens, Welles's parents were, if not actively then certainly symbolically, on opposite sides in that struggle, one of the many divisions in their fundamentally riven relationship.

Welles's father, Richard Head Welles, was in trade. It is as simple as that. It became important for Welles to romanticise his father, for reasons that will become evident. Central to his image of his father was the fact that he was an inventor. He was; but in a very quiet way. Welles's view of him as the Kenosha Leonardo does not, alas, withstand scrutiny. His inventions were largely confined to the business in which he worked, and that was the lamp trade. His first job had been in his uncle George Yule's Bain Wagon Company; he had worked well and hard enough in this enormous organisation with its vast sales force supplying the railroads of the world to be rewarded with a partnership, at the age of twenty-five, in Yule's subsidiary company, Badger Brass. Badger's principal product, invented by E.L. Williams, was the Solar acetylene bicycle lamp – 'a patented wonder of its time, a lamp that made its own gas and burned it', according to a paper of the thirties. By 1901, they were producing a thousand lamps a day; four years later, thanks to the bicycle craze of the period, over a million were in use. Richard Welles was treasurer and general secretary of the firm, an exhausting, responsible job which he did well, balancing the books (no mean task; by 1900 the company was the sixth-largest employer in Kenosha) and liaising with the outside world. *Bicycling*

World of 1901 admiringly reports that 'practically the entire trade is acquainted with R.H. Welles'. His charm was widely acknowledged, and can be glimpsed in photographs, a lazy, sexy smile informing his handsome features.

It would appear that his heart was not entirely in Badger Brass, even if his work was valued. His creative mind was engaged in his inventions – in 1904 he patented an automobile jack, the nearest, sadly, he came to actually inventing the automobile itself, as his son gallantly claimed – while the rest of him was drawn irresistibly to the fleshpots of Chicago. He couldn't have chosen a better time for it. The big city – an hour and three-quarters by rail from Kenosha – was still awash with pleasurable possibilities. In 1912 when the Levee district was closed down, these pleasures would be severely curtailed, or at the very least driven underground, but for Richard Welles, in the hot flush of his young manhood, it was the embodiment of Edwardian shamelessness. 'No other city in the world could boast of so much vice, such elaborate bagnios, such colourful madames, such a phalanx of demi-mondes,' Alston J. Smith exuberantly recorded. 'The madames would drive into the Loop to transact business, wearing extremely low-cut gowns and pounds of diamonds; their equipages would be banked with flowers and if it was at all dusky the lights would be turned on full blaze. In the back seat, wearing the most décolleté of gowns, shining with gems, and painted to a fare-thee-well, would be the youngest, fairest flower of the maison.' Richard Welles, enchanted by all this elegant naughtiness, was a natural citizen of the demimonde, frequenting the splendid musical comedies to be found at Mortimer Singer's various establishments, seducing the young ladies of their choruses. He began what amounted to a double life, Badger Brass by day – by night the Eversleigh club, 'the classiest seraglio in town: if you didn't know you were in a House of Ill Fame, you might have confused the joint with a young ladies' seminary.' When you paid by cheque, it would come back endorsed 'Utopia Novelty Co.' It was here, during these evenings of dining and yarning and delicious debauchery, that he began to drink more than ordinarily socially.

It may be presumed that he went home as rarely as possible – neither to the sober house his mother had provided for him, still less to her own, on the other side of Kenosha's main square. Named Rudolphsheim, it was a squat, massive building studded with beer bottles, in defiant proclamation of her second husband's déclassé profession of brewer. Orson Welles was frank in his loathing of this grandmother, Mary Head Welles Gottfredson; in general, it is hard not to share his feeling. Wagnerian is the word that comes most vividly to mind in describing her: physically tiny, her eyes ablaze, she seems to embody the triumph of the will. Her courtship of Orson's grandfather seems to belong more to the insect world than to that of normal human relations. The daughter of a powerful Kenosha attorney, she had travelled unaccompanied to St Joseph, Missouri for reasons which are unclear (though she seems to have had no doubts about what she was doing). There she met and selected for her future husband an amiably good-looking freight clerk by the name of Richard Wells, whisked him back to her appalled family in Kenosha, and proceeded in frank defiance of them to marry him. She was at the time fourteen and a half years old. No protest of her formidable family would deter her, not even the legendary temper of her father, Orson Head, draconian attorney and sometime senator, one of 'The Pioneer Lawyers of Kenosha County', according to a contemporary publication. His photograph shows him to possess the original of his daughter's thunderous mien. The fourteen-year-old bride and her twenty-six-year-old spouse made their way back to St Joseph where they quickly went through her substantial dowry, returned to Kenosha – with their son Richard, born in 1872 – and set up house, finally moving in with Mary's protesting family after the old District Attorney's death.

By 1881, Richard Senior had had enough and fled, thereafter to pursue a nomad's life, an occasional inventor and perennial bon viveur, just like his son. His was a ghostly existence: last sighted in 1901, he had been declared dead some sixteen years before by his formidable ex-wife to enable her to collect the patrimony conditional on his demise. Once she had consigned Richard to the ranks of the living dead, Mary remarried, this time – scandalising her family for a second time – to the Danish-American brewer Gottfredson, soon giving birth to her second son, Rudolph, after whom she named her ugly, beer-bottle-studded folly. It was in this dismal dwelling that Richard Wells Junior grew up with a stepfather for whom he had no feeling and who had none for him, a much younger stepbrother who was a model of good behaviour and a mother single-mindedly devoted to outraging the family who had so disapproved of her. She took on the role of society hostess, seeming to parody the gracious ways that the family had cultivated; one of her most striking innovations was to charge admission for the parties she threw. Richard Wells escaped this ménage as soon as possible, somehow emphasising his independence by adding an extra e to his name. By

1901, well established in business, he had his own house, a hundred yards down the street from Rudolphsheim, and a reasonable income. Perhaps having the house suggested to him the notion of marriage; at any rate, in 1903, he met – somewhere between Badger Brass and the Utopia Novelty Company – a formidable young woman with whom he fell powerfully in love.

Beatrice Ives's background was, like her suitor's, commercial and Mid-Western: her father had been a prosperous coal merchant in Springfield, Illinois, where she was born in 1882, but had suffered during the coal slump of the 1880s. They continued to maintain an impressive establishment just outside Kenosha, but it was a squeeze to make ends meet; Beatrice Ives and her mother Lucy gave music lessons in order to survive. When this was not enough, Beatrice, according to her son Orson in the beautifully written and almost entirely imaginary autobiographical piece that he wrote in French *Vogue*, in 1982, 'went to work as a "typewriter" (as stenographers were then called) to pay for the completion of her musical training. She was a celebrated beauty, a champion rifle shot, a highly imaginative practical joker, a radical and a suffragette.' With only a small allowance for filial exaggeration, everything in his description is borne out by independent witness. Perhaps 'handsome' is a more precise word than 'beautiful'; her photographs none the less reveal a most striking woman: in one of them she sits at her piano, a hand on the keyboard. Her eyebrow cocked, she looks challengingly out of her huge eyes into the camera. Underneath her fine aquiline nose, the full, wide mouth is unsmiling; a fiercely intelligent face. One would not readily cross this woman – even if she was not as good a shot as Welles claims. His is the only evidence for this gift, but it seems perfectly feasible. Of her practical jokes, there are no recorded instances, either, but her political activity, and her musicianship, are both well attested.

On the face of it, barely a single one of her qualities would seem to recommend her to a sensual, dreamy young man looking for a mate. Neither her music nor her intellect nor her politics would have obvious appeal for him. The gunmanship, perhaps? It may well have been her feminine strength to which he with his masculine weakness was drawn; and vice versa. She, interestingly, had had a tense relationship with her own tough mother, while adoring her gentle, hopeless father. Or perhaps it was just sex; both seem powerfully sensual figures. 'It was because they were both charmers,' Welles told a biographer, Barbara Leaming, vaguely. Different as individuals, they also had very different notions of marriage: he was looking forward to relaxing into it; she saw it as a springboard for a life of achievement – in the arts, in social amelioration, in self-improvement. Freed from economic embarrassment (he was no millionaire, but solidly successful) she could devote herself to her life's work with the intensity that she brought to everything. They married, in November of 1903, in an Episcopalian church in Chicago, and he brought his bride home to Kenosha to meet Mother.

The meeting was not a success. After that first encounter, Beatrice never stepped inside Rudolphsheim again until poverty compelled the young family temporarily and briefly to move in with the old tyrant. By then, they were three. Beatrice had given birth in 1905 to a son, named, a little uninventively perhaps, Richard (the third in a row). From the beginning he failed to please. His mother was disappointed in his apparent lack of intelligence, his father found him dull and withdrawn, and his grandmother – who probably would have been dissatisfied had Beatrice given birth to the Messiah – loathed his slovenly, disobedient ways. The photographs reveal a pleasant-looking young fellow, his features more influenced by his father's regular and balanced looks than the more dramatic ones of his mother. He is found in most of the pictures holding his baby brother, and seems happy to be doing so. As for that brother – no, this is to anticipate. For the time being, they are three: Richard Senior, drinking more and more heavily as he realises how little companionship marriage seems to have bought; Beatrice, increasingly involved in the life of the community, expanding her musical activities and leaving her husband further and further behind both intellectually and socially; and little Richard, failing to bridge the growing gap between his parents, lonely, awkward, seemingly unable to meet with anyone's approval.

Their financial problems can hardly have helped. They moved four times in ten years, always to cheaper accommodations, occasionally having to take in lodgers. Some of the money had gone on Richard's booze; but Badger Brass, like many other Kenosha companies – like companies all over the industrialised world during that pre-war decade – was in the throes of considerable industrial unrest. There were strikes and bomb threats. During those years, the rate of development reached fever pitch; more and more people flooded into the city which grew in ten years from the eighteenth most populous in Wisconsin to the ninth. Housing, education and health provision all became critical. Charles Higham vividly describes the city as 'a microcosm of industrial America at the beginning of the automobile age'. It was Chicago writ small:

Kenosha, like the bigger city, was also divided up into ethnic neighbourhoods more accurately described as ghettoes. What was this huge new labour force making? Iron and brass beds, pleasure and commercial vehicles, harness leather, brass and copper sheet and roll. The factories that made these commodities were the largest of their kind in the world. Eighty years before – a mere lifetime ago – there had been nothing; nothing whatever but sedge and swamp. Now these powerhouses had brought with them a sort of urban hell, with the poor of the world, it seemed, living in their shadow. When the city council offered lectures on The Child, they were given in seven languages: Italian, Russian, Yiddish, Polish, Slovak, German and English.

The city was acutely aware of the crisis. Just as in Chicago, where Jane Addams had founded her visionary Hull House settlement for the relief of the poor, there was a surge of involvement by middle-class women in the question of welfare. Already campaigning furiously for the vote, they were now determined to act effectively, if need be unilaterally, to eradicate the squalor, both moral and physical, of the city. In the forefront of these reformers was Beatrice Welles. In February 1914, she made Kenosha history – and the front page of the local newspaper – by being the first woman to be elected to political office: she became first a member of the Board of Education, then its Chairman. 'Mrs Welles will have as strong support among the men as among the women,' claimed the *News*. They were right: she won by a large majority over her male competitor, and received 171 out of 185 votes cast by the women of her ward. The *News* continued: 'she is one of the most prominent members of Kenosha clubs and societies, and has taken a great interest in public questions.' She had actually founded the Kenosha City Club 'to study civic problems, to seek ways of correcting wrongs, and giving proper support to movements along right lines'. Mary D. Bradford, one of the great educationalists of the period, had occasion to work with her; in her memoirs she wrote that 'she was a very handsome woman, of brilliant intellect and had the courage of her convictions. She was a brilliant public speaker . . . her social prestige aroused an interest among those who had previously been rather indifferent.'

Her passion for music and the other arts was equal to her social commitment; here too, there was an undercurrent of crusade, a visionary impulse towards improvement. Art for Art's Sake was to her a meaningless watchword. In Kenosha she was by no means starved of music. Before the development of the mechanical media, the touring circuit was in full swing. No musician of note considered himself or herself too grand to take to the road; the road was where the bulk of their performances were given. Thus Kenosha, provincial and Mid-Western, was host during the last years of the old century and the first of the new to – among many others – Kreisler, Gieseking, Cortot, Tito Schipa, and Ernestine Schumann-Heink, all of whom could command full houses in any capital in Europe. Part of the ritual of the road was that the artists would be feted, fed and housed by the local grandees. If one was reasonably well connected, one could confidently expect to take supper with one's hero. It was thus that Beatrice Welles came to mix with many of the leading musicians of her day. Her own playing was greatly admired locally; she was, says Mrs Brown in her 1934 study, *Music in Kenosha*, 'among the best-known pianists in Kenosha'. But her fame did not stop there. Frederick Stock, conductor of the Chicago Symphony Orchestra, one of the great men in American music, is quoted as saying that she was the foremost woman pianist he knew – a sexist compliment from a sexist age, but an impressive testimonial, none the less.

The use to which she put her talent was characteristically original and educational: she pioneered a form of lecture recital in which performances of daringly modern pieces by Ravel and Debussy were interspersed with poems and disquisitions on the music. Her speaking voice – 'cello voice' as Welles describes it in his *Vogue* piece – was much remarked on for its beauty, and her programme was held to be a great success. Her constant quest to engage in improving activity is characteristic of the auto-didact – imparting the fruits of her own ceaseless self-improvement with the urgency that comes from knowing that there will never be enough time to learn all that needs to be learned. She was, without being absolutely pre-eminent in any of her spheres, a public figure to be reckoned with – reformer, teacher, artist. Life at home, however, with the two Richard Welleses – Senior lazy and boozy, Junior sullen and slow-witted – can have afforded her little satisfaction. Since 1911, too, after the death of the father she loved, the mother she felt uncomfortable with had moved in, already ill with the stomach cancer which would eventually and agonisingly kill her. Into this complex ménage, George Orson Welles was introduced on 6 May 1915.

He was named after a famous, and famously discreet, gay couple, George Ade and Orson Wells. Wells, a stockbroker, was nicknamed 'Circumnavigation' in acknowledgement of the passion for travel which he indulged with Ade, one of America's best-known humorists. A witty double portrait in cartoon form shows them on the steps of a pyramid, Wells with drink in hand, Ade in flowing Edwardian gown, picture hat and parasol, clutching a handbag on which is written FABLES IN SLANG, the title of his masterpiece. The couple are the first of many gay men who had an influence on Welles at crucial points in his life. It is also entirely possible that he was not named after these two men at all, since George was his great-uncle's name and Orson that of his great-grandfather. Grandmaternal influence may have prevailed. Thus the first question mark in Welles's life hovers over the font. Even that may not be the first: there is an earlier, and altogether unresolvable, question: where was he conceived? Perhaps in order to avoid the derision of having been born in Kenosha, Welles liked to say that conception (obviously a vital incident in the legend of the artist) occurred in Rio de Janeiro. It is perfectly possible. Anyone can hop on a train from Kenosha to New York and a boat from New York to Brazil, and Richard Welles was, Orson always averred, passionate about travel; his father and mother are said, indeed, to have met Ade and Wells on a Caribbean cruise just before her confinement with Orson. This would suggest rather a lot of travelling within a nine-month period. The seriously surprising factor is that they could afford these journeys: at the time of Orson's birth the family had moved to the least impressive of all their Kenosha residences – 463½ Park Avenue; the other ½ was let out to businessmen. Perhaps they were attempting to salvage their relationship by having a holiday in Brazil, Orson was the outcome, and they wanted to celebrate his coming birth with another jaunt.

In any event, what is not at all in question is that he was born in Kenosha, on 6 May 1915. 'Over and over again, this date has been confirmed by the city fathers of Kenosha for the benefit of Sunday supplement journalists hopeful of discovering that Welles is really thirty or thirty-five,' said *The New Yorker* in 1938. 'This scepticism about his age has never angered Welles, but he cannot restrain a sensation of gentle triumph whenever he hears that another reporter has put himself to the useless expense of wiring to Kenosha for a duplicate of the birth certificate.' His mother later told him that because it was six o'clock in the morning – the time Kenosha's many factories started work – whistles and bells had all started blowing at once, as if to herald him; a perfectly appropriate beginning, since most of the rest of his life was accompanied by fanfares of one sort or another.

He weighed ten pounds, and was a roaring success from the

very start. This was the baby Beatrice and Richard had wanted all along: bright as a button, bonny, iron-lunged and lusty. In the face, no doubt, of the adulation heaped on the noisy head of the newcomer, Richard Junior, the failed candidate for family affection, became even more sullen and unmanageable. A decision was taken when he was eleven (a year after the baby's arrival) to send him away to school, an unusual step for an American family; clearly they felt that severe measures were called for. The school they chose brooked no nonsense in the discipline department. The Todd Seminary for Boys had a fearsome reputation for dealing with problem cases. The Rev. Todd had founded the school in the middle of the previous century, but, losing control of his delinquent charges, he had handed over the reins to his deputy, the impressive Noble Hill, known as 'the King'. This Spartan man, born with splendid appropriateness in Economy, Nova Scotia, formulated the Todd spirit in the brochure that Beatrice and Richard Welles must have read: 'it is the spirit of Loyalty, Obedience and Service. There you have the Todd idea in a nutshell. To state it concisely, it is the spirit of obedience, for where you have obedience there will be loyalty and service. There is nothing new or original in my methods,' he added, modestly. 'Without bigotry or cant, I simply follow the methods of The Great Teacher. Like him, I become flesh and dwell among my pupils living the life of sacrifice and service. I drive out all who profane the temple with unholy traffic, and I refuse to attempt any mighty works for those who lack faith in me or my methods.' The little boy in the photographs cuddling his baby brother, or being happily dandled on his mother's knee, seems hardly to have deserved this righteous onslaught. No doubt his blond locks and smiling face hid deep contrarieties; he was, too, approaching 'the difficult age'. None the less, to have been faced with the Holy Terror of Todd seems a little excessive. The regime was in some regards enlightened: corporal punishment was rare 'and then only on the insistence of parents'; locks and keys were unknown and individual and property rights respected. On vacation, none the less, Richard spoke to his young brother in lurid terms of what he endured. 'I knew about Todd,' Orson told Barbara Leaming, 'as criminals know about San Quentin.'

The absence of Richard Junior meant that the infant Orson had the spotlight all to himself, and it beat down on him unrelentingly. The best that could be hoped for Richard was to be saved from a life of vice or crime. Of Orson, there was no limit to what was expected; and he amply fulfilled expectation. It is clear from the infant snaps that whatever else he might or might not be, he would not be ignored. There is about his demeanour, to a degree rare in a baby, a sort of authority; his stare commands the camera. A heavy child, his features – as was widely remarked at the time – have something Oriental about them: not Far Eastern, neither Japanese nor Chinese, but Mongolian, with their burning brown eyes slightly slanted, wide lips and squashy little nose – a face in width, not length. The eyebrows are already, aged two, active, charmingly mobile, lending that forceful visage an irresistible vulnerability. Some of his father's face is there, but the whole feeling of it derives from his mother. Not a handsome child, exactly, but one bursting with character. His mother had firm ideas about what to do with him. Almost before he could speak, she was reading to him – Charles and Mary Lamb's *Tales from Shakespeare*, to begin with, and then the real thing. 'Why,' she demanded, 'should a person at his most impressionable age be shovelled into the sordid company of *Auntie's Nice Kit Kat* or *Little Sister's Silly Red Ball*?' The chairman of the Kenosha Board of Education had original notions on the subject. There would be no reaching down to the child's level, no baby talk. 'Children could be treated as adults as long as they were amusing,' Welles wrote in *Vogue*. 'The moment you became boring, it was off to the nursery.' Or, when you were old enough, to the Todd School. Orson learned his lesson very quickly: the nursery was not a place where he planned to spend much time. A photograph shows him watching with glazed eyes as his brother babyishly labours over a pile of building bricks; not for him. He would master whatever skills were required to keep him at the side of his beautiful, tough mother. A visiting doctor, called in to examine Richard Junior's head – he had fallen downstairs and broken it – was somewhat surprised to be told by the one-and-a-half-year-old Orson that 'the desire to take medicine is one of the greatest features which distinguishes men from animals'. If articulate speech was what was required, then articulate speech it would be, whether one quite understood what one was saying or not.

The effect on the doctor was remarkable. He experienced a coup de foudre. 'I was astounded by the extraordinary mental maturity of the boy,' he told Peter Noble thirty years later. 'He was talking remarkably sound sense at the age of two, and I felt sure, from his appearance, demeanour and receptivity to paintings and sculptures, that he was destined to be some kind of an artist.' In addition to Richard Junior's head, the doctor was treating Beatrice Welles's mother, Lucy Ives, increasingly and agonisingly in the grip of the cancer that would kill her. In the course of his encounters with Beatrice he had fallen under her spell. Now, meeting her son for the first time, he experienced a double cathexis, falling in love with both mother and son. He soon became a regular visitor; another part of Orson's already overcrowded emotional landscape. He awarded Orson the name Pookles, and was in turn called Dadda. The significance of this can have been lost on no one.

His real name was Maurice Abraham Bernstein. He had been born, according to the 1929 edition of *Who's Who in Chicago*, in Russia in 1886; trained and graduated in Chicago where he had practised since 1908, specialising in orthopaedics, but equally at home in hormone therapy, gastrology and infantile paralysis. Three years after graduation he moved, somewhat abruptly, to Kenosha, 'exiled from Chicago', according to Higham, 'because of a scandalous episode in which he was charged with attacking, beating, and leaving injured a clinic supervisor'. Scandal of another kind was never far behind him, either. Immensely handsome in a wolfish way, he was prone to triangular involvements, perhaps believing, with Oscar Wilde's Algernon, that in married life, three is company and two is none. He had been married himself, the year in which he met the Welleses, 1917. His bride was Minna, the rather plain sister of the virtuoso violinist Mischa Elman who had provided her, at Dr Bernstein's demand, with a dowry of $15,000; the marriage had lasted no more than four months, dissolving amidst accusations of cupidity and treachery. It seems fairly certain that he started an affair with Beatrice Welles on the rebound.

The atmosphere in 463½ Park Avenue can only be guessed at. Beatrice was rarely at home. She maintained a heavy programme of public appearances, both musical and political, to such an extent that she briefly considered farming out her explosively ebullient younger son to her childless neighbours, the Andreas. They nervously declined the offer, instead adopting two very sweet but thoroughly normal children, with whom Orson would play, rather roughly. Otherwise he was looked after by his deeply caring nanny, Sigrid Jacobsen. Beatrice meanwhile continued her social work with the dauntingly-named Big Sisterhood Association; this sterling organisation was dedicated to saving fallen girls, of whom there were now a great many more since the further explosion of immigration precipitated by the war – to which Beatrice had been publicly and militantly opposed but which America had now, in 1917, entered as an Associated Power. Germans and Italians flooded the city, straining to breaking point the fledgling welfare system; Beatrice gave herself over to solving their problems. Beatrice's mother, meanwhile, was dying in extreme pain. Sedatives were of little avail and the air was rent with her screams. Richard Junior was away at school, and when he wasn't there, he was in the doghouse. Richard Senior, cuckolded, had relapsed into untrammelled alcoholism, the only restraint on which, his participation in the affairs of Badger Brass, was removed when the company was bought out in that same crucial year of 1917. The CM Hall Lamp Company of Detroit swallowed it whole; Richard's settlement was $100,000, no mean sum – at least a million of today's dollars. He had no need to work ever again, so he didn't. He was forty-six.

A year later, Beatrice's mother Lucy Ives died, and, as if they had been waiting for a signal, the whole ménage moved to Chicago: Beatrice, the two Richards, Orson – and Dr Bernstein. Orson's Kenosha period was over. He only ever returned to visit his dread grandmother. But the sights and sounds of it stuck with him. The area in which he lived – around Library Park – was, and is, an attractive place, a few minutes' walk from the southern shore of Lake Michigan. It has a seaside feeling about it, the regular houses laid out on their grid – balanced, peaceful. Rudolphsheim, on one side of the Park, and the other large house which has become a funeral home dominate, but they don't overwhelm. It is Norman Rockwell territory, porches and gabled roofs; but even more it is Booth Tarkington. Describing his Indiana town in *The Magnificent Ambersons*, Tarkington describes at the same time the elegant part of Kenosha: 'At the beginning of the Ambersons' great period most of the houses of the Midland town were of a pleasant architecture. They lacked style, but they also lacked pretentiousness, and whatever does not pretend at all has style enough. They stood in commodious yards, well shaded by left-over forest trees, elm and walnut and beech . . .' Fitzgerald spoke of it, too, in *The Great Gatsby*: 'That's my Middle West – not the wheat or the prairies or the lost Swede towns, but the thrilling returning trains of my youth, and the street lamps and sleigh bells in the frosty dark and the shadows of holly leaves thrown by lighted windows on the snow.' A part of all that remained with Orson Welles, however far he wandered.

CHAPTER TWO

Chicago

CHICAGO IN 1918 was heaven and hell. Barely fifty years older than Kenosha, Wisconsin, its name celebrating the drained wild garlic swamps on which it stood, it had been galvanised as a city by the fire that had all but razed it in 1870. Its citizens – and more particularly its architects – plunged into a fervour of new building as comprehensive as that of London in 1666, and with the same effect on civic pride. Chicago was full of itself, and America was full of Chicago. The Windy City they called it: not from the gales which certainly do sweep down its streets, but from the unconscionable amount of publicity the city generated to secure for itself the privilege of hosting the Columbian Exposition of 1893 – a celebration of both Americas, North and South, of art, of industry, but most of all, of Chicago. The city's nickname for itself was more self-mocking (a sure mark of confidence) than anything anyone else could come up with: Porkopolis. For this was also the city of Upton Sinclair's *The Jungle*, the centre of the meat trade, awash with the blood of a million animals and of quite a few humans, too. A vast industrial complex and a port, the archetypal megalopolis of the modern world,

> Hog Butcher for the World
> Tool Maker, Stacker of Wheat
> Player with Railroads
>   and the Nation's Freight Handler;
> Stormy, husky, brawling.
> City of the Big Shoulders.

Carl Sandburg's words. Sandburg was Chicago's poet laureate, and it says something for the city that it should have had one. It had, in fact, many, and Chicago proved an inexhaustible topic for them. Gathered round the Old Water Tower in the North Side, these writers – Sherwood Anderson, Max Bodenheim, Edgar Lee Masters, Ben Hecht – collectively took the lead in American letters, making a new language, giving voice to the savage vitality of the city – Chicago the prototype of all urban experience. 'You know my city – Chicago triumphant; factories and marts and roar of machines – horrible, terrible, ugly and brutal. Can a singer arise and sing in this smoke and grime? Can he keep his throat clear? Can his courage survive?' H.L. Mencken, incorruptible arbiter of American literary taste, gave Anderson his answer: 'Out in Chicago, the only genuinely civilised city in the New World, they take the fine arts seriously and get into such frets and excitements about them as are raised nowhere else save by baseball, murder, political treachery, foreign wars and romantic loves . . . almost one fancies the world bumped by a flying asteroid, and the Chicago river suddenly turned into the Seine.'

It was to this city, drunk radiant with contradictions – 'Chicago, the jazz-baby – the reeking, cinder-ridden, joyous baptist stronghold; Chicago, the chewing gum centre of the world, the bleating, slant-headed rendezvous of half-witted newspapers, sociopaths and pants makers', to quote one of its more restrained self-descriptions – that Beatrice Welles brought her family. It was certainly she who brought them: her husband, though enamoured of the stage and its citizens, and partial to fine wine and good food and concomitant fleshly pleasures, showed no sign of needing to move to the source of these things, and Dr Bernstein, according to Orson, only left Kenosha to be near Beatrice. He spoke of it as 'a paradise he'd lost . . . my mother used to make HEARTLESS fun of that.' As for the boys – cosy and comfortable though they surely were in Kenosha, this huge and thrilling city was the biggest playground a child could imagine. This is where Orson Welles grew up, this swaggering, boastful place, which sneered at New York as a provincial cousin. Here was everything and anything they could want – provided they had the money. And, thanks to Richard Welles's golden handshake, they did. Had they not, it might have been a harsh life; they would have shared the squalor and deprivation of a large portion of the city's population, the immigrants in their northern ghettoes, the blacks in theirs on the South Side. For these people, undernourished, brutalised, cold, Chicago was hell. 'For God's sake,' cried Margaret Anderson at the end of her first editorial for *The Little Review*, one of Chicago's many little magazines, 'why doesn't someone start the revolution?' All the conditions were present, enough to make a Marxist despair at its reluctance to occur. But Chicago was still too high on itself. Even the poor were swept up in its undentable confidence, which lasted till the Big Crash – ten years away, in 1929. After that, nothing would ever quite be the same again for Chicago.

In Alston J. Smith's phrase: 'there was the manic phase. Then came the Great Depression.'

The sheer size of the city might have shocked a little boy from Kenosha. Building skyscrapers not, like New York, out of necessity, but from aesthetic conviction, Chicago's great architects Louis L. Sullivan and John Root had filled the tabula rasa that the fire had given them with block upon block of soaring, streamlined buildings, sweeping away any vestige of the Beaux-Arts fussiness and ornament that prevailed in most of America's great cities. Chicago's architects matched the city's spirit in their buildings. There was no Bauhaus imposition of an aesthetic; these men captured the spirit of their time and place and rendered it in brick and stone. And Chicago responded affectionately and wittily: the great wide sweep of Michigan Avenue is both celebrated and teased in its local nickname: Boul' Mich'. Sullivan's masterpiece, The Auditorium, intended for the Opera House but acoustically disappointing, testifies in its sweep and scale to the ambitiousness of its subscriber-patrons. There is scarcely an opera house in the world that could have matched it for sheer grandeur. Art – especially the musical arts, but art in pretty well any form – was all the rage in Chicago. 'A crazy thing happened here with the rich men and their wives at the turn of the century,' wrote Studs Terkel. 'Mrs Palmer Potter and the other wives longed for culture. Whether or not they knew what it was, they wanted it. And so Chicago became a centre for culture because of the wives of the guys who were meatpackers.' 'I want less of steers and less of pork and more of culture,' said one prosperous attorney in 1881.

This is what brought Beatrice Welles here. There is no record of her becoming involved in either politics or social work in Chicago. Perhaps she felt that enough in that regard was being done without her. The Hull House settlement under Jane Addams was a world-famous foundation, ministering to the needs of the disadvantaged. Women in the city were particularly active politically: only three years after they had won the vote, Chicago very nearly elected a female mayor. Beatrice's political skills were not needed here. Her focus was on the arts and artistic circles: the fine arts, the theatre, above all, of course, music. In all of these, she was spoilt for choice. The Arts Institute possessed one of the finest collections in America if not the world; more significantly, the colony of practising artists was enormous, and they maintained a high profile: Boris Anisfeldt, designer for Diaghilev and now a teacher at the Fine Arts Institute, led over a hundred artists in roasting a whole lamb or pig on the great seasonal holidays; Lorado Taft, head of the Institute – Fra Lorado to his followers – held 'Attic processions' in flowing robes to celebrate the muses. And Mrs Palmer Potter and her friends made sure that these artists were feted and fabled. It was fashionable and rewarding to be an artist in Chicago, 1918; the mildly preposterous suggestion widely offered at the time that Chicago was Florence to New York's Rome had at least this grain of truth: the city sought to glorify itself through its artists. Nelson Algren, another of Chicago's laureates, had a harsher phrase for it: 'with the blood and sweat of the arena still on them, they would pause together at the end of the week to sniff shyly at the little flowers of culture.' They did more than sniff; they fertilised.

The theatre, too, boomed. The commercial theatre rivalled New York, with six or seven openings a week; you could catch touring productions like *The Hairy Ape*, *Anna Christie*, *He Who Gets Slapped* and *R.U.R.*: the cream of the avant-garde. Stanislavsky brought the Moscow Art Theatre, with Chekhov, Gorky and *Tsar Fyodor*. The Habimah came; and Mei Lan-fang; Stratford-upon-Avon, under Ben Greet; and, later, Katharine Cornell in *The Green Hat*. And at the Chicago Little Theatre, Maurice Browne, a Craig disciple, and his wife Ellen Van Valkenberg experimented with design and with light and with acting, presenting the symbolists and later Ibsen, a theatre of poetry and image. As for the opera: Beatrice Welles must have been in her seventh heaven. Barely a city in the world, let alone in America, could field a season as brilliant as Chicago's. It owed this in large measure to the desire of the Metropolitan Opera in New York to expel Oscar Hammerstein I from its immediate orbit. He moved his operation to Chicago, bringing with him Mary Garden and her notorious performance of Richard Strauss's *Salome*: 'like a cat in a bed of catnip', said the Police Chief, called in to maintain law, order and public decency, thus immeasurably enhancing the popularity of opera in Chicago. With Miss Garden as (in her own phrase) 'directa' of the company there was an air of temperament and danger about the whole enterprise, and again, a commitment to living, often daunting, composers: Chicago was determined to be in the vanguard, thumbing its nose at New York. Prokofiev's *Love of Three Oranges*, spiky satire clothed in prickly melody and shocking harmonies, was commissioned and premièred by the Chicago Opera, with sets and costumes by the lamb-roasting Anisfeldt. It was well, if uncomprehendingly, received. Visiting stars included Chaliapin, Louise Homer and Claudia Muzio; Adolph Bolm, Diaghilev dancer and choreographer, became the ballet master.

It is worth detailing all these, not merely because of the delight they gave Beatrice Welles, but because Orson, now talking and walking, was exposed to as many of the performances as possible. Beatrice's ambitions for Orson, as for herself, were entirely musical. She became a member of the Lakeside Musical Society; being who she was, she was before long running it. Through Dr Bernstein's connections with the Elmans, she invited the great violinist to address the Society and perform for them; she herself gave her lecture-recital on Spanish music and its 'cantillations and various charming dance rhythms'. Bernstein, who was also musical – he played the cello – had become acquainted with Chicago's leading music critic, Edward Moore, and, more passionately, with his wife, Hazel, creating further troilistic patterns in his emotional life. He was not of as passionate a disposition as these entanglements suggest, being that kind of Lothario who attaches himself with dog-like devotion to the object of his love, while yet being unable to make a complete commitment – hence the preference for a third party. His attentions exasperated Beatrice Welles; stopping the car one day in the middle of Michigan Avenue, she ordered him out. But he was useful to her, and through his connection with the Moores she managed to attract a glittering roster of guest speakers and artists. In a charming fantasy, Welles's biographer Frank Brady has suggested that it was not unusual to bump into Stravinsky and Ravel in her drawing room; the record does not reveal that either of these gentlemen visited Chicago at all during her time there, let alone attended her soirées. It is conceivable that Prokofiev, in town for the première of *The Love of Three Oranges*, may have done so; quite certain that, in the wider social circles in which she moved, she would have met any visiting stars.

Equally certain is that her entire new life was intolerable to poor Dick Welles. This high-falutin', hobnobbing existence was not for him. He must have felt entirely inadequate, unable to tell one painting from another, sleeping through the interminable nights at the opera, unaware of the existence of the latest Bodenheim. He took his pleasure elsewhere. His new little fortune gave him the opportunity to be the person he had always wanted to be: Champagne Charlie – all-round good fellow, friend to restaurateurs, barmen, pretty girls of every size or shape; a clubbable fellow, given to yarning, inordinately fond of travel, but mainly, according to his son, because of his love of the lounges of ocean-going liners: 'the creaking of leather, the cradling seas, the cards he played so masterfully, and a captive audience for his stories'. Welles claimed that his father had actually broken the bank at Monte Carlo. Well, maybe he did and maybe he didn't, although some doubt was expressed in a 1940's edition of the *Kenosha Journal* as to the actual extent of his globe-trotting. 'The Man Who Broke the Bank at Monte Carlo', however, is unquestionably his song; it expresses him perfectly, with its rolling, strolling gait, a spring in its heel and all the time in the world. It is some little way from this to Stravinsky, Ravel and the cantillations of Spanish dance rhythm – or indeed the jazz which he so loved, now, in 1918, having taken up residence in Chicago since being forcibly driven out of New Orleans with the closure of Storyville. Down there on the South Side, he was happily awash with cheap liquor and hot rhythm while Beatrice, Orson and Dadda revelled in Ravel.

He was, by now, an alcoholic. He depended on alcohol; life was not possible without it. His purposeless presence must have been intolerable to the dynamic, frustrated Beatrice. 'I'd see my father wither under one of her looks into a crisp, brown, winter's leaf,' wrote Welles. In 1919, they separated. Beatrice moved, with the children, to a swish North Shore apartment on east Superior Street, a mere two blocks away from the area around the Water Tower: Towertown, the hub of the artistic community. From here, she planned her musical career, now calling herself Trixie Ives – an unexpectedly larky name for this very serious woman; it has the smack of the music hall about it: Miss Trixie Ives and Her Ivory Tricks! One glimpse of her intense features would surely dispel any such fancy. As well as her own musical career, she was planning that of her son, Orson, four years old, and already conversing fluently with the adults to whom she invariably introduced him. So far he had been successful in his evasion of the nursery. To the amusement of her circle, he would stand on a chair and pretend to conduct ('I was surprised she indulged me in this, since she indulged me in nothing else'); in fact, he would do pretty well anything to please an adult. Dr Bernstein, who loved his Pookles with the same devotion and microscopic attention that he extended to Beatrice, had provided Orson with two crucial presents: a magic set and a toy theatre. Quickly mastering these, he gave performances to the properly and politely appreciative visitors in both his new media (though of course, as he was often to say later, to him they represented two sides of the same coin – the theatre of magic, the magic of theatre).

For Dr Bernstein, however, this was no kid putting on a show for Mummy's friends. The fatal word 'genius' had no sooner formed itself in his mind, than he was whispering it in Orson's ear. Verbally precocious Orson certainly was, but in no other regard did he demonstrate prodigious gifts; neither in reading (he was slow to start this), the visual arts, nor – unfortunately – musicianship, the sphere in which success was most ardently willed on him by his mother. 'She was not the musical version of a stage mother, but was simply resolved that whatever I did had to be good if it was to be done at all, and I was made to practise hours on end every day.' Beatrice was not to be defied. In a disturbing story that he told on several occasions with different endings, Welles describes how, 'distracted to the point of madness by endlessly repeated musical scales', he climbed onto the third-floor balcony of the hotel in which they were staying (the Ritz in Paris, he says, a nice, colourful touch) and threatened to throw himself off. The piano teacher, terrified, rushes to get Beatrice. Generally, the story ends with Beatrice gently luring him down off the balcony. In his autobiographical fragment, something quite different happens. 'Well,' says Beatrice to the hysterical piano teacher, 'if he wants to jump, let him jump.' Eventually he came down of his own accord. Welles adds: 'the truth is her heart was in her mouth . . . by the sheer force of her formidable character, she persuaded the spinster lady to muffle her whimpering . . . she was, in all things, as tough-minded as she was loving-hearted.' Years later he told Barbara Leaming: 'I always felt I was letting them down. That's why I worked so hard. That's the stuff that turned the motor . . . my mother and father were much cooler and more distant. I trusted and feared their judgement.' It is to be wondered whether it was both of them, or simply his mother that he felt he was letting down. The word he uses of her – formidable – rings out. No one ever said that of Dick, though of course people create their emotional hold over others in different ways; some do it with a look, and some with a shrug. In their differently blighted ways, the pressure behind both may have been the same: an overwhelming sense of unfulfilment in themselves, a desire to make another live for them.

Despite his disappointing showing at the keyboard, Orson was able to participate in musical performances, but in a way more familiar from his later achievements. Just outside Chicago is a charming lakeside suburb called Ravinia Park, and here, to add to what was almost an embarrassment of musical riches, the entrepreneur Louis Eckstein established what he called 'his yacht' and what more extravagant wordsmiths (no doubt in his pay; publicity was one of the sources of his fortune) dubbed 'the Chicago Bayreuth': a summer opera festival, which ran from 1912 to 1935. Claudia Cassidy wrote of it: 'There never was anything like Louis Eckstein's Ravinia, and there will not be again. The little wooden Pavilion in the flowering park. About 14,000 seats. The little stage with the blue velvet curtains, stars of the Chicago, Metropolitan and Paris Operas, fifty players of the Chicago Symphony in the pit.' The repertory was very much the staple repertory of the time – Verdi, Puccini and the verismo school (contemporary composers: Leoncavallo, Alfano, Montemezzi) and the French repertory whose great interpreters were still alive and really able to do it justice.

Beatrice and Maurice Bernstein, accompanied by Orson, were regular subscribers, as were the Moores, and it is possible that they were able to get Orson enlisted as a non-singing infant, of whom there are a number in the repertory favoured by Ravinia, most notably the role of Trouble, Cio-Cio San's son in *Madame Butterfly*. It is claimed that Orson did indeed essay this role, though it has proved impossible to verify it. In fact, at the period when he might have done so, performances were only semi-staged. Perhaps the diva (Edith Mason and Claudia Muzio both sang Butterfly during this period) had requested a child as a dramatic aid – though most divas would be likely to make the opposite request. At any rate, if he wasn't Trouble in 1920, he has certainly been Trouble ever since, not least to his biographers. There are further unverified and unverifiable reports that he was relieved of his role in *Pagliacci* when Martinelli complained that he had become too heavy to lift, but it is difficult to imagine what role it might be that required him to be lifted. The important thing is that Orson was exposed to and immersed in opera and its special dramaturgy from the earliest possible age.

In addition to these musical outings to Ravinia, there were weekends, and sometimes longer stays, in the tiny town – village, properly speaking – of Grand Detour. These were family jaunts, though somewhat unconventional ones. The Richards, Junior and Senior, would drive in one car, Maurice, Beatrice and Orson in another, and they would stay in separate lodgings: Beatrice's team in the house she had rented, the two Richards at the Sheffield House Hotel. It was – and to some extent still is – an idyllic escape from the big city, a sylvan settlement on the bend of Rock River, opposite a green, fertile island surrounded by smaller leafy islets. This is Davy Crockett territory – almost literally. When Captain Andrus, veteran of the terrible Black Hawk war, pitched his tent here, laying claim to the land, he was watched by 'lounging Indians' as he cooked his meals. The year is 1834; a twelve-month away from the foundation of Kenosha. But the fact that Kenosha became Kenosha, and Grand Detour remained just that, conceals an extraordinary American story that must have given a dark thrill to the Welles boys on their regular visits to the little resort.

The town, once thriving, had been destroyed by a duel of wills between two of its residents, the famous John Deere, inventor of the revolutionary self-scouring plough (necessary because of the over-richness of the local soil), and his dark rival, darkly named, Solomon Cumins, from Vermont, emissary of a consortium bent on wresting the patent from Deere. Cumins started little by little to buy up the entire town, including the newly installed dam, race and saw-mill. Deere, meanwhile, persuaded the Chicago & Northwestern Railroad Co. to lay tracks to Grand Detour; Cumins, gambling on getting Deere to leave town and give up – thus leaving him free to exploit the patent – intercepted the laying of the tracks. The railroaders went instead to Nachusa and Dixon, which throve. Deere left the town and moved to Moline, where his business prospered to become mighty, his self-scouring 'Grandy' ploughs a household name. Cumins, baulked, ruled the town as its embittered tyrant for twenty-five years, allowing no newspaper, no journalist, no photographer to enter it. When he died, his son, Theron, immediately fled to Dixon. Grand Detour, in effect, died then, too. The townspeople finally burnt down Cumins's property; in the 1920s his grave was desecrated. It was believed that he was the devil.

What gave Grand Detour a new, if modest, lease of life – the thing that brought it, no doubt, to the Welleses' attention – was its development into an Artists' Colony. In the late nineties of the previous century, the art boom had led to the foundation of Eagle's Nest Camp on the east side of the river above Oregon as a retreat for writers, editors, and sculptors among what the *History of Ogle County* is pleased to describe as 'an endless variety of towering cliffs and mystic caverns'. Just above Oregon, on a limestone bluff, stands Lorado Taft's '43 foot behemoth' of a monumental sculpture, *Black Hawk* of 1911: 265 tons of concrete, its head and shoulders alone weigh 30 tons; but its heart is in the right place, a decent liberal's apology for genocide. Rock River Valley became popular with Chicago artists: they 'discovered' Grand Detour which, knowing nothing of the lurid story of John Deere and Solomon Cumins, they took for a slumbering nineteenth-century village. Classes from the Art Institute would spend two or three weeks going back to nature, and sketching it. The place they would stay was the Sheffield House Hotel.

> This commodious hostelry has been under the same management for 50 years [boasted the brochure]. It has light, airy rooms, comfortable beds, bathrooms and modern conveniences, and in the dining-room, home-cooking and plenty of it. The table is always supplied with fresh eggs, country butter and cream, vegetables just from the garden, poultry etcetera in such abundance as only Mrs Sheffield knows how to provide. Boating, bathing, fishing, tennis, croquet, all furnish amusement for guests and frequent hay-ride parties are organized for a visit to the famous castle Rock, Devil's backbone, etc. – Boats are furnished free to guests.

It is interesting to note in this blurb from the brochure the tone of nostalgia for pioneer days.

> Bob White whistles in the field and birds and bees revel in clover and orchard bloom. If you love the country, if you would hear again the familiar song of the meadow lark, the bobolink, the brown rush and the whip-poor-will; if you would sit down once more with the same old out-of-door appetite, to meals such as you had on the farm – COME TO GRAND DETOUR. Rooms: $2.50 per night.

In his memoir Welles remembered it as 'Mark Twain, a horse and buggy village . . . a childhood there was like a childhood back in the 1870s. No electric light, horse-drawn buggies – a completely anachronistic, old-fashioned, early-Tarkington, rural kind of life. It was one of those lost worlds, one of those Edens that you get thrown out of.' Solipsistically – he was after all a child when he was there, and childhood is almost by definition solipsistic – he saw it all as somehow deriving from his father. Sometimes he claimed in interviews that his father owned the village; in others that Dick had decreed that there would be no cars and no electric light. There was no electric light, just as there was no running water, not from choice but from sheer bloody necessity. As it was and is situated slap on Route 3, it would be hard to ban automobiles, but there is indeed every possibility that no one there owned one. Decrees from Richard Welles held no force in Grand Detour which had a life very much its own, one which went on quite satisfactorily when the Welleses and the other guests had repaired to the big city after their brief sojourns.

It was certainly a paradise for small boys interested in small boy-like activities; this may not have included Orson. Among the diversions were the annual clam harvesting (for the shells only: they make good buttons) and – during the winter – ice-sawing on the river; still big business in the twenties. Equally picturesque but to be viewed from a distance was the annual Ku Klux Klan meeting, which took place for a week every July in a cow pasture at the bottom of Canal Street known surprisingly frankly as Klan Park. On Whirlpool Rock, a large wooden cross was built and burnt for all to note. One summer, two boys swimming in Klan Park found a new flag-pole. In its base, three human skulls were embedded, emblazoned KKK. Many Americas coexisted in young Orson's head. His father, for his own diversion, would most probably have ended up on Nigger Island, just across the river. Here the eponymous African-American, whose name was Washington, had an apparently unlimited supply of bootleg liquor. 1920 was the first year of official prohibition (though it had been creeping up for some time) and Dick Welles would have been relieved to have discovered such a plentiful supply; a dry holiday would have been no holiday at all for him.

The town was not without its amiable eccentricities. The fine building which dominates the town had been the Grand Detour Methodist Episcopal Building until the man who built it – disgusted with the low attendances of his fellow churchgoers – converted it into a ballroom. In the twenties, the Grand Detour Players staged plays there; local legend has it that Orson took part. It's hard to see how he could have failed to, though his relations with the community were not of the best. He seemed to regard them as rural know-nothings, and took pleasure in proving his superior smartness. 'Do you want to see the stars?' he asked young Bruno Catalina, (now running the Grand Detour bar). On receipt of a cent, he handed the boy a painted tube (with soot on the eye-piece, naturally); as the boy screwed his eyes up, Welles kicked him in the pants. 'Now you can see the stars!' he gloated. This heartless scene is played out in a million playgrounds around the world, but it did nothing to endear the Grand Detourians to him. They found him to be a loner, and taunted him: 'Georgie, Porgie, Pudding and Pie.' Now they remember him as an oddity: curiously attired by his mother in velvet knee-breeches, dressing up all day long, eating, reciting, and showing off the smattering of foreign words that his mother had taught him (allegro con brio, and so on, no doubt).

It's a sad image, but then childhood, for Welles, as he repeated again and again in later life, was 'a prison', 'a pestilential handicap I determined to cure myself of'. He vouchsafed Peter Bogdanovich a very touching glimpse of himself in Grand Detour: 'There was a country store that had above it a ballroom with an old dance floor with springs in it, so that folks would feel light on their feet. When I was little, nobody had danced up there for many years, but I used to sneak up at night and dance by moonlight with the dust rising from the floor . . .' Years later he remembered Grand Detour as a lost paradise, but from all the evidence it was as complicated an experience as anything else in his young life, with his always exigent mother, his father slipping away, both actually and ontologically, and his brother . . . what do we know of his brother? Nothing at all: an unperson, tolerated, fed, clothed, but seemingly allowed no affirmation – never encouraged, never admired, never enjoyed. No praise for him, no laughter; no plans and no hopes. At some unspecified point, he was expelled from the Todd School, but there is no mention of how or why. One of the strict rules of that academy – the downside of the rule outlawing locks – was that theft was punished with instant dismissal. Perhaps the unhappy young fellow had tried to get something for nothing. If he did, it would be all too understandable. It feels as if they were all just waiting for him to go away; which, eventually, almost unnoticed, he did. For Orson, the situation must have been excruciating. His brother should have been his natural ally. He must have felt that siding with him would be a defiance of his parents, and dependent as he was on their approval, how could he risk that? Ten years is an enormous gap between siblings, anyway, but life might have been rather different for both of them had they found in each other a friend.

Back in the city, life continued as before, with one crucial difference. Beatrice began to be unwell. This interfered with her professional life, but she was, true to form, undaunted by it. She continued her single-handed education of Orson, reading to hm from the classics, having him read to her. He started on the course of voluminous though unsystematic reading which persisted throughout his life. 'I was marinated in poetry and to learn right at the beginning, "a sense of awe, wonder and delight." ' Beatrice's regime did not include the sciences, natural, physical or mathematical, nor did he ever make good the deficiency. She taught him the things she wanted to share. What she was looking for was a companion, someone she could talk to on her own level. Dick was gone, but he had anyway been incapable while he was around of expressing an interesting opinion about anything that concerned her. As for Maurice Bernstein, intelligent and cultured though he was, his anxious, cloying devotion was equally useless to her. Unsentimental, longing to stretch her intellectual wings, she turned to Orson for stimulation, and of course, he was a disappointment.

Not only was her own health a source of anxiety, she also had to look after Orson's. Though physically strong, he was plagued by respiratory conditions – hay fever, and, particularly virulent, asthma – which even at the time were acknowledged to have psychosomatic origins. It is interesting to note that outstandingly gifted people very often endure periods of ill health in childhood. The enforced inactivity, the absence of companions and playmates, give rise to fantasy and speculation for which the ordinarily healthy child never has time. They do, moreover, create in a child a sense of specialness, of requiring, and being entitled to, special attention. Asthma and hay fever would never leave Welles; crises would always provoke both. In 1924 came the first great crisis of his life; perhaps also the worst.

His mother, weak for some time, now contracted jaundice, at that time an always terminal, always agonising condition. 'I knew very well she was going to die, and how real that would be, and how very soon it would happen. Whenever she left me, the moment the door had closed, I would burst into tears, afraid that I would never see her again.' Dick Welles and Maurice Bernstein, his two fathers, the surrogate and the real, moved into the apartment. Perhaps this helped Welles; their feelings – rivals in affection for both Orson and Beatrice – may only be guessed at. Bernstein of course attended her as her physician. There is no record of Richard Junior being present, and no one seems to have felt his absence. Expelled from Todd School, he was now drifting aimlessly through life as the great family drama unfolded without him.

On Orson's birthday – his ninth – he was summoned to his mother's sickroom. He describes the scene in his memoir with graphic precision, like a scene from a film, a most wonderfully scripted scene, which tells us the essence of everything that he wanted to carry around with him from the experience, the story that he would tell himself for the rest of his life.

> How much like her it was to have arranged it so that our farewell in that black room was made to seem like the high point of my birthday party. I heard that cello voice: 'Well now, Georgie-Porgie . . .' Mother, who knew about that awful jingle, was teasing me – as she often liked to do. Then I heard her again, a voice in the shadows, speaking Shakespeare:
>
> 'These antique fables apprehend,
> More than cool reason ever comprehends.'

The quotation – spoken consolingly – came from her choice of a primer when she was first teaching me to read.

And now she was holding me in one of her looks. Some of these could be quite terrible.

> 'The lunatic, the lover, and the poet
> Are of imagination all compact.'

Those great shining eyes looked dark by the light of the eight small candles. I can remember now what I was thinking. I thought how green those eyes looked when it was sunny.

Then – all tenderness, as if she was speaking from a great distance

> 'A lovely boy, stol'n from an Indian king,
> Whoever had so sweet a changeling . . .'

What did she mean? Was I, indeed, a changeling? (I have in later years been given certain hints . . .)

'That stupid birthday cake,' she said, 'is just another cake; and you'll have all the cakes you want. But the candles are a fairy ring. And you will never again in your whole life have just that number to blow out.'

She was a Sorceress.

'You must puff hard,' she said, 'and you must blow out every one of them. And you must make a wish.'

I puffed very hard. And suddenly the room was dark and my mother had vanished forever.

Sometimes, in the dead watches of the night, it strikes me that of all my mistakes, the greatest was on that birthday just before my mother died, when I forgot to make a wish.

Two days later, she was moved to the Chicago Memorial Hospital where, on 10 May 1924, she died.

Whatever else this extraordinary scene was – Charles Higham calls it a lesson in mortality, though one might be pardoned for thinking it a lesson in theatre – it was certainly designed to ensure that Orson never forgot her. And he never did. It is not an exaggeration to say that from her position deep inside him, she dictated his actions and influenced the course of his life up to his own death, more than sixty years later.

The Canadian Jungian Guy Corneau has written an extremely informative study of the sons of absent fathers, and has identified certain clear patterns of behaviour. In his account of one of his types, the Super-Achievers (or Heroes, as he suggestively calls them; and there can be no doubt that Orson Welles, whatever failures may have shadowed his career, was heroically, almost superhumanly, productive for much of it) he says: 'Mothers of heroes are not generally affectionate or accommodating as mothers; in fact, they're more likely to be tough no-nonsense types, who are so proud of their off-spring that they try to make them into divine beings. The young hero thus finds himself trapped in his heart of hearts, by the desire to please his mother, to fulfil her ambitions. He tries to satisfy the ambitions of his real mother, then, very soon, he starts aiming to satisfy the highest demands of his society, business, social group, or university . . . he lives for the approval of others. So that every one will love and appreciate him, he performs the most difficult exploits.'

Kenneth Tynan, in one of several profiles of Welles, wrote that 'a perceptive American director once suggested to me that Orson reached a state of perfect self-fulfilment just before his mother's death, and that he has been trying to recapture it ever since'. That certainly is what Welles said, on many occasions. His mother's death was the end of the idyll. It seems that the truth, as it usually is, was considerably more complicated. Welles's first nine years – the years with Mother – were certainly idyllic in the sense that he had her undivided attention, especially in the last five years, with his brother exiled and his father dismissed. But there was nothing relaxing about this attention. It was a focus full of demand: he was expected, required, in fact, to be intelligent, amusing, considerate, sympathetic, grown-up – and to play the piano very well indeed.

Welles and his biographers have all made much of the fact that as soon as his mother died, out of grief he gave up playing the piano (and, it is implied, a promising career). The truth seems to be, however, that he couldn't wait to give up a hated task for which he showed no particular aptitude. Relieved of the task, he carried the guilt around with him for the rest of life; the guilt of never quite having done well enough. Now, in theory, he was free to do as he pleased; his easy-going dad wouldn't force him to do anything he didn't want to. Except that, in a further complication typical of a life in which nothing was ever simple, he now had two fathers. The next phase of his life was dominated by the struggle for power between these two men, who formed an uneasy relationship in the aftermath of the death of the woman they had both loved so unsatisfactorily, to the extent of moving in together, and then going on holiday together to Europe. Orson, meanwhile, was sent to stay with a family friend, Dudley Crafts Watson, a notable educationalist and father of several lively children. Perhaps Dr Bernstein and Dick Welles were trying to restore him to the normal life of a child. If so, it was a question of too little, too late.

Shortly after his mother's death, at Hillside Farm, Syosset, on Long Island, Orson Welles discovered sex. Playing nurses and doctors with the Crafts Watson children, he told Barbara Leaming, he was deflowered. Welles talked a lot to Mrs Leaming about his sex life and she gamely reports what he told her. These are delicate matters upon which it is very difficult to secure reliable evidence; as sex researchers have discovered, pretty well everyone has a motive to lie, or at the very least exaggerate, in one direction or the other, about their sexual activities. At any rate, Welles said that he was deflowered at the age of nine, a couple of weeks after his mother's death. It sounds a very agreeable and friendly initiation; consolatory, perhaps. There is no record of Welles's response to the loss of his mother, except for Maurice Bernstein chiding him for not being more demonstrative in his grief. 'It wasn't that I didn't love my mother; I didn't love her the way HE did.' Bernstein was shattered by her death, piously acquiring her possessions. He redoubled his attentions to Orson. 'I WAS my mother,' Welles said, 'and I kept the flame.' More guilt; and more pressure to do something, or be something, extraordinary.

There was the matter of his education to be considered. Beatrice's regime had left Welles, like *Hamlet*, full of quotations, knowing the high points of the poetic literature, more by sound than by sense, and able to hold forth on any subject without pausing, hesitation or repetition; also, it has to be said, without much thought. Welles later modestly disavowed the delightful claims made for him – that at seven he knew *King Lear* by heart ('er, no, didn't touch *Lear* till later'), at eight he had written *A Universal History of the Drama*, at ten a critique of *Also Sprach Zarathustra* – but he was quite unusually quick to learn, a sharp magpie, picking up brightly coloured fragments of language and information, and arranging them into impressive little orations. What he lacked entirely were any structured habits of mind or behaviour. His two fathers, Dadda and Dick, had different ambitions for him – Maurice Bernstein wanting him to be a living memorial to his mother's greatness, a creative genius and intellectual giant – Dick Welles hoping that he would develop into an amusing sort of journalist. To that end he gave him a typewriter, and, discovering that he had some facility as an artist, tried to push him into the notion of being a cartoonist.

Both men must therefore have been gratified by the headline that appeared in *The Madison Journal* in February 1926: CARTOONIST, ACTOR, POET – AND ONLY 10. Orson had been sent to the Washington School – his first – in Madison; Dr Bernstein had connections there. The piece is Welles's first meeting with the press, and it sets the pattern for all the many, many subsequent encounters. Detailing his achievements, which include oil painting, acting in, writing and directing plays, composing and reciting epic verse, and editing a summer camp paper – *The Indianola Trail* – the anonymous writer whips his story up to a pitch of fervour that verges on self-parody; the claim that Welles held his fellow campers spellbound for three or four hours at a time with his epic poetry makes one doubt the veracity of much of the rest. Orson, the writer maintains, was 'already attracting the attention of some of the greatest literary men in the country' without substantiating it; he was definitely attracting the attention of Dr Frederick G. Mueller, psychologist of Madison State University, and friend of Maurice Bernstein.

Mueller had met the boy at summer camp and had proposed a series of tests on his obviously formidable intellect. The results were somewhat inconclusive, baffling Mueller and his fellow researchers: they detected 'a profound dissociation of ideas'. This seems to be another way of saying that he said whatever came into his head: a rich selection, no doubt, of magpie scraps produced in his mother's drawing room, to enthusiastic applause. He was precocious – verbally, not intellectually; and he was not prodigious. Perhaps the most dangerous thing that can happen to precocity is acclaim – dangerous because the precocious behaviour, confirmed as successful, will be endlessly reproduced. What was startling about ten-year-old Orson was his assurance; his personality, as one might say. He was phenomenal not in what he said or what he did, but in what he was. This process was well underway by the time of CARTOONIST, ACTOR, POET AND ONLY 10. 'The unceasing roar of appreciation from everybody when I was a child', of which Welles spoke years later to Leslie Megahey in interviews for the BBC, seemed to confirm his worth for him – despite the inner voice from his late mother telling him that he was not doing nearly well enough.

The sessions with Dr Mueller came to an abrupt end, Welles told Mrs Leaming, when that distinguished academic attempted to seduce him. Welles escaped out of the window. This is a significant revelation, impossible to evaluate objectively. Its interest is that it is the first of many claims made by Welles to have been, from a very early age, sexually interfered with by men. In his conversations with Barbara Leaming, he passes it off as all in good fun, and he seems in his stories always to escape, either by simply leaving the room, or by some witty ploy, with his honour intact. Nowadays, in the 1990s, such claims no longer seem so amusing. This is something quite different from playing doctors and nurses with your contemporaries. He tells Mrs Leaming another droll story of that kind: drawn into a circle of sexual dabbling under the leadership of a certain forceful girl, they are all discovered in flagrante delicto by her mother, who immediately blames Welles, his verbal precocity having associated him in her mind with Leopold and Loeb, the proto-Nietzschean murderers brought to trial in Chicago not long before. Very funny, and very likely. But to be approached sexually by an adult man, the same age as your father, must have a very different impact on you. No matter how fast-talking and apparently assured, no ten-year-old simply makes an Errol Flynn-like getaway from a fate worse than death, and then has a good laugh about it afterwards.

A ten-year-old, confused by having two fathers, neither of whom is entirely satisfactory – the real one a drifting alcoholic, the other a cloying old fuss-budget with a somewhat religious attitude to one's recently deceased mother – may be on the look-out for other, better fathers, and in so doing may offer himself as vulnerably in need of protection. He may even become aware of the fact that he is sexually attractive to certain older men, and, playing with fire, may use his sexuality to secure their interest. He may, alternatively, want their sexual attention, but be frightened from accepting it at the last moment. Or he may accept their attentions, and later claim that he had avoided them. Finally, if he is simply very unlucky, he may find himself again and again in situations where men force themselves on him. Whichever of these is true, it is remarkable how often Orson Welles reports himself as an object of homosexual desire. 'From my earliest years, I was the Lily Langtry of the older homosexual set. Everybody wanted me.' The young Welles was not a beautiful child, being decidedly fat and rather pugnacious of expression; but he had, and would never lose, when he desired to command it, a seductive charm which could get him most of what he wanted. Perhaps what he wanted above all was to be wanted. This area of sexual ambiguity persists throughout the early part of Welles's life, striking a note of considerable complexity.

No doubt sensing that the boy was developing out of their control, Maurice Bernstein and Dick Welles decided to remove him from the Washington School, Madison – where he had, in fact, been doing rather well scholastically, taking giant strides in what had hitherto been his worst subject, arithmetic – and submit him to the rigorous attentions of Noble Hill at the Todd School for Boys. Dick Welles had been vaguely threatening whenever he misbehaved to send him to Todd – where Richard Junior had been knocked into shape, until they threw him out – while Dr Bernstein entertained equally vague ideas of nurturing his artistic impulses; Todd had a reputation for being strong on music. The nature of what they had in mind may be deduced from the fact that their first choice of school had been Northwestern Military Academy at Lake Geneva. How different might the history of twentieth-century warfare have been had they sùcceeded. According to Dudley Crafts Watson, it was only with some difficulty that they got Orson admitted to Todd; no doubt the memory of the expelled Richard Junior was still fresh, and the staff desired no repetition of that experience. Once Orson was accepted, however, there was great relief among the unofficial committee masterminding his development: 'the school did to him,' wrote Watson, 'what none of the rest of us could.'

CHAPTER THREE

Todd

TODD WAS not quite what they had expected, however. In 1926, when Welles was enrolled, the school was undergoing a subtle change. The Christ-like Noble had decided to hand the reins over to his son, Roger, whom he summoned from a career in advertising to take his place on the staff and prepare himself for the headmastership. Lacking any academic qualifications whatever, Roger obeyed, joining the school as games teacher. In 1921, Noble Hill drew up an agreement handing over ownership of the school to his son, while remaining headmaster; by the time Welles arrived, Todd was evolving quite significantly into radical directions. Roger Hill proved to be an inspired and innovative educator, and Welles found himself in surroundings as congenial to his natural gifts as could have been devised. From being a sort of refined borstal, the school was becoming an establishment not unlike Dartington Hall in England, or Summerhill in Scotland. The ground had in fact been laid by Noble Hill. Once he had secured his authority ('thus with a single blow had I crushed a rebellion and established my dictatorship') he had already introduced a number of enlightened elements into school policy: interschool athletics were abhorred, for example, competition being regarded as unhealthy; every boy was automatically a member of the Literary Society, whose magazine, *The Society Echo*, was edited in rotation by the members. Central to Noble's philosophy was the notion that, in his resounding phrase, 'responsibility is the great educator'. Thus it was that the school's intake ended at tenth grade, making the last two years seniors at fifteen and sixteen – and 'seniority brings responsibility'. Once again Welles found himself in an environment in which childhood as sentimentally conceived was not encouraged.

Building on these notions, Roger Hill gently transformed his stern father's pedagogic principles, till, without knowing where he was going, he had created a school which educated without appearing to do so. His originality sprang from innocence of academic method, and a hatred of its self-importance. 'When, by accident of birth, I became Headmaster of a great school,' he wrote,

'I attempted to cover my shame through some graduate Education courses at Chicago University. How else could I face my peers in meetings of the Private Schools Association? But once I learned to talk their jargon, I found I didn't want to . . . the Association had a predominantly military membership. Many of these institutions were mere reform schools for the rich . . . could I spend years in this job without becoming equally bumptious, overweening? Headmasters are big frogs in small puddles. They constantly speak down ex cathedra.' He carved in the lid of his desk the phrase GOD'S BODYKINS, MAN, the beginning of Hamlet's remark: 'Use every man after his desert and who should 'scape whipping?' defining his own school in the brochure as a place where 'one hundred boys (no more, such is the limit of intimacy) live a joyous communal existence with twenty-two folk called teachers whose birthdays have mounted a bit but whose zest for life has not dimmed; whose sense of humor is intact, and whose feeling of importance and dignity is (Allah be praised) not predominant.'

The man who had flunked his degree at college proposed an approach based not on examinations but on practical experience: theory deduced, if at all, from practice, not the other way round. It was his conviction that doing was the best way of learning, and that his pupils were not merely in transit to adulthood but fully alive and complicated human beings, needing neither to be put in their places nor to be patronised. 'Boyhood is not a preparation for life. It is life itself in one of its most glorious aspects. Text-book training is a part of this life but only a part . . . at Todd we "expose" our boys to opportunities for expression of any inner urge . . . in each one of these the standards must be kept up – way up. Let the boy hitch his wagon to a star. He'll never rise unless he tries . . . modern youth receives too few of the first-hand experiences their forefathers knew. In their place we have substituted the second-hand ones of the bleachers, the movies and – yes, even the text book. But life isn't a matter of reciting things. It's a matter of thinking things; doing things. At Todd we offer boys this chance.'

It was a standing joke in the school that Roger Hill's personal enthusiasms would quickly become part of the curriculum. 'I wonder what new hobby Skipper has that will be GOOD-FOR-THE-BOYS?' But since his passions were all boyish ones, they met with general approval, and were eagerly entered into. He liked flying, so he built an airport at Todd; he liked theatre, so Todd had a theatre. He was fond of dogs, so he set up a kennel. The children learned everything about breeding and training dogs;

they learned the rudiments of veterinary medicine; they even sold dogs to local people from nearby Woodstock. Noble Hill had had a rather different view, but he seems to have accepted his son's innovations. He was still headmaster, still wore his starched, stiff collars, addressed assembly and complained to the boys about the amount of shoe polish that they used. He was perceived as a kindly, harmless old party; whereas Roger – 'Skipper', after his yacht – was simply idolised by his pupils. Handsome, sporty, democratic, and married to Hortense ('Horty') whom he loved with unashamedly public desire and devotion, he was every boy's ideal elder brother. 'The adolescent's adolescent', Hascy Tarbox, one of them, later said.

Welles joined the school after term had begun, and was, unusually, formally welcomed by the Hills. He created a stir from the beginning. 'Other students stuck their head round the corner to see what kind of a celebrity had arrived.' Dr Bernstein (not his father; Dick Welles, perhaps feeling guilty, hardly ever came to Todd) brought Orson to Todd, nervously accompanying him as the boy was shown round the various facilities. Coming to the theatre, Orson is alleged to have protested at its shortcomings. 'But Orson,' said Bernstein, 'if everything was perfect you wouldn't need to change it. Now you can make it over any way you want to. They've promised me that.' And with this surely false promise, he departed, leaving him in the hands of Roger Hill. He and Welles fell for each other almost on sight. 'I fell in love with Roger Hill. I tried to find a way to capture the attention of this fascinating man who fascinates me tonight as much as he did the first day I laid eyes on him,' said Welles in the sixties, in a chat show entitled *An Evening with Orson Welles*. 'He has never ceased to be my idea of who I would like to be.' Roger was, indeed, the father that Welles desperately wanted: strong but not threatening, trustworthy without being dully predictable, many-layered but not complicated. Neither Welles's actual father, amusing but unreliable and emotionally exhausting, nor Dadda, fussing, fretting, loving but leech-like, fitted the bill. In his own phrase, 'a semi-orphan with a surplus of foster parents even before I went to Todd,' he knew that this was the one. As Barbara Leaming tells it, he set about seducing Hill. Seduction was his natural instinct, and he made his overtures on several fronts. Obviously he attempted a sexual seduction. 'I'm the boy you could have had,' he told Hill years later. When that yielded no results, he tried another tack. Only four weeks after his arrival, he appeared in a Hallowe'en concert with a magic act of such ambitiousness that, almost inevitably, it fell apart. The magician did not, however. He held the stage while everything went wrong, engaging the audience with banter and bluster so effective and surprising that he emerged from the experience with a reputation. The person whom he crucially wished to impress – Skipper – was stunned.

'We all recognised almost immediately that Orson was someone very different.' John C. Dexter, on whom had fallen the distinction of being his room-mate, had never met another child like him. Welles arrived with several suitcases and a large steamer trunk full of make-up, wigs, capes, magic equipment, candles, flashlights and assorted stage wear. 'I was informed before he was unpacked that he had been born in it, on stage. He enquired into my knowledge of the theatre, which was nil, and proceeded to relate what a wonderful medium it was.' Switching the lights off he retired into the bathroom, reappearing with a candle, hunchbacked and gruesomely made-up. 'Who am I?' he demanded, to which Dexter had 'a negative reply'. Not for long. His night classes had begun. 'We all had to bathe then change into clean night clothes and lights out at nine (controlled by the dorm marm). Then the Welles little theatre would begin.' After several months, with deep bags under his eyes, Dexter requested a transfer. Welles thereafter had a room of his own, a thing unheard of. In it he would burn incense, and speak, as he often did, of the Mysteries of the East. There, too, he kept a pastel-tinted photograph of his mother. 'He was not one of us,' said Hascy Tarbox, another student. 'Not part of the human zoo.'

Hortense Hill kept a cooler head than her husband. 'When I first saw him at ten years old he was dressed as Sherlock Holmes. I thought he was a cute little round-faced boy. As I got to know him more and found out how demanding he was, I learned how much of a problem it was going to be just to keep him a little bit under.' Welles, a regular visitor to the Hills' house almost from the beginning, at first saw Hortense as a threat to his relationship with Roger; then, under the influence of Horty's practical kindness, and aware – as everybody inevitably was – of their indivisibility, he formed a double attachment to them. Roger was all energy, enthusiasm, optimism: 'he had a kind of youth that I never had,' Welles later said. 'He was always younger than I was.' Hortense was shrewder and, perhaps, deeper. 'Of everyone I've known, she was the most truly passionate. Other great and good souls may be described as warm, or warm-hearted. That's too tepid sounding for Hortense. Warm is a word for comfort or consolation. The word for her is HEAT. Fire.' Arriving at Todd, Welles had expected a spell of penal servitude. Instead he found his first real home, with a perfectly balanced and deeply committed pair of proto-parents. 'It's that Christian marriage we're all supposed to believe in,' Welles told Barbara Leaming. Roger Hill, writing after his wife's death, offered this utterly characteristic observation: 'What's the formula? OPPOSITENESS! POLARITY! The magnetic pull of the negative for the positive . . . a Kiss-Me-Kate alliance . . . sure there are fights. Otherwise, how dull . . . opposites in every way except a shared appetite for life. Is this the polarity that puts the magic in our lives? Certainly,' he concluded, aged ninety-three, 'it is the basis for healthy sex.' Here, for the first time in Welles's life, was a model of normal behaviour to which he could respond.

The idyll was not without shadow, however. 'Orson could talk a good talk,' said Joanne, the Hills' eldest daughter. 'The minute my mother and father listened to him they were fascinated. I was furious. It didn't seem right the amount of attention he got.' Joanne and her sister were outraged by the cuckoo that had suddenly appeared in the nest. 'He didn't look or feel like a twelve-year-old,' said the final member of the family, Hascy Tarbox, like Welles a semi-orphan, similarly taken under the Hills' wings. Hitherto he had been considered something of a prodigy. 'Hascy was as gifted as his schoolmate, Orson, and could have found predictable fame in many fields, acting, singing, writing, painting.' But now, like everyone else, he played second fiddle to the new arrival. Roger became obsessed by Welles, and remained so till the day, some years after Welles's own death, that he died. 'I knew he was going to be a great man, and I tried to structure a life for him at Todd that wouldn't impede his brilliance at all.' Roger Hill's Todd School provided the hothouse in which Orson Welles's exotic talents bloomed. It was a stroke of destiny that put that boy into that school at that moment. 'It was either the best thing or the worst thing that ever happened to him,' according to Hascy Tarbox, 'if he'd gone to somewhere sensible like West Point Military Academy he would have had all that genius nonsense knocked out of him.' Which is as pithy an assessment of the effect of Todd on Orson Welles as could be asked for.

The effect of Orson Welles on Todd was limited, but within

those limits, overwhelming. Because, with the approval and protection of Roger and Hortense Hill, he only participated in those areas of the school's life that interested him, life in general went on pretty much as it had done; but his presence was a highly visible one, since he commandeered all the most public activities: the theatre, the literary society, the school magazine. From an early stage in his school career, he was in control of what might be described as the media. The rest of the school population seem to have taken it lying down.

He did take lessons in the ordinary way, up to a point; but he was not a co-operative student. 'I attacked the textbooks rather than mastered them. I led student revolutions – comic ones.' The teachers that Roger Hill had assembled around him were outstandingly gifted, and, as he made sure, lacking in pomposity, but they were not always able to see the amusing side of these comic revolutions of Welles. He made it his life's work to catch them out. In any area of knowledge where he had some expertise, he was unrelenting. He had become fascinated by Egyptology, but was not an admirer of the works of the leading American authority, the Chicago-based scholar, James H. Breasted. Todd's history teacher revered Breasted. Welles set himself to destroy him, and in class after class, bombarded the unhappy man with evidence supposedly refuting the great scholar. Similarly, in English lessons, he tormented the instructor 'if he even so much as dangled a participle', according to John C. Dexter. Eventually, the instructor resigned. Hill never chastised Welles for these activities. Once, in fact, he publicly endorsed them; trying to catch the teachers out, he said, made the students do a great deal of extra-curricular work, which was all to the good. Complaints from persecuted members of staff were rebuffed by the Hills on the grounds that Welles was a special case, requiring special treatment. 'It was MADNESS!' roared Hascy Tarbox, sixty years later. Nanette Hendrickson tersely reported that 'he had a beautiful voice, a lot of talent, but he was not easy as a person'. She was speaking at the time of his death, of course, and was baffled by the fact that the famous school for which she and her husband had worked all their lives had become simply a small detail in the biography of Orson Welles. Coach Tony Roskie, second only to Skipper Hill as a campus hero, was equally tightlipped: 'He was a good kid, but he wasn't the only one. The school didn't revolve around him.'

His relations with his fellow students seem not to have been of the best, a situation that could only have been exacerbated by his powerful protectors. He was known as a p.c.: privileged character. An air of mutual suspicion seems to have prevailed. There may be some truth in Maurice Bernstein's later remark that 'Orson really looked up to other children. He didn't know how to behave among them and could not join in their childish pleasures. They mystified him, even scared him.' But the effect of this anxiety was to make him arrogant and separate. His one friend was Paul Guggenheim, 'the second genius in Todd's class of 1931', wrote Roger Hill. 'Opposites in every way, theirs was a symbiosis.' Having scored a public hit with his short story after Poe 'The Ingrown Toenail', 'Guggie' was chosen by Skipper to be Welles's best friend. 'I became a man of importance, particularly one worthy of the company of Orson. All the other boys looked on us as VIPs – socially, we were carried around on cotton wool.' They swaggered about like feudal knights, exacting tithes from the other boys' food parcels from home, demanding and getting their share of the other boys' fruit and vegetable supplements. Welles led, Guggie followed. Orson even exacted his feudal dues from Guggenheim; the chocolate that his room-mate got from his Swiss father was generally, and without permission, consumed by Orson, who took pleasure in eating it in front of its rightful owners while he watched them playing football – a game (like most games) he refrained from engaging in. His only sport was fencing, and that for the obvious reason: it had some application to the stage.

When Orson and Guggie were alone together, they discussed philosophy and poetry; or rather, Orson discussed philosophy and poetry. 'Orson was distressed that I seemed to be very logical and not given to appreciating poetry or mythology. He said: "you are an Aristotelian, I'm going to make a Platonist out of you if it kills me." ' He recited to Guggenheim a poem by Lin Yutang that he claimed summed up his personal philosophy:

Parents when a child is born
Hope for it to be intelligent
But I through intelligence having ruined my whole life
Only hope the child will prove innocent of correction, ignorant
and stupid.
He will then crown a long and successful career
By becoming a cabinet minister.

Throughout his life, Welles maintained an implacable opposition to logical thought, preferring to speak in gnomically resonant phrases that he would refuse to explain. There is a curious tension in this, since his was not a poetic nature, nor was he able or willing to propound any coherent vision. He was, in fact, a logical thinker who refused to think logically, in love with the sound of poetry, addicted to paradox and wit, but never with the objective of expressing anything precise. He preferred even as a child, on this evidence, to create an atmosphere of thought and meaning without really saying anything. Jean Clay, interviewing him in the sixties, ran up against a brick wall when he tried to probe him a little. 'Welles does not want to explain himself. When I asked him about one of his sibylline remarks, "Picasso is a son of the sun; I am a son of the moon", he became angry. "I won't answer. No discussions. I haven't got time. It doesn't interest me." ' He had the habits of mind of someone who has been expected to talk coherently before he has anything coherent to say.

Like bright twelve- and thirteen-year-olds anywhere, at any time, young Orson and young Guggie were enthralled by the feeling that they had discovered truths hitherto obscured. 'Our philosophic discussion always reminded me of Raphael's Academy.' They sat in the front pews of the Presbyterian Church every Sunday, snickering and whispering over their copy of *The Bab Ballads*. Again, extraordinarily, no reproach or penalty was forthcoming. Welles's enthusiasm for mythology and poetry clearly did not extend to the sphere of religion.

Guggenheim managed to maintain his friendship with Welles and still be part of the main life of the school. He was a sportsman, a musician, a mathematician. Son of a famous doctor, a distinguished doctor himself now, he had a strong feeling at the time that part of Welles's apartness was to do with sexual complication. He always refused to be Guggenheim's room-mate. 'I always had the feeling that he was bi-sexual, that he didn't trust himself in the immediate vicinity of a friend.' In his first year of high school, Welles related a dream to Guggenheim: he approached a castle in the shape of the Tower of Babel, with a winding spiral staircase which he ascended. On every floor, in every single room, he was greeted with the same sight – a dead man with arms folded across his chest, covered in newspaper, with an unlit cigar in his mouth. Going up to another floor, he would find the identical scene, all the way to the top. After this dream Welles became depressed, stopped talking to anybody; his only contact with the school was Paul – who had to report regularly to Skipper about him: what he was thinking, what he was doing. He carried on with his schoolwork, but cut himself off socially from everyone. 'He told me that his dream made it very clear to him that he had committed "the unpardonable sin". What, he never said – somehow I had the feeling that this had to do with homosexual activity.'

The perpendicular cigar – its phallic associations a commonplace of Freudian dream interpretation – suggests some kind of a rite-of-passage dream; a young man becoming aware of his masculine potency for the first time. The assumption of masculinity predicates the death, symbolically, of the father: which the dream also contains. On the face of it, the dream's central figure is a dead parent – a cigar-smoking adult (Welles's father was not only a heavy smoker, he had a cigar named after him); the sin might then be patricide. Welles told Bogdanovich: 'I've had that recurring dream since I was about 12 – that I murdered somebody and buried him under the floorboards. I wake up and say "Where did I do it?" ' Welles's father was still alive, but Orson may have felt that he symbolically slew him, not once but twice: by in effect adopting Roger Hill as his preferred father, but also, earlier, by siding with his mother, who, on her deathbed, as her parting gesture had sowed a seed of doubt as to Dick's paternity: 'was I a changeling?' No doubt his various guilts merged, as they so often do, into one nameless guilt; whatever its source, it never left him. He scarcely knew an untroubled night till the day he died.

This dark inner world of Welles appears in sharp contrast to the bustling utopia all around him. Set in forty acres of woodland, Todd was a self-contained world, with its own shops, at which every boy had his own cheque account, its printing press, its forge, even its farm. A visiting journalist rhapsodised: 'Todd is the most complete laboratory for self-expression to be found in the land.' After describing the print shop and the music building, he enters the manual shop where a group was building 'an amazingly authentic stage-coach for use in a Western movie they were producing'. Another group was manning the rabbit hutches; yet another rehearsing a play that had been written and planned by a student: 'in the paint shop the boy artist in charge informed me that the flats and boxes which were getting a final splatter coat were "not planned for realism but for symbolic impressionism through the use of mass and line". I hoped my gasp was not too audible to the lad.' It is tempting, and by no means improbable, to think that boy was Orson Welles. But it could have been a lot of other boys. Todd bred them like that.

Only one boy, however, was in charge in the theatre. 'The theatre was totally Orson's,' said Hascy. 'It was a one-man band.' This was Orson's real world: the theatre, refuge of all who feel themselves not to be entirely part of the human race. He took it by the scruff of its neck, and made it into his own special arena. Not immediately, of course. It had flourished for many years before he arrived, the creation of the stage-struck Roger Hill. Like everything else at Todd, it was spread across the whole school, from ages six to sixteen, divided up into separate companies: the Todd Troupers, the Junior Troupers, the Learn Pigeons, the Tiny Troupers, the Slap Stick Club, and the racy Paint and Powder Club (Saturday night entertainments). It was entirely unsupervised by faculty members, the only central directive being that 'our activities are genuine, not artificial. Our standards in these activities are professional, not sentimental. Our viewpoint on childhood is realistic, not maudlin. Our classroom pedagogy relies on mental discipline, not ego building . . . our TODD TROUPERS take to the road to perform for audiences who have paid for tickets and will pay again only if they have been entertained.' Responsibility the great educator.

When Orson arrived at Todd, the school was famous for its musical comedies. They were cashing in on a theatrical aberration of the time: all-male casts of collegians that travelled as girlie shows. 'Soon a whole country was finding hilarity in chorus lines of bony-kneed transvestites kicking up hairy legs.' Roger Hill wrote the lyrics and the book; the music teacher, Carl Hendrickson, wrote the songs. *Finesse the Queen* was their offering for 1926. Orson put himself forward. 'The chubby 11-year-old was just the size and shape for the chorus. Unthinkable, once you had talked to him. The child had an adult presence even then. Also, believe it or not, the same VOICE now recognisable the world over as WELLES.' (Roger Hill, though the identification is no doubt redundant.) Orson was cast as leading man, as well as supervising the make-up of his leading lady, John C. Dexter. 'When he finished with me he kissed me, said he couldn't help it, but I turned out so good. He had a crush on me every time we did that show.' Quite right too; he looks quite lovely in the production photographs. As for the chorus girls: 'Yes, They're Boys – Real Ones, too. This same group won the 85-pound State Basketball Championship.' Orson surveys them wolfishly.

His next role was en travesti, but altogether more serious: he played (despite that VOICE, as Roger Hill would say) the Virgin

Mary in the Nativity play, one of a sequence of roles with biblical overtones. Next was Judas Iscariot in *The Dust of the Road*, followed by Christ in *The Servant of the House*. This is an unusual, perhaps a unique, hat-trick, though to be scrupulously accurate, the character in that very rum piece, *The Servant of the House*, is never specifically identified as Jesus, posing as he does as an English butler rather coyly named Manson (Man's Son). 'Mystic, Ibsenic, Maeterlinckian, symbolic, morality-wise, conscientious, talky, didactic, preachy, at times impressive, and enormously tedious', as Alan Dale wrote, it was not obvious matter for schoolchildren. In this enterprising repertory, Welles seems invariably to have played the leading role: in the musical *It Won't Be Long Now* – like *Finesse the Queen* a transcontinental, transoceanic extravaganza – he plays Jim Bailey, 'a pal with troubles of his own'; in *Wings over Europe* (which he designed, as he did most of the shows) he was Francis Lightfoot, a genius, who discovers how to harness the power of the atom; the British government's greedy response makes him resolve to blow the earth to bits. He is killed before this can happen; the play ends, ominously, with reports of A-bomb planes passing over London. The effect of this piece, a small sensation on Broadway the very year in which the Todd Troupers played it, must have been remarkable with a cast of young teenagers, starring a twelve-year-old as the destructive genius.

At the 1928 commencement, he appeared as The Wife in a short play by William de Mille with a – for him – prophetic title: *Food: A Tragedy of the Future*. Interestingly, at this same event there was a programme of music put on by the music department and among the items (including a Mozart minuet played by Paul Guggenheim) was a Tarantella for piano by Miller, played by Orson. Now pretty well any tarantella is likely to be difficult to play, so it would appear that his abandonment of the piano was not quite as complete as he later chose to remember. It was a year or two before he started directing the Troupers, but he worked with all the other groups. Being directed by him was a fairly terrifying experience, in which democratic consultation was unknown, and ordinary politeness a luxury. 'It was Simon Legree. He never said anything about interpretation. If you had a lead, you did exactly as you were told. He choreographed everything: that's your mark. Don't move. Don't wriggle. He was a martinet. The result,' adds Hascy Tarbox, 'was extraordinary theatre. His vitality swept you away. He drilled us and we became a magnificently choreographed company.' He threw out lines that meant little to the story or the plot, or mumbled insignificant ones, and trained his tiny troupers to 'speak over him but always keep the plot moving', according to John Dexter. 'I can remember a number of times in rehearsal he would stop and explain to one and all the plot, the feeling he wanted, the mood, speed, etc. How he knew it I don't know.'

It is indeed a puzzle. Here Welles is unquestionably prodigious. To be a remarkable actor at the age of twelve is unusual, but not unheard of. To be a director, especially a director in this mould, a Reinhardt, or a Guthrie, a virtuoso, controlling and organising large groups, shaping and orchestrating texts, is entirely unheard of at this age. The most startling thing, the almost monstrous element, is the degree of authority it requires: how does a twelve- or thirteen-year-old acquire that? There have been infant conductors – a Pierino Gamba, say – directing the London Symphony Orchestra at that age. But the LSO is a body of trained musicians: as long as Gamba knew what he wanted, they would follow him. Welles was dealing with kids, not merely untrained but not necessarily even talented. He was their own age, yet they took it, apparently without demur. It can only be because they acknowledged that the results justified it. During his time at Todd, Welles devoted himself to the theatre to such an extent that it almost became a theatre arts degree course – except that he was teacher and pupil, course director and apprentice. He mastered every aspect of production during this time – design, stage management, lighting design, set-building. The campus theatre was a well-equipped two-hundred seater, with a reasonable number of lamps, all on dimmers; a plaster back wall which made possible 'realistic and stunning outdoor effects'; an arras, with a drape setting (the drapes being removable) and a rigging loft equipped with ten sets of lines. He used every aspect to its utmost potential.

He had, at this astonishingly early age, a clear conception of the unifying role of the director, an idea which had not yet taken root in America in practical form. Its first articulate proponent was Edward Gordon Craig, though its lineage can clearly be traced down, through Appia, to Wagner. It flourished in Europe in the work of Brahm, Reinhardt, Copeau. Books were written by or about these men (and of course by their masters, Craig and Appia), and Welles may well have read them, or reviews of them, in, for example, the excellent and well-illustrated *Theatre Arts Monthly*. It is also possible that Orson had seen their work in Europe, when travelling with his father. However he acquired it, at the age of fifteen he had a highly developed notion of a many-pronged assault on the theatre, and was able to write about it with great lucidity: 'The Theatre blends in a common art the talents of the story teller, the poet, the speaker, the singer, the dancer, the composer, the mimic, the artist, the carpenter, and the electrician.' Unlike Craig, of whom this is a liberal paraphrase, he did not name the director as the controlling figure; but it is evident that the blending into a common art must be done by someone, and that someone – even at fifteen – was Welles.

His writing, here and everywhere, was an occasional thing for him; but it is from the start entirely characteristic. In 1928, he was the editor of *Red and White: Tosebo* [= TOdd SEminary for BOys] *Camp Number*: the frontispiece contains a sketch – signed by Welles – of a man carrying a placard that proclaims OUR PLATFORM: A BIGGER, BETTER, SNAPPIER, RED AND WHITE. The first piece is a 'History of Todd' by ORSON WELLES, brisk and clear; then comes 'Item: Senior Literary Society Starts Active Year: "Senior Society has staged some interesting Friday night sessions this fall. Rivalry is keen and some creditable bits of literary work have been produced. Orson Welles's paper of October 19th was the high spot of the term thus far." ' Nothing like editorial impartiality. 'Theatricals' is by Staff Drama Critic, whose tone of voice is oddly familiar. He is reviewing *Sweetheart Town*, at the Woodstock Opera House. One has to remind oneself that it is a thirteen-year-old writing.

'The whole piece was rather loosely put together . . . for instance, *The March of the Wooden Soldiers* was used in a drawing-room setting with no lines either before or after to give it the slightest plausibility. Evidently the producing company had the costumes and figured it was an easy number to stage so in it went. The leads were handled by very competent talent but the chorus work was rather pitiful in spots.' Very strict; a hint perhaps of a note session after one of the young Welles's rehearsals. The Tosebo Camp number 1928 closes with a cartoon, also by the editor, which is in effect the earliest surviving Welles storyboard. 1. Opening two shot, medium close-up; 2. wide shot on boys' backs; 3. close-up on speaker, as other boy disappears, leaving behind only an exclamation mark, a question mark and a puff of dust. His sense of line was highly developed; his father's hopes for him as a cartoonist were not founded on nothing. His confidence leaps off the page. Nothing said is remarkable; nor is it said remarkably. But it is said loud and clear. It expects to be heard.

His journalism went professional that same summer of 1928, while he was staying with Maurice Bernstein in his holiday retreat.

The Highland Park News of 6 July 1928 printed an ominous headline: RAVINIA STARS BEWARE. 'On page eight of this issue,' ran the story, 'we are introducing Orson Welles, our 13-year-old drama critic, cub reporter and what have you . . .' Though the intention is merry, there is something a little disquieting about it. The first article opens in the middle-aged leftover Edwardian style Welles was often to affect in later life.

HITTING THE HIGH NOTES: ORSON WELLES

> 'Cover the opera,' quoth the editor the other evening as he threw down the proof-sheet he had been reading and gave me a professionally 'editorial' look with those beautiful eyes of his. 'Play Ravinia for all it's worth, it's good, interesting news!'
>
> Well, to begin with – there's hardly any opera to write about! Yes, you will remind me that the most reliable of Ravinia's stars have appeared on the stage in costume, that people have flocked to the park, that tickets are on sale at the gate . . . but I will not admit that there has been any real performances as yet, some lovely singing yes, but Ravinia was not half as beautiful last week, as it will be next and the weeks to come.

He goes on in this unlovely vein, revealing how 'Martinelli came near swallowing his moustache which had come off in the heat, or how An Onion [= A. Anian, a leading singer of the day] fell off a stool to the unsuppressed enjoyment of both the audience and singers. But,' he continues, 'I have some dandy jokes planned on the singers for next week, some news that wouldn't get into print otherwise, some verse, I hope some reviews, and – well . . .' He signs off with a prayer that 'both the opera and this column will be improved, I am, Orson Welles.' A familiar sign-off.

The column is so repulsive in tone, it's almost inconceivable that he was asked to repeat it. But he was:

> Last week I insinuated that there had been no real performance of opera in Ravinia and I think I was right.

He goes on to praise the casts of *Lohengrin*, *Manon* and *Trovatore*, reserving his main comment for Montemezzi's Wagnerian verismo opera, *L'amore Dei Tre Re*:

> The incomparable Lazzar! the Mansfield of modern Opera he should be called. If you have gasped when he strangles Fiora and thrilled 'neath the spell of one of America's most glorious

> voices, then I advise you to go to *Fra Diavolo* next week and laugh at the comical hobo who eats spaghetti and does the most convincing murder on the stage with equal artistry.

It is noteworthy that all the specific comment is to do with the acting, not the music. The third column continues the raillery:

> . . . and omitting the accident suffered by Rethberg's 'territory' when a light slithered down from the flys and struck her in the middle of a dramatic area (wherever that is). I would lay down my job and hie myself to the 'eatery' where I would replenish the empty corridors of my bread basket with healthful nourishment. The best I can do is promise a better article next time, and a review of *Fra Diavolo*. Another journalistic tragedy. And so to the printery!

Two ominous signs: he eats when he can't work; and he resorts to that ancient journalistic standby, the column about the impossibility of writing a column. There were two more columns in exactly the same vein. Unpalatable though all this is, it is a passable imitation of what an adult journalist in the same mould might have written, though Welles was perhaps able to be slightly more rebarbative, hiding behind his youth. This is precocity run riot; not a pretty sight. The writing itself is what an exuberant and opinionated thirteen-year-old might jot down in letter form – there are letters of Mozart at the same age which are as bumptious and as callous – but there are few thirteen-year-olds who would commit themselves to newsprint in like vein – few who would want to; even fewer who would be asked to. Maurice Bernstein seems to be behind this: his summer house in Highland Park was near to his beloved Moores and the Crafts Watsons. No doubt a discreet word in the editor's ear had swung it.

When Welles was not with Bernstein (with whom he sometimes travelled; together, in 1927, they took a cruise to Cuba) he was with his father. They too travelled, quite how far and how often it is now impossible to determine; China was on the itinerary at least twice. He later claimed that he led a restlessly peripatetic life with his father, spending part of every year in Shanghai, another part in Jamaica where his father supposedly had a winter residence, at other times flitting from European capital to European capital. The years of wandering are an essential part of the biography of the artist, his meetings with remarkable men, his hidden years. 'I rollicked around my whole childhood,' he told Huw Wheldon.

'What places do you remember most vividly from this early,

globe-trotting period?' asked Kenneth Tynan in 1967. 'Berlin had about three good years, from 1926 onward,' replied Welles (he was then aged eleven to fourteen) 'but the best cities were certainly Budapest and Peking. They had the best talk and the most action right up to the end.' Just how good were Welles's Hungarian and Mandarin, one wonders? To Bazin and the *Cahiers du Cinéma* team he said that he'd seen an enormous number of German stage productions in his childhood, also Russian and French ones; while he told Bogdanovich that he'd seen 'all the great ones, Werner Krauss and Kachalov' (Craig's and Stanislavsky's Hamlet). Then he goes too far: 'this hand that touches you now once touched the hand of Sarah Bernhardt – can you imagine that?' Well barely, since her last stage appearance in America was in 1918 (when Welles was three), and her last onstage appearance anywhere – it was in France – was in 1920. 'The hand I saw was a claw covered with liver spots and liquid white and with the pointy ends of her sleeves glued over the back of it,' he reports, a brilliant and vivid description, as striking when said by Orson Welles as it was when said by Micheál Mac Liammóir, to whom it actually happened.

This little economy with the truth, however, does not discredit all the rest. Dr Bernstein told a journalist that in 1929, he and two other boys went to Europe visiting France, England and Italy. The records of the police in Italian, claimed the not always wholly reliable Dadda, show that Orson was arrested for sleeping in the park and throwing a stunt fit in the streets. There is clear evidence that he was in Munich and possibly Berlin in 1929; he was on a walking tour with the school, sending back to his nurse in Chicago a boisterously boyish card: 'How you'd love it here . . . the beer! Oh, baby!' which is probably what she wanted to hear, not a scene-by-scene account of *Jedermann*. (Later, he reported how he'd been sitting in a Munich beer hall, when some funny little chap in a Charlie Chaplin moustache started to harangue the audience . . . Even Roger Hill, who reports this story, was a little sceptical of Orson's Zelig-like ability to be present at every crucial moment in modern history.)

As often as not, however, Welles and his father would go to Grand Detour. In 1925, the year before Welles went to Todd, Dick had, on an alcoholic whim, bought the admirable Sheffield House Hotel, so glowingly described in its brochure. Evidently Dick's chums, Charles and Lotte Sheffield, who had rebuilt the hotel after it had burnt down at the turn of the century, had had enough; they had been running it for fifteen years. It must have taken some running, too: a sixty-room L-shaped frame building, it had steam heat and indoor plumbing, and boasted a fine restaurant with an excellent cook. There were two waitresses; on Sundays the restaurant pulled in customers from as far as Rockford or Clinton, Iowa. Although not quite what Welles claimed for it – 'America's most exclusive hotel' – it was a splendid place, then surrounded by elms, all of which were wiped out in the 1960s.

Dick approached the business of being a hotelier with unexpected seriousness, sensibly buying the Sheffield General Store; he it was who converted its upper level into the dance hall on whose springy floor Orson danced in the moonlight. He also rented a small unpainted building on River Street and turned it into a giant toy house for Orson, filling it with 'wonderful Chicago-built toys', in the envious words of a contemporary Grand Detourian. Welles liked to claim that his father had bought the hotel because he liked the service, then threw all the guests out. He was also said – by Welles, of course – to have admitted only old music-hall performers as guests; or, alternatively, to have recruited his staff exclusively from vaudevillians. None of this was true: the clientele, actively encouraged, consisted mainly of Chicago artists on their sketching expeditions or casual tourists in the region. The restaurant was frequented by people from miles around; you had to book to be sure of a table. Dick was rarely there; in his absence the hotel was run, profitably and efficiently, by the excellent staff, most of whom he had inherited from the Sheffields. It is entirely possible, none the less, as Orson remembered, that he smoked his own sausages, and that 'you'd wake up in the morning to the sound of the folks in the bake-house and the smells . . .' For Welles Grand Detour was 'one of the Merrie Englands'. He felt that he'd had 'a childhood in the last century from these short summers'. Idyllic though it assuredly was, he remained unable to form any relationship with the people of Grand Detour. Even the man who drove him the four-hour journey to Todd and back in Dick Welles's brand-new, four-door Chevrolet (no *cars*, Orson? Just Daddy's, perhaps) 'never got to know Orson well'.

Dick Welles, on the other hand, seems to have been much liked, and not regarded in the least as eccentric. The only feature of his father's regime worth commenting on was his regular and profound drunkenness. 'Eccentric' is a much more agreeable word than 'drunk'; it is touching of Welles that in order to convince himself of the euphemism, he invented the appropriate eccentricities.

It all ended very suddenly on 28 May 1928. The Chicago artists were sketching in their bad-weather studio over the Landmark restaurant, while the chambermaids were burning some papers in the grate. A few of the burning papers entered the upstairs lumber room; the fire took hold. People poured out of the hotel, including a confused Dick Welles. The building burned to the ground; overnight, someone stole the large boiler from the basement. The next day, Dick Welles left Grand Detour, and never went back. Nor did Orson. Over the years, he marinaded the events of that night, turning them into a charming tragic-comic tale. 'We'd just returned from China, and there was a nice Christmassy fall of snow on the ground the night of the fire,' he wrote in his memoir. The fire actually occurred on 28 May, during the day, and they hadn't been to China that year, nor was Orson present; he was in Highland Park, doling out bad reviews to hapless opera singers. 'The six-mile distance was too great for the Dixon Fire Department which arrived to preside over the smoking ruins of what had been America's most exclusive hotel. At the very last moment, my father (the suspected arsonist) emerged from the flames dressed only in his nightshirt, carrying in one hand an empty parrot cage and in the other, a framed, hand-tinted photograph of a lady in pink tights (an ex-mistress fondly remembered) named Trixi Friganza.' Something stirred at the back of Welles's mind as he wrote this, and he comments on the extraordinary coincidence that both his father's favourite mistress and his mother should have had the same unusual nickname. He does not recall that at the time of the fire he himself had a hand-tinted photograph of that other Trixie, his mother, at his own bedside.

It seems that by this time Dick and Orson were losing each other. Dick would occasionally go to Todd; according to Paul Guggenheim, Orson used to hide from him when he did, saying that he hated him. His drunkenness was impossible to ignore, an unbearable embarrassment in front of his fellow students. So Orson hid. In effect he disowned him. In this he was encouraged by the Hills, who thought him an appalling influence. But Dick in a way disowned Orson, too. Coming unannounced to a performance of *Wings over Europe*, he left before the end of the play, because, Welles told Barbara Leaming, 'he didn't want to admit he was interested in my acting career or some damn thing'. There was nothing Dick Welles could do to bridge the gap between himself and this son whom he so deeply but unusefully loved. For Orson, the theatre,

Todd, and the Hills were his emotional reality. His work on plays continued with unabated intensity. Now – at the age of fourteen – he was designing and directing as well as starring in the Todd Troupers productions. This was a serious business, thanks to Roger Hill's policy. 'I felt that the ordinary audience for school shows was worse than none at all because it consisted of parents and friends who were completely uncritical. So we organised the Todd Troupers and started taking shows out of town. We would rent the Goodman Theatre in Chicago or use some of the suburban movie houses in the area.' Welles also wrote the programmes: 'ANDROCLES AND THE LION: JUNIOR TROUPERS OF TODD together with LEARN PIGEONS PRESENT FOR WOODSTOCK'S WOMEN'S CLUB a special performance of ANDROCLES AND THE LION being an arrangement of the play by G. BERNARD SHAW and staged by ORSON WELLES.' There is an excellent woodcut by Welles on the cover. 'NOTE: A mystery surrounds the author of this delightful satire. Just what is Bernard Shaw, vegetarian, socialist, anti-vivisectionist and Irishman, really driving at? . . . In ANDROCLES AND THE LION, the author flaunts the wormy spots in Caesarism, Paganism and Martyrdom right in our faces. But don't let that worry you. Somewhere in Hertfordshire a blue eye is winking. It is suggested that you wink right back and accept, for this evening at least, the Shavian doctrine of the theatre: "Don't take anything seriously." '

There was nothing makeshift about the productions or the presentation. The good people of Woodstock or the Goodman Theatre's subscribers could count themselves lucky to catch Orson's production of *The Physician in Spite of Himself*, in a full-blown constructivist setting with its naked structure, inclined planes, platforms, wheels, stepladders and stage lights clearly visible, an environment that deliberately forces a playing style of extreme physicality. The set is pretty well a duplicate of Meyerhold's design for *The Magnanimous Cuckold*. But that famous production had been staged only seven years before, in 1922, and on the other side of the world. Its implications had barely been absorbed by the avant-garde of the English-speaking theatre. And here it was, being boldly reproduced by a small boys' school in a small town in the Mid-West of America. Of course the idea was a borrowed one; but Picasso's *mot* about originality is particularly appropriate here: to imitate others is necessary; to imitate oneself is pathetic.

There was, too, a *Julius Caesar*, the entry for the Goodman Theatre Amateur Drama League, hence pared down to sixty minutes. On the evidence of surviving photographs, the design uses the width of the stage but is scenically relatively conventional, the set consisting of boxes shifted around during the action; togas were worn, created from bedsheets the boys stripped from their own beds. Fifteen-year-old Orson played both Antony and Cassius. In the competition, the boys playing these two roles were highly praised, but disqualified because they were evidently older than seventeen, the age limit for entrants. Or so the story goes; certainly a photograph of his Cassius shows him expressionistically intense in his shock wig, with no hint of the schoolboy about him. Welles was evidently very upset to have lost; Dadda Bernstein wrote him a charming note of consolation, containing sentiments that only someone who had never stood on a stage could have expressed: 'even though you did not get the first prize it was worth doing. Applause means little in the long run and not all the things we do that are worth while receive recognition . . . some day when you will be in the eyes of the world doing big things as I know you will, you will look back on this disappointment as having been just a passing experience . . . "Success is in the silence, though fame is in the song." I know your true values and hope to see them grow into fruition. I love you more than all else. Dadda.' Over the years in which Welles sometimes seemed to value the song far above the silence, he never lacked either love or faith.

That summer, in July of 1930, Orson and his father went by sea to Shanghai. Earlier, in the middle of June, he had resumed his column for the *Highland Park News*. No longer music critic for the Festival (after death threats, perhaps?), he had his own chat spot: 'Inklings', with a smart logo (the name of the column being poured out of an ink bottle) designed by himself. The June 30th piece is a vacuous piece of chatter, a word-spinning puff for his editor's forthcoming marriage, replete with middle-aged matrimonial jokes ('All of which goes to show that intelligence and world-wide experience has nothing to do with it. Immunization is impossible! Our brainiest men are acquiring the ball and chain every day. Nothing can be done, Mort has put his foot firmly in the molasses. All we can do is to smile through the tears and yell a hoarse "Congratulations!" ' On July 4th, he announced the Shanghai trip. The column has a new, cunningly fashioned logo showing assorted Chinese heads on a globe over the rim of which a steamer is puffing; there are clouds on the other side; a placard, upside down, says OTHER SIDE OF THE WORLD. At the bottom of this there is a slogan: THE INSIDE DOPE ON CHOP SUEY LANDS.

> More or less (in the manner of the COMING ATTRACTIONS ANNOUNCER of the Talkies) Ladeez and Gentlemen: . . . instead of lingering

> here in HP to prattle weekly – (voice from the gallery: 'weakly is right!' – we are packing up and going far away . . . very, very far away indeed. Even unto the other side of the earth i.e. China and environs – many thousands of miles beneath Central Avenue, to the under-world kingdoms of dog-stew and birds' nest soup . . . we are broadening out, we will write about the East, and we'll spill you the whole business, absolutely everything . . . All the clout, glamour, romance of the Orient will troop in Literary Caravan across the glowing lines of this: your favourite feature of your favourite journal . . . I thank you!!!! (loud sound of escaping steam as we take our bow).

It's school magazine stuff, but fun. The next column, July 11th 1930, describes the journey to Victoria, Vancouver Island, British Columbia, whence the boat departed:

> Dear Readers: We've rattled down out of the cool, clean air of the mountains on to a dry and dusty desert wasteland . . . nothing is particularly desirable today. Gissing would terminate his feverish search for 'where the blue begins' were he here now, for this is where the blue ends, the sky being considerably faded with the heat . . .

Further instalments will come, he says, but fitfully: it takes fourteen days for the mail boat to return.

> We'd write more but there's about a second left for us to get to the gang-plank. And so – Adios!

His slang is more Edwardian, it seems, than 1920s – perhaps because he spends so much time around older people. He seems to want to present himself as an old buffer; an Alexander Woollcott tone prevails. But he paints the scene amusingly, dramatising himself, as he was to do for the rest of his life. He is ever-present between the reader and the subject.

The last column was that of 5 September 1930: headed MIDNIGHT, YELLOW SEA. It is worth quoting at length:

> The heart of the Chinese pirate country: the first day in Nara was an adventurous one to say the least. Nara is picturesque and lovely, one of the most beautiful spots in Japanese Japan and particularly so in the rain. It started to sprinkle just as we left the station in our ricksha and increased in violence as we

rode. There was a thin green mist hanging over everything as we went scurrying through a kind of three-dimensional Japanese print, rattling over little lacquered bridges across willow-bordered streams under huge pines as old as time itself, crunching across temple yards, past age-old pagodas, and on up to the hill to our hotel. The furnishings in our room were typically Nipponese and most fascinating but not sufficiently so to keep us among them, so leaving our Dad to snooze under mosquito netting we stepped out the back entrance and took a walk. It had just stopped raining. You know how lovely it can be right after a summer rain – everything clean and green and glistening? It was like that, just as fragrant as a flower, as warm and wet as the tropics in heaven. The willows wept liquid sunshine into the silver streams, lovely little sacred deer stood in the deep, damp grass, a pilgrim scuffled along the road, his bell tinkling faintly from beneath his great straw coat, and behind the pagodas above everything, there hung a rainbow . . . ! In the park we found an open space in the centre of which was a gayly-curtained platform.

We guessed correctly that it was a temporary stage erected by some company of strolling players. We parted the drapes and peered in. The actors were clustered about a tiny stove eating their supper. They invited us to join in with them and of course we accepted. We shall not forget that meal. How we thanked our lucky stars we had learned to eat with chopsticks! We were the honored guest. Seated in the only chair, we were stuffed with rice, raw fish and 'saki.' And while even our Japanese was more extensive than their English we carried on a successful conversation of three hours' duration entirely with our hands. We taught them a song from a school musical comedy and they instructed us in the art of Oriental theatrical fencing and make-up. It was a truly fascinating experience. Late that afternoon we left, promising to return to their show that evening. We did, but we found ourselves alone in the park. The moving picture industry is hitting the theatrical world even in the East, and it was raining a little. The players laughed long and heartily, and we had tea. We were shocked by their living conditions, their poverty. They told us that they had enough rice for one more day, if no one came the next night . . . They felt hurt when we offered them some money and laughed at our sympathising. They would laugh at death . . . we said goodbye and the last thing we heard as we walked off down the road was the sound of their merry voices singing the American song we had taught them.

It's an authentic cameo, charming and evocative. Naive, pardonably, and still a bit stilted, but the narrative and the images are vivid: the best of his childish writing. The performance is most likely to have been Kabuki, with its mix of music and drama. He must have had occasion to see many varieties of theatre – a whole other world unknown to his contemporaries. If his boyish prose scarcely reflects that, it's hardly surprising, but this Far Eastern journey – and an earlier one, when he was twelve – gave him the certainty that there was a world elsewhere.

Something else his despatches to the *Highland Park News* fail to convey is that he was travelling with a hopeless drunk: his father ('our Dad', snoozing under the mosquito net). This last trip to Shanghai has the air of a farewell voyage: Dick's farewell to travel, to Orson, to life.

It seems that the razing of the Sheffield House Hotel was a psychological blow for Richard Welles. He appears to have done everything he could – the toy house, the smoked sausages – to make it somewhere special for him and his son, away from Todd, away from Maurice Bernstein, away from the theatre, which was sucking Orson in. He would have been only too happy if it had been the theatre he, Dick, loved: vaudeville, musical comedy, the circus. Of all of these he was a connoisseur, known backstage and in the theatre bars. He would take Orson to meet the stars, especially the magicians. Welles said later that love of magic was what bound him and his father together; a curious thought. Magic, both black and white, threads its way through Welles's life and career. He had performed it to delight his mother's guests; he had used it to lasso Roger Hill's affection. It is the theatrical equivalent of fireworks: brilliantly impressive, it leaves nothing behind. It is an end in itself, contentless, inexplicable. It renders the successful practitioner mysterious and powerful, though there is never any doubt in the audience's mind that it is not real. The word trick is significantly central to descriptions of magic. We, the audience, are bamboozled; the magician has got away with something.

Alcoholics are always trying to get away with something, too: hoping – believing – that their condition passes unnoticed; or that it doesn't matter; and, in a brilliant double bind, that if things go wrong, it was only because they were drunk, so that's all right. They didn't mean it or they didn't see it. They, too, are involved in a conjuring act: by taking the magic potion, they make things disappear – the past, the present, the future; pain, complication, loss; the truth. Hey presto! It's gone. So Orson and his father were great fans of magic. There is a story that Richard Welles took Orson backstage to meet Harry Houdini. Orson enthusiastically showed the great conjuror his handkerchief trick, to be told to keep working on it: he must never, ever, perform a trick until he'd practised it in private at least a thousand times. Going back some little while later to show Houdini how much he'd improved, Welles found the great man having a brand new trick demonstrated by its inventor. 'Great,' says Houdini, 'I'll put it in tonight.' A turning point, and a dangerous lesson. Getting away with things is always exciting, of course – until you don't.

Dick Welles was getting away with less and less. Feeling the increasing loss of his favourite son, he cruelly punished his eldest one. Loathing his sullen, uncommunicative namesake, who had continued drifting aimlessly, wandering the country, working as a casual labourer, Dick Welles had conspired with Dr Bernstein to have Richard certified insane (dementia simplex, a form of catatonia, was diagnosed) and imprisoned in the state sanatorium of Kanakee. This terrible act was never alluded to by Orson; when he mentioned his brother at all it was to suggest that he was charmingly eccentric. Various early biographers describe him as a member of a religious cult, and author of a *Life of Jesus*, which must have been something of a family trait, since both Beatrice and Orson have the same pious work attributed to them. These whimsical details mask a grim truth unearthed by Charles Higham: Richard Ives Welles was for ten years – from the age of twenty-five – incarcerated in a lunatic asylum along with four thousand fellow inmates in varying degrees of mental distress, during which time he saw no member of his family except his cousin, Irene Lefkow, appointed guardian in the absence of Richard's father. There is no evidence of his having harmed anyone or caused any breach of the peace; when he was finally released, he followed a slightly erratic career as a social worker, popping up in his brother's life from time to time. His very existence, not to mention his enforced confinement in a state sanatorium when Orson was fifteen years old, can only have weighed darkly on Welles's young heart.

Richard Junior had been expelled from Todd; Dick Welles might have hoped that Orson would be. Treated with contempt when he attempted to visit Orson there, he resorted more and more to the bar-room where, with his ever-open tab, he was everybody's best friend. Orson too discovered this trick, on their first voyage to Shanghai. 'I discovered the magic of money,' he told David Lewin, in an interesting phrase, 'when I crossed the Pacific from China and

Japan to San Francisco at the age of 12. By signing my name on chits for everyone's drinks at the bar, I was able to cause universal happiness. At the end of the trip, my father received a bar bill for $2,700. He said "We've had alcoholics in the family, but no one started at 12." ' That sounds like fun. The replay in 1930 was far from it. This time it was the sheer humiliation of having to replace his father's pants in front of 'the colonial British' with whom he drank. This contrasts horribly with the image of him Orson tried to fashion in his memoir: 'he hoped to be mistaken for one of those he most admired: some sober figure in the world of high finance, and not the idle, hedonistic London clubman he despised – and so closely resembled. He was, in fact, an Edwardian bon vivant. My father wore black spats. His shoes were made for him in London and his hats in Paris. When he travelled by train he carried his own bed linen and a small Persian prayer rug for his feet . . .. as for the spats, they were appreciated by the sort of gentleman who never travelled without his valet, and who had yet to acknowledge that the motor car had already purged the streets of the nuisance of the horse. Spats were mauve, dove gray and even white. That the spats of my father were black should explain why – though his chosen way of life might strike some modern readers as a touch on the flamboyant side – he would be pained to learn that he could never have given such an impression.' The spats were not the problem.

So now, as we all do eventually, Orson had become parent to his parent. He was fifteen years old. The tangle of premature responsibility, guilt and necessary deception held him in its grip for the rest of his life. The consequences for adults of having alcoholic parents have recently been the subject of intensive study. A specialist in this area, Janet Woititz, drew up a list of characteristics of such people: they are strikingly applicable to Orson Welles: 'they guess at what normal behaviour is; they have difficulty following a project through from beginning to end; they lie when it would be just as easy to tell the truth; they judge themselves without mercy; they have difficulty having fun; they take themselves very seriously; they have difficulty with intimate relationships; they overreact to changes over which they have no control; they constantly seek approval and affirmation; they usually feel that they are different to other people; they are super responsible or super irresponsible; they are extremely loyal, even in the face of evidence that the loyalty is undeserved; they are impulsive. They tend to lock themselves into a course of action without giving serious consideration to alternative behaviours or possible consequences. This impulsivity leads to confusion, self-loathing and lack of control over the environment. In addition, they spend an excessive amount of energy clearing up the mess.' Orson Welles, more even than most human beings, was highly individual and not easy to type. It is, however, very interesting that had one drawn up a list of Welles's patterns of behaviour, they might, substituting 'he' for 'they', have looked very like the above. Whatever else he was, Orson Welles was the son of an alcoholic and an absent father. They happened to be the same parent. His mother, though dead, was far from absent. His father, still alive, was, to all intents and purposes, not there. Soon, he would not be there, full stop. And though he lived for another six months, Orson never saw him again. To add to the momentousness of this farewell voyage, Richard Welles staged for Orson a harrowing scene to rival Beatrice's deathbed scene: Dick made him swear solemnly that he wouldn't let them bury him under the ground – he must either be buried at sea or cremated. In case Orson were not sufficiently acquainted with the notion of mortality, Dick spelt out the details.

Small wonder that 'I was, in my childhood, determined to cure myself of childhood, a condition I conceived to be a pestilential handicap.' By 1930, in charge of a child-adult, he was completely cured. He never ceased from that moment on to try to recover the state that he had never really known. When he returned to school, the Hills, hearing of his terrifying journey, made him vow not to see his father again until he had sobered up; in other words, not to see him again, because only death was strong enough to prise him away from the bottle. And that is how it was. Orson behaved as always under pressure: he brazened it out. He gave a talk about his recent travels entitled 'Toilets of the World'. No doubt he had assisted Dick to a great many of them. A paternal connection may have been responsible for his appearance shortly after on the front page of the *Chicago Herald American*. Having dabbled with the suburban press, he was now news in a major regional paper. If it was parental pull that secured this coup, it might have seemed to Dick Welles slightly to have backfired. The piece was written by his friend Ashton Stevens, the paper's drama critic, and one of the most distinguished drama critics in America. Welles always said that the character of Jedediah Leland in *Citizen Kane* was based on Stevens; the *Herald American* was a Hearst paper. The piece he wrote in November 1930 was in his weekly column, and its opening has been widely quoted in articles and books about Welles:

> Given as good an education as will adhere to him at a good college, Orson Welles is as likely as not going to become my favourite actor. True, it will be 4 or 5 years before he has attained his majority and a degree, and I have yet to see him act. But I like the way he handles a difficult situation and to lay my plans long ahead, I am going to put a clipping of this paragraph in my betting book. If Orson is not at least a leading man by the time it has yellowed, I'll never make another prophecy.

Passing over the crucial phrase 'I have yet to see him act', various writers have praised Stevens for his prescience. In the circumstances, this is not so much prescience as clairvoyance. The piece continues:

> This was the difficult situation handled by my young friend. He came into town from his prep school at Woodstock and spent all his money on a matinee. Penniless, hungry, and unable to find either his guardian, the distinguished Dr Bernstein, or the doctor's play-mates, the childless but children-loving Ned Moores, Orson gamely walked into his guardian's club and ordered a meal.
>
> Too young to be a member of the Tavern, and too prosperous looking to be a dinner-snatcher, he caused considerable speculation among the club's employees. Manager Kuhn was sent for. One glance at the youth, who met it with the acknowledging smile of a man of the world and O.K'd Orson to the headwaiter, saying, 'Why that young gentleman's alright; he's the only son of Mr & Mrs Edward Moore.'

Poor Dick Welles, if he was able to read the piece, to find one of his deadly rivals for Orson's affection described as 'his guardian' – and then to read that it was a triumph for Orson to be passed off as another man's son.

In truth, it is unlikely that Dick Welles was in any condition to focus on such nuances. Installed in the Bismarck Hotel in Chicago, denied the presence of his son, even at Christmas, but hopefully surrounded by his bird-cage and the portrait of Trixi Friganza, he died on 28 December 1930. The death is tinged with a certain mystery. The certificate, unearthed by Charles Higham, gives as cause of death, chronic myocarditis and chronic nephritis, respectively heart and kidney diseases, and cardiac failure – all of which is perfectly consonant with what we know of his life. There are persistent rumours, however, that he killed himself; which also seems perfectly feasible. Finally, Orson Welles, in his memoir, claims that he was at the time, and continued to be, convinced that he killed his father, adding: 'I'll try to write about that later.' Understandably, he never did.

In a sense, all three of these claims are true. Clearly, the conditions described on the death certificate account perfectly satisfactorily for Richard Welles's death, and they are commonly found in heavy smokers and drinkers. There is a curious feature, drawn attention to by Higham: both witnesses, Maurice Bernstein and Jacob Gottfredson, Dick Welles's brother-in-law, declare the deceased's father and mother to be 'unknown' – this of Jacob's own mother. There is no apparent explanation for this. As for the suicide theory: Dick Welles drank himself to death. What other course did he have? What was there to live for? Desertion by his child-parent, Orson, was the end for him. There is no record of how the break was made – whether he was given an ultimatum, or whether Orson simply wasn't there any more – but in his alcoholic twilight he would have no reason to expect ever to see him again. It is also, of course, possible that he did actually kill himself, by means undetected in the post-mortem examination, but to have done so seems redundant. He must have known he was on his way out. Orson himself told Barbara Leaming that he thought his father had committed suicide, having lost the tug-of-war with Maurice Bernstein for Orson, but also out of a kind of continuing grief for the loss of Beatrice – lost, as it happens, in another tug-of-war, and to the same man. The first suggestion is really a confirmation of Dick's desperation; the last seems to smack a little of wish-fulfilment, a posthumous reunion of two beloved but estranged figures.

But what of Welles's self-accusation? What matters here is not proof one way or the other (quite obviously he did not physically kill his father) but the fact that he felt that he was, at the deepest level, responsible for his father's death. He was already riven with guilt about him. He had favoured his mother over his father, was her emissary in the world, living out her hopes and dreams. He had given his emotional loyalty to other substitute fathers. He had perhaps wished his father out of the way. Often, in the years to come, he would frighten himself with the destructive power of his will; perhaps he had used it here, with apparently direct results. Above all, however, Orson had, at the behest of others, abandoned his father. Six months is an awfully long time in the relationship of a fifteen-year-old boy to his father. He had never let more than a couple of weeks go by before without seeing Dick. And now he could never see him again. The loss of his mother occurred when he was nine, a child; and besides, he had never really lost her. Now he was a man. The loss of his father was irremediable, a shattering blow. Having never really had him, he searched for him all his days, sometimes trying to be him, sometimes trying to create an image of him that would absolve the disappointment of the past. He remained an absence, a void, a gap deep within Orson which nothing could fill.

His position was desperate. Paralysed with guilt, he felt that both his surviving father figures were somehow implicated in Richard Welles's death: Dadda Bernstein had stolen first Beatrice then Orson away from him; Skipper and Horty had stopped Orson from seeing him when he was in most need. 'I didn't think I was doing the right thing. I simply wanted to please the Hills . . . [after his death] I felt that they had been, momentarily, false gods; that I had followed the wrong adults, you know, and for the wrong reasons.'

For the immediate future, there was more pain to endure. It was decreed, inevitably, that the funeral must take place in Kenosha; arrangements were in the hands of Dick's – 'unknown' – mother, Mary Head Welles Gottfredson. Orson's relationship with her had never been a success. Despising Richard Junior (who for obvious reasons was not at his father's funeral), she was permanently incensed by Orson, whom she regarded as unmanly. Orson fiercely defended his right to aestheticism. Their occasional encounters after the family had left Kenosha were fraught, with Orson defiant – not something to which Mrs Gottfredson was accustomed. Her other grandson Edward recalled that 'Orson once tried to scare Grandma with a rubber dagger and when Grandma refused to become frightened, he dramatically plunged the dagger into his own heart, and died as horribly as his youthful histrionic powers would permit.' 'He was always emoting all over the place,' explained Mrs Gottfredson Junior. 'And egotistical as hell,' added her husband. When Orson arrived, explaining that his father must be buried at sea, or cremated, he was brushed aside. He persisted, frantic and tearful, and was ignored. His brimming cup of guilt must have overflowed. The final betrayal: to break a solemn oath given to a dying man. 'I was in no position to interfere, being convinced – as I am now – that I had killed my father.'

Orson's immediate revenge was in embroidering tales about his loathed grandmother to which he later gave vehement expression in press interviews and most vividly in his memoir:

> The ballroom on the top floor of the old woman's house had,

> at some remote period, mysteriously been converted into an enormous indoor miniature golf course full of wooden hills and nasty little sand traps, still partly covered with rotting green paper. Crowning the highest of the hills there had been erected, at a later date, what was unmistakably an altar. Representing some more recent epoch in Grandmother's spiritual progress, it was no place for Christian sacraments. The feathers of many birds long dead lay about the golf course, and the altar itself was deeply stained with blood.
>
> This dreadful woman – dwarfish, obese, and evil-smelling – was a practising witch. On the occasion of her son's funeral, celebrated in that huge house of hers (where my mother had never been allowed to enter) this hellish creature managed to sandwich some obscure passages into the ordinary protestant service, so that the wretched, weak-willed minister was confused enough to read out during the ceremony some of the more bizarre invocations employed by Madame Blavatsky, and great, reeking dollops of Aleister Crowley.

This startling passage is preceded by an assertion that 'this dreadful woman' had put a curse on his parents' marriage, which is perhaps a clue to the intensity of his rage against her. He was looking for someone to blame for the fact that had blighted his life: the break-up of his mother and father which somehow split him up, too.

As for the truth of the situation: when Welles started telling these stories about his grandmother to journalists, they were reported to her. A 1941 article ('Debunking the Orson Welles Myth'; it was the year of *Kane*) goes: 'Mrs Mary Gottfredson is still living in the family home in Kenosha. She is now 92, blind, quite deaf, and bedridden, but the current stories have been read to her by her son, J.R. Gottfredson. She has been displeased and hurt.' She is a Christian Scientist, the paper reports. There were no dead birds in her house. The funeral was perfectly regular – there were no 'weird obsequies'. (Although Charles Higham was told by the subsequent owner of house that she had found on the top floor a wooden altar, inscribed with Latin text, adorned with pentagram and a stained glass window.) Just as he needed to romanticise his father, he needed to demonise his grandmother. Normally, an artist would have done this on a canvas, a writer in a novel or a film-maker on a screen. Welles avoided the autobiographical mode in his work, preferring to rewrite history in his on-going memoir, the story of his life as relayed to the press of the world over many years.

The local paper published a very decent obituary of Dick headed, erroneously, R.H. WELLS, 55, DIES SUDDENLY, (he was fifty-nine, and he had changed the spelling of his name at the age of twenty) noting his business career and background. 'News of the passing of Mr Wells has caused profound regret among his wide circle of friends and relatives in Kenosha.' They record his life of 'semi-retirement and extensive travel'. A few days later, there was a further small item headed: 'Dr Bernstein is named guardian of Welles's son.' Dick's will had left it to Orson to choose his own guardian; he had immediately asked Skipper, wanting, obviously, to confirm his membership of that family. Skipper persuaded him that he must choose Maurice Bernstein, since it would break his heart not to be chosen. That is probably true, but we can imagine that with his children and Hascy implacably hostile to Orson, he may have had the preservation of his own family somewhat in mind.

So on 1 January 1931, Maurice Bernstein became Orson Welles's legal guardian. Moving in with him, Welles was scarcely entering a haven of peace and light. Bernstein was now married to a remarkable woman: Edith Mason, one of the most distinguished American singers of her day, an outstanding actress and possessor of a voice whose silvery brilliance can be clearly heard on her surviving recordings. She had been married to Giorgio Polacco, an inspiring conductor, held to be Toscanini's equal, but a somewhat diabolic human being. Bernstein had become her lover when the marriage to Polacco had broken down, marrying her in 1929. Polacco seems never to have been far from sight; eventually he moved back into Edith's Lake Shore apartment. At one point, Bernstein, Edith, Polacco (all furiously abusing each other), their daughter Graziella (who loathed Welles) and Orson were all living in the same apartment. Mrs Leaming reports that Polacco, during a pause in the mutual invective, started to approach Orson sexually. Orson fled. This, though, was only the straw that had broken the camel's back. There was a stream of male opera singers visiting the flat, who, pretty well without exception, were – according to Orson – drawn to him like bees to a honeypot, and were, too, soon involved in the laying on of hands. 'You see, the Italians believe any young boy is meat for a quick seduction, and it will have no effect on him or on the masculinity of the grown man,' Orson informed Mrs Leaming, in a perhaps controversial piece of anthropology. 'Everybody wanted me.' His method of defence was traditional – 'I always said I had a headache'

– but apparently effective. 'I was like an eternal virgin.'

According to Mrs Leaming, Welles's mother confessor on all such matters, Orson had by now experienced the full delight of sexual intercourse with a girl on a boat – perhaps while travelling with his father. Thereafter, he had taken to slipping into Woodstock for assignations with the ever-obliging girls from the Presbyterian Church Choir. Somehow or another, some very explicit homosexual pornography had come into his hands: he was particularly troubled by a picture of some sixteen Swedish men sodomising each other – 'in their socks!' The socks were, it seems, the problem: he found them sordid. He had not lost his attractiveness to what he called 'the older homosexual set' and managed, according to John C. Dexter, to get a couple of teachers sacked for mild homosexual advances. He was also attractive, it would seem, to the older *heterosexual* set: a friend's father suddenly laid hands on him in the middle of the night when he and Orson were sharing a bed. Orson, he told Mrs Leaming, hadn't suspected a thing when the older man suggested that they share a bed.

What are we to understand by these incidents, all reported by Welles himself? Apart from anything else, it appears that Welles wants us to know how attractive he was at that age. It is true that he had changed from the plump rather bossy-looking child of earlier photographs. Between the ages of thirteen and fourteen he had rapidly grown to six foot in height, and in doing so had lost much of his plumpness. His large, long-lashed eyes stood out warmly in a face that now had cheek-bones; his full lips added a soft seductiveness, the dainty, almost retroussé, nose a certain vulnerability. And he had a splendid head of hair. His single greatest asset, stunningly complementing the rest, was his voice, quite simply a gift from God, a natural instrument equivalent, in speech, to the singing voice of a Gigli or a Chaliapin.

It is easy to see his appeal to anyone, of any age or sex. His body had caught up with his manner. From being a child who spoke and comported himself disconcertingly like an adult, he was, simply, a striking young man, who could have been anything from sixteen to twenty-one. To desire him was not an admission of paedophilia. No one could have guessed that he was fifteen years old; not until they got to know him a little better, and then they might have discovered that in some respects he was even younger than that.

Pretty well everyone must have felt some sort of sexual frisson in his presence. What happened next is more complicated. It is hard to believe – especially now that he was as tall as a baseball forward, with every appearance of being as strong as one – that men simply made lunges for him. To be blunt: he must have put out certain signals. He was looking for affirmation and approval specifically from men, and this is one of the ways of getting it. So, if you were a middle-aged man, you might have found yourself being looked at through those enormous brown eyes with unexpected intimacy. And you may have surprised yourself with your quickened pulse and tightening chest. It must have given him an enormous, and new, sense of power. Hard to resist. Also: he may have enjoyed it. Not in the case of Signor Polacco, however, and all those lecherous opera singers. Basta was basta. He went back to school.

Returning to Todd was a holiday. He flung himself into his final production. His *Richard III*, sometimes spoken of as *Winter of Discontent*, is strikingly grouped and set, with a lit aperture at the back of the stage, at the top of a flight of stairs. It was an epic in scale: the programme tells us that TODD TROUPERS together with JUNIOR TROUPERS and LEARN PIGEONS Present a play called KING RICHARD THE THIRD. 'Our sixth and final offering of the season,' writes the director, 'is something of a patchwork, a Shakespearean goulash. Four Histories and a tragedy have gone into its making, and of the original kill, only the choicest cuts have been preserved. Has this Stratford pot-pie a precedent? We think so.' Here he quickly surveys the various versions and adaptations, Cibber and Co. 'And so our RICHARD III is a composite of the later histories. Beginning with Edward's return from exile and carrying through his reign and that of his deformed and unprincipled brother Richard, to the beginning of the Tudor line by Richmond . . . and so, we humbly add our little polyglot to the 315th volume of crime and sacrilege committed in the master's name. Our offence is rank, it smells to high heaven, and we robustious periwig-pated fellows, whose names sully its pages, we are the "curst that move his bones", rattle the flaggings in Trinity Church and turn William Shakespeare, gent., to a point of nausea in his grave. Rest, rest, Perturbed spirit!!!' The boy was intoxicated with Shakespeare. In his passion – and it *was* the last production of the season – he had overstuffed the goose. The show ran for three and a half hours and had to be savagely cut shortly before the opening. His make-up as Richard (he was, needless to say, eponymous) out Lon Chaneyed Lon Chaney: his face unrecognisable, as if made from spare parts of several faces stuck together with huge pieces of sticking plaster, it is disturbing and powerful – a botched monster put together by a sadistic Frankenstein.

None of these shows was noticed by the national, or, as far as the record shows, by the Chicago press. In the school, of course, and among those who cared, Welles was thought of as a genius, but geniuses tend to come and go in schools. It is impossible to say, on the evidence we have, how good the shows were. The importance of all the work that Welles had done was that he was able to flex his theatre muscles without limitation of time or labour – his own or anyone else's; to discover what was possible, what would work and what wouldn't. Everything that had been brewing in his head could now be put to the test. Welles was able to allow his talent to develop almost in isolation. Because of the support he had from the Hills, and because of his own driving need to achieve something remarkable, he had done in rather extreme form exactly what Todd was supposed to make possible. He had learned by doing. Had he not gone to such a school, he would never have grown theatrically as he did. He might, on the other hand, have learned something more about adapting to other people's needs, and to external conditions; although to a certain extent, he had created the circumstances in which he flourished. He made sure of the relationship with Roger Hill; he demanded time and facilities, and persuaded the school to extend its ambitions in terms of repertory. In all these things, he got his way. Sometimes, of course, a little resistance is a useful thing. At Todd, he knew none.

There remained the small question of his academic qualifications. Here the estimable Guggie was at hand to coach him. There were limits to what he could achieve – no word of Latin, no term of Geometry would enter that otherwise absorbent brain. The results were a testimony to Guggie's skills as an instructor: both Orson and he made it on the highest honour medal when they were in the 8th grade; both got red and white ribbon representing school colours. In the same year, he and Welles both got the Grand Gold Medal, with two gold bars. Welles was actually one medal ahead of his chum. Unsurprisingly, he won the medal for elocution and acting. He passed summa cum laude. But he was not proud of this. In all subsequent interviews, he invariably attributed any success he had had in the examinations to Paul Guggenheim, who had crammed him. It was an important part of his personal myth, even at this age, that he had had no teachers. And, essentially, it is true. He refused what they had to offer, was by nature and conviction an autodidact. He did it his way. He had no intention of playing their game and being judged according to their rules. This again was willed. He knew that criticism was intolerable to him, so he put himself beyond it. He was a one-off, his own sternest critic, and woe betide anyone who attempted to set themselves up in judgement of him. In essence, Welles remained exactly the same academically at the end of his time at Todd as he had been at the beginning. Maurice Bernstein was desperate that Orson should continue his education. At sixteen, he was too young for university, but Bernstein wanted him to go on to higher education, prior to Harvard or Yale. He offered Paul Guggenheim $1,000 (quite a sum for anyone; for Maurice Bernstein a king's ransom) if he could persuade Orson to go with him to Lake Forest pre-university college. Orson replied: Why should I waste my time going to college and teaching those goddam professors what I know?

The photographs of the period show him a lot jollier than in previous ones. Here he is, short-trousered, standing on a log, throwing back his head and roaring with laughter. However embattled he may have been, regardless of which demons he was wrestling with, laughter never deserted him entirely. He was not in himself an especially funny man, nor an especially amusing boy, but he was, like Lear, always susceptible to being amused. He had a deep love of comics and comedians, having seen and met many of them, no doubt, with his father.

His last contribution to the school as a student was to edit the new catalogue: *The Book of Todd, 1931*. It is his most extended achievement to date in projecting his public persona; it also gives a comprehensive view of the world that he was about to leave behind. He may not have participated in every aspect of it, but it was the cradle of the man he became. He dominates the entire book. The cover (by him) is a boldly executed aerial view of the school, set in its bosky surrounds. The first article introduces not only Todd but its boyish editor.

> HOW THIS BOOK STARTED: THE EDITOR SPEAKS: 'I have a job for you,' said Skipper, one afternoon in May. 'That's fine,' I answered, 'but I've more jobs now than I can finish this year. The murals in the history room are only half-done and that primary play I'm directing – '. 'It isn't exactly your job, it's for the Seniors, but I want you to take charge of it,' he countered, and then of course I fell, for who doesn't like to boss a task?

This is vintage Orson in tone and in content: he advertises both his talents, and his relationship with Skipper. Facing the page is a picture of murals in the History Room (simply stylised, but attractive) 'done by our editor, Orson Welles'.

> We decided not to sign any of the articles or works of art in this book as it would make it even more confusing than it is now . . . however, we are over-riding our Editor's authority in this one spot and stating that he drew the maps of the campus on the cover and is responsible for most of the better written articles in this book. Also he has been our leading light in dramatics this year, acting as Student Director of the Troupers.

It is not hard to imagine the reactions of most alumni to this naked piece of mock-modest self-promotion. He proceeds to a guide to the institutions of the school, most of which are found to be in an advanced state of democracy. Then: the enemy:

> TEACHERS: The 20 men and women who share our life at Todd are all the type one loves to work with, to play with, and to live with. There is a great array of impressive degrees among the group but under the Skipper's humanising influence, they have forgotten about them all and, like the boys, their rating in our life is determined solely by their contribution to its joy and its usefulness.

Certainly faculty members may have been found grinding their teeth as they read this. Orson goes on to describe the school's extraordinary craft facilities, which give Todd the feel of a mediaeval village: the machine shops ('some boys have made complete gasoline engines'), the print shop, turning out the weekly school magazine, and the textile shop with its sixteen looms and facilities for rug designing and making. There were even – to gladden Dick Welles's troubled spirit – facilities for cartooning. The catalogue is littered with talented examples of that art, almost all signed O.W. The articles on sport – evidently wonderfully well catered for – are notably less exuberant than the rest, and evidently by another hand.

It is predictably the theatre that dominates the catalogue. He makes a bold statement, claiming it as the activity of activities, uniting all the school's elements:

> DRAMATICS: The activity that has made the school famous, and the activity that touches every boy here and gives him a chance to express any talent he has. It is not a single activity but a combination of all.

It is a measure of the force of this sixteen-year-old's personality that in a boys' school run by a sports master, sport should have assumed second place to what is generally considered a specialised interest – or at least it did in the catalogue, edited by that same sixteen-year-old. The photographs testify to the originality and sophistication of the boys' work, from the youngest, as Skipper had decreed, to the eldest. Since the standards they aspired to were entirely professional, make-up was a crucial art. The boys were supposed to look like adults – men and women. Orson became a master of this art, and a whole page is devoted to a photo-collage of characters: SOME PRODUCTS OF THE MAKE-UP CLASS: 'The boy in the center is 13 years old and many of the others are younger.' It's an impressive display. By a remarkable act of self-restraint, Orson only includes three photographs of himself out of the twelve: as Richard III, a turbanned, bearded Manson in *The Servant in the House*, and an unnamed character with impassioned, upward-turned face – cunningly lit to conceal tubbiness – the expression questing and apprehensive, full lips barely parted, eyebrows raised from the centre to furrow the brow, nostrils slightly flared, retroussé tip to the nose giving an impression of vulnerability. It is this face, out of all fourteen on the page, which immediately catches the eye: it is one of the essential faces of Orson Welles. He is playing Francis Lightfoot, the genius.

The catalogue was his farewell to the campus. It became 'one of the Merrie Englands', a kingdom of which the king was a boy: him. Before he left Todd, there was one thing to be done: one of the school's hallowed rituals. Each boy on becoming a senior was given a sled, which he kept as long as he was there. When he left, he handed it over to an upcoming senior; solemnly, this is what he did, in May 1931. As far as we know, it was not named Rosebud.

CHAPTER FOUR

Ireland/*Jew Süss*

IN THE immediate hiatus following graduation from Todd, Orson enrolled in Boris Anisfeldt's class at the Chicago Art Institute. He had a very lively talent for sketching; his line drawings are sharp, witty and evocative, especially effective in capturing the essential character in a face. He told Hascy: 'I was never any good, but I could always make it go where I wanted it to.' His gift was for illustration. It is unlikely that he ever expected to cultivate it professionally, though it was politic of him to suggest, as he did now, that painting was his real passion – as opposed to the less respectable, the feared and dreaded, theatre. It can hardly have been by accident that the teacher in whose class he enrolled had been a brilliant theatre designer in his time. At any rate, his attendance at the classes was fitful, as he engaged in the pursuit for which they were, in reality, nothing but a cover.

Billboard for May 1931 carried, under its

'At Liberty
Dramatic Artists'

column, the following announcement:

> ORSON WELLES – Stock, Characters, Heavies, Juveniles or as cast. Also specialties, chalk talk or can handle stage. Young, excellent appearance, quick sure study. Lots of pep, experience and ability. Close in Chicago early in June and want place in good stock company for remainder of season. Salary according to late date of opening and business conditions. Photos on request. Address ORSON WELLES c/o H.L. Powers, Illinois Theatre, 65 E Jackson Bvd, Chicago, Ill.

Orson was rarely out of the Powers Agency that summer, to no avail – pipped at the post, perhaps, by the young gentleman who, in the same edition, advertised himself as having 'some singing-talking specialties' and being able to 'build, repair anything; paint plain scenery, banners'. Chalk talk was no match for singing-talking specialties, and certainly not for a skilled carpenter. Accordingly, the following month a second, more desperate, ad was placed:

> Orson Welles is willing to invest moderate amount of cash and own services as Heavy, Character and Juvenile in good summer stock or repertory proposition. Reply to Orson Welles, Dramatic Coach, Todd Academy, Woodstock, Illinois.

We may assume that Maurice Bernstein was unaware of Orson's plans for himself. Like many a parent or guardian before him, Dadda's suggestion was that Orson should first become qualified academically, and then, with a safety net underneath him (that is the standard phrase), should he still feel the need to act, he could go ahead and give it a try. Clearly this was not going to wash with Orson, his appetite for the theatre raging, and all his juices at full flood after an unbroken sequence of triumphant productions at Todd. Had there been any takers for his adverts, he would have been off like a greyhound out of a trap. But for the time being, in the absence of any openings, he continued to pose as a would-be painter. The question of his future was the sole topic in his guardian's home, which had undergone radical rearrangement. Bernstein's marriage to Edith Mason broke up amid ugly recriminations (including the familiar one that he was a fortune-hunter; also that he was 'and is' a notorious womaniser). 'I told her before she married Dr Bernstein, who though a capable surgeon is a Russian Jew, and therefore a hybrid as I see it,' wrote Mason's brother, Baron Barnes, in a comprehensively politically incorrect letter written during an earlier breakdown of the marriage only a year after it had been entered into, 'that she'll do just as she pleases – get the divorce amid worlds of mud as publicity, probably marry that damn dago again and cut her throat in the end with her decent-minded American public and be fini'. He was right in everything except the last prediction; Edith Mason became one of the most admired and respected singers America has produced. But there was mud, and she did remarry the damn dago, Polacco. Losing no time at all, Bernstein resumed his relationship with Mrs Edward Moore; when Moore died, she became the third (and last) Mrs Bernstein. An altogether calmer figure than La Mason, she rather went to the other extreme, being something of a hygiene faddist. Orson preferred to spend most of his time back at Todd, where Skipper let him have a room of his own. From time to time, however, he would visit Maurice and Hazel at their spotless residence in Highland Park and address the equally vexed questions of his legacy and his future: intertwined problems, in fact.

Dick Welles had made his will in 1927. It contains a startlingly brutal paragraph about his son Richard ('the irresponsibility and ingratitude of said Richard I. Welles') who was reduced to inheriting one seventh of the estate which should be administered to him until his thirty-fifth birthday (it was never paid to him); the rest went to Orson, likewise being administered to him until his twenty-fifth birthday. Richard's one seventh amounted to $6,500; Orson's portion was $37,500; these sums are worth approximately ten times the amount at current rates. Maurice Bernstein, as trustee, was responsible for the administration of the estate. Richard, incarcerated in Kanakee, was allowed niggardly sums for clothing and upkeep. Orson hardly found it easier to extract money for his needs. According to a 1940 article in *Saturday Evening Post*, Bernstein never let Orson know how much he had inherited, suggesting that it was little or nothing. 'He feared his ward might never do anything useful if he learned that an inheritance was hanging over his head. To let him know of his inheritance would be like letting an Osage Indian know that he had struck oil.' This is conceivable; whatever the case, there invariably hovers over any financial dealing concerning Dr Bernstein a question mark – with both his previous wives, with Richard Junior, with Orson – even with Beatrice, from whom it is suggested that he expected, erroneously, to inherit. There is no doubt of his love for Orson, but there is a possibility that he tried to cheat him, too. A further complication for the boy.

As for his future: the goal was always Harvard or Cornell. The most Orson could hope to do was to stave off the hour at which he would be obliged to enrol. In August, he managed to buy, as he saw it, a little time.

> Three days of particularly vicious domestic warfare . . . ended in a roundtable conference which found all the principal powers as determined as ever [he wrote to Roger Hill]. Dadda had thought the matter over and decided he could not permit my having ought to do with the diseased and despicable theatre. The deuteragonist and the tritagonist questioned the educational value and the chorus (everybody about) was uniformly and maddeningly derisive. Things went from bad to worse. Alternately I defended and offended. My head remained bloody but unbowed and my nose, thanks to the thoughtful blooming of some neighbouring clover (which I assured the enemy was ragweed!) began to sniffle hay-feverishly, and the household was illusioned into the realisation that something had to be done.
>
> It was then that Dadda arrived at a momentous decision – and in the spirit of true martyrdom chose the lesser of two great

> evils. Going abroad alone is not quite as unthinkable as joining the theatre – and so . . . I was whisked out of the fire into the frying pan. Four days later I was in New York!
>
> A few months of walking and painting in Ireland and Scotland . . . and then on to England where there are schools – and theatres!!!!!!

It is curious that in later life Welles liked to suggest that really he had just drifted into the theatre. His work at Todd was simply to impress Skipper; he had really wanted to be a painter; it was all a charming accident which took him by surprise. In fact he was fanatically devoted to the idea of the theatre, immersed in its lore and its terminology (even his account of a domestic battle is analysed in terms of a well-informed knowledge of the Greek theatre), and deeply ambitious. Perhaps he had come to believe his own propaganda, the pretence that he was obliged to maintain for Maurice and Hazel Bernstein. There was no need to conceal his glee from Skipper, who wanted nothing more for him than to follow his heart. It was to Skipper that the above letter was addressed, from on board the *SS Baltic* the night before disembarking at Galway.

If Welles felt the slightest anxiety at the prospect of being alone in a strange country, he doesn't betray it. In fact, his despatches and the journal that he kept betray nothing but youthful exuberance, delight in the new world that he was discovering and unqualified joie de vivre. His life at home – whether at Todd or at the Bernsteins' – was of such continuing complexity that it must have been a liberation simply not to be there. He was also strongly and romantically drawn to Ireland, infected by the twin charms that rendered it such a magnet for romantics in the first couple of decades of the century: on the one hand, its timeless and unvarnished beauty, on the other, its nationalist revival, both political and cultural. The idea of Ireland – passionate, oppressed, mystic – was in every way the antithesis of the old tired civilised post-war world. 'Get out your Don Byrne and your Synge and your gallic ballads – you can't trace my wanderings on the map!' he wrote to Skipper, that last night on board the *Baltic*.

He carried with him in his pocket a copy of *Field and Fair*, by Pádriac Ó Conaire: *Travels with a Donkey in Ireland*, and he seems to have accepted its invitation:

> Come with me, O friend of my heart, and let us enjoy the sight of majestic mountain peaks and dark pine forests; let us stroll by musical streams, past cool brooks where dwell thousands

> of birds; come along for Spring is at hand, and fresh blood is flowing through your veins and mine . . . come along with me, my friend, and we shall travel till night overtakes us. We shall pass thro snug little villages with a light in every house, and a messy fire will be seen through the open door, and the bean-a-tighe busy preparing the meal, or minding her baby, or having a chat with her neighbour . . . up, friend of my heart, and come along with me till I have cured that dark disease that afflicts your mind . . . delay not, but come along.

Intoxicating stuff: a perfect remedy for late-adolescent accidie, sense of self-disgust and self-weariness, oneself ever-present, unavoidable, impossible to ignore, Ó Conaire's 'dark disease that afflicts your mind'. And Ireland lived up to Ó Conaire: it did not disappoint. In fact, it inspired Orson to pages of prose every bit as high-flown, and in their own way, as contagiously charming as those of his model. It was of course in the back of his mind that he might return not merely with a number of masterpieces on canvas (he had come laden with the accoutrements of the career he pretended to espouse) but also with a slim volume of travel writing. He kept a journal, and wrote letters to Hortense and Roger Hill and to Dadda. The latter have a more studied quality, as if for publication; indeed, Dadda being Dadda, the moment they arrived they were typed up and passed around among interested parties. It is the most extended correspondence Welles undertook, and along with the private matter of the journal and the chatty tones of the letters to Roger and Hortense ('the Skippers', as he calls them) it gives a very agreeable picture of the sixteen-year-old Orson, footloose and fancy free. It is still to some extent an official account; there are no intensely private revelations. Even on holiday, and to his most intimate circle, Orson presented a public face.

> Our very landing was dramatic – the tender pulled up to the side of the ship full of luggage and relations – everyone aboard it seemed to me was Irish – men and women got on their knees, weeping with joy, there was much craning of necks and pitiful waving and then little cries of recognition as first one passenger and then another picked out their 'Paddy' or 'Michael.' A fine tall man with flowing silver hair and a face like Wotan brandished his silver-headed cane fiercely over our heads crying in a voice like thunder – 'Sure it's God's own country.' I looked out over the rolling indigo sea into the misty mountains, blue and gold at the

> horizon – they were singing 'The Wearin' of the Green,' and on the tender people separated for years were locking and locking in the intricacies of an Irish jig. 'Home is the sailor, home from the sea, and the hunter, home from the hills.' I unarmored, as Wotan, leaping madly down the gang-plank sang out for the hundredth time – 'Sure, and it's God's own country.'

He decided impulsively to disembark at Galway, making up his own itinerary.

> I must say I don't regret it. If I had gone on to Cobb, I should have missed Connacht entirely – the West Coast of Ireland is unknown and unbelievable. In all Europe and the Western Hemisphere there is nothing to approach it – in this Americanised three-quarters of the globe, it is unique – the last frontier of romance.

The writer of this was not a topographical ignoramus: at the beginning of this letter to Dadda Bernstein he says 'surprises I have had in my travels – countries like Japan and China have exceeded my expectations, but in sixteen short, very full years of living, nothing comparable with Galway – or the West Coast of Ireland – has loomed so unexpectedly – so breath-takingly on my horizon'. The sense of awe and excitement never seems to have left him. He relates his adventures with comic awareness of his own situation; the country, its people and its customs seem glorious to him: Ó Conaire himself could not have celebrated them more. Despite fetching up in Galway at the height of the turfing season, he manages to acquire the regulation donkey; her name, after 'a certain species of fairy', is Sidheoghc (pronounced – and thereafter spelt – Sheeog) and together he and she embark, in classic Robert Louis Stevenson fashion, on a month's adventuring.

> We travelled a good per cent of Ireland together, Sheeog and I – from Galway to Donegal and the giants' courseway, and nearly back, at night we camped at the roadside – Sheeog feeding on the mountain grass and I cooking over a turf fire, and when the stars were out, Sheeog went to join the 'sidhe' – the fairies – and I curled myself up under the cart and fell asleep. There were nights, too, spent in the cottages, wakes, weddings, and match-makings . . . my week with the band of gypsies, my mountain-climbs, my night in a quagmire, and finally, the auctioning of Sheeog at the Clifden fair – should all make tolerably interesting after-dinner tales.

He found a welcome in the small, comfortable communities scattered around the countryside. He was a stranger, and therefore fascinating. He evidently had no fear, which people as well as dogs can spot in an instant. He also seemed to assume, which is more surprising, that people would treat him generously; so of course they did. What it was in his experience that led him to such an assumption is not easy to know, although, despite the myriad complications of his emotional life, he had never known rejection, and rarely encountered malice. He had been greatly loved: by no means always wisely, but very well. And it seems that there was never a time in his life that Orson Welles joined a group of people, expecting them to dislike him.

As for the gypsies . . . well, why not? He was obviously ready for anything. Like many people whose home life is for whatever reason unsatisfying, he was always able to become part of a different clan with ease: to identify with them, to join in, to be one of them. This too was a repeated pattern. At various times in his life, Welles would become immersed in black life, in Spanish life, in Arab life. Lacking a family of his own in the usual sense, he had no identity to lose; he was thrilled to belong to a new one. Of course, he would then move on. So a week with the gypsies would be par for the course. Having sold the donkey, his next move was to the Aran Islands, a yet more intimate community than that of the West Coast, and one with which he identified even more easily and closely. Synge, it would appear, was the lure, initially. His love affair with all things Irish had not entirely made him forget his first and one true love, the theatre. He found his way to it with unerring instinct. In Galway, Professor Liam O'Briain had, with a little government money, established the first Irish-speaking theatre, the Taibhearc. Their initial production had been *Diarmuid and Gráinne*, by the young actor and designer Micheál Mac Liammóir (who had, uncredited, illustrated the copy of *Field and Fair* in Welles's pocket), and they were eager to recruit young Irish-speaking actors. Hearing of this, Welles applied for a grant to learn the Irish language – on the Aran Islands, for preference – and then return to act at the Taibhearc. His application was turned down; they didn't have that sort of money. So he made his way to the isles of Synge on his own.

> John Connelly who sells stout and plug tobacco built a slate roof on his house thirty years ago. Fifty years before, the English government performed the remarkable engineering feat of erecting a coast-guard station – (which has gone out of use, and which I use

> as a studio) – and a light-house. There too, there is a priest who braves the waves when the Sundays are fine – to say Mass, but despite these vague hints at civilisation, Inisheer remains as it has been for many centuries – the most primitive spot in Europe.

He describes the history of the isles – 'these people who produced and flourished in Tut Antkahmen's time – and kept alive the flame of Christian culture in the days of Genghis Khan' – in excitable language: 'it is almost beyond belief that two days' journeying from the world's greatest metropolis brings one to a land where an intelligent and aristocratic people live in archaic simplicity, surpassing anything in Homer!' He calls the island 'their paradise'. It is notable that Welles's view of human history, and of life in general, is very severely polarised into the innocent and the corrupt. For him, very little exists between evil and good. The West of Ireland was for him pre-lapsarian. Writing to Hortense Hill, he says that

> here life has attained a simplicity and is lived with an artistry surpassing anything – I am sure in the South Seas . . . somewhere there may be a forgotten land where eyes are as clear and hearts as open, but nowhere is candour so remarkably combined with intelligence, an intelligence which results from nearly five thousand years cultural background. Being then fully cognisant of these several underlined wonders – you may gather that my wanderings have brought me to a kind of lost Eden rich in romance and of bounteous beauty . . . I shall find it very hard to leave my little cottage by the sea for the world of tram-cars and leather shoes I used to know.

He visits the Donahues, to see Mrs Donahue's new-born.

> I know and love every spot and every soul on these isles . . . I left Donahue's after a time and spent an hour or so lying in the sand listening to the sounds of the night – afar off the crying of dogs and donkeys – the mournful note of a Gaelic ballad and nearer me the wailing of the gulls and the 'wash-wash' of the quiet sea. It was a clear night tonight – so clear that as I walked back to my village I could make out the brighter stars in the wet strand at my feet.

And then there was the other side of the coin; Dionysos's part in the Homeric paradise. To Maurice Bernstein he wrote, in the accents of his hosts:

> a shindy is a great thing, and scarcely an evening goes by but what one of us doesn't rout the old fiddlers out and stage one. You would hardly recognise your Pookles – or 'Paddy' as everyone here calls him, jigging away into the wee small hours! Irish dancing is not delicate, but it is a hearty, joyful, genuine expression of the dance impulse. It is a great sight to see the kitchen of, let us say, Maggie Flaherty, (dealer in the mountain dew) – sichh! – cleared of impediments and full of fine Erin men in indigo and homespun and beautiful (I use the word unhesitatingly) and smiling colleens in nice red skirts and sienna jackets, all whirling about in the intricacies of 'the stalk of barley,' and stamping their leathern slippers on the flaggings as the orchestra lays on into the night. It was fine tonight, and when the dancing was over, there were ballads sung, and stories told, as is usual – and a long walk across the moonlit strand brings me here.

He submitted joyfully to a view of Ireland and the Irish – especially the islanders – that merged in his mind with what he had read. He had clearly *not* read Liam O'Flaherty, then a very angry young Irishman indeed.

> The Irish peasant . . . is in process of transformation, and goodness only knows where he may get to and what he may become . . . those literary hirelings that still dishonour our country by trying to persuade us that the peasant is a babbling child of God, who is innocent of all ambition, ignorant of guile, midway between heaven and earth, enveloped in a cloud of mystical adoration of the priests and of Caitlin ni Houlihan, the raparee with a pike in his thatch, the croppy boy confessing his sins on the way to the scaffold to suffer a patriotic martyrdom, a violent primitive who runs wild, naked and raving mad, once the gentle hand of the priest is raised from his back, a cold sexless ascetic whose loins never cry out for the pleasure of love, a quantity as fixed and unchangeable as the infallibility of the pope.

O'Flaherty's fierce and furious *Tourist's Guide to Ireland* of 1930 tells the other side. But for Orson, romantic American child of his time, he had discovered Shangri-La. He had frankly given up most pretence of sketching. The oils had tumbled out of his rucksack on the first day, and most of them had been sent on to Dublin to await his arrival. With the rest he had managed to execute 'precisely ten terrible landscapes . . . the almost unearthly quality of the countryside and the mountains in the West and North completely stumped me. I cannot tell you of the bitterness associated with those ten futile efforts – I actually wept aloud at the realisation of my own incapacity.' Four went to pay for lodgings, the remaining six destroyed. 'Ireland is really a watercolour country,' he says, going on quite accurately to identify his talent as being exclusively for still-life composition, design and portraiture. But there he is stumped, too: 'I shall carry away with me perhaps half a dozen portraits – most of them will be good likenesses, but as portrayals of that indefinable Erin spirit they will be dismal failures . . . there is a twinkle that dances in an Erin eye – an *intelligent candour* – and something more . . . to paint *that* is to paint *God*.' As for the writing: 'I am really drinking too deeply of Ireland to write well about it . . . I have lingered in these parts so long I have almost ceased to be a traveller.' Drily he adds: 'neither of us could write an amusing article on Kenosha from the tourist's standpoint.'

Inevitably his letters to Dadda end with the eternal refrain: send money! Rather jarringly, at the end of his last letter written from the Isles, he alludes to his incarcerated brother: 'the point is an old one, and one which you are much accustomed to hearing, the same blood that flows in Richard's veins flows also in mine . . . I am desperately in need of money!!!!!! Unless financial aid awaits me in Dublin, I shall never be able to leave that city alive, but will die a swift and painful death by starvation.' How much was left of the $500 he started out with is unclear, but he made no bee-line for Dublin, deciding instead to mess about in a boat on the River Shannon, travelling with Michael Conroy, whom he had met in Galway. Conroy was Pádraic Ó Conaire's brother, and they seem to have had a delightful time of it. He makes regular appearances throughout the journal as Mr O'Connor, a more sober counterpart to Orson's madcap self.

Welles is often moved by what he sees. 'The glory of the Shannon scheme and the wonder of it are suddenly overshadowed by the great beauty of ordinary nature. I think of the much quoted and mis-quoted phrase of Joyce Kilmer – and whisper it to myself as we glide on into the dusk: "Only God can make a tree." ' The adolescent emotionalism of this passage is duplicated throughout the journal, and is as much to do with literary tone as with real feeling – shortly afterwards he 'notes with alarm a subtle hint of autumn in the air'. At Limerick he disembarked, heading for Dublin on a newly acquired bicycle named Ulysses, spelt throughout as Ulysees, especially in reference to their Oddysey. Penelope gets a mention too, but classical allusions are abandoned as he realises 'what a really long way it is to Tipperary'. Boarding another barge to travel up the Shannon again – 'in as adventurous and I fear as mad a manner as has characterised the whole of my movements in Ireland' – the account begins more and more, no doubt unconsciously, to have a Jerome K. Jerome feel about it. There are disasters with the bicycle – and the comic refrain 'I really must get my brakes fixed' – odd semi-encounters with young Irish women (who seem rather to fancy Mr O'Connor), dark suspicions of madness in entire village populations. 'I feel a part of all this joyous world about me!' he exclaims.

In the margins and sometimes across the page he sketches the barge, the countryside and especially the faces of his fellow travellers. These are vivid, brilliant in some cases. His sketch of the head bargee – 'he looks and acts like General Lee's elder brother' – is a fine creation in the manner of Jack B. Yeats. His prose becomes livelier, too, whenever another human being enters it. His immersion in plays and playing had given him that: a keen sense of character – an external view, but sharp, well observed.

They finally arrive in Athlone, the end of his peregrinations. The next stop is Dublin, which he enters by bus – the bus drawn in the journal, bowling merrily along into the sun. Over it he has scrawled: 'a great deal happened here of which I have not written' and below it: 'I am riding into Dublin thinking glad thoughts about Ireland.' They did not last long. Having surrendered to the warmth and generosity of country people, he experienced the shock of the Big City. The journal suddenly loses its hello-clouds, hello-sky blitheness. 'I am grateful that the electricity was off when I came back to my room that first evening in Dublin two days ago. If there had been light I would have sat down to this desk then and poured out the anguish that was in my soul – and it was anguish – the despairing ready-for-the-river anguish one experiences when unknown and alone in a big city and apparently forgotten at home.' No one knew where the American Express office was; when he finally found it there was nothing there for him. ' "Nothing," I shrieked – so loudly that traffic stopped on College Green to see what was the matter, "Nothing for W-E-L-L-E-S????!!!" The agent eyed me with Christ-like tenderness. "There was a post-card," said that gentleman, "for *Wallace* – but it was claimed!!" '

Even allowing for the shock of arriving in a city after a bucolic couple of months, Dublin in 1931 could well have been very daunting. Not by comparative standards a *very big* city, it had, and has, a swagger and a splendour all its own. The layout is that of a great city, some of its buildings rival those of Berlin or London, but its juxtaposition of shoddiness and splendour is more abrupt than in most great cities, its beauty intermittent, its dignity easily compromised. When Welles first crossed the Liffey (the 'dirty water' after which the city is named) the marks of the uprising of only fifteen years before were clearly visible on the great monuments of O'Connell Street, heroic scars added to noble features. Layers of history would have immediately been apparent, an essentially English Georgian city somehow subverted by its context, intimate and rural, a capriccio of curious juxtapositions, both a village and a metropolis. Small though it actually is, its character is so powerful as to be intimidating, for all its wit and vigour and good manners. Neither Kenosha nor Chicago – and certainly not Galway and Limerick – not even Tokyo or Shanghai – could have prepared Orson Welles for this maelstrom of sophisticated mullarkey.

At least he spoke the language; and – better still – there were theatres to haunt. The troubles were far enough in the past, the Free State for the moment securely enough established, to lead an uninformed visitor to believe that Dublin was still one of the capital cities of the United Kingdom. A prime date on the number one circuit for visiting theatre companies hotfoot from London, it offered sensational fare. *Bitter Sweet* straight from the West End; Will Rogers topping the variety bill upon which those sterling performers Kafka, Stanley and Mae (artists in paranoia?) were also featured. The musicians of the world played in its concert halls: Paderewski, no longer Prime Minister of Poland, was still dazzling audiences with his prodigious pianism; Conchita Supervia was in recital; and the Shakespearean rear was brought up by Sir Frank Benson and his cricket-playing thespians. The now world-famous Abbey Theatre, still presided over by Yeats and Lady Gregory, was the home of both the most vital group of national playwrights in the world and the most distinguished group of players, even eclipsing the Moscow Art Theatre in fame. It also boasted a brilliantly lively and audacious art theatre, the Gate.

The Abbey Players were in the midst of a world tour, currently playing (Orson may have been vexed to discover) in America, shortly to open in Chicago. So, forgoing the charms of *Bitter Sweet*, Polish pianists and Spanish sopranos, Orson took himself on his second evening in town down O'Connell Street to the old Rotunda, the converted eighteenth-century concert hall in which the Gate Theatre had taken up residence, to see a play distinctly not of the

Abbey School: *The Melians: A Tragedy of Imperialism*, by Edward, Earl of Longford, in which Ireland was Melos to England's Athens, a characteristically intelligent and powerful piece, not perhaps in the last resort theatrically persuasive: certainly not in the view of the young American visitor. '*New* and *native* and to blame for a stupid production', Orson told his journal. The leading part was played by the theatre's star actor, designer and co-director, Micheál Mac Liammóir, author of the Galway Taibhearc's *Diarmuid and Gráinne*. But Welles's attention was taken more excitedly by a young man playing a small role: Cathal Ó Ceallaigh, whom he had met on his travels in the North. In some excitement he went backstage to see him; they met and spent some time together wandering around Dublin. Eventually, Ó Ceallaigh invited – was persuaded to invite? – Welles to meet him at the theatre, and there he bumped into Hilton Edwards, director of *The Melians* and of the Gate itself. Before their chat had got very far, Welles boldly put himself forward for a job. Edwards 'was gracious and candid. He would be delighted, he said, but the budget would not permit of another member. He could find me a small part in *Jew Süss* just going into rehearsal but I would have to work on amateur's wages – which are just a gesture. If I cared to stick it and if we got along together bigger parts might come and he might even persuade the committee to pay me an extra guinea if I accepted.' On this basis, he started work at the Gate Theatre. The exuberance of his letters is absent from his private journal, which speaks of 'the loneliness, boredom, terror and hopes that the VERY BIG city of Dublin has caused me' and of his shame that 'the amount of things accomplished or pleasure gained in the last (nearly) three weeks is so little that an account of my squanderings of time and money would only prove depressing reading in the years to come. In a nutshell,' he rather mournfully continues, 'I have landed a job in the Gate Theatre and I *plan* to work there and go to Trinity until Christmas at least.'

Welles had been sent to Ireland, like a foreign legionnaire, to forget; in his case, the theatre. Now here he was, about to take a job in one, albeit a rather inglorious one. Then his luck changed. Charlie Margood, actor, press agent and assistant scene painter suddenly left the company and 'I am *hired*' – the words PROFESSIONAL BASIS, ringed round, are placed above 'hired' – 'in his place to fill the various departments in which he functioned'. He was, as his letters reveal, employed as a factotum, with the possibility of small roles, privileged to be involved in the work of the theatre and graciously awarded an honorarium which would barely cover his expenses. The prospect filled him with bliss. 'Step back John Barrymore, Gordon Craig and John Clayton,' he crowed, 'your day has passed, a new glory glows in the East. I am a professional!!!' The last word is underlined six times. On the following page he has drawn a cartoon of a soigné figure with a cane leaving the stage door, as flowers cascade around him. It is obviously meant as a far-fetched joke; in the event it was not so very different to what actually happened.

His arrival at the Gate Theatre was a supreme example of his being in the right place at the right time. By chance, the directors of the theatre were in a serious spot. They had announced a play – *Jew Süss* – without having an actor for the crucial second leading part, Duke Karl Alexander; Orson was one of a stream of aspirants being allowed to try for the role. 'Tomorrow is casting. I have been promised Karl Alexander, the second largest role (and thereon hangs a tale!)' He understates.

What followed has been the subject of as many variants and baroque elaborations as a Nativity Scene or an Annunciation; two of the participants were fabulists of Olympic standard and the third was loth to spoil a good story. Here is Orson's contemporary account, in a letter to Roger Hill: 'There are two big parts in Jew Süss. One is the George Arliss title role and the other is the half Emil Jannings, half Douglas Fairbanks contrast to the Jew, Karl Alexander, the Duke. I read the play, decided I had no chance as Süss and though I scarcely dreamed of getting it learned Karl Alexander. My first audition was a bitter failure. I read them a scene and being terribly nervous to please and anxious to impress I did a J. Worthington Ham with all the tricks and resonance I could conjure up.' Mac Liammóir, in his autobiography *All for Hecuba*, elaborates memorably:

> Hilton walked into the scene dock one day and said: 'Somebody strange has arrived from America; come and see what you think of it.'
>
> 'What,' I asked, 'is it?'
>
> 'Tall, young, fat: says he's been with the Guild Theatre in New York. Don't believe a word of it, but he's interesting. I want him to give me an audition . . .'

The scene of Orson's audition as Mac Liammóir describes it is a masterpiece of comedy, which needs to be read in its entirety. But it is shot through, too, with a sense of the mystery both of acting and the human personality that is entirely characteristic of its author, and powerfully perceptive of its subject, whom he never ceased to regard as a phenomenon of nature compounded equally of the monstrous and the sublime.

> 'Is this all the light you can give me?' he said in a voice like a regretful oboe. We hadn't given him any at all yet, so that was settled, and he began. It was an astonishing performance, wrong from beginning to end but with all the qualities of fine acting tearing their way through a chaos of inexperience. His diction was practically perfect, his personality, in spite of his fantastic circus antics, was real and varied; his sense of passion, of evil, of drunkenness, of tyranny, of a sort of demoniac authority was arresting; a preposterous energy pulsated through everything he did. One wanted to bellow with laughter, yet the laughter died on one's lips. One wanted to say, 'Now, now, *really*, you know,' but something stopped the words from coming. And that was because he was real to himself, because it was something more to him than a show, more than the mere inflated exhibitionism one might have suspected from his previous talk, something much more.

Hilton Edwards (who, according to Mac Liammóir, had throughout that audition, been 'shaking with silent guffaws and throwing out his hands with broad Italianate gestures as if to encourage our new friend to further frenzies') brought Orson down to the stalls. 'Terrible, wasn't it?' said Orson. 'Yes, bloody awful,' Hilton answered. 'But you can play the part . . . that is, if you make me a promise. Don't obey me blindly, but listen to me. More important still, listen to yourself. I can help show you how to play this part, but you must see and hear what's good about yourself and what's lousy.' 'But I know that already.' 'Then act on it.' Hilton's little speech presumably was made after the second audition; Orson wrote a rather different version of it to Maurice Bernstein:

> 'You're already at the point a matinee idol arrives at when it's got on in years and people are writing plays around his little tricks and capers. But that won't do here. We have nobody to write nonsense for you to show off in. You have a gorgeous stage voice and a stage presence in a million, and you're the finest overactor I've seen in aeons, but you couldn't come in and say "Milford, the carriage awaits" as well as Art, our electrician . . . you couldn't say "how do you do?" behind the footlights like a human being. You handle

your voice like a singer, and there isn't a note of sincerity in it.'

Perhaps that's what Edwards said after the first audition. Either way, his words were worth their weight in gold. Orson somehow knew in his genes what all amateur actors know: ham acting, a style which they cannot possibly have seen practised on any professional stage, harking back as it does to the start of the melodrama of the previous century. But his physique, voice and personality rendered it more striking than it would have been in most people. Edwards's advice was perfectly judged; to the extent he was prepared to take it, Orson was a good, and sometimes a superb, actor. It, and whatever other advice he received during his time at the Gate, was the only training he ever received.

Later it became very important for Welles to believe that he had strolled into the Gate, claimed to be a star of the Theatre Guild, and immediately been awarded a starring role. He wanted to suggest that he had never really had any ambitions as an actor; that becoming one was all an accident. This is, at first glance, rather modest of him. What it actually betokens is a desire to affirm his universal giftedness, but also to avoid being judged too harshly: after all, folks, I just kind of drifted into this. He told David Frost: 'I had no desire to be an actor. If I had, I would have said: "Could I have a spear to hold?" But it was ridiculous that I would be an actor, so I just said: "I am a leading actor." I played a star part the first time I ever walked on stage and I've been working my way down ever since.' Even more grandly, he told Peter Bogdanovich, 'I said I was a star already. I lied like a maniac . . . I was from America, and in Ireland, back in those distant days, anything American was possible. I informed the directors of the Gate Theatre that I was that same Welles they must have read about. Just for the lark of it, I told them I'd enjoy the experience of playing with their company for a play or two – that is, if any leading roles were available.'

At the time, of course, it was a different matter: 'need I tell you,' he wrote Skipper Hill, 'how happy I am in the arrangement? Here is the opportunity I have been praying for.' Sometimes in later years his common sense baulked at the idea of a shrewd and cosmopolitan man of the theatre like Hilton Edwards believing that a sixteen-year-old lad was a Broadway star: he told Dilys Powell in the sixties that 'Hilton can't have swallowed all that, but he was nice enough to pretend to, and he did start me at the top with leading roles.' But later, when Leslie Megahey asked him, on BBC television, 'is it reasonably true that you claimed to be a big star?' Orson replied: 'Yeah, I did. And what's true is that Hilton believed me.' Eventually, in his frustration at the persistence of scepticism about this crucial part of his myth, he played his usual trump card: the lie audacious. Of Mac Liammóir's account in *All for Hecuba* he said (also on the BBC): 'It's a wonderful description, when you consider that the author was in London at the time this was happening in Dublin. Micheál was in London the first six weeks that I was in Dublin and I got my job only with Hilton and Micheál never saw any of the stuff he writes about.' During this period, far from being in London, Mac Liammóir was playing the leading part in *The Melians*; when that failed he revived the Capek brothers' *R.U.R.*, translated *Arms and the Man* into Gaelic and directed it, and designed and built the set for *Jew Süss*. It can hardly have been possible to fail to bump into him wherever you turned at the Gate that September. And no decisions affecting the theatre were ever unilateral; Mac Liammóir and Edwards were involved in everything at every level, and both would have expected to approve Charlie Margood's replacement.

The crucial thing about Orson for both Micheál and Hilton was that someone of real force of personality had entered their lives. As an actor, assuming he could be contained, he was exactly what they had been waiting for. In *All for Hecuba*, Mac Liammóir laments that 'everywhere in Dublin among the younger members of the profession, among the students, the amateurs, the boys and the girls who want to go on the stage, one found the same complacent apathy, the same cheerful and careless approach, the same lack of passion. They showed it in their pleasant, untroubled faces, in their heavy hands, in their cheerful, colourless voices, in the prim lines of their bodies and feet. One looked in vain for some young ardent face, for an eye that showed a dilated pupil, for a quivering nostril; one listened for a catch in the breath, a break in the voice; one waited for a sudden smile, a nervous frown, for any unexpected small sign; but no, they were nice fellows and charming girls, and there was the end of them.' Orson was an answer to prayer. 'We found . . . a very tall young man with a chubby face, full powerful lips, and disconcerting Chinese eyes . . . the voice, with its brazen transatlantic sonority, was already that of a preacher, a leader, a man of power; it bloomed and boomed its way through the dusty air of the scene dock as though it would crush down the little Georgian walls and rip up the floor; he moved in a leisurely manner from foot to foot and surveyed us with magnificent patience as though here was our chance to do something beautiful at last – yes, sir – and were we going to take it? . . . and all this did not come from mere youth . . . but from some ageless and superb inner confidence that no one could blow out. It was unquenchable. That was his secret. He knew that he was precisely what he himself would have chosen to be had God consulted him on the subject at his birth.'

His conversation was hardly a disappointment, either: 'I've just told Mr Edwards some of the things I've done, Mr MacL'móir,' he said, 'but I haven't told him everything; there wouldn't be time. I've acted with the Guild. I've written a couple of plays. I've toured the States as a sword-swallowing female impersonator. I've flared through Hollywood like a firecracker. I've lived in a little tomato-coloured house on the Great Wall of China for two dollars a week. I've wafted my way with a jackass through Connemara. I've eaten dates all over the burning desert and crooned Delaware squaws asleep with Serbian rhapsodies. But I haven't told you everything. No; there wouldn't be time.' Mac Liammóir's 'almost totally inaccurate report of his monologue', as he admitted, none the less has an authentic ring to it. 'And then he threw back his head and laughed, a frenzy of laughter that involved a display of small white teeth, a buckling up of the eyes into two oblique slits, a perplexed knitting of the sparse darkly coloured brows, and a totally unexpected darting forth of a big pale tongue.'

The physical impact of Orson Welles, a thing attested to again and again, has rarely been more vividly evoked than here. The sexual undercurrent in Mac Liammóir's account is not exclusive to those, like him, of homosexual persuasion. Orson, young and old, had a way of invading you that was nothing to do with the sheer size of him, but to do rather with a knack of immediate intimacy that was one of his greatest assets. Mac Liammóir and Edwards were far from unaware of or indifferent to the sexual charm of this sixteen-year-old; but that, too, was part of his impact as an actor. The pressing question now was, precisely: could he be contained – either as an actor or as a person?

He had, by luck, or destiny, stumbled upon an extraordinary theatre, and two formidable men whom he would continue to know until the end of his life. It was not, and never would be, an uncomplicated relationship, but in some ways they, and their theatre, formed him. Mac Liammóir was, to the naked eye, the more extraordinary of the two, at the age of thirty-one sporting a jet-black toupee of rather uncertain fit, his face painted with a fine layer of flesh-toned greasepaint, eyes lined with kohl, a touch of rouge on either cheek. It was as if he were permanently onstage, attempting to play a juvenile lead in front of a groundrow of footlights. This is perhaps what a contemporary journalist meant in describing him as 'an Irishman of the high art type'. Despite all this – certainly not because of it – he was strikingly handsome, beautiful even, in a sultry, Spanish sort of a way. Hilton was as English as a side of beef, his head like an elephant's, small-eyed, with an olfactory organ of uncommon dimensions. He claimed that when he gave talks at girls' schools, he used, to avoid the snickering that his face provoked, to deliver his words from behind a screen. To all intents and purposes he was bluff and business-like. What, people would wonder, could possibly have brought these two men together? The answer is simple: love – for the theatre, and, above all, for each other. Initially a sexual passion, it had quickly modulated into a marriage of minds and hearts, fuelled by stupendous rages and fierce protective urges. In the end, perhaps, their greatest achievement was the relationship itself; but the Gate was their child.

They had met in the fit-up company of Mac Liammóir's brother-in-law, the legendary Anew McMaster, immortalised in Harold Pinter's memoir *Mac*: the last, probably, of that breed of touring actor-manager who banged around the countryside (of Ireland, mostly, in his case) playing the great classical roles in productions graced with maximum light and minimum design, in which, night after night and to barely literate audiences, they stormed the heavens, unleashing prodigies of emotional and physical power. Mac was the greatest of all these. Hilton had joined his company from the Old Vic where he had played middle-ranking roles; it was simply another stepping-stone in his career, whereas Micheál was in the process of reinventing himself. If Welles over the years tried to rewrite his own history in public, Micheál Mac Liammóir had gone further down that road than would be thought possible. Born Alfred Willmore, in North London, the son of Kentish people, he had become a child actor, the most successful of his time, playing Oliver Twist to Beerbohm Tree's Fagin in the West End of London. When his voice broke, he spent a year in Spain, then came back to England to study art at the Slade College. He was successful in his new métier (*The Star*: 'To have attained some measure of success both as an actor and as an artist, is an achievement beyond the powers of the average youthful prodigy . . . 3 weeks ago a clever drawing from his pen appeared in *Punch* . . . and he is still in knickerbockers, a merry boy, with tousled hair and inky fingers'), but while he was studying, he became possessed by a new enthusiasm: Ireland and the Irish language. Inspired by what he had seen of Ireland when touring there but above all by Yeats's exhortations to the new artists of Ireland, he learned the language, and determined to become Irish. First he settled in Howth with his ailing cousin Máire; then they toured Europe together as she moved from one sanatorium; eventually they returned to Ireland, where she died. Micheál (having rechristened himself several times) took the final form of his name, like a nun taking the veil, and shyly resumed his old trade of acting in the shelter of his brother-in-law's company. He now boasted a complete command of the Irish language and a rich accent that became the epitome of an Irish acting voice, though in truth it was unlike any Irish voice to be heard in the streets – and certainly not the streets of what he now claimed was his native city, Cork.

He was by temperament emotional, intuitive and impulsive; sexually compulsive; a dreamer, a poet, and glorious company – funny, fantastical, eloquent and inescapably exotic. As an actor he was equipped with a slight, graceful physique, a viola voice darkened by sixty cigarettes a day, and a distinct charisma. He was also prone on stage to self-hypnosis, bewitched by his own cadences, and to a certain overemphasis of his profile. There was vanity there, but also a spellbinding mystery that was his soul's natural element. Hard in writing of Micheál not to talk of soul.

Hilton, as far as his background was concerned, was what he seemed (though ironically he *did* have a strain of Irish blood in him). Onstage he was a solid, experienced English actor, powerful of lung, intelligent and authoritative. But his appearance and manner belied his soul – otherwise how could Micheál and he have been together? Behind the effectiveness and the efficiency lay a passionate, wildly fluctuating nature, prone to despair. Micheál calls his temperament Russian. Welles described him in a letter as 'our dynamic, hot-tempered and golden-hearted Lord of Lords'. Even at sixteen, Welles was well enough experienced in emotional politics not to have been overwhelmed by the tornado that Micheál and Hilton together constituted; but it is to be wondered how much input a youthful psyche can endure. His capacity was unusually high. He wrote to Skipper that 'there's not a "ham" nor an "arty" among us. I really didn't think such a company existed – where people were serious-minded and highly intelligent and well-educated and combined those virtues with the more cardinal sense of humour – wholesomeness – and a rationality and sense of value.' Wholesomeness is an unexpected word to come across in this context – Micheál took a demonic delight in outraging conventional expectation ('have you never been to bed with a woman, then, Mr Mac Liammóir?'

asked a journalist, to which he replied that he'd been accused of a lot of things, 'but never of being a Lesbian') – but basic decency was at the heart of their lives and work. 'We are a kind of Irish Theatre Guild – that is to say an Art Theatre on a commercial basis,' Welles wrote, and so they were, up to a point.

'We wanted,' wrote Hilton only a couple of years later, 'a first-hand knowledge of the new methods of presentation discovered by the Continental experimental theatres. We wanted ourselves to discover new forms. We wanted to revive, or at least take advantage of, and learn from the best of the discarded old traditions. And, not least, we wanted to put at the disposal of our audiences all the riches of the theatre, past, present and future, culled from the theatres of all the world and irrespective of their nationality. A theatre limited only by the limits of the imagination. In spite of all the efforts of pioneers . . . Appia, Craig . . . and except for . . . the work of such producers as Robert Atkins and Théodore Komisarjevsky, the contemporary theatre of Europe was still in the thraldom of naturalism . . . the art of the theatre has become indistinguishable from the art of the camera.'

This is very interesting in the light of Orson Welles's subsequent career in the theatre: he too was enamoured of experiment; he too associated this with a return to the past. Aware of the encroachment of the moving picture, Hilton described the theatre's unique contribution: 'when the theatre once again makes its audience conscious of the presence of its art, people will go to the theatre to see and hear a theatrical performance, and to the cinema to see a cinematic one. The theatre will be the theatre precisely because it is theatrical.' From an entirely different (specifically, an aesthetic rather than a political) perspective, the Gate Theatre arrived at a philosophy similar to Brecht's, rejecting the creeping naturalism of the 1880s which, paradoxically, became the territory of the movies. 'The theatre,' Hilton wrote, 'has lost the individuality it once had; therefore we seek, not for something new, but for something once possessed and now mislaid, and that is the conscious realisation of the presence of the audience . . . the stage picture must step once more out of its frame and become three dimensional; and it must live, not by its semblance of reality but because it *is* reality – real actors speaking real words to real audiences. There is your realism for you, whatever the method of its presentation.'

Welles, in the mid-sixties, said of Hilton and Micheál: 'They gave me an education. Whatever I know about any of the stage arts today is only an extension of what I first knew from them.'

He learned his lessons well, but the substance of his thinking was formed here. The Gate was only three years old when Welles arrived; the ideas that lay behind it were still fresh. They were still fulfilling their manifesto, consciously opposing themselves to the Abbey Theatre, now no longer the poets' theatre of Yeats's dream, though he was still running it. They disdained that theatre's present policy of 'peasant and other domestic dramas' performed in an acting style that according to Micheál was merely 'behaving – their behaviour was Irish and not English, but neither was it acting'. The Gate believed fundamentally in Coquelin's dictum that 'the arts differ according to the nature of their medium; well, the actor's medium is – himself.' Micheál had his own variation: 'The actor works with himself as surely as a philosopher does with his brain, or a prostitute with her body.' The crucial word is work. However exotic a bloom Micheál's personality may have been, it was the outcome of strenuous and continuing cultivation, pushed so that it was naturally and fluently able to express more and more interesting states of being; and this it was that they both tried to impress on the sixteen-year-old barbarian who had just joined their company. High spirits and a striking presence were not enough.

Rehearsals with Welles were alternately inspiring and dismaying: 'There were moments that held one breathless with excitement, and there were sometimes hours together when we would look dumbly at one another with pursed lips and wagging heads thinking, "This sort of thing will never do." ' The role of Karl Alexander is not without its pitfalls, to put it mildly. Welles was right to describe it as the fattest of the two parts in the play – 'it runs the gauntlet of fine temper scenes, drunks, daring seductions, rapine, murder, heart attacks and death.' Adapted by Ashley Dukes from Lion Feuchtwanger's novel, it is the story of how a rich and cultured Jew assists to power the minor nobleman Karl Alexander, distantly related to the incumbent Duke. Enthroned, Karl Alexander depends entirely on the Jew, until he turns against him, tracking him down in his private hide-away. Discovering that Süss has a daughter, he attempts to rape her. She evades him, but in so doing, she falls from an upper window and dies. The Jew has his revenge which precipitates Karl Alexander's heart attack. Süss is taken away to his death. – The play ('a tragic comedy') is, unlike the novel, melodrama. The whole interest lies in the character of the main antagonists. Had the actor playing the Duke failed, the play would have failed, for all that Süss is the central character. Süss watches, comments, flicks a scene this way and that. Even in extremity, his passion is controlled, filtered through thought. Matheson Lang, with his extraordinary presence and other-worldly voice had managed the two sides of Süss – cunning sophisticate and deeply religious father – with notable success in the London première; but it was Frank Harvey as Karl Alexander who had made it possible. The role, Orson accurately observed in a letter home, is 'all positives'. Unexpectedly he adds 'I prefer dealing with negations' – a reference, I suspect, to his shrewd awareness that in a role like that of the Duke, one can do all the work while allowing the other actor quietly to steal all the glory (particularly since Hilton was playing the Jew).

The directors of the Gate had taken an enormous gamble in hiring him for such a pivotal role. Welles seems to have had no doubts of his ability to play the part, but then he was being kept very busy in the paint shop and the press department as well as in the rehearsal room, so can barely have had time for doubt – Micheál pictures him at the time: 'He had indeed that unwavering energy of those that are born for the stage, and after rehearsing the Duke all day and raging round the town from show to show, from Jimmy O'Dea at the Olympia to some earnest young group of Left players reciting *Roar China* in a gaslit garage, he would gobble supper in Noonan's or the Kitchen or harangue a group of Trinity students or Gaelic Leaguers or the like until the small hours, when he would return, if we gave him the permission and the keys, to paint flats for us at the Gate until somebody fished him up from a bucket or down from a ladder or gave him breakfast.' Whatever misgivings Micheál and Hilton may have had there was no going back: on 10 October 1931, the play was announced, including the following: 'A newcomer to the large cast will be Orson Wells [sic] who served his apprenticeship to the stage at the Goodman Memorial Theatre in Chicago under the direction of Whitford Kane, formerly of the Ulster Literary Theatre.' Perhaps he found he could sustain a story about the Goodman better than one about the Theatre Guild – he had after all acted on its stage, though not as part of its company, and never under Kane's direction. The mention of an Irish name was a smart move. In his long letter to Roger Hill (with a mock formal frontispiece saying A SERIES OF PARAGRAPHS DEALING SOLELY WITH MYSELF) he writes on the last page: 'Tonight is the first dress rehearsal and the day after tomorrow night I make my *professional debut* (ahem!) – in a foreign country – and in the most accent-conscious city on the globe!' At the top of the page is a sketch of his periwigged head; above it, in a bubble, the words OH! YEAH!

OH! YEAH! indeed. 'In all the striving years since my debut,

I have never achieved such an ovation,' Orson said, and for once, this may be the unvarnished truth. The first night of *Jew Süss* was Orson's night, one of those occasions – theatrical and operatic history is full of them – when a newcomer creates an excitement verging on hysteria that the greatest artists at their height cannot create, and that they themselves can never duplicate. The effect is perhaps even more startling in a small city (Dublin's population was a fraction of London's, and it had perhaps a tenth the number of theatres) and in a small theatre. The Gate held just over four hundred people. For this occasion, it was packed: the Abbey was away on tour, and, more importantly, the company had, for the first time since moving to its new premises, established a regular audience that it could rely on. They were rooting for the show, which was anyway quite a hot property, a London hit of only four years before, never seen in Dublin. It was a Big Night and no mistake.

Previews were a thing of the future: in Dublin, in 1931, the First Night was the *first* night. Hilton's technical rehearsals were legendarily long-winded affairs, sometimes going over two days. He was something of a pioneer in lighting, an absolute innovator in the Irish theatre, but a restless experimenter by any standards. There is every chance that there had never been a full run-through of the play until that first performance. Adrenalin must have been running at dangerously high levels. Orson often claimed that he had never known stage fright until that night, but his appetite for the fray surely converted such nerves as he had into raw energy. An audience never fails to respond to that appetite, that need, which has a kind of innocence, naked in its lust to perform. He uttered a prayer to Ming Huang, the Chinese patron saint of actors, and entered the stage, as he later said, 'in the bliss of ignorance, like a baby on a trapeze'. His first sight of the audience, he said, confirmed Edwin Booth's description of it as a 'crouching and invisible beast'. Then he began, scattering his oafish insults and libidinous glances, 'a full-blooded soldierly figure in field-marshal's uniform', fully thirty-five years younger than the character he was playing.

MANAGER

I beg you to respect his highness's privacy.

KARL ALEXANDER

Privacy – trash! We live in a royal window, and the rabble
are welcome to rub their greasy nose on the glass . . . we
are used to be stared at, as a soldier is used to fire and a
pretty woman to kisses . . . they have seen me before, for my

> picture hangs in all their kitchens to be smoked between a pair of hams.

'When Orson came padding onto the stage with his lopsided grace, his laughter, his softly thunderous voice, there was a flutter of astonishment and alarm, a hush, and a volley of applause,' Mac Liammóir wrote. Hilton, as was still the custom, brought Orson forth at the first short interval, then again at the second. 'Hilton said some words of praise and introduction. Orson swelled visibly. I have heard of people swelling visibly before, but Orson is one of those who really do it.' The play resumed. Orson was by now very high indeed. Betty Chancellor as Naomi had her big scene with him; a love scene. 'His extraordinarily mature acting fell apart. He was then obviously embarrassed and unsure and he tried to hide this by gripping me with such violence that I nearly lost my life but certainly not my virtue.' During the second act, he murmured the phrase 'A bride fit for Solomon. He had a thousand wives, did he not?' and was so fazed by a cry from the audience of 'that's a black Protestant lie!' that he mangled his next line: 'Ring the canons and fire the bells!' Before anyone could interrupt, he hurled himself down the steps, and was greeted by an even greater ovation than he had received before. 'Dubliners, besides being very keen critics, are also generous with their praise, and I don't suppose that anything like that frenzied back-flip had been seen on the shores of the Liffey before.'

He took his final curtain call to a roar of acclaim. At the back of the theatre, or perhaps lurking in the wings, all unknown to Orson, was Micheál Mac Liammóir (who had designed the play but was not in it), observing and judging.

> Orson bows slowly, sedately; that they should realise him like this merits a bow, so slow and sedate the head goes down and quickly up again, up higher than ever, for maybe this is all a dream, and if the eyes are on the boots, blood rushing to the ears, who knows that sight and sound may not double-cross and vanish like a flame blown out, and Orson be back at school again, hungry, unsatisfied, not ready yet for the world? No, the people are still there, still applauding, more and more and more, and back goes the big head, and the laugh breaks out like a fire in a jungle, a white lightning slits open across the chubby sweating cheeks, the brows knit in perplexity like a coolie's, the hands shoot widely out to either side, one to the right at Hilton, the other to the

> left at Betty, for you don't mean to say that all this racket is for Orson? What about Hilton and Betty? And anyway there's Ashley Dukes, and there's a man called Feuchtwanger, isn't there? But whoever it's all about it goes on and on, then trickles back a little like a sea slowly receding, receding, curling away like a fire burning out, fading inexorably, emptying itself hollow; and God damn that stage manager anyway. Couldn't he easily steal a couple more of them before the thing dies down? Take that curtain up again, you silly son of a bitch; to taste the last, to drain it dry, no meat left clinging to the bone: no, no! listen! three pairs of hands keep on, then two, then six, then sixty, and then – ah! – then the whole house again, and up goes the curtain once more and the light shoots like a rainbow through the eyes and the unappeasable head rears up round as a cannon ball: no bowing now, no boot-licking booby tricks, *let them have me as I am and so. And so.* And the jaws snap, crunch, and then the foolish curtain closes down. For the last time. The last time.

The violence of this passage leaps off the pages of *All for Hecuba* with disturbing savagery. Clearly Mac Liammóir was angry at the eclipse of Hilton and Betty Chancellor: 'Hilton's beautiful performance of Süss with its suffering pallor, its agonised repression, the slow-mounting horror of its martyrdom and pain was approved and taken for granted, and so was Betty's exquisite Naomi, all amber and carved ivory.' But there's more, something darker and deeper than that in this account, written, or at any rate published, some fifteen years after the event. There's a real loathing, if not of Orson, then of an aspect of him: his crude lust for applause, ruthlessly vainglorious. It's not the only time in *All for Hecuba* that Micheál, avowedly a friend, turns a remorselessly harsh light on the boy (still, let us not forget, sixteen years old, and in his first professional job). Was there a sense in which Micheál envied what he saw in Orson – a sort of hugeness of appetite for public approval, a capacity for fame on a scale that Micheál had explicitly renounced by establishing himself in Dublin, an obscure corner of the English-speaking theatre? Did he (by no means oblivious to acclaim) see himself unattractively mirrored in Orson's shameless stimulation of the audience? The note that seems to underlie the raillery is one of disappointment; a feeling that Orson had somehow betrayed himself, and perhaps betrayed Micheál too.

The complexity of the relationship between Micheál, Hilton and Orson needs to be considered for a moment, though nothing definitive can be said on the subject. Orson in later life – after their deaths – spoke very differently of the two of them, seeking to derogate Micheál, and to endorse Hilton. Micheál was, in this late view, a shrieking, screaming queen, ridiculous in his make-up, insatiable in his desires and full of malice. Hilton was a terrific chap, trusting, warm, good-natured, who should really have been heterosexual. ('He just fell under the spell of Micheál, you know, who ruled him like the Queen of the Night,' he told Leslie Megahey on BBC television.) Preposterously, he told Barbara Leaming that Micheál felt threatened by Orson's friendship with Hilton – 'the friendship of two *men* with no sexual overtones' – fearing that Hilton might be restored to heterosexuality, a laughable insistence by Welles that his heterosexual orientation was so powerful as actually to be contagious. In fact, Betty Chancellor noted that Orson at that age was abnormally immature in any kind of sexual discussion 'or even in playing a part that called for a romantic side'; scarcely a good role model for Hilton's wavering orientation. What seems more likely is that Orson was drawn to Hilton as a father-figure – not the first time this had happened – and that he had used his uniquely seductive charms to gain Hilton's affections.

If Hilton had betrayed so much as a flicker of interest in the boy – whether emotional or sexual – Micheál would certainly have moved in on him with the speed and the venom of a black mamba. Micheál may even have known what Orson was attempting before Orson himself did. There was something witch-like about him, as he freely admitted, with his intuitive, thought-reading faculties. Talking about Micheál's alleged absence from his first six weeks in Dublin, Orson cited as proof that 'Micheál would have seen through it, you see, and Micheál didn't like the fact that Hilton had that kind of gullibility. Micheál hated the fact that I had put over anything on them.' It may even be that Orson had tried to charm Micheál. Hortense Hill had written to Orson: 'The only thing that might happen is that you might meet a brilliant person that was fascinating company that – ' 'What dire threat were you about to make and what sinister power stayed your hand??????' wrote back Orson. 'Seriously, my purse and my virtue are intact and will remain so long as I confine myself to my present company.' If he did try to charm Micheál, he was taking on more than he could handle. Micheál was passionate and elusive, emotional and unwavering, skittish and savage. He was all of these things by turn, sometimes all at once, and he knew it; knew himself with awful familiarity, and he was able to bring all these things to his acting, though he was just as capable of substituting for it a much inferior high-flown manner. His writing – the very account of Orson's first night – was, for all its beguiling wit and fantasy, sometimes possessed of a startling ugly honesty. Perhaps he saw, and deplored, to what extent Welles was substituting energy and exuberance for his real self: a self, despite Orson's denials ('I am like Hilton; I believe anything anyone tells me'), not entirely dissimilar to Micheál's.

None of these complexities could have clouded Welles's delight in his notices for *Jew Süss* and his continuing acclaim in the role of Karl Alexander. 'Tonight,' he wrote to Hortense Hill, 'I took 6 curtain calls alone – with the gallery and the pit shouting and stamping and calling out my name. This sounds like an *appalling* boast, and so it is.' Understandable, and forgivable: every single notice praised him, in detailed terms. *Dublin Opinion* reported that 'the young American actor received nothing short of a personal triumph', *The Herald* pronounced his impersonation 'interesting at every moment', while *The Independent* found 'a touch of humanity and simplicity in his swinishness which in less expert hands might have been lost . . . Orson Welles captured it magnificently.' Everywhere the performance was held to be 'a notable success' and 'excellent'. That shrewd, spinsterish self-appointed commissar of the Dublin theatre, Joseph Holloway, confided to his diary that Welles 'looked the uncouth, hard-drinking, loud-voiced brute the author intended him to be and made quite an impression by a clever character study. He was blustering and sensual and repellent.'

The Dublin critics did not, none the less, abandon all sense of proportion. *The Irish Times* struck a cautionary note that was repeated elsewhere: 'It will be necessary to see him in other parts before it can be said that he is the accomplished actor that he seemed last night in a part that might have been especially made for him.' 'Whether it is that there has never till now been a character like Karl Alexander portrayed at the Gate,' wrote 'N' in the *Weekly Times*, 'or whether Welles is really a brilliant actor, remains to be seen.'

No such reservations were made in what was for Welles the most important of these notices. J.J. Hayes, the *New York Times*'s man in Dublin, nailed his colours to the mast in his report: 'the Duke is played by a young American actor, 18 years old, whose performance is astonishingly fine.' Hayes then offered a brief synopsis of Welles's Irish expedition, dangerously recycling a legend to which some of his American readers would have been able to give the lie: 'Welles, who had appeared occasionally at the Goodman Theatre Chicago and in small parts with the Theatre Guild in New

York . . .' Reporting the first night triumph, Hayes outlined the prodigy's future plans: 'Dublin is eager to see him in other roles . . . his coming will probably lead to the production of *Coriolanus*, which was shelved . . . because a suitable man could not be found for the title part . . . 35 years since it was done in Ireland by Sir Frank Benson.'

Now this really is publicity of a kind indispensable at the start of a career. How fortunate that he should have had a tremendous admirer in the Gate's press office: one Orson Welles. There is no question that Welles made a smash at the beginning of his time in Dublin, but the continuing waves that his name created owe not a little to the fact that he was in constant contact with the press, and able to feed them stories whenever things were a bit slack. The *Coriolanus* story is a real novelty; actually not such a bad idea: Aufidius's scornful 'boy' would have had a peculiar resonance. Nothing came of it, probably because it had just entered his mind at that moment, and went out of it a moment later.

'People began to talk about Orson,' wrote Mac Liammóir. ' "Young Welles" they called him, with that curious bantering sense of self-congratulation the public feels when its new idol has not reached the age of twenty; and many Dublin matrons had a proprietary look in their eyes when they praised him as though they had given him birth and were vaguely responsible for the wayward and unexpected qualities of his talent.' He became the toast of Dublin, when, that is, he was not painting flats, catching midnight matinees, and rehearsing for the next play. 'It will delight you,' he wrote to Hortense Hill, 'who so long have lamented my social delinquencies, to know that I am now found in the society of young femininity and that I blossom in starched shirt front once or twice a week, to the edification of various Dublin "sets"!' He made the acquaintance of the Gate's principal supporters, later arch rivals, the Earl and Countess of Longford, Edward – the Earl – revealing that 'his favourite words were virile, pronounced virral and futile, pronounced footle. "Life is footle, Lord LongFORD," he used to say; "life is footle." He was a great man at a party. When he thought a party had gone on long enough, he would say, "Take me out to Kilmashogue to see the fairies!" I don't know that anyone ever did.' His sheer Americanness fascinated everyone: Denis Johnston wrote in his diary about 'the new American boy Orson Welles playing what he calls "The Dook".' Lady Longford, wit and novelist, was given the full guided tour: Orson Welles, The Early Years: 'The extraordinary thing about Orson was that he became a legend almost at once. Everyone started talking about him . . . that he had walked round the Great Wall of China; that he had played in Greek plays in Greece and had Turkish baths in Turkey. He was said to be eighteen at first, and later seventeen. But one thing was certain – he could act. There was no doubt about that. And another thing was, he was as nice and friendly as could be.'

Quite apart from the cocktail circuit, Dublin in 1931 was an extraordinary place to be. The Irish Free State, newly established, was conducting its affairs with some panache. The terrible beauty born in 1916 had transformed itself into the forms and structures of regular government: Denis Johnston recalled the lavish viceregal hospitality of the period, remembering 1931 as being 'a time of balls and parties'. The city's life was a curious blend of the stately and old-fashioned with the politically historic. V.S. Pritchett, just a few years before, noted that 'people had tea parties. They lived on cake. One was back in Mrs Gaskell's country world; and at the same time was thrown forward into the first conflict of colonialism.' The heroic figures of the recent past were very much present: as recently as 1929, Maud Gonne MacBride had been arrested. 'British or Irish Free State seems to make no difference. She is still evidently considered a stormy petrel,' wrote Joseph Holloway. Pritchett was alarmed, taking tea with Yeats, to see him go to the window and 'swoosh the tea leaves into Merrion Square, for all I knew on the heads of Gogarty, AE, Lady Gregory, James Stephens – who might have popped over from the library or the Museum.' Yeats remained a commanding figure in the community. The theatre – despite the temporary absence of the Abbey – was still a central event in its existence, whether the plays were actually attended or not. The debates over O'Casey were still raging: was his picture of Irish history and the Irish character acceptable? It was a mere two years since *The Silver Tassie* had been turned down. St Stephen's Green was daily agog with the events of the previous night on stage, a sort of living newspaper; the various factions were regulars in the soap opera that was Dublin's daily life. So the arrival of a very young American actor at the still controversial, the still radical and daring, Gate Theatre, was an event.

And Dublin was always ready for a novelty. 'It is astonishing,' wrote Pritchett, 'to see how watchful Dubliners are of each other. This is said to be because Dublin is a village where everyone knows everyone else; certainly a rural ethos prevails. Every word uttered in the pub or at dinner will be repeated and added to; so that one is living in a web of gossip, usually with a malicious edge to it;

you can see your friends eagerly alerted for it and you know they are teasing it out of you. Malice they love. It keeps their gifts alive, establishes their distinction, and sharpens what they most care for: their personality.' That was what Orson most cared for, too. He took to the attention he received with almost indecent relish. Again, Micheál Mac Liammóir was on hand, observing and judging. 'When the demon of showmanship was on him, he would be intolerable; something dark and brutal swept through him when a stupid audience surrounded him, and he would use them mercilessly, without shame or repulsion, blaring out his impromptu opinions and trumpeting his jungle-laughter as one tinsel fable followed another, and the circle of fish-eyes watched his antics spell-bound like children at a country fair . . . it was the shameful sight of Ariel borrowing the tatters of Caliban and wearing them with such naive complacency that made one blush and look away.' The note of disappointment sounds again. It was that public self that Micheál hated in Orson; in private he was someone else. 'With theatre people he was at his best, good nature bubbling irresistibly out of him sweet as wild honey in a young bear's paw. He was charming, almost invariably charming, and full of generosity, giving little parties for us all and suddenly asking for advice like a penitent child who has been fractious when there were strangers in the house.'

Most of his time he was with theatre people, so this best side of him must have been frequently on display. He seems to have plunged into every available activity; as if his multiple duties at the Gate (especially in the Press Office) were not enough, he became Head of Design for an enterprise ('an art-theatrish stock company quite distinct from the Gate', he wrote to Roger Hill) run by, and starring, his chum William Sherwood. They played at the Peacock Theatre, the Abbey's Studio, available for hire in the absence of the resident company. 'I am kept in a state of perpetual sweaty bliss.' Sherwood was an ambitious fellow, and the list of plays in the weekly repertory that he and Orson got on is impressive. Their first, *Alice in Wonderland*, adapted by Sherwood, called for twenty-two settings. It opened the day after Boxing Day, 1931, and was liked by *The Independent*. 'The settings, designed and decorated by Orson Welles are attractive and appropriate . . . in the true spirit.' That stern judge, Joseph Holloway, was not so impressed: 'The whole show gave one the idea of being hastily strung together and lacking in vitality . . .' which, if true, is not entirely surprising, since it was the day before the Gate opened Pádraic Colum's Persian fantasia *Mogu of the Desert*, in which Orson had a small but crucial role. His productivity, possibly at the expense of excellence, was thus established at a very early age. He liked, in later life, to quote Chesterton's remark that if a thing is worth doing, it is worth doing badly, but it is doubtful whether Chesterton intended an endorsement of sloppiness, rather an encouragement of attempting tasks beyond one's apparent abilities. For Orson, it would seem, the sensation of being urgently occupied was often more important than the satisfaction of completing things to the best of his ability.

His season at the Gate was progressing interestingly, but perhaps not thrillingly enough for him. The Duke proved a hard act to follow. Ovations can prove dangerously addictive, and there was little in what came next that could provide them. Nor, it is reasonable to assume, did the directors of the Gate particularly wish to provide them. Theirs was a serious theatre, with radical aspirations. They had two leading actors, Edwards the character lead, Mac Liammóir the romantic, and their programme was to provide a blend of modern and classical plays, performed in a stimulating style. They were also trying to develop a company of actors who had a sure sense of style and a sure sense of themselves. In those terms, it would not only have been strange, it would have been disastrous both for the theatre and for Welles if they had sought to provide a series of vehicles for him. It is understandable that Orson should have regretted this attitude, but peculiar that so many of his biographers have also accused Edwards and Micheál of jealousy and spite in not promoting his career more spectacularly than they did. In the event, they handled the sixteen-year-old well and generously.

The press department (a.k.a. Orson Welles) continued to push him in the direction of journalists. Just before *Jew Süss* closed (it was extended for an extra week) the London *Daily Express* felt compelled

> while on the subject of the Gate Theatre to mention the fact that after all we have the 'bright boy' of the American stage, Mr Orson Welles, with us until the end of the Gate Season, which is certainly good news, for . . . he has descended on Dublin and taken it by storm.

Almost wearily he adds

> As this young man's amazing life and adventures are now everybody's property I will not say much more; but when I hear him mention his trip alone across Manchuria, experiences in Canada,

> life in a barge on the Shannon, acting in California, painting in Connemara and the Aran Isles, I would like to give him a good shake and say: 'How dare you have done all these things when you're not even twenty years old. It isn't fair when the rest of us lead such dull, prosaic lives.'

He may not have been the only person in Dublin who would like to have given him a good shake.

His next show for the Gate, *The Dead Ride Fast*, was a bizarre farrago by David Sears set in The House of Shame, where Fintan O'Driscoll, a Black Magician, wreaks terrible things with his Book of Knowledge; Welles played an American millionaire who happens to be passing by. Mary Manning in *The Independent*, liking his performance, wrote that he was a great acquisition to the Gate but that 'he must not be given too many aged parts, as they keep him in a state of permanent semi-intoxication. We all want to see young Mr Welles without a wig!' Joseph Holloway grumpily dissented: 'I didn't like Orson Welles; his American accent on top of his big gruff voice was hard to understand.'

Only Holloway read Holloway's diary; Welles's most enthusiastic notice was by far the most important, and the most widely read: Hayes in *The New York Times* again. Welles brought to his portrayal, America was told, 'qualities of subtlety sufficient to make him mystically sinister without approaching the grotesque. Irish drama is reaching out,' said Hayes, 'and Mr Sears has brought it far.' Percy Robinson attempted to take it even further in the Gate's next offering, *The Archdupe*, with its punning title about the Archduke Maximilian, Napoleon III's puppet Emperor of Mexico. Hilton played the eponymous patsy; Micheál was Napoleon III. Again Welles (General Bazaine) played much older than his own age. He was settling into a line of parts for which his physique, his voice and his taste for broad characterisation largely achieved by intensive application of make-up well suited him: he was becoming, at the age of sixteen, the supporting heavy.

There was in the Irish Theatre in general and particularly at the Gate a dearth of such actors – those occupying the middle ground of the cast list, the solid underpinning of the play. These roles do not often bring glory to those who play them; General Bazaine in *The Archdupe* was no exception. Still, on the whole, his work was admired, though now critical voices were heard. J.J. Hayes remained steadfastly loyal, and did not fail to tell the readership of *The New York Times* that 'at the première, the young American actor Orson

Welles scored heavily . . . as the French general he succeeded in maintaining that balance which left in doubt whether Bazaine was a traitor or merely indolent and procrastinating.' Whatever the merits of the plays or the performances, Welles was certainly gaining solid experience; and he was working very hard.

The Archdupe closed on Saturday 5 December. The next day, before rehearsals for Pádraic Colum's *Mogu of the Desert* started on the 7th, he managed to slip in a performance in a Sunday night production at the Abbey (his only appearance on that stage): Somerset Maugham's *The Circle*. It was an amateur production in which he had taken over the leading role of Lord Porteous at the last moment. 'He had put most of the contents of his make-up box on his face in order to look sixty,' the producer recalled. 'We had to scrape him off while the other actors waited at curtain-rise.' *The Independent* applauded his 'hirsute, cantankerous and rather simian peer'. Holloway, by now very suspicious of the young actor, was, on the contrary, highly critical: Welles, he said, was made up 'with a pantomime head placed on square shoulders, and arms and legs that behaved like the penny wooden dancing masters where one pulled the string! He seemed completely out of the picture. His voice is gruff and his manner uncouth. He made quite a hit in *Jew Süss* as the rogue, the old Duke, as all his mannerisms suited the role, but in all his characters since he has only repeated himself till one is inclined to think him a grotesque instead of an actor.'

In the 1970s, Welles, talking to the BBC, remembered the event in a different light. 'My greatest success was at the Abbey, playing Lord Porteous in *The Circle*, who was a sixty-year-old man and I played such a terrible, hateful parody of an upper-class Englishman that the entire Irish public took me to their bosoms.' To compare the modest appreciation extended to the Sunday-night performance of *The Circle* with the blast of praise that greeted his Karl Alexander in *Jew Süss* is absurd; but Welles was by then intent on minimising the importance of the Gate Theatre in his life. 'At the Gate,' he said, 'I got less and less good parts and I saved myself by going over to the Abbey,' which is scarcely less absurd. He had not 'gone over' to the still-touring Abbey Company, but simply played in a Sunday-night amateur production in their theatre while continuing to be a member of the Gate company. His next appearance for them was in *Mogu*, another example of the Gate's inability to find new plays of distinction, a fact which Mac Liammóir's ambitious design in the manner of Hafiz failed to conceal. Welles's performance was itself a triumph of appearance over substance. His make-up was a marvel, involving, according to Mac Liammóir, 'several pounds of nose putty, a white turban at least two and a half feet in diameter, and three-inch fingernails of peacock-blue and silver'. His work brought forth a double-edged comment from *The Irish Times*: 'His performance is good enough to keep one still doubting'; they were still doubting.

The play failed and the run was curtailed, the company immediately plunging into yet another new play, *Death Takes a Holiday* by Walter Ferris, from an Italian original. Welles had a more substantial and more glamorous role in this, giving his second Duke of the season: Duke Lamberto who escapes Death (in the guise of the Russian Prince Sirki: Mac Liammóir, of course) thanks to the love of the dreamy Grazia. *The Irish Times* finally started to come off the fence about the young actor: 'Mr Orson Welles did much to satisfy those who have had doubts of his possibilities.' Immediately *Death Takes a Holiday* opened (in January 1932) rehearsals began for *Hamlet*, with Mac Liammóir in the title role, one for which he became famous. Welles was the Ghost and Fortinbras. In his spare time (which was considerable: the two roles together occupy about ten minutes of stage time), he designed Jules Romains' play *Dr Knock* for Sherwood's Peacock Players; his work was admired by *The Independent* for the 'hints at Cézanne in his modernist treatment of the landscape'.

Hamlet was an enormous success for the Gate. They needed one. Produced by Hilton Edwards in what would now be regarded as a straightforward manner, it was for the time revolutionary in eschewing heavily realistic scenery and in its swift, conversational style. Mac Liammóir went against tradition by playing Hamlet like a man communing with himself; Edwards had used light to speed the action from one location to the next, so that the play was released as the mercurial, ever-shifting dramatic poem that it is rather than the series of historical tableaux favoured by the Victorians and Edwardians. In the general glory, Welles was frequently singled out: particularly for his Ghost: seldom, said *The Irish Press*, 'can the Ghost have been more movingly portrayed'. Even that old curmudgeon Holloway acknowledged that 'Orson Welles made the speech of the Ghost almost human as well as awesome.' No doubt he was able to invest the figure of the dead father with a singularly personal urgency. 'Remember me!' It was a good note on which to go out. He did a final design for the Peacock Players (*The All Alone*) and then took off for London, on his way home.

We may take it as preposterous (as has been suggested by some of his biographers) that Welles left Ireland in a huff because he was not offered *Coriolanus* or the part of King Magnus in *The Apple Cart*. It is conceivable that he might have asked to be allowed to play some such huge play-carrying leading role (compared to which even the Duke in *Jew Süss* is a bagatelle), but he cannot have held out much hope. He had done well, wonderfully well, but as the reviews increasingly suggest, he was more of a phenomenon, an adolescent Roscius, than a member of the ensemble that Micheál and Hilton were trying to establish. Somehow, in order really to develop, he would need to start again, to wipe the slate clean of his freakish success, build his craft and his understanding. As it was, he was eager to leap onto the stage with half the contents of his make-up box on his face, putting on voices. It is to be doubted whether he had, in his heart, accepted Hilton Edwards's sterling advice: 'listen to yourself . . . you must see and hear what's good about yourself and what's lousy.' It was very hard for Welles to develop. He preferred only to go further, which is not at all the same thing. Having rather splendidly got away with a couple of supporting parts, he now wanted to hurl himself at the great roles. If not physically, then technically, it is as dangerous for a young actor to take on those huge roles as it is for a singer. You will only get through them on tricks; and you will find it almost impossible to unlearn those tricks, especially if, as is likely, you will be acclaimed, simply for having had the courage. To be acclaimed for giving a good performance 'for a sixteen-year-old' is a bad precedent. It became hard for critics from this point on to assess Welles's work on its merits. Already they knew too much about the person behind the work; there was always an element of special pleading, over and above it, an element of the phenomenal.

Dublin had spoiled him, to an extent. It is hard to imagine a city in the Western World – outside, perhaps, an Italian one – where he could find an audience so vocal, so parti pris, so excitable. He had thrilled them to the marrow, then of course both he and they wanted more thrills. Mac Liammóir watched him keenly, oddly perturbed by the sight of a unique personality and outstanding gifts somehow subordinated to a cruder, grosser, unrelenting other self: 'of course it was said in Dublin that he never did anything half as good as the Duke again. It was, I think, untrue. Everything he touched took on a queer and gruesome magic, a misshapen and indescribable grace . . . through the turbulent vapours of his temperament there flows a broad river full of stars . . . all with Orson was theatre; the radiance that shone from him was the light never seen on land or sea, but invariably on painted flats and proscenium arches. He seldom,

I think, noticed the wind in the chimney-tops, or the moon on the water, or the rain on the roof; seldom wandered in his mind to the shadows of the woods or tasted solitude on the mountain-tops; all in his world was bustle and authority, a laughing, easily fought battle in the heart of the traffic. He was born for success, big, rapid, and decisive; people excited him and beautiful things aroused his passion, but people and things must all be flung together and hurled into boxes and crates and swept away to make room for new ones at a moment's notice, and he would sail through them all or cast them into the sea or shatter them into fragments and, sitting straddle-legged over the debris, start to work again whistling and laughing and all in the highest spirits.'

And yet, months before, he had been lying on his back on the Isles of Aran, watching the moon and feeling himself part of a great lost civilisation. Dublin and the Gate and Duke Karl Alexander had been the drug that had hooked him for life, which is what he meant when he had John Houseman say of him (in his autobiographical 1982 screenplay *The Cradle Will Rock*, never filmed):

> In Dublin, when he started in the theatre he was just sixteen and claiming to be what he is now – twenty-two. In effect, this was a pact with hell; he sold his youth for grown-up glory. As a result of which we are inflicted with these flashes of that delinquent adolescence which he appears to have bartered away.

He had always aspired to the theatre; it was his dream and his goal. Actually experiencing it had made it, as it does for so many people who make their lives in it, a focus and a release for all the many conflicting and sometimes intolerable aspects of his personality. It is both liberation and affirmation; one is no longer trapped inside one's murky self, because one offers it to other people. The Gate was a particularly exhilarating experience for him because he had before him the example of theatre people who worked in every branch of the craft: Micheál as actor, writer, translator, designer, occasional director, Hilton actor, director, lighting designer. And how they worked! These homosexual aesthetes were unendingly engaged in the nuts and bolts of their job, Micheál actually applying the paint himself to the sets he had designed, Hilton wrestling with the lamps that he so inventively deployed. They staged a hundred plays in their first six years, every one designed by Mac Liammóir, many of them translated by him and three actually written by him. He and Hilton between them shared huge leading roles; Hilton took it upon himself to create acceptable standards of discipline in a country notoriously easygoing. In his own words: 'in reaction against the conditions it found at its birth, the Gate Theatre was inclined to overstress the visual, the abstract, the international and the less naturalistic attitude to the stage. It tended also perhaps to over-discipline productions in contrast to the too-casual attitude that then prevailed.' This had a great influence on Welles; as did his deployment of light, and his belief in 'the desirability of continuity, swift-moving scene changes, and the possible elimination of intervals'.

He learned a lot about design, too, from Micheál. Despite, in his own words, 'the fatal influence of Beardsley and Bakst' on his work, Mac Liammóir had integrated these elements with Celtic motifs to forge an original language. This was not something that Welles absorbed, nor should he have done. What he did take from his contact with Micheál was, first of all, the practical craftsmanship (reinforced by his experience in the paint shop as 'assistant assistant scene-painter', of which he drew a charming cartoon); but also of another influence on Micheál: the Berlin theatre of the day. Micheál and Hilton had just come back from Germany in the summer of the year in which Orson appeared at their stage door to pay his compliments to his chum Cathal Ó Ceallaigh. 'It was Berlin with its Russian influences that taught me how unnecessary the British fetish of the customary masking-in was becoming, Berlin that broke my growing obsession with Playfair's symmetry, that freed my brain from a thousand tyrannies of visual convention,' wrote Mac Liammóir. 'Yet I began to wonder if the . . . splendour could not be achieved with a lighter and more suggestive method – a street scene . . . could be suggested by a sloping ramp, a solid wall, a lamp-post, and a black space; a woman's room by a gigantic bed, a lustrous festoon of drapery, and a hanging lamp; a moonlit garden by darkness and a green stone fountain.' That lighter, more suggestive method was what Welles took back home; that, and an experience of acting that stayed with him to the last.

It was not provided by Edwards, nor even by Mac Liammóir, whose romantic self-consciousness he admired but never sought to emulate. It was Anew McMaster who left the indelible impression on his imagination. He saw him whenever he could; McMaster stayed in his mind as the embodiment of what an actor might be. 'Anew McMaster,' wrote Bridges-Adams, 'is an unashamed exponent of the heroic style in acting – without which, be it said, no heroic part can be fully played. We may trace his art back through Booth, Salvini and Barry Sullivan in his prime, back even to those superhuman performers who made melody of Dryden's torrential verse at Drury Lane. It is an art which our stage must sooner or later discover if it is not to lose itself in subtleties and pettiness.' The Irish actor and writer Gabriel Fallon elaborated: 'Anew McMaster convinces us that he knows more about ACTING Shakespeare than thousands of others who concern themselves merely with UNDERSTANDING him . . . he has the sound sense to read the simple and wonderful line not like an actor who would be a savant but like an actor who would merely be an actor. It is impossible that Kean did otherwise . . . he possesses that mesmeric quality which is one of the marks of a great actor, a quality which proceeds from the constant "forcing the soul" to the imagination's bidding. Most of the other actors we have seen in our time are but puny whispers against him.' Where else but in Ireland could Welles have seen such a creature, out of time and out of place? Even in England, which produced in Donald Wolfit one of the century's few tragedians, there was no genuinely heroic actor to be found. This was the line which Welles sought to join; inappropriately, as it happens, but whenever he wrote of his ideal actor, it was McMaster he described, whether he named him or not.

It is so easy to forget that Welles, complex, almost monstrous, though he sometimes might be, was also a sixteen-year-old boy who was perfectly capable of simple emotions such as homesickness. For him, home was Todd ('which is just another way of spelling your names', he touchingly wrote to the Skippers). Less convincingly, he had written to them on the wave of his great success in *Jew Süss* that he was only 'crowing so loudly . . . to make more forceful my assurance that if ever you could find a place for me at Todd, I'd take the next boat!!!' He was not hoping to lead the life of a schoolmaster; but evidently he missed the warmth and unstinting support of the Hills. He made jokes about keeping his accent, despite having learned proper English stage diction. His pretence, at the outset of his Dublin sojourn, to be enrolling at Trinity – he telegraphed Skipper: 'have job at the gate theatre and courses in trinity college wire objections' – was abandoned by stages. Clearly his destiny did not lie in Dublin, a city in which familiarity breeds, if not contempt, then at the very least scepticism. His legend, unsustained by further miracles, had dwindled into mild celebrity. He began to speak of his plans back in America: he told Joseph Holloway that he was returning to do *King Lear*. Holloway evinced no surprise. Admittedly, he thought that Welles ('who drifted into Dublin a few months ago from world travelling . . . an American who left the States for adventure and to write a book thereon') was twenty but even that seems a little young to be attempting the ancient king. Holloway adds a queer little comment: 'When Kernoff tried to see the stage behind Welles's broad back, I said, "You can't see through Welles; few can." And Welles said, "That is very true . . ." '

Dublin and the Gate remembered him affectionately: the Gate brochure (of 1934) gives him a little section to himself: 'ORSON WELLES is a young American actor who paid a memorable visit to the Gate Theatre in its fifth season. He gave a magnificent performance as the Duke in JEW SÜSS, and in HAMLET was an impressive Ghost and a virile Fortinbras. In DEATH TAKES A HOLIDAY he played an Italian Duke with mature dignity; and he was a poetic Persian king in MOGU. He is now playing in America.' In the PHOTO by ROSS, he looks exactly, and only, sixteen years of age. Among the Gate actors he was a different sort of legend. Arriving a couple of years later, Geraldine Fitzgerald was told tales of this extraordinary young man 'who could be thirty though he was only sixteen, had this stupendous voice and knew every dirty trick in the book and played them on Micheál – who we had proudly regarded as the past master of the dirty trick. Welles had no guilt; there was nothing furtive about it. He walked on the end of everybody's lines and moved in front of them and things like that. All the younger actors were awed that someone as young as themselves dared to be so alarming to the brass.' All for glory. That was not to be had in Dublin. At the end of February 1932, he set out for home, by way of England.

CHAPTER FIVE

Hiatus/*Everybody's Shakespeare*

IN THE absence of letters or other evidence, it is hard to determine just what Welles did during his London stay. He was now in a position to concentrate exclusively on executing the plan so exuberantly outlined on his way to Ireland: to visit 'theatres!!!!!' London was, as it still is, endowed with more of these than any other city in the world, and he could have seen a wide range of work, from Max Reinhardt's *Helen!* starring Evelyn Laye to a revival at the London Gate Theatre, (after which Edwards and Mac Liammóir had named theirs), of its greatest hit, Kaiser's *Morn to Midnight*, the quintessence of theatrical Expressionism. In between these poles of high art and delirious froth was a range of agreeable work encompassing plays by Ben Travers and James Bridie, Edgar Wallace (*The Green Back*, starring Gerald du Maurier) and Clifford Bax (*Rose without a Thorn*, a Henry VIII play). The West End was at its most urbane with well-turned performances in well-made plays; no one of comparable audacity and originality had replaced the recently departed Charles Laughton. The theatrical waters were becalmed. Most pleasing, no doubt, to a Bard-struck young actor was the unusual amount of Shakespeare on offer, though again, to someone who had seen McMaster, not to mention having just acted opposite Mac Liammóir, the general level may have seemed somewhat sober. None the less, it was an opportunity available to him neither in Ireland nor America to see a large number of the canon in solid, well-spoken productions. At the Old Vic or Sadler's Wells (plays and operas were still alternating in the two houses) he could have caught *Twelfth Night* with Edith Evans's exquisite Viola, or either Robert Speaight or Robert Harris alternating in the title role of *Hamlet*. Had he made the journey to Stratford-upon-Avon, he could have seen the first productions in the new Art Deco Memorial Theatre, among them Bridges-Adams's straightforward productions of *Henry IV*, both parts, *Julius Caesar*, *As You Like It*, *A Midsummer Night's Dream* and the play in which he had already announced himself, *King Lear*. This last was a startling production by Théodore Komisarjevsky; at last a taste of the theatrical revolution.

The West End itself fielded quite a number of productions of Shakespeare, with Sybil and Russell Thorndike in the midst of a big season at the Kingsway Theatre, which included, on successive nights, *Macbeth*, *The Merchant of Venice*, *Twelfth Night*, *The Taming of the Shrew*, *Romeo and Juliet* and finally, *Hamlet*. At the St James's Theatre, he could have seen *The Merchant of Venice* again, with Ernest Milton as Shylock. Apart from the intrinsic interest of that famous performance, Welles may have derived some hope from the spectacle of a San Francisco-born actor accepted as among the most distinguished Shakespeareans of the English stage – because, needless to say, Welles was not in London simply to be a spectator. He presented himself, notices in hand, to the managers of the various theatres; but this was not Dublin. There was no dearth of eager, trained and talented young men just waiting to prove their worth without the inconvenience of having to get a work permit – always a difficult thing, but in the midst of recession (and, despite the apparently thriving theatre, the West End was having to fight to make ends meet) almost impossible.

At this point, it seems that Welles went to Paris, where he had never been before. (He had been in London in 1929, on his way to Bavaria for his walking holiday – 'the beer! Oh baby!' – and on his last visit had seen the Old Vic Company: 'the best in the world'). Frank Brady maintains that he spent his time in Paris dining, drinking and attending parties. He had a knack of landing on his feet, and particularly of striking up friendships along his way, but his inability to speak French and his lack of any contact in the city would, one might imagine, have made an extensive social life unlikely. He presumably went to the theatre, despite the language barrier, but Brady's claim that while he was in Paris he struck up a warm friendship with Brahim, the eldest son of the legendary Thami el-Glaoui, Pasha of Marrakesh, strains credibility. Returning to England, he is said by more than one of his biographers to have had an even grander encounter: with George Bernard Shaw, perhaps the most popular and certainly the most immediately recognisable author alive. Welles is said by Brady to have managed this by 'enthusiasm and perseverance, combined with some letters of introduction'. From whom exactly he could have acquired letters of introduction that would gain him admission to Shaw's presence is difficult to imagine. Welles himself was still talking about his meeting in the fifties, when he spoke to Peter Noble, but after that we hear little of it. This is what he says to Noble: 'I recall the way in which he received me, listened to my idea on the Theatre, gossiped about Dublin and shared a joke with all the enthusiasm of a schoolboy. I remember his walking me down to his gate and talking to me with the greatest simplicity as if I were as grown up as he. Shaw was a great man – and like all great men essentially kind and simple.' This is suspiciously general; another, modest, variant on *Christ among the Doctors*: the sage of the Western World chats with an unknown seventeen-year-old American boy.

The source of all this, it may be suspected, is a revival of *Heartbreak House*, which opened at the Queen's Theatre in April 1932, provoking a deal of press coverage in which Shaw enthusiastically participated. Edith Evans forsook the sea-coast of Illyria in order to play Lady Utterword ('Magnificent, Superb, Stupendous, Surpassing, Masterly, Delightful, Overwhelming and Better-than-the-part. It saved us from shipwreck. In short, quite good,' Shaw wrote to her) and Welles would surely have seen the production and read the newspapers with their interviews with Shaw. No doubt he *felt* as if he'd met him. Certainly when, six years later, he applied to Shaw for the rights, neither party alluded to any earlier meeting. In fact Shaw's telegram on that occasion said: 'Who are you?'.

Welles set off for America by ship, arriving in New York in June of 1932, ten months after he'd left. He stayed in the city for a while, again trying to capitalise on his Dublin experience, but if he found the London managements a tough nut to crack, New York's were worse. The 1931–2 season just coming to an end had been a bad one, with five flops for every success. The turnover was fast and furious; there were always shows to replace the ones that had just closed, but of increasingly cheap quality. The big managements were taking no risks. Welles attempted to audition for the Shuberts' September revival of the 1928 British spinechiller, *Silent House* (presumably for the role of the sinister Dr Chan-Fu; nothing else would have suited him, apart from the juvenile lead), but he failed to get beyond the outer office, where he was addressed as 'Kiddie', and told, in so many words, to push off. It can't have been easy: a blow to his amour-propre. The *Saturday Evening Post*, in an article some years later, put it rather amusingly:

> After being a celebrity at sixteen in Dublin and London, he had returned home expecting to be a Broadway celebrity. But he got to the Algonquin without being mobbed. He discovered people in the lobby not talking about him. In Times Square he found large groups of people not mentioning him. A celebrity has a negative or an inverted sense of hearing; he can hear his name not being

> mentioned at forty paces. Everywhere he went, nonmention of his name drummed on his ear. He was bewildered. Through all his years as a cosmic tot, people had sought out Orson. By rights, the Shuberts should have met him at the docks.

He must have returned to Chicago, and then Woodstock, with his tail rather between his legs. He was plagued with hay-fever and asthma as usual in the summer, and in a moment of inspiration, Roger Hill suggested ('to get him out of my hair') that he take a trip to Mercer in the cooler area up-state Wisconsin near the lakes, and try his hand at writing a play. Hill promised to start the play off. Orson happily agreed. They decided to take the controversial figure of John Brown, unilateral anti-slaver, as their theme; he was much in the air, the subject of two recent biographies, a play, and an epic poem: an emblem of muddle-headed, or perhaps pig-headed idealism that seemed to touch a chord in depression America. Orson made for the North. Once again he sent a generally exuberant set of letters which record his adventures, chronicle his observations of nature – and human nature – and blush for shame at asking – again! – for money. Their special interest is that they record his progress on the play, showing something of his developing grasp as a writer and editor. The letters are fun; he seems to have had a delightful time.

On the train he had the good fortune to bump into the Meigs, friends of the Hills; they had a summer home in the area of the Chippewa Indian reservation at Lac du Flambeau, and invited him to stay with them, at the bottom of their pine-grove. 'How delightfully unexpected everything turns out for me! In the seventeen kaleidoscopic years of my existence I have not once successfully predicted any one minute of my following future!' He got some 'squaws and a few antiques of the neuter gender' to put up a wig-wam ('or more correctly, a "wig-ii-wham" ') and settled in for the duration. Immediately his 'tortured nasal passage and bespasmed bronchial tubes' improved. He hadn't entirely gone native – he ate with the Meigs and their 'rosy-faced and multitudinous' children – but he abandoned himself to the reservation's picturesque charm: 'A tuneful country, this . . . woodland sounds from the wild where the Chippewa hunt bear and deer, silver sounds from the lake and sunny insect-sounds at mid-day. A little sad, perhaps, the song the marsh-folk sing, and sadder yet the endless dirging of the wind in the fir-trees. At night there are stealthy little sounds, and always the unbelievable; ceaseless, in the air, the throbbing of medicine drums.' Mac Liammóir wasn't entirely right that Orson failed to give himself over to nature; but he wasn't entirely wrong, either: his descriptions have the feeling of stage directions about them. Hardly surprising, since he was here to write a play, a matter to which – with occasional lapses – he applied himself very seriously.

Roger Hill sent him the first act immediately, nonchalantly claiming to have written it in a day; this galvanised Orson, and he boasts quite soon to his 'beloved co-author' that he is writing furiously to produce what he spells as a 'first draught' so that they can see the thing whole, like 'a great uncut diamond'. He offers advice to Skipper on his first act: 'it's mighty damned good. Personally I think it's *great*. Wonderful!! And with this opinion clearly understood may I offer the inevitable criticism?' He finds that Thoreau is made too interesting: 'if he remains as he is at this writing nothing on earth will persuade me away from him into playing John Brown!' He tells Skipper that some of the speeches he's written are too good. 'We don't want to be accused of bombast. I think neat lines are a fault of mine, too, we must both beware, for that way lies floweriness . . .' Everything that he writes seems shrewd and practical.

Halfway through his sojourn, as autumn started to threaten with an east wind blowing up and a prolonged rainy season imminent, he moved across the lake, to share a lodge with a silent and solitary archer by the name of Larry to whom he paid a few cents for board. There he stayed till he returned. When Larry had done his bow and arrow work, he sat at his typewriter, Welles sat at his, and so the play got finished. Welles's ability to team up with companions in this way – Mr O'Connor on the Shannon expedition is another instance – is interesting; interesting, too, that he was happier with his silent friend than in the bustle of the Meigs' noisy hearth. He was, after all, to all intents and purposes an only child; solitude *à deux* may have suited him better than the competitive atmosphere of a big family.

He succumbed to the charms of 'the crystal lakes and timberlands and all that sort of thing, well-stocked, understand, with the leaping trout, the bounding deer, the scudding muskie and the grunting Indian, all rampant, so to speak and in great abundance' and occasional trips to the movies with the Meigs ('the movie tonight was distressingly adequate on the subject of skyscrapers . . . may the show business flounder until producers cry out in agony for the return of the mov*ing* drama (*D*rama) for the return of the good old lengthiness, the romance and the real melo-drama!'); mostly, though, he was plugging away at John Brown, and also at another play: *The Dark Room*. 'It's a natural, a positive honey! . . . every

English-speaking repertory company on the globe will be doing that show, mark my words!' It concerns a representative group of people – a gangster, a society-queen, a financial leader, a diamond-merchant, the mayor of the town and others – who assemble for a seance (an early appearance of the supernatural figures in Welles's work). 'And through all of this exciting, rapid-fire, *sure-fire*, melodrama, moves the sinister shadow of Dr Marvel! . . . then for the last time, the lights go out and The Voice speaks! The answer to that is a wow, a perfect wow . . . it could be produced for the price of a theatre rental, the set is in every scene dock in the world – a new coat of paint . . .' From this description, it would not have been entirely out of place in the Gate's repertory.

He could hardly wait now to get back, with his two thrilling properties in his rucksack. He looks forward to returning to civilisation, 'in the sunshine of your enthusiasm', in less than a week. He expresses himself to Hill ('Skip') with absolutely direct affection, signing off 'Love without end'. From time to time he worries in a letter that he hasn't heard from him and fears that he might be in his bad books: 'you aren't angry, are you? Are you?' Generally these anxieties concern his constant requests for money: but since 'Doctor', as he refers to his guardian, is so unforthcoming, what can he do? He signs off his last letter from Lac du Flambeau – 'the merest word from Woodstock would send me into perfect triologies of delight' – then throws in his joke of the moment, repeated in more than one letter: 'I can ride a canoe, canoe?' Skipper brought out the boy in him.

Not another word is ever heard about *The Dark Room*; but the John Brown play – which they called *Marching Song* – filled them with excitement and hopes of a production. Once they'd rewritten it, Skipper sent it to an old acquaintance, Samuel Raphaelson, who wrote back 'Stick with this boy! . . . Any three pages of this script sing. But any 20 pages fall apart. Tell your star pupil to either turn this into a novel or teach him that stage plays are tight little miniatures' – not a lesson that Orson Welles was ever going to learn, thank God. They decided that they needed to be on the spot if they were to place it; Hortense and Roger Hill and Orson travelled to New York in what they liked to call the 'land-yacht', the caravan bus in which the Todd Troupers toured, 'complete with its chauffeur-cook'. Once in New York, they rented a suite at the Algonquin (not cheap at any time, least of all at its zenith in the early thirties) and approached as many producers as they could. They had scant success. Even Dwight Deere Wiman, an ex-Todd man, Skipper's contemporary, and America's most prolific producer, turned them down, as did the almost equally prolific William A. Brady. Depressed and out of pocket, the Hills returned to Woodstock; Welles moved into a cheap room on West 77th Street, off Riverside, and continued to peddle the play around town. Ben Boyars read it, and he was at least kind. 'It's a swell show,' he told Welles. 'It makes good reading. It would be a good book. I think maybe it's even a good play. But that doesn't matter. It won't make money. It isn't a commercial piece. At least that's what I think.'

Maurice Bernstein wrote to him in New York: 'I do hope you won't continue to waste your youth aimlessly.' Then, in the absence of any reaction, sent a telegram: 'leave play with agent and come home'. Which he did, after a final rebuff from yet another manager who read the play, declared it 'unsuitable' and then charged him $5 for the opinion. 'Unsuitable' for what, one may ask; but he was not wrong to reject it. Ben Boyars hits the nail on the head: 'it makes good reading.' It's a good solid slog through some tangled history, but except for a few interesting moments of stagecraft is dramatically inert. It is in fact the stage directions which quicken the pulse, suggesting that the authors were not born dramatists but perhaps born directors; one of them, at any rate. The subject none the less has considerable resonance in Orson Welles's life and even in some of his future work.

The play takes the form of an inquiry into Brown, his motives and the value of his actions: was he self-motivated? A genuine idealist? A clever strategist? A megalomaniac? Or simply mad? The play starts and ends with journalists trying to answer some of these questions, questions posed in his lifetime, and still not satisfactorily resolved. The play's subject is the paradox that whatever the answer to these questions, he became, especially after his death at the gallows, an emblem of the anti-slave movement, and a vital rallying point. 'His soul,' in the words of the great song he inspired, 'goes marching on.' On being told that abolitionists were planning to spring him from jail before his execution Brown responded 'Let them hang me. I am worth inconceivably more to hang than for any other purpose' – a remark (not in the play) which reveals an acute sense of the value of publicity. It is this that fascinates Welles. Brown's conduct at all times was highly theatrical, and reported on by a permanent phalanx of journalists. Even as he lay on the grass after being beaten unconscious with the hilt of a marine's sword, he gave interviews. Q: What was your object? A: To free the slaves from bondage. His trial, during which he lay on a cot, was a magnificent piece of stage-management; a show-trial, in fact, but one in which the accused was putting on the show for his own benefit, and that of his cause.

The press coverage was the first newspaper great campaign of modern times. The theme of Brown's possible madness, coupled with that of the power of publicity obviously had considerable resonance for Welles; as did the additional theme of the vanity of the man who believes he is God's vessel. Brown was certain enough of his own destiny to have ordered one of his men somehow to procure George Washington's sword, with which he then proceeded to lead the battle. This hubris of his is given great weight in *Marching Song*, which is essentially a political piece; in no way does it resemble Stephen Vincent Benét's great poem, 'John Brown's Body', with its complex lament for a vanished culture.

The canvas is enormous: its eleven scenes convey dense action; there is a cast of twenty-six, plus three children. Characterisation is clear and detailed closely following historical fact; the one character who has been somewhat extrapolated from recorded reality is John Brown's son, John Junior, who suffered a nervous breakdown witnessing the Potawotomie Massacre – the event that precipitated his father's commitment to the cause. Welles and Hill have made him 'an idiot, with a loose, wet mouth and saucer eyes'. He laughs and giggles, until suddenly tormented by the imagined sound of marching; he identifies passionately with the suffering slaves. There is a Jacobean feel to his presence in the play; frequently he burbles on at the side of the action, apparently irrelevant. It is hard not to be reminded of the fact that Welles's brother Richard Junior was, as he was writing the play, still repining, hungry and unclothed, in Kanakee Mental Asylum.

JOHN JUNIOR

Inspiration! Inspiration! You don't understand! You don't know what inspiration means! . . . I've been inspired . . . I can tell you about it . . . inspiration don't mean being crazy . . . not . . . not exactly . . . inspiration is a kind of happy song, it's like a spring rain shower falling soft and sudden on young leaves . . . it's like a ray of dawn sunshine smiling, and pointing at the mountain-tops . . . and mostly, mostly it's like my dreams . . . the dreams I have I can't tell you about . . . take that marching, now . . . the sound of that marching . . . believe me that sound isn't crazy . . . it's a fine wild kind of music . . . a Call . . . it ain't insane, I tell you! It ain't crazy! It's the footsteps of a whole nation, marching in the

> chains they was born in! . . . you don't have to be simple to hear that echoing and echoing in your heart, do you? . . . John Brown hears it and he knows what it means!!!

Clumsy though it is as writing, it has real feeling; the idealism, the hysterical identification with the oppressed, is unmistakable. Throughout, despite the reckless proliferation of exclamation marks, elevated states of emotion are powerfully conveyed. Belief is a central question, and the issue of Brown's prophetic inspiration is not dodged:

> JOHN BROWN
>
> THE SWORD OF THE LORD AND OF GIDEON!
>
> *(Suddenly a great unearthly light falls full upon him. He is transfigured . . . his arms have been stretched sideways in triumph and now a strange thing happens to them, they are momentarily paralysed . . . with a shock we realise that the attitude is no longer that of triumph but of crucifixion!)* O my Father, if this cup may not pass away from me, except I drink it. *(Kagi and Anderson sink to their knees, awed and prayerful.)*

In a Victorian sort of way, it is all quite powerful; the Christ image boldly undertaken. There are reminiscences of *The Servant in the House* (also about a man who would be king). No irony seems to be intended, nor is it told from Brown's point of view. The moment of transfiguration simply happens, *tout court.* In the penultimate scene, the journalists discuss Brown outside his cell, where he's giving interviews and writing pamphlets. Is he mad? Or what? A soldier passes by, producing an article by Abraham Lincoln condemning Brown. The soldier gives his name: Booth – John Wilkes Booth, who was, indeed, there.

The final scene shows Brown ascending the hill to the gallows (a theatrical and symbolic transposition; the reality was a wooden structure in the middle of the square at Charlestown, Virginia). He hears, alternately, the marching we've heard throughout the play and the mad laughter of John Junior. He makes his famous speech from the top of the Hill. Then: 'the sound of marching feet grows louder, louder, louder. But the note is gradually changing. The chains are gone and a martial ring has taken their place. The drum and bugle insinuate themselves. The tempo has quickened and the cadence is now that of a great army of free men – marching. Marching – Marching – Indomitable . . . now the bugle sound has melted into a vaster harmony, the full chords of a song . . . and as the play ends the whole theatre is filled with the song. JOHN BROWN'S BODY LIES A'MOULDERING IN THE GRAVE, BUT HIS SOUL GOES MARCHING ON.' This is the overlap of play and production.

Welles's use of sound is everywhere in evidence, from the beginning, played with voices off for nearly the whole of the scene, through the constant marching, to a number of felicitous touches – offstage choruses, Schubert's *Serenade* playing underneath a scene and so on. Welles's setting, of which he draws an exuberant sketch, shows the essentially straightforward four-walled set divided two ways – by a full curtain which functions as a front cloth (he calls it THE GRAND DRAPE 'in the *grand manner*. Note cut-out tassels!') and by traverse curtains, clearly made from something light and loose, white cotton or silk. These curtains are drawn between scenes, and serve as a screen for projections of kaleidoscopic images 'depicting newspaper headlines and views of immediate surroundings' from an implement called a stereopticon. Elsewhere he refers to the stereopticon as a magic lantern, which suggests he may be attempting a form of Victorian theatre – a form contemporary with the events depicted. It is also of course a version of techniques being developed in Berlin by Piscator.

It is all very ambitious. Welles never saw it staged, though in the 1970s, by an irony that both of them will not have failed to appreciate, his arch-enemy Hascy Tarbox, then teaching at Todd, designed and directed a trimmed-down version in the Opera House at Woodstock. It was a modest success. The only reason that it was staged was, of course, because of Orson's co-authorship, though from that point of view it must have proved a disappointment for anyone looking for traces of his hand. With the exception of those few elements noted, it is essentially impersonal, a public play depicting public events. The newspaper headlines, and indeed the presence in the play of investigative journalists, inevitably seem to pre-echo *Citizen Kane*, but the structure of the play owes little to them; they convey information neatly and confirm the emblematic value of Brown. The mystery, the void at the centre of *Kane*, is nowhere to be found. But in the marshalling of the material and the increasing mastery of the narrative, he had learned an enormous amount. The very fact that he had risen to the challenge that he set himself was no mean achievement.

At the same time as he was writing this public play, and the shamelessly commercial *Dark Room*, he was writing, during this remarkably productive summer, a third play which is among the most curious and personal documents of his that we have: *Bright*

Lucifer. Set on an Indian reservation, full of the local colour mentioned in his letters from Lac du Flambeau, it contains as malign a self-portrait as can ever have been written. The play is in three acts, in a single simple setting: a holiday cabin on the reservation in the North Woods. There are three characters: Morgan Flynn, addressed as Jack, a star of horror movies; Bill Flynn, his elder brother, editor of the *National Weekly*; and Eldred Brand, Bill's ward, who is on the reservation because of his hay-fever. Bill has come up to the North Woods for a break ('Haven't had fish like that in four years, and AIR. They breathe gas in Hollywood'). The air is heavy with the throbbing of the drums, the drums. Bill frets that the furniture is meagre: an army cot doesn't seem right for a movie star. Jack: Are you calling your brother a sissy? They laugh, then discuss Jack's broken romance: his girl ran off with a cameraman. Took dope, too. They also discuss Eldred. Is Bill, Jack wants to know, as fond of him as ever? Suddenly he asks why Eldred hates him; Bill poo-poos the idea. They bicker. The drums insist. Somebody must be dead or dying, says Bill; the drums are supposed to scare away the DEVILS. Jack laughs; surely Bill can't believe in Devil drums?

As he says this, Eldred comes in. He stands there, silent, unseen. Jack and Bill discuss devils and whether they exist. The atmosphere is uneasy. Bill, seeing Eldred, asks him what he believes. I don't believe in anything, says Eldred. I only believe in myself. To break this impasse Jack heartily asks Eldred what his preferences are, to which he replies: I like them high-breasted and virgin. I like them in wet silk dresses licking my galoshes. Understandably, *there is*, says the stage direction, *a silence*. The subject goes back to ghosts. Jack describes a seance he attended at which he played a spirit . . . 'like a magician discovering that the beautiful lady in the box is really cut in half'. Jack says that he has always wanted to scare people on a big scale: a huge practical joke. Eldred quibbles about something; Bill asks him why he always gets everything wrong? Somebody's got to, says Eldred, since you're always right. *Bill throws his head back and laughs. His big, wonderful laugh*, the stage direction tells us. He goes to bed. Eldred eggs Jack on to describe the practical joke he had in mind, to scare the fishermen. Jack's idea, it transpires, is to dress up in a black robe, sitting in the back of a boat with a muffled motor, then to ask the fisherman the time: not the hour – the year. *Eldred shrieks with shrill hard laughter. Then abruptly he stops*. Eldred suggests that it might be fun to try it on the Indians. He knows that Jack has his make-up with him; why not use it? Jack demurs; he's played too many monsters. 'And you've got to get it out of you,' says Eldred. 'Not run away from it.' By God! says Jack, I'll show you! He laughs: forced and just a trifle frenzied, then leaves. Eldred laughs, then, again, stops suddenly. 'By *God*?' he asks, blowing out the lantern. Enter Bill, who tells him, forgivably, that he's crazy. You've said that once! says Eldred. They fight about Jack. Don't be silly, says Bill. Eldred screams back: WILL YOU STOP INSULTING ME?

Then ensues an extraordinary scene in which Eldred accuses Bill of loving Jack more than him. He's my brother, says Bill, to which Eldred replies: 'you never miss a chance, do you, to remind me that I'm an orphan, an adopted orphan? . . . if it had just happened that you were my father instead of the man that beat you to it . . . you've tried to be just like a father to me, haven't you? All those years tucking me into bed. I have my mother's eyes, haven't I? I used to wear bangs and we went on little walks together and you taught me the alphabet.' Bill weakly protests that Eldred has no right to – at which Eldred again screams: 'I have no right! I have no right to anything; money, friends, anything. I haven't the right to breathe, have I, my adored old stepmother?' He calls his guardian his step*mother*; which is exactly what Dadda with his fussy loving must have felt like. Eldred continues, of Bill's wife Martha: 'She hates me! . . . she's jealous of our love for each other. So's Jack.' Bill sternly tells him that they have to cheer Jack up, and goes. There is a gust of wind; drums; the click of a latch; the door opens slowly. it's The Ghoul. *The thing is dark and hairy, the head like a great crazy, cracking egg, punctured with two blind eyes. The nose a greedy claw, grabbing the hungry mouth that grins under it, full of red, dripping teeth.* Eldred screams; Bill runs in. Eldred has cut his own hand to justify the scream. Where's Jack? asks Bill. I thought it was Jack coming out. Eldred: GOD, BILL, I HOPE IT WAS. Act One curtain.

Act Two takes place early the next night: there are shouts, yells, and a low excited murmur off. Jack is drinking; Bill comes in with a lantern. They can't find the body. 'Eldred's loving this,' says Bill. Jack asks what school he's going to. None, says Bill. 'He doesn't believe in them. I don't know what he wants to do. Hasn't made his mind up yet . . . he's young.' There's nothing young about Eldred, says Jack. 'He's as old as Egypt.' There isn't a generation or a world for *busy little bitch boys*!' There is a curious, sexually charged atmosphere between Jack and Eldred throughout the play. Jack seems on the brink of a revelation (Bill: Eldred's my boy. Jack: *Your boy!* I've half a mind to tell you –) when Eldred returns. Bill walks out. Eldred and Jack discuss what's happened:

Jack as The Ghoul has terrified the mourners; the body of the dead squaw they are mourning has disappeared. 'My God,' says Jack in one of many seeming anticipations of *The War of the Worlds* furore, 'the whole country's up in arms.' Jack describes how The Ghoul took him over. '*Delicious*,' says Eldred. 'The Brands were always mad.' *After a moment, Jack laughs wildly. Eldred joins him and the sound of his laugh stops Jack. Eldred stops laughing.* There are several of these laughing duels in the course of the action. Eldred prescribes 'a grain of reality' to cure Jack's raving. He offers him another drink. Jack: 'You're a persuasive little bitch.' *Eldred smiles.* Bill comes back, tries to josh Jack, who storms off. Bill and Eldred discuss spirits. Eldred says:

> There's evil on this earth! In holy days, men fought it – there were charms and chants and bells and books and candles, and good men fought for good. But now they don't believe! Vampires fatten, were-wolves range and witches go unburnt – they aren't believed! Thicker and quicker flows the force and tide of evil. Strong with a million years' momentum, since the great flaming fall when all the hosts of Lucifer showered down out of the sky like comets . . . they *are* – *everywhere!* . . . there – there, behind you! Or there –

There at the door The Ghoul appears. Bill rushes out. Jack, without mask, returns. Eldred asks if Bill's laughing. 'No,' says Jack. 'He's dead.' Curtain.

Act Three starts with Jack raving, wanting to know what he looks like, unable to find a mirror. (Much play is made throughout of the lack of a mirror; an allusion to Dracula, presumably.) 'If there was a mirror and I looked in it . . . what would I *see*?'

> ELDRED
> Nothing . . . [you're] a ghost . . . I'm the host – The master of ceremonies. I call the dances . . . the heavens are bright, I see – my star. I must follow it. Last night there was no power on earth but me. Nothing anywhere, I stowed the cosmos in a casserole of my five senses. I made a Morse Code of eternity and got a mess of blots and blurs. That was my world . . . Tonight I'm sane. I see! Now that Bill's dead. He left a hole to see through in the night. And Jack Flynn left a reflection . . . I see my face in it, but something more – behind – bright as my star and big as my shadow – leaning over me and whispering a reason.

Jack realises (not perhaps the quickest, our Jack) that Eldred has manipulated all these events – that he killed Bill. Eldred: *(Very quietly)* 'Perhaps. *(Almost to himself)* I had to. I loved him so. *(Almost musingly)* Bill was destroyed with love. *(Very sincerely)* I loved – him so much – he had to die.' Jack understands. *He has become, finally, a new man.* He goes to get a pistol. Eldred hands him a box of shells. *The drums, the drums.* Jack returns with his loaded gun. Eldred: 'I show you all the kingdoms of the world in a moment of time. And I say unto you, all this power will I give thee, and the glory of them: for that is delivered unto me; and to whomsoever I will give it. And I'll throw in some immortality . . . if thou therefore wilt worship me, all shall be thine.' 'ASMOEDELIUS!' screams Jack. Eldred: 'It was God's apple! His bastard – whining! The wriggling Christ! Snivelling and screaming on the cross! Let's make him pay!' – Jack shoots him: 'You're losing Eldred Satan Brand.' Eldred's dying speech predicts eternal restlessness for Jack. '*The whole world will be your haunted house* . . . devils don't [die] – *I won't. The evil that we do lives after us . . . my demon will never die.*' Jack shoots and shoots and shoots. He stands motionless. Across the lake, sound of the jazz band *but the notes come over the distance strangely, weirdly, piping like a gnomes' accompaniment to some tiny cabal.* The door opens slowly: it's The Ghoul. Jack runs after it, shouting hysterically Eldred! Eldred! *The drums, the drums. Something old and dark has got its way.*

Eldred, the bitch boy, is one of the most breathtakingly unpleasant characters in the whole of twentieth-century dramatic literature. What makes it doubly disturbing is that it is so self-evidently a detailed self-portrait; the intensity of the feeling, the loathing for Dr Bernstein and his wife are absolutely real. Of course, it may be said that it simply betrays a lack of invention and a lack of imagination: he reached for events, people from his own life and squeezed them into the plot of his melodrama. But whether accidentally or consciously, he has summoned a degree of emotion that is quite shocking. It seems to be self-loathing that Welles is expressing in his delineation of Eldred: he is the guilty one, the inhuman, the not as others – tainted, or just monstrous? The autobiographical elements of the play sing out: in the details, but also in a more general sense of evil, of nightmares, of self-loathing. Until the final twist, Eldred is a Nietzschean figure, rejecting love as weakness, asserting his independence of morality and religion. He exists to destroy. His instinctive grasp of Jack's weakness enables him to use him as his puppet – to do his evil for him. This could be mere fantasy of adolescent omnipotence; or some deeper more personal feeling of Welles's that a fundamental weakness and dependency in himself needed to be overcome. He had, after all, from an early age, been dependent on people other than his parents. The most shocking thing in the play is Eldred's hatred of his guardian; one can only hope that he never showed it to Maurice Bernstein.

Stylistically, it's fevered, stagey, exclamatory – naive, larded with quotations and echoes. But it has real and disturbing power, fuelled by the personal feeling that runs through it. There are theatrical effects, particularly sound effects, of some imagination. But the feel is immature, both confessional and sensational. He continued working on the play for some years. The bulk of it was written when he was seventeen; but he was still talking about mounting it as late as 1939. '*Bright Lucifer* is a likely sounding piece about a Hollywood horror actor, a sort of Boris Karloff, who eventually gets to the point of believing he is an honest-to-god menace,' said *The New Yorker*. 'This delusion seizes him on an Indian reservation, and the Indians get him. Welles still thinks it might make a fine play.' Significantly he makes no mention of the central character.

No doubt it was something he had to get out of his system. James Naremore in a brilliant analysis observes that 'a great deal of Welles's work can be explained in terms of the conflicting demands of his humanism, personified in this case by Jack, and his romantic rebelliousness, represented by Eldred. It is as if characters like Eldred give him the opportunity to express an anger that the more rational side of his personality then corrects and criticizes. But clearly his imagination and passion were fired by the notion of the tragic outlaw; usually he makes such characters the victims of some kind of determinism, and in so doing he gives a certain humanity to their rebellion.' The anger is unmistakable: rage at dependency, containment. It is harder to see the weak and hysterical Jack as an embodiment of humanism. The real issue in the play is between Eldred and Bill, his guardian, and it is over the question of absolute love. Bill has to die because Eldred loves him too much, which renders him weak. Love kills. Orson was very well capable of expressing himself lovingly, and clearly had an overwhelming need for affection and affirmation ('the sunshine of your enthusiasm'). But love was also a complicated thing, a source of guilt, disappointment and fearful vulnerability. Often he would seem to need to kill the love that he had provoked. He had, after all, killed his father.

Mrs Leaming, it should be noted, has an entirely different

conception of the play. The tone, she maintains, is comic, and the self-portrait is ironic, portraying Welles as others portray him, only with preposterous exaggeration – but who then had ever portrayed him as diabolic, or haunted? It takes, I would suggest, a very particular sense of humour to find the wantonly destructive action of the play or its violent language amusing. It is, rather, *A Portrait of the Artist As a Young Demon*, once read, hard to forget. It is a disturbing glimpse into a very old and dark side of Welles's mind.

After the disappointment of *Marching Song*'s failure to interest New York producers, Welles was restless again. Again Skipper came to the rescue. 'I needed a new project to absorb this boy's bubbling energy; to satisfy that constant creative urge.' The boy really was now at a loose end, neither working nor studying. He had scarcely wasted his time; Dublin and the work he did on *Marching Song*, particularly, were highly educative, if not strictly speaking educational. He told Peter Bogdanovich that he had a scholarship for Harvard, but even if that were so, the academic year was well under way by now; he would certainly need something to fill his time until the following fall. The charm of writing plays without prospect of production may have begun to pall, and nature-watching had its limits, too.

Maurice Bernstein, feeling baulked at every level, had an extraordinary suggestion: that Welles should take to the Chatauqua circuit, just like his mother, offering a similar programme of music and poetry, interspersed with explanatory comments. No doubt he would have handled the poetry and, especially, the commentary with relish; but quite apart from the question of his musicianship (last heard of three years before at the school concert) the *hommage* to his dead mother is most uncomfortable – everything to do with Bernstein, and nothing to do with Welles. Skipper's notion was infinitely more attractive: 'Write a Shakespeare book. Tell other teachers some of the tricks we used at Todd to make the Elizabethan popular in the classroom as well as the stage.' They would call it *Everybody's Shakespeare*. As before, Hill would kick things off, writing an introduction and editing the texts: Welles's chief task was to illustrate the characters and the settings, and through stage directions provide an impression of how the plays might appear in performance to a spectator.

For Skipper it was a way of killing two birds with one stone: occupying Welles, and using the Todd Press, professionally dormant since the last printing of Skipper's once brilliantly successful basketball primer. For Welles too, the venture had two purposes:

he would be doing something productive which might have a fair chance of making him rich and famous (and put an end to dependency), and it would give him an excuse to get out of Chicago. He'd had enough of home – with its comforts but also its demands. Even more than most seventeen-year-olds, he was a man but not quite an adult. He had lived and worked in the real world, earning his way, being judged and assessed and, on the whole, not found wanting. His play had been read by important New York producers, and though it wasn't optioned, it wasn't altogether dismissed either. He had achieved a great deal already. And yet he had no real independence. Sitting around unemployed and unregarded except by his immediate family circle was intolerable. So he set out – not merely away from the North West, but out of America, and indeed out of the Western World. He booked a second-class passage on the American Export Line freighter for Morocco, the *Exermont*.

Maurice Bernstein forked out the price of the passage. As always, he was willing to underwrite any activity that seemed to push Welles away from the idea of acting. Curiously, whenever Welles appeared to be cultivating his abilities as an artist (surely an even less secure and generally less remunerative calling than the theatre), 'Doctor' approved, perhaps subconsciously aware that it had been Richard Welles's ambition for the boy. It is also remarkable that he gave his blessing to what was, in 1933, a wildly exotic adventure, fraught with unknown peril. To most Americans, Africa was an unimaginably distant world, much more so than the Far East, which had had, for at least a half a century, close commercial connections with the United States. The fearlessness with which Welles contemplated the voyage is equally remarkable. The large cities of Morocco – Tangiers, Casablanca, Fez – were accustomed to European visitors (Tangiers in particular was included in many guide-books on Spain, as if it were an island off the mainland) but the interior had been inaccessible to all but the most intrepid for centuries. Welles, whatever else he was or was not, was intrepid. The simple act of embarking on such a journey is almost as extraordinary as anything that may or may not have happened to him there, the subject of some of his most inventive yarns.

It is useless to pretend that we really know what did happen. In all heroic myths, voyages occupy a special place, and this one of Welles's is no different: the secret journey of the hero, his hidden half-year, both initiation and self-discovery. In the absence of any publicly reported activity (he appeared in no plays in Rabat, nor was there a *New York Times* correspondent in Fez), and with few letters to go on, we can only examine the tantalising fragments of his adventure there that he would from time to time bring out. In this case, his fabulating gifts had fairly free rein, uninhibited by the existence of witnesses. Some of the stories are delightful in themselves; often they tell us something about his state of mind. What is certain is that he got a glimpse of yet another world, and that the seventeen-year-old who ventured on such a journey on his own was no ordinary lad.

It all started with his customary boyish exuberance. The letter that he wrote to Skipper on board the *Exermont* is full of holiday high spirits – a tone familiar from all his letters to him. Like most good correspondents, Welles reserved particular personas for particular people; for Skipper he always wrote cheerily, punningly and lovingly; generally he apologised for being behind with the work, whatever it was; and as often as not he asked for money. He always wished Skipper were there. 'Of the work in progress on *Everybody's Shakespeare*: You'll find grotesqueries in my stage directions, repetitions and misfirings. You'll have to do a clean-up job. I'll be relieved when I can get this off in the mails. The mere presence of Shakespeare's script worries me. What right have I . . . ? What a nerve I have . . . ? I wish to high heaven you were here to reassure me. Mainly I just wish you were here. You'd love it! Everyone from the captain down is a real character.' He had with him paper, pen and ink (the illustrations were to be marginal line drawings), a Complete Works, and, he told a journalist in 1938, 'a trunkful of Elizabethan dramas'. The *Exermont* brought him to Tangiers. At least, that is what he generally said. From there, according to several of his interviews, he travelled to the Atlas mountains to meet up with his Paris chum, the Kaïd Brahim, son of the fabled Lord of the High Atlas, Thami el-Glaoui. Once there, he was treated to lavish and exotic Arab hospitality. Next he went to Casablanca, and thence to Spain. It is worth considering this baldly recited itinerary in some detail, because if true, it must have been a simply astonishing experience; and it is not necessarily not true. Certainly the *Exermont* docked at Tangiers, and it is entirely likely that Welles decided to stay there.

If he did, he would have stepped into a scene from the Arabian nights. Benn's Blue Guide in the 1929 edition (which Welles may well have consulted before setting out) describes the street scene. 'Moors in flowing robes and red fezes or in white-hooded burnouses, Jews in dark dresses, and negroes of every shade, throng the streets, off which open the dark little shops of merchants.

Though West here meets East, though motorcabs hoot at biblical strings of laden camels, the atmosphere is oriental, and to wander through the narrow twisting streets and lanes, often vaulted, and to visit the animated morning markets is to leave Europe behind.' To say nothing of Highland Park, Illinois. Its proximity to the Spanish mainland made Tangiers an accessible introduction to the Muslim world for European visitors, and of these there were plenty, admirably catered for in a number of hotels and cafés; the powerful French influence since 1919 had ensured a modicum of what were held to be civilised amenities. Nor would Welles have been the only American in Tangiers, either. In the last few years, there had been quantities of young American artists of one persuasion or another in Morocco, travelling about and meeting up. Perhaps Welles had got a whiff of this, and that was his reason for choosing to go to Morocco in particular. Paul Bowles had been there a year before in 1931; his first view of the city was a revelation.

> If I said that Tangiers struck me as a dream city, I should mean it in the strict sense. Its topography was rich in prototypal dream scenes: covered streets like corridors with doors opening into rooms on each side, hidden terraces high above the sea, streets consisting only of steps, dark impasses, small squares built on sloping terrain so that they looked like ballet sets designed in false perspective, with alleys leading off in several directions; as well as the classical dream equipment of tunnels, ramparts, ruins, dungeons and cliffs. The climate was both violent and langorous.

Another traveller, Edward Hutton, at nearly the same time – also describing what he saw as dream-like, 'as though suddenly you had half-remembered something that for a lifetime you had forgotten' – wandered through the streets till he came upon a gate:

> A noble-looking old man in soutane and turban, with bare feet and legs and beautiful expressive hands recited to a listening circle of people the acts of the prophet. Every now and then he would pause and play a little desert air, the formless tune of a nomad people, on his tiny Arab guitar . . . it was Homer that I saw in the midst of that attentive throng, Homer reciting 'The Wrath of Achilles' to the people of Chios, in days that we cannot forget. Not far away I found the snake charmer piping to his swaying servants . . .

Such sights must have spoken deeply to the aspect of Welles

that had fallen in love with the Aran Islands and their vanished civilisation. For Welles, who was there to illustrate the plays of Shakespeare, it may have occurred to him that this culture had more in common with the Elizabethan world than the Elizabethan world does with our own: a structured world, one in which simple tools performed the daily tasks, where the community existed as a living whole, and where religion audibly and visibly penetrated every moment of the waking day. He'd seen China, Japan, rural Ireland, he'd spent time on an American Indian reservation. Here was yet another manifestation of human culture, entirely different again. If travel really does broaden the mind, few people of his age can have had greater breadth; few people of any age.

So far, so credible. The story now modulates into the Thousand and One Nights mode. Welles-Scheherazade told Barbara Leaming (and no one else) that travelling around Tangiers and its outskirts in buses, having presumably seen and tired of the Souk, the Casbah and the seemingly unending beach (the second longest in the world), he bumped into an elderly Dutch miniature water-colourist, a curator at the Rijksmuseum. They palled up and travelled together for some weeks. This is a familiar pattern: Mr O'Connor in Ireland and Larry the Archer had been previous travelling companions. The elderly Dutchman, it transpired, was expected at the court of Thami el-Glaoui, Pasha of Marrakesh, so they headed in that direction. In doing so (assuming they did) they would have been taking a route that had only recently been opened up and was treacherous to negotiate. The Hachette Guide to Morocco of 1924 firmly pronounced, under the heading TOURING AND EXCURSIONS AMONG THE NATIVES that 'the time for distant trips in the mountains and in the Sahara has not yet come: it is necessary to wait till the political situation has improved in those parts, and the still rebellious tribes have made their submission'. By 1930, the same guide was cautiously looking forward to 'the possibility' of travel to the mountains. A year earlier, a dogged young Englishman (Richard Hughes, later author of *A High Wind in Jamaica*) had with great difficulty reached the same destination by donkey. But it is just possible; let us assume that our odd couple, an enormous plump American, laden with Elizabethan dramas, pen, paper and ink, and an elderly Dutch curator with his artist's materials, arrived together in Marrakesh.

The sight that greeted them would have made Tangiers seem like a rather ordinary resort. 'It was the year 1346 of the Mahometan calendar,' wrote Hughes, 'but it might as well be 1346 A.D.' Gavin Maxwell has a fine passage about it: 'Much as Europeans visualise the Baghdad of the thousand and one nights, but more beautiful than Baghdad ever was, for Baghdad lacked the savage glories of the Atlas as a background to the jewels of palace and garden, orchard and lake, and the glittering green-tiled minarets of the mosques.'

The old Dutchman, according to Leaming, then introduced himself to the legendary Pasha and his household, and he and Welles were extended full hospitality. They were taken on picnics; every night after feasting and music and dancing, the Europeans retired, six to a tent, where they shared among them one of the concubines.

It is hard to tell whether it is the way Mrs Leaming tells these things (she may simply be transcribing what Welles told her) but these stories lack the ring of truth. They sound made up. The crucial encounters are missing: what happened when Welles himself met the Glaoui? Was he reunited with the Glaoui's son, his bosom friend? How did he feel about having sex in front of five other men? And what about the Dutchman with whom he roamed this exotic and rather frightening country for weeks on end? What did they talk about? Did they keep in touch later? And when and where and how did Welles do the drawings (because he did do them)? Mrs Leaming simply reports the seasoned travelling companions parting with a mere formal goodbye.

If the account of Welles's stay at the court of the Glaoui is true, it is quite extraordinary how little Welles was affected by these amazing experiences: in his subsequent letters he still seems the lively boy, extrovert, full of beans, not specially sophisticated. No Rimbaud, he. Perhaps precocious experience does not, in fact, produce maturity. Perhaps, in fact, someone who has at an early age run the gamut of experience is keen to recover the youthfulness that his experience denies; perhaps, as it is impossible to integrate the experience into everyday life, it is imperative to behave as if it hadn't happened, so Welles's encounter with the great warrior-chieftain was compartmentalised, along with his other exotic experiences. A simpler interpretation suggests itself: Welles had heard some of the many stories current about the Glaoui and absorbed them into his own traveller's tales. The Glaoui was a much publicised figure not only in Morocco, but in France, too. 'In the 1920s,' according to Gavin Maxwell, 'T'hami became, among many Europeans, a fashion, like American jazz, or the Charleston dance, or the new art form of cubism. To be aware of "The Glaoui", and to be able to speak of him with familiarity, was equivalent to what was known forty years later as being "with it".' The publication of the scurrilous *Son Excellence*, a detailed but ignorant denunciation of him by the French left-wing lawyer of his exiled enemy, had created a sensation in Paris at exactly the time of Welles's post-Dublin trip there. The book and the furore surrounding it would certainly have made an impact on Welles. It would be a natural and not altogether reprehensible instinct, in telling tales about his Moroccan sojourn, to put the Glaoui into the story. And when he met the old Dutch curator, and they chummed up, Welles put *him* into the story, a little narrative link to explain his encounter with the Glaoui. Later he may have thought that meeting the Glaoui's son in Paris would be more credible; when in reality, none of these stories makes him more interesting: the mere fact of a seventeen-year-old loose in Tangiers in the early 1930s is quite fascinating enough in itself. Roger Hill wearily admitted in an interview in the early forties that pretty well all the stories about Welles originated with Welles himself: a magnificent Münchhausen, Skipper called him. In an interview in the late thirties, Welles recounted a modest version of the el-Glaoui stories, adding rather sadly: 'But no one believes me, so I've stopped talking about them any more.' The boy who cried wolf.

If he did stay in the royal palace in Marrakesh, he would have had a stupendous experience, and if he had met the Glaoui himself, he would have encountered an unforgettable figure. 'Vast banquets,' writes Maxwell, 'hospitality that included the bestowal of almost priceless gifts; a delicately handled air of omnicompetence . . . to Europeans T'hami gave, literally, whatever they wanted, whether it might be a diamond ring, a present of money in gold, or a Berber girl or boy from the High Atlas.' The Glaoui had sedulously cultivated his personal myth; it was an essential factor in maintaining his rule. His regime was perilously sustained; its survival was a feat of theatrical illusion, backed up by a wide and ruthless intelligence network which ensured that inconvenient people were simply rubbed out, although he did not, disappointingly, kill his own son with a bow-string, as Welles liked to say, nor did he, as Mrs Leaming reports, put an enemy in a cage, like Iago at the beginning of Welles's *Othello*. That was someone else.

The Glaoui was quite Jacobean enough, though, as eye-witness reports of the man himself confirm. Harris, the correspondent of the London *Times*, described how he had once stripped to show off his scars: there was hardly enough of his body unscarred for Harris to be able to put his palm on. 'The curious droop of his mouth is due to the severing of a tendon on his face . . . the truth of his withered hand . . . was that Glaoui was once besieged in a fort which was about to fall to the enemy: he evacuated his men and remained behind alone to blow up the powder magazine as the enemy entered, and that was how his hand was rendered useless.' In his contradictoriness, simultaneously savage and suave, he was the sort of man whom Welles would later delight to depict; an Arkadin or a Mr Clay. This was the world, then, that Welles would have known as a guest of the Glaoui. He would have had experiences unlike anything life had prepared him for. Such experiences would not be calculated to increase his sense of reality; it would be like taking LSD. These were the stories with which he regaled his actors during breaks in rehearsal; these are the stories with which, later, he regaled Mrs Leaming. They amount to a reverse mirror of his Merrie Englands: a brutal, savage, but somehow chivalrous world in which men were men, and life was lived with pure, fierce intensity. Whatever the reality, his imagination had certainly lived that life, and it was one he would over the years try to put on the stage or the screen.

He gave another version of his time in Marrakesh to a New York journalist in 1938: 'I went to Africa – to the High Atlas mountains – taking a trunkful of Elizabethan dramas with me. It sounds crazy doesn't it? But I swear that is what I did. I stayed at a castle in the mountains; it belonged to an Atlas chieftain, and the name of the place was unbelievable – Glaoni, pronounced Glowny. Nothing happened in that romantic spot except that I read my way right through the Elizabethan period. You see, I went there to write my book on Shakespeare. I didn't do much writing, after all . . . but I did a lot of reading – and that was when I got my admiration for the Elizabethan theatre.' This has a ring of truth about it; but how did he get to the mountains? Did he meet the Glaoui? If not, why not? The only person who could have told us is Welles, and it seems that he no longer knew what was true and what was fable. From Marrakesh, at any rate, he went, briefly, to Casablanca, and thence to Spain, to Seville.

There is a radically alternative version to all this, comic in its difference, told by one of the most diligent promulgators of Wellesian myth: Professor Frank Brady. According to the good professor, Welles arrived, not in Tangiers at all, but in Casablanca, and there he stayed till – for 'unexplained reasons' – he made for Tangiers, and thence Spain. While in Casablanca, he stayed, courtesy of Brahim el-Glaoui, in a house maintained by the Coca-Cola company, of which Thami el-Glaoui was vice-President; which, indeed, he was. This is a version of his Moroccan sojourn that Welles never put about.

What is not in question is that he went to Spain, which in its way was every bit as extraordinary and exotic as Morocco, its people possessed and obsessed with pride and honour. Seville itself – birthplace of Velázquez and Murillo, with its Catedral, Giralda, and Alacazar among the most famous buildings of Spain, its religious functions unrivalled even by those of Rome – was proudly separate from the rest of Spain, and on another planet from the rest of Europe. This is the Spain of the imagination, the Spain of *Carmen*, and certainly must have seemed so to Welles, since he went to stay in the Triana, the gypsy quarter. There is an interesting and admirable tendency on his part – it may have been to some extent financially dictated – to avoid hotels and touristic quarters. He did it in Ireland: he did it in Lac du Flambeau; now he was doing it in Seville, seeking to become part of the life of the community. He placed himself right at the centre of it by staying over a brothel. The Triana was at once picturesque and squalid, the industrial quarter which has been noted since early antiquity for its potteries. Čapek, in Spain two years before, described the district: 'There are some tiny cottages with clean patios, with a regular gypsyish abundance of children, mothers suckling their babies, almond-eyed girls with a red flower in their blue-black hair, slender gypsy-lads with a rose between their teeth, a peaceable Sunday crowd taking its ease on its doorsteps . . . suddenly, in the distance a clatter of castanets became audible, and through the narrow streets of Triana glided a high car, dragged by oxen and festooned with wreaths and an abundance of tulle curtains, canopies, trimmings, flounces, drapery, veils and all sorts of other fallals' – a scene that can equally be seen, minus the castanets, in Morocco, where a wedding procession, led by a garlanded cow, will suddenly erupt through the alleys. Life is on the streets, not behind closed doors, another distinctly unAmerican phenomenon. Across the river from the Triana, and impossible to ignore, was – *Carmen* again – the Tobacco Factory: 'They are employed, some five thousand of them, at the Fabrica de Tabacos, a huge building between the Jardines del Alcazar and Jardin del Palacio. It is like a harem, this immense house full of women, and certainly the most melancholy and distressing spectacle in Seville,' wrote Hutton, 'it is a herd, a legion, an army that is broken.'

Welles supported himself, he said, by writing pulp fiction for which he got paid well enough to live 'like Diamond Jim Brady'. Whenever the cash ran out, he just sat down and knocked off another story and sent it back to Chicago. This is to place a great deal of faith in the mail, but no doubt it was better then. The stories concerned a young detective living with his aunt in Baltimore, he told Barbara Leaming, 'expressly based on what Orson imagined his father's youth to have been like'. It would be interesting to see the stories; they have, alas, disappeared. With the profits from them, he entertained his neighbours, 'buying drinks,' as he put it, 'for half Andalucia'. Whatever was left over he spent on bulls. He had been reading Hemingway's just published *Death in the Afternoon*, and was determined to participate in the primitive masculine rituals it describes. There was of course no question of him training formally to become a bull-fighter. His only chance of getting into the corrida was the way Hemingway had managed it: at the amateur free-for-all bull-fights held each morning, where the bulls' horns were padded. Carlos Baker in his life of Hemingway has a passage about it which may closely resemble Welles's experience: 'wearing white pants and waving a red cape, he made the legitimate bull-call – HUH, TORO, TORO! – and the animal charged. Ernest manfully grabbed the padded horns and succeeded in bulldogging the animal to the ground . . . they performed each day before 20,000 fans . . . the whole town split into two factions, humanitarians who wanted them to quit while they were alive, the rest to make certain that the Americanos would appear.'

Welles could also have pitted himself (for a small consideration) against the cows used in training torreros. *Death in the Afternoon* gives an idea of what this was like: 'sometimes with naked horns, sometimes with the points covered with a leather ball, they come in as fast and lithe as deer to practice on the amateur capemen and aspirant bullfighters of all sorts in the capeas; to toss, rip, gore, pursue and inspire with terror these amateurs until, when the vacas tire, steers are led into the ring to take them out to rest in the corrals until their next appearance.' Having read this passage, Welles would have had no doubt about the real violence and danger involved in the sport. Even if he did it only once, it betrays a degree of physical courage and nimbleness, from someone noted for neither, that is breathtaking. Was he persuaded as a dare to get into the ring? Or did he force himself to do it? Must he, like Hemingway, 'prove himself'? It is interesting that the bull-fight is the very embodiment of that quintessentially Spanish ideal, majismo, a working-class reaction against the perceived effeminacy and decadence of eighteenth-century Spanish middle-class life. Unlike the effeminate Europeans, Spanish men must be men, and Spanish women must be women. Hemingway's attraction to the concept has always been felt to betray some underlying anxiety; perhaps Orson ('the bitch boy') too wanted to prove something to himself. Perhaps, on the other hand, he was just in it for the hell of it. He came out with a wound, which must have been very gratifying, though the wound – in the familiar way – tended to travel a little. Sometimes it was on his lip (Barbara Leaming), sometimes on his thigh (Tynan).

He said an interesting thing to Peter Bogdanovich on the subject of his career in the corrida. 'I'd never have got myself out there on the sand in front of the twisted horns of a perfect cathedral of a becerro (calf) – and before audiences of short-tempered and super-critical Andalusian bull experts – if I'd really been *scared*. No, what made that little taurine caper possible was what had made it possible for me, a year earlier, to launch myself in show-business not as a spear-carrier but as a star. What got me up there on stage and out there in the bull-ring wasn't a lack of nerves, it was an absolutely perfect lack of ambition. I saw no glorious future for myself in either episode.'

Clearly he had no ambition to be a bull-fighter. It is interesting that he felt obliged to insist that he had no ambition as an actor, either, when every letter he wrote suggests the exact opposite. It is possible, though, that as long as he wasn't at home, he could put off the insistent demands, both his own and those of others, that he get on and do something, be somebody. Every indication that we have suggests a blazing ambition, an enormous compulsion to cut a swathe in the world. It may be that he was trying to escape that nagging, imperious demand by travelling. At least he would be able to say when he returned that he hadn't wasted his time: he'd proved himself in the bull-ring.

He returned to Chicago. Once back there, he was unable to deliver very many drawings. 'All that hot summer of 1933 I had kept Orson slaving in a Chicago Rush Street "studio" just large enough for one small bed and one oversize drawing board,' wrote Roger Hill. 'There he turned out literally thousands of detailed sketches, most of them crumpled and thrown away in angry frustration by a self-critical young artist. But I saved over twelve hundred and these went to press.' And if this were not enough to eat up Welles's energies, Skipper invited him to direct the Todd Troupers in *Twelfth Night*, in Hill's own edition, for the Chicago Drama League. He played Malvolio – in a somewhat swashbuckling, Italianate make-up if the photograph is anything to go by – and designed it, too, after a picture-book design for an earlier production by Kenneth MacGowan, Robert Edmond Jones's collaborator. It's unlike Welles simply to copy another man's work. The suggestion was Skipper's; if this lack of creative contribution indicates a certain half heartedness on Welles's part, that would be understandable. From the High Atlas Mountains and the corrida to the Chicago Drama League must have felt like a retrogressive move.

However, he was fond of the play (he often announced productions of it: as late as 1960 he was laying plans to do it in London) and may have derived some satisfaction from standing in front of an audience again: it had been eighteen months since his final performance in Dublin. The open-book setting, hand-painted by Welles, has some charm: the page turns to give a new scene, opening with the words A PLEASANT CONCEITED COMEDIE CALLED TWELFE NIGHT or WHAT YOU WILL, going on to ORSINO'S CASTLE (with distant sea), OLIVIA'S GARDEN (with cypress grove) and so on, with a pleasant, light use of stylised perspective. In the Toby Belch/Andrew Aguecheek scene, Maria and Malvolio, both in nightshirts, seem suspended in the air at the side of the book-leaves. The costumes are largely Elizabethan in feel, apart, perhaps, from Maria's polka-dot nightshirt and semi-mediaeval head-gear. Welles had over half of the high school boys in the cast, typical of Skipper's policy of pupil participation; Hascy Tarbox, now resident genius, played Aguecheek.

They won first prize – 'at last', in Roger Hill's words. It is always better to win than to lose, but it can't have meant very much to Welles, after the sort of dreams he'd been entertaining: *Coriolanus* and *Othello* in Dublin; *King Lear* on Broadway. His trophy may even have seemed to mock his ambitions: a schoolboy prize. Certainly by the time a few weeks later that he was moodily drinking cocktails at a party thrown by the salonnière and musician, Hazel Buchbinder – a Todd parent – he told one of the other guests that he was 'a writer'. Perhaps he said that because his interlocutor was a writer himself: Thornton Wilder, Professor of Literature at the University of Chicago, author of a couple of admired novels, and some experimental plays though not as yet the ones by which he would become internationally famous. Welles and he had a rather flirtatious conversation around the piano – Wilder: 'Do you play?' Welles: 'Yes, but not on the piano' – which may be the basis of Welles's later report to Barbara Leaming that his first reaction was to think 'here's another queen'. Wilder was gay, but scarcely a queen (in later life, Welles seems to have used the term synonymously with homosexual). 'A mixture,' according to Alexander Woollcott, 'of poet, prophet, hummingbird and gadfly'. Wilder was that curious phenomenon, a shy party-goer.

'By some surprising "jump of association" – I really had no idea who he was' he asked Welles 'Are you the young American actor who made such an extraordinary success in Dublin?' He had heard about him, not via *The New York Times*, but from his sister whose friend Lady Longford had written about him in a letter from Dublin. Welles admitted to being the very same young American actor, but poo-poohed his acting. Wilder poo-poohed his poo-poohing and tipped him off that his friend Katharine Cornell, for whom he had translated *Lucrece*, (one of her few flops), was looking for a young actor to play Marchbanks on her forthcoming tour. Wilder would introduce him to Alexander Woollcott, who would introduce him to Miss Cornell and her husband-director, Guthrie McClintic. 'Get on a train tomorrow.' He did; the train's name was the Broadway Ltd, and on it he sped to his next date with destiny, the eighteen-month hiatus in his career suddenly terminated.

The letter of introduction Wilder wrote to Woollcott gives a new version of Welles's Irish career: Welles, he reports, had been lending some friends a hand in painting the scenery for *Jew Süss*, heard about the desperate search for a Karl Alexander, presented himself and was cast. 'The reviews were so astounding that he was kept on to play Othello and Hamlet' – which may have been what Welles said. Wilder describes Welles as round-faced with a lock of hair always falling into his eyes, and prone to affect an abstract pose. He did not affect it for long in Woollcott's presence. No doubt he was trying out various personas for size: wisely, since he was about to enter the very big league of personality players. Woollcott, through his journalism, his radio work, but above all through his ceaseless social networking, was one of the key figures of pre-war civilised Manhattan. Fat and fruity, his personal legend reached its apogee in *The Man who Came to Dinner*, in which he was depicted as the imperious and infantile Sheridan Whiteside. (It had its apotheosis when he himself appeared in the role on stage.) Of indeterminate sexuality, friendship was his delight and his gospel. He took particular pleasure in advancing not only his and his friends' reputations, but also in creating those of talented newcomers. Almost unheard of now, advancement through personal recommendation was one of the principal ways in which the theatre functioned: 'who you knew' was often the open sesame for young actors. Talent was not the ultimate criterion; a family connection or a chance introduction at a party would do it. Without influence, simply getting through to one of the big Broadway figures like Guthrie McClintic would be all but impossible; a young unknown from Chicago, Illinois wouldn't even begin.

Welles instinctively grasped this. 'You have given me a whole ring of keys to this city, and I've been busy all week excitedly fitting them into their locks and opening important doors,' he wrote to Thornton Wilder. 'If I don't cover myself with glory now you've opened up this New York to me, why then there's nothing to cover.' In introducing him to Woollcott, Wilder had put him in touch with the single most influential man in New York; Welles set about charming him with great dedication. Soon he was 'my hulking prodigy'. Alexander King gives a glimpse of their relationship at the period: 'I remember shortly after Orson Welles arrived in New York I was living in Woollcott's apartment . . . Welles suddenly showed up looking terrible. Woollcott immediately dressed him from head to foot; he gave him all the clothes he could spare. Then he took him out and got him shoes, which were hard to find because his feet were so big. Then he introduced him to Katharine Cornell.' The chronology may be out, but the relationship is clear: Welles had found himself another daddy, as he was to do so often in his young manhood. He needed, and unerringly found, someone to look after him. If luck is defined as opportunity plus readiness, he was always ready; he knew how to make the most of the gifts destiny so generously threw his way. To put on someone else's clothes is a very intimate thing to do, suggesting great trust and a certain degree of identification: if I can wear your clothes, I must be awfully like you. There was in him – and this was only intensified by his great bulk, the copious scale on which he was constructed – an ability to provoke protectiveness in others; Woollcott extended his protection in very practical ways. Things moved fast. Immediately after his first, highly successful, meeting with Welles he secured an interview for him with McClintic; later that night the exhilarated young man wrote to Roger Hill from the Algonquin Hotel:

> Just a note on a night of triumph. *I've signed the contract. I am to play Mercutio – Marchbanks and Octavius with Katharine Cornell.*
>
> *Mr McClintic hasn't even asked me to read!* There may be a worry in that but *Mrs Robert Edmond Jones* formerly the great (she's still great) *Miss Corrington* who *made John Barrymore's 'Hamlet'* HAS

> *heard me. Enthuses pretty much. Will coach me.* – looks pretty much like the saga has begun. – All my love – Orson.

He was quite right; it had.

CHAPTER SIX

Wonder Boy of Acting/ *Romeo and Juliet*

DADDA BERNSTEIN had finally been out-manoeuvred. All his efforts to steer Welles away from the theatre had failed. His resistance to Welles's chosen career was not unreasonable; joining a hard-pressed, overcrowded, underemployed profession during the worst slump in America's history would not normally be considered a shrewd move. As if he were writing at the specific behest of Bernstein, the distinguished New York critic Burns Mantle wrote, in the *Chicago Tribune*, that same year of 1933, 'If I did not know how useless they are, I should start a campaign of discouragement directed at those young people who insist on a stage career. Now that the summer theatres are in full blast and considerable local talent is being employed, the urge to act is again sweeping the country and the requests for advice are piling in . . . for every six or eight letters I have from ambitious actors, there are at least two from various actor charities. Listen, for example, to this: "The emergency, to some extent, continues . . . more than $94,000 has been given out to the needy in all branches of the theatre. More than 6,000 men, women and children have received help and about $700 a week is being distributed at this time." ' But Welles was all right; he started, as he so often did, at the top.

His engagement to play Octavius Moulton-Barrett in *The Barretts of Wimpole Street*, and Marchbanks in *Candida*, and, particularly, Mercutio in *Romeo and Juliet* is one of the most extraordinary breakthroughs in theatre history. His exuberant telegram to Maurice Bernstein ('just signed contract with mcclintic to do mercutio marchbanks octavius with katharine cornell stop biggest and best debut in america for me') was no word of an exaggeration; but the cautionary note then sounded was also wise, in view of the enormity of the gamble: 'dont rejoice too loudly i can be kicked out during rehearsals'. It is a great indication of Welles's personal impact even at the age of seventeen that he got the job. It was *only* his personal impact that had secured it, since they had never seen him act, didn't ask him to audition nor even to read. It is also an indication of McClintic's considerable faith in his own judgement. A great deal was at stake in this season.

The production company that McClintic and his wife ran was Broadway's flower; Welles was joining a team which epitomised the refined best of American theatre. Built round its star, this was none the less a company which aspired to an overall excellence at every level. Katharine Cornell was already, at the age of forty, a prime contender for the title of First Lady of the American Stage. There was no First Gentleman: the theatre of the early thirties was, as Brooks Atkinson liked to say, a matriarchy. Cornell's fellow actress-managers Helen Hayes and the Australian-born Judith Anderson were her principal rivals, but she, in close partnership with McClintic, was a more adventurous manager than either. Her range as an actress was remarkably wide, encompassing flappers and dutiful daughters, killers and Candida, though not as yet any classical role. Taller than actresses were then supposed to be (five foot seven inches in her stockinged feet) she had a unique presence, ethereal and passionate, exotic and ordinary. Bernard Shaw had written at the time of her first Candida: 'fancy my feelings on seeing the photograph of a gorgeous dark lady from the cradle of the human race. If you look like that it doesn't matter a rap if you can act or not. Can you? – GBS'. She could; despite feelings of discomfort and sometimes actual physical pain when acting, she was entirely devoted to her craft. She and her husband had met in Jessie Bonstelle's Detroit stock company; there they had learned excellent habits of work and a sense of responsibility to both the theatre itself and to the audience – especially the less wealthy section of it: 'it is an old story that the balcony and the gallery are the true support of the theatre. They have done well by me throughout the years and I in turn feel an obligation to them,' McClintic wrote. Their partnership, a *mariage blanc* (he was homosexual), was one of fierce commitment in which their mutual and unquestioned support enabled them to challenge each other unceasingly. Their lives were their work; the theatre was their faith. It was very serious and it was great fun, within formal limits. Even fun had to be disciplined.

From *Candida* to *The Green Hat*, from *The Letter* to *The Age of Innocence*, Cornell's work for other managers had been consistently striking and varied; when she and McClintic took the plunge into management, they had an enormous success with its first venture, *The Barretts of Wimpole Street*. *Alien Corn* which followed had been a comparable triumph. Typically, instead of looking for another vehicle, she was now taking on a challenge she had nervously avoided: Shakespeare. It was a challenge for McClintic too. He had proved himself a master craftsman in staging the well-made plays (frequently adaptations of novels) in which his wife triumphed. *Candida* was the nearest to a classical play that he had come; and that is a long way from the conventions and freedoms of Elizabethan theatre. When it came to Shakespeare they were both very unsure of themselves (though not of each other); they prepared very thoroughly, McClintic immersing himself in scholarly editions and critical literature, feeling obscurely inadequate in the face of what he saw as the ultimate challenge. Nervous of presenting their work to the New York critics, they planned for *Romeo and Juliet* a year-long tour of the United States, to give themselves a chance of getting it right.

He was particularly keen to surround himself with actors experienced in Shakespeare. When his friend Alexander Woollcott, that great pundit, on the recommendation of Professor Thornton Wilder, sent him a young man of imposing stature, startling self-confidence and an impressive knowledge of – not to say easy familiarity with – the Collected Works, McClintic must have jumped. He was not an easy man, and not easily impressed; but this was something he wanted in his company. 'It was obvious to me that this extraordinary-looking young man with his beautiful voice and speech was a "natural" for a part in *Romeo and Juliet,* and it seemed at the moment he was the best to play Mercutio.' In addition, he asked him to play Chorus, speaking the first lines in the play. Katharine Cornell was equally impressed: 'We were all struck by his beautiful voice and speech and always provocative acting methods. It was obvious from the time that he gave his first performance with us that he was a tremendously talented boy.'

It remains remarkable that a key role in a huge new production of a play about which both Cornell and McClintic were anxious should be entrusted to a 'boy'. It is no less surprising that McClintic should have cast him in the role of the quintessentially romantic young poet Marchbanks in *Candida*, 'a strange, shy youth of eighteen, slight, effeminate, with a delicate childish voice, and a hunted tormented and shrinking expression that show the painful sensitiveness of very swift and acute apprehensiveness in youth', according to Shaw's stage directions. 'He is so uncommon as to be almost unearthly.' No one could accuse McClintic of type-casting. However, both Cornell and he knew the play intimately, and were prepared to take a risk. As for stammering, stuttering Occy in the revived *Barretts of Wimpole Street*, that again was at the very least

PRODIGY

The Badger Brass Manufacturing Co.

:::: MAKERS OF ::::

SOLAR, GAS, OIL AND ELECT

For Motor Cars, Cycles, Carriages, Bo

Badger Brass, where Orson's father Richard was treasurer and general secretary before turning to other pursuits. *Right* Great-grandfather O. S. Head

Beatrice Welles

Richard Welles

Preceding page Orson Welles at fifteen

Top left Orson as a baby and *right* featuring in a newspaper story under the headline 'Cartoonist, Actor, Poet – and Only 10'
Above Orson (left) with his older brother Richard Jr.

A school group at Todd. Welles is in the middle of the second row

The main building of the Todd School for Boys

From the 1936 Todd yearbook, 'The seniors in their formal dinner clothes.' Welles is in shorts

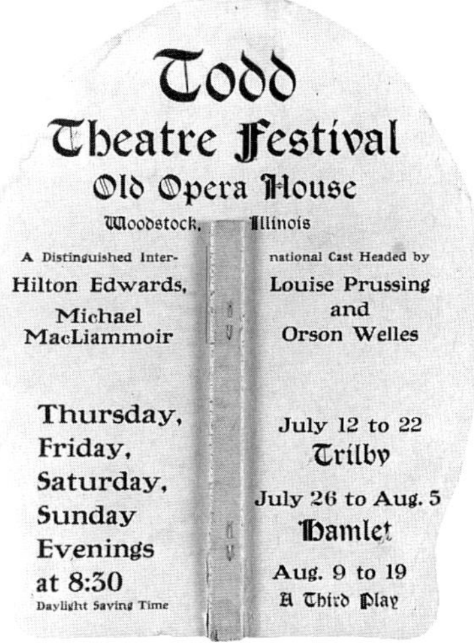

Above A souvenir fan from the Todd Theatre Festival

Left Todd headmaster Roger Hill with his wife Hortense and their daughter Joanne

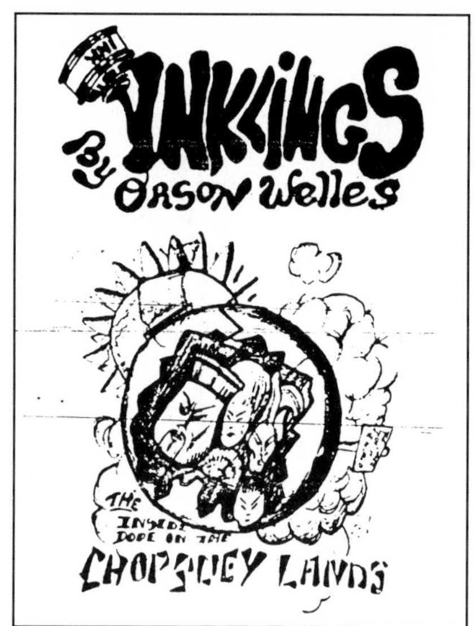

Some of Orson's artwork: *above* cover for a Todd catalogue;
right headpiece for his column in the Todd *News*;
below sketches in a letter to Roger Hill from Dublin

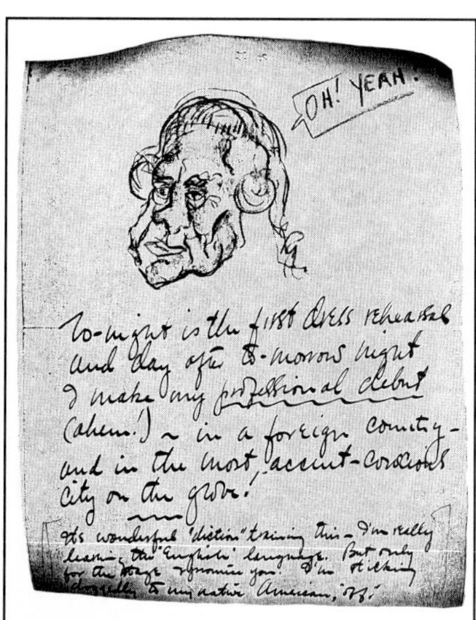

To-night is the first dress rehearsal
and day after to-morrow night
I make my professional debut
(ahem!) — in a foreign country —
and in the most accent-conscious
city on the globe!

It's wonderful "diction" training this — I'm really
learning the "English" language. But only
for the stage I promise you. I'm sticking
doggedly to my native "American," O.W.

Above Taking a break during the Todd Theatre Festival in Woodstock: Welles and Hilton Edwards at edge of pool, Micheál MacLiammóir on diving board. *Below* Welles (right) as Claudius to MacLiammóir's Hamlet at Woodstock

Photographed for a publicity release at the age of eighteen, Welles is described as 'a young Chicagoan of amazing precocity'

Right Welles's own drawing of the Gate Theatre in Dublin, where he launched his professional career

imaginative casting, though not so extreme. It was a part for a young actor simply to be pleasant in. In fact, Welles tried to get out of playing it; he would rather do nothing than play such a minor part, according to the company manager, Gertrude Macy. The contract was conditional on his accepting all three roles, so he gave in. It would have been a wonderful break for any other young actor to be offered Octavius in such company. But Welles had the smell of glory in his nostrils.

Rehearsals were not without incident. McClintic was a painstaking, demanding director, innovatory in his methods. His staging was tasteful and skilful, essentially conventional; he surrounded himself with the best talents – for *Romeo and Juliet* he engaged Martha Graham to stage the dances, which she did without a whiff of innovation, simply exercising her considerable taste and skill. His work with the actors, however, was probing, designed to ensure freshness of response and freedom from hackneyed formulas. Using neither the Stanislavsky method nor any other theory, his was a very different approach to that of the block-it-and-run-it Broadway directors of his day. 'He began,' according to Mary Henderson, 'by having his cast sit around a table and read the play over and over again for a week. He did this to allow the actors to get to know the script and each other, and to convey to them the kind of performance he wanted.' 'Talkative, nervous, very witty,' said Burgess Meredith of him. 'He'd spend half the time during rehearsals telling you stories, to get you into the spirit of the theatre, of the play, of your part. Then he would get these flashes for the high points of the play, and act them out for you. He did it in a kind of broad caricature, so that you wouldn't imitate him.' Meredith found McClintic 'an extraordinarily effective director'. He was also volatile, passionate and intolerant of resistance. Stories of his towering rages are legendary.

It is evident that he and the seventeen-year-old Welles did not see eye to eye. The sort of elegance and psychological verisimilitude that McClintic was after were elusive to Welles, both by instinct and experience. The poetic theatricality of Mac Liammóir and Edwards —their curious combination of an atavistic acting style with radical staging methods – and his own flamboyantly rhetorical manner were things that needed, according to McClintic, to be eradicated. 'Orson at that time always played to the top row of the third balcony, both in make-up and projectivity,' according to a fellow actor, John Hoyt. McClintic disapproved of Welles's 'hammy ways'. And Welles, buzzing with the avant-garde influences and full-frontal theatrical assault he had known at the Gate, his mind still teeming with the ideas about staging he had been evolving in *Everybody's Shakespeare*, can scarcely have been excited by McClintic's sedate production, either. Nor were relations with his fellow actors of the best. Basil Rathbone, the English actor who had already played Morell to Cornell's Candida in an earlier revival and was now her forty-two-year-old Romeo, vividly expresses the animus he felt against his young co-star in his autobiography *In and Out of Character*: 'Orson Welles had come to our company via Dublin, Ireland, Thornton Wilder, and Alexander Woollcott and was supposed to be a boy wonder verging on the phenomenon of genius. With this type of advance publicity much should be forgiven him.' It is understandable, if not altogether attractive, that the highly trained, brilliantly skilful older man should have resented the prominence accorded to the callow young Welles. Welles had no time at all for Rathbone. But he reined himself in. He knew which side his bread was buttered on. And McClintic and Cornell seemed to have sensed that, whatever the artistic disagreements, the buzz that he brought with him was in itself an asset.

His touch with the press had not deserted him. Shortly before the launch of the tour, his debut was announced, in some style, to the waiting world. YOUNG ACTOR TO PLAY MERCUTIO AND MARCHBANKS, said *The New York Times*. A photograph of Welles, noble and concerned, hand in pocket, dominates the theatre page. This is the sort of publicity coup that a young actor dreams of. The legend, exposed to the national press for the first time, was already evolving. The copy by Wilella Waldorf claims that Thornton Wilder saw Welles on stage in Dublin and wrote to Woollcott who wired Cornell. 'She has agreed to the selection and Orson Welles is therefore enrolled as a leading member of her troupe.' The now standard story of his arrival at the Gate is duly retold, with an addition: 'from the Gate he went on to the famous Abbey Theatre, where he had the distinction of becoming a featured performer – the first foreign player so honored. Ruth Draper was the second.' This imaginative information can only have come from him; rather risky, one would have thought, since the Abbey were at that time touring America – about, indeed, to arrive in New York at any moment. He was nothing if not bold. Of course, nobody had heard of the Gate, and everybody had heard of the Abbey. 'Returning to America about a year ago, young Mr Welles decided to become a writer. His play, *Marching Song*, will be produced in November at the Gate Theatre in Dublin.' It had, in fact, been flatly turned down by them. At this early stage, it is evident that Welles had a great gift for providing good copy, a quality always endearing to the press. If what had actually happened was a little dull, he would obligingly spice it up; at a pinch, he would invent something altogether new. Of course, journalists will always simplify and italicise, but they had a wonderful collaborator in 'young Mr Welles'.

The Cornell tour was anyway a major event for the press, even without his help. Starting in Buffalo, it was to end in Brooklyn, after covering 16,538 miles, having played 77 cities in 7 months: a total of 225 performances. This represented a tremendous act of faith in the idea of touring; an idea whose time, it was widely believed, had gone. The rise of radio and film had closed many of the regional theatres; the majority of the rest had been converted into movie houses. There were now no more than four or five companies a year on the road; the country simply didn't get to see the big shows. 'In the 1930's Broadway began to assume its overwhelming importance to American theatre,' wrote the great lighting designer Jean Rosenthal. 'The objective of all productions became the New York run.' In Ethan Mordden's striking phrase: 'all the rest was just dead wire'. Cornell and McClintic boldly bucked the trend, and, treading where only third-rate touring companies like those of Fritz Leiber (a sort of Donald Wolfit *manqué*) and Percy Vivian dared to venture, they offered their highly wrought, richly costumed and strongly cast shows to an America starved of quality theatre.

Buffalo in New York State was where they chose to open the tour, not with *Romeo and Juliet* but with *Candida*. Cornell's performance (of which John Mason Brown had earlier written that it 'glows with the radiance which is so uniquely Miss Cornell's own. Its pictorial qualities are at once arresting and unforgettable') was again warmly received; Welles's performance was the subject of some controversy. Rathbone was very clear about it: '[Miss Cornell] was so beautiful and so desirable that had she murdered Morell and married Marchbanks we would have forgiven her – or almost – because in this production Marchbanks was played by Orson Welles, whose performance was so fatuously unpleasant that Morell became, by contrast, a deeply sympathetic character.' Welles had his revenge years later when he told Leslie Megahey on BBC television: 'Basil Rathbone . . . had to shake me as I said: "You shook me like a rat." It's pretty hard to be shaken *by* a rat – you know, Mrs Campbell said he was two profiles in search of a face . . . a very thin, slight figure and we did it behind a couch and I sort of crouched. And of course, it always came out as a terrible,

terrible campy thing . . . one of the poorer moments in the American theatre.'

McClintic was terse about Welles's performance: 'His Marchbanks to my way of thinking was never right.' Even Roger Hill considered him hopelessly unsuitable in the part: 'He could play *Jew Süss* but not a normal sixteen-year-old boy.' Enthusiasm for his performance came from a surprising quarter: Gertrude Macy, the company manager, whose life he made something of a trial: 'He was flamboyant, exciting, hammy . . . he gave an excellent performance. He should have been slight & delicate; yet he was enormous and clumsy.' His appearance may have contributed to his strange impact: he had had his hair permed. 'People gathered six-deep outside the beauty shops to sneer,' according to Welles. Interestingly, Macy adds that 'he appealed to the general run of audiences who weren't tied to a preconceived concept of the role.' Marchbanks has always been a problem role; few actors since Granville Barker have been able to render Shaw's poet convincingly; only Rupert Graves in recent times has succeeded. Despite Macy's enthusiasm, it may be doubted if Welles's performance really made sense; nor does it seem that he tried very hard. McClintic's final verdict contains some of his irritation: 'That he got by was by no means enough.'

The Barretts of Wimpole Street was another triumph for Miss Cornell and another damp squib from Welles. Cornell's performance was already legendary. 'By the crescendo of her playing, by the wild sensitivity that lurks behind her ardent gestures and her piercing stares across the footlights she charges the drama with a meaning beyond the facts it records,' wrote Brooks Atkinson in *The New York Times*. 'Her acting is quite as remarkable for the carefulness of its design as for the fire of her presence.' Behind the evident tastefulness of her performances was both latent temperament and painstaking, sometimes painful, work. Everything was considered and refound night after night. The casualness of Welles's performance as Octavius must have been deeply offensive to her. 'He was just adequate, always reading his lines intelligently, but sloppy and careless as a member of that well-disciplined, strictly ordered family,' according to his defender, Gertrude Macy. He was unwilling to submit himself to the ensemble feeling that both Katharine Cornell and Guthrie McClintic strove for. Where was the glory in that? 'I personally believe that his sprained ankle on the day of our Los Angeles opening was contrived so that the audience would not have to see him in that very subordinate role.' (Macy again.) He played the part under sufferance, which is the most destructive possible attitude to bring, undermining the play, the other actors, and, ultimately, oneself. It is also short-sighted; there are, of course, no small parts, only small actors: when Burgess Meredith played the role in a revival of the same production, the *New York American* said of him 'his performance begins to confirm the suspicion that he's just about the most able and versatile of the younger actors'. By his own lights, however, Welles was right: he wanted to establish himself, immediately, as a leading actor. He was interested neither in developing his craft nor in exploring his range. He was sublimely confident of his right to hold the centre of the stage, and his readiness for it, and he was impatient to be allowed to get on with it. Not for him the profound need to lose himself in another person, nor the desire to expose himself in public, nor even the compulsion to dazzle and thrill.

It is a curious feature of Welles's personality, this: it would be wrong to describe him as merely ambitious, or simply arrogant. He simply knew that he was formed by temperament and physique to be a leading actor, so he would do the job. This strange conviction lies behind the casualness of so much of his work as an actor. Neither in interpretation nor in execution did he push himself very hard; he made a good strong decision about the character, devised the appropriate make-up and performed. That was that. The physical impact was all. Tom Triffely, seeing *The Barretts* in New Orleans, was overwhelmed: 'his entrance was so strange, so extraordinary, like a Martian. He towered like a Buddha with a wig on' – an unexpected description of Elizabeth Barrett's tongue-tied little brother. After his barely adequate showings in the season's two revivals, it is as well that he found his stride in *Romeo and Juliet*. In the role of Mercutio his odd charisma and the part he was playing came together.

The production over which McClintic had laboured so intensely was received with respect ('it is admirable Shakespeare, offered with a lavish hand to the playgoers of a period that has been treating the noblest heritage of English-speaking drama with shocking neglect'); Woodman Thompson's solid design was admired for the way in which 'he has created a glowing spectacle of the romantic period that serves as a background for Shakespeare's greatest love story'; Cornell's radiance was routinely praised, the ensemble acclaimed – 'a marked improvement over the Shakespeare that the American stage gave its patrons in the much-lamented "good old days" . . . they were Shakespearean giants in those days but the aforesaid giants too often held sway over courts of pygmies.' But it was Welles, particularly in his home town, who elicited the golden plaudits. 'Passing over Basil Rathbone's Romeo, already described as handsome but cold,' said the *Chicago Tribune*, most gratifyingly, 'attention focuses on Orson Welles's Mercutio – a new treatment of the character, abundant in vitality. . . I had never seen him acted in a style that approached my conception until young Welles swaggered out to prove that the critics of Dublin who hailed him as a wonder-boy were not crazy. Welles is flamboyant, some will say – but so is Mercutio. Welles violates tradition by wearing a half-fledged beard – but it gives his boyish face a definite Tudor look. He reads the Queen Mab speech with merry flourishes, and he plunges into the duel scene with a fine fury of swordmanship.'

A photograph of Welles in the role suggests a robust, piratical figure, ear-ringed and bearded; more like the traditional image of Petruchio. It can well be imagined that Welles's size and force could have made for an original and startling Mercutio, quite unlike the jolly jester of Victorian tradition ('that indestructibly happy part', Stark Young called it, as late as 1923), or the neurotic ectomorph of current fashion. The contrast with Rathbone's Romeo ('which seemed to meet with McClintic's and Cornell's approval, as later it was to do with every critic throughout the country', in his own modest phrase) must have been rather striking; Rathbone forty-one years old, Welles eighteen.

Chicago's press, at any rate, was in no doubt that a star had been born. The *Tribune* followed up their enthusiastic notice with a feature on their theatre page, headed WONDER BOY OF ACTING. The page is dominated by a fine photographic portrait by Vandamm with Welles in mid-profile, a looming shadow on the wall, his right hand hanging expressively down. He looks fifteen at the most. 'Orson Welles, who has scored a hit as Mercutio in Katharine Cornell's production of ROMEO & JULIET,' reads the caption, 'is a young Chicagoan of amazing precocity. A prep school lad, at the age of 18, he takes a leading role with the power and skill of a veteran.' The allusions to his 'preppy' manner are confirmed by contemporaries; he was still recognisably a middle-class boy from the Middle West. The manner made the myth even more remarkable in the eyes of his early chroniclers. The romance of the Irish sojourn takes another leap forward; here he is 'the David Garrick of the Irish Free State'. Reality has long been left behind. The more recent past, too, is endowed with a legendary touch: as he prepares for rehearsals with the famous drama coach Miss Dorothy Corrington, she hands him a copy of *Hamlet*. It is inscribed 'John Barrymore'. She taught him, too. 'It was a favourable omen.' The essential elements of Welles's public profile had now been established: precocity, direct succession to the great ones of the past, possession of special insights gained from foreign wanderings. His curriculum vitae thus presented bears a striking resemblance to that of Jesus Christ.

It is worth mentioning that Welles's father and Roger Hill both had close contacts with Chicago's journalistic fraternity; Ashton Stevens was Dick Welles's best friend, and most of the other arts journalists took a lively interest in Todd School. Many of their children studied there. Welles would not have been given any attention had he lacked talent or news value; but chums in the press were very happy to fan a spark into flames.

Meanwhile there was the tour, with its twelve cities a month; three moves a week, all three plays in each city. The organisational effort required to make this happen was enormous, with large and elaborate realistic settings to be transported and installed, lighting facilities varying from house to house and having to be adjusted to, the actors (over thirty of them) to be accommodated and looked after. The Cornell management was famous for its generous treatment of the company and crew; Welles, though not exactly handsomely remunerated – his salary was described by the company manager as 'small', so it really must have been – stayed at excellent hotels throughout the tour. Discomfort was minimised; Cornell and McClintic were good if demanding parents of their 'well-disciplined, strictly-ordered family'. This was not anything that Welles knew about, and sure enough, his role in the family rapidly became that of black sheep. Touring is traditionally an adventure playground for young actors and those who would remain young past their first youth; oats are sown, hell is raised, candles are burned at both ends. The twin excitements of a new town and an almost unbroken succession of first nights, every one a triumph of adrenalin over adversity, added to the curious sense of truancy involved in being away from home, create an emotional wildness that Orson Welles was the last person on earth to be able to resist. In a sense, he was living out his adolescence – for once, slightly later than most people. Though he had adventured way beyond his years, both mentally and geographically, he had done so as a loner. Until the *Romeo and Juliet* tour, he had been a stranger to the intoxicating company of his contemporaries. In fact, as John Hannah has sharply pointed out, he was living offstage the life of the Veronese youth that he and his companions in carousal (always excluding the tremendously proper Basil Rathbone, of course) were playing each night onstage.

Miss Cornell and Mr McClintic were not amused. 'He was

at all times during this long tour an arresting, stimulating and at moments exasperating member of the company,' said McClintic, and one can hear his teeth grind as he speaks. The theatre was not fun and games to Kit and Guthrie; it was life and death, not to mention bread and butter. They put their every penny and all their dreams into the work; they strove unceasingly, if not always blithely, to improve its quality and to enhance the status of the theatrical profession (a note in the programme for the tour says 'to aid the Actors' Fund of America, Miss Cornell makes a charge of 50c for her autographed photograph. The entire sum is given to the fund'). It was her public comportment as much as her professional prowess that earned her the title of First Lady (and, as Tynan wittily commented, Last Lady) of the American Theatre. She and McClintic had come about as far from roguery and vagabondage as it was possible for actors to come. Welles, by temperament and by conviction, as well as by sheer youth, embraced the contrary idea of the actor as a law unto himself, anarchic, antinomian, born for the exception, not the rule. Drinking and dining all day and all night, he was frequently in danger of failing to fulfil the actor's absolute minimum obligation: turning up on stage in time for one's entrance. Missing his last train for one touring date, he was obliged to charter a plane to make the show, which he did by the merest hair's breadth; Miss Cornell was furious. Miss Cornell was often furious. When he and a chum wearing false beards and heavy cloaks, posing as foreign dignitaries, paraded round a restaurant in San Francisco in which she and some friends were dining, she was so furious that she ordered him to go to bed immediately. This is high spirits mixed up with teenage rebellion. McClintic and Cornell were very satisfactory authority figures against whom to hurl himself; better than any of the various alternately pliant or anxious adults, the Daddas and the Skippers, by whom he had been brought up and whose method was to nag, and then to indulge. There was small satisfaction in rebelling against them.

He wrote an interesting letter to Katharine Cornell after one of these misdemeanours:

> About twice a year I wake up and find myself a sinner. Somebody slaps me in the face, and after the stars have cleared away and I've stopped blubbering, I am made aware of the discomforting realities. I see that my boots are roughshod and that I've been galloping in them over people's sensibilities. – I see that I have been assertive and brutal and irreverent, and that the sins of deliberate commission

> are as nothing to these. – This of course is good for me, coming as I am, noisy and faltering out of the age of insolence – just as the discipline of the tour is good for me.

This is the first of many, many such letters in his collected correspondence. 'Sorry, I behaved badly – but I didn't mean to' is the burden of them all; 'I'm just a kid, after all.' And all these letters have something else in common: they are apologies which aren't really apologetic at all. The transgression to which the above letter is a reply is not recorded, but there is one offence which is indicative of the gulf that separated their attitudes. He had had his hair permed for *The Barretts of Wimpole Street*, as he told a reporter, and he felt a fool in it. 'I couldn't bear it after a while, so I had my hair cut short – and nobody except Miss Cornell noticed.' You bet she did. His casual destruction of a detail of the production carefully thought about and agreed upon must have been anathema to her, a slap in the face. Her work, and McClintic's, depended entirely on an accumulation of detail. Lose any detail, and the whole show suffered; that was their credo. It could not have been further from Welles's, neither then nor ever. The big gesture, the overpowering effect, the glorious surge of adrenalin: these were the ingredients of Welles's bank-holiday approach to the theatre, gratifying for the performer, thrilling for the audience, however temporarily. For the McClintics it was a daily and painstaking re-creation of what had once been painfully established, an exhausting but necessary uphill struggle, all too liable to fall short of excellence. Perpetual vigilance was the price of this approach. (Small wonder, when Edith Evans joined them for the New York revival of *Romeo and Juliet*, she felt so in sympathy with their attitude that she volunteered a cut in her salary.) Welles's very existence was an offence to their values. 'I found myself wondering skeptically,' wrote Alexander Woollcott, 'if Mr Wilder and I had done well by Miss Cornell.'

The impression he made on the rest of the company was not much more favourable: Brenda Forbes, the Nurse in *Romeo and Juliet*, said later: 'He was gauche and tiresome. He was always talking about plans for his own theatre, or else wanting to "take over" any group he joined.' He was, of course, frustrated. He felt awkward in *Candida*, loathed being in *The Barretts of Wimpole Street*, and though clearly enjoying himself enormously in *Romeo and Juliet*, he was dead by the interval; there was another two hours to go, and McClintic absolutely refused to allow him to skip the curtain call. His prodigious energy was underused. He had no regard for the production, either, whose tastefulness seemed to him the opposite of the conception of the Elizabethan theatre that he and Skipper were evolving for *Everybody's Shakespeare*, on which he continued to work during the tour. The final straw came early on, in February of 1934: *Romeo and Juliet*, for all its respectable notices, was failing to draw the crowd. This was partly because 'on "Big Time," so to speak, Shakespeare had been a box-office graveyard since Barrymore's HAMLET and Jane Cowl's JULIET twelve years before,' as McClintic put it ('when we substituted *The Barretts*, the business leapt to capacity') but also because there was something, he couldn't quite put his finger on it, not right with the production. They would not, he decided, show it to New York, or certainly not this year; it would end at Cincinnati, where they donated the set, all $11,000-worth of it, to the local Little Theatre. The tour continued, miserably for Welles, with *Candida* and *The Barretts*.

'That cooks my Manhattan opening that had been held out to me,' wrote Orson to Skipper from Detroit. It also seems to have scuppered another venture because 'it alters all plans for Central City . . . [Katharine] Carrington has called off previous plans and she and [Robert Edmond] Jones will do (God dammit!) *Othello* with a whole milky way of Big Stars. That hurt for a while . . .' The tone of this letter is very different from that of the roustabout most often found standing sheepishly on Miss Cornell's carpet. There is serious career consideration here, steely calculation. The tone is properly, even alarmingly, grown-up. 'Now that I've begun to cool off, it seems to me that the free summer might be made to mean a great deal for us both. I have an idea.' He pursued this idea with extraordinary vigour, and in the end pulled it off with real flair. It was, he told Skipper, 'an old idea of yours jazzed up some, and improved and made practical, I think, by an addition'.

CHAPTER SEVEN

Woodstock/*Romeo and Juliet* Again

ROGER HILL's original notion which Welles was about to jazz up had been to hold a summer drama course at Todd. The school was often used for similar purposes; the drama course idea seemed to Hill an excellent way of achieving his perennial objectives: making money and keeping Welles busy. The addition which Welles proposed in his letter was a professional repertory company in residence at Todd: nothing short of an integrated school and company. It was to be 'not simply another school, or a Summer Repertory Theatre in another barn, doing last season's light comedy successes and sometimes trying out next season's but (by High Heaven!) A Chicago Drama Festival, devoted to the production of representative classics, that majority of the very greatest that nobody's done in living memory . . . and those new plays which are both too good and too exciting or courageous for anyone to dare to do anywhere else.' Among these might be, he tentatively suggests, their very own *Marching Song*, despite – or because of – the flop of a recent Broadway play on the same theme. He suggests a tie-in with Ravinia, his old stamping-ground; but no, better to centre it on Todd's nearby town of Woodstock with its quaint charms, its lovely old Opera House and adorable tree-shaded square.

Once the idea had seized him, suggestions pour out: combined dinner-and-show tickets, for example, with meals whipped up by 'some picturesque black chef'. As he plans the publicity campaign – 'both intensive and extensive' – he begins to write like a press release. 'Theatre-goers will be urged to make pilgrimages to the charming old festival town of Woodstock, to dine al fresco on the campus of Todd, world-famous preparatory school for young boys.' He instructs Roger Hill to get to work on the Woodstock Chamber of Commerce to secure their 'delighted co-operation'. There will be, in the square, 'a certain amount of festooning, some gala sort of illumination . . . and above all, in the bandstand, a rousing local band'. This goes on, he hopes, 'merrily', for a month, then, assuming the success of the professional productions (the student productions won't be for public consumption) the whole thing transfers to Chicago for a fortnight.

How will it all be paid for? Welles will chip in a thousand dollars which he thinks he can save from his salary, they'll charge the students for their tuition, of course, and 'a little more money should be quite easy to get hold of by organising a company or something'. The question is not how, much less if: when? is all he wants to know. – Poor Roger Hill! His solid and practical idea transformed into a dream of megalomaniac speculation. But he couldn't refuse. Welles was his favourite, almost as a Roman emperor or a Stuart monarch might have one. There was nothing Skipper could deny him. And indeed, few people could when he was in this vein. His passion for the idea, his inventiveness, his need all add up to an unstoppable impulse. There is something heartless about the way in which Woodstock, Skipper, the school, even the as-yet-unformed company, are all bent to his will – but then it's so self-evidently for their own good! And for the good of the theatre! And indeed, it was, on the whole. It all came to pass, pretty well as he laid it out to Roger Hill in that first letter, with an important subtraction: the original idea.

Meanwhile, he was planning, drawing more people into the net. His first approach was to Whitford Kane, under whose direction he mendaciously claimed in the Irish press to have acted. A distinguished Ulster actor who had played an important part in Chicago's theatrical life, directing and acting at the Goodman, he had been the first actor to play O'Casey's Captain Boyle in America. Welles and Roger Hill knew him from the Chicago Drama League; he and his protégé and lover Hiram 'Chubby' Sherman were on the panel which had singled out Welles for his performance in the dual roles of Cassius and Caesar, and had protested when he failed to win a prize. Welles wanted Kane to be the Director of Studies for the Summer School. In describing the set-up to him, Welles says that he's hoping to get Hilton Edwards and Micheál Mac Liammóir to come over as the mainstay of the professional company; he hopes to do *Doctor Faustus* and an Arthur Schnitzler play. As for funding, he writes, shamelessly: 'Roger is putting up most of the money. He figures the idea is a good publicity stunt for his school . . . he has a good many publicity connections. He has been in his time a tophole advertising man and I have every confidence he will be able to sell the idea to a large and desirable group of young people.' He offers the job to Kane for 6 per cent of every tuition fee (about $300) and a salary – 'here I blush a little' – of $25 per week. It must have felt strange to be thus (in Welles's own words) propositioned by someone who was as far as Kane was concerned only yesterday a schoolboy, but the tone of authority is compelling, the wooing direct and shameless. 'The smart magazines are going to begin flaunting advertisements of the Todd Summer School of the Drama pretty soon and we want to be able to put "Under the direction of Whitford Kane." Well, how about it?' For good measure he throws in an offer to Sherman – 'there's a job for Chub' – lest the thought of being separated from him might have stopped Kane from agreeing.

Kane's letter back is cautious: his Broadway play is doing well, but even if it closes, he fears he's going to have to go to Hollywood to make some cash. He might spare a week or two to do one production. He's due to teach a little at the University of Michigan, so this might fit in. He doubts whether Welles will be able to afford to bring over Hilton and Edwards, as he calls them. On the strength of this really rather uncertain commitment, Welles immediately had leaflets printed emblazoned with the promised phrase Under the direction of Whitford Kane; the paragraph detailing the members of the faculty concludes: 'This is too brief for the proper consideration of Whitford Kane. His epic career as player and producer on both sides of the Atlantic is an important chapter in the history of the stage and the outlines of his career need no rehearsal. Of all our blessings, perhaps the chiefest is the privilege of heading the constellation of the school faculty with that illustrious name.'

Welles had meanwhile got in touch with Mac Liammóir and Edwards who had been somewhat amazed to receive an urgent telegram: 'Would you both join me for summer season at campus in Woodstock, Illinois? 3 plays running for a fortnight each stop HAMLET for Micheál, TSAR PAUL for Hilton, something for me so far undecided stop I am trying my hand at production stop lovely school to live in and small Victorian theatre stop can pay your expenses of course and whatever is going stop now do say yes it will be a kind of a holiday and lots of fun stop love Orson.' Their plaintive request for particulars was met with a torrent of enthusiastic persuasion: 'With the idea of founding in America a Festival theatre in the European spirit and tradition, Woodstock, fifty miles from Chicago by easy motor drive, is to become the scene of a good deal of theatrical hysteria during the months of July and August . . . each production will have careful, painstaking and leisurely consideration, so that by the time the critics get at them they won't need either the apology of the summer repertory theatre, or the older apology of the first night.' Rehearsals were to start on 1 July; the first play to open 12 July. So it was not exactly the Moscow Art Theatre. In his mind – or in his publicity, which often amounted to the same thing – the season was a fulfilment of the wildest dreams of the most inspired visionaries the theatre has ever known. He then supplies Micheál and Hilton a list of the company which includes Kane, Sherman, Brenda Forbes (the Nurse from Cornell's *Romeo and Juliet*) and others, not one of whom actually appeared. His list of plays includes, in addition to *Hamlet* and *Tsar Paul*, *Doctor Faustus*, Schnitzler's *Living Hours*, *Bleak House*, *The Idiot*, *Brothers Karamazov* – and 'SOME NEW PLAYS.' The enterprising list reflects the reading of nineteen-year-old Welles: a typical late adolescent's discovery of the great, dark classics, all meaning a great deal of work for the Dubliners, already exhausted by a long season. Surprisingly, however, they said yes. Hilton had been against it, but Micheál was swayed by an encounter with a mystical American acquaintance: 'Hail to thee, blithe spirit!' she said. 'I wanted to tell you you're a Navajo Indian. Yes! Isn't that splendid. Now, here's what I've just had revealed. It's the loveliest thrill; you're going to America.' Bludgeoned by Orson's exuberance, and cornered by the clairvoyant, they seem to have set out with few artistic expectations, in a mood of resignation rather than anticipation.

Welles immediately cabled them for pictures: 'Our publicity man is particularly partial to Sex Appeal (note the capital letters) and costume. You and Micheál together, apart and under every sort of lighting and wig.' Hilton and Micheál too may have been somewhat astonished at receiving such urgent and authoritative instructions from the cumbersome and boyishly brash lad who had hurled himself so prodigiously across their tiny stage two years ago for a few months. If they had remembered the amount of publicity he had engendered during that brief stay, they might not have been so surprised. Here, from hotels across America (the Cornell tour still rumbling inexorably on) Welles masterminded The Selling of Woodstock, Summer of '34. His instructions to Skipper were clear and detailed. He started with the folder: 'this folder should have a good deal about me in it,' he decreed, magnanimously adding 'as well as the others and stuff about Woodstock and the Opera House and the Festival idea.'

The first formal announcement spoke of Roger Hill conducting the summer school of the theatre with Whitford Kane as its director. Then there was a list of plays, some of which he had mentioned to his various collaborators, others of which had obviously been thrown in on the spur of the moment. Reciting lists of plays is a favourite activity of artistic directors; it was a sport at which Welles excelled throughout his career. *Spring Awakening*, *The Constant Nymph* and Strindberg's *The Father* made their first, and last, appearances here, as did 'one of the Beaumont & Fletcher comedies'. The mailing list received this: 'Here is the most important dramatic news of the decade for the Chicago territory – the founding in the middle-west of an American Festival Theatre of genuine distinction. Probably no finer acting company will be assembled on the continent during the summer than the acting group headed by Orson Welles, Louise Prussing, Hilton Edwards and Micheál Mac Liammóir.' The billing is interesting. Under *Hamlet*, Mac Liammóir's 'first appearance on this continent in his phenomenally successful interpretation' is welcomed. 'Mr Welles is doubling for the first time in the history of the play, as the Ghost and his brother the King.' The third play is to be either Dmitri Merejkovsky's *Tsar Paul* or a first production of *The Master of the Revels*, Don Marquis's four-act comedy written that year and set in Tudor times.

Inside is Welles's account of himself: 'Chicagoans have read for years of the acclaim accorded their own Orson Welles both abroad and throughout the wide reaches of the continent. Now for the first time they will have the opportunity to see him at home. The return of the only foreign artist to be starred in the Irish Abbey; the only actor of recent times to be cast simultaneously in such divergent parts as Marchbanks and Mercutio, is a genuinely important event. Within recent months every important critic has lavished praise on this young actor's portrayal of leading roles opposite Katharine Cornell.' There are equal extravagances for Louise Prussing ('another Chicagoan who journeyed far from home to meet honor and rich reward. After 4 glamorous years in London where she was leading lady for such luminous names as Gerald du Maurier, Arthur Bourchier, Leslie Faber, she came back to New York'), for Mac Liammóir and for Edwards, and including the odd grammatical howler: 'Todd School, one of the most unique educational institutions in the world. Vacant in the summer months, Mr Roger Hill, its headmaster . . .' There was no danger of Roger Hill being vacant *this* summer.

The leaflet discloses the names of the distinguished COMMITTEE OF FRIENDS OF THE FESTIVAL: the CHICAGO PROMOTION includes Lorado Taft, Mr & Mrs Dudley Crafts Watson; more significantly, the PROFESSIONAL ADVISORY panel includes Charles Collins, Ashton Stevens, Lloyd Lewis – the three most influential critics in Chicago, with all of whom Welles was on first-name terms. He shrewdly made sure they were on the festival's side telling Hill to invite 'Ashton, Charlie or all the critics' to sign a circular letter advertising the season. But he had a much more ambitious proposal for harnessing their power: 'they to decide on the plays and launch the whole festival as their peculiar pet and beloved creature, it being first impressed on them that after the launching they are to sit back and be as cold-bloodedly critical as critics can be . . . I therefore propose you give a great dinner for them all in the Tavern, bringing with you photographs, your winning way and the proposition. Are they willing to be organised as a jury, will they give their very hearty approval to something that will really mean something to the Middle West? If a company of really fine actors are placed at their bidding it should be worth their bid. They are offered the entirely unique opportunity of genuinely representing the public by planning the plays they're to see and giving a fine project their personal blessing. If the performance and execution of the plays are not to their liking they are under no responsibility or obligation.' A likely story. There is something a little chilling about Welles's determination to make this thing work by whatever means. 'I expect you to shine brightly at that great dinner,' he says to Skipper, ominously.

Skipper, in fact, was beginning to feel very frightened by what he had unleashed. Welles's cavalier attitude to money bordered on the callous, considering it wasn't his own that was at risk. The school had been hit by the continuing depression and attendances were down; Skipper was committed to bringing Mac Liammóir and Edwards over from Dublin; the only way ends could possibly meet would be if the season was 100 per cent sold out. As a casual aside in his first letter to Whitford Kane, Welles had written: 'The only person that can possibly lose is Roger, and he is ready for that.' To Skipper himself he wrote: 'I don't blame you for feeling a little worried about money, particularly if the school isn't filling up as it ought to and no money is coming in by way of enrolments. Perhaps,' he helpfully adds, 'you'd better look for some outside money from somewhere.' Then: '*I've* spent over $300.' Skipper's anxiety turned to real panic when he consulted John Clayton, social director of the faltering Chicago magnate Samuel Insull, on how best to shift the seats. Clayton was a communications wizard whose income had suffered badly during the depression; his children were at Todd on scholarships. 'My God, Roger, do you realise what you're up against?' he said. 'There's a World Fair out there on the lake front with a million dollars' worth of ballyhoo and a dozen publicity men to feed stories to papers all summer.'

Chicago had made an almighty effort, in the midst of economic despair – and Chicago's depression was among the worst in the country – to put a brave face on things. 'It exhibits the spirit that enabled Chicago to overcome all obstacles,' said a local politician. 'It is typical of Chicago for it was achieved in the face of great obstacles. In Chicago there is no backward step.' It looked to Roger Hill as if he himself were about to take a giant one. But Clayton was resourceful: 'There's one way we might pull it off . . . the society gals. They all owe me favours.' He persuaded Skipper to spend yet another $1,000 on a party to launch the Festival; together they drew up a list of intellectually respectable patrons and made sure that they had invited le tout Chicago. Clayton addressed them: 'Roger and Hortense Hill will lose their shirts unless you give them a big send-off.' Roger Hill wrote in his memoirs: 'The party had cost a fortune by depression standards and seemed to us only a moderate success. Then came the Sunday papers!! We read them in utter disbelief. It was our first lesson in the phoneyness of "society" as portrayed in the press. Anyway we were gloriously launched; a flaming rocket in the sky. The glow lasted all summer. Marshall Field ran a full-page ad on what to wear at our final opening night.'

Hill was in no doubt whatever that the success of the season (and the aversion of financial catastrophe for him personally) was entirely due to Clayton's activities. At one remove, Welles's umbilical relationship with publicity continued apace. As soon as the Cornell tour came to an end, he was able to contribute personally; there was no holding him back. 'Orson Welles,' burbled the *Chicago Herald and Examiner*, 'says that the festival will be in spirit at least something of a combination of Bayreuth and a strawberry festival . . . a revival of great plays, rather than a try-out of new ones or a rehash of recent B'way successes, is planned.' So SOME NEW PLAYS had been dropped. 'Most everyone knows Orson Welles' history . . .' Indeed. Meanwhile, the society pages were in full thrill: 'Not to be taken in by anything that might not measure up to the social standard of the summer repertory companies at Newport, Southampton etc in the east, a great many of our sophisticates have been going a little slow . . . until they heard more about it. Now that they're quite convinced it's going to be one of the gayest things to do, to go to the Theatre Festival, there's no end of talk about routes to Woodstock. And on July 12th it'll be THE THING to drive out to the Op'ry House in the pretty sleepy little town.' When the local paper reproduced this item, its headline ran: TRILBY WILL BE FIRST PRODUCTION AT OPERA HOUSE/TODD SCHOOL THEATRE FESTIVAL OPENS HERE FOR THE SUMMER ON JULY 12/JUST THE THING/WRITER IN CHICAGO PAPER SAYS FASHIONABLES FROM NORTH SHORES WILL DRIVE OUT, which seems to contain an understandable note of apprehension. An invasion was under way.

First to arrive were the aspiring students. Skipper's original Big Idea, the notion of a real intensive summer school of drama, had become a mere appendage to the Drama Festival; financially speaking, it was its foundation. 'Anyone who had 500 big depression-time dollars also had a child with a talent we were anxious to develop,' wrote Roger Hill, despite the brochure's claim that 'enrollment is extremely limited and the remarkable attractiveness of this offer makes possible the strictest exclusiveness and the very highest standards of admission requirements.' In fact, they had reduced the fee to $250, when it seemed that the higher figure would be prohibitive, finally selecting twenty 'students' – Roger Hill's inverted commas – 'a mixed bag including a professor of Drama at Iowa and a bevy of stage-struck high-school kids'. Welles took the auditions; among the successful candidates was Virginia Nicolson, a friend of the Hills girls, a pretty, sassy young woman, whose recitation of a large section of *Henry IV, Part One*, convinced Welles that she was steeped in the Complete Works – something which enhanced the attraction he felt for her. They began, as the phrase had it, 'seeing each other' shortly afterwards: his first acknowledged girlfriend.

The next invasion consisted of what Roger Hill called the Dublingate boys. This invasion may have amazed Woodstock considerably more than that of the visiting students. Their departure from Ireland had been noted in the New York press; the *Chicago Tribune*, once they had arrived, hailed them under the heading DUBLIN FLAVOR TO DRAMA FESTIVAL. 'The work of Mac Liammóir and Edwards at the Gate Theatre has attracted international acclaim,' the writer averred, which was not exactly true yet, but would be. They arrived in New York on 25 June; Welles was there to greet the travellers at the quay – a rather different Welles from the one they had last seen two years before. 'Orson began to swell again. Now he had added to the swelling a new habit of towering . . . a looming tree, dark and elaborate as a monkey-puzzle, reared above your head, an important, imperturbable smile shot down at you from afar.' His manly persona was beginning to take, ousting the boyish one they had known. This was a Welles in charge – his charm a necessary mask for his authority, an integral part of his public self. The gauche show-off of the Dublin days, alternately exasperating and endearing, had modulated into this new figure: the master of the press conference, both intimate and magisterial, his omniscience qualified by a carefully controlled vulnerability. This mask stood him in good stead for many years, until it began to crack under strain in middle age, resulting in curiously ugly outbursts. By the end of his life, however, something like serenity had returned.

Here, now, in Woodstock in 1934, the 'important, imperturbable smile' was brilliantly effective, especially when accompanied by that irresistibly self-humorous dent of the eyebrows that spoke of fathomless frailty. Mac Liammóir and Edwards were disconcerted by the new Welles, and even more disconcerted to find themselves in the midst of what was in effect an American summer camp with a theatrical theme; disconcerted to find themselves the centre of so much ill-informed enthusiasm; disconcerted, most of all, to find their former junior company member displaying them to his public – the massed press of Woodstock and environs – with an unattractive mixture of exaggerated awe and inappropriate mockery. 'Micheál Mac Liammóir talked the least of the actors' – a sure sign of something being not quite right – 'seeing him sitting at his head of the table, so handsome in his dinner clothes, it was easy to believe that he was the last actor ever invited to speak at a certain girls' boarding school. "Devastating fellow," reported Mr Welles.' To add to the homely feel of this little fireside chat of Welles, his cousin, Mrs Dudley Crafts Watson, chipped in with 'You were play-acting when you were scarcely able to talk, Orson. And you're still making those funny faces.'

Mac Liammóir and Edwards must have felt that they had strayed into a suburban nightmare. They may not, either, have been best pleased to realise that the Woodstock Summer Festival was in reality a celebration of the life and work of Orson Welles. 'A great-grandson of Gideon Welles, the black-eyed young director is the star alumnus of Todd School . . . Orson Welles, the boy actor from Racine, Wisconsin.' A convincing report states that 'he relieved everyone at his end of the table of the responsibility of talking'. His frame of reference could hardly have been grander; Woodstock was already, in his mind, an event of international significance. 'As in the Salzburg drama festival and the musical festival in Beirut, the performers live in the town and become a part of it during the festival.' It was Orson, Orson everywhere, organising, giving interviews, a whirlwind of promotion: self-promotion, particularly, but the effervescence of it all is contagious. It's brilliant, breathtaking, delightful: one of the greatest one-man publicity machines ever created. Did he have any real vision, though, or did he simply say whatever would go over best?

'Young Mr Welles has brought forth another idea for this dramatic festival,' reported a slightly exhausted Ashton Stevens. 'He now thinks that now is the time to revive Romance in the form it took when Woodstock's op'ry house was young. He now believes that there are comparatively recent classics or near-classics that need only spirited reproduction to attest their worth.' Welles thereupon, without pausing for breath, dashed off a list of those plays: *Trilby*, *The Only Way*, *Under the Red Robe*, *In Mizzoura*, *The Girl of the Golden West*, *The Rose of the Rancho*, *The Third Degree*, *Arizona*, *The Great Divide*, *If I Were King*, *The Thief*, *The Copperhead*, *Raffles*, *Romance*, and *Davy Crockett*. So much for the scheme to do the great masterpieces of the past, not to mention new plays too new or courageous to be attempted by a commercial management. But of course, the season no more consisted of a systematic examination of Victorian and Edwardian American melodrama than it did of Beaumont and Fletcher or intractable modern plays. Welles instinctively knew what would appeal to the journalist to whom he was speaking. In the event, he was, inevitably and rightly, governed by practical considerations. Out of that list, produced like hankies from a conjuror's hat, he selected one play, *Trilby*, with which to start the season. It seems that it was originally included in the programme to lure Whitford Kane into appearing in a play as well as directing the students. When Kane finally decided that Hollywood and its pay cheques were more attractive than a summer in Woodstock, Welles took over, as both director and star.

There can have been little reluctance on his part. Melodrama was always close to his heart, with its opportunities for extravagant displays of acting not too closely linked to intimate emotions, its limitless opportunities for theatrical effects, and its stark opposition of good and evil. The role of Svengali, moreover, offered limitless opportunities for another of his enthusiasms: make-up. 'He will do Svengali in a long black beard and with his own thick black hair marcelled,' one of his many interviewers was thrilled to report. Mac Liammóir and Edwards were a little less thrilled at the choice of opening play, though it was not without sentimental resonance for them; they played the same parts – Little Billee and Taffy – that they were unwillingly about to play for Welles when they had first met as members of the Anew McMaster company. Rehearsals in that sweltering summer of 1934 were conducted al fresco and en déshabillé: swimming costumes all round (Micheál's of unexampled brevity), which must have made the experience even less like any form of professional theatre in which they had ever been involved before. Welles told Mrs Leaming that Micheál and Hilton spent the entire time in Woodstock hating him. If this was the case, it was presumably because of their changed status in relation to him. He further alleged to her that Hilton refused to help him with his debut production itself, maintaining that the very idea of Welles as a director was absurd. 'It was a real vendetta against me,' Welles claimed. Even Roger Hill, normally reliable, says 'They were really, I think, rather mean to Orson.' Meanness was not something of which they were incapable, but if things were so wretched between them, it is mysterious that until Mrs Leaming's biography, Welles had seized every opportunity to praise them and their work to the high heavens, to work with them again, to send them letters and even, during the war, food parcels. Whatever the truth of this, their attitude can hardly have figured largely in his consciousness. He was acting, directing, designing, scene-painting, prop-making, furniture-borrowing, costume-fitting, and having an affair with Virginia Nicolson – not to mention masterminding The Selling of Woodstock.

Woodstock was in two minds about Orson's view of it. 'Like a wax flower under a bell of glass, in the paisley and gingham County of McHenry is Woodstock, grand capital of Victorianism in the Mid-West. Towering over a Square full of Civil War monuments, a bandstand and a spring house is the edifice in the picture. This very rustic and rusticated thing is a municipal office building, a public library, a fire department and, what is more to our purpose, an honest-to-horsehair Opera House.' This celebration of quaintness (purportedly written by Thornton Wilder, who was in residence that summer, but bearing the unmistakable stylistic fingerprints of the young Welles) was far from what the people of Woodstock wanted to hear: they saw themselves as citizens of a small and rapidly expanding city, proud of their typewriter factory and Alemeite plant. Mac Liammóir saw the place in yet another light: 'To us it looked like any short screen comedy, new and glistening with white wooden houses and open lawns and barbecues and druggists and a procession of ice-men and plumbers who always seemed to be on the brink of calamitous comedy.' That is certainly the impression that the town makes today. Welles's version was another triumph of publicity over truth.

The excitement was building. DRAMA IN HINTERLAND, said Charles Collins in the *Tribune*, no doubt to the further displeasure of Woodstock. 'It represents, chiefly, the conjurations of a 20-year-old lad who appears to be a striking specimen of adolescent genius of the drama. His name is Orson Welles, and his story has often been told . . .' The opening night of the festival was stage-managed as carefully as anything that happened on the boards. India Moffett of the *Tribune* painted the scene for Chicago stay-at-homes: 'It is a gala occasion, perhaps the most exciting the little town of Woodstock ever has had and certainly the most thrilling it has had in many a day. The whole town was out to watch the guests assemble in front of the theatre and the square in front of the theatre was as gay and crowded as it is on Saturday night.'

That it was not a strictly dramatic occasion is made clear by Miss Moffett's last paragraph. 'It is delightful to sit and be thrilled by Orson Welles's Svengali and be reached by Louise Prussing's helplessness and loveliness as Trilby and every now and then to glance out through the windows and see the green leaves moving gently in the last glow of the twilight.' The auditorium, sweltering in the absence of air-conditioning, was a-flutter with the swish of fans thoughtfully provided by the management and printed with details of the remainder of the season. Small children ran around; dowagers ate ice creams. All this was grist to Welles's mill: 'altho he disclaims a "purpose" in his artistic venture, feeling that "the instant a 'purpose' is introduced to art, it becomes propagandistic and the true spirit of art disappears," young Mr Welles wants, he says, to help recapture the fun which should accompany our going to the theatre. "What I should like is for them to come joyously as schoolchildren going to a fair. Theatre is the only social art left which brings all sorts of people together." '

The marketing had triumphed. Woodstock remained suspicious. Lloyd Lewis told his readers in the *News*: 'the natives sat, early on the opening evening of the festival, watching the reputedly great folk from Chicago arriving in limousines to pay the incredible price of $2 a ticket. Among these sceptics it was being enviously whispered that the jailbreak of Woodstock convicts last Sunday was inspired by the prisoners' fear that some kind-hearted warden intended to make them see the show. But I am confident that the citizens will in time find the town's dramatic prominence as did the reputedly "great folk" from the big, wicked city.'

It was a brilliant operation, brilliantly mounted; and there was more. A note at the bottom of the programme said: 'A buffet supper with the cast will be served on the campus of the Todd School after the performance. Reservations are necessary.' Hortense Hill presided at these events ('she was a harried gal that summer') which would go on for hours, while the cast performed for specially invited celebrity guests, including Hedda Hopper and other figures from Chicago's beau monde. The society angle was doggedly maintained; Marshall Fields ran full-page advertisements featuring gowns for Woodstock opening nights. And though society had ensured the house full notices on which avoidance of bankruptcy depended, there was an equally important – for Welles's purposes, more important – section of the community that needed to be considered: the critics. Skipper arranged for the school bus, his 'land yacht', to pick the critics up in Chicago. 'A man of impeccable social standing was aboard to serve drinks en route,' wrote Hill, still evidently bewildered by the manipulatory ploys in which he found himself conniving. 'On the way back he provided them with typewriters for their fables.'

Their fables were, on the whole, (surprise surprise), favourable, though not without an element of persiflage. 'I could only quail and shiver as Mr Welles, striding the antique stage of the opry house added a horrendous Dracula touch to his performance. Svengali has made enormous hams out of some of the best veteran actors in stage repertory . . . so there is plenty of excuse for Mr Welles who is only 19,' said Lewis of the *News*. Mrs Henry Field of the *Herald and Examiner* held that 'he played the villain last night with great success . . . his acting has great bravado, and his voice booms,' an equivocal sort of a compliment. His make-up was much commented on: 'Welles' friends and fellow alumni of the Todd school, where his career started, would fail to recognise him. He has a striking gift for make-up and the tricks that go with the trade of character acting. Too much Franco-Yiddish accent and too hurried diction were minor flaws in his performance.' Claudia Cassidy, later Chicago's most powerful critic, confided to her diary: 'Orson's Svengali was a cadaver after Du Maurier, with an operatic flair out of the music master in *The Barber of Seville* and Dr Miracle in *Tales of Hoffmann*. He could trick you into thinking his chubby youth the shell of weakness.'

The role is so extravagant, so exotic and fantastical, that it is hard to imagine what a young actor could do with it but cover himself in make-up and run his personal gamut of effects. 'Wunderschon!' cries Svengali, on first hearing Trilby sing. 'It comes straight from the 'eart; it has its roots in the stomach – pardon, mademoiselle, will you permit that I look into your mouth? Ach

Himmel! Wunderbar! Mon dieu, the roof of your mouth is much like the dome of the Pantheon. The entrance to your throat is like the middle porch of Saint Sulpice when all the doors are open on All Saints' Day.' Only a Laughton might have taken the part seriously and discovered its broken heart, rendering the charismatic monster a part of the human race. Welles was not in the job of reclamation; adrenalin was the name of his game. The thing that he brought to the part was size: not just his height and bulk, but the physical impact (that booming voice). 'Even his fakes were on a Titanic scale. His Svengali lacked grace and humour, he was a lowering barbarian,' wrote Mac Liammóir, who had vivid memories of Beerbohm Tree in the role.

As for the production: 'Due obviously to this youth's fervour for the eccentric, the whole revival of this 45-year old melodrama is so bizarre as to become more mystery-farce than Victorian museum piece. Weird lights playing upon Svengali's staring eye, savour not so much of old-time atmosphere as of hokum murder movie technic. As played . . . the melodrama is all Svengali . . . the other characters were puppets moved around so that the occult impresario might have effective moments.' Mac Liammóir – who might not have been best pleased by this last detail – wrote that 'the production was disappointingly vague and indefinite, but that was because he could know nothing at that period of love, of intimacy, of Paris.' Mac Liammóir is surely right: the play hinges on tenderness and youthful romanticism to which the monstrous Svengali is a counterpoise. It seems likely that Welles was simply trying to pull out all the stops for his first show – as much to impress Hilton and Micheál as anyone. His curtain speech at the last performance gracefully drew attention to his guests' main contribution: *Hamlet*. 'Joseph Jefferson made a curtain speech here, 65 years ago. Since then the speeches have been of lesser and lesser importance. But I can say without any maidenly blushing, that our next play will be really good.'

It was. Abandoning the arch smiles appropriate both to melodrama and the efforts of the boy wonder of acting, the critics approached the masterpiece of masterpieces on bended knee. They were scarcely less respectful of Mac Liammóir. The *Tribune* gave advance notice that he was 'said to be one of the few first-rate Hamlets of this generation', adding that 'a conservative historian of Irish drama' believes it will be recognised as the greatest of our day. Hamletolatory, rife in England, was even more strongly established in America. The number of Shakespeare's plays actually performed was small: when Maurice Evans played Richard II in New York it was the first time the play had been given professionally since Edwin Booth's 1878 performance. The same few plays recurred over and over, *Hamlet* more than any; there was frantic competition to say who was now the best exponent of the leading role. John Barrymore in 1923 had set the benchmark, which was not to be seriously challenged until John Gielgud in 1936. Meanwhile, the 'young Irishman' (he was thirty-five) was keenly anticipated. As Hilton Edwards's production note indicated, the production was 'a replica of that directed by myself at the Gate Theatre in Dublin in 1932 and 1934. After 300 years of almost continuous performance,' he continued, 'it seems not only difficult but inadvisable to attempt anything new in the performance of *Hamlet*. Rather we have deemed it necessary to discard much that this play has accumulated through the ages . . . [we have chosen] a method that allows the scene to change and the action to proceed with the swiftness of speech and light . . . we have put our faith in color, movement, and above all in a faithful and vital interpretation of Shakespeare's words.'

These were the words of a member of the modern tendency of Shakespearean production. Micheál's designs were evocative but minimal, a far cry from Woodman Thompson's solid, monumental settings for the *Romeo and Juliet* in which Orson had just been appearing, but equally seeming to owe little to Craig's epic linearity, on view in Robert Edmond Jones's famous designs for Barrymore. It was a chamber approach, as befitted both the intimate dimensions of the Gate Theatre and Mac Liammóir's own susurrated performance, which the audience seemed not so much to hear as to overhear. 'I fancied at times . . . to have penetrated to strange moods, strange perfumes, strange shadows in the depths of his mind, as when the soul, shuddering before that welter of mortal sorrow, sought release in temporary expansion of the spirit, and wandered alone and undismayed in a freedom the body could never know. Like a disembodied being indeed one could imagine him pacing amid the wintry cloisters on that pale interminable afternoon in which the first part of the play is steeped before the dreadful night of action begins.' His performance was perhaps like his prose: dreamy, diffuse, richly and sombrely coloured.

It was received with respect, but not excitement. Immense stress was laid on his youthfulness, which reminds us that it wasn't until John Gielgud's sensational performances of the thirties that the tradition of elderly Hamlets was swept away. HE KNOWS A HAWK FROM A HANDSAW, said the caption over a strikingly posed photograph of Micheál, arms upraised, palms flat. 'A Hamlet of metropolitan stature and a distinguished addition to the meagre Shakespearean annals of the contemporary stage,' said Charles Collins. 'Mac Liammóir has youth and the romantic qualifications for the great role – a sensitive and poetic face which wears the mask of tragedy nobly . . . slowness of pace is Mac Liammóir's handicap.' And it is true: celerity was not Micheál's strongest suit; a measured relish was responsible for some of his finest effects, but the mercurial aspect of Hamlet, in which Gielgud was supreme, was not attempted by Mac Liammóir.

Welles's performance as Claudius was so much clearer and easier to respond to. 'Into this version of the world's most interesting drama, Orson Welles, the bright morning star of Woodstock drama, fits himself with zest. He views the fratricidal king as decadent and monstrous enough to make the situation between uncle and nephew as melodramatically simple as that between Oliver Twist and Fagin. With the courage of his 19 summers and the impact of his own vigorous imagination, Mr Welles plays the king much as Charles Laughton played Nero, lasciviously, swinishly. With no beard to hide a sensuously made-up face, and with bangs half-obscuring his sidelong eyes, this king is frankly degenerate. So much of an eye-catcher is this king that he at times hampers the play . . . [during the play within the play] he allows the audience to be conscious of nothing but the king, for during the major part of the scene he is busy making love to his queen. Sitting with Miss Louise Prussing, who obligingly bared one shoulder to make the most seductive Gertrude in my experience, Mr Welles exchanged caresses, ripe plums, California grapes and lawless looks with her, interjecting so much amorous business as to fairly hog the scene. It is brilliant technical character work, but it flattens the drama, which, as Hamlet remarks, is the thing.'

It sounds as if it might have led to an outbreak of justifiable thespicide from either of the distinguished professional players whose production Orson had thus invaded, but no: 'his King was outrageously exciting,' wrote Mac Liammóir. 'Had he kept control and given the performance he promised in rehearsal' – before he invented the make-up, perhaps? – 'it would have been the finest Claudius I have seen, but Orson in those days was a victim of stage intoxication: the presence of an audience caused him to lose his head; his horses panicked, and one was left with the impression of a man in the acute stages of delirium tremens.' Even the amiable, ice-cream licking, fan-waving, buffet-supper chomping Woodstock audience was in two minds about it . 'Some of the Woodstock patrons have been proclaiming that they didn't like him, which merely means that they didn't like the character. That was young Mr Welles' intention . . . the speech that contains the lines "there's such divinity doth hedge a king" was fat meat for the elder Thespians. They made a play to the gallery with it. Welles takes that speech and shrewdly molds it into his treatment of the king as a wheedling, cajoling scoundrel. Trembling inwardly, he pours out his oily rhetoric and bluffs Laertes into submission. This is a new idea, cleverly carried out; and it deserves a cheer.' Mrs Henry Field confessed her doubts to the readers of the *Herald Examiner*: 'Orson Welles departed from the orthodox king and we have not yet decided exactly what we think of his new departure.' Claudia Cassidy well describes the knife-edge on which the performance existed: 'he thumbed a flat nose at convention, achieving a make-up somewhere between an obscene old woman and the mask of lechery that visits Dr Faustus. Decadence is here in a thicket of curls hung from a bald pate, with voluptuous mouth confirming the evil glimpsed in heavy-lidded eyes. Almost a caricature, this face, but rescued from absurdity by the command of the voice that is the Welles passport to stardom.'

It is clear from this description that his performance was a melodramatic one, again: he created an ogre, a nightmare figure. It is hard to imagine what else, at his age, he could do – other than play safe and dull. He could hardly create a credible middle-aged, adulterous, guilt-haunted, manipulative politician-king. Instead he did something in broad strokes which made a strong impact, sustained, always sustained, by that mighty organ, his voice. The voice is the focus of so much comment on Welles's performances, early and late, that it is worth observing that any huge natural endowment is a double-edged sword for a performer. The temptation to rely on it to get you out of trouble is overwhelming, and can prevent proper development. The greatest artists – Olivier and Margot Fonteyn spring to mind – are those of modest natural endowments who have worked and worked to extend them, thus developing in themselves disciplines and hard-won strength which open up worlds of expression and imagination unknown to those who had it all for nothing. In his performance, Welles was going for broke – throwing in everything that he knew, exhausting his make-up box and rolling the verse on his tongue like vintage wine. These are the excesses of young actors with courage, appetite and ambition. What is odd is that the performance should have been given opposite actors – Louise Prussing, Hilton, Micheál – of great experience and consummate technique. It also odd for the performance to have been reviewed by critics of major newspapers.

That, however, is what Welles had engineered for himself. His desire to shortcut the usual processes, had the usual consequences: forcing growth is a risky business.

Welles repeated his Ghost from the original Dublin production. 'An unhorrific old ghost, gentle and grandfatherly, and almost a crooner,' said Lloyd Lewis. It is interesting to compare this comment with the notices he received in Ireland two years before: 'he made the speech of the Ghost almost human as well as awesome.' Perhaps his father's death was now more distant, and the sense of urgency that he had found in Dublin had gone from the performance. The production in general was liked; Hilton mildly praised for his Polonius, greatly admired for daring to include so much of the text, and for his directing and lighting. It was another opportunity for Welles to examine at close hand Edwards's immense skill in these departments. He learned his grammar of stagecraft directly from Hilton: what he had to say was different, as was his way of saying it, but the swiftness of transition, the economy of action and precision of focus that characterised Hilton's work were all to inform Welles's work as a director. Less influential, perhaps, were Hilton's manners. 'Would it be reasonable,' Hascy Tarbox reports him as saying to a student actor, 'do you think it might help, if you moved HERE?' Orson's way was to be a little more direct.

The third and final offering of the season, *Tsar Paul* by Dmitri Merejkovsky, was designed to show Hilton off as an actor. He had had a substantial success with the piece in Dublin; it had created a stir in London, too, when Laughton played not the title role but the part, Count Pahlen, Welles was to play in Woodstock. This was its first staging in America. 'This comment on the life of the mad Tsar Paul I,' said the production note, 'should prove apropos at a time when so much attention has been focused on the life of his mother, Catherine the Great of Russia.' Interestingly, it got the best notices of the three plays, and Welles, too, came out of his relatively unshowy role crowned with laurels. Both Mac Liammóir and Welles may have been a little miffed to read of their supporting performances in *Tsar Paul* that 'Hilton Edwards, Orson Welles and Micheál Mac Liammóir all three appear to better effect than in their earlier summer's work.' Edwards was praised as expert and intelligent, which may not be the ideal combination for conveying lunacy, but was clearly technically impressive. Mac Liammóir's Tsarevich was held to be properly touching, but the reviews concentrated on Welles's Pahlen. The make-up box had again been raided, of course: 'he achieves the effect of vigorous and cunning old age with a make-up that suggests a death's head,' said Charles Collins in the *Tribune*. Enough already with the make-up, Orson! one is tempted to cry, but it is evident that in this role, at any rate, he didn't lead with his false nose. 'The surprise of the performance is Orson Welles as Pahlen. Mr Welles hides his 19-year-old face behind a make-up that is a cross between the saracen Saladin and General Pershing, a swarthy, weather-tanned face of sixty, military, stern, zealously patriotic. Restrained within the monosyllabic nature of a soldier, Mr Welles is an exceedingly good actor. The overboyish exuberance which made him caricature Svengali and the Danish king, is witheld here by Pahlen's self-discipline. Mr Welles has, for the moment at least, quit trying to scare his audience to death, and is the artist, making Pahlen come alive by thinking and moving as Pahlen would think and move. Welles catches the chained fervour of Pahlen so perfectly.'

Mac Liammóir, too, admired his performance. 'His Count Pahlen kept all the essentials of the part and extended the limitations of its framework.' He added – an important comment – 'in the second of the two productions which he put in Hilton's hands, he was superb.' The diagnosis for this young actor with a case of uncontrollable overacting would be, first, a steady diet of Pahlens; second, put yourself in the hands of a skilled director. Welles was fatally drawn to roles in which he could experience the rush of adrenalin that comes from eating up the stage. A few of these from time to time in a career is a fine thing, but regular exposure to them can only lead to diminishing returns. Secondly, although directing and acting in the same show is a feat that has been triumphantly achieved, and not merely by barnstorming actor-managers – Louis Jouvet, Stanislavsky and Harley Granville Barker to name but three great artists have all done so with success – it is not recommended at the very start of one's career. One thing at a time. This was a lesson Welles would never learn, or, more to the point, a proposition he would never accept. But it seems clear that his best early performances were those given under the direction of someone else.

Too often his own central performances were the last element in the production to which he turned his attention. His Pahlen is a glimpse of the different sort of actor that he might have been. Claudia Cassidy had no doubts about him whatsoever. She told her journal: 'His variety and range are amazing and his youth has nothing to do with the matter except to hint at genius. The man is an actor and I think one of our major theatre pages will have fine things written in his name. Perhaps the Todd Festival's chief achievement will be to permit a lot of people to say of Orson Welles, "I saw him when." '

Getting the plays on had been the overwhelming priority; but with performances on only four nights a week (Thursday, Friday, Saturday and Sunday at 8.30) there was plenty of spare time, both for the students and for the faculty. The advertised curriculum never existed except in the brochure; had it done, it would have been rather marvellous: 'Todd presents its students with a two months' comprehensive apprenticeship on both sides of a fine working theatre . . . experiment, major production . . . every student will receive careful personal attention . . . acting, voice, scene and costume design, make-up, journalistic criticism . . . a long series of visiting lecturers . . .' There was little evidence, apart from a late-night performance of *The Drunkard* and the après-show cabarets, of any student productions; instead, taking a cue from the conveniently flexible first line of the blurb ('Favouring a less formal and a practical rather than a theoretical approach to dramatic education') they put the students to work as an adaptable army of theatrical helots, either as stage hands, set builders, or bit-part players, fit to start a scene, swell a progress. There could be worse educations.

For the rest, it would appear that any remaining time was filled, in time-honoured fashion, with sex. Whether the unthinkably politically incorrect occurred, and the faculty and the students canoodled together, or whether each kept to his own, is hard at this distance to determine. Welles himself certainly crossed the divide, in his relationship with Virginia Nicolson. As for the other professional actors: the rather grand Louise Prussing is unlikely to have consorted with the student body, the Horatio, Charles 'Blacky' O'Neal and Ophelia, Constance Heron, were married to each other (a union that was eventually to give Ryan O'Neal to the world). As for Micheál and Hilton, Welles painted a lurid picture of their campus activities for the benefit of Mrs Leaming, some of which may be true but which reads as an act of revenge, a posthumous character assassination. 'Oh it was wild because these fellows were at the absolute high pitch of their sexuality! They went through Woodstock like a withering flame. NOBODY was safe, you know. Down the main street of Woodstock went Micheál, with beaded eyelashes with the black running slightly down the side of his face because he could never get it right, and his toupee slipping, but still full of beauty. Hilton couldn't keep his hands off his genitals.' No doubt they were knocked sideways by the summery beauty of young American manhood – always breathtaking at first sight to Europeans, particularly at a time when European youth kept itself properly covered no matter what the temperature. It is certainly true that Mac Liammóir cut a bizarrely theatrical figure wherever he went. But – as Orson acknowledges elsewhere – his taste in men was essentially for 'vigorous, non-homosexual types', in Welles's own phrase. He was not a sexual omnivore, though he could never have too much of what he liked. It is highly unlikely that he would have found that among the students, and to claim as Mrs Leaming does that he chased Hascy Tarbox is laughable: Hascy as a grown man had a pixie-like quality, almost feminine, though resolutely heterosexual. As a boy nobody on earth would be a less likely object of desire for Mac Liammóir. As for Edwards, discretion was his middle name. To describe him, with his demeanour of a bank manager or a senior civil servant as a 'roaring pansy' is simply a piece of vulgar inaccuracy. The tendency of this entire passage is to render both men laughable and pathetic. Why did Welles feel the need to do this?

At the time – despite his claim to Mrs Leaming that they 'hated him' all that summer – he spent a great deal of his spare time with them, indulging Micheál's passion for the movies (*Whom the Gods Destroy*; *Martyred by his Love*; *Little Man, What Now* were the hits of the day). They were at the movies the afternoon John Dillinger was gunned down by the FBI, only a few blocks away from the cinema they were in. They visited the World's Fair, though whether they attended the reproduction of the Globe ('In Merrie England, world's fair grounds, tabloid Shakespearean and classic plays, daily at 2, 3, 4, 5, 6.30, 8.30 and 9.30') is unrecorded. There were meals, and parties, and long and passionate conversations with Thornton Wilder, who seems to have been in residence most of that summer. As far as Mac Liammóir was concerned, writing some ten years later, the whole period had become suffused in a golden glow of reminiscence: 'Our season at Woodstock ended for us all amid whoops of youthful triumph, and for me with two offers of film-tests for Hollywood . . . but the thought of not returning to Dublin was unbearable: I would have a few weeks more in this marvellous, unreal country, and then I would inevitably wake up, and when I woke, I would have to continue what I had begun. To leave a house half built in a land of ruins was impossible. So it was at last over, this early venture of Orson's, and on the last regretful night of *Tsar Paul* amid the lantern-lit trees in the courtyard of the school we drank his health and swore lasting friendship with them all.' They packed up and departed for home, pausing only to become involved in an extravagant Gaelic Pageant in Chicago, written by Mac Liammóir, staged by Hilton Edwards, which they ended up doing for nothing, the management having decamped. Then they returned to Dublin to continue what they had begun; they continued it till the day they died.

As a sort of end-of-term romp, Welles and assorted Woodstockites hired a camera and made a little film, a wild parody of avant-garde film styles to which they had recently been exposed at a local film society. *Hearts of Age*, they called it: Welles claimed in later life that it was his satire on Bunuel and Cocteau, but the real influence is *The Cabinet of Dr Caligari*. Jerky, grotesque, melodramatic and full of the imagery of death, it is, for all its technical limitations, a highly distinctive piece of work. Welles is of course the central character, made-up like something out of E.T.A. Hoffmann, high-domed and wild-eyed, with a steeple-top hat, cane and prancing gait. Virginia is a mournful old lady, little Egerton Paul appears in blackface as a servant, Keystone cops come hurtling through, as Welles is coming down the stairs three times in a row, leaping onto the roof, moodily playing the piano with bent fingers. Bells toll, candelabras gutter, Virginia dies. The final sequence shows a selection of tombstones, the last one of which, of course, is inscribed THE END. The images stick in the mind. Even with a cumbersome old 16 mill camera, Welles was able to frame interesting shots, and the action he unleashed for the camera to record is nightmarish and alarming. The angles of shooting are Dutch and distorted, from low down and high up, odd, glancing shots. The entire film (which would gain him immediate admission to a film school today) is full of life and imagination, highly theatrical, but keen to exploit the freedom and the tricks of the cinema; in these regards it bears an uncanny resemblance to Eisenstein's first film, *Even a Wise Man Stumbles*, shot for insertion into a stage production of Ostrovsky's play. The influence of *Caligari* is equally strong there; considering that that famous film is more or less lifted straight from current German expressionist theatre practice, the appeal to both stage-struck young men, Welles in Woodstock, Eisenstein in Moscow, is understandable. It was to surface again in both men's mature work.

The students (including Virginia, with whom Orson was now intensely involved) went back to their homes; the socialites and the critics departed. Woodstock breathed a sigh of relief, and Todd went back to being a school. For Welles (though presumably no offers of film-tests had been forthcoming) the season had been an enormous personal triumph, as actor – less so as director – as organiser, as front-man and not least as publicist. Skipper was reasonably content and not financially disadvantaged. They scarcely had time to think about it, because, in the midst of the season, their earlier joint venture, *Everybody's Shakespeare*, was rolling off the school press. It is typical of the density of Welles's life, now and always, that two of his most ambitious enterprises should have occurred simultaneously. And *Everybody's Shakespeare* is an extraordinary achievement by any standard.

Extracting illustrations from Welles had been like pulling teeth; Roger was still nagging him while *Romeo and Juliet* was lugging itself round the country: 'plug at that book. Work will be impossible later . . . finish first – and soon – the Malvolio lock-up scene. We must get forms for the introduction and first two plays to the press to send to prospective foreword writers. Then we must finish the book and circulate literature before the closing of the schools – a better time to introduce a text than the fall.' Skipper was as ever trying to make practical, financially feasible sense of the venture. Without him, it wouldn't have existed at all. But he was content to function as Welles's handmaiden. He beavered away in research libraries to provide the academic apparatus for the edition, but claimed no creative contribution whatever: 'it is a mystery to me and will be a blank to you how I could spend the immense amount of time on a mere detail to make a dummy from your work.' Orson was eighteen; Roger Hill was forty-one, his teacher and surrogate father. Yet there is no mistaking where the power in the relationship lies.

They had chosen to publish three plays: *Twelfth Night* and *Julius Caesar*, both of which, in truncated form, Welles had directed, and *The Merchant of Venice*, which he had not. Skipper's original notion was 'to make the Elizabethan popular in the classroom as well as the stage'. The whole venture must be seen in terms of an American theatre where Shakespeare was relatively rarely seen – where neither actors nor audiences had much experience of his work, and where there was consequent terror of it. 'I found,' wrote Margaret Webster as late as 1942, 'that actors were plainly frightened of Shakespeare, particularly of the verse, and were initially disinclined to regard his characters as real people. Audiences were frightened, too.' There must be, it was felt, some mystery about Shakespeare that was beyond them. It was this cultural and intellectual inferiority complex that Welles and Hill wanted to challenge. They believed that it started in the classroom, and that if you could alert school-kids to the excitement of Shakespeare's plays, you would have them hooked for life. The texts attempted to evoke live performance as much as possible, since there was a serious shortage of it on the contemporary stage.

Their first modest volume, green with a soberly calligraphed gold label saying

SHAKESPEARE
TWELFTH NIGHT
HILL – WELLES

is prefaced with a quotation from the distinguished scholar, Brander Matthews, averring the indispensability of actors to an understanding of the plays: 'No commentary on *Hamlet* . . . would be a more useful aid to a larger understanding of his character than a detailed record of the readings, the gestures, the business employed in the successive performances of the part by Burbage, by Betterton, by Garrick, by Kemble, by Macready, by Forrest, by Booth and by Irving. They have been compelled by their professional training to acquire an insight into this character – an insight to be obtained only in the theatre itself and hopelessly unattainable in the library even by the most scholarly.' This is partly what Welles and Hill set out to provide, by means of illustrations and stage directions. The non-academic bias is stressed again in Roger Hill's lively introduction:

ON STUDYING SHAKESPEARE'S PLAYS

> Don't!
> Read them. Enjoy them. Act them.
> . . . he wrote plays to amuse audiences in the theatre and he never bothered to have them printed. But luckily they were and the wide world has been joyfully reading them ever since. Internally or externally, however taken, the plays of Shakespeare are among the wide world's major joys; in the theatre, in the library, even in the schoolroom.
>
> After you have read and re-read his plays; after you have come to loving terms with them; after their music sings in your heart and their characters are part of your intimate acquaintanceship, then is time enough for the literary dissecting table.

This is pure Todd, pure Roger Hill, the inspired natural pedagogue, full of love and passion, loathing academic procedures. He takes the students' side. At the top of this page, Welles has drawn a cartoon of an angry book, frisking its devil's tail, in full pursuit of some academics. At the bottom of the page, a smiling book, with a halo, holds the actors' hands as they take their curtain calls. The next page brings a *Biography of William Shakespeare (No 1,000,999)*, a chatty sympathetic account, followed by a short essay on the quartos and folios, THREE WEIGHTY CHAPTERS REDUCED TO SUBHEADS: THE PLOTS, THE CHRONOLOGY, THE LITTLE MATTER OF GRAMMAR and finally SOME COMEDY RELIEF: BACON IS SHAKESPEARE. All of this in the unmistakably breezy and genial style of Skipper Hill.

Orson's contribution, too, is unmistakable. ON STAGING SHAKESPEARE AND ON SHAKESPEARE'STAGE: ORSON WELLES.

> Shakespeare said everything. Brain to belly; every mood and minute of a man's season. His language is starlight and fireflies and the sun and the moon. He wrote it with tears and blood and beer, and his words march like heartbeats. He speaks to everyone and we all claim him but it's wise to remember, if we would really appreciate him, that he doesn't properly belong to us but to another world that smelled assertively of columbine and gun powder and printer's ink and was vigorously dominated by Elizabeth.

This is the first fully fledged example of the characteristic Orsonian manner: sweeping, rhetorical, perfectly adapted to his own cadences, knowing, lofty, echoing with other men's phrases, infectiously exhilarating. It is, in fact, actorly – but like a fifty-year-old actor. Eloquent, certainly, but perhaps a little too instantly eloquent: verbal monosodium glutamate. It is interesting to note that this platform – the essentially Elizabethan nature of the plays' world – is diametrically opposed to the productions he made his name with. The important thing is its assertion of the stageworthiness and irrepressible vitality of the plays. (An example of how foolishly Welles was overpraised is Thornton Wilder's remark, reported by Skipper, that the above paragraph was 'the greatest thumbnail summation of Shakespeare's genius ever written'. If he believed even half of what was said about him, he was in serious trouble.) ON STAGING SHAKESPEARE continues:

> The curtain, which 'discovers' an act and 'descends' at the end of it, leaving everything in the middle of the stage and in the middle of a situation, came in with scenery and scene-shifting a number of years after Shakespeare when people had forgotten how to write plays. If you think the Elizabethans had a pretty primitive way of putting on a play I don't blame you. The show-business has been

> certain of it for two hundred years but lately it is beginning to wonder.

Good, provocative stuff, punchy but seductive, flattering the reader. The omnipresent first person singular is striking in its confidence, and its ease. The voice of the school magazine is still present, occasionally modulating into that of an after-dinner speaker. 'Femininity makes for other forms,' he writes, talking of the introduction of actresses to the English stage. 'The Drama in England, hitherto strictly a man's business, was now for a while scarcely a manly one. And to this very minute the ladies have maintained on us, as in all matters in which they're importantly interested, an emphatic edge.' Somewhat ironically, in view of his later innovations in the field both of light and settings, he inveighs against developments in scenic arts. 'Poetry has since then been neither necessary nor possible because when you can make the dawn over Elsinore with a lantern and a pot of paint there's no call for having a character stop in the middle of the action and say a line like, "But look the morn, in russet mantle clad, walks o'er the dew of yon high eastern hill," even supposing you could write a line like it. You can't see and hear beauty, fully, at the same time.' He redeems this dubious apophthegm with a witty drawing in the margin: 'How to make the morn in russet mantle clad without resorting to poetry.' 'I feel,' he continues, 'that one of the very wisest ways to play Shakespeare is the way he wrote it . . . I believe he wrote it that way not because he didn't know better but because he knew best. So I entreat you who are going to use this book for producing these plays to try at least one of them utterly without impediment. Fix up a platform in a class-room, a gymnasium, a dance-hall or a back-yard and give Shakespeare a chance. I think you'll find him more literal than anybody's paint brush. For those of you who are students, if I may be permitted another personal opinion, I do think that in studying these plays you ought to act them out, if only in the theatre of your own mind. Mr Hill, who is a scholar and a teacher and ought to know, agrees with me.'

Noting that there are a thousand different Shylocks – his sketch shows a line of Shylocks stretching back to the crack of doom, arms outstretched to heaven, heads bowed in despair – he hopes that the reader will 'jump in and fill the holes with ideas of your own. This is a book of ideas and whenever it inspires other ideas it will have value. Your idea is as worth trying as anyone's. Remember that every single way of playing Shakespeare – as long as the way is effective – is right.' Except, presumably, with realistic scenery, a curtain etc. The tone he finally settles on is of an enlightened high school senior addressing high school juniors. It's a very attractive and unthreatening approach. His final injunction (as 'the actor-half of this editorship') is to urge 'the study of these plays by acting them. This is because I think the theatre the pleasantest, speediest and safest way to that zealous and jealous love which most intelligent people, once exposed to him, must inevitably feel for Shakespeare.' There never was the slightest doubt of the jealousy or zeal of Welles's love for him.

The bulk of the book is, of course, taken up by the text, judiciously pruned by Roger Hill. The cuts are fairly standard; obscurity is eschewed, all but the most obvious quibbles are out, including some fairly ripe stuff. Welles writes: 'Elizabethan plays are not played in their entirety any more. This is partly because the language has changed and certain passages have become meaningless, and partly because modern theatre audiences are unaccustomed to sit through more than two hours of actual performance.' In later editions the following is added: 'although thousands of pilgrims to the Todd Theatre Festival last summer sat enthralled before Dublin's Micheál Mac Liammóir in the ole Opera House at Woodstock and looked at their watches in amazement after the final ovation to realise they had been under the spell for four hours'. Even pruned, their edition was fuller than most that contemporary audiences would have seen. Understanding and enjoyment of the plays is immeasurably enhanced by Welles's stage directions, even more by his illustrations, obviously the work of someone who has been personally and closely involved with the plays himself. Sometimes they are cartoons, sometimes straightforward line-drawings with vividly animated matchstick people, often very skilful realistic illustrations of a particular actor in a role – Hampden as Shylock, for example – or a set – Emil Orlick's and Ernst Stern's design for Reinhardt's production of *Merchant of Venice* (which Welles might just possibly have seen), or Belasco's 'costly failure', starring David Warfield.

What he provides is in effect a story-board narrating the action, a performing history, and a textual commentary, all rolled into one. It anticipates by some fifty years the highly successful cartoon Shakespeare books of the recent past. He creates delicious fantasias in the margins, and is especially good at conveying the dynamics of group stagings. Allowing himself great freedom in conveying a character, he doesn't limit himself to one version of it. Sir Toby Belch, for example, is fat in several different ways –

sometimes he seems massively fat, avoirdupois incarnate; another time, he's helium-filled. Welles uses different styles to convey this: pure cartoon, imitation print manner (a very successful impression of James Lewis in the role, for example), complex crayon sketch (a striking representation of the floored knight, caterwauling), brush strokes with no outline. The stage directions – supplemented by illustrations, suggestive, vivid, like designers' preliminary sketches – don't describe the concrete world referred to by the author in the play: they discuss possible stagings, and describe past ones.

An example from *Twelfth Night*: Act I, scene ii, shows a transfigured ship's mast: 'Characters and cut-outs of sky and ship silhouetted against drop – suggestions of clearing storm – lit from behind.' Alongside the sketch, Welles has written: 'entrance from below, exit to side'. It is as if he were taking the reader into his confidence, saying: 'this is the effect we want, and this is the way we go about it.' There is no pretence of three-dimensional realism, no suggestion that it is anything but a stage. He continues:

> The wreck of a ship may be in evidence. Some thunder and lightning, representing the last of a violent storm, often opens the scene. Viola is sometimes carried on in the sea captain's arms, just awakening from semi-consciousness. The seamen who enter with her, bedraggled and dripping and obviously exhausted, establish the mood of ship-wreck. But Viola is the first lady of the play and more often she is given a 'good entrance' which is perhaps just as well. That means that she enters first, walking to the Centre, where she stands making a picture in the attractive tatters of her dress and the sweep of her improvised sail-cloth cloak. Viola herself is attractive; often dark and always of the same physical type as her brother . . . she waits silently as two or more sailors, staggering under a great sea-chest and such gear as might have been salvaged from the wreck, come up with the captain. Sometimes she enters last, after a pause, and after the men, lowering their loads to rest, have turned in her direction.

The stage sense of the nineteen-year-old Welles is revealed here: quite old-fashioned, thoroughly aware of hierarchies of character ('Viola is the first lady of the play') and of effects ('she stands making a picture in the attractive tatters of her dress'). The production suggested in these words is a very straightforward traditional one: that is partly his purpose, to show how these plays are normally staged. His character descriptions, too, are detailed and conventional: 'Sir

Toby is the Countess Olivia's uncle, and, we may assume, a cousin of some sorts to Sir John Falstaff. He is a fun- and liquor-loving old gentleman, very fat and very hearty. He swaggers in valorously-hatted and gauntleted, carrying a whip. He is in high spirits, which is natural for Sir Toby, but he seems to be sober. Maria is Olivia's first maid, a little plump perhaps, or a little vixenish, but certainly a pretty little mischief, a bit wicked-looking and marvellously gay even in the household's mourning. Malvolio is the steward . . . a stork-like, wry, dry, complacent and sallow-faced personage; monumentally dignified, excruciatingly refined, and fanatically infatuated with himself.'

The one departure from normal practice is to be found at the beginning of the play: OLIVIA'S APARTMENT: 'This can be simply set on a shallow stage; perhaps a plain row of drapes.' Then, rather sensationally, Feste is heard off, singing 'Come away, come away death' from Act II, scene 4. The curtain rises on him, followed by Orsino and the court. That's quite a big directional decision, already. There's no explanation of why he's there, or where he goes. Perhaps Welles saw a production in which this happened and was impressed. This is almost the only instance of a reordering of the text in *Everybody's Shakespeare*. There are, however, interesting and revealing additional comments. In the introduction to *The Merchant of Venice*, for example, he writes, in explanation of his interpretation of Shylock's character: 'personally my guess is that Shakespeare wrote the play for just what it is usually made – a story of craftiness outwitted and true love triumphant . . . it was an age of intense self-righteousness among the Christian nations. The American Indian could be tortured and enslaved with the blessing of God if he was first "converted" . . . to the average patron of the Globe it was essentially noble for a Christian to act with diabolical cruelty to a Jew . . . just a Boy Scout doing his good turn daily. But Shylock must be MERCIFUL. And a million high school students must learn the speech and recite it without laughing.'

There is a flicker here of the beginnings of Welles's liberal political views. He has not yet politicised *Julius Caesar*, not specifically, anyway. 'It was inevitable that Shakespeare would dramatise the assassination of "the foremost man of the world . . ." ' He adds in some extracts from Plutarch and in doing so becomes uncharacteristically schoolmasterly: 'compare each incident in the two versions and gain a new appreciation of the Dramatist's divine power with words.' 'WHAT'S IN A NAME?' he asks. 'Commentators say the play is misnamed. *Brutus* should be its title . . . I disagree

. . . the personality of Caesar is the focal point of every line of the play.' The stage directions tell us that 'CAESAR is richly robed; a majestic figure, kingly and dignified. His handsome, almost feminine face is oldish and cut with wrinkles, but the eyes are clear and steady and the mouth is firm. CASSIUS a thin, keen-eyed, active man. MARCUS BRUTUS is a fine patrician type, his face sensitive and intellectual.' All of this is of interest in view of his subsequent, sensationally successful production of the play. Despite a change of period, his essential view doesn't seem to have altered.

The illustrations to *Caesar* are of exceptional quality. The looseness of the togas makes for sketches of great fluidity, especially in group scenes, which are often brilliantly composed. The setting for 'Friends, Romans and Countrymen' is an especially striking composition, with a huge shadow of Antony on the wall behind him – a configuration that seems to look forward, not to his famous stage *Caesar* but rather, if anything, to *Citizen Kane*. Surprisingly, Welles suggests ending the play with Antony's 'Mischief, thou art afoot, Take thou what course thou wilt', to avoid all those awkward battle scenes, an extraordinarily radical proposal which gives a glimpse of the editorial ruthlessness he was later to employ to such effect. Somewhat whimsically at the end of the edition proper, he quotes a favourite poem: Eugene Field's 'With Brutus in St Jo':

> Oh happy times when sounded in the public's rapturous ears
> The clink of pasteboard armour and the clash of wooden spears!
> O happy times for Jack and me and that one other supe
> That then and there did constitute the noblest Roman's troop!

– an instance of his fondness for old theatrical lore, in which he was steeped. His informed affection for it never left him, a nostalgia for what he'd never known, an entirely mythical golden age of actor-laddies: outrageous hamming, occasional flights of glorious inspiration, camaraderie, competition, upstaging and all-round outlandishness. They were actors then! is a theme which recurs throughout his life, the theatrical equivalent of the Merrie Englands with which he associated Grand Detour and other haunts of his youth.

Everybody's Shakespeare was well reviewed. Chicago's Krock and Brentano store filled its Wabash Avenue window with a special display, including originals of Welles's drawings. This brought publishers with offers; Hill and Welles chose Harpers 'for its prestige and also its willingness to let our school shop continue the manufacture. It was a foolish choice.' Fortunately Harpers sold their school business to McGraw-Hill, who kept selling the texts, in various guises, till the mid-seventies. 'No other school texts have ever approached that record of longevity,' wrote Hill with justifiable pride. The credit for their excellence belongs equally to him and to Welles, a lasting monument to their extraordinary relationship. It was Roger's inspiration, and its spirit is that of the Todd school's revolutionary attitude to learning. But Welles's sense of theatre, the wit and point of his drawings and the articulate enthusiasm of his approach make *Everybody's Shakespeare* one of the outstanding achievements of his entire output.

It was pioneering work, and must have turned on generations of schoolchildren to Shakespeare as he really is, making the plays seem fun without undermining them in any way. This, more than many more celebrated aspects of his output, arriving modestly in the world, stayed the course quietly and unassumingly. The 'tributes' quoted in an early reissue, though quite possibly fabricated by McGraw-Hill's publicity department, are not misleading: 'That our boys are actually buying copies for themselves is evidence of its appeal . . . I believe these texts will revolutionise the teaching of Shakespeare . . . I find my students reading them for fun and that is indeed an achievement.' If they have finally been superseded, in presentation and in theatrical reference, their spirit remains infectiously attractive.

It was not, however, going to pay the rent. Although he wasn't out of pocket as a result of the Woodstock Season, he had no capital of his own. Dadda was no doubt as reluctant as ever to hand over Welles's patrimony to him, and he now had a girlfriend to entertain. So when Guthrie McClintic approached him to rejoin the company for a New York run of *Romeo and Juliet*, he must have been privately grateful. Gratitude may quickly have turned to rage when he realised that he was not being asked to repeat his Mercutio, but to move sideways – downwards, in fact – to the role of Tybalt. McClintic later offered differing reasons for this demotion, and they are both quite credible: that he wanted Brian Aherne to play Robert Browning (as he had done some years before) in the planned revival of *The Barretts of Wimpole Street*, and Aherne's terms for doing so were to be allowed to play Mercutio; and that 'Orson's extreme and obvious youth in such an important part might make certain other members of the company appear older than they should', which is perfectly feasible (the representations may have come from Rathbone – who had just returned from Hollywood where he played Mr Murdstone in *David Copperfield*, as uncommon a double with Romeo as can be imagined). It must have been humiliating for Welles, a blow to his self-esteem, particularly after the summer's triumphs, but he had little choice. He needed the money, and he wanted a New York opening; so – despite his lack of enthusiasm for McClintic's approach to Shakespeare – he accepted the part.

In fact, in the interim, McClintic's approach had completely changed to something much closer to that of *Everybody's Shakespeare*. In his book *Me and Kit*, he describes in compelling detail and with great frankness the evolution that he and the production underwent. Disappointed with what he had done the first time round, but unable really to put his finger on what was wrong, he overheard one old lady say to another, on seeing the Capulets' tomb: 'I knew it! When the curtain went up on this show I knew it would have a bad end.' This crystallised for him what was wrong with his approach: he was presenting the play as a solemn drama whose outcome was never in any doubt, instead of telling the story the way Shakespeare had written it, in all its breathless variety. His first move, having already scrapped Woodman Thompson's lumbering design, was to commission Jo Mielziner, with whom he had just worked on *Yellow Jack*, to provide new ones: 'I told him of my newly conceived decor: light, gay; hot sun, hot passions; young, swift.' Mielziner, taking his inspiration from Giotto's paintings 'with their high colour and total lack of sophistication in their story-telling . . . beautifully organised within the master's great sense of design – design not for decoration but in order to give expression to the story he was imparting' produced a decor that was absolutely fluid and at the same time shockingly real – 'ending with a marvellous dark Capulet tomb . . . Paris actually needed a torch – one couldn't tell which tomb was Juliet's . . .' The new costumes, in which they rehearsed to learn how to move in this new world, were equally dazzling to behold and full of individual character – except, it appears, for Katharine Cornell's. 'She seemed a person apart – more a star than one of the girls.' Exactly the effect that most leading ladies of the period – or perhaps any period – would have actively sought. Dyspeptic with frustration, as was his way, McClintic approached one of the girls in the ensemble, told her to 'go into Kit's dressing room and divest herself of her charming frock and then told Kit to put it on. It was perfect.' Cornell's two rejected dresses had cost between them $1,000; the one she wore, $85.

The changes required an outlay of $43,000. But the new scenery and costumes, though the most expensive elements in McClintic's new approach, were by no means the most radical. He decided to play a virtually full text, something almost unheard of on either side of the Atlantic. His delight in the play he thus rediscovered is still touching, sixty years later: 'how fine the play was when left intact and played with speed, energy, humour and honesty! What a good play it turned out to be when it wasn't amputated . . . the events of the entire play take place in just 72 hours! Here was a drama of hot blood, high passion and exhilaration! Tragedy springing from recklessness – from youth's fervour – its refusal to turn back – to pause and reflect; had either one of the lovers stopped to think, there would have been no tragedy. This was no museum piece to be steeped in tradition. Its two-hours' traffic must be breathless with headlong action, not an actor's holiday – a play to be played as written.' Among the traditional cuts which he restored were 'Gallop apace you fiery footed steeds' (not played since Adelaide Neilson in the 1870s); all the vignettes of the preparation for Juliet's wedding to Paris; the scene in which the Nurse discovers Juliet's body; the one just before the finale in which Friar Laurence learns that his letter to Romeo was undelivered.

McClintic was not a particularly sophisticated man, nor a particularly clever one, but he knew when a thing was wrong. He had applied himself diligently and dutifully to the task of tackling the great cultural monument, studying the variora, and all the promptbooks of previous productions he could get hold of: 'all during the rehearsals of *Romeo* the menacing cloud of Shakespeare's commentators hung over me – the dictatorship of tradition had imposed on me a boundary which I felt it treason to cross.' It didn't work. Instead of abandoning the whole thing, and endlessly reviving the shows which did work, he determined to get it right. The revelation, when it came, was blindingly, banally, simple: trust the writer. He discovered, as so often, that cutting, whether it be literary, dramatic or cinematic, is often a counter-productive exercise; that a restored work of art, though longer by the clock, often, if the original is sound, feels shorter. And this principle of trusting the writer extended to the actors, as well. McClintic's work always began and ended with them.

'The actors must be made to forget that they are playing Shakespeare. That look that comes on the average actor's face – what happens to his body – when he starts reading Shakespeare is something that has to be seen to be believed.' A great deal of what he now believed about Shakespeare was identical to what Welles the editor had recently proclaimed, and what Welles the director would shortly practise: 'Overlapping scenes – pace – kill applause,' McClintic wrote, telegraphic with excitement. 'No stilted pauses to let an audience be depressed by the fact that they are witnessing a Shakespeare production; warmth, gaiety – JULIET IS THE SUN! – and there must be no waits between scenes. I was staging an exciting new play by a man named William Shakespeare.' Unfortunately their philosophical agreement was not matched by an improvement in their working relationship. All was not well in rehearsals: McClintic may have regretted ever offering the part to him. There was an explosion caused by Welles's belief that he was trying to teach him how to play Tybalt; McClintic was growingly convinced of his new approach, which clashed with Welles's deep-seated certainty that he, Welles, knew more about Shakespeare than anyone living. He matched McClintic temperament for temperament: a dangerous thing to do.

McClintic was not the only one to find him difficult. Brian Aherne, the new Mercutio, wrote: 'Orson seemed friendly and good-natured about losing Mercutio, but secretly, I am sure, the actor in him could never forgive me. In the famous duel scene I often had the impression that he slashed at me with unnecessary venom and twice he broke my property sword off at the hilt.' A stage manager who had the temerity to chastise Welles for being late (an ingrained personality defect of his) had a teacup thrown at him. Somehow or another, no doubt by means of extravagant acts of contrition, he managed to remain in the company, and in due course, set out with them on the brief pre-Broadway tour.

The New York Times despatched a reporter to put a foot in the water. The result was positive, despite the curious wording: 'Audience warm in its commendation of the most pretentious Shakespeare representation here since Belasco's *Merchant of Venice*'. It was equally successful in Cleveland, Pittsburgh, and Toronto, before finally opening triumphantly in New York. Every aspect of the production was praised in terms which McClintic must have relished: 'It was a performance at once resonant and vibrant; neither "modern" nor archaic; but infinitely human; a performance which glorified neither the star, the actors, nor the director, but all three together, and therefore the play.' That was his purpose, in a nutshell. 'Guthrie McClintic has somehow managed to persuade all the members of the cast that the word Shakespeare is one which need not freeze the lips.' Edith Evans, who had just played the Nurse successfully in London for the first time, was universally lauded, her performance simply described by Brooks Atkinson as 'a masterpiece'. (New York only saw her for a week before she returned to England, her husband having suddenly died.) Rathbone was reasonably well reviewed, as was Brian Aherne.

It was, above all, a great triumph for Katharine Cornell, one for which she had worked with unrelenting application. 'Miss Cornell has kept faith with her audiences by giving *Romeo and Juliet* a thoroughly gifted performance. She has kept faith with herself by acting Juliet with the humility of an artist who respects her material. Fortunately she is a great actress, and that is why her Juliet is a deeply moving realisation of fate.' Moving as is McClintic's refusal to be beaten by the challenge – not to take any short-cuts to success – Cornell's painstaking realisation of each moment for the role, her slow development of complete belief in herself as Juliet is a model of artistic dedication. Her biographer, Tad Mosel, reports her standing in the wings for ten minutes before her entrance clenching and unclenching her fists, her arms in the air, to give her hands 'the smooth, veinless look of a young girl's'. Invisible from anywhere further than the third row of the stalls, a glimpse of veins would have interfered with her belief in herself.

As for Welles: he didn't do badly at all. Atkinson in *The New York Times* noted his Tybalt, (along with Moroni Olsen's Capulet and others) as 'instances of minor parts played with something more than minor authority'. The *New York American* more enthusiastically described his Tybalt as 'a performance to watch and applaud: there was never a Tybalt so feline and subtly hateful'. There was no avoiding it, however, he was playing a supporting role, not merely in *Romeo and Juliet*, but in what was the greatest drama of McClintic's and Cornell's careers. It was an intersection of two radically different approaches to life and art. There was hardly a point of meeting. For the McClintics, this had been a crusade, for Welles simply a stepping-stone, a stage in his career. For the McClintics, this First Night was a mythic moment, for Welles a bit of a humiliation. He can hardly have shared McClintic's excitement, so vividly conveyed in *Me and Kit*, though he was physically part of it: 'Before our beautiful green sage curtains with the crest of the Capulets embroidered on one side and the Montagues on the other, Orson, resplendent, shielding his face with a gold Benda mask, came through and in his magnificent voice began the Prologue: "Two households both alike in dignity . . ." When he finished, his spot went out and there was the first scene exactly as I had wanted it to be.' One senses Welles's separateness from the rest of the company. McClintic even had to insist that he took the curtain call. There is something sad about this, because it was obviously a great event for the audience and for the actors. He had not really been part of it. It was, none the less, a turning point in his life, though he could scarcely know it, on that December night, in 1934, at the Martin Beck Theatre as he stood scowling in the line of actors while the audience roared its approval and the curtain went up and down, again and again.

Part Two

WHITE HOPE

CHAPTER EIGHT

Houseman/*Panic*

THE INSTRUMENT of Welles's destiny that night was a stocky, balding thirty-three-year-old Jewish-Alsatian Anglo-Rumanian, born Jacques Haussmann and renamed John Houseman, which perfectly suited his accent and bearing, those of an English gentleman. His view of what he had just seen on stage was rather different from that of his cheering fellow spectators: 'that glossy and successful evening,' as he referred to it in his memoirs, written some thirty years later, 'with Brian Aherne's Mercutio exuberantly slapping his thighs as he strutted through Jo Mielziner's bright Italianate scenery . . . Basil Rathbone's polite, middle-aged Romeo.' His nodding attention was galvanised when 'the furious Tybalt appeared suddenly in that sunlit Verona square: death, in scarlet and black, in the form of a monstrous boy – flat-footed and graceless, yet swift and agile; soft as a jelly one moment and uncoiled, the next, in a spring of such furious energy that, once released, it could be checked by no human intervention. What made this figure so obscene and terrible was the pale, shiny child's face under the unnatural growth of dark beard, from which there issued a voice of such clarity and power that it tore like a high wind through the genteel, modulated voices of the well-trained professionals around him. "Peace! I hate the word as I hate Hell!" cried the sick boy, as he shuffled along, driven by some irresistible interior violence to kill and soon, inevitably, himself to die.'

This electrified response to a performance that had passed largely unremarked by either critics or audience came from a man who was quite as complex and needful as Welles himself. His life, though without the dramatic contrast and colourful incident of the younger man's, had taken him through a startling variety of experiences and incarnations and was based, like Welles's, on an early emotional background both conflicting and confusing. Born in Bucharest, as a child Houseman spoke French, German, English, and Rumanian. His early life was erratic and peripatetic; his parents distant, glamorous figures who handed him over to a succession of governesses. At six he was in Istanbul, where his father was stationed. At seven he was sent to Clifton College in England; while there, his father died. He was perceived to be 'a fat French boy named fat Jack . . . a spoiled only child who arrived from Paris with a beautiful mama'. His fellow students set about knocking all delusions of self-respect out of him, along with any traces of foreignness, all of which delighted his Anglo-Welsh mother, who also urged him to convert to the Church of England. This confused and upset him: he felt that he was betraying his Jewish father, and himself. His mother saw no conflict, actively urging a policy of dual consciousness at every level: 'she believed that by combining the healthy austerity of my life in England with the glamour of her own cosmopolitan world, she was giving me the best of all possible lives. It didn't work out that way . . . divided between my two worlds, I belonged to neither.'

Having won a scholarship to Trinity College, Cambridge, he took a year off to work on a farm in Argentina; while there he discovered his mother's desperate financial straits, and, in a spirit of guilt-induced self-sacrifice, forwent the campus for the high pampas. There he made enough money to put her affairs on a more secure footing. Returning to England, he anglicised his name, but the basic duality of his existence continued, as he reviewed books for *The New Statesman* by night while selling grain in the exchanges by day. His firm sent him to America; after two years of listlessness in the job, he suddenly discovered 'some inherited, long-buried Alsatian trader's instinct' and overnight became a brilliant success as a businessman – whereupon he gave up the job and, by now married to an actress, devoted himself to his dream of being an artist. He co-wrote a play (which was performed), collaborated on a series of translations and adaptations (which were sold), had a brief period as one of a team of writers on a Hollywood movie (which was made) then, dissatisfied with his own efforts, drifted back to New York where he became part of that city's thriving salon society. At one gathering, he met Virgil Thomson who, taking a shine to him, invited him to direct the world première of his chef d'oeuvre, the Gertrude Stein opera *Four Saints in Three Acts.* This production of all the talents (Ashton choreography, Florine Stettheimer designs, Lee Miller photography) was a huge success, admirably co-ordinated by Houseman; after it, the toast of Hartford and later Broadway, he was unable to repeat his success, nor even find his niche. Feeling less confident with every fresh attempt, he emerged 'with an almost total lack of faith in my own creative ability'. No existing group seemed to have a place for him, with his inflated reputation and diminished sense of identity. What he needed was a sense of purpose and a channel for his own unrealised gifts. He had reached an absolute impasse – a writer lacking the courage to write, a director terrified of entering the rehearsal room ('my shame and fear were almost unbearable, my ineptitude so glaring that I could conceal it from nobody – least of all myself'). He needed a solution to his life.

For no reason he could articulate, he knew that this electrifying Tybalt contained the answer. A first-night guest of the Mielziners, he went backstage to congratulate them. 'I looked around in vain for a glimpse of the red and black costume. I left without seeing him; yet in the days that followed, he was seldom out of my mind. My agitation grew and I did nothing about it – in much the same way as a man nurtures his sense of excited anticipation over a woman the sight of whom has deeply disturbed him and of whom he feels quite certain that there will one day be something between them. He postpones the meeting until it can no longer be delayed.' The nakedness of the language, which is repeated throughout Houseman's account of his relationship with Welles, makes it quite clear that he knows the nature of his feelings for Orson: he experienced a submission of his whole being to another. In this there is certainly a sexual component, but its objective and conclusion is not sex. The emotion is the classic one described by Plato's Diotima: the longing for something in another which one feels oneself to lack, mingled aspiration and abnegation, hope predicated on hopelessness; the desire for completion by one whom one perceives already to be complete.

No two men on the face of the earth could have been less alike, and yet they might have been made for each other. They formed one of the classic working partnerships of the modern theatre; even its bust-up was classic. Both partnership and bust-up are brilliantly documented in a work which is itself a classic, though of necessity, since its author was one-half of the partnership, a somewhat biased one. Conceived on the Rousseau model, John Houseman's three-volume memoir is a confessional and critical self-portrait, frank – sometimes blush-makingly so – detailed (he drew on his extensive personal archives, diaries, letters and documents) and stylish. He observes with a novelist's eye, he dramatises with a playwright's skill, and analyses with a psychologist's precision, sparing neither himself nor anyone else. The first and best volume of the memoir, *Run-Through*, is dominated by Houseman's account of his relationship with Orson Welles, a relationship which ended in recrimination, and, on one memorably reported occasion, violence.

It is enthralling and convincing; but it is his version of events.

Welles, of course, left no autobiography. Thus Houseman, to Welles's immeasurable rage, won the war of words. His book must be quoted with caution, but its often unlovely portrait of Houseman himself lends it the stamp of truth. Welles used Barbara Leaming to pass on to posterity his side of the story. Chivalrously taking up cudgels on his behalf, she seems to think that she's found Houseman out; but he knew exactly what he was saying, and how he was saying it. Self-knowledge is above all else what differentiates him from Welles. On the other hand, spontaneity is not his chief quality. He observes, others and himself, with hawk-like eye; but it is almost impossible for him to surrender to impulse without pre-meditation. In Sartre's famous phrase about Baudelaire, he is a man without immediacy: like a child, as Sartre says, who plays in front of adults. Behind this lies fear. Of himself he says: 'to anyone as frightened of life as I was . . .' Orson Welles must have seemed absolutely unafraid of life, or any aspect of it. Talking to Peter Bogdanovich, who had gingerly opened up the subject, Welles said: 'Let's not talk about Houseman; I want to enjoy the afternoon, and he's one of the few subjects that depresses me so deeply, it really spoils my day to think of him.' That was in 1965. Twenty-five years later, Houseman, who generally expressed himself on the subject of Welles in terms of ironic bafflement, declared, literally on his deathbed, that 'meeting Welles was the most important event of my life'. From the first, he makes no attempt to conceal the violence of his attraction. 'Orson Welles's initial impact – if one was sensitive or allergic to it – was overwhelming and unforgettable.'

He continues the description of their first meeting in *Run-Through*: 'The period of my waiting, during which the conditions of my meeting with Orson Welles were ineluctably shaping themselves, was about three weeks, but the event which finally brought us together had been germinating for months.' Happily for Houseman, he had a project at hand with which to engineer an encounter and then, perhaps, a collaboration. *Panic*, Archibald MacLeish's apocalyptic verse play about the death of a capitalist, had been doing the rounds, but nobody would touch it. Conceived as an unequivocally left-wing response to criticisms of his contentious first play, *Frescoes for Mr Rockefeller's City*, it was a bold attempt to create a demotic – and specifically American – poetic language, an attempt which condemned its author to find favour with neither realists nor classicists. This neither-one-thing-nor-the-otherness immediately commended it to Houseman, feeling himself to be in exactly the same boat. Ignoring the small detail that he had never met MacLeish, or had any communication with him on the subject, he announced in the press that he would be producing the play; this audacity led to a meeting, and finally to his securing, for a very modest sum, the rights to the play. Joined by his roguish partner, the publicist Nathan Zatkin, he determined to set up a new producing organisation: the Phoenix Theatre. With $500 in the kitty they opened offices over a burlesque house on 42nd Street and proceeded to generate excitement over their new property, inhibited in their efforts only by their inability to cast the huge leading role of McGafferty, the prototypical man of Capital. Their offer of the part to Paul Muni had been greeted with silence. It was then that Houseman saw *Romeo and Juliet*, and various strands of his life began to come together.

The idea that the nineteen-year old Welles, who had struck Houseman as a 'monstrous boy . . . with his pale, shiny child's face', would be able convincingly to play the sixty-year-old, all-powerful McGafferty in Archibald MacLeish's *Panic* was, to put it mildly, a long shot, but Houseman became convinced of its rightness. Thus it was that the 'feared and eagerly awaited moment . . . with its predictable consequences' arrived. Houseman, relishing every deliciously romantic moment, paid a 'secret visit' to Welles during a performance of *Romeo and Juliet*. He found Tybalt (by now dead) half in and half out of costume and character, beardless and naked to the waist, but still covered in greasepaint, still falsely nosed. Houseman noted the discarded costume, 'stiff with sweat', the extraordinarily beautiful hands 'with enormous white palms and incredibly long, tapering fingers that seemed to have a life of their own', the play 'about the Devil' that Welles was working on. They agreed to meet at a bar across the road. When Welles arrived, Houseman was amazed by his boyish appearance; it was his 'shuffling, flat-footed gait' that identified him as Cornell's Tybalt. His physical features indelibly impressed themselves on Houseman; he writes of them, not necessarily with admiration, but with startling precision. He was obviously hypnotised. He describes 'his pale pudding face with the violent black eyes, the button nose with the wen to one side of it and the deep runnel meeting the well-shaped mouth over the astonishingly small teeth'; he is struck again by those mobile, expressive hands; above all, he is stirred – as so many had been before, and so many, many would be again – by the beauty of the voice 'that made people turn at the neighbouring tables'. As Houseman acutely observes, it was not the volume of the voice that made them turn, but its 'surprising vibration'. The power of the speaking voice is widely underestimated. Welles's was an instrument like that of Steiner's Hitler, a siren voice to which Houseman succumbed completely.

During the three delicious weeks of waiting, Houseman had 'eagerly absorbed' the already considerable legend surrounding Welles: from it he would have expected to meet a dazzlingly precocious, multi-talented budding actor-manager of genius, a teenaged combination of Leonardo da Vinci and John Barrymore. Instinctively recognising the successor to Dadda Bernstein and Skipper Hill, Welles presented himself quite differently to Houseman. Coming on as the Boy Wonder of the Western World would not have created the emotional commitment that he required of those who provided him with the supportive context without which he could not function. He needed to create intimacy. So, applying his usual strategy, he offered himself with a mixture of deference and demand, to which Houseman immediately responded. He was both flattered and appealed to, wooed and honoured, swept off his feet and placed on a pedestal. His first impression of Welles's power was thus tempered by a desire to protect and nurture the rare spirit who had revealed himself so completely and sweetly. Houseman gave him a copy of *Panic*, and arranged a meeting with MacLeish. 'After he had gone, I was left not so much with the impression of his force and brilliance as with a sense of extreme youth and charm and of a courtesy that came very close to tenderness.' 'At first,' Welles plaintively told Barbara Leaming, 'he fell in love with me.' He says nothing about his own emotions, as ever. He had always to present himself as the passive and innocent recipient of love or hate, just as it was important for him to believe that his career had simply happened to him, a series of happy accidents. But in these crucial relationships, he was a very active partner, and their trajectories are often identical to those of intense love affairs.

Interestingly, this particular relationship was opposed from the beginning by the woman who, the day after the opening night of *Romeo and Juliet*, became (at a glamorous candle-lit ceremony in Llewellyn Park, New Jersey, attended among others by Katharine Cornell, Guthrie McClintic and Thornton Wilder), the first Mrs Orson Welles – Virginia Nicolson, friend of Skipper's daughters, apprentice actress at Woodstock, and Orson's first girlfriend. In fact, in order to satisfy the stuffy landlord of the boarding-house in which they were living together, they had already been married in a secret ceremony some six weeks before. The match was opposed by Virginia's wealthy father Leo (who, faced with the inevitable, tried to persuade Orson to join the Stock Exchange as a broker; a somewhat surreal notion) and actively encouraged by Hortense and Roger Hill, anxious that he should find a legitimate channel for his burgeoning sexuality. (They acted as witnesses at the first wedding; as a consolation prize, Maurice Bernstein was best man at the official ceremony.) All this cloak-and-dagger business, the real wedding and the false wedding, was greatly to the taste of the bride and groom, to whom getting married was essentially something of a lark. There was no suggestion of high romance. In his screenplay for *The Cradle Will Rock*, written in the 1980s, Welles has given himself the following speech: 'you know what she said to the Minister? Practically on the steps of that cheesy little altar? "Reverend –" she said, "because of our youth we're being forced to do this in New Jersey, and it's all rather irregular, isn't it? What I want to know is – will there be any trouble if we want to get divorced?" ' And elsewhere in the same screenplay he says: 'the only reason she married me was to get away from home . . . I was the first train out of town.' As usual, he says nothing about his own motives or feelings, but there is no reason to assume they were anything other than those of a lively and highly sexed young man. Fun was the basis of their early relationship. Even at this stage, they were scarcely equals professionally; in fact it might be said that the considerable newspaper coverage received by their marriage (the official one, of course) was the first and last time she ever stole the headlines from Orson: VIRGINIA NICOLSON BECOMES A BRIDE *The New York Times*, 24 December. They had no money, which might have been a problem: 'I promised her the Great White Way, and glamour – and, you know – the whole megillah. And instead, when she got here we were splitting up Horn and Hardat's 25c daily blue plate special, half and half, and filling up with water and free bread.' They had found a tiny little duplex on 14th Street which was considerably more modest than any home either of them had lived in before. But they were together and in New York when New York really *was* New York and everything seemed possible.

Unusually, when Welles went with Houseman to meet MacLeish, Virginia came along too. 'A delicious child with blond, reddish hair and ivory skin', Houseman found her to be. MacLeish was more concerned with Welles, also, to all outward appearances, a child. How could he possibly do justice to that Lear of Wall Street, McGafferty? The poet – still, according to Herbert Kline, 'slim and graceful of movement, as he had been in his days as an Ivy League football star halfback, holding himself ramrod straight from his military service as a World War One hero' – expressed impatience. Then Welles read. 'Hearing that voice for the first time in its full and astonishing range, MacLeish stared incredulously. It was an instrument of pathos and terror, of infinite delicacy and brutally devastating power.' In a daze of mutual excitement, Houseman beaming with nearly parental pride in his discovery – his protégé – it was agreed that Welles would play the role. He was very happy to give two weeks' notice to the Cornell company. In the event, it was unnecessary. Despite those glittering notices, *Romeo and Juliet* had not sold out, and McClintic terminated the run after nine weeks, replacing it, again, with *The Barretts of Wimpole Street*, which, with Brian Aherne as an unlikely but popular Robert Browning, played to capacity houses. Thus ended Orson's involvement with establishment Shakespeare. With *Panic* he came in contact for the first time with the radical political theatre of his day.

MacLeish's conversion to the left was something of a sensation in its time. He had had a reasonable claim to being the foremost American poet from his early twenties, when, under the influence of T.S. Eliot, he had articulated 'the voice of the hopeless individual in a chaotic postwar world', in, among other works, his verse drama, *Nobodaddy*. Returning from Europe, he opened himself to American influence and heritage, finally, with the depression, becoming actively politicised. This development was the more surprising in view of his parallel career as an editor of *Fortune* magazine, and author of *The Young Men of Wall Street*, an admiring account of the Stock Exchange. Neither a Marxist nor even, formally, a socialist, by the time of *Panic*, he had become convinced of 'the symbolic death of capitalism'. His shift was hailed in an article for *New Theatre Magazine*: HOW ARCHIBALD MACLEISH JOINED THE NEW THEATRE MOVEMENT, which then went on to publish scenes from *Panic*. Neither the play nor MacLeish were greeted with unalloyed enthusiasm by the serious left-wing theatre. His statement, being largely apocalyptic, lacked both diagnosis and prognosis, and his artistic method was ambitious to the point of elitism. But for Houseman, unable, as he felt, to function within the patterns of the existent commercial, social or art-theatre set-ups, 'it had become necessary for me to create the image of a man who would undertake what no one else would venture. *Panic* was the perfect vehicle for such a demonstration.' Houseman was wryly able to identify with the crash of a capitalist; but he doesn't try to conceal the fact that the whole venture had more to do with his personal ambition than any political impulse.

He assembled an immensely strong production team: Jo Mielziner and Martha Graham (both fresh from *Romeo and Juliet*), Abe Feder to light, Virgil Thomson to write music and control the choral speaking; the cast consisted of twenty-five principals and a chorus of twenty-three. The Imperial Theatre was hired. Understandably, Houseman withdrew from directing the play, since to mount a piece of this scale on a budget of $3,000 – two-thirds of which had come from the poet himself – demanded full-time cajoling, wheedling, charming, calling-in of favours and pledgings of eternal gratitude. Before handing over the actual staging to Martha Graham and James Light – a recruit from the Provincetown Players – Houseman, Mielziner, and Abe Feder ('pale-faced, garrulous, exhaustingly eager and ambitious') devised a setting of monumental simplicity, a sharply raked stage with a great trench just beyond the regular footlights which, filled with powerful lights, and supplemented with others from above, created a wall of light, an effect which later became almost synonymous with Welles's productions at Project 891 and the Mercury Theatre. Rehearsals, scattered across the city, proceeded with great intensity, particularly the choral sections under the galvanising command of Martha Graham. The individual scenes – the ones which concerned Welles as McGafferty – were under the control of James Light, who proved to be somewhat frail under pressure. Welles, onstage almost continuously, became the solid foundation of the whole enterprise: contradicting his 'hair-raising' reputation, his conduct was 'from first to last, perfect'. Patient with James Light, considerate with his fellow actors, 'to his own part . . . he brought us, as a free gift, the strength, the keen intelligence, the arrogance and the prodigious energy of his nineteen and a half years.'

The production and Welles both received full marks for trying; Welles was held by the *Times* to be 'excellent' while the *New York American* remarked that 'for such a young actor as Welles to play McGafferty as ruthlessly, as interestingly as he did was a genuine feat and puts him up as one of the most promising artists of our day.' One imagines his performance may have been rather like the middle-aged Kane; certainly some of his text could be Kane's:

The Revolution!
That kind!
The sick souls

Herding like hogs in the hang of the dark to be rid of the
Man's burden of living their forefathers won for them! –
Rid of the liberty! – rid of the hard choice! –
The free man's choosing of the free man's journey!

Welles excelled from the earliest age at playing monolithic patriarchal figures, halfway turned to stone – Mount Rushmore on legs. His noble lower register, trombones doubled by cellos, would make sense of the vigorous, ugly verse if anyone could (as later, in MacLeish's acclaimed radio play *The Fall of the City* he was to do with great success). He evidently took McGafferty on his journey from ascendancy to collapse and ultimately silence and suicide with complete conviction. For him, *Panic* was a triumph; as it was for most of the performers. The play itself was more controversial: greeted with respectful admiration by *The New York Times* ('the work of our protean poet'), it was excoriated by the *Evening Journal*: as 'a pretentious bore'. More kindly, Edith Isaacs believed that 'the words of the play were packed too tight for the use of a theatre not used to the gaunt fullness of poetry'. The fledgling Phoenix Theatre deserved congratulations, Brooks Atkinson told the readers of *The New York Times*, for 'reviving an impulse that our middle-aged stage has long been lacking': the theatre of public debate.

In truth, the opposite seems to be the case. *Panic*, as written, reads like the work of a middle-aged aesthete trying to rejuvenate himself by grafting the monkey-gland of political commitment onto his art; as performed, in contrast to the work of other radical groups of the time, its experiment seemed aesthetically motivated, its expressive devices not functional but decorative – imitatively decorative at that. With its vatic Blind man, its jagged stagecraft, and its powerfully obscure statements it is almost parodistically Toller-like. It is a little hard to determine, for example, what *exactly* is meant by the triumphantly shouted final line ('Man's fate is a drum!'). The truth, as Houseman swiftly realised, was that *Panic* was already vieux jeu both in its artistic gestures and in its preoccupations: America wanted to forget what *Variety* memorably described in its review as the 'busto-crusto days of 1933'; there were new crises, other battles.

Of public debate there was none – in the play, that is; in the auditorium there was a great deal, on the exciting third and final performance. The first performance, a preview, was a subscribers-only show, consisting, according to Herb Kline, of MacLeish's rich friends, who were respectful. The second performance was the Press Night, with the usual awkward mix of the curious, the committed, and the critical. The third performance, however, sold for $1,000 to the New Theatre, was, as Houseman wrote, 'swept by one of those groundswells of excitement that were characteristic of the period . . . the theatre became far more than entertainment or even artistic release'. The excitement was real; but it was also stage-managed by the American Communist Party. It was intended as a Marxist equivalent of a Gospel meeting; the climax would be the public conversion of 'our protean poet', MacLeish himself. The post-show 'discussion' was carefully marshalled towards this end. 'To accomplish this, the heads of the party's cultural apparatus assembled their strongest and subtlest forces on the stage of the Imperial Theatre for a ceremony which seemed to fall somewhere between an exorcism and a conversion, a kidnapping and an auto-da-fé.' Houseman's description, a masterpiece of comic writing, details the elephantine engagement of the party with aesthetics, precisely catching the ponderous theatricality of its procedures and the self-righteous pomposity of its tone, embodied in the Chestertonian person of Party Secretary, V.J. Jerome. 'His face was pale, his eyes sorrowful, his voice gentle and cultivated with a faint trace of a Whitechapel accent. The hiss of the bourgeoisie is the applause of the proletariat! – Was it not Lenin who said "The bourgeoisie does not fall. The Proletariat drops it!"?' He was a familiar part of the theatrical landscape of these immediately pre-war years.

MacLeish, unsurprisingly, failed to succumb to Jerome's Victorian rhetoric. Declaring himself, in carefully chosen words, for decent living conditions and for social justice, he eluded the Party's net. Welles, reluctantly in attendance, was much amused by the proceedings, even indulging in a little good-natured barracking. The issues were not ones with which he had so far concerned himself. In time, he would come to be an eloquent spokesman for the liberal cause, especially in its anti-racist, anti-fascist manifestation; but his relationship with the Communist Party was always an uneasy one. Soon, however, both he and Houseman would be obliged to reach some sort of entente with the Forces of Progress: the times had forced the theatre out of its ivory tower and into direct engagement with events, and the Party was experiencing one of those rare periods when the national temper brought it into the mainstream of political consciousness. As a vocal and highly organised division of that loose-knit army, the Broad Left, it claimed and received serious attention. For the time being, however, *Panic* quietly died down, with MacLeish a free agent, the Phoenix Theatre, $35,000 in debt, immediately consigned to the flames again, and Welles and Houseman at loose ends.

Welles had at the very least gained critical kudos, if nothing else. To go from a respected Tybalt to an acclaimed McGafferty was excellent progress for a nineteen-year-old. There was something else, too: an apparently insignificant side-effect of *Panic* which soon developed into a major thread of Welles's life and work. Houseman – or more likely Nathan Zatkin, the tireless publicist half of the partnership – had arranged for an extract from the play to be recorded for a radio arts programme. Thus Welles had his first important introduction to a medium which he was soon to make peculiarly his own, and which might have been invented for him; from a practical point of view, it introduced him to the possibility of making a substantial income.

He had already been hired by Paul Stewart to appear on *School of the Air of the Americas*, where he had met the twenty-nine-year-old Joseph Cotten. With them it was laugh at first sight; coming upon a line, in a programme about colonial administration, which referred to 'barrels and barrels of pith', it had been almost impossible for them to get through the show without collapsing. A different Welles was glimpsed by Dwight Weist, one of the most versatile and hence most in-demand of radio actors of the period. He was there when Welles came to record the extract from *Panic*. 'I saw this very strange guy dressed in a strange ill-fitting suit and he walked very funny. He never moved his shoulders, arms hanging limply by his side and sort of getting off in a corner by himself. And he was a strange-looking man. He looked like a Eurasian with a head that seemed to be too big for his shoulders, a mouth almost too small for his face which was sort of round, rosy cheeks. And I thought "What is this guy going to sound like when he gets in front of the microphone?" Then all of a sudden he gets in front of the microphone and you get the famous Orson Welles voice, and I thought, "Oh, OK." ' The 'surprising vibration' that Houseman had noted during their first meeting was superbly apt for the microphone, allowing its owner to create an uncanny intimacy with the listener. Compared to this facility, his other gifts – his command of phrasing, his latent power – were unimportant. From the beginning, he was able to use his voice in a way that flattered and stimulated. The smile in his voice is positively audible, as is the arched eyebrow. Welles has also been praised for his versatility, but compared to a Dwight Weist, this was low down on his list of accomplishments.

His command of accents was general, and though he could vary the pitch of his voice, its timbre gave him away every time. 'He impressed them with his voice really – he was a reasonably good actor – I don't think anyone has said he was a great actor – but he was a personality,' thought Weist. 'From the very beginning when he was starting out there was never any question in Orson's mind that not only was he a great personality but he was going to get there and he never had any doubts about himself and his ability.' The story goes that while *Panic* was being recorded at an adjacent studio, *Time* magazine's highly successful programme *The March of Time* which specialised in dramatic reconstructions of the day's big news stories was doing a feature on the quintuplets just born to a Mr and Mrs Dionne. Needing somebody to impersonate the babies, they roped Welles in, and he did all five.

He began very soon to be part of what the *Saturday Evening Post* described as 'a select group of anonymous radio artists who shuttle about from station to station taking part in many programmes every day'. The radio boom was at its height, commercially speaking, still holding its own against the fledgling talking-picture industry (a mere eight years in existence in 1935). Welles was very happy to dash from studio to studio, making a great deal of money. Within six months he was earning an average of $1,000 a week, a sensational sum for almost anyone in depression America; for a twenty-year-old tyro actor, it was prodigious. The motive for working quite so hard was more than simply financial. Dwight Weist was on one occasion part of a pool of actors who were, along with Welles, vying for roles. 'The director was auditioning people for *Shadow Play* – I don't think anyone had heard Noël Coward – and Orson said "I AM Noël Coward!" and he stepped up and in his very loud voice proceeded to do something which didn't sound anything like Noël Coward at all but which was Orson Welles doing his idea of an English accent and he got the part. Why? His showmanship. He had this thing in him which got the part . . . it was very important to him . . . we didn't get any more money if we played one part or a dozen parts. For the abdication edition of *The March of Time* Orson was not chosen to play Edward – it bugged him – not that he didn't get the part but that he wasn't the best.' Not to be the best was always intolerable to Welles; the never entirely silent voice of Beatrice Welles, sounding deep in his cranium, forbade it.

Welles's radio career built up steadily over the months following the recording of the *Panic* extract. Meanwhile, he and Houseman consolidated their relationship. For Houseman, it was a heady time, and there is no reason to doubt that the same was true, in different degree, for Welles. Encountering what appears to be a kindred spirit is always exhilarating, perhaps especially so when sexual consummation is not a part of it. In this instance, Houseman's unqualified admiration for Welles, and the openness of his enthusiasm, powerfully endeared him to Welles, who throve on approval, and was lost without it. He ensured that he made himself entirely available to the older man. When Houseman first visited him at his duplex ('a curious one-room residence') he was still in his bath, 'his huge, dead-white body appeared swollen to gigantic proportions. When he got up, I discovered his bulk owed nothing to refraction.' The bath, with a plank on top, doubled as the marriage bed. Mrs Leaming characteristically assumes from Houseman's description of Welles's physique, above, that he was phallically fixated on him; but what, one wonders, does she think Welles was up to by meeting Houseman in his bath? Trying to impress him? To dominate? Or perhaps simply to wrongfoot him – to discombobulate and disorientate him.

If he thought that Houseman was possibly bisexual, and sensing how intensely the older man was drawn to him, he may have wanted to put it to the test. Or perhaps, more innocently, he was simply proud of his physique and wanted to show it off. The only clues we have to any of this come from Welles's divulgences to Barbara Leaming. In her openly hostile account of Houseman and his relationship with Welles, she seems to blame Houseman for being attracted to him. Her implication is that Houseman was erotically and psychically obsessed with him, and that the seeds of his later destructiveness (her word and Welles's) was present from the start. On the other hand, she admits that Welles saw how useful Houseman could be, and shamelessly seduced him. The crucial difference is that she seems to think that perfectly reasonable: Houseman deserved it, in some unnamed way (for being a repressed homosexual? for being a manager and not an artist?). Or perhaps she simply thinks – as, obviously, does Welles – that it was the duty of everyone he came across to advance his career and expect nothing in return. Houseman's crime is that he wanted to be, not an ancillary, but a partner.

Perhaps wisely, they rarely met in each other's houses, instead spending hours 'drinking coffee in odd places'. This period has the same place in their relationship as the legendary meeting of Nemirovich-Danchenko and Stanislavsky at the Slansky Bazaar. Houseman and Welles became so excited by their shared dreams that they repaired to a suite at the top of Sardi's (the key furnished by

Nathan Zatkin) to continue their fevered exchanges in the office of the Mendelssohn Society of America. Under the bronze and surely disapproving gaze of that very proper composer, they spent hours 'talking, dreaming, laughing and vaguely developing schemes for making bricks without straws. Each was an improvisation, an inspiration or an escape: our response to an emotional impulse rather than the considered execution of a plan . . . we were seized with a sudden, compulsive urge to produce a play together.' The play they chose was *'Tis Pity She's a Whore* (with *Doctor Faustus* as a possible alternative). 'Orson's dominant drive, at this moment, was a desire to expose the anaemic elegance of Guthrie McClintic's *Romeo and Juliet* through an Elizabethan production of such energy and violence as New York had never seen.' He produced a design which he demonstrated 'on and in the bath' at the Riverside Drive duplex. It showed a complex Italian street scene, 'a theatrical crossroads where the physical and emotional crises of the tragedy converged'.

Houseman's admiration for Welles was coming dangerously close to hero-worship; Houseman was thirty-four, his hero nineteen. 'I watched him, with growing wonder, take as mannered and decadent a work as John Ford's tragedy, bend it to his will and recreate it, on the stage of his imagination, in the vivid dramatic light of his own imagination.' It is again Welles's extraordinary fearlessness that thrills Houseman – in this case in the face of The Classics. During these fevered and passionate weeks, he was exposed in its purest form to the strange combination in Welles of seductively submissive, rather female charm with other, very masculine attributes: mastery, bending to his will, recreating, re-shaping. 'To me those weeks together were a revelation . . . in my working relationship with this astonishing boy whose theatrical experience was so much greater than mine, it was I who was the pupil, he the teacher . . . what amazed and awed me in Orson was his astounding and, apparently, innate dramatic instinct. Listening to him, day after day, with rising fascination, I had the sense of hearing a man initiated, at birth, into the most secret rites of a mystery – the theatre – of which he felt himself, at all times, the rightful and undisputed master.' Welles had a similar certainty in the area of verse-speaking: unemployed young actors would drop round on their way to or from auditions; in addition to tea and biscuits 'we set them – for their benefit and ours – to reading Elizabethan verse'. Welles, veteran of a grand total of two professional productions of classical plays, offered spontaneous tutorials on the delivery of iambic pentameters. How different from poor Katharine Cornell's dread of verse, and Guthrie McClintic's dogged determination to master its rules. Welles regarded it as his natural inheritance. An unfriendly observer at the time spotted him in a restaurant: 'He would, by voice and presence, make everybody ask "Who is this man?" Saying "Shakespeare and I." '

He did not intend to appear in *'Tis Pity She's a Whore*. He saw it as above all a vehicle for Chubby Sherman 'of whose talent he was so fanatically convinced that he would not rest till he had proved it to the world'. Chubby was to play Poggio; casting and verse exercises were held in the basement on 14th Street which he shared with Whitford Kane. Miriam Batista and Alexander Scourby were to play the incestuous siblings. The role of 'a venal courtier' was to be played by one Francis Carpenter, a friend of both Orson and Virginia, thought of by those who remember him as camp beyond the dreams of Quentin Crisp, someone who, at a time of rigid sexual typing, flaunted his outrageousness without inhibition. His audition, Houseman observes, was of 'prodigious obscenity'. Both the Welleses were deeply fond of him; in Welles's case there may have been more than simple friendly affection. William Alland, as close as anyone to Welles shortly after the period under discussion, avers that without question Welles and Carpenter had had a sexual relationship, and were publicly prone to furious rows and extravagant reconciliations. Whatever the truth of this, Carpenter remained part of Welles's loose-knit theatrical family almost to the end, finally appearing in *King Lear* at the City Centre in 1956. During the Second World War he astonished his circle by performing acts of conspicuous gallantry on the battlefield, for which he was much decorated – a notion which amused him no end.

He it was that had secured finance for the projected *'Tis Pity*. An eccentric old lady of his acquaintance was prepared to underwrite the show. On the strength of this, Houseman and Welles hired the Bijou Theatre, a run-down six-hundred seater. When the $10,000 from Carpenter's protectress finally came through, it did so with a stipulation that it must be spent on sand-blasting the façade of the theatre – and nothing else. They laughed; it seemed the funniest thing in the world to them. The production and the Bijou Theatre were abandoned in gales of good humour. 'We parted friends – without promises or commitments, and with no particular reason to believe we would ever be associated again.' As if in direct contradiction of that last thought, he writes: '*'Tis Pity* served its function . . . through it we learned each other's language and laid the foundation and set the form and tone for our future collaboration.'

Orson and Virginia meanwhile went off to join Carpenter at his 'palatial Long Island Estate', which turned out to be a crumbling, run-down and foodless mansion, from which they retreated to New York, checking in at the Algonquin. The radio income had presumably not started in earnest, since Skipper Hill was importuned for money to settle the bill. Why they should think that they could afford an expensive hotel when they patently couldn't is mysterious; can they really have thought that Roger Hill with his schoolmaster's income was able to bail them out? The clue to this may be in Welles's comment in *The Cradle Will Rock* screenplay: Virginia expected a better standard of living than he was yet able to provide. Or possibly it was just a mad, unthinking impulse, something they promised themselves as they shivered and starved in Carpenter's ghastly country retreat, and to hell with the cost! Except that in the real world, someone has to pick up the tab: a concept with which Welles had great difficulty all his life.

Not only was there no money, early that summer: there was no work. The Broadway season ended, as usual, on June 15; the new one wouldn't commence till September. Welles's inherent restlessness overcame him, and, as so often in the past, he looked to Skipper to satisfy it. He sent him *Bright Lucifer*, but Skipper wisely declined it. Welles next suggested a version of *Tom Sawyer*, himself in the title role; Skipper was equally reluctant. A national tour of the Todd Troupers under Whitford Kane? Impossible. Instead, he went back to Todd and staged an impromptu production of *Uncle Tom's Cabin*, in which he didn't appear. He continued to return to Todd for reaffirmation until well beyond the time that he was an international celebrity; Roger Hill maintained that when the school was finally wound up in the 1960s, Welles, having lost his sanctuary, went into a deep depression, and thereafter never mentioned the place again. It was, obviously, home. Skipper, like any parent with a fractious child on his hands, desperately sought affordable diversions. His solution was to hire a cabin for Orson and Virginia at nearby Lake Geneva, just over the state border in Wisconsin. There Welles tinkered at *Bright Lucifer*, at an Irish travel book, and at a slightly premature volume entitled *Now I Am Twenty-one*. Finally, they motored back to New York in a car belonging to Skipper, driven by Virginia (Welles was not allowed to drive: 'I'm one of those people,' he said in an interview, 'who are so terrified in a car that they put their foot down on the accelerator and never take it off').

New York offered more lucrative radio work; his career in that medium – still anonymously – began to take off. But for him, as he freely confessed to an interviewer a little later, though 'he admires radio as a medium, in his own case he calls it hack work, about which he is very casual'. A dangerous thing to say; an even more dangerous one to think. But it was the precise truth: the theatre, as always, was his overriding obsession. The question for him, as for Houseman, was where would he fit in? The New York theatre of 1935 was bewilderingly diverse and in a state of tumultuous ferment; but there seemed to be no obvious opening for his unusual gifts.

The depression had shaken the theatre as roughly as it had every other aspect of American life, with similar results: a huge reduction in consumption and manufacture, and widespread politicisation. The twenties had been the theatre's boom years: 'more shows were produced in one city in a ten-year span than ever before or since in the history of the world', wrote Sam Leiter in the *Encyclopaedia of the New York Stage*. 'Two dozen Broadway theatres were created in the blink of an eye.' In writing (especially new American writing) there had been almost an embarras de richesses. The Theatre Guild, having done proud by Eugene O'Neill, continued to promote new dramatists; the Little Theatres pursued experiment, especially in the visual sphere. The Community Theatres throve: the Yiddish Art Theatre, the Lafayette Players in Harlem. Nor was there any feeling of parochialism, or chauvinism. Germany, Russia and Ireland sent their companies, pioneers of intense realism and extreme stylisation, the epic theatre and the domestic. Harold Clurman and his fellow students watched wide-eyed. 'We saw Reinhardt's productions of *A Midsummer Night's Dream*, *Danton's Death* and *The Miracle*. We not only studied these productions, we debated them with passion. We sought out exotic examples of theatre craft. We visited the Chinese theatre in the Bowery, and led our friends down to Grand St to see the Sicilian Giovanni Grasi, who exemplified a violent emotional acting that positively stunned us . . . all this was done with eagerness and deliberation . . . it never occurred to us to say: "This is our world and it bodes no good." '

The Great Crash in 1929 changed all that. Art for Art's Sake ceased to be a watchword; it was necessary to engage with life, and experiment must be harnessed to that engagement. For the commercial theatre it was a question of engaging with financial reality. The legendary managers (Belasco, Ziegfeld, Cohan, and Winthrop Ames) were dying out. Despite the arrival of new names like George Abbott, Billy Rose, and indeed Kit Cornell, in the 1930–31 season there were 190 productions, a drop of fifty compared with the previous season. Only three new theatres opened during the thirties, compared to thirty in the previous three decades. Paradoxically, the number of new productions picked up enormously as the decade wore on, due to the prodigious number of closures. There were the usual consequences, familiar in both London and New York today: with a couple of exceptions each season, shows became smaller. Sets were less and less spectacular; there was less use of stars; casts got smaller; there was a miraculous increase in the number of one-set plays offered for production; there were cheap revivals of recent successes. The Shuberts, hitherto the most prosperous of theatre owners, went into receivership; having negotiated a loan, they used it to import London hits and revived – 'the usual last resort', in Howard Taubmann's words – *The Student Prince* and *Blossom Time*. The attempt to revive the touring circuit failed; producers started to take advantage of summer stock for try-outs (the very thing against which Welles had pitted himself at Woodstock). These theatres became something like Off- and Off-off Broadway laboratories of later years.

Even gangsters couldn't be sure to make money out of the Broadway theatre; the well-known bootlegger who payrolled *Strike Me Pink* (which was neither agitprop nor gay, but a frothy revue starring Jimmy Durante) lost his entire investment. Hollywood became for a while a major investor in shows, buying rights for future use, but after a dispute with the Writers' Union, this involvement slacked off. In fact, Hollywood's principal impact on Broadway was the negative one of creating a drain of both writers and actors to Los Angeles. Sound in movies had created an urgent demand for actors with trained voices; financially the theatre could not compete. Apart from stars absolute who could, with royalties, make up to $3,000 a week, according to the indispensable Sam Leiter, the theatre was poorly paid: at the other end of the scale, the minimum for actors with less than two years' experience (that would include Welles) was $25; for more experienced actors, the minimum was $40. An average actor of repute could expect from $75–$125; while a minor star might manage between 200 and 500 dollars. All these actors were, of course, the lucky ones; in the profession at large there was despair. The Stage Relief Fund was founded to raise money to pay out-of-work actors' bills; at the Actors' Dinner Club you could get a meal for $1, if you could afford it. If not it was free. One winter 150,000 meals were served, according to Howard Taubmann, and 120,000 of them were free.

Welles had good reason to thank his lucky stars for his involvement in radio; he could eat, copiously and well; he was comfortable.

But his hunger for work in the theatre gnawed angrily at him. Broadway seemed unpromising. He had not enjoyed his stint with the McClintics; *Panic* had been a sojourn with the sort of Art Theatre to which he was not drawn. He hadn't, despite a reasonable amount of exposure, made a name for himself yet, was not even 'a minor star'. Besides, he was erupting with energy and ideas; a long run in a supporting role on Broadway was not really what he had in mind, even if it were possible. He was young, but not a juvenile; he was powerful and imposing, but not a leading man. It is hard to know where he would have fitted in the Broadway of 1935. On the other hand, the alternative seemed even less possible for him. The period, theatrically speaking, has been dubbed, not inappropriately, The Decade of Revolt; it was dominated by its response to political and social circumstances.

Immersed as he was in dreams of a theatrical golden age when actors were really actors, filled with visions of the Elizabethan and Jacobean theatre in all its harsh and lovely vigour, and almost equally obsessed by the magical possibilities of modern stagecraft, he found very little in the current scene towards which to aspire. He abominated Broadway. The political theatre, amateur or professional, had no hold on him, despite its astonishing new-found vitality. The outburst of agitprop, generally playing to workers' union meetings, inventing a shorthand language of theatre to make points as stirringly and economically as possible, passed him by. Mainstream theatre people made their way to these performances to admire their 'beauty'. Welles was unimpressed by the level of excitement at these performances, feeling, in Ethan Mordden's words, that 'there was excitement because the communion of stage and house was perfect; but it was perfect because everybody agreed'. Nor was he impassioned to help create a viable theatre for working-class audiences, which was the Theatre Union's platform. He was not hostile to these things; they were simply out of his sphere, not to his taste. He would certainly have described himself as belonging to 'the left': a term, as John Gassner pointed out, 'attached to anything critical of war or fascism and favouring social reform – no Marxist or other specific political platform implied. Marxist theory was just one more piece of driftwood afloat in the current of fashionable intellectualism, along with amateur Freudianism and hazy bourgeois romanticism.' Certainly no Marxist, and abhorring Freudianism, both amateur and professional, Welles's world-view at that time might best be described as ebulliently tragic, marinaded in the Nietzsche of *The Birth of Tragedy* and bearing some family connection with the great American writers, Melville and Hawthorne, whose theme of expiation chimed well with Welles's sense of personal guilt; this view he sought to express in grand theatrical forms. He would scarcely have responded to what Goldstein describes as 'the overriding dramatic topic of the decade: the individual's problem of maintaining dignity and self-esteem without harming others'.

That topic, of course, was the special province of another of the dominant theatrical forces of the day, the Group Theatre, from whom, both in theory and in practice, he also felt himself distant. Like the Playwrights' Company, a breakaway from the Theatre Guild, their equal commitment to socially aware scripts and to the theories of Stanislavsky, made them highly unattractive to Welles. Quite apart from his dislike of method of any sort, Stanislavsky's insistence that the actor search his own experience for his performance was entirely unacceptable; Lee Strasberg's elevation of an early stage of Stanislavsky's work, with its belief that emotion is the beginning, middle and end of acting, into the Group's central tenet made it positively repugnant. Another of the founding members of the Group, Harold Clurman – Danton to Strasberg's Robespierre, or perhaps Lenin to his Stalin – expressed a further aspect of their credo which would have held no charms for Welles: moral fervour. This was the influence of Copeau. 'We expected,' wrote Clurman, 'to bring the actor much closer to the content of the play, to link the actor as an individual with the creative purpose of the playwright . . . in our belief, unless the actor in some way shared the playwright's impulse, the result on the stage always remained somewhat mechanical . . . our interest in the life of our times must lead us to the discovery of those methods that would most truly convey this life through the theatre . . . since we were theatre people, the proper action for us was to establish a theatre in which our philosophy of life might be translated into a philosophy of the theatre . . . there were to be no stars in our theatre . . . the writer himself was to be no star, either . . . the director was the leader of the theatrical group, unifying its various efforts, enunciating its basic aims, tied to it not as a master to his slave but as a head to a body. In a sense, the group produced its own director, just as the director in turn helped form and guide the group.'

It is impossible not to be moved by Clurman's passion and his idealism, while acknowledging the serious difficulties inherent in his approach. The position of the director, in particular, needs to be articulated much more clearly than Clurman is prepared to do. As expressed above, it sounds suspiciously like the old revolutionary notion that the leader somehow embodies the will of the people; and we know to our bitter cost what *that* unfortunate principle leads to. Welles was in no doubt as to who was going to be the star, in whatever capacity; nor what the powers and function of the director were going to be: absolute. As it happens, perhaps the most violent of the many arguments that shook the Group throughout its brief life concerned the position of the director. It was an argument that was much in the air in the early thirties in America, and it related to a development in the American theatre that helps to explain something of Orson Welles's sensational impact on it in what was to be the very near future.

The leader of the revolt in the Group was the actor and director Robert Lewis. He prepared and read a paper on what he considered to be its limitations: 'I say that Group productions lack music, colour, rhythm, movement – all those other things in the theatre besides psychology, and all the things which in theatrical form clarify and make important one's psychology – not that colour, movement, rhythm etc are not present one by one on our stage – they are, but they are not fused into a single style which in each production is peculiar to the expression of the talent of the particular author.' There were limits, evidently, to what could be achieved democratically. In a piece in *Theatre Arts Monthly* on the rise of the director, Edith Isaacs, one of the clearest-headed theatrical analysts of the day wrote: 'twenty years ago, the director was an apologetic person whose business it was to evoke a harmony between an egotistic actor and a stubborn playwright. Tact and patience and humility were his chief requisites for success. Today he is the guiding, unfolding, unifying spirit in the theatre. The greatest men in the theatre today are all directors.' She was speaking of the European theatre. In a lengthier analysis of the American scene, John Mason Brown summed up (in 1930) the current crop of directors: 'the painstaking love of detail and the infinite patience of Mr Belasco's work . . . the less certain but far more imaginative contribution of such a man as Mr Hopkins . . . skillful but unobtrusive practitioners such as Guthrie McClintic, Gilbert Miller, Dudley Digges; uncanny showmen: the three Georges: Abbott, Cohan, Kaufmann. Jed Harris's jubilant toughness; Mamoulian's gift in handling crowds'. Despite all this talent, something, he feels, is missing. 'The touch of our directors is varied, even if their virtuosity is small. It is in the scope of their ambitions rather than the limits of their power that our American directors differ from their European contemporaries. Their talents are of a lesser kind, and their originality is less marked. Unlike the directors who dominate the stage of the continent they feel that their first duty is the intention of the author rather than the interpretation they may bring to it.'

Enter Orson Welles. With his first professional production he created, at a stroke, and for better or for worse, the 'concept production'. It was Houseman who offered him the job, but the framework for it was something much bigger than both of them; one of the most extraordinary events in theatre history, in fact: the creation of the Federal Theatre Project. Orson Welles's achievements in the theatre of the thirties can only be understood in the light of it.

CHAPTER NINE

FTP/*Macbeth*

THE FEDERAL Theatre Project was an offshoot of Roosevelt's second New Deal programme. The first New Deal programme (1933–5) had initiated various relief schemes, one of which included a scheme for unemployed theatre workers; but the second programme (1935–9), including the creation of Harry Hopkins's Works Progress Administration, sought to implement a much wider-ranging policy of productive redeployment. 'For the first time the skills of the worker and his self-respect became the cornerstone of a relief programme,' write O'Connor and Brown in their history of the project, *Free, Adult and Uncensored.* There was a Federal Music Project, a Federal Art Project, and a Federal Writers' Project in addition to the Theatre Project; together they employed 40,000 people. As head of the Theatre Project, Hopkins appointed, in the face of considerable opposition, a forty-five-year-old theatre academic, Hallie Flanagan, head of the Experimental Theatre at Vassar Women's College, and author of a survey of the European theatrical revolution, *Shifting Scenes.* Hopkins's instinct was sound, not to say inspired. She brought to the job a sinewy strength, undentable enthusiasm and a very clear brain; but the quality above all that she contributed was vision, and it is that which transformed the Project from a practical and a useful undertaking into a crusade whose generosity of spirit and breadth of purpose still has the power to move.

From the start she insisted that, though 'the arts projects were being set up to deal with physical hunger, was there not another form of hunger with which we could rightly be concerned, the hunger of millions of Americans for music, plays, pictures, books?' The Theatre Project would bring jobs to as many out-of-work artists as possible, but the opportunity would be seized to create a national network of easily accessible theatres in places where there had been none before, for people who had never dreamed of attending one. At a time like the present, when the notion of state support for the performing arts is being quietly dropped even in those countries where it has from time immemorial been an unspoken assumption, her vision is especially moving. 'Belief in the theory that the work of the artists was a part of the national wealth America could not afford to lose, belief in the new pattern of life this work could create for many people – these were the passionate affirmations underlying the alternate despair and laughter of those gargantuan days.' The size of the task never seemed to trouble her. What she was proposing was the establishment of a national health service of the theatre arts – to benefit audience and performers in equal measure.

The range of work that she sponsored is astonishing: in some cases she sought to revitalise an ailing branch of the performance arts (the circus, for example), in others to create something entirely new, like the theatre of the blind in Omaha. There were, across the country, vaudeville projects, and variety projects; there was a special division for marionettes. Educational projects were part of every production; old and young artists were brought together in apprentice-master relationship. 'Perhaps,' as O'Connor and Brown say, 'the real measure of the Federal Theatre should not be the now-famous names, but rather the thousands of unknown people in rural towns, CCC camps, and city parks who saw live theatre for the first time, and the hundreds of people who had given their lives to the theatre, who were able to end or continue their careers with pride, doing what they were trained to do and did well.'

At the time, there was immense scepticism on all sides. The Project was seen as a) utopian and naive, a further waste of taxpayers' money (boon-doggling, in the expressive phrase of the period); b) liable to draw people away from the legitimate, unsubsidised theatre, since prices were pegged at 75c or less; c) in danger of fostering tenth-rate work, since only the unemployed were being used, and good actors were never unemployed for long, were they? Above all, the Project was perceived, like the New Deal itself, as another form of 'creeping socialism'. If the theatre couldn't survive without government aid, then too bad; let it go to the wall. This perception was reinforced by the nature of much of what was produced: Hallie Flanagan didn't bother to conceal her conviction that 'the theatre must become conscious of the implications of the changing social order, or the changing social order will ignore, and rightly, the implications of the theatre'. Every FTP show had something to contribute to the national debate; it was a truly public theatre. Plays by the people, of the people, for the people; being an actor, a writer or a director did not stop you from being a citizen.

For Hallie Flanagan, the Federal Theatre was a part of 'the tremendous rethinking, redreaming and rebuilding of America. Our people are one, not only with the musicians playing symphonies in Federal orchestra; with writers recreating the American scene; with artists compiling from the rich and almost forgotten past "The Index of American Design"; but they are one also with thousands of men building roads and bridges and sewers; one with doctors and nurses giving clinical aid to a million destitute men, women and children; one with workers carrying travelling libraries into desolate areas; one with scientists studying mosquito control and reforestation and swamp drainage and soil erosion. What has all this to do with the theatre?' she asked, and then ringingly answered herself: 'It has everything to do with the Federal Theatre. For these activities represent a new frontier in America, a frontier against disease, dirt, illiteracy, unemployment, despair, and at the same time against selfishness, special privilege and social apathy.'

There were plays about syphilis, and about housing, about the conditions of the agricultural industry, the history of labour unions, and public ownership of utilities. There was a marionette play about careless driving (*Death Takes the Wheel*); even the children's plays were socially conscious. Of *Revolt of the Beavers*, Brooks Atkinson wrote in *The New York Times*: 'Mother Goose is no longer a rhymed escapist; she has been studying Marx.' Flanagan was very firm about the political neutrality of the Project, but there was no mistaking the progressive – as Gassner would say, the leftist – bias of the great majority of the work. For precisely this reason, it would not be tolerated for long. The rumblings started very early; when the time was ripe, the Project had made enough enemies on the right for it to disappear virtually overnight.

But in 1935, heaven was still there for the storming. Not that it was easy. The alliance of the arts with public services was an uncomfortable one. 'Imagine an organisation producing in a season nearly as many plays as all the commercial theatres on Broadway,' wrote the former head of production services for the FTP. 'On top of that, imagine that organisation being required constantly to adapt itself to the same rules and regulations set down primarily for engineering projects. Then imagine those rules and regulations enforced by people completely without a knowledge of the theatre and theatre practice – and you have precisely the position of the FTP.' Flanagan herself gave an example of the failure of the organisation to grasp the nature of its tasks: a theatre which had spent the entire rehearsal period trying to secure a loaf of bread for each performance of a projected run of thirty, received, on the first night, thirty loaves.

In view of the scale of the operation, and the suddenness of its development, she and her lieutenants were none the less miraculously successful in achieving their goals. The New York Project presented problems of its own; inevitably. It became 'the best and the worst of Federal Theatre. It presented the widest range of productions, talents, taste, attitudes, races, religious and political faiths. It was everything in excess. In short, it reflected its city . . .' New York had six Project theatres, and a number of first-time ventures: a bureau of research and publication; a Federal Theatre Magazine; the Living Newspaper, in a way the most famous and characteristic of all the Project's enterprises; and the Negro Theatre Unit.

John Houseman was appointed to run this; and he, naturally, approached Orson Welles to direct a play for him. Houseman's appointment was not without controversy: within the black acting community there were distinct factions, some of whom (notably the former members of the now defunct Lafayette Players) believed that the director of the unit should be black, while others (the intellectuals, teachers, social workers and so on) believed that, realistically speaking, 'a white man was needed to guide the project through a white man's world'. Among the latter was the great black actress, Rose McLendon, star of *Porgy* and Langston Hughes's *Mulatto*. If the leader of the Negro Theatre project were to be black, she was the natural choice; and she, having admired Houseman's skills as co-ordinator on *Four Saints in Three Acts*, in which she had appeared, nominated him as the person she felt most likely to make a go of things – at which point, she died of the cancer with which she had struggled for years, and Houseman was appointed, unopposed; endorsed, in fact, from beyond the grave. He ran the Negro Theatre project, in the not unadmiring words of a black colleague, 'like a colonial governor'.

He surrounded himself with talent. His black team consisted of the writers Countee Cullen, Zora Hurston Neale; the dancer Clarence Yates; the designer Perry Hopkins; Eubie Blake, Joe Jordan, Leonard de Paur, musicians. All of them were already distinguished in their respective spheres, and as a result of the Federal Theatre Project, became part of the mainstream of the theatre. White colleagues included Houseman's friend and now house-mate Virgil Thomson, Abe Feder, the lighting designer of *Panic*, and a new colleague, the designer Nat Karson who had created sensational extravaganzas at Radio City Music Hall. All were paid exactly what Houseman himself was paid: $23.86 per week. As assistants, he chose Carlton Moss – 'bitter, but brilliantly clear about "the negro mind" ' – Edward Perry, his stage manager from *Four Saints in Three Acts*, and, as his secretary, the 'plump, pink-cheeked, bouncing Jewish virgin' Augusta Weissberger. For the rest – for the personnel of the unit, actors, stage-hands, set-builders – he held open recruitment sessions. The result was pandemonium. Just as with any other division of the Project, the Negro Unit was inundated with applications from people who, desperate to work, were often only vestigially connected with the theatre – if at all. Since so many black performers were driven to pursue their careers in a sort of twilight zone out of the professional mainstream, it was especially difficult to determine whose application was legitimate, and whose was not. Carlton Moss, with his bitter brilliant clarity, was particularly ruthless in weeding out the pretenders.

The arrival of the Negro Unit in Harlem was greeted with controversy. On the one hand, any activity, any sign of hopeful life, any possibility of employment and confidence, was to be welcomed in that desperate quarter, so recently the scene of riots. With a population 80 per cent of whom were out of work, endemic prostitution, gambling and bootlegging, and with rents, as Houseman observes, 'double those for the equivalent white dwelling', it was a very different place from the Renaissance Harlem of even ten years before, where there had existed for the first time in America a black community of artists, intellectuals and entrepreneurs – businessmen, property owners, responsible politicians – a life unforgettably recorded by the camera of the great black photographer James Van Der Zee. This black Montmartre and Champs Elysées rolled into one had disappeared pretty well as suddenly as it had arisen, a casualty of the depression; and no amount of 'momentary tranquillisation by the New Deal Relief' could compensate for the loss of dignity and self-respect. There remained, of course, the clubs and the dives, frequented by down-there-on-a-visit whites; Harlem was not yet a no-go area. But the place was seething with anger and despair.

What was the purpose of this Negro Unit, Harlemites wanted to know. Was the Unit, provocatively taking up residence in the Lafayette, scene of the most successful attempt to create a permanent black company (where a wide range of plays had been attempted, from *Othello* to *Dr Jekyll and Mr Hyde* taking in on the way *The Count of Monte Cristo* and sentimental Yiddish comedy) intended to cater to a white audience or a black one? Would it preserve an image of black people as 'handkerchief-headed' savages, whether noble or mentally sub-normal, violent or comic, or would the slow slow process of legitimisation of the black profession be advanced?

Here and there, hopeful signs were visible: since Charles Gilpin, a veteran of the Lafayette, had created the title role in *The Emperor Jones*, it had begun to be possible for the occasional black actor to be taken seriously. Robeson had continued along Gilpin's path, as had others in the small outcrop of (mostly white-authored) black dramas, of which Dubose Heyward's *Porgy* was the outstanding example.

As well as the perennial revues, such as the *Blackbirds* series, there were all-black versions of recent Broadway hits – Nicholson's and Robinson's *Sailor Beware!* and Hecht's and MacArthur's *The Front Page*, and the curious genre of the adapted folk-play, most famously Marc Connelly's *In Abraham's Bosom* (in which God's first entrance is preceded by a cry of 'here come de Lawd!') and, more enterprisingly, Paul Green's *Roll, Sweet Chariot*, 'a symphonic play of the Negro people'. Another striking Broadway drama of the late twenties had been *Harlem*, by a black author, Wallace Thurman, featuring a cast of sixty black actors and a lone white one. An 'Episode of Life in New York's Black Belt' it was described in an admiring notice by George Jean Nathan as affording 'a dozen and one vivid hints of niggerdom at its realest', a phrase which fairly neatly sums up the situation of the black drama in the third decade of the century. Did black life exist, as far as the theatre was concerned, simply to be held up for examination by well-heeled white audiences, for amusement or gratifying shock? Was it better not to work in the theatre at all, rather than be subject to the squealing scrutiny so well parodied by Ben Hecht in the late twenties: 'My set has discovered something too marvellous for words. Negroes! Oodles and oodles of them! Big ones and little ones! Harlem, way this side of the zoo.'

Virgil Thomson helped to clear Houseman's mind. When they had cast *Four Saints in Three Acts* with an entirely black cast, he reminded him, the only consideration in doing so had been aesthetic: voices, movement, diction. There was no political statement involved; nor had they adapted the text in any way to make sense of the performers' negritude. They found black performers more beautiful and more expressive. No more, no less. With this highly radical principle in mind, Houseman decided to divide the work of the Unit into two categories: '1. Plays by blacks, for blacks, with blacks. 2. Classical plays, performed by black artists "without concession or reference to colour".' The former category he handed over to his black colleagues. They would open the theatre with an example of new black writing; the classical play, whatever it might be, would take more time to prepare. Without hesitation (though as far as he knew he had only ever previously directed school productions) Houseman invited Orson Welles to direct it. Without hesitation, Welles accepted the invitation.

The fact that most of his actors would have no experience whatever of blank verse, and that indeed many of them would have very little experience of acting, tout court, was only a further recommendation to him. His abhorrence of the polite approach to Shakespeare was absolute; rather complete ignorance than *that*. Professionalism per se had no appeal for him; he realised – as Houseman must have done – that there was no question of turning the Negro Unit into the Old Vic and that what was required were not tutorials in the iambic pentameter but leadership of a galvanising, inspirational kind. The only question was which play was best suited to the actors at his disposal. Houseman reports being roused at 2 a.m. by a telephone call from Welles passionately eager to convey the inspiration that Virginia – as a result of conversations with Francis Carpenter – had had: they must do *Macbeth*, and set it at the court of the early nineteenth-century Haitian Emperor Henri Christophe. Houseman was delighted, and Welles and Nat Karson set to work with passion, researching the period and the curious figure of the gigantic Grenadian slave who had become an emperor. Leader of the Haitian forces of insurrection, he was first elected President, then, after a furious civil war, Napoleonically crowned himself. As Henri I, his vigorous rule was marred by avarice and cruelty; eventually his people revolted, and, cornered, he shot himself. The subject of Aimé Césaire's great poem 'La Tragédie du Roi Christophe', he is an extraordinary figure, not least in the mannered extravagance of his court, anticipating the excesses of the Emperor Bokassa in the Central African Republic; the parallels with Shakespeare's hero are clear enough. For Welles the element in the transposition that really attracted him was that Haiti's voodoo culture enabled him to make the supernatural scenes a credible centre of the play.

It is to be questioned whether this approach quite fulfilled Houseman's and Thomson's criterion of using black performers without reference to the colour of their skins, or 'any other cultural factor'. It may be questioned, in fact, whether it constituted an interpretation of the play. What it is, essentially, is a *concept*: a way of doing the play which makes you think about it afresh. Concepts, almost by definition, only apply to existing work, generally with a long performing tradition. They are by their nature corrective. What Welles wanted to do – what he always wanted to do in the earlier part of his career in the theatre – was to break the mould. He may, in his heart, have longed to see Elizabethan productions of Elizabethan plays (that was certainly the message of *Everybody's Shakespeare*, only two years before); but in practice, he felt he needed to shake off the performing stereotypes of recent tradition. Admiring above all the magnificently timeless performances of an Anew McMaster, and being strangely old-fashioned himself, in practice Welles felt compelled to use shock tactics to restore the immediacy of the texts. For the most part that meant taking an explicit and monothematic line on a play, and that meant cutting and reshaping it to give it surface vividness at the expense of digging into its meaning and discovering its organic structure. It is this that made Mary McCarthy, most ruthless of his critics, say, in the late thirties, 'Mr Welles has the idea that an Elizabethan play is a liability which only by the most strenuous showmanship, by cutting, doctoring, and modernising, can be converted into an asset. Mr Welles' method is to find a modern formula into which a classic can somehow be squeezed.' The fact that generally speaking he realised his concept with electrifying brilliance deflected attention from the superficiality of the approach, and with concept, as opposed to interpretation, the execution is all. That said, electrifying brilliance is not such a common commodity that it can be lightly dismissed; it cost him a great deal of effort and inspiration, and never more so than on this *Macbeth*.

The human material with which he had to work was varied in its abilities, but eager, enthusiastic, energetic, expressive and, especially en masse, emotional. There were no more than five professional actors in the company, which otherwise consisted of a group of voodoo drummers assembled by the Sierra Leonian Asadata Dafora Horton (who had not so long before scored a Broadway hit with his show *Kyunokor* based on the courtship rituals of his country) and over a hundred individuals with more or less glancing relationships to one or other of the performing arts. Welles sought to shape them into a highly drilled troupe. What he had in mind was almost choreographic – literally so in the case of the scene where Banquo's ghost appears, which Welles had re-conceived as a sumptuous ball. Every scene was shaped and moved with dictatorial precision. Some of this work was handed over to an assistant, Tommy Anderson ('I rehearsed them on a count of ONE move here, TWO move there') but for the most part it was Welles, exhorting, demonstrating, haranguing and generally risking his life. These Harlemites were not accustomed to being bossed around by preppy young whites (Brooks Atkinson described him at the period as being 'a round-faced child prodigy who had almost reached voting age') and from time to time he had to be gently taken aside by his Lady Macbeth ('Orson, don't do that; these people will take your head off') or have his Macbeth read the riot act ('So get back to work! You no-acting sons of bitches!' a speech that nearly provoked the riot it was intended to head off). But he was shrewd enough – uncannily shrewd for a middle-class twenty-year-old who had almost no experience whatever of working with black people – to temper his autocracy with fun and charm and crate upon crate of beer. (Himself he fuelled with whiskey, until Virgil Thomson advised him that if you do that, 'you fall'; whereupon he switched to white wine.) There was certainly no liberal crap in his dealings with the company; that might have been really offensive. He had the strength, wrote Houseman, 'but also the kindness and loving patience – and a capacity for total concentration. He kept them going by the sheer force of his personality. His energy was at all times greater than theirs; he was even more mercurial and less predictable than they were.'

With his principals, he rehearsed separately and more calmly. They were a powerful group: Edna Thomas as Lady Macbeth, Jack Carter, Macbeth; Banquo, Canada Lee, Maurice Ellis, Macduff; Eric Burroughs, RADA-trained, as Hecate, so often cut from the play altogether, now placed in a pivotal position: 'the charm's wound up!' was in Welles's version the final line of the text. 'I don't know what this guy's up to,' said Burroughs, 'but he's a genius.' Welles formed particularly close relations with Edna Thomas and Jack Carter. Thomas he treated with the deference due to a great lady of the theatre, and that is indeed how she was perceived by the company, though in truth this owed more to her manner than to her career. A discreet and rather statuesque lesbian, she stood apart from the company, but had great authority, with which she endorsed Welles, a crucial support. Jack Carter, his Macbeth, was an altogether different character, 'the most furious man I have ever known', wrote Houseman. He was six foot four inches tall, had bright blue eyes, and 'a skin so light he could pass as white anywhere in the world, if he'd wanted to. He didn't.' His background was as swathed in myth as Orson's – was he born in a French château, not knowing that he was a negro? Or did he really come from Harlem? Certainly he had a history of violence. Despite creating, to great acclaim, the role of Crown in *Porgy* and the eponymous *Stevedore* (one of the biggest hits of the Theatre Union) he didn't work much as an actor, instead making a living through underworld connections in Harlem. Everybody, according to Houseman, was nervous about how he would behave in rehearsals. But: 'From the moment at the first reading when Orson threw his arms around Jack, his eyes brimming with tears of gratitude and admiration, a close and passionate friendship had sprung up between these two giants.' 'I always seduce actors,' he told Barbara Leaming, 'I make them fall in love with me.' According to Houseman, 'Orson spent a quarter of his radio earnings on loans and handouts to the company; a quarter on props etc; a quarter on meals; and a final quarter on Jack Carter.'

Carter needed a lot of help with his performance. His great gift was for living as dangerously on stage as in life. He was weak vocally and without technical skills. Welles worked unceasingly and tenderly on his performance, which brought them even closer together. The frustration that Welles must have suppressed during this work is evident in the notes (CORRECTIONS, it says at the top of the page) that he dictated to Virginia on 3 April (the first night was 14 April).

Jack's turn before cross to steps should be fixed up.

First half of 'If it were done' speech needs fixing.

Cripples entrance cue must be settled on.

Cut 'ughs' of cripples

'Hath been' lost

Edna should have a look over shoulder as she crosses ramp.

Jack's turn on 'He has asked for me' wrong.

Too long a pause before 'When Duncan is asleep.'

Pick up 'Would it not be received' and 'who dare receive it' more

Work on 'I am settled.'

Fix Canada's turn.

Jack should look more into air.

JACK, FOR GOD'S SAKE LEARN YOUR LINES, AND TAKE THE WEARINESS OUT OF YOUR BODY WHEN YOU GO UP STAIRS.

JESUS CHRIST.
PACE, pace
pace
pace
pace . . .

Christ – first half of scene needs ENORMOUS amount of work.

Jack too casual.

'Stay there till we call' – get that move right, for Christ's sake.

Jack not audible enough in 'tomorrow and tomorrow'.

Phil –
Jesus Christ
God
damn
it.

Though he no doubt modified some of his comments in delivering them, these notes, hissed out in the stalls in the dark, give, to judge from other reports, a fairly good impression of Welles's directing style. The precision of his staging is very clearly revealed. He rarely dealt with ideas in his work with actors; what he loved was to engender adrenalin, then embody it in the physical life of the scene. This skill – also one of the supreme gifts of Reinhardt, though Reinhardt was more interested in psychology than Welles – was one of his greatest natural endowments as a director.

Rehearsals – which went on for a staggering four months in, Welles told a reporter, 'this theatre, auditoriums, hallways, fire escapes, paper bags, coal scuttles, trash barrels and my apartment' – started late and generally went through the night, to the fascination and sometimes consternation of the neighbourhood, as the voodoo drums pounded through to dawn. This impossible schedule partially accounts for the heightened levels of emotion flying around the rehearsal room. The eccentric hours were mostly to accommodate Welles's radio schedule, which would have been hard to fulfil even without *Macbeth*. 'For several days running he was never out of his clothes, but this ended with his breakdown at a radio recital of a poem of Browning's,' a contemporary profile reported. 'He got not only every word wrong but every syllable wrong and the station cut in with an organ recital. Welles always tries to top everybody; on this occasion he succeeded in adding obscurity to Browning.' Houseman computed that he was working twenty out of the twenty-four hours. The remaining four were spent with his Macbeth, not, as we may presume, giving him notes. According to Houseman, they hit the Harlem clubs and brothels.

One is immediately struck again by Welles's fearlessness, and his sense of adventure. These forays could actually have been quite dangerous, although Carter with his underworld connections was as good a protector as anyone could have been. Welles needed to hurl himself into the heart of danger; to associate himself with risk and recklessness. This middle-class boy, steeped in literature (dramatic literature, at any rate), music and art, needed to earn the respect of tough guys. He was not macho himself – everyone speaks of his gentleness, despite the occasional rage which was impressive but passed quickly – yet he was drawn to hell-raising. There seems to have been a need to keep high: the essential motivation of compulsive behaviour. Anything – for the alcoholic, the drug addict, the glutton, the satyriasist – not to lose the adrenalin. Here, with Jack Carter, he seems to have indulged in all of those stimulants, alcohol, food, drink and sex. It is from this period that his real intemperateness dates. There is little record of it before; hereafter he maintains a constant level of indulgence. Despite his asthma – which always threatened to return – he had a massively strong constitution and pushed his body beyond any normal limits. When nothing else worked, he took pills. Throughout the thirties, he chewed amphetamines as if they were candy.

His relationship with Carter seems even more complex than most of his relationships. It is hardly possible that they saw themselves as a couple of likely lads, this lumbering but brilliant white boy and the raging, physically magnificent actor-criminal who were, in the rehearsal room, teacher and pupil: the boy teacher of the man. And here in the fleshpots of Harlem? Were the positions reversed? In some ways they seem to be classic buddies: whatever they did with the women, the real relationship was between the men. Male companionship in this rather simple form was rare with Welles. His instinct to seduce precluded it. Perhaps with Jack Carter he underwent the masculine rites of passage that seem somehow hitherto to have eluded him. 'I never really knew how much of all this was director's strategy,' wrote Houseman, 'or how much it reflected a true and urgent affinity between these two troubled and dangerous men. (I used to wonder, sometimes, seeing Orson return from these nocturnal forays, if they did not perhaps evoke some echo of those other long, wild nights he had spent as a boy, with his father in the red-light districts of the Mediterranean, Hong Kong and Singapore.)' Houseman writes about all of this with a sense of doleful exclusion, like a dog left at home when his master goes out. He has the manner of a perpetual gooseberry, forever doomed to be dropped when things hot up. His own relationship with Welles was confined to making it possible for him to continue working as he wished to, and to prevent him 'from being murdered in spite of their admiration for him'. He was not admitted into the rehearsal room, Welles claiming it would make him self-conscious.

While Welles worked his secret magic with his actors, Houseman had been vigorously establishing the unit. The Lafayette, 'a sordid, icy cavern when we moved in . . . was transformed in a month by the zeal of black technicians who had had nowhere to work, and who were denied the right of unionising themselves.' This was to be his experience at every level: finally allowed to function, black theatre-workers excelled themselves. Houseman fought an important battle early on: the white stage-hands' union tried to apply the Jim Crow principle at the Lafayette. Houseman said, 'I'd be delighted to hire union stagehands if you'll furnish me with black ones, or allow my black ones to join your union.' They said, 'No we can't do that, but you are going to hire union stagehands; otherwise we'll picket this theatre.' He said, 'If you seriously think you can picket a Negro theatre in Harlem for hiring Negroes, just come and try it.' There was no picket. His skills in manoeuvring were highly developed; he was, said Mrs Flanagan, 'our most original and imaginative mind'.

While *Macbeth* rehearsed, the Negro Theatre Project was suddenly thrust into the limelight. For fear of offending the Italian government, Washington had enforced the cancellation of the FTP's first production, which was also to be the first Living Newspaper: the anti-Mussolini show *Ethiopia*. Elmer Rice, the director of the New York Theatre Project, resigned (thus nearly closing down the whole operation) and Houseman's first show was rushed forward to become the very first show staged under the auspices of the Federal Theatre Project: *Walk Together Chillun!* by Frank Wilson (the original Porgy), no masterpiece, but a play by a black, for blacks, with blacks. It was a modest success; the refurbishment of the Lafayette Theatre was admired, as were the technical innovations, and the band. The second play, *Conjur' Man Dies*, written by a Harlem physician and novelist and directed by Joseph Losey, was fun and a smash hit, locally, though snootily received by the press. The FTP was still on probation. No one could doubt their productivity or their range. In a breathless three weeks they managed to stage with respectable success *Everyman*, *Chalk Dust*, *Conjur' Man Dies*, *Triple-A Plowed Under*, and the American première of *Murder in the Cathedral*, reaching entirely new audiences; Hallie Flanagan maintains that many people went to the last-named play 'thinking they were going to see a murder mystery'.

Nobody quite knew what they were going to see when they

bought tickets for *Macbeth*. Universally known in advance as The Voodoo *Macbeth*, it had generated a great deal of controversy, which as far as Houseman and Welles were concerned was splendid. In smart circles it was patronised, in Harlem it was whispered that it was 'a campaign to burlesque negroes'. Even within the Negro Unit, it was controversial: rumoured never to open, it was believed, said Houseman, that 'so much of the project's money had been spent by me on my boyfriend's folly that all future productions of the negro unit had been cancelled'. The casts of other plays at the Lafayette watched with envy and resentment as they glimpsed the splendid costumes being assembled in the wardrobe, and they cursed when they were obliged to shift their own sets forward to make room for *Macbeth*'s. Welles had been working as intensely with his collaborators as with the company. He revealed, according to Houseman, a 'surprising capacity for collaboration. For all the mass of his own ego, he was able to apprehend other people's weakness and strength, and to make creative use of them.' Nat Karson, the Project's head of design, had devised a very simple, unchanging setting for the play: a castle laid in a jungle. The exotic plants and trees were to be created in a series of backcloths of great boldness: this, Houseman says, is essentially what Welles had modelled in Plasticine on top of his ironing board at West 14th Street when he first described the idea of the production to him. Welles had very strong instincts, both visually and structurally. He had, after all, designed, painted and built his own and other people's sets since he was ten. Any designer who worked with him could expect to be realising Welles's concept, to a large extent. Costume was an area in which he had less expertise, but equally strong opinions. That is not to say that his designers were mere executants; realising Welles's ideas was by no means always simple.

Nat Karson wrote an interesting little essay about his work on this production which suggests their general approach: their basic question was 'what would the negro interpretation do to Shakespeare? Would the characters in the accepted version of *Macbeth* remain the same with a negro cast or would the characterisations take on a different form and alter the basic rhythmic patterns of the play?' Their decision, in Karson's words, was to create 'a series of pictures in a chromatic ascension of color, each picture with its own series of climaxes, but essentially a part of an integral whole'. They stared off 'in an extremely low key in the first scene, in muddy reds and blues . . . and as one would draw a chart or graph the colors in the following scenes mount in intensity and brilliance till we come to the ball which is the mathematical centre of the play . . . from that point we descend in key until we reach the sleep-walking scene . . . this is played in a misty haze of light . . . in the last act, I intensified this misty haze.' He and Welles were attempting an exceptionally ambitious integration of all the production elements to create an emotional progression that, we can assume, may not have been present in the performances of the untrained company. They took the question of how best to serve the pigmentation of their actors extremely seriously; this affected every area of the work. 'This necessitated a scene painting that would absorb the type of lighting, rather than reflect.' There was, he says, the same problem with costumes: 'I found that a touch of light color at the wrist line and the collar did a great deal to offset the particular person's coloring . . . I resorted to painting various fabrics . . . the period was simple. However, the danger was to avoid it looking like a musical comedy and for this reason I exaggerated only the costumes of the people appearing in ensembles . . . I hope that I arrived at an almost architectural form, the shoulders of the men representing the capital of a Greek column with its attendant decoration and tapering to the waistline.' He became convinced that because of the predominance of the voodoo scenes in this version, 'the actual scenery should at all times have an eerie, luminescent quality'. Clearly a great deal of the effect he and Welles intended was dependent on light, and they had in their collaborator Abe Feder an extraordinary innovator; he was also a uniquely prickly personality.

Feder was one of the first of the full-time lighting designers. Theatre lighting as an art was in its infancy; hitherto, it had been the province of the designer, the stage manager or the director. Feder started work in the theatre at a time technical developments were transforming the possibilities and demanding special skills. He was one of the earliest lighting designers to have access to high-wattage incandescent lamps, enabling him for the first time really to direct and focus the light; the subsequent arrival of remote control consoles worked by single operators made possible the development of complex lighting plots. He had tubular bulbs, whose beam could be projected in any direction; spotlight bulbs (birdies, perfected by Clarence Birdseye, the frozen food man), smaller in size, and much more flexible; fluorescent light, still then difficult to control; a range of up to seventy-five colours in the recently improved gelatins; and dimmers, newly developed in movie houses, which used them front of house 'with all the fancy coloured light trimmings in the theatre proper'.

This was a formidable array of technical facilities. But Feder was never simply a mechanic of light; he saw himself as an artist. Initially inspired to go into the theatre by the magic act of The Great Thurston (a bond between him and Welles, you would have thought, but no) he was always interested in the overall expression of the play. His alphabetical *Steps in Lighting* (A. READ THE PLAY) reveals a degree of interest in the process of rehearsal unusual in a lighting designer of the period. E. is ATTEND REHEARSALS: 'Soak up the show. Watch it for mood, and visualise the effects you will want to create.' G. (FIRST REHEARSALS) warns: 'the director will start arguing about effects. Keep him happy, and make the necessary changes.' For *Macbeth* he considered his approach particularly carefully. 'Nat Karson set the play in a castle laid in a jungle actually using only one set for the entire play. The limitations of a one-set play and the small size of our stage made it difficult to create the illusion of distance and perspective. And this production offered other difficulties; the physical structure of the castle was real enough, but the background was a stylised design of huge tropical leaves.' So much for the practical challenges. In this case, too, there were special demands, made by an unusually exigent collaborator. 'The director required that at times this setting should take on all the mysticism and fantasy of Negro spiritualism.'

And of course, there was the question of the actors' skins, difficult to light because of the light-absorbing properties of darker pigmentation. In collaboration with Nat Karson, Feder devised light-friendly make-ups and a series of gels specially suited to the actors' pigmentation; the rule of thumb hitherto had been 'Amber for negroes'. Thus the light too, was politicised, helping to break down the dehumanising visual stereotypes. 'It will be seen then, that because the director and the designer deviated from the original script, it was necessary to light this classic in a manner that would create a balance of fantasy and realism in light.' This is the reality of the work that underpins a directorial inspiration. As always, too, the theatre's overwhelmingly practical nature means that there is a constant negotiation between the vision and the possibility, so that pretty nearly everything that appears before the public has evolved into something quite different from what was originally envisaged; sometimes it is better, and sometimes worse.

As far as can be told, Karson had an amicable relationship with Welles. This was not the case with Feder; perhaps Welles decided that the best way to get good work out of him was to enrage him. Either way, he took delight in publicly goading and abusing him; this, Houseman felt, was good for the troupe: seeing a white man abused by another, which is taking work psychology to machiavellian lengths. Feder was, in Houseman's words, 'a garrulous masochist', though there was no doubt of his brilliance as a lighting designer. His assistant, Jean Rosenthal, later a famous light designer herself, called him 'gadget-happy and opinionated'. This was calculated not to appeal to Welles. He had strong ideas about light – as about everything else – and was not interested in any sort of competitive one-upmanship in technical matters. He knew what he wanted, and he expected his collaborators to give it to him. As it happens, Feder had a great deal to give him – and gave it, despite the persecution; his contribution to Welles's success as a director was crucial. Fifty years later, he was not in a forgiving mood: 'Orson Welles? It was just like the *Wizard of Oz*, with Houseman cranking up the loudspeaker. He was just a kid of 21, part of the flim flam of the thirties. He had an enormous voice, but his ideas were all pedestrian. He knew nothing of the nuts and bolts of the theatre.'

Sensing something strange about the unrelenting nature of the goading that he received from Welles, Feder came to a curious conclusion: 'Welles was a glandular case – he had a glandular malfunction, which had a lot to do with the madness he was perpetrating from 35–38.' There is no medical evidence whatever for this, nor any likelihood of it; but it says something about the impression made by Welles's terrifying dynamism, sweeping all before it. (Feder had little time for Houseman, either: 'Houseman was a grain merchant when he was young and when he died he was still a grain merchant.') Embittered he may have been, but his contribution to the lighting of these early productions of Welles was unarguable. He knew as much about light as anyone in the American theatre, and took the art some large strides further forward, partly thanks to the demands that Welles made of him; a man deeply curious and exploratory by nature, he was set challenges and given demands by Welles that no one else would have even thought of. Welles was the catalyst.

In the case of the music, Welles more than met his match as far as temperament was concerned. Welles's seductive charms had no effect on Virgil Thomson, so it seems he decided instead to bluster. 'My other close director friend, Jo Losey, could not bear him,' wrote Thomson, 'but Houseman scenting brains and temperament, brought him to our flat. That Welles could be so overbearing at eighteen was in his favour; that he had directed plays in Dublin we did not believe.' They had to work together, however, as they were both officers of the Negro Unit. 'Orson and I never quarrelled; but we never really agreed. He was extremely professional and he knew exactly what he wanted. He knew it so well and thoroughly that I, as an older musician with a certain amount of pride, would not write him original music. I would not humiliate myself to write precisely on his demand. On the other hand, I respected his demands dramatically. So, as Houseman's employee, I gave him sound effects and ready-made music – trumpet call, battle scenes and percussive scenes when he wanted them – and of course, the waltzes for the party scene.' In Welles's conception, music and an organised sound score were crucial. His aim was to render the play as a sort of symphonic poem.

'*Macbeth* was staged as a romantic tragedy,' Thomson says. He describes the musical approach: 'There was a sizeable pit orchestra . . . also there was a percussion group backstage made up of bass drums, kettledrums, a thunder drum, a thunder sheet, a wind machine – also these not only for stimulating storms, but also, played by musicians and conducted for accompanying some of the grander speeches. In this way, on a pretext of rough weather, I could support an actor's voice and even build it to twice life size . . . the music consisted altogether (outside its voodoo realisms, its offstage storms and battles) of familiar suspense-conventions, of pathos passages almost *Hearts and Flowers*, and, in the ball scene, of Lanner waltzes . . . the whole production was melodramatic to the utmost.' Thomson of course uses the word melodrama in its specific, technical connotation: speech underpinned by music. It is, as he implies, a heightening device, which can also very effectively conceal weakness in a performer; almost anyone sounds better with music under them. But it amounts, in Welles's treatment, in conjunction with the other elements, to a new art form, somewhere between dance and play.

With his curious mixture of Kansas City bluntness and Parisian sophistication, his hatred of pretentiousness and his nose for talent, Thomson didn't like Welles, but he respected his work. 'Orson Welles knew nothing about musical ideas. He was virtually without musical interests; but he was very quick to know what he didn't want. Orson knew about matching sounds to the voice . . . He knew his business. God knows where he learned it.' Leonard de Paur, the distinguished black conductor who was Thomson's assistant, said that 'instead of telling you in musical terms he'd say: this is what I want to accomplish. Ninety-nine per cent of the time he was right.' The most sensational element of the score was provided by the drummers under Asodata Dafora. Their first demand after being given the job was to request black goats, which were then ritually slaughtered in order, they said, to make skins for their drums. Their leader, Abdul, was a genuine witchdoctor, (Welles, unwisely, one cannot help feeling, insisted on addressing him as 'Jazbo') and their chants consisted of real African spells. Somehow, they didn't sound sufficiently menacing; eventually they admitted that the spell they were chanting was medical: a safeguard against beri-beri (Shamkoko, Shanwable, O beri-beri). They agreed to darken their imprecations somewhat; next time he overheard them rehearsing, Houseman was sure he heard them chanting 'Mr Houseman, Mr Welles'. He refrained from reporting this to Welles because 'he was ridiculously superstitious' and haunted by *Macbeth*'s evil reputation, which Welles later confessed to Peter Bogdanovich. 'When you do that play, it has a really oppressive effect on everybody. Really, it's terrifying – stays with you all day. The atmosphere it generates is so horrendous and awful that it's easy to see how the old superstition lives on.' This sense of oppression can only have contributed to the driven feeling that Welles emanated throughout the rehearsals. In fact, said Houseman, this was the only show they ever did together in which Welles didn't sprain an ankle or sustain some physical damage to his person. He did none the less have, almost literally, a close shave very near to the first performance: walking through the foyer, he was attacked by a black man with a razor taped to his wrist, allegedly put up to it by the black communist faction. Fortunately he was with his Banquo, the ex-boxer Canada Lee, who overpowered and disarmed the man.

Agitation and expectation gripped Harlem as the first night approached. *The New York Times* sent their man, Bosley Crowther, to the spot to interview the director: 'Why had they mustered the audacity to take the bard for a ride?' his readers wanted to know. After a few minutes with Welles, he was convinced that 'this was no striving to accomplish a freak production just for the sake of sensation. They had good, sound reasons for it.' Giving a quick tour d'horizon of Welles (including the new claims that he had directed *Othello* and *The Tempest* at the Royalty Theatre in London; every interview advanced the legend a notch or two), he quickly allowed his subject to take over the interview. 'You've heard that the locale we've chosen is Haiti? Well, it isn't Haiti at all. It's like the island *The Tempest* was put on – just a mythical place which, because our company is composed of negroes, may be anywhere in the West Indies.' That was, of course, the party line: 'without reference to race or colour'. Orson doesn't try to square that one (he couldn't; there's a real and significant conceptual inconsistency there) so he tells a lie. Then he makes a joke: 'The only point in shifting the scene from Scotland was because the kilt is naturally not a particularly adaptable costume for negro actors.' Finally he comes clean: 'The witch element in the play falls beautifully into the supernatural atmosphere of Haitian voodoo. We've taken full advantage of that. Instead of using just three witches, as most productions of *Macbeth* conventionally do, we have an entire chorus of singers and dancers. And Hecate, who is seldom presented, is the leading spirit in their midst – a sort of sinister Father Divine – a man witch who leads the others.'

Crowther asks about the quality of the acting. Welles, happily mounting his hobby-horse, replies 'You see, the negro actors have never had the misfortune of hearing Elizabethan verse spouted by actors strongly flavoring of well-cured Smithfield. They read their lines just as they would any others. On the whole, they're no better and no worse than the average white actor before he discovered the red plush style.' Crowther reports that 'Mr Welles said that he found the present acting company a whole lot more comprehending than any troupe of professional whites that he had ever seen.' One in the eye for Katharine Cornell, or for that matter Hilton Edwards and Micheál Mac Liammóir. The *Times*'s man was impressed, though, and came down firmly on the side of the project and the Negro Unit, and against the suspicious chorus of doubters, who could see nothing in this venture but free-loading loafers. 'Every one of the actors seemed as alert and enthusiastic as they must have been the day – or night – they started. The New Deal, not only in the theatre but in Shakespeare, was meat and drink for them. And any actor who will rehearse from midnight to dawn, the rosy-fingered, every night for eleven weeks must be interested in something more than a pay check.'

The anticipation and controversy among the smart audience were expertly maintained by both Houseman and Welles; in Harlem, things were in the hands of Houseman's assistant, Carlton Moss, who had forged good relations with the community, building the local audience with patient propaganda, then, nearer the opening night, capping it with stunts like the luminous stencilled logos of MACBETH that appeared all over the neighbourhood, while garlands and balloons festooned the Tree of Hope. A free preview drew 3,000 more spectators than the theatre could hold; police had to disperse the crowd. When the first night itself arrived – on 14

April – all northbound automobile traffic was stopped for more than an hour while from trucks in the street, floodlights flared a circle of light into the lobby, and cameramen took photographs of the arrival of celebrities. The massed forces of the brass bands of the Monarch Lodge of Benevolent and Protective Order of Elks played, marching over the painted footsteps on the pavement – another of Moss's stunts. Hallie Flanagan, proud and exhilarated at having instigated an event that was as brilliant as any Broadway opening and at the same time a genuinely popular occasion, wrote a sharp impression of that night: 'Flash of ten thousand people clogging the streets, following the scarlet and gold bands of the Negro Elks, marching with flying banners, bearing the strange device: MACBETH by Wm Shakespeare – flash of police holding back the crowds, of newsreel men grinding their cameras on soundtrucks – flash of jewels, silk hats and ermine.' The result of all this extra-theatrical activity was that the curtain went up an hour late, at half past nine; the mood inside the theatre was unlike that for any Shakespeare anyone had ever known. Perhaps it was a little like an audience at the Globe Theatre, one afternoon in 1600: rampant with expectation, oblivious of theatrical etiquette, keenly following the story.

'Negroes have taken Shakespeare to themselves,' wrote Martha Gellhorn, 'Macbeth wore military costumes of canary yellow and emerald green . . . women came on and off the stage in salmon pink and purple. The impression was of a hot richness that I have almost never seen in the theatre or anywhere else. The audience sat and watched and listened as if this were a murder mystery by Edgar Wallace, only much more exciting.' The production inspired a great deal of excited prose. This is Hallie Flanagan: 'African drums beat, Lady Macbeth walked on the edge of a jungle throbbing with sinister life, Hecate with his bullwhip lashed out at the witches, Macbeth, pierced by a bullet, took his terrific headlong plunge from the balustrade.' Houseman, viewing the proceedings with an equally passionate but more calculating eye, was able to say that 'within five minutes, amid the thunder of drums and the orgiastic howls and squeals of our voodoo celebrants, we knew that victory was ours. The next scene to stop the show' (a slightly unexpected phrase in an account of *Macbeth*) 'was the Macbeths' royal reception, shimmering couples swirling with wild abandon . . . then suddenly, a wild, high, inhuman sound that froze them all in their tracks, followed by Macbeth's terrible cry as the spirit of Banquo, in the shape of a luminous death mask, suddenly appeared on the battlements to taunt him in the hour of his triumph.'

The final moment of the production, the arrival of the army in the form of Birnam wood, was greeted with a roar of approval: 'the floor became a moving forest above which . . . Macbeth shot then . . . kicked the cream-faced loon, for an 18-foot drop, into the courtyard below – a moment later Macbeth's head came sailing down from the battlements.' There was no doubt in the actors' mind whose triumph it was. 'At the conclusion of the performance, Orson Welles who adapted and staged the play, was virtually dragged out of the wings by members of the company and forced to take a bow,' reported *The New York Times*. 'There were salvoes of applause as numerous bouquets of flowers were handed over the footlights to the leading players.' The applause went on for a quarter of an hour. It meant more than the success of *Macbeth*: its real significance was that the Negro Unit, the Federal Theatre Project, John Houseman and Orson Welles were all endorsed.

The press reaction the following day was, for *Macbeth* at the Lafayette, no longer crucial. The show was already the most enormous success. For Welles and Houseman, it mattered a great deal. They both had reputations to make. All the first-string critics had attended the first night (one of them asking not to be seated next to negroes), and for the most part, they were enthusiastic. While regarding the whole event as a curiosity from a Shakespearean point of view, they could hardly fail – simply as reporters – to acknowledge the excitement engendered. Every single notice, good or bad – there were no indifferent ones – makes you long to see the show. Brooks Atkinson of the *Times*, a friend of the Project, was saddled by his sub-editor with a headline which bore no resemblance to his copy. It is a good indication of the degree of racism, both latent and blatant, that informed most of the notices: MACBETH OR HARLEM BOY GOES WRONG. He starts (as perhaps Welles did) with the witches' scenes. 'They have always worried the life out of the polite tragic stage: ship the witches into the rank and fever-stricken jungles of Haiti . . . raise the voices until the jungle echoes, stuff a gleaming naked witch doctor into a cauldron, hold up negro masks in the baleful light – and there you have a witches' scene that is logical and stunning and a triumph of the theatre art.' He admired Nat Karson's costumes and settings, and Feder's light. 'They have turned the banquet scene into a ball at a semi-barbaric court, heralded it with music and crowded it with big, rangy figures dressed in magnificent court array. Put that down in your memory-book as another scene that fills the theatre with sensuous, black-blooded vitality.'

His (more or less) innocent racism is revealed in every phrase.

'Jack Carter is a fine figure of a negro in tight-fitting trousers that do justice to his anatomy.' Then Atkinson turned to Carter's performance. 'He has no command of poetry or character . . . Edna Thomas has stage presence and a way with costumes, and also a considerable awareness of the character she is playing. Although she speaks the lines conscientiously, she has left the poetry out of them.' This is an assertion which is constantly made about Welles, his productions, other people's performances in his productions, and his own performances: that they lack poetry. There seems to be some truth in it. He had a passion for verse, but he wanted to eliminate Poetry from the classical theatre, considering it an obstacle to the life in the plays, a veneer that needed to be stripped away. And yet he was no realist. He wanted the majesty without the poetry, the tone without the music. What he offered instead was Orchestration; colour and sound, largely devoid either of meaning or of melody. 'Since the programme announces *Macbeth* by William Shakespeare, it is fair to point out that the tragedy is written in verse and that it reveals the disintegration of a superior man who is infected by ambition. There is very little of that in the current Harlem revival,' wrote Atkinson. But, he concluded enticingly enough, 'as an experiment in Afro-American showmanship the *Macbeth* merited the excitement that rocked the Lafayette last night. If it is witches you want, Harlem knows how to overwhelm you with their fury and phantom splendour.'

Burns Mantle in the *Sunday News* had much the same message, less attractively expressed: 'This is not the speech of negroes, nor within their grasp . . . with the spoken lines, though they are modestly and sensibly spoken, the coloured *Macbeth* becomes a good deal like a charade.' The costumes, generally admired, were also held to be somewhat fantasticated. 'Extremely vivid, though a bit bizarre,' wrote Richard Lockridge in *The New York Sun*. 'They are prodigious, running wild-eyed through the rainbow and being of such strange shapes that one can only guess that Nat Karson, who did them, was one time frightened by a costume ball . . . Macbeth's costume is like a football player's outfit, with great padded epaulets; Duncan's crown madly sprouts feathers.' Percy Hammond, in a notice which was less a review of the production than an expression of personal affront at being unable to file his copy on time, took the anti-Federal Theatre Project line. 'The production is only as interesting as could be expected – one of your benevolent Uncle Sam's experimental philanthropies . . . an exhibition of deluxe boondoggling . . . the actors sounded the notes with a muffled timidity that was often unintelligible . . . the personnel of the Negro Theatre is magnificent in its titles and numbers. It contains, one learns from the playbill, a managing producer, a casting director, a stage manager with four assistants etc, some experts in voodoo chants, and a superintendent of the chorus to say nothing of the ticket takers, the ushers, the press representatives, and as pathetic an orchestra as ever misunderstood the wood-winds, cat-guts and brasses. Despite the competence of this large army of Federal officials *Macbeth* could not get its curtain up until 9.30 p.m. – so I, as a punctual reporter, had to desert the performance before Miss Thomas, as Lady Macbeth, walked and talked in her sleep. The *Macbeth* of the Negro Theatre and the WPA is as interesting as can be expected, a unique example of the New Deal's friendly processes.' This dyspeptic irrelevance cost the critic dear; according to legend, either Welles or Asodata Horton were particularly incensed by its tone, and conveyed their displeasure (crying, perhaps 'who will rid me of this meddlesome hack?') to Abdul, the show's witchdoctor, who then stayed up all night cursing Percy Hammond with a particularly virulent chant. His notice appeared on the Tuesday, he took ill on the Thursday, and was dead by Sunday. Gratifying though this story is, its veracity may be doubted. As Sam Leiter points out, there were far worse notices than Hammond's – though critics should note that nothing is more calculated to render homicidal the person criticised than a refusal to engage with the work done, instead of some external factor; liked or loathed, it should be the work that is reviewed, nothing else. Perhaps Percy's notice and his sad, if apocryphal fate, should be conveyed to all critics at the outset of their careers.

The few black critics were enthusiastic, without gushing. They saw the event in a different light, of course. The militant journalist Roi Ottley wrote in the *Amsterdam News*: 'In *Macbeth* the negro has been given an opportunity to discard the bandana and burnt-cork casting to play a universal character . . . we attended the *Macbeth* showing, happy in the thought that we wouldn't again be reminded, with all its vicious implications, that we were niggers.' More simply, Errol Aubrey Jones in the *New York Age* wrote: 'Hallie Flanagan and Phillip Barber must have felt proud for their protégé after it all was over. We were. The theatre lives again! Hurrah!' – an important vote of confidence from the community.

Mainstream critics felt impelled to return to the subject. More or less reversing his original judgement, Brooks Atkinson in his weekly round-up declared that the production was not *Macbeth*: 'it turns out to be a colorful and rousing voodoo show . . . an amusing show shop lark.' This word keeps cropping up: 'amusing'. Unexpected in a review of *Macbeth*; rather refreshing, though it is scarcely intended as a compliment. Many of these notices represent, in fact, the reverse side of American anxiety about Shakespeare. Now they're worried that they're enjoying it too much. John Mason Brown in the *New York Post* offered A FURTHER CONSIDERATION OF THE WAY IN WHICH ORSON WELLES FAILED TO DEVELOP AN INTERESTING IDEA. The piece makes some interesting points about the production, and about Welles: 'In a moment of inspiration, Mr Welles apparently saw the three weird sisters of Shakespeare's text not as fantastical hags lurking in the shadows of a Scotch heath, but as mumbo-jumbo agents of a fearful witch doctor in the jungles of Haiti. The next step in his thinking . . . was to imagine a Macbeth who would be appropriate for these witches; who would be subject to the spell of black instead of white magic; in other words, a sort of Brutus Jones Macbeth, whose heart would quicken to the beat of voodoo drums.' This is exactly what most critics claim to have seen. Not according to Mason Brown.

'Unfortunately,' he continued, 'Mr Welles seems to have lost his nerve just when he needed it most . . . he has introduced a few fairly tame voodoo scenes into a wretchedly cut and stupidly altered version of *Macbeth* that, in spite of being acted by an all-Negro cast, is still laid in Scotland . . . it is merely a conventional production with unconventional features which is less well acted than are most indifferent Shakespearean revivals of the same traditional sort.' The concept, Mason Brown is saying, is merely a gimmick. 'One wonders why Mr Welles lacked imagination enough to adapt the language of the play to the locale he had selected for it and the actors who were to speak it. It is not the absence of orthodoxy but its presence that one objects to in this *Macbeth*.'

This was the sticking point for the hostile critics: they would, they imply, have liked it better if it hadn't been called *Macbeth*, and if the actors hadn't used Shakespeare's text. Equally, they would have been happy if Welles had held classes in the iambic pentameter and produced a troupe of medal-winning verse speakers. The point is that the Negro Unit (that is to say Houseman, and, behind him, Hallie Flanagan) wanted to make a bold statement of intent: black actors, they were saying, will be confined neither to folkloristic tweeness nor to Broadway slickness (both offering stereotypical views of black performers) but will create something thrilling and bold which will rival anything that the white theatre can offer. The works of Shakespeare, part of the store of common culture, provided a useful starting point.

Whatever the critics' cavills, the beau monde took up the show in a big way, as did theatre people (John Barrymore, Welles claimed, saw the show every night of its ten-week run). But its fame went beyond the theatre. 'No event in the art galleries this week,' wrote the *New York Times* Art Critic, 'could hope to rival in barbaric splendour the transmogrification of *Macbeth* by members of the Negro Theatre . . . the stage pictures at any rate constituted a sumptuous pageant of colour, form, pattern and movement, keyed to the pulsebeat of voodoo drums.' Whatever the original intention, Orson Welles had staged a highly original and exciting event, an integration of light, sound, movement and decor which had an overwhelming sensuous and visceral impact, a barbaric cabaret. The effect on its audiences must have been something like that of the Ballets Russes in Paris, 1911. Feder's lights, in conjunction with Karson's Douanier Rousseau backcloths, revealed 'a tragedy of black ambition in a Green Jungle shot with such lights from both heaven and hell as no other stage has seen', in the fevered words of a contemporary critic; the lights were co-ordinated with the sound score and the stage action to a degree never before experienced by an American (or any other) audience.

Virgil Thomson invited Jean Cocteau, in 1936 making his trip around the world in eighty days, to the production. 'Cocteau did not understand the constant lighting changes. His classical theatre mind found them distracting till he had seized their function in the spectacle as contributing to the climate of violence . . . he perceived a Wagnerian aspect to the proceedings.' This is a precise perception: the totality of expression, the gesamtkunstwerk, of Wagner's aesthetic, is exactly what Welles was after. It is hardly surprising, given his immersion in grand opera from his earliest years (it was the first form of theatre to which he had been exposed) that his work should aspire to its condition. The integration of motifs – the aspiration towards the organic – is entirely Wagnerian. Reinhardt's designer, Ernst Stern, who was in town to design (of all things) *The White Horse Inn*, left a vivid account of one instance of this: 'When Macbeth and Lady Macbeth planned the murder, their plottings were accompanied by the background throbbing of the drums. It merged naturally into the knocking on the door: "Wake Duncan with thy knocking! I would thou could'st." Sometimes the throbbing was subdued, like the insistent throbbing of a guilty conscience, like a steady pulse-beat; sometimes louder and more insistent, according to whether it conveyed the memory of past horrors or the suggestion of new horrible deeds to come.'

The influence of *The Emperor Jones* was felt by many spectators, especially perhaps in this insistent use of drums. Welles, like many an artist, a Stravinsky or a Picasso, stole anything that was germane to his purpose. He was not, in fact, a great innovator at all; he was a great fulfiller. Pragmatic rather than visionary, he was supreme as a doer. Houseman felt that Welles had been initiated into the mysteries of the theatre. If we say, rather, that he seemed innately to have an absolute mastery of the skills of the theatre – of its hokum, so to say – and all the whorish skills involved, a shameless, unabashed determination to give immediate gratification, it may be closer to the truth. It is an astonishing, an uncanny endowment, not liable to produce the greatest art, but still formidable. Not yet twenty-one years old, Welles had it in him to be the greatest manufacturer of theatrical fireworks ever known. Mary McCarthy, unrelentingly pursuing him, wrote, two years later: 'The Harlem *Macbeth* is now far enough in the past so that even those who enjoyed it can see that it was at best a pleasant bit of legerdemain.' Contemporary accounts suggest a different adjective; a staggering piece of legerdemain.

Cocteau, plagued with doubts and reservations, finally abandoned his objections and allowed himself to submit to the spell wrought by Welles. 'I like *Macbeth* and I like negroes. Where then is the gap? The voodoo violence of the witches' scenes stifles the plot of the tragedy. Macbeth and Lady Macbeth become an American household in which Macbeth trembles and his wife wears the breeches. The terror of the king haunted by Banquo's ghost turns into negro panic in a cemetery, and I deplore the omission of the physician hearing the sleep-walking Queen's confessions and also that the ghost does not occupy the throne at the ball that replaces the banquet scene. But what does it matter! The play's the thing! The Lafayette puts on the sublime tragedy that no other theatre is playing, and negro enthusiasm transforms the end, which is always somewhat confused, into a superb ballet of ruin and death.' Mary McCarthy noting that 'it is significant that our white culture has had to draw so heavily on the negro for the revivification of its classics' somewhat fancifully suggests that 'as in the days of the Empire in Rome, it is the son of the freedman who believes most in the national past, and the elite must depend on the feelings and energies of its ex-slaves to experience its own artistic inheritance.' Certainly there was an explosive energy that came from the actors finally being allowed access to this supremely stimulating work; a process comparable to the explosion of Jewish artistic activity once Jewish artists had been admitted to bourgeois society. This liberated energy was what Welles and Houseman had begun to tap.

For the critics the question was whether this *Macbeth* should be assessed as Shakespeare, or as a show. To expect inexperienced black actors to be able successfully to perform a play which has defeated (as several reviews pointed out) highly trained and experienced white companies was unreasonable; to judge the production purely as a diversion not only seems patronising, but also misses the main point, which is that something big and splendid had been brought off in a section of the community which had been made marginal. It may not have been good Shakespeare, but it was very good Negro Unit, though even here there is a question of whether in the long term it had a beneficent effect. It proved impossible to top The Voodoo *Macbeth*; nor was it a fruitful vein of work to pursue. For the Negro Unit, it was a one-off maroon, a great big noise to say 'we're here!' Welles had an interesting suggestion to follow it up, a *Romeo and Juliet* with black Montagues and white Capulets – a really explosive notion for a New York stage that had just survived its first inter-racial kiss. But by then, he and Houseman had moved on. Welles's artistic Don Juanism starts here.

For him, of course, *Macbeth* was an unequivocal triumph – even though at the time there was some uncertainty about the extent to which it was his sole work. Even Hallie Flanagan, writing five years later, wrote 'it was difficult to tell who was responsible for what'. The programme even contains the phrase 'the production supervised by John Houseman'. To Welles's fury, *The New York Times* had coupled his name with Houseman's in the review, which led to their first row – 'a brief, violent, personal row on the sidewalk' – a taste of things to come. Welles was quite right to claim entire responsibility for the production – it was his, from beginning to end; Houseman had not even been allowed into rehearsals until the very end (another cause of friction: mild now, later to become severe). But it was Houseman who had given him the opportunity, and Houseman who ensured that he was able to make the best of it. Phillip Barber, the head of the New York division of the Federal Theatre Project, said in an interview: 'Welles has all the gall that you can possibly conceive of any human being ever having in all of time, and he always had it. And Jack Houseman is one of the most astute and clever managers that ever lived on shore. And he used Orson and in a sense protected him. He had to fight him to the point of separation practically . . . to prevent him from doing things. But he kept that force contained and moving in a direction, and there was nothing like that.'

The deep underlying knowledge that this was the case – that he needed Houseman, and that somehow this detracted from his glory – grew from this tiny spat on a Harlem pavement into an obsession. It was not unilateral. In an interesting passage from the early part of his memoirs, Houseman describes a relationship that he had with a school-fellow, Eric, the son of the headmaster. The seven-year-old Houseman shared a room with him. 'It was here that my first male relationship was formed – an intimacy based on inequality and fear . . . (it was) HIS house . . . HIS room . . . through HIM the hope of acceptance and the menace of rejection were kept in constant suspense. This created a pattern of insecurity that has persisted through most of my life and . . . left me incapable of parity – a prey to competitiveness in its most virulent form. More than once, at some critical point in a working relationship, I have had the uncomfortable feeling that I was following the emotional curve of that first ambivalent children's intimacy of long ago.' The sense of inequality and aspiration, his desire to be liked and affirmed, simultaneously fearing both rejection and domination, that lurked beneath his surface calm and confidence, was a fertile soil for Welles to sow his seeds of, alternately, affection and resentment. Their relationship was, in fact, a classic instance of what has come to be called co-dependency: an addiction to the power struggle at the heart of the relationship.

This was to come. For the time being, they were the toast of Harlem ('I was really the King of Harlem! I really was,' Welles told Barbara Leaming) and the wonder of Broadway. The show sold out for all of its sixty-four performances; on the opening night it was announced that on Monday evenings, two-thirds of the seats would be set aside for 'persons on home relief who would receive tickets on presentation of relief identification cards'. At 9 o'clock on the first Monday, the box office manager announced that all seats had been filled. The queue, stretching back a whole block, continued to push forward, however, and a pane of glass was broken at the theatre entrance. A year ago, the same crowd had been burning cars and smashing shop windows; now the peace was broken in the name of theatre tickets. Progress of a sort.

At the end of its run at the Lafayette, the show transferred to the Adelphi on West 54th Street, where it played for eleven performances. Jack Carter's self-restraint broke down; he started to drink heavily during a show. When Edna Thomas burst into tears on stage, he simply walked offstage to his dressing room, then out of the theatre, and was seen no more. The Macduff, Maurice Ellis, took over, and it was he that led the subsequent triumphant nationwide tour: Bridgeport, Hartford, Chicago, Indianapolis, Detroit, Cleveland, Dallas; something of a feat. 'You have to take into account that this was 110 black people,' wrote John Silvera, the company manager. 'And travel for black people at that time . . . was not the most pleasant or easiest thing in the world. We were living in a strictly Jim Crow situation where hotel accommodations for blacks were non-existent in many cases. But there were no incidents.' In another way, then, the Negro Unit had blazed a trail. A hundred thousand people of all races saw the show. In Indianapolis, an event occurred that might have set back the cause of black theatre by many years. Maurice Ellis fell ill; his understudy too, was sick, nor did the new stage manager know the role. As if it was what he had been waiting for all along, Welles jumped onto the next plane and took over the role, playing it in blackface. This well-attested event is best contemplated in awed silence.

CHAPTER TEN

Horse Eats Hat/Doctor Faustus

ONCE MACBETH was running, Houseman did some quick, hard thinking. The Negro Unit's next play – partly the work of Gus Smith, one of Houseman's associate directors, who also directed and starred in it – was *Turpentine*, a dramatisation of the plight of Negro workers in the Florida pine woods. Decent but dull, it ran for as long as *Macbeth*. By contrast, Zora Neale Hurston, one of the writers attached to the Project, produced a version of *Lysistrata* so inflammatory that it was impossible to stage. Bored by the one and frustrated by the other, Houseman began to reconsider his position. He acknowledged to himself that, however worthy the Negro Unit may have been, there was only one person with whom he wished to work, and that was Orson Welles. The excitement, however complicated by their separate expectations of each other, proved addictive. Welles gave Houseman the sense of creative exhilaration that he was unable – yet – to muster on his own. Without it he felt dull; felt the way he looked: solid, smooth, middle-aged. In the screenplay for *The Cradle Will Rock*, Welles describes him as follows: 'Now in his early thirties he conveys an impression of greater age by virtue of a magisterial air, wholly natural and unforced, and already impressive.' He must find an honourable way to extract himself from the Negro Project.

There is something both admirable and appalling about the frankness with which Houseman analysed and then served his needs: 'I must leave the Project on a note of triumph, abandon my position with the Negro Theatre (turning it over to those to whom it rightly belonged) and risk my whole future on a partnership with a 20-year-old boy, in whose talent I had unquestioning faith but with whom I must increasingly play the combined and tricky roles of producer, censor, adviser, impresario, father, older brother, and bosom friend!' It's hard to admire his cavalier attitude to the Unit: he *could* have stayed on; *could* have found other producers who could have brought up standards, if he had really believed in it. For the negro profession, the Unit wasn't a career move, or an excuse for getting away with amusingly outrageous productions: it was a once-in-a-lifetime opportunity to break down social and artistic obstacles that destroyed the hope and dignity of many millions of Americans. He was fully aware of the shallowness of his attitude (as he was fully aware of every one of his shortcomings) and admits to it in one of the bleakest sentences in his autobiography. 'At the last moment, I was filled with that sense of loss and sorrow and of guilt that I have felt with each of the many departures and desertions of which my life is the sum.'

But there was no going back; he was led by a sort of compulsion towards Welles, addicted to the adrenalin Welles engendered, and impelled towards the great fame and theatrical excitement that he knew were beckoning. He was not, of course, unaware of the strangeness of this move in personal terms: 'if I did subordinate myself, consciously and willingly, to a man twelve years younger than myself, it was the price I was willing to pay for my participation in acts of theatrical creation that were far more stimulating and satisfying than any I felt capable of conceiving or creating by myself . . . I must immediately supply those new theatrical opportunities of which he dreamed and find fresh scope for Orson's terrible energy and boundless ambition, before someone else did and before he became wholly absorbed in the commercial success-mill which was beginning to grind for him.' He was aware that to launch out into the commercial theatre of 1936 was an impossibility; somehow he must find a way of keeping within the bounds of the Federal Theatre Project which, for the time being, could provide them with everything they needed.

Harking back to those sessions at the top of Sardi's a year before, when Houseman had first been exhilarated by Welles's approach to the classics, they conceived the notion of a Classical Unit within the FTP. It was not difficult to persuade Hallie Flanagan – herself immersed in the classics, especially the Elizabethan classics, which would inevitably form the cornerstone of the repertory – of the value of such a unit; 'the Federal Theatre,' she wrote, 'was committed to the belief that a people's theatre could be occupied in no better way than by production of the classics.' She had, moreover, exactly the right theatre on her hands, the Maxine Elliott on 39th Street, which the WPA had just rented from the Shuberts. So Houseman and Welles got exactly what they wanted, when they wanted it. It was a bold decision of Flanagan's, since the Federal Theatre Project, having survived the early crisis of *Ethiopia* and to a large extent confounded the Cassandras who had predicted mediocrity and incompetence, was now, after a year of existence, coming under increasing fire from a right wing implacably opposed both to the perceived radical persuasion of most FTP shows and to the very notion of subsidy in the arts. Essentially the opposition to the FTP was a branch of opposition to the New Deal. As long as Roosevelt was strong, the Project had a chance of survival, though from this point on it was always under threat, from within and without. There had already been cuts in the budget, sufficient to provoke a one-day strike by FTP workers. The fall of 1936 was the run-up to the crucial December election, Roosevelt's bid for a second term. His critics were on the attack, and the Federal Theatre Project, a minor but highly visible example of the New Deal in action, was a prime target.

Harrison Grey Fiske led with a comprehensive assault in the *Saturday Evening Post*, in August 1936, under the punning title THE FEDERAL THEATRE DOOM-BOGGLE. At the bottom of the page is a cartoon showing a smiling Roosevelt waving a Promissory Note: 'We, the undersigned, promise to pay the national Debt of $35,000,000,000.00 with interest. Signed: American parent, American youth.' FDR leans on a MORTGAGE ON AMERICA. Fiske immediately discerns a conspiracy: first to kill the National Theatre (a bill to create such an institution had been passed by Congress days before the establishment of the Federal Theatre Project, after which the National Theatre was quietly dropped); second to destroy Broadway. He quotes Elmer Rice: 'The finish of the commercial theatre predicted by me for two decades is now in sight and inevitable. The present system is archaic and its ability is the only test of a play's worth.' Then there were the freeloaders. 'Scores of impostors made the pay rolls. These included amateurs, office workers, "singing waiters" from village joints, miscellaneous Harlem negroes, idle welfare workers and plumbers. An especially hospitable welcome was extended to communists and those of radical leanings, white and black.'

Fiske detects subversion. The Living Newspaper comes under particularly savage attack: 'And so, in this perfectly natural way that has been told, it happened that a play in which a member of the government is personated attacking the US Supreme Court, and the radical party in the audience is delighted with a tableau that represents the Communist International Program for this country – a work of playwrights employed by the government – was produced in a NY City theatre rented by the government, acted by actors hired and trained by the government, with an official government symbol on the door.'

Even the Project's triumphs are denounced: 'On April 14th *Macbeth* at the Lafayette: floodlights, a big brass band and thousands of excited Harlemites gathered in the streets, blocked traffic and necessitated a detail of police to open a lane for visitors. Thus the initial Shakespearean foray under government auspices was ushered in.' Welles and Houseman were in the line of direct fire: 'It proved to be a shameless degradation of the cosmic tragedy, the scene of which was transferred to Haiti, and its profound metaphysical background was converted into a frenzied voodoo jamboree. Not a vestige of the power, beauty and meaning of the titanic work remained.' How Welles and Houseman must have hugged themselves.

Fiske then stops pussy-footing around: 'the Federal Theatre's hair is full of communists . . . they found inspiration in the fact that Mrs Flanagan cherished the ambition to Russianise our theatre, to transform it into "the true theatre which reflects the economic forces of modern life." ' His triumphant conclusion reports that the Theatre Veterans' League had accused Mrs Flanagan and her colleagues of using the FTP primarily 'as a means of disseminating communistic propaganda . . . Helen Arthur, head of the Manhattan Theatre, has invited the cast to tea in the lobby, for the purpose of studying the Soviet Theatre and the theory of government back of it.' Somehow, tea in the lobby is to Fiske as sinister as the Soviet system itself. When the Veterans' protest was made public, Flanagan simply pointed to the track record.

Of course it is true that there were communists in the Federal Theatre Project, and it is certainly true that the work was broadly left wing. Harry Hopkins had roundly declared that they were 'for labor, first last and all the time. WPA is labor – don't forget that.' And there is no question but that Mrs Flanagan had swallowed the vision of Soviet Russia as a nascent utopia, especially in matters theatrical. However, she was no more a Marxist than Roosevelt himself. They shared a belief in the mobilisation of labour, and sought to correct what they perceived as a flaw in the capitalist system. Neither desired to overthrow it, much less to replace it with a system absolutely alien, as both of them believed, to American history and the American way of life. Their critical view of the capitalist system was strongly in tune with the times, both in the population at large and within the artistic community. While Broadway ran ever further into the past, or cloud cuckoo land, the Federal Theatre Project insisted on relating everything to the present, regarding it with a challenging eye, believing that it was the job of the theatre not to anaesthetise, but to stimulate, the citizenry. It was naturally regarded as a threat, at many levels. Against this background, Hallie Flanagan must have greeted the notion of a Classical Unit with pleasure and relief.

Confident that Welles and Houseman would turn out challenging work, she was none the less grateful that the plays they would choose could scarcely be accused of being left wing. As it happens, the first play that the Classical Unit chose to do was neither classical nor left wing; it almost defies categorisation, particularly as staged by Welles. In fact, it wasn't even put on by the Classical Unit, because both Welles and Houseman hated the name. Receiving a government document formally initiating the unit, they were delighted to discover that their official designation was Project 891; that became the title of their organisation. The incongruity of their new home, the Maxine Elliott Theatre, delighted them too. Built for the mistress of the financier J.P. Morgan, it was a 900-seat jewel-box: 'For eight years I have cherished consistently – though I am a woman,' Elliott wrote, 'the dream of building a theatre that should be small and intimate; that should be beautiful and harmonious to the eye in every last detail; that should be comfortable for the spectators, and, behind the scenes, comfortable and humane for every last player.' There was gold silk on the auditorium walls; English veined marble lined the lobby walls; the façade was of Dorset marble.

Until recently it had been the home of Lillian Hellman's long-running *The Children's Hour*. It is a measure of the starkness of the times that the Shubert organisation had little faith in their ability to find a successor to it, preferring to lease out the theatre for an exiguous sum to the Federal Theatre Project. Miss Elliott (who had long ago retired but was still alive) might have been a little surprised to find her exquisite pink dressing room commandeered as Welles's office, and even more surprised to see passing through its doors the procession of 'ageing character actors, comics and eccentrics that delighted Orson's heart . . . middle-aged, garrulous ladies with bright coloured hair whom nobody else seemed to want and a number of bright young ladies' all auditioning for a place in 891's first production, Labiche and Marc-Michel's vintage farce, *An Italian Straw Hat*. The play had been chosen specifically to mop up the pool of performers left without anything to do after the dissolution of their units. The vaudevillian faction was predominant, which tipped the balance in favour of opening with Labiche; at the same time they announced their second play, *Doctor Faustus* (with its own – more limited – opportunities for knockabout comedians). Shamelessly, they justified the inclusion of *An Italian Straw Hat* by claiming, no doubt accurately, that nineteenth-century French farce was a genre taught in schools – a fact which is none the less hardly a basis on which to construct the repertory of a classical company.

Behind this show, influencing it in innumerable ways from the beginning, was Virgil Thomson. It had been his idea to do the play in the first place, and his was the inspired title of their version, *Horse Eats Hat.* Thomson suggested both the translator – the poet, dancer and librettist Edwin Denby, another American denizen of the Left Bank and habitué of Miss Stein's salon – and the composer, Paul Bowles, not yet a writer (not yet, in fact, a composer, properly speaking, but he had Thomson's imprimatur, and that was all that seemed to matter, on this project). When Denby and Welles went about adapting the translation – which they did in the manner that seemed best to suit Welles, writing all through the night, one taking it in turns to doze while the other wrote, then Welles reading it out loud – the end result was an extraordinary mixture of Paris and the Middle West: precisely the combination that made Virgil Thomson himself so striking. As far as the music was concerned, Thomson advised Bowles at every turn, and finally orchestrated what he wrote, since the younger man had no experience in that sphere. He was at very least a godparent to the show, and took properly godparental pride in it. His contribution was made for his own amusement, and out of affection for Houseman. Welles continued to irritate him, but he was fully aware of the size of his talent and the prodigiousness of his energy. He simply found him intellectually insubstantial, socially gauche and lacking in proper seriousness as an artist. Apart from that, he liked him a lot. 'Working with him in his youth was ever a delight,' he wrote, 'also a lesson that might be called Abundance in the Theatre.' Notwithstanding, he took pleasure in pricking Orson's bubble. He and Houseman made a point in conversing in French whenever he was around, which infuriated him, as it was meant to.

This was a small tension in what were, by all accounts, wildly amusing rehearsals. Denby and Welles had taken the wonderful old play (which had been seen a decade before in a production by Richard Boleslavsky for American Laboratory Theatre, when it was greeted with bewilderment) and seized on its almost surreal progression from incident to incident to create something which owed a great deal to American vaudeville and almost nothing to the French genre of the same name. It became in their hands all form and no content: a delirious string of gags bearing only the most tenuous relationship to the basic situation, thus somewhat tampering with the nature of the original play.

French farce is utterly unlike English farce, which is an extension of the nonsense tradition, also nightmarish but a child's nightmare, nor does it bear much resemblance to American farce, which is usually a celebration of eccentricity and tends towards unbridled zaniness. French farces, especially those of Feydeau and Labiche, are rigidly rooted in a real world, and their plots have a grinding relentlessness that has been compared, not without justice, to those of Sophocles. They devolve without exception on sex – either the longing for it, or the illicit consummation of it. Real sex is entirely absent from both English and American farce.

What Denby and Welles did to *An Italian Straw Hat* was to turn it into an American farce, a wild farrago of the incomprehensible in pursuit of the unbelievable. Maintaining the Parisian setting, Denby and Welles none the less make all the characters unmistakably Mid-Western: Fadinard is Freddy, Nonancourt his father-in-law to be is Mugglethorpe, Beauperthuis, the husband of the woman whose hat is eaten becomes Entwhistle, Trouillebert is called Little Berkowitz, 'better known as Gumshoe Gus, of the pantry school', and so on. The incongruity of these people apparently perfectly at ease as their carriages (or rather cars, since the piece had been updated to the Edwardian era) whizz past the Eiffel Tower only adds to the general barminess of the action. The text has been thoroughly Americanised: DAISY (the maid): 'What's the bride like?' JOSEPH (the valet): 'Oh . . . countrified . . . but plenty mazooma.' Characters are given to Will Rogerisms like 'What in Sam Hills is the matter with her?' and 'Creeping Jesus!' (which got them into hot water with the censors). Sometimes the script becomes positively surreal, as when the guests for the party are announced:

> Dowager Lady Sucker
> Duchess O'Grady
> A large piece of pastrami
> A simple tick from Siam
> The three little pigs
> The teeth of Gloria Swanson

This text, full of corny jokes, dadaist riffs and schoolboy double entendres (the second verse of Mugglethorpe's song about his rubber plant went 'And when of an evening your mother/Unbuttoned her blouse and began/She fed one and I fed the other/With the aid of my watering can') was simply the pretext for a non-stop demonstration of physical theatre of a kind that can rarely have been attempted before or since. Only the resources of the Federal Theatre could have made it possible, and only someone given an absolute free rein could have carried it to the extremes to which Welles took it. His production was, in effect, an anti-production: everything that could go wrong, did go wrong, not for the characters – for the show. Labiche's universe of treacherous conventions and devastating coincidence was replaced by treacherous scenery and terrifying mise-en-scène: collapsing proscenium arches, collapsing chandeliers (fifty years before Andrew Lloyd Webber attempted the same thing), and, particularly hair-raising, collapsing actors, occasionally hurtling to what seemed to be their deaths. Where Labiche's characters are trapped in the remorselessness of the plot, Welles's actors are overwhelmed by the physical production.

Welles was at his most jovially demonic in rehearsal, possessed by a spirit of almost unstoppable invention, regardless of life or limb. As well as the ex-vaudevillians and broken-down tragedians, he had surrounded himself with friends and contemporaries – Joe Cotten, Arlene Francis, Paula Laurence, Chubby Sherman – and with them any trace of inhibition he may once have had disappeared. Like a huge child, he romped gloriously through rehearsals, cheered on by the company. Welles's ability to laugh at himself, at life, at almost anything at all – never deserted him; any of his collaborators or friends, before listing the torrents of rage or the storms of inspiration, will first cite laughter as the predominant memory of time spent with him – laughter which was often quite silly, and which could leave him (and you) helpless, with tears streaming down your faces. But there was hard, disciplined work, too. For things to appear to be going wrong, it was essential that they went absolutely right, and this required drilling, not only of the technical crew, but of the actors. 'He fed them every line, every inflection. It was like Reinhardt mouthing Schiller,' said Edwin Denby.

Welles was very sweet with the older actors, the ex-vaudevillians, the broken-down tragedians, the one-time showgirls. People who had been subjected to his whirlwind ways were astonished at the gentleness of his dealings with this senior citizenry of the theatre. For the younger actors, he delighted to give them ever more amusing and audacious business. 'Everyone,' said Paula Laurence, 'had their own aria.' 'Can you faint backwards?' he asked her one day. 'I said of course – so I did. I'd never done anything like it in my life before – but I just went straight back, and I was six inches from the floor before Joe Cotten caught me.' The prop-maker and puppeteer Bill Baird had dropped by to deliver part of the eponymous horse just as

Welles was trying to get Hiram Sherman to fall into the orchestra pit. 'Hiram said he wouldn't do it. So I went, "Whoop!" like that, and did a flop and landed on my back in the orchestra pit. Everybody applauded and Orson said, "Mr Baird, you're hired." I wasn't on the Project. I didn't get paid. I was just a stage-struck kid.'

There was only the mildest tension between the relief artists and – slightly more of them than the statutory 10 per cent – the non-relief players, those who had separate incomes. These included Joe Cotten and Arlene Francis. Francis, in her own words then 'Queen of radio soap operas', arrived for rehearsals one day wearing a suit with orchids; one of the reliefers wisecracked: 'WPA orchids, I suppose.' Despite the occasional touch of persiflage, Welles had bound his disparate company into a whole. The only sign of resistance came from Virginia Welles, who one day dared to say: 'I don't think this is right.' 'But I do,' replied Orson, whereupon she threw a milk-shake at him. He would accept any suggestion from anyone; but to have a suggestion of his own refused (particularly by his own wife) was unacceptable, smacked of criticism. That was intolerable to him. Of course, Virginia's outburst may not have been unconnected with the nights without number he spent away from their duplex, nights when he preferred to adapt plays, or rehearse, or carouse or simply disport himself elsewhere. And maybe she was struck from time to time by the irony of being cast as Myrtle, the hapless would-be bride of Freddy, humiliatingly condemned to trail round after her man, uncomprehending, as he pursues she knows not what.

The only other serious check on Welles's high spirits was Houseman. There is a photograph of the two of them standing together in the stalls of the Maxine Elliott: the black rage on Welles's face is only matched for intensity by the look of miserable concentration on Houseman's, all conversation having clearly come to a complete standstill. It was Houseman's unhappy lot to point out the realities of the situation to Welles – any situation. He may have done so with more or less tact, but whatever he said would have enraged Welles who was only interested in possibilities, not in limitations. Houseman's job, in Welles's view – his function in Welles's life – was to make things happen, not to prevent them from happening. Even a suggestion to the effect that he was going to be denied something was enough to awaken oceanic feelings of emptiness and impotence; the immediate outcome of which was rage. The tragic situation that Houseman had constructed for himself was that he had allied his destiny to someone who profoundly resented the only gift he could offer: his sense of what was practical. Houseman wanted something: he wanted to be a part of Welles's work. This was intolerable to Welles. He gladly accepted the input of his collaborators; it was absorbed and integrated into the concept. But Houseman wanted partnership; shared credit. Welles's sense of his own worth was insufficient to share any credit. He needed his achievement to be endorsed unequivocally; like Walt Whitman, his cry was 'O if I am to have so much, let me have more!'

With the rest of his team, by contrast, he was relaxed and happy, and they liked him. Denby told Aaron Copland that Welles was the 'most talented man in town'; Paul Bowles, a man so unsensual (pretty well, according to Thomson, asexual) that it is hard to imagine him and Welles in the same room together, let alone in the rough and tumble of rehearsal, was first amazed by, and then impressed by, him: 'Within ten minutes of our meeting, Orson shocked me by remarking coolly that he saw no hope of there being anything but fascism in Spain. How right he was!' Welles's certainty in his theatrical instinct was beginning to be matched by a general assurance in worldly matters. For his startling young boss Bowles wrote, or rather assembled from existing scores ('in that way one can have varieties and richnesses of texture almost never available in music run up rapidly' according to Thomson) a delectable series of 'overtures, intermezzos, meditations, marches, even a song or two'; Nat Karson, goaded by Welles, produced as bold a visual language for Americanised Labiche as he had for Haitian *Macbeth*. Since the deconstructing scenery was to be the central theatrical event of the production, he was faced with a double challenge. It had to be beautiful; and it had to fall apart. He provided a gorgeous series of Paris backdrops and front cloths including rooftops, the Champs Elysées, Montmartre, la Pigalle, and that indispensable element of farce, doors, of which he had provided seven in a single flat, and a practical fountain; not to mention a plethora of brassy American vaudeville outfits. Karson was of course in charge of all the special exploding scenic effects which Bill Baird built; at one point, moreover, there are five two-dimensional cars onstage. The lighting was more straightforward; bright and sharp, as befits comedy. With Feder, of course, there could never be harmony. The screaming matches continued, to Welles's delight and Feder's inexpressible fury. It seems that Welles could never resist goading him. He was lucky not to have been hit; Feder had been banned by the union for a while after striking one of his subordinates. On the other hand, Edwin Denby, suddenly shouting at Feder one day, found that he crumpled completely. Whatever his personal crisis, however, he made his usual distinguished contribution to Welles's tightly organised mayhem.

The show had been announced in *The New York Times* under the headline WPA PREPARES A NOVELTY. Apart from informing its readers that the show was the newest variation on 'the old Labiche–Michel French farce of 1850', that Orson Welles and Edwin Denby had adapted it, that it had been placed 'in the peg-top pants period' and that 'Mr Welles will also be leading man, playing his favorite role, an old gaffer', the nature of the novelty was unexplained. The *Times*'s short paragraph is indicative of a certain confusion as to what to expect from this latest manifestation of the already bewilderingly diverse Federal Theatre Project; the first night was a leap in the dark for all concerned, actors and audience alike. The only clue offered by a glance at the programme was the scale of the enterprise; on that level, only the FTP could possibly have produced it.

There were seventy-four actors on the bijou stage of the Maxine Elliott Theatre for that first night, including, in addition to the named characters, the world's grandest countess, its most corrupt valet and an ageing cuckold with the gout; wedding guests, party guests, a bevy of Tillie's girls (the Giggling Girls) and two regiments of Zouaves; a maid on roller-skates. In the pit there were thirty-five musicians; an additional women's orchestra played in the boxes during the interludes. The prop list requires, amongst other things seventy-two hat-boxes and five hundred pounds of rice; the show opened with a prologue (not in Labiche) in which the original equine crime is re-enacted: the horse eats the hat. Bill Baird had made the horse – body in brown plush; head papier mâché; roller skates attached to its hooves – and very splendid it is. A photograph on the first night shows it entering a taxi. Operating it were Edwin Denby 'and Carol'. 'If *Macbeth* had in Orson's hands turned negroid and Wagnerian, this classical French vaudeville became a circus,' wrote Virgil Thomson. Marc Connelly saw the show a little way into the run. He describes that same Act One finale in vivid detail:

> The last scene of the first act was a ballroom in a Paris mansion. It was crowded with guests waltzing to the music of an improbably large band of zimbalon players, augmenting the conventional orchestra in the pit. The dancers floated around a fountain in the centre of the ballroom. (You must remember another object of the FTP was to provide jobs for technicians.) The fugitive hero of the piece, played by Joseph Cotten, whom we had seen being chased

> by half the population of Paris, dashed onto the stage pursued by gendarmes. The dancers and the music stopped as the hero leaped like a gymnast to the branches of a chandelier. As it swung back and forth, pistols were whipped out from full-dress coats and décolleté gowns. Everyone began firing at the young man on the chandelier. Simultaneously the fountain rose yet higher, drenching the fugitive until the chandelier, on an impulse of its own, rose like a balloon out of range. While the shooting kept up, 10 liveried footmen made their way through the crowd. As the curtain began to fall they announced to the audience with unruffled dignity: 'Supper is served.' At that moment the curtain shut off the scene –

Which itself fell clean onto the floor, to be followed by the final descent of the house curtain. At that carefully planned and diligently rehearsed moment, Muriel Draper, inveterate collector of theatrical events, was heard to cry, according to Virgil Thomson, 'It's wonderful! They should keep this in the show!' The evening was by no means over. Marc Connelly continues:

> a lady cornetist in a hussar's uniform appeared in an upper box and offered a virtuoso demonstration of her skill –

Houseman takes up the story:

> – a loud and brilliant solo of Paul Bowles's variations on the *Carnaval de Venise*, with *Hiawatha* as an encore. Hardly had her well-merited applause begun to diminish when, in the upper stage box opposite, a mechanical piano broke furiously into *Rosy O'Grady*. The noise must have broken the sleep of a drunken guest, a member of the Countess's ill-fated party, who now appeared, lost and leering, from behind the pianola, seemed to feel himself trapped up there and started to climb out over the edge of the box into the auditorium . . . with a great cry he slipped and fell and remained hanging, head down with one foot caught in a railing, swinging like an erratic pendulum over the heads of the audience while the mechanical piano switched to Liszt's *Hungarian Rhapsody No 2*.

Marc Connelly met up with John Dos Passos at the interval. Tears of pleasure were running down their faces; they had been the only two people in the packed auditorium who had laughed at all. Returning for the second half, they sat together, and again screamed with laughter; again, they were the only people in the building to evince the slightest pleasure in the proceedings. Joseph Losey saw the production, too, and thought it 'imaginative, vigorous and delightful, and I hadn't expected it'. That's real praise: from an enemy. 'I was so impressed by this production that I went home and sent Welles a three-page wire . . . I thought it was the best theatre production I had ever seen in the United States. After this telegram I never heard from him.' (Welles was convinced that Losey was pulling his leg.) Hallie Flanagan, though she had reservations about the 'odd too physiological moment', pronounced it 'inspired lunacy' and felt sorry for those who didn't see it 'and even sorrier for those who didn't enjoy it'. Flanagan's pleasure on the first night was redoubled by the sight of Harrison Grey Fiske (of the *Saturday Evening Post*'s 'doom-boggling' article) 'rigid with horror making notes in a little book'. The (Hearst-owned) *New York American* was equally aghast: 'dozens of young men and women are compelled by stress of circumstances to participate in this offensive play that represents a new low in the tide of drama. An outmoded farce has been garnered with sewage in an apparent attempt to appeal to devotees of filthy drama sufficiently to overcome the stupidity of plot and ineptness of production.'

For the most part the reviews expressed genial mystification at so much effort being expended to so little effect. 'It looked as though somebody from Montclair High School had just been to a performance of the Swedish Ballet, just read a manifesto by Meyerhold on the idiocy of all idioms of the stage – and had just had a sore case of the colic, with acute caterwauls and all the other sounds of physical distress duly and direly indicated . . . I for one would say them hooray if they'd been sufficiently funny about it for anything like a single minute.' The *Brooklyn Eagle* sharply suggested that 'this sort of calculated nonsense requires a much sharper calculation than they are equipped to give it. It asks for the expert and there is not a single expert on the premises.' (It is absolutely true that a variety artist of the past would have spent years honing a ten-minute routine; in *Horse Eats Hat* there was the equivalent of a hundred such routines.) Watts in the *Herald Tribune* was harsher yet, writing of 'that dismal embarrassment which comes to one when actors are indulging in a grim determination to be high spirited and there is nothing to be high spirited about . . . I found it of surpassing interest that one of the adapters plays the rear section of the play's highly engaging horse.'

When they wanted to be pleasant, like Lewis Nichols in the *Times*, they tried to be as whimsical as the production: 'It is as though Gertrude Stein had dreamed a dream after a late supper of pickles and ice cream, the ensuing revelations being crisply acted by giants and midgets, caricatures, lunatics and a prop nag.' Nichols ends his review: 'Half the audience was pretty indignant and the other half quite amused. It can be fought about at a top price of 55c.' Which they did; the production was sold out, and its more fanatical devotees returned as many as twenty times during the course of the run.

It is extraordinarily hard to assess the production of *Horse Eats Hat*. Some descriptions (even favourable ones) make it sound like an evening of unmitigated hell: an unrelenting series of visual gags piling up one on top of another while actors rush about dementedly, pulling faces, affecting funny voices and funny walks (Welles the worst offender). It may have been that worst of all possible things, a comedy in which the company shrieked with laughter during rehearsals. Laughter is a very serious business, a science. The important thing is to give the audience pleasure, not to have pleasure yourself. The sheer quantity of invention, the Abundance of it (as Thomson would say), is rather admirable, in the abstract, though no doubt exhausting to sit through, a sort of teenaged romp of genius. Put like that, it sounds more interesting. There is yet another way of thinking of it: as an entirely radical project, a dada deconstruction, a demonstration of the absurdity of bourgeois plays – of the notion of theatre itself. Jarry meets Labiche. In that case, laughter would hardly be the object of the exercise, simply exhilaration at watching the whole edifice of expectation blown up before one's very eyes.

Or perhaps it was just zany without being funny, *Hellzapoppin* four years ahead of time, without the talent or the script, a jeu d'esprit carried to insane lengths. Whichever of the above is true, or none, it's an extraordinary phenomenon to have sprung out of the twenty-one-year-old brain of young Mr Welles; and there is no doubt that despite the Virgil Thomson influence, and the brilliant efforts of all his collaborators, it was his, and his alone. 'What started as my idea,' Houseman rather wistfully writes, 'had turned into Orson's private joke.' It was all the more extraordinary for coming immediately after the Voodoo *Macbeth*: eclecticism bordering on promiscuity. It is hard to grasp the nature of the brain that would produce both of these extravagant projects in such swift succession – except in their very extravagance, and in the degree to which the productions are mounted on top of the plays, rather than being realisations of them. In the discredited old formula: it is hard to know what Welles was trying to *say* with either of these productions, except (and this is not an insignificant proposition) that the theatre is a place where extraordinary things should happen, where the audience should be continuously assaulted and stimulated. Here he seems to overlap with Antonin Artaud (who, unbeknown of course to Welles, and purely coincidentally, had only the year before founded his Theatre of Cruelty). It is only an overlap, however, not an identity; the spiritual, apocalyptic dimension of Artaud is quite lacking from Welles. He simply wanted the theatre to be a temple of adrenalin, a place where the audience was electrified out of its mundane life. In this, surprisingly, he was a prophet, not so much of The Living Theatre, but of latter-day Broadway, where any cessation of movement, colour or noise is anathema, an obstacle to the evening's goal: the standing ovation. His ancestors, theatrically speaking, are the nineteenth-century purveyors of melodrama, with its non-stop orchestration of tension and atmosphere. Thrills! Spills! When his approach and the play were in tune, he was among the most consummate practitioners of the century.

As far as the acting in *Horse Eats Hat* goes, it was, for the most part, indistinguishable from the general mayhem. The one actor to emerge from it with real credit was Joseph Cotten 'who will no doubt be sought after by commercial producers', as *The New York Times* correctly predicted. Welles had conceived an enormous affection for Cotten, something very like love. He was everything that Welles would have liked to have been: soigné, good-looking, graceful, balanced – normal. Though he was not deluded about Cotten's range or power, there was a truth at the centre of his temperament and his work that Welles deeply admired. In their personal relationship, from that first radio encounter with the barrels and barrels of pith, laughter had been the bond. But when the laughter stopped, Cotten could find himself being lectured by the younger man, suddenly magisterial, on what was wrong with his life: 'I'm afraid you'll never make it as an actor. But as a star, I think you might well hit the jackpot.' There was laughter in this, too, of course, but a shrewdness and determination that left the older man feeling naive. In *Horse Eats Hat*, Welles gave him his first break; he continued to nurture his career until Cotten no longer needed him. It is one of the few relationships of Welles's life in which he was the servant and not the master; and in *Horse Eats Hat*, he served Cotten very well.

As for his own performance: 'Mr Welles plays the bride's angry father with false nose, false stomach, false voice and false hair, until very little of Mr Welles seems left,' the *Times* said, with some bewilderment. It was generally considered to be something of an aberration. It is worth a little consideration, however, this minor performance in his output as an actor, since it is in a recognisable line of characters created by him; and when an actor finds a type of character with which he feels comfortable, it is always revealing. Richard France (whose study of Welles's theatre is indispensable, detailed and shrewd) suggests that Welles based his performance of Mortimer J. Mugglethorpe, 'a fiercely independent businessman', on his father. This hardly describes the real Dick Welles who retired at forty-three after an increasingly desultory career in order to concentrate on whoring and boozing, but it well enough describes the romanticised Richard Welles that Welles had posthumously invented. 'A prototypical American businessman of a kind that is going out of existence,' Welles said to Martin Gabel of Mugglethorpe. Just as well, perhaps; as written by Denby and Welles, he is a sentimental hick. A photograph of Orson in character suggests someone of baroque and decrepit appearance – a forerunner of his Ben Franklin make-up from *Si Versailles M'Etait Conté*, fifteen years later. As the piece in *The New York Times* had said, the old gaffer was a favourite character of his, one with which he felt very much at home; it is interesting that this recurring character should be identified with his father. In reality, Dick Welles was slim and dashing; even at the end (when he was, after all, only fifty-eight) he remained debonair through his dissipation. The problem was his ungraspability, his ultimate elusiveness. No, this other father, substantial, rather ponderous, but definitely *there*, was a projection of something else, a desire for solidity and groundedness that eluded Welles quite as much as it eluded his father. It is interesting to note that frequently actors most successfully project the thing they least are but would most like to be – to the confusion both of their loved ones and themselves.

As far as Welles personally was concerned, he was far more prominently featured in the reviews for *Horse Eats Hat* than in those for *Macbeth*. Mostly this attention was in order to disparage the present effort: 'His versatility and enthusiasm make him a person worthy of consideration and respect. It comes as a sort of anticlimax, therefore . . .' and he could have written the rest himself. 'It is a government-subsidised release of all Mr Welles's inhibitions . . . Mr Welles, the triple threat of the evening . . . Mr Welles (wonder-product No. 1 of Project 891) . . . Mr Welles, an unusually gifted young man of the theatre of several nations.' He was news now, whatever he did. They hadn't quite decided whether he was a good thing or a bad thing, but he was definitely a thing to be reckoned with. He had arrived, but as a phenomenon, not as an artist. No one doubted his intelligence, his talent, his personality: the question was: what would he do with all these things?

Horse Eats Hat did not hold Welles's attention as an actor for long, nor did it have to. He intended to play the part for no more than the first week of the run. Not sufficiently stretched by the manic rehearsal schedule of *Horse Eats Hat*, plus his never-ending round of radio quickies, even before the opening of the Labiche, Welles had started rehearsing in another play: *Ten Million Ghosts*, by thirty-year-old whizz-kid Sidney Kingsley, prestigious author of the Pulitzer prize-winning *Men in White* for the Group Theatre, and *Dead End*, an enormous hit, for which Norman Bel Geddes had created one of Broadway's most famous designs, a slice of street life whose verisimilitude caused gasps. The new play, based on documentary material, was an attack on the munitions industry; Welles was to play the hero, a radical poet who reveals that the German and French munitions manufacturers were in collusion during the First World War, conspiring together to prevent bombing of their plant, thus prolonging the war. The play ran for no more than two weeks; had it run for longer, presumably Welles would have continued to direct for Project 891 but not to act.

Curiously, the moment he and Houseman had established the Classical Unit, they both looked for work elsewhere: Welles to act, Houseman to direct. In Houseman's case this may have had something to do with money (he was still on $2.86 per week) but this was hardly the case with Welles, whose earnings were rising astronomically as more and more radio programmes sought his services. In fact, in both cases their sudden absenteeism had deeper motives. For Welles, the part of André Pecquot, poet and aviator in *Ten Million Ghosts*, was the sort of role a young leading actor should be playing: romantically doomed and passionate. His attitude to acting was always equivocal. He rarely admitted to enjoying it, and, as Virgil Thomson indicated, his mind was not often in it. 'Welles, as an actor, for all his fine bass speaking voice, never did quite get into a role; his mind was elsewhere. He discovered many an actor's talent; his own he seemed to throw away.' None the less, he felt that he needed to prove himself – especially in the great roles, but also, particularly in the earlier part of his career, as a young star. 'I was obsessed in my hot youth,' he told Leslie Megahey on BBC television, 'with the idea that I would not be a star.' And elsewhere, he told Peter Bogdanovich – modestly refusing to compare himself with John Barrymore – that 'what I do have in common with Jack is a lack of vocation. He himself played the part of an actor because that was the role he'd been given by life. He didn't love acting. Neither do I. We both loved the theatre, though. I know I hold it, as he did, in awe and respect. A vocation has to do with the simple pleasure you have in doing your job.'

A further reason for accepting the part was that it was a major production on Broadway of an eagerly awaited new play. So far, Welles's triumphs had been decidedly off-Broadway. Neither of these motives seems to have been sufficient to animate him towards the venture. As often in the future, he was present in the flesh, but absent in spirit. Charles Bowden, the stage manager, observed that 'the moment rehearsals were over, Orson would disappear. Sidney Kingsley started ranting and raving. "Where the hell is Orson?" We discovered he was running two blocks down to rehearse *Horse Eats Hat*, shouting as he went "Got to get rid of this Broadway crud, get down to 891." ' Once *Horse Eats Hat* had opened, Orson handed over his role in it to his chum, Egerton Paul, who had up till then been playing Augustus, and operating the nickelodeon. Paul was a tiny, dapper man, which may have resulted in a shift of emphasis in the play. Whether anyone would have noticed as the scenery crashed around the characters' ears, is, of course, another question. Down at the St James's Theatre, where rehearsals for *Ten Million Ghosts* had now transferred, Sidney Kingsley had installed a cot with pillows in the stalls, in order to snatch a nap during the immensely elaborate and much extended technical rehearsals. Not to be outdone, Welles brought one along, too. 'We had to climb over these two cots,' reports Charles Bowden.

The opening night was shifted several times giving rise to rumours that the government was going to ban it. In fact the delays were due to the complexities of Donald Oenslager's design: it was enormous, comprising ten realistically detailed sets, requiring two eighteen-foot revolves to operate; a cannon in Act Two; and elaborate effects like having a midget far upstage in one scene to suggest depth. In addition there were, according to Sam Leiter, a panoply of mixed-media techniques: 'a flashing screen of headlines, bulletins, newspaper clippings, photographs, cemetery crosses, and so on'. No wonder Kingsley needed his cot. Welles was not at his most helpful during the technical rehearsals. There was, according to Chuck Bowden, a moment in the play when Welles's character wanted to show a film. There were, as part of the setting, two large china blackamoors at either side of the screen. Welles refused to act with them; but Kingsley was adamant. Welles gave in surprisingly easily; at the dress rehearsal he simply smashed the figures in the dark during a black-out, sweetly enquiring, 'How did that happen?' They were never replaced.

Even the first night was dogged with disaster: the curtain stuck halfway up for the whole of the first scene; there were problems, as there always are, with the revolve. The reviews, though respectful, were poor. '*Ten Million Ghosts* is not the sort of play a man can politely ignore, nor rise up from in a composed state of mind,' said Brooks Atkinson in the *Times*. 'Nor can he honestly ignore the fact that the characters are placard stencils and that the drama is a cumbersome snarl of story. On his biggest subject Mr Kingsley has written his least spontaneous play.' Richard Watts in the *Tribune*, echoing Atkinson's reservations, pointed an accusing finger in one direction: 'Nor can I say that the acting of Orson Welles in the role of the disillusioned young lover is of help to the drama.' He does, at any rate, look unexpectedly handsome in the moustache that he affected for the role; it is unlikely that this afforded him much consolation.

One scene which struck reviewers as effective is commented on by Welles, quoted in Peter Noble's book *The Fabulous Orson Welles*: 'At the end of the second act, the munitions makers are in a private theatre, watching newsreels from the battlefields showing wholesale slaughter. As the newsreels show innocent young men being needlessly butchered, I, as the idealistic youngster, rose to my feet and protested against the whole bloody affair. The munitions makers also rose to their feet and, silhouetted against the scene of butchery, they retorted, "But this is our business!" Second act curtain.' The suggestion is that this scene may have had some influence on the celebrated scene at the beginning of *Citizen Kane* when the reporters watch newsreels of Kane. 'That is one of the biggest pieces of schweinerei I've ever heard in my life,' roared Welles when Peter Bogdanovich put the suggestion to him directly. 'In *Ten Million Ghosts* there is a scene in which a home movie of war atrocities is run off in an apartment somewhere in Europe. I never saw the scene because I was in my dressing room during the six days that the play ran.' Another Wellesian mystery. He adds, 'I fell asleep onstage on the opening night, but that's another story.' Perhaps it was during the home movie scene – in which his character certainly does appear – that he fell asleep.

After the eleven performances of *Ten Million Ghosts*, Welles came back to the Maxine Elliott, unable to resist from time to time the temptation of taking back his old part of Mugglethorpe. Houseman had not yet returned from his leave of absence. While they had both been otherwise engaged, the Project had undergone a small, interestingly significant crisis: the wife of a certain Congressman Dirkett had come to a performance of *Horse Eats Hat* and been scandalised by its bawdiness; Congressman Dirkett immediately denounced it as 'salacious tripe', and put in a complaint to the WPA, which had duly sent a representative to investigate. This was one of the perils of working for a government agency. In the American theatre at large – the private sector – there was no censorship and there never had been. An attempt only a few months later to introduce it was repulsed by all sides of show business. Yet here were the investigators (admittedly somewhat apologetically) picking over the minutiae of *Horse Eats Hat* in a way that will bring nostalgic smiles to victims of the British Lord Chamberlain's office, or indeed of the Hayes Office in America. MEMO: LESTER SCHARFF TO PHILLIP BARBER (Head of the New York division): OCT 26 1936: '1) Joseph (the servant) places his hand on Daisy's (the maid) knee and lightly strokes her leg . . . this is somewhat unfortunate in occurring so soon after the rise of the curtain as it has a tendency to key the audience for this sort of thing. 2) 'It's nice to see a pretty little pussy' . . . should be immediately deleted. 3) 'It is alright; they're cousins.' This is obviously one of the lines which fall into the inoffensive category, but the audience undoubtedly read into it a double meaning. 5) Mugglethorpe . . . makes use of the expression 'Creeping Jesus.' This is unquestionably funny, but I am afraid we can anticipate difficulties and possibly hear from the more religious members of our audience. 13) 'I don't care what shape it's in; it's bound to fit.' In this dialogue we have one of the most definite examples of double meaning and the audience again, of course, chooses to place a soiled construction on it . . . it is a pity,' the commissioners conclude, clearly embarrassed by their task, 'that plays of this kind should be subject to emasculation because the minority choose to consider them "dirty." But since I know of no way of purifying the mass of auditors before they enter the auditorium, I am afraid it will have to be considered for deletion.'

The phrase 'emasculation' in this context may have afforded the acting directors of Project 891 a merry laugh. They replied with perfectly straight faces. TED THOMAS AND EDWIN DENBY MEMO TO PHILLIP BARBER: '1) Business considered objectionable has been deleted. 2) "It's nice to see such a pretty pussy" becomes "lassie." 7) Business referred to has been deleted. Queeper has definite instructions never to make any gesture below the waist line.' They appended a note: 'In the absence of Mr Welles and Mr Houseman, we wish to state that we do not consider the implication of salaciousness in this play justifiable . . . we believe that much of the fun of the play lies in the madness of many of the lines which are certainly laughed at in all innocence. Several of the reviews, in fact, made reference to Gertrude Stein in this connexion.' Their lack of practice in outwitting the censor shows in the absence of horse-trading (two damns for a bloody): the whole affair is quite understandably bewildering to them.

Shortly afterwards, Welles was back, and Houseman was not far behind. Both of them had wounds to lick. It is as if they had had affairs which hadn't worked out and had rather sheepishly come back to the marriage. Houseman had been directing Leslie Howard in *Hamlet*, and it was a more or less unmitigated disaster, certainly for him. True to the rules of a clandestine affair, he had managed to avoid letting Welles know anything about it until it was inevitable, 'since the mention of any theatrical activity except his own provoked in Orson an automatic reaction of ridicule or rage'. As if there were a curse on it, everything about the production had gone wrong from the beginning. Leslie Howard chose his own cast, including some duds, and he hadn't learned his lines. Virgil Thomson who was writing the music fought incessantly with Agnes de Mille who was responsible for the dances; Stewart Chaney's huge eleventh-century settings dwarfed Howard and forced him into a heavy-handedness which betrayed his natural gifts. The production and Howard were both critically slaughtered in the wake of John Gielgud's triumph in the same role only a month before, which was still running. Houseman retired, hurt. If he had expected sympathy from Orson, none was forthcoming. 'Orson had chosen to regard my *Hamlet* activity as I had regarded his appearance in the juvenile lead of *Ten Million Ghosts* – as a sort of absurd and shameful interlude of which the least said the better. It was more than two years before I undertook any new theatrical work of my own. For now, I was completely committed to my partnership with Welles and happier within the creative collaboration of that partnership than I could be, by myself, on the outside.' He had, as the saying goes, got it out of his system.

Welles had returned to Project 891 chastened, too: but not reconciled. While Houseman now blissfully proceeded as if their relationship were stronger than ever, Welles was restless. For the time being, however, there was the next play: *Doctor Faustus*. This had been on Welles's mind for a long time; it was one of the plays proposed for the Woodstock Festival two and a half years before. It contained two elements that were always close to his heart: magic, and high-flown verse. As far as the verse is concerned, Welles might have been born to play Marlowe. As a Shakespearean actor, he lacked access to the pressure of the verse, and to its breathtaking variety; intelligent and beautifully spoken though his performances of Shakespeare invariably are, he is inclined to fall into a sonorous, monochromatic mode. He lacks rhythmic flexibility. What he has is superb tone and a wonderful command of legato, perfect attributes for the rendition of what has been called Marlowe's 'mighty line': great arcs of verse that soar and swoop, arias independent of character or situation. This essentially rhetorical writing suits him perfectly, and he fulfils it as few other actors of our time have been able to do, a notable exception being the late Richard Burton, another rhetorical actor. Both Burton and Welles when they play Shakespeare attempt to make him rhetorical; it soon becomes dull, as if a singer were to attempt to sing Mozart like Wagner. All the bubbling and varied life becomes subdued in the attempt to make a splendid noise. Marlowe was his man.

There is no doubt, either, that he felt special kindred to the character of Faustus himself. 'There was a deep personal identification which, across a gulf of three and a half centuries, led him to the heart of the work and to its vivid re-creation on the American stage,' wrote Houseman. 'The truth is that the legend of the man who sells his soul to the Devil in exchange for knowledge and power and who must finally pay . . . with the agonies of eternal damnation was uncomfortably close to Welles's own personal myth.' It might also be said that Faustus, last of the long line of Marlovian 'over-reachers', was, like Welles, driven to achieve ever more, unable to rest content with what he had done, and intolerant of any restriction on him. There is a chilling resonance for Welles in the lines from the Prologue which compare Faust to Icarus:

> Till swoll'n with cunning, of a self-conceit,
> His waxen wings did mount above his reach
> And melting, heavens conspired his overthrow!

The identification goes even deeper, and darker, according to Houseman: 'Orson really believed in the Devil . . . this was not a whimsey but a very real obsession. At twenty-one Orson was sure he was doomed . . . he was rarely free from a sense of sin and fear of retribution so intense and immediate that it drove him through long nights of panic to seek refuge in debauchery or in work.'

> And long ere this I should have done the deed
> Had not sweet pleasure conquered deep despair.

'Quite literally, Orson dared not sleep. No sooner were his eyes closed than, out of the darkness, troupes of demons – the symbols of his sins – surrounded and claimed him . . . in retribution for crimes of which he could not remember the nature, but of which he never for a moment doubted he was guilty.' It is interesting to note that Houseman was himself no stranger to haunted sleep; but he had dismissed his demons. 'My nightmares grew to such an unbearable pitch of violence that I knew I had to break through them or go mad. When they finally scattered and dissolved, they drained away some of those other, deeper terrors – of rejection, poverty, death and annihilation – that haunted me for so many years of my life.' Welles seemed unable to. Perhaps he never tried, for fear of what he would actually discover. Maybe like many another artist, he was convinced that his demons were the source of his art. They were certainly, if we are to believe Houseman, the driving force behind it; perhaps they also destroyed it, finally, by forcing him ever on and on.

Only Houseman and a very few others saw Welles in this light. To most people he was a conquering hero: Tamburlaine rather than Faustus. He laid into this production with overwhelming energy and intensity. His concept of *Doctor Faustus* was intimately bound up with magic, and he focused his considerable ingenuity and industry on realising that aspect. Magic was not only a theatrical diversion; it was a metaphor of both power and delusion. The magician has control over nature and the elements, but what he secures for himself is insubstantial. Faustus uses his magic for banal purposes, as much as for exalted ones; similarly Welles used theatrical magic for the crudest low comedy (the Pope's procession, with meats flying up into the air, a pig dancing an obscene dance, hats flying off, and then the entire scene disappearing, leaving Faustus alone), and for effects of breathtaking beauty. In *The Cradle Will Rock* screenplay, he describes the scene of Helen's appearance.

> FAUSTUS *opens his arms as though in a gesture of ritual, and out of the murk there appears* HELEN OF TROY, *high in the filmy air, as though riding a cloud. He looks up at her dark form and as he looks, takes wing and flies up, through the air to* HELEN*'s side.)*

FAUSTUS

O thou art fairer than the evening air
  Clad in the beauty of a thousand stars!

(Now, as Faustus rises to her, HELEN *is aglow with new light . . . we realise that she wears a mask.* FAUSTUS, *embracing her, raises the mask . . . Her head falls back, loosening a great fall of reddish-blonde hair. It reaches almost to the ground above which she floats.)*

FAUSTUS

Her lips suck forth my soul – see where it flies!
  Come, Helen, come give me my soul again.

(The kiss is obviously real, and held for longer than is customary on the stage. The instant before a first titter might be heard, he drops her head – her body – There is nothing there! Nothing but her cloak – FAUSTUS *himself falls down from the sky. He hits the floor hard. (It is almost like an accident.)*

And now, at the sound of a tolling bell, he raises his head and we see he is no longer the young man (nor the mature scholar) – He is suddenly old . . . This is the last midnight, the hour when DOCTOR FAUSTUS *must keep his dreadful bargain . . .)*

A bravura description of bravura effects, thrillingly reported from the front line. The first element in the creation of these effects was light: Feder's department. Grumpily observing that 'the performance was run continuously with no intermission, putting the whole burden of changes in tempo and space into the realm of the worker in light', he continues: 'A very curious phenomenon appeared in this production. In the past, light had been the tool to illuminate what was to be seen; now light itself was to take the place of the object that was to be illuminated. The stage took on a new freedom, because by means of its very darkness one could light up a scene at the back of the stage, and with nothing intervening, the entire foreground space disappeared.' So many lights were hung from the grid that it broke under the weight, according to Richard France; the cast had to abandon the theatre for a week. There was, or appeared to be, no set; the light was the set. In order for this principle to work, the stage was made into a black shell; the floor was painted black, too. Bill Baird, now doing the job for which he was trained – making puppets of the Seven Deadly Sins – described the apparatus required to make the effects work: 'He had miles of black velvet and tubes of about five foot maybe twenty foot long on the inside of which he had lekolites – and they made columns of light . . . it is one of the first times they used these long tubes with light in them . . . they just came down and hit the floor – and they wouldn't be more than five foot wide.' The techniques were those of variety magic acts from time immemorial, allied to the new lighting skills that were being developed day by day.

Paula Laurence, who was playing Helen of Troy, reports the use of columns of black velour 'to produce Living Statues as in the circus'. The stage was mined with trapdoors: 'The stage manager of that show must have lost his mind. I think they had fifteen trapdoors, with all kinds of effects and smoke pots and everything.' So many holes had been cut in the stage that it had to be reinforced. Further to facilitate the transitions, Welles commissioned Paul Bowles to write linking passages for the unearthly combination of oboe, saxophone, clarinet, trombone, and harp that, in Stark Young's words, 'can often float you into the scenes' Elysium'. Sound, as always, was a crucial element in Welles's production: radio speakers were used to amplify the voices from hell.

Rehearsals took place at night to allow construction by day, and they had to be onstage, with the lights. 'Going into the Maxine Elliott during rehearsals was like going into the pit of hell,' wrote Hallie Flanagan. 'Total darkness punctuated by stabs of light, trapdoors opening and closing to reveal bewildered stagehands or actors going up, down and around in circles; explosions; properties disappearing in a clap of thunder; and onstage Orson, muttering the mighty lines and interspersing them with fierce adjurations to the invisible but omnipresent Feder. The only point of equilibrium in these midnight seances was Jack Carter, quiet, slightly amused, probably the only actor who ever played Mephisto without raising his voice.' Welles had taken another gamble on Carter; on the understanding that he would stay with him and Virginia in the duplex on 14th Street for the duration of the run. The rest of the cast were recruited from *Horse Eats Hat*. Chubby Sherman was playing Robin, the principal comic servant; in the role of the clown, Welles cast the ancient vaudevillian Harry McKee. He put Edwin Denby in charge of him.

'Go across the street and make a dance for him,' Welles told Denby. 'I want him to have a dance.' 'And I said, "What kind of a dance? You mean a morris dance?" He said, "Yes, yes, anything you want" . . . I didn't know what to do because I realised he was an old man . . . so I said to him, "What could you do?" and he said, "Well, I have this bauble and I could play golf with it." And I said, "OK" . . . one time he spat on the floor and pretended it was a golf ball. It was really in the spirit of an Elizabethan clown.' Just as Denby had been roped in to teach an old man how to morris dance, so Paula Laurence and Virginia Welles were sent off to the public libraries to research the costumes, tracing out the patterns for Welles to choose from. His costume drawings (based on what they found and straightforwardly Elizabethan) are skilful and witty; they give, as the best costume designs do, vivid intimations of character, practically useful to the actor. Welles's adroitness in this area has been little commented on, but it is clear that had he wished to make his living as a designer, he could have done. The industrious wardrobe mistress for Project 891, charged with making up the costumes from these sketches, was Beverly Juno; with her face 'like a chocolate-box blonde' she had once been a showgirl. Now she had a bad leg. 'She liked a drink. I'd go and see her in the wardrobe and she'd say: "Anybody who doesn't like this life is crazy!" I sure agreed with her.'

In addition to her ancillary activities as costume researcher, Paula Laurence (the leading lady, after all, however brief her appearances) was told by Welles to make a mask for her character, shiny clown white. She got hold of some plaster of Paris, and duly made a life-mask of herself: a tricky business. Welles then came along and painted it with a faintly green tinge, applying brass clippings to it. 'Orson designed everything you saw on that stage. Everything originated in Orson's head; it was the duty of everybody to fill it out – it was presented with such clarity.' 'Hands-on' is a phrase that might have been invented for Welles; it is part of what gave these rehearsals such excitement, an excitement generally absent from a professional theatre in which each department's activities are strictly demarcated, and the director is an umpire, adjudicating, occasionally advising, but almost never actively participating. On another occasion he demanded a thunder drum; none in existence was terrifying enough. He gave instructions for one to be built: 'Here was one of the goddam biggest bull-skins you can imagine. They stretched it wet over a frame made of four-by-tens. It was so strong that it pulled the corners of the frame apart. But you never heard a thunder drum like it . . . all you had to do was take a hammer and just touch it, and you get a sound that went all through the theatre. You could even feel it in your seat.' The palpable sense of creativity, not so much striking while the iron is hot, but making the iron hot by striking it, was everywhere, and unforgettable to those involved. No wonder Jack Carter was drawn to it, simply to sit and watch; no cabaret, no mere entertainment could have been as enthralling as watching the show being made before his very eyes in the furnace of Welles's Promethean art. There was no calmly premeditated master-plan; Welles made it up as he went along. This is the source of its validity. It may also have denied it the solidity which only comes from well-laid foundations.

The journalist Helen Ormsbee, who was often to write about Welles, came to interview him in the midst of all this activity. Under a typical headline (ACTOR, WRITER, DIRECTOR AND NOT QUITE 22) she described the scene: 'Orson Welles is a young man to delight the heart of the original Doctor Faustus, that legendary magician of the sixteenth century. For Welles practices the art of acting with the aid of strange processes. He appears and disappears on stage amid blinding flashes of light, he directs rehearsals by talking into a machine that carries his voice wherever he wants it to; he knows his way about those resorts of necromancy known as broadcasting stations.' Orson told her that 'our aim is to create on modern spectators an effect corresponding to the effect in 1589 when the play was new. We want to rouse the same magical feeling, but we use modern methods . . . I think Marlowe would be delighted . . . every production of our classics should make its own impact in its own way . . .' Then his fascination with his new toy bubbled over: 'the production's greatest novelty is the use of the radio method of directing. It was a big timesaver. Whenever I wanted anything or anybody, I spoke into a microphone, and my voice reached the remotest parts of the building. People came running as if they had heard Gabriel blow his trumpet.' Another form of magic, giving delusions of God-like power proving equally insubstantial when the current is switched off. Perhaps this is what gave Feder his image of Welles as the Wizard of Oz.

Welles was keen to tell Ormbee about another of his innovations: a thrust stage, the first ever in a Broadway theatre. 'The performer frankly admits that the audience is present. Sometimes he talks to it, whereas with the picture-frame, the audience is assumed to be non-existent.' Like the skilled magician he was, Welles loved to insist that there was nothing up his sleeve. This apparently Brechtian notion was not so much a verfremdungseffekt as a ploy to take the audience into his confidence, only to pull the carpet from under their feet. (He made a curious observation about the apron stage, quoted by Richard France, which, like many of his sayings, is bewilderingly the opposite of the truth. 'The apron causes the actor to use a larger manner and more voice than when he is separated from his listeners by the proscenium arch. The nearer you are the bigger you must speak, to hold attention.' Gnomic remarks of this sort – he had, all his life, a weakness for obiter dicta – make one wonder how much he really knew about acting. It may be that the thought is only half formed, released before it had reached its definitive meaning; it is certainly true that you need as much *energy* if you're in close proximity to the audience, but you most certainly don't need more voice, or a bigger manner. This is just wrong.)

The technical rehearsals were held after the stage crew and the actors had gone home, leaving only volunteers (generally including Jack Carter, 'girlfriends', and Virginia) to stand under the lights while they were focused. There was much shouting, mainly by Welles and Abe Feder. Around four, hamburgers, milkshakes and brandy were brought in; they would break at 8 'because we couldn't see any more, but also because Welles usually had a radio call at nine . . . despite their satanic complication, I remember those unending electrical sessions with pleasure as a time when we were all very close together – in our work and in our lives.' Houseman well describes the pleasure of technical rehearsals when everything is practical, and things begin to happen before your eyes: effects dreamed of now actually being realised, others unimagined suddenly occurring as if by divine intervention. Though often fraught, these sessions are the first real intimation of what it is you might all have been striving for. Especially if they run on into the small hours – in Welles's case, the larger hours – there is great intimacy in the camaraderie of the team effort, everybody tiring together, surrounded by the debris of the production, empty coffee cups and cigarette butts, all the usual rules of conduct in the auditorium suspended.

As Welles went off to his first radio job of the day Houseman would then go home to his girlfriend (who as it happened was born, Houseman does not fail to note, with appropriate irony, on the same hour on the same day in the same month of the same year as Welles) and they would make love, have breakfast, and sleep; then he would go back to work again. To Mrs Leaming, this identity of the birth dates of his mistress and his partner is scandalous, proof positive of his unhealthy interest in Welles. To Houseman, it is entirely appropriate and agreeable, a symptom of the rightness of things at this period. He was – ten, or even fifteen, years late – living out his youth, through and with Welles. This was the epoch of their greatest closeness, though never at any time was there anything remotely resembling harmony. As the first night approached, Welles became more tense and neurotic, 'pathologically reluctant' to expose his work to Houseman, whose judgement he trusted. The relationship was always most strained when Welles was, as now, playing the leading role. 'At such times, I became not merely the hated figure of authority, to be defied and outwitted as I refused further delays and escapes, but the first hostile witness to the ghastly struggle between narcissism and self-loathing that characterised Orson's approach to a part.' After that he was welcome again.

'It became my main responsibility to preserve him from exhaustion and confusion, to disentangle the essentials of the production as he had originally conceived it from that obsessive preoccupation with insignificant detail in which he was inclined to seek refuge when fatigue or self-doubt had begun to wear him down.' He *was* tired; dangerously so, kept going by tobacco and alcohol and pills. He could have taken a little time off from the radio shows, at least during the period of technical and dress rehearsals, until the play had properly opened. If anything, he seemed to increase his workload, to flog himself on near to the point of collapse. 'Welles's dress rehearsals and previews were nearly always catastrophic – especially if he was performing. I think he enjoyed these near disasters; they gave him a pleasing sense, later, of having brought order out of chaos and of having, singlehanded, plucked victory from defeat . . . suffering more than the usual actor's fears, Orson welcomed and exploited . . . technical hazards as a means of delaying the hideous moment when he must finally come out onstage and deliver a performance.' On one occasion, Welles, backstage, overheard two familiar voices: the painter Pavel Tchelitchew and his friend Charles-Henri Ford. He summoned Houseman, refusing to perform unless they were removed. As they left, reports Houseman, 'I could hear Orson's voice from behind the curtain howling triumphantly of Russian pederasts and international whores.'

The first night was on 8 January 1937, and the audience had been well primed for the show by the advance publicity:

ANNOUNCING

A production extraordinary!

The first great Elizabethan play

THE TRAGICAL HISTORY OF DOCTOR FAUSTUS

The Magic of MACBETH   The Humor of HORSE EATS HAT

Salesmanship at its most ingenious: the result was an enormous success (it ran for 128 performances, having been seen by 80,000 people, including 3,600 standees), the most admired, with *Julius Caesar*, of all of Welles's and Houseman's work in the theatre. There was remarkable unanimity among the critical fraternity. The few dissenters either disliked or dismissed the play (Burns Mantle, describing the play as 'nothing but a curio' went on to say that it seemed to him that 'the people's theatre would be better employed, considering the greatest good for the greatest number, in producing plays of timely significance . . . a modern play of social import . . . would have achieved far more in the way of clarifying and stimulating a puzzled people's thought') or they abhorred Welles's techniques – 'arty and ineffective', said Gabriel in the *New York American* – but then he was Hearst's man, and the Federal Theatre Project was high on his hit list. With unexpected vehemence, Edith Isaacs in *Theatre Arts Monthly* wrote that the acting, 'including that of Mr Welles, is so bad that it is better without comment'. But these were rare. Most reviews vied with each other in praising the production, and describing its effects.

'The prologue is spoken in complete darkness with only a lantern held up by the chorus to illuminate his face,' said the *Catholic World*, welcoming the play, evidently delighted to see important matters like the salvation of the soul once again under serious consideration in the theatre. 'Then far away at the back Faustus is disclosed surrounded by his diabolic books . . . from the velvet shadows [of the stage] emerge the brilliantly costumed players, while spotlights illumine certain spaces . . . intimate scenes are played on the apron . . . Mephistopheles first is seen as gigantic horrible eyes which Faustus conjures into a human head.' Brooks Atkinson (invariably crediting both Welles and Houseman with the production) wrote that they have 'boldly thrust an apron stage straight into the faces of the audience and the settings reduced to a somber background of hangings. Modern stagecraft is represented by the wizardry of lighting; the actors are isolated in eerie columns of light that are particularly well suited to the diabolical theme of *Doctor Faustus* . . . the modern switchboard is so incredibly ingenious that stage lighting has become an art in its own right . . . when the cupbearers of Beelzebub climb out of hell, the furnace flares of purgatory flood up through a trapdoor in an awful blaze of light, incidentally giving the actors a sinister majesty. On an unadorned stage, the virtuoso light gives the production the benefit of one modern invention that is most valuable to the theatre.'

Feder ('whose name,' wrote Stark Young, 'seems one of the attendant spirits or demons of the piece') was warmly and universally praised, and the scenic simplicity that the novel use of light had made possible was hailed by Atkinson in the *Times* as revolutionary and beneficial: 'on the whole it is an invigorating thing to strip Elizabethan drama of all the gorgeous things that silently plague the acting . . . Project 891 has done us all a major service. By adding a little originality to a vast fund of common artistic sense it has shown us how an Elizabethan verse drama can be staged without becoming a formal ordeal . . . it is hoped that the Federal Theatre will stage some of the less familiar plays of Shakespeare in the same original and exhilarating fashion . . . after a brisk hour or so in the presence of *Doctor Faustus* . . . I am inclined to believe that our recent Shakespeare revivals have been on too large a scale for the good of the acting, and that the settings have been too imposing. They have competed with the acting.' This revelation was an unexpected bonus of the FTP. 'Being primarily an emergency labor enterprise with a good deal of artistic latitude, the Federal Theatre has an enviable opportunity to try some of the mad things that are forever whirling through the minds of restless rehearsal people, and the case of *Doctor Faustus* is an experiment that has succeeded brilliantly.'

The acting was liked, but not acclaimed – apart, that is, from Harry McKee, the clown. 'Harry McKee was the best clown I have ever seen in Elizabethan revivals,' wrote Stark Young, 'the brain really seemed to chase about with the lice he talked of.' Jack Carter was acknowledged for his originality, but not for his technique. 'He brings something to the part,' said Young, 'that the ordinary actor of the rant school might miss; he needs only to feel like troubling himself to study the vivid meanings written there.' As for Welles, 'he finds in the title role the opportunity for which he has apparently been waiting. He misses, perhaps, some of the music of the noble lines, but he gets resounding drama into them, and in the final scenes where he listens to the striking clock and waits to pay his soul to Lucifer, his acting has great emotional force.' Many other notices spoke, not entirely enthusiastically, of his deliberate pacing and articulation. Atkinson: 'Mr Welles has a heavy and resonant voice that takes possession of a theatre; as Doctor Faustus he gives a performance deliberate enough to be understood and magnetic enough to be completely absorbing.' Stark Young had him speaking the poetry 'far above average' and credited him with 'some veritable triumphs of reading, not least those passages that hang in the air by almost less than a thread.'

There is little sense in the notices of what Houseman and others detected in Welles's performance: a feeling of personal identification. Paula Laurence said: 'There were so many dark sides of Orson's nature, his belief in evil forces, that suited Faustus.' Neither this, nor the intensity of his relationship with Jack Carter's Mephostophilis, were remarked on. For Paula Laurence, 'Jack Carter, that hostile, troubled, violent man, played Mephostophilis with a tenderness towards Faustus that was totally riveting and unexpected.' Houseman, in describing the scenes between them, reveals his deep love of Welles's work, his involvement in it, and his precise observation of it. In his account, one senses his eyes riveted on the stage, night after night. 'Their presence on stage together was unforgettable: both were around six foot four, both men of abnormal strength capable of sudden, furious violence. Yet their scenes together were played with restraint, verging on tenderness, in which temptation and damnation were treated as acts of love. Welles was brightly garbed, bearded, mediaeval, ravenous, sweating and human; Carter was in black – a cold, ascetic monk, his face and gleaming bald head moon white and ageless against the surrounding night. As Orson directed him, he had the beauty, the pride and the sadness of a fallen angel . . . he listened to his last gasping plea for respite . . . with the contemptuous and elegant calm of a Lucifer who is, himself, more deeply and irrevocably damned than his cringing human victim.' Faustus's sin was the terrible sin against the Holy Ghost: 'pride and despair, inextricably linked, must be so called', in Roma Gill's words: the very combination that made Jack and Orson soul-mates.

The private relationship of the two men seems to have lost some of its intensity. Partly this was because they were off-Broadway rather than in Harlem – Orson's territory, not Jack's. Welles no longer needed to prove himself, as a man or as a director. The screenplay of *The Cradle Will Rock* includes a curious exchange between the two:

JACK CARTER

Folks'll start thinkin' that old rumour was true.

ORSON WELLES

What rumour? . . . You and me? Whoever believed that?

JACK CARTER

About me and your wife.

(Orson stares at Jack.)

JACK CARTER

He's so dumb he has to use both hands to find his ass.

I wish it *had* been true. But now word's out about your Jewish pal –

ORSON WELLES

Marc and me? . . . or Marc and Virginia?

JACK CARTER

The combination of your choice, Bubah.

Some of the complexity of their relationship is suggested by this exchange; it must have informed their work onstage.

Critical feeling emphasised that the play had been released to a new audience, and with it perhaps the whole corpus of Elizabethan theatre. Atkinson in his re-review of the production in the *Times* says: 'By being sensible as well as artists, Mr Welles and Mr Houseman have gone a long way toward revolutionising the staging of Elizabethan plays.' Robert Benchley, in his bright and breezy *New Yorker* way, seems to have hit the nail on the head, as he often did: 'The old Marlowe opus trimmed for modern times – you would be surprised what a good show it makes. It seems like one of the best general entertainments in town.' The 'trimming' was substantial; the play ran for just under one hour and fifteen minutes. No one missed those sections of what was widely acknowledged to be a play of mixed inspiration – and indeed, authorship. It is interesting to note exactly how Welles cut and rearranged the play, a much more thorough reworking than the modest revisions of *Macbeth*.

Taking the old play by the scruff of its neck, he fashioned it without inhibition to his own purposes. Its critical reputation, as a play, has never been high; it lacks unity of theme or tone. In the etymologically pedantic sense, it is a satire (satura, a medley). Veering from the sublime (some of the most sublime utterances in all of English dramatic literature) to the childishly prankish, it combines morality play with Renaissance tragic-heroic drama, and was the work of many hands, including Rowley and Bird, incorporating passages from contemporary works, both prose and verse, while the clown John Adams wrote his own jokes. Welles became, in effect, a posthumous collaborator. Not that he wrote any text – he never, in any of his adaptations, did that – but by omission and substitution, created a new play. The nub of this approach is that he didn't interpret the text: he used it. His intention was direct effectiveness, abandonment of obscurity, and vivid juxtaposition of events. There was no political point to this (indeed, a handful of militants had cancelled their seats because the show lacked 'a social slant', prompting Hallie Flanagan to write to her husband: 'I suppose they wanted Lenin's blood streaming from the firmament'). Nor was there an intellectual, much less a philosophical, purpose. Immediacy was the only aim.

After the prologue, with its Icarus image, Welles plunges straight in with Faustus's first line: 'Che sarà, sarà! What will be shall be!' thus cutting Faustus's restless consideration of the intellectual disciplines, and particularly of divinity (in which he detects an absolute fatalism). With this cut, Welles excises the man's essential character and dilemma, reducing him – or enlarging him, as you will – from a questing intellectual to Everyman. The opening speech, recklessly cut about, makes little sense, completely transforming the original from its meaning, 'metaphysics of magicians' is so placed that it appears to refer to medicine, not to necromancy. The provocative phrase 'Get a deity' is rendered 'gain a deity'. Substitution is rife, and it is not always clear why. Sometimes for euphony, sometimes perhaps to justify business. All this, of course, is perfectly Elizabethan practice; the two editions of *Doctor Faustus* are clearly the result of two different productions, in which the actors have recorded their own improvements.

In Welles's version, indisputably authentic Marlowe is hacked about just as much as any of the rest, partly due to an awareness of the limitations of the actors: the longer speeches are cut up and distributed among several voices; surprisingly, his own longer speeches are also altered and cut, at the loss of some remarkably fine passages. He cuts 'Now that the gloomy shadow of the earth, Longing to view Orion's drizzling look, Leaps from th'Antarctic world unto the sky, And dims the welkin with her pitchy breath' starting the speech 'Faustus, begin thy incantations.' He moves all the astonishing exchanges of Faustus and Mephostophilis in their first interview ('How comes it then that thou art out of hell?' 'Why this is hell, nor am I out of it') to after the Seven Deadly Sins, and cuts 'This word "damnation" terrifies not me' – a sop to the Christian faction in the audience. From the soliloquy in scene five, astonishingly, he cuts

> Away with such vain fancies and despair
> Despair in God and trust in Beelzebub!

and also

> The god thou serv'st is thine own appetite
> Wherein is fixed the love of Beelzebub!
> To him I'll build an altar and a church

And offer lukewarm blood of newborn babes!

Too strong, presumably, for New York 1937. There are innumerable small changes to suit the production. Faustus agrees to give his soul to Mephostophilis immediately.

MEPHOSTOPHILIS
Tell me, Faustus, shall I have thy soul?
FAUSTUS
What says Lucifer thy lord?
MEPHOSTOPHILIS
That I shall wait on Faustus whilst he lives
So he will buy my services with his soul.
FAUSTUS
Ay Mephostophilis, I give it thee

which is undeniably exciting and moves things along, but loses out on Faustus's insatiable curiosity, his maggoty intellect, and the haunting lines (admittedly in Latin) about the miserable denizens of hell loving company, so sardonically witty and bleak. Of course, Welles was tailoring the part to his actor. He cuts the spirits' dance – rather crucial, one might have thought, to his dalliance with the spirits, culminating in Helen's appearance. Inexplicably he changes the location of the place – Wittenberg, with its Hamletian associations – to Wertenberg (perhaps he was harking back to *Jew Süss*, in which he played the Duke of that principality). He cuts the long interview with Mephostophilis about the cosmos, including

MEPHOSTOPHILIS
Where we are is hell
And where hell is, must we ever be
FAUSTUS
Come, I think hell's a fable

and Lucifer's intervention, going straight to the comic scene with Robin (Chubby Sherman) to which he adds the scene with the Vintner, then plunges straight into the Seven Deadly Sins, each of whom is allowed only a line or two. After Lechery, Mephostophilis says, 'Tell me, Faustus, how dost thou like thy wife?' The audacity is breathtaking – is it brilliant? or cheap? – then, somewhat jarringly, has the conversation about Lucifer and hell – 'What is that Lucifer thy lord?' – from Faustus's first encounter with him. He cuts Lucifer's stupendous reappearance ('Christ cannot save thy soul for he is just') including his grim parting line – 'Think of the devil and nothing else' – and therefore the invitation to his infernal cabaret, the Seven Deadly Sins. The effect of this is also to lose the crucial theme of Faustus's weakness for sensual diversions, something in which one might have expected Welles of all people to be interested. The Emperor, and the Duke, and the horse-courser are all cut, mercifully, and the scene of Faustus's final night on earth is slightly trimmed; only Pythagoras' metem-psychosis is cut from the final aria, neither Pythagoras nor the migration of his soul being part of the intellectual baggage of the average twentieth-century play-goer. The argument about substitution or omission of obscure phrases has been neither won nor lost; but we always lose something. Every generation of theatre-goers has had to learn the meaning of Macbeth's 'incarnadine' and been the richer for it. As far as Welles was concerned, there was no argument: it was all academic humbug. The play was for the theatre; if the play-goer didn't understand what was said there and then, everyone had wasted their time.

All this is now very familiar practice. No Fringe or off-off Broadway company would think twice about merging characters, redistributing speeches, intercutting scenes. Even in 1937, it caused little stir. The assumption was that Welles had simply cut the boring bits. Far from it; he's ruthlessly got rid of the gold and embellished the dross for reasons of pressing theatrical need. The celestial drama – the fight for Faust's soul – is much less urgent and chilling in Welles's version and Faust's own mercurial nature, with its violent mood swings, is made much more stable and dogged – as suits a rhetorical actor. (A typical cut is 'What walking, disputing, etc . . . But leaving off this, let me have a wife, the fairest maid in Germany, for I am wanton and lascivious, and cannot live without a wife'.) As so often, Welles's approach harks back to an earlier precedent, and forward to something more modern. Welles's way with *Doctor Faustus* recalls Henry Irving's version of the same story, based on the Goethe play (but only just). Irving too used the existing text for his own purposes: to generate atmosphere and theatrical thrills in a series of set-pieces, and to provide a framework for his own unique gifts (he of course played Mephostophilis).

Welles's version is in the great tradition of actor-managerial theatre, the play used as a vehicle for the leading actor's particular talents. But equally it is clear what his version is, in all its essentials: a screenplay, complete with intercutting, lightning transitions, dissolves, wipes and, in the use of the apron stage, an equivalent to the close-up. It succeeded triumphantly. Despite various sententious utterances, Welles was no theorist: he was a pragmatic operator, and *Doctor Faustus* worked, in exactly the way he wanted it to. Nothing that he subsequently did in the theatre – not even the famous *Julius Caesar* of the following year – was more completely achieved. The success was not necessarily in terms of the acting (which was, said Brooks Atkinson, 'not sublime') but in its total effect. For Paula Laurence '*Doctor Faustus* is the definitive Orson Welles theatrical production – it embodied all the things that were special to him: the sense of mystery, the sense of magic, and the majesty of his own gift as an actor . . . he played Faustus in a baroque style that illuminated the text.' Even Mary McCarthy, who had no intention of letting Welles get away with anything, acknowledged that '*Doctor Faustus* was truly successful, for here the formula actually corresponded in a way to the spirit and construction of the original, and one saw a play that was modern and, at the same time, *Doctor Faustus*.'

The new 85c-a-head audience that the Federal Theatre Project had brought into the theatre was agog. Welles himself said that 'the audience was fresh. It was not the Broadway crowd . . . even less was it the special audience one has learned to associate with classic revivals. One had the feeling every night that people were on a voyage of discovery in the theatre.' Paula Laurence noted that '*Faustus* played to just people, you know – they were not intellectually prepared for the arguments. Orson knew how to grab them in the best ways.' Stark Young wrote that 'the audience's attention was such that I have not seen elsewhere in the theatre this year.' In the *WPA Audience Survey Report* for *Doctor Faustus*, in March 1937, the OCCUPATIONAL CLASSIFICATIONS are instructive: PROFESSIONALS account for 284, including 134 teachers, 27 lawyers, 1 weatherman, 1 X-ray technician, 1 aviator; THE ARTS for 117 including 45 writers, 1 dancer, 1 puppeteer, TRADES for 45 including 5 domestics, 1 lifeguard, 1 milkman, BUSINESS for 63. There were 153 OFFICE WORKERS, and 192 MISCELLANEOUS including 134 students, 1 shopper, 1 travel agent.

The reaction to the play was overwhelmingly affirmative: 940 people admired it; 143 preferred not to comment and only twenty were negative about it. It is clear that the Federal Theatre Project had tapped a new, responsive, eager audience. Small wonder that Paula Laurence and her fellow actors felt that 'we should have had a national theatre and Orson Welles should have been the head of it'. This was a notion frequently mooted, in one form or another, during the next couple of years. The idea was beginning to be formed that

Orson Welles was going to be the saviour of the American theatre. His failure to fulfil that expectation was a hard blow for many people.

Welles himself had no intention of forming any national theatre, which is, to put it mildly, a full-time job, allowing of few extra-curricular activities. With the success of *Faustus*, his appetite for work, any work, seemed redoubled. Not only did the run of the play fail to hinder his ever-increasing involvement with radio, the performance itself wasn't allowed to interfere with it. Barely pausing in his headlong rush from one studio to another, Welles arrived at the theatre as Chorus was starting to speak the opening lines of the play, during which he would throw his costume on, arriving on stage just in time for 'Che sarà, sarà!' There was another radio show to do at 8.30 p.m., so as soon as his first scene with Mephostophilis was over he would climb – in costume and substantial make-up – into an ambulance specially hired for the occasion and speed through the streets of New York, bells ringing, to the studio, for twenty minutes giving his all to the radio audience, thereupon returning to the theatre, to watch Christ's blood stream through the firmament. Clearly Welles was of the 'just get up and do it' school of actors. Any notion that some preparation might be useful for what is, though not the longest, by no means the least demanding of roles in the classical repertory, was alien to him.

Actors differ wildly from each other on the question of what is most helpful to them before they actually stand on the stage, some needing silence and sleep, others chat and companionship. Some must eat, while others insist on starving. Yet others need a stiff drink, though their closest colleagues won't let a drop pass their lips till the curtain falls. Welles, unsurprisingly, did not belong to the latter group. In the screenplay of *The Cradle Will Rock*, he sweeps into the theatre and calls out to Augusta Weissberger:

> Tell your mother God sees everything she does and writes it down in a book, and make me three very double martinis. Two of which are for Mr Blitzstein.

There is no point in piety about alcohol in the theatre; for some it is a useful warm-up, for others disaster. It can bring freedom, but also, often, a loss of objective judgement. Its most likely immediate effect is to induce slowness of pace. In the case of Welles, this would not be an advantage. Already prone to measured utterance, he was liable to fall into impassioned (and sometimes inaudible) monotony. His capacity for alcohol was large, as large as his consumption. There were no crude outward effects of intoxication; he did not slur, or fall down. But alcohol cannot possibly increase the actor's responsiveness to impulse or his agility of thought or word, and the emotional freedom produced is likely to result in feeling that is generalised and self-referential. It is a chain of association familiar to all alcoholics: the consumption of a drink leads to a sensation of ease and effectiveness, so is forever after associated with those conditions. For Welles, there was the ever-present longing to produce and sustain adrenalin. If the ambulances and the panic of unprepared performance couldn't do it, perhaps alcohol would.

It helped him overcome his boredom, which set in very early on. The loss of excitement is the beginning of professionalism. The thrill of standing on a stage, of receiving the audience's attention and admiration, the release of becoming someone other than yourself: all these stimuli are transient and superficial. They must be replaced by something much more deeply rooted which takes as its starting point the audience's experience rather than your own. It is to be doubted whether Welles ever reached this point. His lack of proper preparation, either in rehearsal or before the performance, condemned him to insecurity and made it impossible for his work to grow, thus denying himself the real satisfaction of the job. His restlessness as an actor was observed by Norman Lloyd, an admirer of the production of *Faustus*: 'Orson was very well aware of his physical presence and his great voice. I never thought he was a good actor in the theatre . . . he was trying to be Herbert Marshall one night, John Barrymore the next.' Chubby Sherman reports that one night Welles wanted to see a movie after the show, so he urged his fellow actors to 'play it for the record books'. His relationship to acting was paradoxical: he was immersed in its lore and unusually well equipped, physically, to practise it, but he never allowed himself to discover its deep rewards. Like someone who confines himself to casual uninvolved sex and never experiences a real act of love, Welles's acting was statistically impressive, but deeply fulfilling neither for himself nor his audience. Once the immediate sensual thrill was over, nothing was left for either partner. His lack of communion both with himself and with the character he was playing made this inevitable. His idea of acting was purely cerebral; when that is the case, the god can never enter in.

His restlessness was not confined to performances; the Federal Theatre itself began to frustrate him, with its proprietorial behaviour. For them, he was both the jewel in their crown and a thorn in their flesh. He broke every rule of the organisation, and when challenged, pointed to the fact that he was in effect affording them relief: he put a great part of his $1,000 weekly income into the shows, as he had done with *Macbeth*. He thus felt above criticism. Moreover, he was acquiring friends in high places. Harry Hopkins, ultimate boss of all the relief organisations, had met Welles backstage, and had invited him to Washington, where he had introduced him to Mr and Mrs Roosevelt. Restraints imposed by Hallie Flanagan and her henchman Houseman (as Welles saw him) were violently resented. Like a schoolboy whose father's best friend is the Chairman of the Board of Governors, he felt that he had a right of appeal above all their heads. In fact, as he was to discover, this was scarcely true, but it contributed greatly to his increasingly intemperate attitude. He was, of course, completely unable to understand that the Federal Theatre as idea and organisation was something that needed careful cultivation – that his fireworks might, unless carefully contained, set fire to the whole damn thing. There were difficulties within the Federal Theatre Project: for one unit to be perceived as ahead of all the others was very bad for general morale. The input of Welles's personal money (whether known of or not) made for problems of jealousy with other units struggling along on a cough and a spit.

There were even internal problems on 891, with all the other actors having actually to survive on $2.86 per week, while Welles lived the life of a young lord. He and Virginia had left their duplex on 14th Street which they occasionally shared with chums like Paula Laurence and Francis Carpenter ('Hello, this is the maid, Francis') and taken a house at Sneden's Landing, up the Hudson, twenty miles away from Times Square, where his neighbours were such swells as Katharine Cornell and Dorothy Thompson. Coming into town, he would take a motor boat across the water, where he would be greeted by a chauffeur-driven Rolls. Lunch would be at Jack and Charlie's '21' (which might have been named for him, since he at twenty-one was the twenty-one-year-old to end all twenty-one-year-olds). Shaved by a barber at the club, and manicured – his elegantly tapered nails are prominent in a famous contemporary photograph – he adopted the manner of a soigné leading man, an Alfred Lunt or a Bob Hope. 'I see myself in those old stills, and I see somebody that could very easily be thought of as a faggot,' he told Barbara Leaming. 'It was wild camp.' What he seems to be saying is that he had a phase of behaving like a Broadway star actor, something rather different from the combination of the Duke of Saxe-Meiningen and a Burbage de nos jours that had hitherto been his image. He was a compulsive chameleon. Who shall I be?

he seemed to be asking. Of course he was only twenty-one. But the process of self-invention was a life-long habit with him, preferably in public, into a journalist's tape recorder. He kept trying things on for size, convinced people of his new skin, then felt uncomfortable in it – ontologically itchy.

The fact that every penny that had led to the current transformation was personally earned would not have counteracted the impression of private wealth being used for personal satisfaction. The workers in Project 891 shared the general anxiety that relief programmes were in danger of being suspended. Roosevelt's landslide at the end of 1936 on a national as opposed to a purely Democratic ticket had the opposite effect to the expected one: relief programmes were cut by 20 per cent. With the depression apparently receding, there was intense pressure on the government to abandon them altogether. The left, anticipating cuts, rallied, denouncing Roosevelt. In this atmosphere, Hallie Flanagan took personal charge of the highly visible New York arm of the Federal Theatre Project, trying to contain and secure its work. Her strategy was both to limit unnecessary expenditure and to prevent undue provocation: a delicate line to tread, requiring the utmost co-operation from her colleagues at every level of the Project. Her dealings with Unit 891 arose from this strategy, which Welles resented.

The brunt of his resentment was borne, naturally, by Houseman. Added to his habitually hare-like impatience with tortoise Houseman, he now perceived him as an ally of the establishment. That establishment was in fact an embattled anti-establishment, under threat from powerfully organised right-wing forces; but to Welles, it came to seem a bureaucratic conspiracy against freedom of artistic expression – *his* artistic expression, to be precise – and he began to look elsewhere for his creative outlets. Poor Houseman, believing himself to have found a perfect partner – Welles giving him what he hadn't got, and needing him for what he had – while all along, Orson was looking for an out, looking for the opportunity to betray him with someone else. They had desultory conversations about what they should do next. Ben Jonson's *The Silent Woman* was mooted, in a half-hearted sort of way (just as well, perhaps, that they didn't attempt it, in view of the dauntingly difficult text); other proposals were *The Duchess of Malfi* and, more seriously, *Julius Caesar* in modern dress.

There are many claims for the authorship of this notion. It hardly matters whose it was – the idea was clearly in the air – but it is worth noting that the playwright Sidney Howard (author of *They*

Knew What They Wanted) wrote to Houseman in February of 1937 shortly after the opening of *Doctor Faustus* to say that 'Marlowe is pretty exciting to begin with, and you have made him beautiful and lively . . . I could wish that you and Welles would turn your attention to *Julius Caesar* in modern dress (I have such fine ideas on that if you want them). Not the modern drama, I admit, but I have always believed that the best way to stimulate the writing of good modern plays is to keep the classics part of what goes on.' The letter is a testimonial to the perceived importance of Project 891 in feeding the needs of the theatre at large. As it happens, Welles and Houseman agreed that neither *Caesar* nor *Malfi* could be cast from within the Project; and it is true that their first two shows had been unusually amenable to casting from a large pool of miscellaneously talented people. Nothing much for jugglers, puppeteers or vaudevillians in *Julius Caesar*.

The Project drifted. Workers on it continued to feel threatened as Welles and Houseman seem to have lost energy and purpose. The situation was suddenly transformed by the arrival on their laps of Marc Blitzstein's 'workers' opera' *The Cradle Will Rock*. Welles had met Blitzstein after a performance of *Horse Eats Hat*; Blitzstein had immediately fallen for him, and impulsively offered him his new work to direct. 'When I played *The Cradle Will Rock* for Orson Welles, he was just twenty-one, but already an extravagantly brilliant and magnetic theatre man. He fell in love with it straight off and made me promise that no matter who should produce it, he would do the staging, and I was glad to agree.' Just as Virgil Thomson had resisted Orson's combination of girlish vulnerability and masculine exuberance, so Blitzstein fell for it absolutely; Welles took to the composer with equal enthusiasm. They decided to stage the piece for the Actors' Repertory Company. Scenting something new and dangerous, Welles was immediately recharged.

CHAPTER ELEVEN

The Cradle Will Rock

MARC BLITZSTEIN, author of the piece that had so ignited Welles, is a curious figure in American musical life; a curious figure altogether, one of whom Welles was deeply fond. There are innumerable testimonials to his charm and integrity from people as different as Leonard Bernstein and Virgil Thomson, but none of them are able to bring these personal qualities to life. Even his biographer, the admirably thorough Eric Gordon, fails to convey his much proclaimed attractiveness. From this distance he seems merely cold, intellectually ruthless and blinkered. Born in Philadelphia, the son of a banker, he was a child prodigy as both pianist and composer. He studied at the Curtis Institute under Scalero and Siloti (Tchaikovsky's friend and editor, perpetrator of the barbarically cut version of the Second Piano Concerto). In 1926 he took what was the well-beaten path for an American musician of the period to Nadia Boulanger's door. She found him to be a 'born musician' who 'gives the greatest reasons to believe he is to become a *true* great artist'. More daringly he then proceeded to Berlin, and Schoenberg. Loathing the twelve-tone system, he nevertheless found of his teacher that 'as an opposing force to test one's own quality against, he is superb'. Schoenberg finally gave up trying to convert Blitzstein to dodecaphonia with the gracious words: 'Very well, compose your Franco-Russian pretty-pretty music – but stay in the class. You play the piano so well.'

In Berlin he absorbed all that the Weimar Republic at its pluralistic height had to offer, sexually and musically. His sexual orientation was homosexual with occasional heterosexual lapses; musically he was drawn to Hindemith's gebrauchsmusik (utility music) and gemeinschaftsmusik (amateur music for community binding), about as far from Franco-Russian pretty-pretty music as can be imagined. It chimed very well, however, with his new-found Marxist affiliations. He returned to America, where he taught, then came back to Europe; in 1933, he married the Marxist critic and novelist Eva Goldbeck. They adjourned to Majorca, where he composed string quartets admired by his fellow composers, but heard by few others.

Rebelling against the loneliness and, as he came increasingly to see it, the elitism of the life of an Art Composer, he turned his attention to 'that most resistant of all musical media – the musical stage', as Aaron Copland put it. 'His purpose was not merely to write the words and music of effective theatre pieces; he wanted to shape each piece for his own ends, to shape it for *human* needs. He took a certain pleasure in needling his audiences; in telling unpleasant truths straight to their faces.'

It is this needling quality that seems most characteristic; obviously to those contemporaries who valued him so highly, it betokened a moral position that was impressively uncompromising. Welles wrote of Blitzstein, in his unproduced screenplay *The Cradle Will Rock*, that he 'could be described as fine-tuned rather than highly strung. His is the attentive stillness of some birds – one of the predators – a gyrfalcon. Serious rather than solemn, he brightens a room when he enters it.' The conductor, Lehman Engel, wrote strikingly of him: 'He was nervous, full of laughs, somehow "tight", impatient, and – it was always my feeling – bent on self-destruction or failure . . . often his music was almost brilliant, but when it became too promising, Marc seemed to need to prevent its successful conclusion: he would do just about anything to frustrate a desirable resolution.' His emotional life was kept hermetically separate from his professional and social lives; after his wife's death (from self-induced starvation) he was exclusively gay, but he never formed a full sexual-emotional relationship with a man, knowing only one-night stands, preferably with rough trade, until his death in 1964 at the hands of three merchant seamen in Martinique.

The Cradle Will Rock, Blitzstein's best-known work, had followed immediately on the death of his wife in 1936. Now a member of the Composers' Collective, his works up to this point included a Piano Sonata and a Piano Concerto and two operas: *The Condemned* (concerning the anarchists Sacco and Vanzetti), and *The Harpies*. Meeting Brecht, he had played him his song 'Nickel Under Foot', written for a workers' revue. Brecht, impressed, urged him to expand it into a full-length piece about the varieties of prostitution – 'the press, the church, the courts, the arts, the whole system'. Suddenly galvanised by the death of his wife, he set to work furiously on *The Cradle Will Rock*, putting some of his grief into writing it. The result is taut and fierce, but buoyant and funny, too, the work of an absolutely individual voice. Copland, ever generous to his fellow musicians, wrote that 'he was the first American composer to invent a vernacular musical idiom that sounded convincing when heard on the lips of the man-in-the-street. The taxi driver, the panhandler, the corner druggist, were given voice for the first time in the context of serious drama.'

It thrilled Welles. 'Orson was excited by the challenge of this, his first contact with musical theatre,' wrote Houseman. 'I remember listening jealously, with an ill-concealed sense of rejection, to Orson's enthusiastic comments about the piece (which I had not heard) and to his ideas for casting and staging it, which he elaborated for my annoyance.' As usual, Houseman is quite frank about his feelings. When, to his quiet satisfaction, the American Repertory Company folded, Houseman, taking his time, eventually suggested that if they'd play the piece to him, he might find it suitable for Unit 891. They did; and he did. The next step was to play it to Hallie Flanagan. 'Marc Blitzstein sat down at the piano and played, sang and acted,' she wrote, 'with the hard hypnotic drive which came to be familiar to audiences, his new opera. It took no wizardry to see that this was not a play set to music, nor music illustrated by actors, but music + play equalling something new and better than either.' Blitzstein exuberantly reported this in a letter on 3 March: 'Hallie Flanagan . . . is crazy for it, says it's the biggest best etc – and is also terrified about it for the Project. She'll take no responsibility, but is having us – Orson, Houseman and me – fly down to Washington . . . I've apparently turned out a firebrand that nobody wants to touch.' It is a measure of the newly charged political situation that it was deemed necessary for producers and directors to clear their choices of work with the central government. Houseman was convinced that though Hallie Flanagan was fully aware of the dangers of programming such a potentially explosive piece, 'she was determined to fly into the eye of the storm'. As for himself and Welles, the more controversial the better, of course. The distinguished Welles scholar Richard France maintains that Welles and Houseman were eager to escape from the Federal Theatre's confining embrace, into that of the organised left, where they perceived their audience to be. They deliberately chose the show, he believes, because they knew it would be provocative – too provocative for the Federal Theatre Project. If so, they miscalculated, because they had support within the Project from the highest level from the beginning.

The piece itself is unusual in form; in content it is absolutely explicit, a call for unionisation. The story is set in Steeltown, USA, in the throes of a union drive. Moll, a prostitute, is arrested by Dick because she refuses to come over with free sex. She's taken to the night court, where she meets Harry Druggist, once respectable but now a lush. In the same cell are the members of the anti-union Liberty Committee – all of whom, including Harry, are revealed in a series of flashbacks, to be in thrall to Mr Mister, the steel boss who controls Steeltown: 'there is not one of these eminent, deserving citizens who isn't just as guilty as Moll is,' writes Blitzstein. The Rev Salvation was prevailed upon by Mrs Mister to preach peace or war, according to the needs of her husband's business; Editor Daily has printed a phony exposé of Larry Foreman's activities; Harry kept quiet when he knew a young worker was being framed; Yasha, the violinist, and Dauber, the painter, have been bought out by their rich patroness Mrs Mister; President Prexy of the college has supplied academics to support the National Guard; Dr Specialist has falsified medical reports on a steel-worker crushed by a machine. In the final scene, Mr Mister tries to bribe Larry Foreman to join the Liberty Committee; in the heroic finale he is mocked, and the triumph of Labour is hymned. The anonymous names were not present from the start; originally Blitzstein was going to call characters Morgan and Lewis, after industrialists of the day; at some point there was to be a pro-union farmer called Sickle who united with a worker called Hammer.

Dedicated 'to Bert Brecht: first because I think him the most admirable theatre-writer of our time; secondly because an extended conversation with him was partly responsible for writing the piece', it is not a work of great political complexity. Eric Gordon calls it a lehrstück in the manner, presumably, of Brecht–Weill pieces like *The Exception and the Rule*, in which the necessity of strict submission to the Party line is demonstrated; but it doesn't actually have that form – no one learns, except perhaps the moll, no one is changed. And of course there is no Party. It's more a simple cartoon, a rallying piece: a pro-syndicalist cantata, in fact. This dismal description is belied by the lyrics, succinct and vivid, and especially by the music. 'I used whatever was indicated and at hand,' Blitzstein wrote in *The New York Times*. 'There are recitatives, arias, revue-patters, tap-dances, suites, chorals, silly symphony, continuous, incidental commentary music, lullaby music – all pitchforked into it. There are also silences treated musically, and music which is practically silent.' Kurt Weill is the obvious reference (indeed, after the première of *The Cradle Will Rock* Weill went around saying, 'Have you heard my latest musical?'), but the American popular influences that for Weill are exotic and ironic are here entirely idiomatic – there is real jazz, plus hymn tunes, à la Ives. Like Weill, Blitzstein sometimes has recourse to Bach. A lot of the score, in fact, is underscoring to spoken text;

but the songs proper are varied and immediate in their appeal, from the austere ecstasy of the 'Gus and Sadie Love Song', to the chippy satire of 'The Rich' and the tango with riffs of 'Ask Us Again'. 'Art for Art's Sake' enables him to have fun with Beethoven's *Egmont*; while the title song is appropriately punchy. The great number of the score is the one that was the starting point for the whole piece, 'Nickel under Your Foot', a real hit song, the ache in the music quite palpable, intensified by the square accompaniment under the soaring tune, the cleverly simple lyric richly fulfilled.

MOLL
Oh you can live like Hearts-and-Flowers,
And every day is a wonderland tour.
Oh you can dream and scheme
And happily put and take, take and put . . .
But first be sure
The nickel's under your foot.

Go stand on someone's neck while you're talkin';
Cut into somebody's throat as you put –
For every dream and scheme's
Depending on whether, all through the storm
You've kept it warm,
The nickel under your foot.

'The Cradle Will Rock' with its staccato, surging energy and irresistible rhythm is electrifyingly reprised for the finale, ending with the words THE – CRADLE – WILL – ROCK – blasted out by the ensemble.

LARRY FOREMAN
That's thunder, that's lightning.
And it's going to surround you!
No wonder those stormbirds
Seem to circle around you –
Well, you can climb down,
And you can't sit still!
That's a storm that's going to last until
The final wind blows –
And when the wind blows –
The cradle will rock!

Thrilled as always by a new medium, Welles planned to stage the show on a grand scale. He designed huge glass wagons to create the different scenes; the scene plot reveals four parallel moving platforms, screens, a traveller for the moon, and one for hammocks. There were, too, a double-quarter revolve and an ingenious aperture curtain. There was a large cast of solo performers, forty-four members of chorus, black and white, and twenty-four musicians. From the middle of April, the orchestra rehearsed five days a week, five hours a day. The taut, gritty workers' opera was being done to all intents and purposes like a Broadway musical, an odd paradox that troubled a number of people (Hallie Flanagan wrote: 'I didn't see why they needed any scenery'.) Welles produced a leaflet for the show ('opening on June 1st') which is oddly inappropriate; it looks as if it's advertising a rather jolly university revue. The words *The Cradle Will Rock* are boldly written over music staves, with a dancing matchstick-man fiddler (Yasha, presumably), thunder and lightning in the bottom right-hand corner, and, looming above it all, an inexplicable figure with a mortar board and a pile of papers, bearing some resemblance facially to Welles. It is, to say the least, odd. But Welles was in the full flood of his driven youthful energy, increasingly so as the first night approached.

'Even during those early years he was driven to being overbusy. When he was not busy, he was lonely and miserable,' wrote Lehman Engel, the conductor of *The Cradle Will Rock*, adding: 'he was, always has been, and still is, a boy: a Peter Pan too heavy for flying . . . despite his youth Orson was in full charge of whatever he undertook. When he was inclined to lag, Jack [Houseman] sped him on his way. He was inventive, witty, alternately lazy and energetic, and knowledgeable. His thinking was bold and his work usually produced sensational results . . . he never tired of going over the smallest details a hundred times in order to have it precisely as he wished it. He would start at ten in the morning and not leave the theatre. He might dismiss his cast at four the next morning but when we would return at noon, we would find Orson sleeping in a theatre seat . . . Augusta's mother Anna Weissberger . . . would rush down the aisle carrying chicken soup.'

He maintained his usual pattern of pushing himself to extremes in order to engender what he considered to be the necessary levels of adrenalin. If not precisely like Peter Pan, he was certainly, in the white heat of rehearsal, flying like a kite. 'Orson was in a regular fever heat of creativity,' recalled his stage manager, David Clarke. 'And I remember him turning to me and saying, "Did you get that?"

And I'd say, "Yes, I think so," and he'd say, "Well, you'd better, you know," because he couldn't remember ten minutes later what he had done . . . he gave them so much stuff that they couldn't possibly use it all, and still it was just rolling out of him.'

Rehearsals were conducted with the usual substitute props and furniture, the changing positions of the moving trucks marked out on the floor with chalk or tape. It was nevertheless a shock when, at the technical rehearsals, the set arrived. Howard da Silva (Larry Foreman) recalled in an interview that 'as actors, it diminished our size and feeling because the production of the thing just overwhelmed us'. Hiram Sherman says much the same; it is clear that the actors, not for the first time in the history of the theatre, loathed the set. They were already unhappy with the orchestrations, of which, said Sherman, Blitzstein was not yet a master; it had sounded so much better with the piano accompaniment. With the chorus in the basement, singing under the stage, and loudspeakers throughout the auditorium, while the illuminated glass blocks trundled back and forth, the effect may well have been overwhelming in quite the wrong way. Blitzstein's tough little piece had turned into a monumental theatrical statement. David Clarke estimated that 'the production would have cost at that time in the commercial theatre $150,000' – the equivalent in today's prices of $1,000,000.

While all this was inexorably proceeding through a series of typically strenuous and explosive technical rehearsals towards the dress rehearsal and the first public performance, events both within the Federal Theatre Project and in the real world beyond were becoming critical. The economic situation was making it increasingly difficult for Roosevelt to sustain the public programmes which had characterised his earlier period of office. Already anticipating cuts, on 27 May there had been a one-day city-wide stoppage of all WPA work; 7,000 out of 9,000 came out. Hallie Flanagan, addressing a meeting of the American Theatre Council that day, had defended them: 'Federal Theatre workers were striking for what was once described as life, liberty, and the pursuit of happiness . . . if we object to that method I feel that some word should come from this gathering as to a better method.' The blow fell on 10 June, just four days before *The Cradle Will Rock* was due to open: Mrs Flanagan was instructed to cut the Project by 30 per cent; in effect, as Goldstein points out, 'to do so meant issuing pink slips to 1,701 workers'. This was accompanied by an instruction prohibiting 'because of the cuts and the reorganisation' any new play, musical performance or art exhibition to open before 1 July. There was no question in the minds of Welles, Houseman or Hallie Flanagan that this directive was specifically aimed at *The Cradle Will Rock.*

Their assumption was that the show would be considered too touchy politically. Since the beginning of rehearsals, the labour situation had become explosive – specifically in the steel industry. In Chicago, communist-led industrial protest had been met with police gunfire; ten workers had been killed. Blitzstein's show seemed transcribed directly from the daily headlines. Government uneasiness is understandable. Three years later, the *Saturday Evening Post* expressed this in its habitually trenchant fashion. 'Before this date, the WPA chiefs had been fairly audacious in backing pink propaganda, but they became thoroughly frightened when congressmen and others began to murmur. The Blitzstein operetta was supposed to have all the dynamite of Beaumarchais's *Marriage of Figaro,* which was supposed to have touched off the French Revolution.' It is interesting to observe how distant the turbulent events of the period seemed by 1940; in June 1937 there remained a genuine expectation – as there had been since the great crash in 1929 – of revolution.

Roosevelt was quite consciously playing two sets of extremists off against one another. Welles and Houseman had tried to secure themselves against government intervention by inviting Flanagan and the WPA bigwig Lawrence Morris to a run-through; 'magnificent', he had pronounced it. There was enormous interest in the show, mainly from leftist organisations; the theatre had already, a week before the start of public performances (an unusually large number of previews, thirty-one, had been scheduled) sold 18,000 tickets. Welles and Houseman were determined, directive or no directive, that *The Cradle Will Rock* must open. Had they not done so, it would inevitably have seemed that they were bowing to government pressure.

Their first move was to arrange a public dress rehearsal, which duly took place on 14 June, in front of New York's most fashionable and progressive elements. The show itself, plagued with technical problems, went somewhat flatly; the singers were still battling with the thirty-piece orchestra. None the less, the audience went wild at the end of it; a gesture of solidarity. Another dress rehearsal passed without incident. The following day, the 16th, was the scheduled first public performance. The house – 600 seats of it – had been sold to benefit the Downtown Music School where Blitzstein taught; everything was ready for the show to open. But, according to Houseman, 'the customary telegram authorising the production never came'. Instead what he called the WPA's 'Cossacks' were guarding the theatre with instructions to see that no government property was removed. 'The theatre was sealed. Neither the audience, which had gathered outside, nor we, the performers, could enter it,' recalled Howard da Silva, Larry Foreman in the show. 'I made a big fuss, threatened to storm the barrier single-handedly, principally because my new toupee was in my dressing room and I loved it.' Will Geer and Howard da Silva entertained the audience in front of the theatre, Geer singing mountain songs while da Silva, 'continuing to rehearse', gave them one of Larry's speeches about the difference between closed and open shop.

'And now,' wrote Marc Blitzstein, 'the irrepressible energy and lightning drive of Orson Welles revealed themselves. He called us all together . . . in the only green room we had. It was actually the ladies' powder room downstairs. I remember an unexplained pink mannequin standing in the corner. Welles said to us, "We have a production ready; we have a fully paid audience outside. And," said Welles, "we will have our première tonight." ' For Blitzstein, Welles was the uncontested hero of the hour: 'Welles proceeded to solve the problem with an ingenuity, a speed and a daring I can almost not believe as I tell it.' Houseman's account of events is more detailed (some details have been contested) and suggests that Welles was as much at the mercy of minute-by-minute developments as anyone else. The problems were twofold: the simple physical problem of how and where to perform the show; the second, how to do so legally. The musicians' union had stated categorically that if the show were to be done in a commercial theatre, then its members must be paid at regular commercial rates; the actors' union had insisted that the material belonged to the Federal Theatre Project and could only be performed under their auspices. The irony of a pro-union show being blocked by the unions of the people performing it was lost on no one. These objections were at any rate academic in the absence of a suitable theatre. The 'Historical Background on *The Cradle Will Rock*' prepared by Unit 891's press office three days later details the search: 'The Comedy and the 49th Street, it developed, were not union houses. The Empire was done up in mothballs. The seats at the Guild were torn up for a repainting job. The National was too expensive. During much frantic telephoning a smallish man in a dark hat had been trying to tell the boys something . . .' Finally, when they had abandoned any hope of finding anywhere, 'the little man in the dark hat spoke up. "Why not take my theatre?" he asked. He was the renting agent for the Venice.' According to Blitzstein, Welles told the actors: 'you may not appear onstage, but there is nothing to prevent you from buying your way into whatever theatre we find, and then why not get up from your seats, as first-class American citizens, and speak your piece when your cue comes.' The actors then trooped down the several blocks to the old theatre in company with their excited audience (who had been regaled outside the sealed theatre with pamphlets saying YOUR FRIENDS HAVE BEEN DISMISSED! YOU MAY BE NEXT!). Along the way they picked up interested passers-by, while the technicians started to prepare the building for the show. Jeannie Rosenthal finally delivered the piano she had been driving around until the theatre was confirmed.

The Venice (formerly Jolson's 59th Street Theatre) was much larger than the Maxine Elliott: with its 1,700 seats and huge stage (eighty foot by forty-five foot), it had been home to many musicals (*The Student Prince* amongst them) but its history encompassed seasons with the great Shakespeareans Southern and Marlowe and the famous twelve-week visit of the Moscow Art Theatre who played *The Cherry Orchard*, *The Three Sisters*, and *The Brothers Karamazov*. Having somewhat fallen on hard times, the theatre was only used now by an Italian company at weekends; when the audience for *The Cradle Will Rock* finally entered the auditorium, they found the Italian flag draped over a box, an emblem of Mussolini's state which was then swiftly torn down to a huge roar of approval. The audience was now performing itself, everyone knowing beyond doubt that they were present at an event. Welles and Houseman too were elated by the drama of it all.

'Like partners in a vaudeville team, Orson and I made our entrance together from the wings onto the stage.' Houseman's brief speech expressed his gratitude to Hallie Flanagan and the Federal Theatre Project for backing a show that no one else would but insisted that the show had to open. Then, according to Lehman Engel (who had stuffed Blitzstein's score down his trousers to smuggle it past the guards at the Maxine Elliott Theatre), Welles 'made a too-long speech to explain the situation, the scenes, the deficiencies of this kind of presentation'. He insisted that they were making an artistic protest, not a political one, and, having described the production as it would have been, he finally announced: 'We have the honour to present – with the composer at the piano – *The Cradle Will Rock*!' At that moment, Welles handed the show back to Blitzstein; it now belonged entirely to him. Feder's spotlight swung round to pick him out, sitting in shirt sleeves and suspenders at the piano, its back removed for increased volume, chewing peanuts as he continued to do throughout the show. He started to play and then to sing his score 'as I had done so often for prospective producers – we used to call it my Essex House run'. After a line or two Olive Stanton (the Moll) from her place in the stalls joined her voice to the composer's, giving courage to all the others who, one by one, joined in. Eventually, the actors got up, stood in the aisles, even danced a little. Then the chorus, sitting behind Lehman Engel, started to sing. The only instrumentalist who turned up, the accordionist, Rudy, joined in whenever appropriate.

'At the end of the first act,' wrote Blitzstein, 'the poet Archibald MacLeish sprinted backstage to say "a new day had dawned in the theatre, the stagnant and supine audience had been killed forever" and he had to make a speech about it. And so he did, after the final curtain.' That final curtain (there was of course no curtain as such at all) had provoked a storm of applause. 'Even that moment had its particular theatrical flair. MacLeish wore a Palm Beach suit, and when Welles held up his hand and finally stopped the roaring pandemonium that greeted us, saying, "We will all now sit down, and the one man left standing will be Mr Archibald MacLeish,' there stood the white suit gleaming conspicuously, and we were told we had witnessed a historical event.' It is hard not to share Blitzstein's sense of the comedy of the liberal poet. 'The chief accomplishment of the Federal Theatre Project,' said MacLeish, 'has been to return the arts to the artists and to the people who love them and to bring artists and their audiences together. Mr Blitzstein was perhaps as good a composer two years ago as he is now but two years ago he could not have found a relationship with an audience which he has tonight and of which you have had a part.' For MacLeish it was the dawn of a new golden age – the rebirth of that very Greek figure, the public artist, performing his own work. For Blitzstein, it was the opening salvo in a revolutionary war.

Elsewhere in the city that night, there were other demonstrations of defiance against the impending threat to the Project: after a performance of *The Case of Philip Lawrence*, and, somehow bizarrely, after an all-Brahms chamber concert, there were sit-down strikes; later there was a night-long sit-down strike for the WPA Music Project. Events at the Maxine Elliott Theatre had been reported in *The New York Times* the following morning.

> STEEL STRIKE OPERA IS PUT OFF BY WPA: Persons who heard the opera's score and extracts last night carried away no very clear impression except that its theme was the steel workers should join a union.

> There was a song (uncomplimentary) about military training in colleges, one about Honolulu, and one about 'the freedom of the press,' the purport of which was that there isn't any . . . when the opera ended after about two hours, Mr Welles made another speech saying the performance was 'not a political protest but an artistic one'. Archibald MacLeish made a speech in which he praised the 'vitality' of the FTP.

There was no show the following day while everyone tried to deal with the consequences of that heady first performance. Hallie Flanagan had asked Blitzstein and Welles to go with her to Washington to speak to Hopkins, to try to retrieve the situation, but Orson had decided to go unilaterally, which he did that day, the 17th. Barry Witham has uncovered the transcripts of the meeting that took place; they give a vivid impression of the gap between the two sides. Welles's position was simple: the show was ready to open. It was bad for morale, and bad for the show not to do so. The WPA position was equally clear: all units within the project had to pull together. They were all under threat; if they co-ordinated their efforts in conjunction with the WPA itself, the damage might be contained. Welles was indifferent to this line of argument. He was sorry, but he had a show which was ready to open, and for which he had already sold a large number of tickets. His interlocutors – David Niles and Ellen Woodward, both people, as Witham makes clear, of impeccable New Deal credentials, fighters for school meals and public health facilities, and passionate supporters of Mrs Flanagan – were genuinely hurt by his lack of esprit de corps: 'I cannot get out of my consciousness the fact that if we do have any trouble, I will never be able to forget the fact that the people whom we counted on to make our troubles a little easier dropped this additional burden upon us,' said Niles.

It is impossible to see how there could have been any compromise between the two sides. It was essential for the WPA that if an order were made, it should be obeyed by all the many troubled sections of the Project; for one unit to break ranks would have threatened the entire delicate structure. From Welles's and Houseman's point of view, failing to open for another two weeks would have brought them obloquy from the left (from which most of their audience was drawn) and restlessness from within the Unit. The ease, however, with which Welles proposed that they take the play away from the Unit and present it commercially (and despite his insistence that he would be happy to see the show open at the Maxine Elliott) suggests that he had no great attachment to the Federal Theatre Project. It presented him with nothing but constraints; its ideals were not his ideals.

Hallie Flanagan gave her view ten years later in a letter to Marc Blitzstein: 'Important as the issue raised by *The Cradle Will Rock* was, it was not the only issue facing us. The thing that people on the New York Project never cared about, never understood, and never took the trouble to find out, is that this is a big country. The Federal Theatre Project was bigger than any project in it. It included not only *The Cradle Will Rock* but the theatre for the children of coal miners in Gary, Indiana, the enterprise for vaudevillians in Portland, Oregon, the negro theatre in Chicago, the research being done in Oklahoma.' What did Welles care for any of these? He had a show ready to open. The meeting in Washington ended with Ellen Woodward saying: 'if you decide to go ahead with a commercial production of the play, I see no reason for Mrs Flanagan not to drop this thing.' Witham and Richard France before him quite correctly point out that there was never any discussion at this meeting of political censorship, no suggestion on the part of the government representatives that the subject matter of the piece is regrettable, nor any attribution to them by Welles of that motive. Nor does Welles complain of the sealing of the theatre, of the presence of the so-called 'Cossacks'. The political theme came later; the immediate issue was one of discipline within the Project.

As soon as Welles (who had been alone, accompanied neither by Houseman nor by MacLeish, as some reports suggest) returned to New York, he and his partners swung into action; they released the piece for commercial presentation, and gained two weeks' leave for WPA members, all of whom now joined Equity, as did Blitzstein. Helen Deutsch, normally press agent for the Theatre Guild, chipped in $1,250 towards the $2,305 needed to put up the Equity bond and pay back dues. It was decided to play a fortnight at the Venice, under exactly the circumstances fortuitously evolved at the first preview; the ticket scale was to be from 35c to a dollar; by error, a roll of 25c tickets was purchased, so WPA members were admitted for 25c. Business was slow to begin with, due to a bad notice (of the dress rehearsal, set and all) in the *Daily Worker*, and an absence of notices anywhere else. The box office at the Maxine Elliott was busy denying its existence. Eventually, however, after coverage in several magazines including *Time* (where Lillian Hellman said of it 'There is good contemptuous laughter behind *The Cradle Will Rock* and that laughter gives the play its vigor') and the denunciation of the CIO, America's Communist Party, by the head of Little Steel, there was standing room only. They then went on tour, principally to steel towns, where business and reactions were variable.

Meanwhile, the WPA in order to prevent any use of FTP property in the commercial staging of the play, had sent its officers into the Maxine Elliott and smashed up the set. Johnston and Smith described it three years later in their most vivid *Saturday Evening Post*-ese: 'The formerly audacious left-wingers of the WPA turned out to be a lot of stuffed shirts under the skin. In their zeal to save America from the WPA theatre, the WPA sent an ax brigade to chop and smash their own settings in their own padlocked playhouse. Big glass pillars full of neon lights and the other expensive equipment of *The Cradle Will Rock* were destroyed in a Carrie Nation raid.' Welles resigned from the Project; Houseman was dismissed under a rule forbidding non-American citizens to be employed by the Works Progress Administration. Unit 891 folded overnight. It had, after all, been created entirely to provide an outlet for Welles's creative needs, and was now redundant.

The whole incident is a curious one. Welles and Houseman having set out to create a company dedicated to classical theatre, inaugurated their first season with a mid-nineteenth-century French farce transposed into a surreal Mid-Western romp, then, having proceeded to what was their legitimate business, an Elizabethan masterpiece, they lurched suddenly into a straightforward piece of agitprop, which, instead of simply taking its place alongside all the many other more or less controversial offerings of the FTP became, due to a series of unforeseen circumstances – crisis within the project, crisis in the steel industry – a cause célèbre, which ended in Houseman and Welles defying the Project, and breaking away on their own. The journey from their original starting point was rapid and complete. But *The Cradle Will Rock* is entirely uncharacteristic of their work, together or apart. In particular, what appeared on the stage of the Venice Theatre owed nothing to Welles. It was to evolve still further; further and further from the original conception. It is probable that had the production gone ahead as Welles planned it, it would have had nothing like the success it achieved. Lehman Engel wrote in *This Bright Day*: 'Orson – serendipity at work – was never to be debited with this nightmare production.' What happened instead was that his name was more than ever linked with notoriety, never a bad thing, as far as Welles was concerned.

It may have winded him a little, privately, to realise that all that ingenuity, all that energy, all that inspiration was dispensable: the show worked anyway. Better, in fact. There is a strange sense of Welles withdrawing, of no longer being needed. The great director withdrew in the face of the primitive relationship between author and audience. He was, in fact, saved by the bell – as, perhaps, was Blitzstein, who said, speaking to the *Daily Worker*, 'I can't regard this work purely from the viewpoint of the artist – I believe firmly in what the play stands for and an audience of steelworkers represents a new public, wide-awake and extremely critical,' a perfectly Brechtian point of view. Welles's approach, as expressed in his production, had it seen the light of day, was the opposite. It sought to overwhelm the audience with theatrical effect. Happy Blitzstein, saved from his director! In fact, Blitzstein had been delighted at every turn with Welles's work (he was fond enough of him to dedicate the next piece – his radio play *I've Got the Tune!* – to him), but *The Cradle Will Rock* is too slight a piece to have survived all the genius Welles was eager to lavish upon it.

Oddly enough, and with that insatiability for new projects that is characteristic of Welles at this period, he had begun rehearsing another piece of musical theatre at the same time as *The Cradle Will Rock*. Planned on a much more modest scale, and premièred three months before it, the staging and presentation had almost presaged the final form of Blitzstein's piece. This was Aaron Copland's children's opera, *The Second Hurricane*, libretto by Welles's *Horse Eats Hat* collaborator, Edwin Denby: 'Once in a while something happens, something exceptional. Have you ever had an adventure? Have you been a hero?' The opera's theme is the building of character among a group of youngsters who have volunteered their services in flood crisis. Finding themselves marooned on a scrap of land, they give way to terror, quarrel, fight and eat the food reserved for flood victims. As their innate heroism asserts itself, however, they sing jazzy and patriotic songs, laugh and joke and generally come through with flying colours. With its representative cast of leading characters – Gwen, Butch, Lowrie, Fat, Gip, Queenie, Jeff (who is black) – it's a sunny version of the *Lord of the Flies*. 'Denby and I,' wrote Copland, 'had agreed from the start that all the stage business was to be simple and natural, and that we would keep before us at all times the premise that this opera was for American youngsters to relate to in their everyday lives and language. Orson's ideas for staging were original. The two choruses were onstage, and the orchestra was placed on a platform at the rear with the conductor facing the audience.' In fact, once rehearsals for *The Cradle Will Rock* hit their stride, Welles handed the work over to Chubby Sherman who conscientiously executed his ideas.

The reviews were largely favourable. Some detected levels of theatrical sophistication that may or may not have been present: 'The fact that the orchestra in every-day dress sat behind the performance and that no scenery was employed smacked strongly of the Chinese theatre, as did the occasional use of simple props with practically all else left to the imagination . . .' More extravagantly, the *World Telegram* proclaimed that 'there is here the suggestion of the Fokine staging of *Coq d'Or*'. It is somewhat surprising that it didn't cross Welles's mind, as he slaved over his epic production *The Cradle Will Rock*, that there might be a simpler, more striking way, but it took a fight with the government to point that way to him.

From the wider perspective of the Federal Theatre Project itself, the débâcle over *The Cradle Will Rock* marked, as Houseman said, 'the end of the honeymoon for the New Deal and the theatre'. Hallie Flanagan herself wrote that 'it was more than a case of censorship. It marked a changing point of view in Washington.' The Project's magazine, which was often more drastically critical of FTP productions than outside critics, and though it was virtually self-supporting, was dropped, and its abandonment was a harbinger of a larger dismantlement. 'Gradually the real reasons began to come out, not all in one conversation, but a little at a time. Was it true that the magazine was on sale in workers' bookshops? Wasn't the editor . . . a communist? . . . Wasn't there too much emphasis on poor audiences, too many pictures of squatters in Oklahoma and shirt-sleeved crowds in city parks – was this the kind of audience we wanted? We wanted our plays to be good enough for any kinds of an audience, but our chief obligation was to people who weren't able to afford other theatre-going. Wasn't that still the idea? Or was it?' This chilling account of the subtle turning away from the original ideals is Hallie Flanagan's. The Project's short, sensational life was nearly at an end. Within two years, in disturbing circumstances, it was on the scrap-heap of noble dreams.

As for Welles and Houseman: 'we had little to say to each other. Our immediate emotional response to the success of *The Cradle Will Rock* was the usual need, on both our parts, to prove that each of us could exist without the other.' Welles was some leagues ahead of Houseman in independence; his radio work had made him entirely secure financially, and it had given him another artistic life, quite separate from Houseman. Radio ceased to be merely a source of income and had begun to fascinate him with its possibilities as a medium. His radio work took a number of important strides forward in 1936 and 1937. From being an anonymous and much disguised voice for hire, he was cast in a regular role which made that voice nationally famous; and he started directing for the medium. He had already, in the autumn of 1936, adapted, performed and directed a thirty-minute version of *Hamlet* (is there a character in the whole of dramatic literature for which he was less suited?). Under the aegis of Irving Reis's Columbia Workshop, he then turned to *Macbeth*, which introduced him to one of his most significant collaborators, the composer Bernard Herrmann, although the collaboration on this occasion was less than happy. Welles insisted on bringing into the studio a Highland bagpipe (Haiti having been left far behind), leaving Herrmann fuming at his podium in front of a redundant studio orchestra; the production as a whole was further vitiated by such musical cues as Herrmann was able to add to the all-pervading drone of the bagpipes being one behind throughout the programme. This chaos was, of course, transmitted live. But Welles was beginning to turn his mind to the challenge of radio; shortly he would apply himself to it with his usual all-consuming intensity, and the results were appropriately startling.

His opportunity came from Mutual, a company hitherto best known for its *Lone Ranger* series. Despite the disaster of his radio *Macbeth*, they asked him to adapt *Les Misérables* as a seven-part series, which he embarked on immediately after the heroic events surrounding *The Cradle Will Rock*. In terms of adaptation alone, the huge complex sprawl of Hugo's novel is reduced to three and a half hours of air time with great cogency and fierce narrative grip, simplified, but denied none of its resonance. Purely as a professional achievement, this is breathtaking, more impressive than many of his more highly publicised feats. To take a thousand pages of text and effectively to convey its essence in brief episodes – to do so, moreover, using the medium at full stretch – is a skill that often eludes radio adaptors of many years' experience; on what was virtually his first outing as a radio director, Welles at twenty-two produced a show that could rival any by the most seasoned practitioner.

He had a strong personal response to the material: its theme of absolution was close to his heart, from the beginning of his career to its end. If you've worked out your punishment, are you absolved? Society says no, to Jean Valjean at any rate. 'No man had ever touched him but to bruise him.' Welles's growing political awareness informed both production and adaptation with intense compassion for injustice (he prefaces the series with the

WHITE HOPE

Left 'Bride of Young Actor' – Virginia Nicolson's wedding picture as it appeared in a newspaper announcement

Above Orson, Virginia and their baby Christopher

Preceding page Orson Welles as Faustus in his production of the Marlowe play

Above Welles and John Houseman confer during a rehearsal of *Horse Eats Hat*.
Below Joseph Cotten and horse in *Horse Eats Hat*, the first Project 891 production

MACBE
MiTEE MONARCH
ELKS
NIGHT
Every
THURSDAY
STANDING
ROOM
ONLY

Above A scene from Welles's sensational production of *Macbeth* with an all-black cast
Left Outside the theatre on opening night and *below* backstage

As Mercutio in *Romeo and Juliet*

'George Orson Welles: Shadow to Shakespeare'

Below Some of Welles's costume sketches for *Doctor Faustus* and *Macbeth*

Pages from *Everybody's Shakespeare* with drawings by Welles

46—The Merchant

ACT IV
Scene I
VENICE—A Court of

(The court is assembled; officia
guards are at their posts; and th
stands with his friends, Bassan
erio. The Duke enters wi
mounts the platform and sett
Duke: What, is Antonio here
Antonio: Ready, so please y
Duke: I am sorry for thee.
A stony adversary, an in
Uncapable of pity, void
From any dram of merc
Antonio: I have heard
Your Grace hath ta'en
His rigorous course; b
And that no lawful
Out of his envy's re

Twelfth Night—7

ACT I
Scene II
ILLYRIA—The sea-coast.

The wreck of a ship may be in evidence. Some thunder and lightning, representing the last of a violent storm, often opens the scene. Otherwise soft music until Viola speaks. Viola is sometimes carried on in the Sea-Captain's arms, just awakening from semi-consciousness. The seamen who enter with her, bedraggled and dripping and obviously exhausted, establish the mood of shipwreck. But Viola is the first lady of the play and more often she is given a "good entrance," which is perhaps just as well. That means that she enters first, walking to Center where she stands making a picture in the attractive tatters of her dress and the sweep of her improvised, sail-cloth cloak. Viola, herself, is attractive; often dark and always of the same physical type as her brother, Sebastian, who is her twin and must be very like her. She and a part of her crew have missed him in the wreck of her ship. She waits silently as the two or three sailors, staggering under a great sea-chest and such gear as might have been salvaged from the wreck, come up with the Captain. Sometimes she enters last, after a pause, and after the men, lowering their loads to rest, have turned in her direction. She looks curiously about her.

Viola. What country, friends, is this?
Captain. *(He is a great grizzly man)* This is Illyria, lady.
(The men throw themselves wearily to the ground)
Viola. *(With a sad little smile)* And what should I do in Illyria?
My brother he is in Elysium.
(Hopefully)
Perchance he is not drown'd: what think you, sailors?
Captain. It is *perchance* that you yourself were saved.
Viola. O my poor brother! and so perchance may he be.
Captain. True, madam: and, to comfort you with chance,
Assure yourself, after our ship did split,
When you and those poor number saved with you
Hung on our diving boat, I saw your brother,
Most provident in peril, bind himself,
Courage and hope both teaching him the practice,
To a strong mast that lived upon the sea;
Where, like Arion on the dolphin's back,

The man behind *The War of the Worlds*

novel's epigraph 'So long as these problems are not solved, so long as ignorance and poverty remain on earth, these words cannot be useless'). But beyond this, he demonstrated in his production three qualities indispensable in radio: ingenuity, intelligence and flair.

He had an instinctive feel for the medium; he had been aware, from as early as his own plays, *Marching Song* with its military tattoos and *Bright Lucifer*, throbbing with Indian drums, of the power of sound in the theatre, having a highly musical sense of its effect on the action and its capacity for heightening dialogue; whole stretches of the Harlem *Macbeth* had been saved from monotony in this way. The medium of radio, moreover, perfectly suited his temperament, both as actor and director.

It is a medium of technical solutions for technical problems: how do you suggest this aspect of the character, how do you evoke that landscape, how do you get from here to there? He was prepared to experiment with anything; in *Les Misérables*, in order to create life-like sewers, he dragged his crew into the men's room, where Ray Collins and Everett Sloane played their scene over a urinal. For both the actor and the director, the medium has less to do with feeling than with thinking. For the actors, clarity of phrasing and diction evoke emotion in the audience far more than if they had deeply felt those emotions; the task of the radio actor is to make the audience see what he's talking about. As long as the story and the images are clearly in the actors' minds, their work is then uniquely available to improvement by externally induced intensity. Even in live broadcasting, there comes a point in the curiously unreal, hermetically sealed world of the studio when everyone engaged on the programme, standing around the microphone in their suits and spectacles, has to be galvanised into a sense of the urgency of the characters and situations.

No one in the history of the medium has ever unleashed such tidal waves of adrenalin as Welles. *Les Misérables* is electric from start to finish, his own gruff and very credibly aged Valjean leading the excellent group of actors (Agnes Moorehead, Ray Collins, Martin Gabel, Everett Sloane, Chubby Sherman). His narration is afflicted with the solemn tremble with which he liked to indicate sincerity, and makes no attempt to create anything like the tone of Hugo's own narration, but it is personal and passionate, far from the manner of the studio linkman who would normally have filled in the plot. Years later, Welles was under the impression that he had experimented with first-person narration in this production; he didn't. The narrator is not a character, he is simply the voice of the author. The important thing is that everything in the programme has Welles's stamp on it. Already in *Les Misérables* Welles's omnicompetence was being sold: 'The distinguished young author, director and actor Orson Welles presents the story,' says the introducer. No one else is credited – neither actor nor technician. This solipsism is as unrealistic on radio as in the theatre; more so, perhaps: the technicians alone, especially before the development of the higher technology, were brilliantly skilful and resourceful. But there is no question, in this first of his major radio productions, of who is in charge. Within the small world of art radio, his name became one to take note of.

Hollywood, too, began to take note. Welles was approached by Warner Brothers with the offer of a contract to develop scripts for them – but the offer didn't promise enough money, enough power, or enough freedom. In any case, it was not his world. The world he had always craved, the world of the theatre, should have been at his feet. But it was not. Having been invited by the progressive impresario Arthur Hopkins to direct and star in *King Lear*, with designs by Pavel Tchelitchew ('the Russian pederast' whom Welles had insisted must leave the audience of *Doctor Faustus* before he would consent to appear onstage), he called a premature press conference, unilaterally announcing the production. Hopkins huffily withdrew, an unusual case of Welles's instinct for publicity backfiring on him. He was again at a loose end, theatrically. Houseman was at a loose end, too, and was grateful, and rather flattered, to be asked by Hallie Flanagan to take over her job at Vassar College for Women for a year. Dropping in on the Welleses at their place at Sneden's Landing, Houseman reported this unusual appointment to them. Virginia, he says, screamed with laughter – a deep, complicated laugh, it would appear. By now she was bewildered by the way in which the thrilling boy she had married had turned into a driven megalomaniac, and angered by the small amount of himself that he was prepared to allow her – mostly on those occasions when at the end of a hard day of eating, being shaved, having manicures, acting on stage and radio, being driven from job to job by ambulance, drinking, directing, camping it up with the boys and fornicating, he would go home, driven by the chauffeur, then ferried by the boatman, to her, and she would walk barefooted down his naked back to relax him. Still in love with him, but humiliated and lonely, she felt jealous of anyone who shared what appeared to be his real life, the part of it that did not concern her; in Houseman she observed someone who was equally dependent on him, and equally denied his full attention. Houseman's news about his job at Vassar obviously suggested to her – though she can scarcely have seen him as a rival to her in physical terms – there was something not altogether masculine in Houseman's dependency on Welles.

That the dependency was not all on Houseman's side is clear though from Welles's moody question to him as he walked him back to his car: 'Why don't we start a theatre of our own?' Houseman's reply – 'Why don't we?' – is equally downbeat; a curious start to a brave new venture, like lovers who have decided to give their relationship another chance simply because they haven't been able to find anyone else.

CHAPTER TWELVE

Mercury

IF THE initial impulse towards their new theatre was somewhat desultory, the reunited partners rapidly threw off any complicated feelings they may have had in a burst of brilliant energy, organising and publicising as only they knew how. As usual, Houseman expresses himself in the language of infatuation: 'I did not go home that night or the next day or the day after that.' The new venture's name – so perfectly apt – was casually assumed after their first planning meal when their eyes idly lit on a two-year-old copy of the bracingly radical magazine edited by H.L. Mencken and George Jean Nathan, *American Mercury*; their winged feet barely hit the ground thereafter. Houseman and Welles announced their PLANS FOR A NEW THEATRE in *The New York Times* on 29 August 1937, only a few days after that first meeting. They staked their claim to the FTP audience in unequivocal terms: 'When it opens its doors . . . the Mercury will expect to play to the same audiences that during the last two seasons stood to see *Doctor Faustus*, the Negro *Macbeth* and *Murder in the Cathedral* . . . people on a voyage of discovery in the theatre . . . people who either had never been to the theatre at all or who, for one reason or another, had ignored it for many seasons.'

Quoting from the FTP questionnaires they noted that the overwhelming majority of the requests was for 'more classical plays', and 'great plays of the past produced in a modern way', so that is what they would do: 'preferably those which seem to have some emotional or factual bearing on contemporary life'. Forestalling criticism from conservatives, they insist that 'there will be no substitution of social consciousness for drama'; equally aware of the demands of radicals, they promised to produce new plays. To encourage this they announced the foundation of the Worklight Theatre to play on Sunday nights. New works would be performed for two or three performances, 'fully rehearsed with music, etc, with everything but the physical side of the production'. It is an almost ideal prescription for a theatre company, the sort of thing that was triumphantly successful for brief periods in the English theatre at the Royal Shakespeare Theatre under Peter Hall, for example, or the Royal Court under George Devine, a mixture of classical and new writing, with an experimental studio to whose productions 'none of the traditional inhibitions or hesitations will apply'. No such integrated theatre had ever existed in America. As so often, Welles and Houseman anticipated the development of theatrical history; or rather, their manifestos did.

Ever mindful of the need to create an audience, they addressed themselves, a few weeks later, to the readership of the *Daily Worker*, appropriately modifying their pitch: 'AGAIN – A PEOPLE'S THEATRE; THE MERCURY TAKES A BOW: When the Mercury Theatre opens its doors early in November, we believe another step will have been taken towards a real People's Theatre in America.' The objective of the Mercury, they claimed, was 'to widen the cultural and social base of the people's theatre'. Praising the WPA and the new audience that it had found, they make an interesting point about their own approach. 'Aesthetically, this new fresh public, entering the theatre as on a voyage of discovery, succeeded in re-establishing the audience as an organic part of the theatre. And again, as in all the great theatrical periods, the audience is becoming a live, participating force to be taken into account by playwright, actor and director.' The abolition of the fourth wall was certainly a crucial element in their aesthetic. They thoroughly rejected the notion of a play as something comfortably ensconced behind the proscenium arch, to be admired and applauded; they expected their audience to be critically engaged participants.

The repertory they announced was bold. It was bold then; it would be bold now. The list consisted of *Julius Caesar*, *Heartbreak House* (with Aline MacMahon), *The Duchess of Malfi* ('one of the great horror plays of all time'), William Gillette's nineteenth-century classic of American farce, *Too Much Johnson*, and Ben Jonson's *The Silent Woman*, (which proved, as it turned out, to be too much Jonson; they never did it). The plan was to play in repertory with no more than two plays a week. Top price was $2; there were four hundred good seats at 50c, 75c and $1 every performance. By comparison, standard Broadway prices were $3.30, $4.40. In the *Daily Worker*, *Julius Caesar* was announced by itself 'in a modern production by Orson Welles. This tragedy (which might well be subtitled Death of a Dictator) is the most contemporary of all Elizabethan plays. In our production the stress will be on the social implications inherent in the history of Caesar and on the atmosphere of personal greed, fear and hysteria that surround a dictatorial regime. The modern parallel is obvious.

For those who saw his *Doctor Faustus* and the Negro *Macbeth*, there should be no question as to the violence and immediacy which Orson Welles will give to the present-day production of *Julius Caesar* and Marc Blitzstein (author of that storm-centre *The Cradle Will Rock*) has written the music for it;' (just in case there were the slightest doubts about their left-wing credentials.) The publicity blitz was well received; *Commonweal*, comparing the Mercury's philosophy to that of the Old Vic, declared that 'it is the duty of all who love the theatre to rally back of them'. Brooks Atkinson in the *Times* confirmed their continuity with the Federal Theatre, which, he observed, 'has already given Mr Welles and Mr Houseman an opportunity to revise a good many professional shibboleths about the theatre'.

They had the press on their side from the start. What they didn't have was any concrete financial basis for their bold announcement. The purpose of the publicity was above all to attract investors; it was a typical ploy of Houseman's to announce a thing in order to make it happen, a ploy he had last used when he announced *Panic* without having even secured the rights. For the first time since then, Houseman was faced with raising money by his own efforts; this time he was not blessed with a living author who also happened to be a millionaire. They had no money themselves: Welles, typically, had spent the large sums he earned as soon as he had got it; Houseman was struggling on his small salary as Hallie Flanagan's understudy. The sum they needed was small (barely more than $10,000) but without it, they couldn't even begin. If the gamble failed, they would simply have to swallow all their brave words. Houseman's first move was to secure a theatre (the Comedy, very cheap) and install a telephone. It never stopped ringing, but not with investors, only theatre-workers wanting work, and theatre-goers wanting theatre. This was, in its way, encouraging (they were filling a definite need) but no basis for creating a new company. Houseman began to despair; finally, out of the blue, a perfect stranger, George Hexter, called offering to put up $4,500 of the $10,500 they needed, and the ball started rolling. With Hexter's sum on the table, the remainder was quickly found; without it, they would simply have had to give up. The Mercury came into existence by the skin of its teeth, and it remained in existence on the same basis. Houseman quickly assembled his team from friends, old FTP hands and newcomers; from the beginning there was a shrewd emphasis on selling: in addition to the usual technical team (stage manager and company manager) there was a press and public relations officer (Henry Senber), a special promotions division (Sylvia

Regan) and a special department devoted to student subscriptions. They knew from the start that they must build a loyal Mercury audience. The Theatre Guild had its subscribers, plump and middle-class; the Mercury would have to be more streetwise. Having identified their constituency, they immediately set about reaching it. All this is very modern, a strong indication of Houseman's organisational flair, and an essential part of the enormous impact that the Mercury made.

Under the masterful control of that steel waif Jean Rosenthal as technical director, the theatre was swiftly converted to their purposes. As well as commanding her own troops, she used her particular elfin qualities to enlist support: she 'inveigled some wonderful night watchman into feeding us heat from a bank across the street when we couldn't pay our heating bills'. The transformation of the Comedy was more radical than the one they had wrought on the Maxine Elliott, only a block away. While that boudoir of a theatre had somehow retained its dainty character through the alternately magical and surreal proceedings unleashed onto its stage by Welles, the Comedy was, in Houseman's phrase, 'made functional'. The stage and its needs were favoured over those of the 623-seat auditorium, which was rather left to fend for itself – as it had been doing for some years. Once the home of the Washington Square players and scene of Ruth Draper's debut, it had become the centre of a scandal with the steamy drama, *Maya*: the theatre was closed down for immorality and padlocked; the actors, held responsible for the content of their roles, were threatened with legal action. The resulting outcry forced a revision of the censorship law; this turned out to be the high point of the Comedy's career. Thereafter, it led a twilit existence, with occasional visits from amateur companies from Newark. Now it was rudely awakened from its slumbers by the Mercury's army of labourers knocking it into shape; Houseman watched the transformation through a peep-hole in his office, the old projection booth left over from the Comedy's brief and unsuccessful spell as a movie-house. Once the job was done and the conversion complete, there was a moment of jubilation as the company gathered to watch the old COMEDY sign being taken down, and the new neon MERCURY erected in its place.

The work was done with remarkable speed, as was the entire creation of the Mercury. Houseman remarks in *Run-Through*, that the same process would now require 'a million, months of discussion, major real estate operations, City, State, Federal participation and that of two or more gigantic foundations'; and he was writing twenty-five years ago. Welles meanwhile was assembling his company of thirty-four – another unimaginable statistic in the present age, when only the very largest subsidised theatres can think of casts of even double figures. No longer obliged to absorb the assorted vaudevillians and superannuated tragedians that formed the FTP's standing army, but equally unable to afford a standard Broadway company (they offered $40 per week, with $25 for junior members, on no binding contract; anyone was free to leave at two weeks' notice), Welles made a statement of intent which was seen as a sort of clarion cry to the non-established profession: 'We are enlisting the co-operation of those actors and musicians who, whether they have had theatrical experience or not, seem to us best suited to work in the theatre. We hope to develop a company of actors who will be prepared to revitalise the classics and be able to turn from them more keenly attuned and aware, to handling great plays of the contemporary scene.'

Over the course of the season, more than 3,000 people auditioned for the thirty or forty available jobs. Welles never ceased insisting that the actor was the central unit of his theatre, and the dream of a company in the European manner, such as America had scarcely known, each actor being nurtured and challenged not at the expense of but to the greater glory of the whole group, exercising itself on a repertory of the world's masterpieces, was one of the most potent parts of the Mercury's appeal within the profession. Welles had seen the great companies with his own eyes on their own territory; he knew what he was talking about. But did he know how to create a company? The ambition alone, the mere vision, were remarkable enough in a twenty-two-year-old. If he could actually lay down the foundations of a genuine ensemble, then he would be not merely prodigious, but a master.

Welles's actors were drawn from pretty well the same pool as Houseman's: the Federal Theatre Project, chums and new recruits, plus a number of people he had encountered in radio studios. These last included Elliott Reid, at seventeen years already, like Welles, a veteran of *The March of Time*, Martin Gabel (whose 'gravid voice had made him, in his early twenties, one of the country's most successful and sexy radio actors' according to Houseman), and the fifteen-year-old Arthur Anderson, star of a show in which Welles also appeared as The Big Ham, a wandering actor-manager, veddy British and querulous unless he has his kettle and teapot. The presence of these radio actors in the Mercury company was not accidental: Welles placed enormous and, even in 1937, old-fashioned stress on the importance of the voice. 'Emphasis has been placed on infusing language with as much beauty as the actors can lend through voice and expression. Language never lives until it is spoken aloud,' he said in an interview early in 1938. He favoured actors with classical experience, including two actors from the London Old Vic, George Coulouris (who was English) and the Austrian actor Stefan Schnabel (son of Artur); a RADA-trained American actor, Joseph Holland (who had a photograph of Irving on the wall of his tiny one-room apartment); and John Hoystradt, who had toured with Welles in *Romeo and Juliet*.

The two female members of the company, Evelyn Allen and Muriel Brassler, had solid stock experience. Joseph Cotten was invited, of course, and Chubby Sherman, and Francis Carpenter; and an unexpected recruit, Norman Lloyd, leading actor of the Living Newspaper, star of its big success, *Power*, an actor equally versed in the theories of Stanislavsky and Brecht, and, like many of his generation, suspicious of what he felt to be Welles's actor-managerial ways and 'chin-up-to-the-balcony' acting. For these actors, the great innovation of the age was that for the first time the audience – whether lower-middle-class Jewish (as at The Group) or working class (the Federal Theatre Project) – actually saw themselves onstage. Despite *The Cradle Will Rock*, clearly the main thrust of Welles's work was away from this. 'Orson,' says Lloyd, 'was still on the old line.' Lloyd, surprised at being invited to meet Welles, and prepared to dislike him, had instead, like all the new recruits, been entirely captivated; the stage direction from *Doctor Faustus* 'Faust charms him dumb' might have been coined for Welles. He had assembled for *Caesar* a group of actors that were diverse, opinionated, talented, ready, willing and, for the most part, young. They had the feeling that they were in on the start of something big, that they were world-beaters. They knew that Welles was in charge, and that they would be executing his will, and that was fine by them, for the time being. The Mercury was now ready for action; Houseman had created the structure for Welles to create extraordinary theatre. It is interesting to know how the young man thus empowered saw his job.

With only four major productions behind him, Welles was, at the age of twenty-two, already fully formed as a director, in his precocious prime. He had already thought a great deal about both directing and acting, and put some of his thoughts into words in an address that he gave to the Theatre Education League just over a year after the Mercury was created; it was later put out as a leaflet under the title *The Director in the Theatre Today*. Somewhat wild and sensational, partly defensive, wholly combative, it is, for all its incoherence, a uniquely revealing statement of Welles's practice and a striking revelation of some of his deepest preoccupations. It is also, in its unguarded rashness, highly revealing both of the man and the artist, simultaneously a manifesto and a confession.

'The director,' he says, 'is the servant of that aggregation of talent, of personality, of force and of potence which is a theatrical company.' It is the director's job to make everyone as good as possible within the framework of his particular conception of the play. Unexceptionable sentiments. But, he says, echoing the paradox that Harold Clurman found himself struggling with, he must be not only the servant but also the master. And he finds resistance to his masterfulness. 'The whole business of producing today,' he says with barely concealed impatience, 'has made a new aristocracy in the theatre of great men who used to have to say "Yes, sir" and shut up. Someone eventually has to say shut up.' And who are these talkative aristocrats that need to be silenced? The composer, the lighting designer, the set designer, the choreographer and 'the actors in the sanctity of the Pennsylvania Drug Store', all trying, he says, to decide on individual conceptions of the play. This is impossible; it would result in chaos. Unexceptionable, again, if perhaps a little aggressively put.

The set designer draws his full wrath. 'The director is exasperated and perpetually hindered today because of what the scene designer has done to his art. A director wants a designer because he is a painter, for no other reason. The director is the man of the theatre. He knows how to build scenery and paint it, make it fit, and make it change. If he does not, he should not be a director. The good director knows all about these things and he can plan them for the scene designer. What he wants from a scene designer is painting – artistry; but the man is incapable of anything but blue velvet. He is such a charlatan craftsman that he is of no human use whatever.' After this sudden outburst, the much put upon twenty-three-year-old testily declares that he would be better off with 'a youngster fresh from the academy or studio'. Far from backing down from this extraordinary expression of contempt for the skill of one of his prime collaborators, Welles explicitly asserts his superiority to the lot of them. 'The director must be better than his scene designer, better than his lighting man – better than all of these people in the field of production at least.'

This frank claim to übermensch status out-Craigs Edward

Gordon Craig. The designer's offence, it would seem, is impertinence: he wants to have a say in the look of the production. That cannot be, because the production, at every level and in every detail, must be the result of one man's vision: the director. In adumbrating this notion – the auteur theory of theatre direction – Welles goes on to define, very specifically, what has come to be known as the *concept production*: 'The great field of the director is of course, in conception . . . one director, for instance, presenting a Molière comedy may decide that the whole play shows the fundamental hardness of the world.' This leads him to erect onstage 'a setting of stainless steel which he decorates with rose leaves to show a kind of hopeless beauty and a sort of basic cruelty'. He admits that the effect of this 'may be somewhat mysterious to the audience who sees nothing but a group of steel erections and some rose leaves; but this nevertheless is the man's conception – and it is a valid one.' If this sounds familiar, it is because it is the story of the art of theatre of the last thirty years.

Welles is momentarily checked in his vision. There is, he acknowledges, a limitation to this approach: 'The script of a play in most cases, unless it is a Greek Tragedy, or one cast in the highest tragic mould, is a wandering and loosely knit affair embracing many plays.' If the director is good enough, he says, he can use all of these many plays and force them into a single evening's entertainment; if he has a special point to make, he will select only one or two. 'Ideally he owes it to his audience to give them everything the playwright intended.' Having clearly scored an own goal, Welles uneasily justifies the failure of the work of the modern directors (and by implication, his own) to reveal the plays in all their richness by invoking 'the disastrous effect of passing time due to the fact that audiences today become restless after a certain volume of words'. He is unable intellectually to justify his unwillingness to engage with the whole play, wandering and loosely knit though – like *King Lear* or *Hamlet*, *The Cherry Orchard* or *The Weavers* – it may indeed be. His work in the theatre faithfully followed this youthful programme of isolating the elements in the author's work that interested him and discarding the rest, as it already had in *Macbeth*, *Faustus* and *Horse Eats Hat*. He never seriously attempted to serve the play; only ever to master it.

The relationship with the actors was a slightly different matter. There was mastery here, too, though he liked actors, as a race, and never ceased to think of himself as one, albeit an actor-manager; the director's main job was 'to make of acting a better thing'. Laudable aim! How is it to be achieved? He never says. Instead he outlines an ideal of acting to which he himself aspires. Just as Craig's work seems to exist in the shadow of Henry Irving, whom he revered as a god, for Welles the figure of the old-time star hovers behind a great deal of what he thought about the theatre and about acting. He and his fellow directors, he says, have failed in the past fifty years to do anything to equal their standard of performance. 'Women do not scream when Othello cuts his throat any more. Everything is nice and artistic today, but no one is really getting under the skin and scratching the nerves of an audience any longer.'

This goes somewhat beyond the usual nostalgia of actors for work of the generation before the generation before one's own. Like Craig, Welles believed that there were Actors then, with Voices: colossuses who bestrode the stage; perhaps he was thinking of McMaster. Like Craig, however, instead of addressing the decline of acting, he proposes a form of theatre in which a controlling figure organises the regrettably less remarkable human material currently available into interesting patterns and shapes.

Elsewhere, in some fragmentary notes on acting jotted down in the form of lecture notes, he observes that 'everything in the theatre depends on a great personality. There is nothing so valuable, or lasting, or interesting as its stars. In the last analysis, there is no interest in the theatre without some kind of star.' Pursuing this argument to startling lengths, he says, 'Let us remember this – the theatre is nothing but an actor – it is not only nothing without an actor – it is nothing but an actor. There is nothing in the theatre of great moment but Shakespeare. Audiences don't need Shakespeare, but the actor does. The function of the playwright is to furnish language for the actor. When acting is good enough, it becomes a substitute for a good play. There are no playwrights today because there are no great actors. And there are no great actors in the theatre today.'

Historically, this is bunk, of course: the Golden Age of Great Acting – that of Garrick and Kean and Macready – was the lowest point of dramatic writing in the last four hundred years. On a poetic plane, however, what he says bears some resemblance both to Artaud and to Craig in their hysterical insistence on liberating the actor from the obligation to be figurative, from the human scale: a longing for prehistoric supermen, dinosaur actors; a yearning for some fantasised Primal Force of Nature to sweep through the theatre and obliterate So-Called Civilisation. 'Great acting is to give an audience a height and awareness of their own being . . . to give it an exultation in a spiritual or aesthetic sense. The most important spiritual mission of the actor is to make the audience aware that they belong to the human race. Great acting isolates the auditorium from the rest of the world . . . and by so doing isolates an audience and intensifies its perception of beauty, of emotion, of being alive.'

How is this thrilling result to be achieved? He rejects modern theory – 'the great contributions to the art of the theatre have been great assaults on the art of acting' – and denounces all modern forms of acting. English acting is neurasthenic; French acting is worthless: pure style with no real vitality. He decisively rejects psychology as the proper study of actors, and even more completely rejects the notion of transformation. 'It is absolutely impossible to give a great performance and have a single characteristic that is not the actor's own. It is impossible for a great actor to be anything but the same in every performance – absolutely impossible. A man may come out as an old man, saying he's King Lear, but he's still the same. If he disguises his personality, he cannot be great. He can disguise his general attack, but he cannot disguise himself. He can eliminate from his own personality certain things which are wrong for a particular role, but he cannot add.'

Personality, he believes, is fixed, immutable – and true. One is who one is, and that's that. He does not admit of the possibility that personality is a selection of elements shaped by education or experience, consciously or not, into a socially acceptable and effective pattern; that one is many different people according to one's circumstances or the people one is with; that 'personality' is a limitation, albeit a socially necessary one, and that the actor's gift is to be able to release the discarded or repressed possibilities dormant within himself. Welles won't allow of that, because he daren't. The mask *is* the face, he insists. It mustn't be questioned. You can hide parts of the mask, but you can't go beyond the mask, much less take it off. This refusal to go beyond the public front denies the possibility of the actor being taken over by the character. 'It is through elimination that you create a true thing.'

Welles offers an interesting little parable of the birth of acting. 'An actor is a story teller. They are actors because there is an urge on the part of the community to exhibit themselves.' He seems to be describing two completely different things: 1 The urge to tell stories; 2 The urge to exhibit oneself. The urge, therefore, to tell stories in public? But that's simply a professional story teller; you don't need to be an actor for that. 'Then somebody else jumped up, wanting to be the tiger, or the bison, or one of the characters in the story.' *Now* he's talking about acting. Up till now, he's been describing the writer and/or the director. The urge to impersonate, in its most literal sense, is surely the essence of the actor: to become somebody else. This is not an attractive idea to Welles, who had worked so hard to become what he was. He will accept – has to accept, since so much of his living came from it on the radio – that the urge to *imitate* is part of being an actor (which it certainly is) but *impersonation* is something else again. Impersonation is the aspect of the actor's art which is responsible for the historic distrust of the profession: stealing someone else's soul, and giving up your own shape: forcing the question: Who are you, really? Impersonation is to be taken over, to give in – but Welles must dominate. He has to be on top.

'It is impossible to be a great actor unless you deal with your audience,' he writes. 'You can deal with them contemptuously – but you must deal with them . . . a great actor is no greater than what he does to his audience.' He seems not to admit of the possibility that the audience can influence the actor's performance: that thanks to them he could transcend himself completely. No. He says: the actor controls the audience totally, that's what's so great about it. Equally, he is saying that actors are born, not made, and that there is no system of work on oneself or one's art that can produce great acting. 'And there are no great actors in the theatre today.'

In their absence, who then is to control the audience? Why, the director, of course. Noting that the old-time star went out at the same time as the director came in, he observes that 'nobody has read the last chapter of the detective story and discovered that this old-time star did not go out. He merely sits in the fifth row and is the director.' As a matter of fact, the old-time star was a director, too, like Irving or Tree; but the point is well made. The director is now the star. Welles rebelled against this idea, while at the same time embodying it to a greater degree than anyone, perhaps, in the history of the theatre. The show was always the star in a Welles production. But Welles doesn't really approve of 'the director' – the others, that is. He berates those 'American, English and Continental directors of excessive eccentricities imposing their tastes and their inhibitions, their inordinate love of various obscure theatrical elements, on an entire pattern of theatrical culture'. He believes that the director 'so far has done more harm than good in exact proportion to his ability'. As elsewhere in this little booklet, Welles seems to be arguing with – and often against – himself, both as actor and director, mentally struggling to justify a gut instinct that seems to him somehow wrong. Great actors are *this*, he says, and then seems suddenly to wonder whether it describes him; directors shouldn't be *that*, he says, and then wonders whether he hasn't just described himself.

The Director in the Theatre Today is a curious document: the work of an arrogant, talented young man, intoxicated with the power of his gift, dreaming of a theatre which would transcend everyday reality and offer astonishing visions, it is fundamentally confused. He longs to be a great actor himself, but postulates a notion of great acting so exalted that no one, including himself, could possibly fulfil it. He clearly believes himself to be a great director, but disapproves of the very idea of directing as a feeble substitute for the great acting that should properly be holding the stage. He loves great writing, but believes that that, too, is secondary to great acting – if only there were any about. This obsession with the Great Actor, or the Old-Time Star, seems (as, again, it did for Craig) to have a little something to do with a longed-for Father, the superhuman, lordly figure, whom one aspires to be. There is a lurking feeling that what he himself wants to be is not a director at all, but an old-time star. If only one were an old-time star, people would respect one, one would be *someone*. Many years later, interviewed for the BBC by Leslie Megahey, he said, 'I have a kind of personality which requires that I play certain kinds of parts, or I discombobulate the scene . . . there used to be a form, a division of actors in France, in the Comédie Française, who were called king actors. And I'm a king actor, maybe a bad one, but that's what I am, you see. And I have to play authoritative roles.' He adds: 'but Truffaut was quite right when he says about me that I show the fragility of the great authority, and that's the thing I do.'

This comment of Truffaut's is a dazzling aperçu, a key to all of Welles's acting; his power, while undeniable, seems assumed, put on – like a false nose – and thus vulnerable. It seems as if behind the king, there is a little boy rather desperately playing at being a king. Thus his portrayal of power comes to seem a critique of power: man, proud man, drest in a little brief authority. There is something unself-convinced, both about the role and the actor. It is doubly poignant; a kingly personage whose authority is questionable, played by an actor whose own claim to greatness is not believed in by himself. He could only be, in his own eyes, a great actor, if he was to be an actor at all; and yet he feels shifty about making the claim. It is as if it were a reluctant and unsuitable destiny; like Barrymore, in a remark already quoted from an awkward exchange with Peter Bogdanovich, he 'played the part of an actor because that was the role he'd been given by life'. The notion of acting – great acting – as a burden he'd been born to, willy-nilly, is a common one with Welles.

He confessed to Harold Stagg in the *New Haven Ledger* only a year after he had started the Mercury: 'I've given myself terrific parts in my plays. I've built myself upon big roles, and I've imposed myself on the public as a star.' Welles tried to make himself a great actor simply by playing leading parts one after another. That is not the way to do it; certainly not in the full glare of *The New York Times*. It is as if an amateur pianist, having a wide span and a nice touch, were simply to play all the towering masterpieces of the piano repertory one after another – not bothering to practise, not spending time studying the scores – all on instinct and enthusiasm. As Virgil Thomson observed, he never gave his mind, let alone his heart, to his work as an actor. Did he want to be one at all? He still seemed unsure forty years later. 'I was obsessed in my hot youth,' he said on *Arena*, 'with the idea that I would not be a star. And I was in a position to promote myself as a star and I should have. I should have gone back to New York and played Hamlet and . . . as long as it was going I didn't. I had this idea that I wanted to be known as a director and that was that.' He seems to have been insecure about the idea of himself as a star, or even perhaps as a leading man. The idea of being a director – the big boss – somehow struck him as having more weight. Welles was constantly trying to give himself weight, solidity. He succeeded beyond his wildest ambitions, and not at all: always feeling small, despite girth and glory.

The conflicting and highly emotional ingredients of his artistic agenda go some way towards explaining why, half-audacious modernist, half-archaic dreamer, reluctant totalitarian and self-doubting star, he created such an extraordinary impact in the world of the American theatre of the thirties. His agenda was often irrational, and always explosive. Now, with his new theatre, he was poised to put it into effect.

He girded his loins and set about staging *Julius Caesar* in September of 1937. Just before starting work on it, and having polished off the last episodes of *Les Misérables*, he was asked by the same company, Mutual, to take the leading part in the relaunch of their sensational success, *The Shadow*. Hitherto the mysterious law-enforcer had merely narrated; in the new version, his adventures were to be enacted. Moreover, he was now to have the supernatural gift of invisibility (hitherto he had merely lurked in, well, yes, the shadows). The final innovation was that he was to have a double identity: by day, Lamont Cranston, 'a wealthy young man-about-town'; by night, The Shadow, who, 'using sophisticated methods that may shortly be available to regular law-enforcement agencies', fights an unceasing war on crime, aided only by his side-kick, the lovely Margot Lane. The character was a prototype for those subsequent split personalities, Batman, Superman, and Captain Marvel; Welles was the first Cranston but the fourth Shadow. Curiously, the famous opening sequence, with The Shadow's trademark, a bass chuckle (oddly sinister for a law-enforcer), and his endlessly imitated warning (under the sound of a whirlwind blended with Saint-Saëns's welling theme from *Le Rouet d'Omphale*), 'Who knows what evil lurks in the heart of man? The Shadow knows . . . the weed of crime bears bitter fruit. Crime does not pay! The Shadow knows!' was not his; Mutual preferred his predecessor's rendition of it, so one of Welles's most famous performances – as well known and as closely associated with him in its time as the Harry Lime theme would be twelve years later – was actually given by Frank Readick, Jr.

Welles plays Cranston rather leisurely and mild, with careless charm in the more or less English accent still synonymous with a private income; there is about the interpretation a suggestion of silk dressing gown and cigarette holder: *this* was his Noël Coward performance. All his love of melodrama informs his performance of Cranston's alter ego, The Shadow himself. In a curious resonance for Welles, this other self was the result of 'a youthful trip to the Orient', where Cranston had learned 'a strange and mysterious secret . . . the hypnotic power to cloud men's minds so they cannot see him'; the *real* him, in Welles's case, perhaps. Jungians everywhere will raise a smile, perhaps a slightly serious smile, at the personification of one of the great analyst's key concepts: the shadow is 'that part of us we fail to know or see' – which, if unacknowledged or denied, destroys us. Another resonance. Initially, the actor's identity was kept secret – but nothing to do with Welles could remain a secret for very long. It added, over the couple of years in which he played the role, to an irresistibly growing fame. But meanwhile, there was *Caesar* to prepare for his new theatre.

CHAPTER THIRTEEN

Caesar

PRESUMABLY IN the belief that *his* eccentricities were not excessive, *his* love of obscure theatrical elements was not inordinate, and that *he* would not be imposing his tastes and inhibitions on theatrical culture, Welles began his work on *Julius Caesar*, withdrawing to the country just as Stanislavsky had to prepare his production of *The Seagull* in the opening months of the Moscow Art Theatre. Once he had assembled his cast, he set off for New Hampshire to work both on *Caesar* and – a late addition to the repertory which Welles had realised would be a superb vehicle for the talents of his chum Chubby Sherman – *The Shoemaker's Holiday* by Thomas Dekker. He returned two weeks later with edited texts, models and drawings for *Julius Caesar* which he presented to his creative team: Jean Rosenthal as lighting designer, Sam Leve as set designer, Marc Blitzstein, composer.

His interpretation of the play was extremely clear, and, as we have seen, not particularly original. Not only had both Hallie Flanagan and Sidney Howard already separately suggested the idea of a modern dress, fascist *Caesar* to Welles and Houseman, but Arthur Schintzer, head of the Federal Theatre Project at Wilmington, Delaware, had actually done one earlier that year, 'a not-too-complimentary satire on premier Benito Mussolini and fascist Italy', said the *Newark Post*. Schintzer had been inspired not by political purposes, but by the familiar FTP problem: having a number of veteran (male) vaudevillians on his hands, he needed a play with a large, largely male, cast. *Julius Caesar* fitted the bill nicely. Realising that 'these old boys would look silly in togas', he decided to dress them in blackshirts and khaki. News of Delaware's *Caesar* had not reached Manhattan, nor was Sidney Howard's Collected Correspondence publicly available, so the idea seemed to have leaped fully fledged out of Welles's brain. Questions of originality and authorship were to plague Welles throughout his career, largely because of his insistence on sole responsibility for his own work and his increasing need to appear as an original genius, a quite unnecessary and largely unsustainable claim. In media as miscegenated as the theatre and film, an original idea is the least of it: the realisation is all. The best idea in the world, poorly executed, is dead in the water; the real creator is the person who can liberate an idea's potential. And by that criterion, Welles had few rivals.

In the case of *Julius Caesar*, he served the idea absolutely, better, perhaps, than the play itself. His version of the text was heavily cut and rearranged: a performing version, and no mistake. During rehearsals, he continued cutting and rearranging; this process only stopped by Press Night. He had come a long way from his resounding affirmation in *Everybody's Shakespeare*: 'one of the very wisest ways to play Shakespeare is the way he wrote it . . . he wrote it that way not because he didn't know better but because he knew best.' He had changed his mind about a number of things since that precocious essay. 'What's in a Name?' he had asked then. 'Commentators say the play is mis-named: *Brutus* should be its title . . . I disagree,' he wrote. 'The personality of Caesar is the focal point of every line of the play.' By 1937, though he didn't go so far as to propose changing the title, he had come to the conclusion that Brutus was very much the central figure of the play. *The Mercury*, the weekly bulletin that was in effect Welles's mouthpiece, stated: 'As those familiar with the play are aware, *Julius Caesar* is really about Brutus.' Welles himself added: 'Brutus is the classical picture of the eternal, impotent, ineffectual, fumbling liberal; the reformer who wants to do something about things but doesn't know how and gets it in the neck in the end. He's dead right all the time, and dead at the final curtain. He's Shakespeare's favourite hero – the fellow who thinks the times are out of joint but who is really out of joint with his time. He's the bourgeois intellectual who, under a modern dictatorship, would be the first to be put up against a wall and shot.'

He had concluded that the play was 'about' the anguish of the liberal in an age of dictators. This emphasis meant that a great deal of the political complexity of the play was sacrificed in order to focus on one man's dilemma. The version Welles fashioned by no means fulfilled Houseman's claim for the production that 'the stress will be on the social implications inherent in the history of Caesar and on the atmosphere of personal greed, fear and hysteria that surrounds a dictatorial regime' or indeed Welles's own claim at the same time that 'it's a timeless tragedy about Caesarism and the collapse of democracy under Caesarism.' Lepidus was axed entirely; Octavius and Antony downgraded, and the mob, so graphically individualised by Shakespeare, relegated to a largely choric function – in the text, that is.

Its function in the staging was heightened, streamlined; but it became a many-headed hydra, losing the dynamics of individuals in a crowd. 'Here we have true fan psychology,' he told *The New York Times*. 'This is the same mob that tears the buttons off the coat of Robert Taylor. It's the same mob, too, that hangs and burns negroes in the South, the same mob that maltreats the Jews in Germany. It's the Nazi mob anywhere.' Significantly Welles's version starts, not with the scene analysed by a million schoolchildren ('Hence! Home, you idle creatures, get you home!') but with Caesar silencing the crowd. 'Bid every noise be still!' We are in the presence of the Great from the start; there is no context. Rome is its leaders; a distinctly bourgeois reading of history.

Whatever the interpretation, the result was nothing if not effective; a great deal of the Mercury version, in fact, was devised for no other reason than to generate theatrical excitement. The text gives every appearance of having been shaped to accommodate the production, rather than the other way round. His adaptation is exactly comparable to those reviled eighteenth-century adaptors, Garrick and Cibber, his purposes exactly the same as theirs: to exploit the possibilities of their stage-craft and to fit the play to the temper of the times. 'In drastically cutting the last twenty minutes of the play,' wrote Hank Senber in *The Mercury*, 'Welles was working to clarify the personal aspects of the tragedy and to liberate the play from such concessions to Elizabethan tastes as drums, alarums and mock battles on stage.' And of course, those things did look and sound ridiculous when the warriors in question were wearing long black leather overcoats and jackboots. Welles certainly wasn't going to lose the stunning effectiveness of the uniforms because some of the play didn't fit. Cut it! The lurid theatricality of the regimes of Mussolini and Hitler was an essential element in choosing the context for the play, and the physical look of the production was absolutely clear in Welles's mind from the beginning. There seems, however, to have been some conceptual confusion. If the play – or at any rate the production – is a critique of Caesarism, what does Antony represent? He, surely, is the demagogue, not Caesar: he's Hitler, he's Mussolini. Is Caesar then Hindenburg? Somewhat defensively, Welles told *The Mercury*: 'I produced the play in modern dress to sharpen contemporary interest rather than to point up or stunt up present-day detail. I'm trying to let Shakespeare's lines do the job of making the play applicable to the tensions of our time.' It was a general feeling of contemporaneity that he was after; not a blow-by-blow parallel.

His absolute certainty about the physical realisation of the concept made his collaborators' work quite cut and dried. Jeannie Rosenthal wrote: 'Welles dictated very clearly and exactly the kind of look he wanted the production to have, a very simple look, based on the Nazi rallies at Nuremberg. The patterns implied in the Nuremberg "festivals" were in terms of platforms, which were the basis of the scenery, and light which went up or down. The uplight was really taken from the effect the Nazis achieved.' (And which Houseman had used before in *Panic.*) Welles described his concept of the physical production in *The Director in the Theatre Today* the following year: 'I wanted to present *Julius Caesar* against a texture of brick, not of stone, and I wanted a color of red that had certain vibrations of blue. In front of this red brick wall I wanted levels and places to act: that was my conception of the production.' Welles's visual confidence is rare among directors. His own skills as a graphic artist, coupled with his experience in designing and building for the Todd Troupers and the Gate Theatre, made him a daunting prospect for a designer. Young Sam Leve, fresh from triumphs with the Federal Theatre Project and the Yiddish Art Theatre, in his own words '*oozing* imagination', found that Welles was uninterested in his suggestions. In order to get them even considered, he had to convey them to Houseman, who might, if he liked them, pass them on, a 'humiliating process' for the young designer, in his own words. However, when Welles asked him for sketches, from the hundreds Leve would produce, on Leve's admission he would unerringly choose the best, dismissing the less good ones: 'Sam, you can do better than that.' The two men were exactly the same age, but as usual Welles immediately and automatically assumed command.

'At the Mercury,' wrote Jean Rosenthal, 'nobody else had any identity for him at all. You were production material. If he liked you, the association could be pleasant. If not, it was injurious. As a director, he approached other talents as he did his gargantuan meals – with a voracious appetite. Your contributions to his feast he either spat out or set aside untouched, or he ate them up, assimilated them, with a gusto which was extraordinarily flattering.' And fun: 'the initial stages of anything with Orson were immensely entertaining, which carried everything along . . . he never counted the cost of anything to himself or to anyone else.' Rosenthal, who became one of the crucial figures in the development of American theatre lighting before her early death in the sixties, was keenly aware of the growth of the power of directors, and identified Welles as one of the first to dominate every single aspect of a production.

Rosenthal avoided confrontation with Welles, but he never doubted her strength, demanding much of her within a framework of respect. Her final judgement, though, on her work with him is a chilling one: 'I do not think Orson made the utmost use of his collaborators' talent, although he often inspired their achievements. He did make the utmost use of his talents at the beginning, but perhaps his lack of respect for others accounts in some measure for the ultimate dissipation of his multiple talents.'

For the time being, the actors were not complaining. Few of them would have been aware of his philosophical baggage. What they saw was a man with very determined ideas putting them into practice with a disarming combination of ruthless drilling and amiable anecdotalising, plus a good deal of horseplay. Exuberant, in some ways still a very young man, almost a boy, he dictated the pace and regularity of work according to his personal mood. 'When he felt like rehearsing, we rehearsed. When he felt like sleeping, we didn't rehearse. If he felt like rehearsing from 11.00 at night to 6.00 in the morning, damn stage-hands' overtime, full speed ahead,' according to his then stage manager Howard Teichmann. 'He was a brilliant, inventive, imaginative, director . . . in a class all by himself. He would sit generally at a table in the centre aisle behind the table, and he would have a microphone on the table. And he would whisper his directions into the microphone. This table also served as his dining table. When he was hungry, he would send people out and they would bring in the steaks and the french fries and the ice cream and pots of coffee a foot and a half high, which he would consume with great relish. And when he was tired, he would say, "All right, children." Now mind you, he was younger than most of the people but we were his children.'

'There was no doubt in anyone's mind that Orson was the big star,' said Teichmann. 'He was a year or two older than I am, and he was slim, with a big head and round cheeks and very boyish. And "boy genius" was a term if he didn't create, he didn't fight it off . . . You had to be a certain kind of a personality to work with Orson. You either had to worship him or you had to meet him on an equal level, or you had to crumble. And a great many people, you know, would end up with ulcers and he was a great one for giving them. He loved everybody, but, boy, he was tough. "Who me, tough? I'm a pussycat." You know, that was his thing . . . he played people off against each other.' His manner was calculated to be humorously high-handed, shouting out admonitions – 'shame on you!' a favourite – if the actor's work wasn't to his liking. He was not averse to having a whipping boy: young William Alland, later famous as the producer of *The Creature from the Black Lagoon*, and known to movie buffs as the shadowy reporter in *Citizen Kane*, had, when the Mercury was being set up, more or less thrown himself at Welles's feet, and that's more or less where he stayed, as actor, stage manager, gofer and pimp. Welles would roar his name out, abusing and cajoling him. It was good-humoured, but only just: a throw away from bullying. If you weren't on the receiving end, it could be fun; to Peg Lloyd it was cheap: 'he seemed a prep school boy with the cheap humour that preppies have. A genius preppy, that's what he was: the ringleader of the bullies on the corner.'

Rehearsals for *Julius Caesar* took place, initially, not in the theatre (the stage was still being reconstructed) but in an abandoned movie studio in Fort Lee, New Jersey, 'the place where the movie industry began' in the words of Elliot Reid. Under a couple of worklights, while the incessant rain dripped into strategically placed buckets and the plaster tumbled from the roof, Welles arranged his cast on the platforms which Sam Leve had found in an old Shubert warehouse, and which were the essential element of the set that he and Welles had devised. There were four platforms: the first fourteen foot deep (the downstage playing area), the second a narrow high step, the third an eight foot deep plateau, the last a narrower platform rising to a total height of six and a half foot above stage level; there were two flagpoles on either side of the stage. Within this framework, Welles laboured to create the images that he had in his mind. Despite the great informality with which he worked, the stories and the atmosphere of wild, almost boyish fun that he engendered, he was always straining towards a specific and precise visual notion, what Norman Lloyd (playing Cinna the poet) described as 'the shot'. 'Every scene had to have a production idea. Is it a shot? Is there something interesting in it?' He improvised the physical action, constantly altering the moves to achieve the desired shape; the scene wasn't worked out in advance, in the Reinhardt manner, every eyebrow, every sniffle planned. But the effect was much the same: there was no discussion of character or motivation, simply a dedication to discovering what Brecht had called the 'gestus', or the gesture, of the scene.

Debate over his methods constantly raged amongst the company, though rarely to his face. Moody, sardonic Coulouris (who during breaks from rehearsals would throw tennis balls against the wall, muttering 'Be a singer, be a singer! Don't be an actor! Acting's horrible') openly challenged Welles, but he became, Jaques-like, a sort of licensed melancholic within the group. For the most part the actors worked happily at the service of Welles's invention. Nor was he intent simply on imposing his ideas on them. Norman Lloyd reports Welles as saying, 'I may not be able to direct actors very well, but once an actor gives me something, I know how to stage it.' Lloyd himself fretted over the absence of any sort of methodology, feeling that the essence or the truth of the scene was sometimes sacrificed to effect; he was none the less delighted by the opportunities Welles's staging afforded him. Welles's instinctive sense of how to release an actor and a scene in physical movement was the equal of his English contemporary, Tyrone Guthrie, with whom he shared a revulsion for dealing with the inner life of the character, or indeed, of the actor. 'Your problem!' Guthrie would briskly tell his actors as they wrestled with difficulties of this kind; the phrase could just as easily have come from Welles.

The concomitant of this external, linear approach was that if the scene was effective, it succeeded; if it wasn't, it was nothing. Welles struggled for weeks with scenes which resisted his best efforts; this process continued up to the very opening. One such was the scene in which Cinna the poet is killed by the mob. There was from the start a disagreement between actor and director over interpretation, Welles seeing the poet as a version of Marchbanks, all long hair and floppy ties, Lloyd, playing the part, seeing him rather as the sort of man who wrote letters to *The New York Times*, a prototypical liberal, brilliantly able to see both sides of the situation, congenitally incapable of deciding between them; Archibald MacLeish, in fact. Lloyd hoped to achieve, as he says, an 'essence'. 'I thought you could say "this is what it is to not take a position." ' Welles quickly gave in over the characterisation, because he was obsessed – 'consumed' is the word Lloyd uses – by an idea of how to stage the scene, a musical, a choreographic conception of how to show a mob destroying an innocent man. First of all he needed more lines than Shakespeare had provided, so, after experimenting with improvisation, he drafted in a few from *Coriolanus*; then he enlisted Marc Blitzstein to orchestrate the voices using a beating drum to indicate the rhythm. Welles rehearsed 'this goddam chanting and boom boom boom' for over three weeks. Sometimes Blitzstein took over; neither of them spent any time on the characters or the acting as such.

As for Welles's own performance, it was a low priority. A stage manager stood in for him throughout rehearsals. The result was that by the time of the dress rehearsal, he had barely acted with his fellow players (which can scarcely have helped them in creating their own performances); nor, never having run the scenes himself, was he very clear about where he should actually be standing. No one knew where he would be coming from or where he would be going to and he was frequently shrouded in darkness. To add to the uncertainty, he was very shaky on his lines, having scarcely uttered them during rehearsals. Throughout his career, on film and on stage, he was never entirely in command of his texts. He was not a quick study and rarely had the time or the inclination to ensure that the words were so securely lodged in his memory that they would spring spontaneously to his lips at the appropriate moment. Fortunately, he had considerable powers of iambic improvisation, and could sonorously if meaninglessly coast along for minutes at a time until a familiar line would, to the relief of the actor who was waiting for his cue, emerge. Since he had not rehearsed the part of Brutus, he had of course no opportunity to explore the character, to experiment with his approach, or to open himself to anyone else's view of his work. He had decided at some earlier time who Brutus was – who *his* Brutus was – and simply slotted it in to the production. Brutus, he said on several occasions, was above all intelligent (the character description for Marcus Brutus in *Everybody's Shakespeare* reads: 'he is a fine patrician type, his face sensitive and intellectual'). It was Welles's belief that he had a special gift for playing 'thinking people': not, as he expressed it in an interview with Peter Bogdanovich, 'that they're thinking about what they're saying, but that they think outside of the scene . . . there are very few actors who can make you believe they think . . . that's the kind of part I can play.'

Happy the actor who knows his own gift. He has at least a chance, given a moderate amount of luck and a shrewd choice of work, of playing straight down the centre of the character to create a vivid and clear image of a particular human being. If he is struggling against type, to express things not in his personal experience or make-up, then he will almost certainly miss the core of the character, however interestingly he may embellish its surface. Though Welles was unquestionably intelligent, the most striking feature of his acting persona is not intelligence but power; he described himself, quite accurately, as 'he who plays the king'. Curiously enough, his portrayals of 'thinking people' often lack intellectual conviction: what he demonstrates is thoughtfulness. Partly this stems from a lack of structure in his own thinking; mostly it derives from the simple technical fact of not having completely mastered the text, and thus the thought. Welles, instead of actually thinking, acts it.

It would seem that what really drew Welles to the role of Brutus was not so much his cerebral nature, but rather his nobility: this dark, wild, immature, titanically possessed young man wanted to present himself as the very soul of dignity and responsibility. His method of doing so was – according to his own formula – simply to suppress the ignoble parts of himself. Easy.

This cavalier attitude to his own performance is partly explicable by absorption in other responsibilities; but there is a strong suggestion that he became involved in his other responsibilities in order not to have to immerse himself in his own performance. He didn't want to evolve his performance; he didn't want to talk about it, or to think about it. In Lehman Engel's acute words: 'His own performances happened suddenly for good or ill. They were or were not at the very outset.' In none of his utterances on the subject of acting does Welles ever speak of the work that goes into a performance. The assumption is that you can either play the part or you can't; if you can, then that's it: you play it. It is a complex matter: he seemed to want to be acclaimed for his acting, but not to have to work on it. He expected to be acknowledged as a major actor, while insisting that acting wasn't a terribly important thing anyway.

His Brutus was barely glimpsed before the dress rehearsal. When the company were finally able to enter the theatre, the physical aspect of the production dominated totally. Every rehearsal was a technical rehearsal. Once the lights started to appear, Welles would move actors into their most effective groupings; he and Jeannie Rosenthal would spend hours moving the actors or the lights to achieve the images they were striving for. They were in a state of constant experiment, Welles improvising as more and more lamps appeared, Rosenthal trying to make possible what he wanted. Despite the advances in technology and the brilliant innovations of McCandless and Feder, the art of lighting was still an approximate one. Houseman maintains that only 50 per cent of cues plotted would materialise as envisaged. In order to combat this, Rosenthal invented a complex system for recording them which immediately enabled the Mercury to be more ambitious in terms of light than any other theatre. The theatre groups of the thirties were in the vanguard of the development of lighting design, not initially for aesthetic reasons, but from necessary thrift. 'The idea, the actor and a pool of light to focus interest on the performing area were used to convey the essence of meaning as never before. These pools of light,' wrote Jean Rosenthal, 'alone could create theatricality. Varied as directed, downward or angled from back or front, left or right, high or low, each position produced its own plasticity and pattern.'

This was very much the form of light identified with Welles's stage productions; as Rosenthal became over the remaining twenty-five years of her life the dominant lighting designer of the American theatre, her view of light predominated too. 'Jeannie considered the most important lighting was lighting air, not scenery or people,' wrote her friend Lucia Victor. 'The air in one of Jean's shows vibrated with the emotion of whatever the particular scene was about.' Welles's view exactly. In order to achieve it in *Julius Caesar*, they needed an enormous amount of equipment which they didn't always have; the only solution was to replug the lights three times during the (interval-less) performance. 'Every elaborate effect had to be created by hand,' reports Andrea Noryeh. 'Rosenthal stood on a catwalk to synchronise the counts for dimming two distinct spotlights. She tapped on one crew member's shoulder with one rhythm and on another crew member's shoulder with a different one.'

There was a third member of the team, poor downtrodden Sam Leve, and he made his contribution to the lighting (it was he, for example, who realised that the famous Nuremberg lights would only work if the actors brought smoke on with them, an effect achieved by stationing smudge pots in the wings). His claim, however, that the light-plot was his alone, executed to his prescription by Rosenthal, seems unlikely. He, Welles and Rosenthal all had strong ideas; Welles created an atmosphere where everything seemed possible. No one was tolerated who expressed caution or anxiety; neither time nor money were held to be acceptable limitations. But there was no master-plan. The whole thing, once the basic line had been established by Welles, was open to negotiation, and to happy accident. 'One effect, spoken of as stunning and innovative, was a marvelous accident,' wrote Rosenthal. 'During a dress rehearsal someone forgot to turn out the bald, overhead work lights – whose sole purpose is to illuminate the grid from which the scenery ropes and pulleys are suspended – and they continued to shine down during the blackout just before the orchard scene. The pattern criss-crossing the stage, conveyed an impression of ground beneath bare branches. Paradoxically in view of the hard thinking and planning I believe in, accident is often the source of inspiration.' A similar happy accident had occurred with regard to the platforms. The original plan had been to pad the hollow platforms to stop them from amplifying the sound of the conspirators' heavy boots; this plan was abandoned due to cost. The boots' drumming sound, urgent and menacing, became one of the production's most distinctive features. Welles's ability to exploit mishaps remained one of his enduring traits. He was galvanised by them; the rush of adrenalin that they brought often redeemed what threatened to be dull work. Of course in October 1937 he was in no need of additional infusions of adrenalin; he was made of the stuff, and without even trying to, sent it pumping through the veins of anyone who came near him.

As far as the costumes were concerned, the production concept dictated uniformity. Welles's friend Millia Davenport refused to work on the show: too dull, she said, for a costume designer. In the event, they hired a job lot of olive-green military outfits which had been used in Maxwell Anderson's 1924 anti-war play *What Price Glory?* The conspirators wore gangster-like clothes. The fascist feeling was startlingly underlined by Marc Blitzstein's score, a series of grinding processional interludes scored for a band consisting of trumpet, horn, percussion and Hammond organ, freely quoting Mussolini's anthem, the 'Giovinezza', making Welles's cheeky claim in interviews that he had intended no specific parallels rather hollow. In addition to his regular percussion, Blitzstein had somehow managed to locate a vast thunder drum constructed for the initial run of *Chu Chin Chow*, which was used to suitably shattering effect; at the other end of the scale, he composed a delicate Kurt Weill-ish lute song for Lucius to sing to Brutus, a setting of *Orpheus with his Lute*. There was, too, an immensely complicated and endlessly troublesome sound score devised by the radio producer Irving Reis, of the *Columbia Workshop*. Apart from simple effects (crickets, owls, railway trains) played on gramophones, sound in the theatre was virtually non-existent. Welles and Reis were experimenting with the sort of ambitious collages that radio engineers were starting to develop; the theatre's speakers were not designed to cope with the levels of sound that the engineers provided, and piercing shrieks and incomprehensible rumbles were the only result.

The company were reeling under the weight of all this additional input. The dress rehearsal is always a difficult moment in any production. The actors must desperately hang on to what they've achieved in the rehearsal room, and use the new elements to enhance and expand their work. The danger, especially in a non-realistic conception, is that they will be disorientated by the physical production, and sink under its weight. It takes some runs of the show for the actors to rise above all these new factors and turn them to their advantage; particularly difficult if the director, as in this case, is given to constant modification of every single aspect of the production. Some things suddenly became thrilling: Caesar's death, for example, as he rolled down the diagonal line of conspirators till he came to Brutus, hanging on to his lapels, and gasping Et tu Brute. 'The way they came up the ramp to greet Caesar was wonderful,' Norman Lloyd recalled. 'Everybody had a real dagger: the lights caught them beautifully. Orson went upstage to stab Caesar. The first time we did it, Orson's knife stuck in the stage and quivered. Jesus! it was unbelievable.' But just as many things made no sense at all. In the prevailing confusion, Welles managed to fall fifteen foot off one of the platforms; miraculously, he picked himself up and carried on changing everything. Still there had been no dress rehearsal. Finally, it took place and was a desperate shambles. Welles found himself faced with a mutiny: Norman Lloyd refused to play the Cinna scene, the scene on which they had worked obsessively week in and week out, on the grounds that they had never really rehearsed it – not for its acting content. Welles acceded; at the first preview, to replace the scene, stage-hands wheeled a large brute light to the foot of the stage and shone it into the audience's eyes. This – matinee – performance was an unmitigated disaster: the primitive sound system became completely unmanageable. At the end of the show there was no applause. Henry Senber, the press officer, went backstage, aghast and said to Welles 'My God, we didn't even get a curtain call.' Quite understandably, Welles spat in his eye. Senber was about to strike him. Welles begged him to spit in *his* eye, which he did. Life went on.

The show, however, did not. The next few previews were suspended, while they set to work on solving their problems. Houseman, who, stealing time from his teaching schedule at Vassar, had been at Welles's side, on his insistence, twenty hours a day during the entire period of technical rehearsal, kept calm, which is exactly what a producer should do. It is unlikely that his outward demeanour was an accurate reflection of his inner state. The Mercury Theatre had been in crisis since its inception, a bare six weeks before. By November 1st, the money initially raised had run out. At the box office, the cheaper seats were doing well but the carriage trade was resistant. The ticket agents were openly scornful of them as 'amateurs'. The first investment had rapidly disappeared; only a fortnight before the official opening of *Julius Caesar*, Rosenthal and George Zorn presented Houseman with a union labour bill for $2,000 which he simply didn't have. The reality of life away from the comfortable, labour-intensive Federal Theatre was made rudely apparent. Thanks to a chance meeting, Houseman was able to explain his plight to the playwright Clare Booth and her husband Henry Luce, proprietor of *Time* magazine: they chipped in $2,500, a bagatelle for them, the difference between life and death for the Mercury. Houseman's old flame Mina Curtiss put in another thousand, and they were in business again. It all hung by a thread, though. *Caesar* must be a huge success, or the Mercury would fold as soon as it had opened.

These anxieties of Houseman were scarcely tempered by his relationship with Welles, or indeed the company. Typically, the actors were suspicious of and in some cases actually hostile to 'the management'. He was perceived as financially stingy, and was, from time to time, quite prepared to cut the actors' salaries. The company joke was that they'd bring a horse into Houseman's office. He wouldn't mind, the joke went, he'd just persuade the horse to take a cut in its oats. Welles did nothing to explain his function or support him. Norman Lloyd, later a close friend, shared the general view: 'In those days we never took him very seriously. We thumbed our noses at authority – and Jack was the boss. He lacked Orson's charisma, he totally lacked confidence. He stuttered, he stammered. His English accent was against him because it made him affected; he wore a suit. We felt what's he doing in the theatre? Little did we know that he was an essential part of Orson's success.' Years later, Lloyd said to him, 'You were scared to death in those days,' to which Houseman replied 'the fear was infinite.' Teichmann describes him as living 'in anguish, fear and righteous indignation'. Welles – 'this creature, this Frankenstein that he had built' – had taken over. 'Orson hired press agents, Orson gave interviews, Orson was photographed, and Houseman was left there to run the operation.' Goostie Weissberger was aware of Houseman's desperate need of Welles. 'He was the most insecure man you ever knew, terribly afraid of doing or saying something that would sever their relationship.'

This anxiety did not prevent him from engaging with Welles in huge rows, one of which Welles describes in his screenplay for *The Cradle Will Rock*: 'the entire theatre is treated to the alarums and discursions of a classic HOUSEMAN–WELLES difference of opinion. As an actor, trained to project iambic pentameters to the furthest reaches of large rehearsal galleries, ORSON is, inevitably, the noisiest and therefore sounds the more aggressive . . . HOUSEMAN is busily, but quietly, kindling the flames . . . if ORSON can roar like a lion, JACK HOUSEMAN has a smiling mouth which "biteth like an adder".' But the relationship was as complicated for Welles as it was for Houseman; Welles required approval, as is made clear in a speech a little later on in the same screenplay:

> ORSON
> And Jack, it's all done with these small pieces of glass – An elegant solution; and you – you don't even deign to look.

This is fairly frankly stated: Daddy, look at me. Houseman's one card was to withhold his approval, while giving Welles pretty well everything else he wanted.

At this precise moment, however, after the catastrophic first preview of *Julius Caesar*, both men were equally frightened, and set to work to salvage the show. The sound score was dropped; various other technical modifications were made. There were more cuts to an already very slim text including most of the Octavius/Antony scenes, perhaps because Francis Carpenter, as Octavius, couldn't handle the part of the ruthless emergent emperor. The crucial scene that required work was, of course, that of Cinna the Poet. They sat down, Welles at his desk, his steak in front of him. 'Orson would argue with you as he ate, and you got angrier. I thought we'd reached an impasse,' says Norman Lloyd. 'But no – he went my way. And *when* he went your way! – I played the first part of the scene for pantomimic comedy. Got a lot of laughs. Just becoming aware of this crowd and thinking they had recognised me as a celebrity. Stuffed my pockets with these poems. He seized that right away. They moved in to kill – I was playing it as the poet laureate. He moved these guys in one by one – and the lighting was fantastic – blood red – the set was red too. The way he moved me – there were laughs, and then the laughs got chilly. Taking out these poems. Orson's direction: the last thing I scream is THE POET. Rush down the ramp – I just disappeared – just this hand, bathed in red light.'

As so often, solving a particular scene had clarified the entire production. The scene became, in Welles's word, the fulcrum of the show: by creating a moment of absolute realism, the concept was made to pay off brilliantly, in a way that stretched both backwards and forwards through the rest of the production. The rage of a roused mob, their destruction of an innocent, rather foolish creature, someone immediately recognisable from real life, gave the whole production its authenticity: 'Its great success was as a political drama written the night before,' as Lloyd said. 'It was Costa-Gavras.'

The previews resumed; every performance was better than the

one before. It needed to be.There was no euphoria; indeed,Coulouris stood in the wings on the penultimate preview, predicting that by Saturday, the Mercury would have folded. It was this preview, a matinee, that, by special dispensation, John Mason Brown, the powerful critic of the *New York Post*, attended. After the show, he went backstage (unusual behaviour for a critic) and expressed himself enraptured. 'When he started acting out the whole play, we knew we were a hit.' Even more unusually for a critic, he made a suggestion: that the show should end with Antony's elegy for Brutus. He had clearly grasped the idea that Brutus was the central character. Exhilarated by his enthusiasm, they agreed; Octavius' final entrance was cut. At the official première that night (in 1937, a first night was crucial: virtually the entire critical fraternity was present) Mason Brown's response was confirmed: the production became itself, fully, for the first time. From the moment the audience walked into the auditorium to find the New York city fireman required to be present by law, actually onstage, to Coulouris's ringing delivery, an hour and three quarters and no interval later, of his second funeral oration of the evening ('And say to all the world this was a man') the audience was held breathless, erupting at the end in wild applause. Detaching himself from the carousing which followed the triumphant curtain calls, Houseman went out to Times Square to catch the early editions of the newspapers; finding that every one was a rave, he tried to find Welles. Failing to do so, he drifted into a bar, picked up a girl, and took her back to his apartment, where they made love, as he tells us in *Run-Through*, 'without a word' – a characteristically vivid and somehow embarrassing detail: it seems as if he were making love to the wrong person.

The reviews were indeed overwhelming. Though by no means unanimous, they all testified to the fact that something unmissable had happened in the theatre. The reconstruction of a theatre event is always a hazardous matter, but in assessing the reviews of *Caesar*, we have a useful point of reference. Nearly a year after the first night, Welles and the company recorded as part of the Mercury Theatre of the Air radio series a severely truncated version of the play, interspersed with readings from Plutarch by the leading political commentator of the day, H.V. Kaltenborn. The cast was essentially the same as onstage, (Blitzstein's music was used, too) and from it we have a fairly good indication of certain aspects of the production. The physical impact, such a vital feature of the show, is obviously absent, but we get a strong sense of how the actors used the verse, and to some extent, how they characterised their roles:

Welles is quiet, measured, meditative – a little soporific, in fact; Gabel (Cassius) is intense, neurotic; Holland (Caesar) is stiff and plummy; Coulouris, as Antony, is electrifying: harsh but charismatic, nowhere more so than in the funeral oration over Caesar's body, which he strikingly orchestrates. All speak in more or less English accents; all handle the verse straightforwardly, with little sense of music – not that *Caesar* is an especially melodious text. Except for Welles, there is a great urgency about the reading; there is a feeling that space is being made for Brutus's temperate and considered utterances. It may, of course, have been very different in the theatre. Most reviewers, anyway, were more interested in describing the physical aspect of the production than the acting; above all they were taken by the concept, the energy and the daring. *Variety* got the mood in its headline: BARD BOFFOLA!

True to his backstage effusions, John Mason Brown led in the *New York Post* with the sort of review that guarantees queues round the block: 'Of all the many new plays and productions the season has so far revealed, this modern-dress version of the mob mischief and demagoguery which can follow the assassination of a dictator is by all odds the most exciting, the most imaginative, the most topical, the most awesome, and the most absorbing. The touch of genius is upon it.' He might have been quoting from Skipper Hill: 'Shakespeare ceases at the Mercury to be the darling of the College Board of Examiners. Unfettered and with all the vigor that was his when he spoke to the groundlings of his own day, he becomes the contemporary of all of us who are Undergroundlings.' Finally, he did the nicest thing a critic can do: he created of his enthusiasm a few memorable phrases that made his readers feel that they would have failed in their duty to themselves if they had missed the show. 'Something deathless and dangerous in the world sweeps past you down the darkened aisles at the Mercury and takes possession of the proud, gaunt stage. It is something fearful and ominous, something turbulent and to be dreaded, which distends the drama to include the life of nations as well as of men. It is an ageless warning, made in such arresting terms that it not only gives a new vitality to an ancient story but unrolls in your mind's eye a map of the world which is increasingly splotched with sickening colors.' He says, in effect, that what happens on the stage of the Mercury is more important than a mere play. Above all, he seems to be exhilarated by Welles's sense of freedom in telling the story his own way; a freedom which is, nowadays, the underlying assumption of any production. 'If the play ceases to be Shakespeare's tragedy, it does manage to become ours.'

The acting was widely liked. *The New York Times*'s Brooks Atkinson (describing the production as 'modern variations on the theme of Shakespeare's *Julius Caesar*') thought Welles's Brutus 'an admirable study in the somber tones of reverie and calm introspection: it is all kindness, reluctance and remorse.' (Mason Brown similarly had written of Welles's uncommon gift for speaking great words simply: 'the deliberation of his speech is the mark of the honesty which flames within him. His reticent Brutus is at once a foil to the staginess of the production as a whole . . .') Once the physical impact of the production had been absorbed, Atkinson – returning to the play the following week – found himself troubled by something, something which troubled many others: the political meaning of the production. What was Welles saying? And was it what Shakespeare was saying? 'In the Shakespeare ethic, Brutus is the murderer of a ruler . . . Shakespeare was in no mood to champion revolutions against the established government . . . and this fact has the somewhat ambiguous effect on a modern-dress *Julius Caesar* of implying that there is no use rebelling against a fascist state – which may be true, although a great many people hate to think so.' The *Daily Worker*, while delighted by the demise of Brutus – 'a wavering liberal' – complained that the idea of one dictator following another was a fascist notion; the production was guilty, he found – using the language of Moscow and Lunarcharsky – of 'formalism'. Especially regrettable for the *Worker* was the 'slanderous' picture of the masses. Political analysis was outside the scope of most critics (though Stark Young made a strong point about Welles's failure to grasp Shakespeare's notion of aristocracy). The great thrill was that the Mercury had made Shakespeare seem newly written: 'It is as if,' according to John Anderson in the *New York Journal American*, 'a great poet had risen in our midst only yesterday, a poet who seems to understand the movies as profoundly as he does the human heart.'

Of the acting, Anderson (sharp and sometimes hard to please) said, with careful choice of words, that it was 'the complete expression of the idea'. He was not unaware of limitations in Welles's acting, while admiring his Brutus. 'His stage effectiveness lies almost entirely in his voice, for while his mannerisms are less noticeable than they used to be, they do touch the portrait, though they put no blemish on such magnificent passages as his speech in the forum.' Coulouris and Gabel ('hardly the lean and hungry Cassius, is altogether admirable as a short and stoutish one') are singled out for praise.

By violent contrast (and it must be remembered that virtually all criticism, then as now, is hyperbole, in one direction or the other), Richard Lockridge in the *New York Sun* wrote that the more successful scenes were those which permitted mass movement; these went 'with electric quickness'. 'It is,' he continued, 'when the play turns to individuals that its tempo slumps, perhaps because the method is essentially opposed to individualism, perhaps merely because the actors are not as expert as the electricians.' For Lockridge, the 'somber tones' and conversational reticence of Welles's Brutus – so admired by others – were an obstacle; he identifies a life-long tendency of Welles's acting in a neat phrase. 'Mr Welles directs for the theatre, but he acts for literature, and the two have never seemed further apart . . . it is Mr Welles who puts the brakes on, and if the production drags, I'm afraid it is his fault.'

The critical impact of the cutting was sharply assessed by the influential Edith Isaacs, writing in *Theatre Monthly*. 'With most of Antony excised to keep the character of Brutus always as the focus of attention, this elimination of contrasts dulls the interest, releases the grip of the story before the play is done. It seems as if the slow and over-thoughtful pacing of the performance might, to emotional advantage, well have been hastened to make room for more of the actual play, which is not a philosophic study but spirited melodrama.' Perhaps it might have been franker if they had called the play *Brutus*, after all.

For the most part, even the severest critics allowed the production its vitality, even Stark Young, the most respected of current practitioners, but he was none the less 'on the whole pretty much disappointed'. What has happened, he says, putting his finger precisely on Welles's method, is 'the hitting of one of Shakespeare's fundamental themes and freeing it from certain conceptions, motifs and qualifications, so that it is thus brought straight out into the audience, the present-day American audience, watching it there in the Mercury Theatre.' But this, he implies, is not enough.

Even less was it enough for Mary McCarthy, writing in the little magazine, *Partisan Review*. McCarthy (somewhat dauntingly described on the blurb of her collected reviews – 'the pathology of the New York Theatre' – as 'quite possibly the cleverest writer the US has ever produced') regarded Welles from the beginning with suspicion. Despite this bias, her accounts of the productions are invariably illuminating. She applies a lethally sharp critical mind to matters which are generally the subject of rhetoric, and, as noted above, hyperbole, positive or negative. 'The production of *Caesar* turns into a battleground between Mr Welles's play and Shakespeare's play. Mr Welles has cut the play to pieces – turned Cassius into a shrewd and jovial comedian; Caesar into a mechanical, expressionless robot; Antony into a repulsive and sinister demagogue.' As for Welles's performance, she goes for the jugular. 'Cloying and monotonous, his performance seemed to be based on the single theory that if you drop your voice two registers below those of the other actors, you will give an impression of innocent saintliness.'

Her peroration decisively rejects Welles's approach to the play, and to plays in general: 'if the classics are to play an important role in the American theatre, their contents ought at least to be examined. To encrust them with traditional ornament or to cut them up into newspaper headlines is to shut them off from the world and the theatre. Acting as an art cannot exist by itself; it must feed on the material of the plays.' This was the essence of the critical debate which centred on Welles (George Jean Nathan made the point more jokily in *Newsweek*: 'playing *Julius Caesar* in modern dress strikes me as being of a piece with playing *Room Service* in togas'), and it is one which still rages today: do you use a play, or do you realise it? For Welles, there was no question.

Nathan had a more serious point to make in his *Scribner's* piece on the production; hoping that 'the hysterical critical endorsement' visited on its initial offering would not turn its head, he put their achievement in perspective. 'For a similar employment of lights, let the critics be reminded of the productions at least twenty years ago of Linnebach and Pasetti in Munich. As for a similar employment of platforms of different levels, let them be referred to the productions of Jessner and Pirchan in Berlin at about the same time. As for the bare walls, let them be prompted on the earliest productions of the celebrated Habima troupe. Good luck, Mr Welles and Mr Houseman, and don't let 'em hear you chuckle.'

Mr Welles and Mr Houseman were, indeed, chuckling fit to bust. The show was an enormous success, and so was their new theatre. The show's triumph was absolutely associated with Welles's name. Earlier productions at Project 891 and in Harlem had seemed to be somehow a joint effort (though no one was quite sure who had done what): *Caesar* was Welles's alone. Jean Rosenthal wrote a slightly bitter little paragraph on the subject: '*Julius Caesar* opened with tremendous éclat. Houseman explained, exactly how I have forgotten, that despite the incidental courtesies of the profession, it was important that Orson be given sole credit for everything. However, it did get around in the profession that Sam had designed the scenery and I had done the lighting.' John Anderson had written at the beginning of his notice: 'Let it be set down at once, without "ifs" and "buts" of a niggling season, that this is the most exciting event in our theatre . . . it would have been a fascinating experiment even if it had failed. That it succeeds so splendidly is enough to blow the hinges off the dictionary. Since Orson Welles is the moving spirit of this new group, and this *Caesar*'s deeply affecting Brutus, his must be most of the credit.' He was absolutely right: Welles was the moving spirit: his was the audacious approach, his the ceaseless invention, his the adrenalising inspiration. As in any collective activity, however, no one person is responsible for the end result.

Collective achievement is hard to personalise. It is in the nature of the press and its hand-maiden, the press office, to simplify things, to seek and to some extent create larger-than-life, uniquely gifted and effective individuals, to build them up even further – and then to break them, which makes an even better story. This was a process which found a willing ally in Welles. Six months later, in a *Time* magazine profile (MARVELOUS BOY), events surrounding *Julius Caesar* had become mythologised in the paper's unmistakable prose: 'After a succession of muffled death-rattles backstage, the Mercury came to its first play's first night. On November 11th it produced *Julius Caesar.* On November 12th the public was informed that Shakespeare's five-act classic had: 1) been turned into a one-act cyclone, 2) on a bare stage, 3) in modern dress, 4) with modern meaning, 5) gone over with the loudest bang that Shakespeare lovers could recall. And decidedly First in Rome had been Director Orson Welles for managing the entire production, Actor Orson Welles for making Brutus come alive in a blue-serge suit.' The 'muffled death-rattles' became a distant memory; it was as if everything had proceeded according to a preordained plan. Welles was interviewed and photographed everywhere; no paper could afford not to carry news of the latest phenomenon.

MR ORSON WELLES SAYS IT WAS LIKE THIS by John K. Hutchens was *The New York Times*'s contribution: 'If they are still complaining around The Lambs club that actors no longer look like actors, they should be willing to settle now for Orson Welles. Mr Welles looks very much like an actor, which, indeed, he is. No hat covers his longish hair, he gestures when he talks and he smokes a pipe.' The *New York Post* (ORSON WELLES, WHO PUTS SHAKESPEARE'S ROMANS IN FANCY DUDS, DISCUSSES RUFFIANS PAST AND PRESENT) was eager to describe his appearance, too: 'Mr Welles looks the way musicians used to look. He has the shiny Byronic brow, the clover-sniffing head-tilt, the flowing mane that trade-marked musicians until Mr Jascha Heifetz got a haircut and placed the profession on a business basis. It wouldn't surprise you if from a deep pocket of that cloak-like coat of his he produced a yellowed ivory and started piping a pastoral.' He was depicted in photographs as moody and intense; cartoons showed him bug-eyed and bizarre. His physiognomy was everywhere remarked on. Alfred Kazin wrote about it in *Starting out in the Thirties*: 'Welles was so masterful that his face swelled and brooded over the empty stage like an inflated goblin's . . . he was more the actor than anyone else we had ever seen, he was the fat, ugly crybaby face that was yet the ultimate in stage Svengalis.'

When the fascination with his physical shape and manner had been exhausted, reporters canvassed his views on life and art. He had this to say about *Caesar*: 'I believe in the factual theatre. People should not be fooled. They should know they are in the theatre, and with that knowledge, they may be taken to any height of which the magic of words and light is capable of taking them. This is a return to the Elizabethan and the Greek theatre. To achieve that simplicity, that wholesomeness, to force the audience into giving the play the same creative attention that a mediaeval crowd gave a juggler on a box in a market, you have to enchant.' This is a very clear statement of an aesthetic position: very close, in some ways (the attention of the audience, the clarity and simplicity of the staging, the frankness of the theatricality), to that of Brecht, though naturally without the German's political attitude. It seems however to bear little resemblance to the production of *Julius Caesar* that he had just directed, whose principal impact as described was in sheer theatrical power engendered by the manipulation of light and dark and sound: in atmospherics, to be precise.

Whatever its philosophy, all eyes were now on the Mercury. At one level, there was fascination with the possibility of creating thrilling and visually breathtaking theatre at a fraction of the cost of a Broadway show. Fortuitously, Tallulah Bankhead and her then husband John Emery had just attempted to stage *Antony and Cleopatra*; it had opened only days before *Julius Caesar* to a shower of abuse verging on derision. It had cost $100,000 against the Mercury's $6,000. The comparison was lost on no one. 'Strange things are happening in the theatre,' wrote Robert Benchley in *The New Yorker*. 'Old-line producers have been shaking their heads sadly at the way their expensive shows have been flopping right and left to the tune of a pretty penny . . . then along comes young Mr Orson

Welles who opens up the old Comedy Theatre and puts on *Julius Caesar* in modern dress and on a bare stage with nothing but lighting to make you think you were in a theatre (and of course, some help from the text). What happens? They are playing to standing room.'

They had, indeed, an enormous box office hit on their hands. This presented its own problems, or rather, temptations. The Mercury's box office manager begged Houseman and Welles to hold off the next production (*The Shoemaker's Holiday*) and extend the run of *Caesar* indefinitely (which current demand suggested was quite possible), or at least until they had accumulated a reasonable fund as a guarantee against failure. They stuck to their guns. As usual, Houseman is startlingly honest about his (and Welles's) motives. 'We thought of the Mercury as an instrument of artistic expression and a ladder to fame and power. We had gambled and won: intoxicated with success, we were moving much too fast, with our own special kind of reckless, whirling motion, to stop for any reason, good or bad. To Orson the prospect of coming to the theatre nightly for seven months to play the part of Brutus was abhorrent, just as it was impossible for me to think of myself sitting in my projection booth day after day with no other activity than to administer the stable and lucrative routine of a successful Broadway run.' Instead of exploiting their hit, they announced a programme of expansions. 'A NEW SORT OF ENTERTAINMENT – NON-STOP CLASSICAL AT THAT' announced the *Herald Tribune*, only two weeks after the triumphant opening of *Caesar*. Houseman is quoted as saying: 'We want to operate seven days a week, because Welles and I feel strongly that the theatre is a growing plant and, at the same time, a social unit. To regard a theatre simply as a piece of real estate into which you slap a hit if you happen to have one and show it eight times a week seems to us too low a view. The theatre will be a focus, we hope, for the literary, musical and theatrical life of a certain kind of audience in the city. We want the people to get in the habit of knowing that at the Mercury – no matter what night it happens to be – there will always be a good show at reasonable prices.' The Mercury was setting the pace, not simply in terms of the show they were presenting, but the whole concept of what the theatre might be. And they were here to stay: 'He also admires films and would like to direct for the screen,' Hutchens wrote in his profile of Welles. 'But not for a while. You can count on him and Mr Houseman being Broadway managers for at least five years, because they have taken the Mercury Theatre on a four-walls basis for that length of time. "We'll still be there," he said, "even if we wind up giving a flea circus." '

CHAPTER FOURTEEN

Shoemaker's Holiday/ Heartbreak House

THE ARTISTIC directors' reckless confidence transmitted itself to every level of the theatre. 'George Zorn (the box office manager) grew resigned to the fact that he was working for a pair of madmen and made the best of it,' wrote Houseman. 'In fact, this air of dedicated insanity came to permeate the entire organisation: from the stage to the boiler room morale was ridiculously high during those first few months of our operation.' In addition to rehearsals for *The Shoemaker's Holiday*, they created plans for their experimental Studio/Youth Theatre. 'THE STUDIO OF THE MERCURY THEATRE. PURPOSE: To establish a permanent apprentice group to the Mercury Theatre. ORGANISATION: To furnish the theatre with new talent . . . to be composed of all the non-equity extras appearing in Mercury Theatre repertory. FEES: $150 for 6 months. SPONSORS: Antoinette Perry, Gertrude Lawrence, Katharine Cornell.' Essentially, this was the framework for the Worklight Theatre described in their earliest announcements. Chubby Sherman was made head of the Acting Bureau, and a new play, David Howard's *Dear Abigail*, announced as first offering. This enlightened scheme existed more on paper than in reality. There were fitful rehearsals resulting in an apprentice production of *Julius Caesar*; work was done on Lope de Vega's *The Well*, and *Abraham and Isaac* from the York Mystery Circle. In its lack of proper training, organisation, or structure, and its exaction of fees for what was in effect extra work, it is strikingly reminiscent of the 'training course' accompanying the Woodstock Festival of three years earlier: a ruse, in fact. But even as a proposal, it was symptomatic of the brave new world of theatre that Houseman and Welles were conjuring up.

The one official production of the Worklight Theatre ('which is designed to give auditions to unusual pieces that are homeless') was a revival of *The Cradle Will Rock*, the extraordinary commercial potential of which, in the wake of its sensational debut, had never been adequately tapped. (The press office made the most of this history, promoting it as THE SHOW THAT MADE THE FRONT PAGES.) Initially, after two Worklight Theatre performances, the show was scheduled for four Sunday performances (part of the new seven-day policy) starting on 5 December; but it proved to have more life in it than that, transferring on 3 January to the Windsor Theatre for a run of 108 performances ('Suppressed by the government! Acclaimed by the critics! Demanded by the Public! Now on Broadway!' screamed the handbills). This was, of course, the first time that the piece had been formally reviewed; it was greeted with nearly unanimous enthusiasm. 'It is the best thing militant labor has put into a theatre yet,' according to Brooks Atkinson of the *Times*. Richard Watts Junior, another conservative critic, was as enthused: 'A savagely humorous social cartoon that hits hard and sardonically and must be set down as one of the most interesting dramatic events of the season.'

In fact, the show was a rather different one from the astonishing improvised evenings at the Venice Theatre the previous year. Those performances had little to do with Welles apart from his courage and showmanship in enabling them to happen. His design and with it his production had been scrapped; what happened onstage had simply happened, with fortuitous appropriateness. The attempt to preserve the form that had accidentally evolved at the famous first performance was not viewed with favour by the Musicians' Union, which demanded that ten musicians be hired even if they didn't play. This absurdity was calmly accepted by the pro-syndicalist composer, who even felt moved publicly to express his acquiescence in it. 'I am in complete agreement with this ruling, and I resent any implication that by it or by our technique either the union or myself is overstepping the boundaries of our respective jurisdictions. Marc Blitzstein.' That he preserved a flicker of irony, none the less, is revealed by his response when an official approached him on the composition of his phantom orchestra. He asked for four cornettists, three flute players, and three trombonists. 'That's not an orchestra,' the official protested. 'That's the orchestra I want to have not play my opera,' Blitzstein replied.

For the revival, Welles had handed the show over to Blitzstein who formalised and structured what had happened that night. The result was neither as spontaneous – how could it be? – or as passionate as before. Alistair Cooke (an enthusiast of the piece) described the evening with masterly precision in an NBC broadcast: 'I only wish that the present production did not bear the marks of its early martyrdom. In the beginning they put this on in a bleak way out of desperation. There is just a suggestion that now it goes on that way out of religious zeal . . . people who can overlook the slight strain of evangelism will recognise that in *The Cradle Will Rock* there is the constant echo of a clarion call, not only to American writing, but to American life.'

Mary McCarthy, *not* a friendly witness, had already, in no uncertain terms, taken against Blitzstein himself: 'His acrid personality is, in fact, the whole show. He, as insolent and sardonic entrepreneur, sits downstage centre at the piano; the actors behind him are his marionettes. The timing and precision of the cast's performances have the cold, military precision of the dance routines of the Radio City Rockettes. *The Cradle Will Rock* is a triumph of theatrical goose-stepping. The drama has become de-humanised; it has been made into a marvelous mechanical monster which begins to operate with great efficiency whenever Mr Blitzstein pulls the switch.' None the less, the show, and its presence on Broadway, further confirmed the image of the Mercury as the most dynamic outfit in town.

Rehearsals for *Shoemaker's Holiday* had started shortly after the opening of *Julius Caesar*. Welles lost interest in playing Brutus very early on. Virgil Thomson reports a telling incident during the early part of the run: seeking to persuade Welles to let him, rather than Blitzstein, write the music for the projected production of *The Duchess of Malfi*, he took Welles and Virginia to supper at Sardi's before the show for 'a blow-out'. Welles ate oysters and champagne, red meat and Burgundy, dessert and brandy, before he pulled himself into his canvas corset for playing Brutus. 'It's lucky I'm playing tragedy tonight, which needs no timing. Comedy would be difficult.' He had discovered that there were two points during the show when he had just enough time to go to Longchamps Diner down the alley behind the theatre and have a substantial snack, generally a triple-decker steak sandwich washed down with bourbon. The assistant stage managers Bill Alland and Richard Wilson were deputed to ensure that he returned on time, which he quite often did, arriving in the wings panting and sweating, somewhat incongruously for the noble figure he was trying to portray. Not surprisingly, his performance began to lose such vitality as it had originally had, to the point where one night someone in the audience had called out 'Louder!' Often he would lose his way during the longer speeches. He claimed humorously to have lost belief in the production after Mrs Patrick Campbell had come backstage and asked him 'Why do you have everybody dressed up like chauffeurs?' 'And it's true!' Welles told Peter Bogdanovich. 'It spoiled it for me. Ever since then, it looked like a whole convention of Rolls-Royces.'

There were the usual number of misfortunes during the run: the occasional unscheduled appearances onstage of people having wandered in from the alley; the accidental unleashing of the fire-sprinklers by a bored Arthur Anderson, fiddling with them backstage. 'Ladies and Gentlemen,' said Welles, 'there seems to be water on the stage.' Anderson was fined $50, plus 50c a show for a permanent bodyguard. At one performance, possibly a little the worse for wear, Welles became overexcited during the assassination sequence and plunged the dagger that had so gratifyingly stuck in the floor deep into the flesh of Joseph Holland, playing Caesar. The actor, a professional to his fingertips, lay motionless while blood poured from his veins, crawling off at a convenient blackout and only then collapsing. He was in hospital for some months. All this was part of the fun (except perhaps for Holland). The mood in the company was one of triumphant exhilaration. Even rival groups admired the work. Clurman of the Group Theatre reluctantly admitted that '*Caesar* had a dash of originality, a boyish zip' and Sandy Meisner, bumping into Norman Lloyd, told him: 'I saw the production – very clever.' Lloyd then 'knew we were good. It felt great.' The show was an enormous hit, the talk, not only of the town, but of the world. Its fame (more particularly that of its director) had even reached England, courtesy of the globe-trotting C.B. Cochran who tried to persuade the Shakespeare Memorial Theatre at Stratford to take the production: 'It is the best thing I have seen for a long time,' *The Daily Telegraph* reported. 'There is no fake about it. It is real theatre. Mr Welles starts where Reinhardt left off.' He wanted to play the production at the Albert Hall. 'I say this in all seriousness. Mr Welles seems to me to be the white hope of the English-speaking world.' Christmas of 1937 found him at one of the peaks of his young life, emotionally as well as professionally; his card that year reveals that Virginia was pregnant. He had it all: fame, money, respect, wife, incipient fatherhood – and mistresses, two of them, in fact, both ballerinas, to whom his impassioned attentions did not cease during (and indeed after) his wife's pregnancy. It seems that it was important for his self-respect to be attached to lithe, glamorous beauty; his wife no longer fell into that category.

He also had – equally necessary for him – a new production, *The Shoemaker's Holiday*, for which rehearsals were now well in hand. The cast were, to put it mildly, working at full stretch: most of them (including of course Welles) were putting in regular appearances on radio, doing eight performances a week of *Caesar*, and then – starting at ten thirty at night and often working through till three or four in the morning – rehearsing *The Shoemaker's Holiday*. The core company of *Caesar* was supplemented by some newcomers; a couple departed (the two women, most notably). After the success of the first production, the flood of applications from actors had become a tidal wave. Chubby Sherman (who was increasingly becoming a crucial Mercurian), already cast as the clown, Firk, was appointed casting director. Welles was not to appear in the play; in the part that he would normally have considered his (Simon Eyre, the shoemaker who becomes Lord Mayor of London) he and Chubby cast Whitford Kane, Chubby's lover. At fifty-seven, he was a very different person from the elderly gents who had graced certain of Welles's productions; though not exactly a star, he was a powerful leading man, a famous Volpone, Falstaff, Bottom and held by some to be a definitive Captain Boyle in *Juno and the Paycock*.

Another newcomer trailing glory was Vincent Price, only twenty-six, but with highly successful runs in the West End and on Broadway in *Victoria Regina*, in which he had created the role of Prince Albert opposite Helen Hayes. A student of art history who had drifted into the theatre, he had gone instantly almost to the very top of the tree. He knew, however, after his subsequent Broadway run in *The Lady Has a Heart* (for which he received, in Sam Leiter's words, 'several stinging notices for comically ponderously playing') that he needed experience, a thorough grounding in his craft. Seeing *Julius Caesar* convinced him that the Mercury was the place to get it: the only place. In order to do so, he was prepared to take a drop in salary from $1,000 on Broadway to $125 at the Mercury, signing a seven-play contract. 'We were all very serious actors, desperately looking for our identification with the classics.' Though an enthusiastic Anglophile and connoisseur of English acting (he had seen John Gielgud's *Hamlet* twelve times) he was, like so many of his contemporaries, frustrated that '90 per cent of the American classical theatre was English actors who were very jealous of American actors invading the American theatre'. The Mercury seemed a way of creating an independent and vital American classical theatre that owed little to the British example.

In *The Shoemaker's Holiday*, Price was cast as the predatory Master Hammond; his then wife, Edith Barrett, was Rose. She was one of the prodigiously high number of actresses who applied for the usual miserably small number of female parts. Both she and Ruth Ford (Jane) had begged to be cast against type, and so they were. The amply constructed Marian Warring-Manley, on the other hand, was cast triumphantly in character as Simon Eyre's forthright wife, Margery ('but let that pass'). Coulouris was the King, Joe Cotten a young gentleman, Norman Lloyd and Elliott Reid Firk's fellow apprentices. There were rich pickings for everyone, despite Welles's trimming of the text to a running time of just over an hour. This is astonishingly bold; slightly less than half of the text is left intact. Perhaps even more astonishing is the decision to do the play at all. Virtually unknown on the American stage, even in England only occasionally played in student productions at Oxford or Cambridge, it was, Welles claimed, part of his reading while he was the guest of the Glaoui in the Atlas mountains. In an interview whose title is itself like an undiscovered play by Dekker – *Everything Old Was Once New* – he told the interviewer, Helen Ormsbee, that besides *The Shoemaker's Holiday*, he had read *The Roaring Girl* and *If This Be Not a Good Play, The Evil Is in It.* 'How do you like that for a title?' Then there were *The Humorous Lieutenant*, Jonson's *Bartholomew Fair*, and Heywood's *A Woman Killed with Kindness* and *If You Know Not Me, You Know Nobody*. He seems to be naming the plays simply because he likes the titles.

'*The Shoemaker's Holiday* is a glimpse,' he continues, 'of the kind of domestic drama that was popular at the very time Shakespeare was writing.' Welles was no archaeologist of the drama, however; it was the curiously modern feeling of these old plays that fascinated him. 'Of course, plays of the present are first in importance to audiences of the present. That is always so. But once you dip into the past there is no drama that can equal the Elizabethan for universal appeal, humanity and richness.' Dekker's play, first performed on the first day of the seventeenth century, brimful of uncontrollable life, interweaving the classes, with a plot loosely revolving around the advancement of Simon Eyre, the legendary Lord Mayor of London, is so human, so rich and so universally appealing, that it can be taken in many different ways. Rosamond Gilder found a parallel in modern life: 'Simon Eyre is the prototype of all the lads who make good; the industrious apprentice who becomes Lord Mayor of London or President of the United States; the poor boy who earns a fortune but never forgets his friends;' Eleanor Flexner, writing in *New Masses* found quite another: 'The play is laden with sentiments for the times: a passionate democracy of the spirit, a hatred of wars, which tear families asunder, reverence for the men who toil with their hands, and an abhorrence for the fetishes of wealth and position.' Both are right; both are wrong. Welles, having read the report by his literary manager, Alexander Campbell, initially thought to emphasise the class conflict (which is plentifully present); instead, Andrea Nouryeh reports him as choosing to celebrate 'democracy, brotherhood between the classes, and the rising power of the bourgeoisie'. This is without question the spirit of the play, even if the letter can be variously interpreted. In practice, what he made of it was something altogether different: a non-stop riot of gags.

His adaptation took as its spine, not the glorious, rambunctious Eyre and his rise to office, nor the machinations of the aristocrats, but rather the antics of Firk, Eyre's apprentice. Welles had long sought a vehicle for Chubby Sherman's comic genius, from as far back as the first planning sessions for Project 891; this, he knew, was it. Not only did he prune out large sections of text, considered either obscure or tedious, but he reshaped the dialogue to increase its comic possibilities. These devolved to a great extent on double entendres sometimes present in the original, sometimes not. A characteristic sequence is taken from the scene in which young Roland Lacey, in love with Eyre's daughter, disguises himself as a Dutch cobbler, and is taken on as an apprentice. The incumbent apprentices quiz him. In Dekker's text, Firk does all the questioning, as follows:

> FIRK
> And hark you, skomaker, have you all your tools – a good rubbing-pin, a good stopper, a good dresser, your four sorts of awls, and your two balls of wax, your paring knife, your hand- and thumb-leathers, and good St Hughes' bones to smooth up your work?

Welles distributes the questions, and the laughs, among the apprentices:

> HODGE
> Hark you skawmakers, have you all your tools?
> FIRK
> A good rubbin pin, a good stopper, your four sorts of awls, and your two balls
> LACY
> Yaw, yaw
> FIRK
> Of wax

On this showing, Dekker and Welles might have been the scriptwriters that the late Benny Hill was waiting for. Sherman noted that 'All the groupings and firkings were like children's horseplay. We were children saying dirty words.' A great deal was made of the homonyms: firk/fuck and, stretching it a bit, firk/fart; firk is, it must be admitted, a rather Clouseauesque fuck. All this is not by any means alien to the Elizabethan mind, though it was only a fraction of it, and only a fraction of Dekker's play.

Rehearsals were, even more than usual with Welles, a riot, interspersed with strict drilling. Lehman Engel describes his method. 'He rehearsed with military discipline. He might laugh at something, then have an actor do a piece of business that he'd devised ten times until the actor knew it mechanically.' Arthur Anderson recalled one such moment: 'One day accidentally Hiram ran into the curtain – he and Orson built a gag out of it. He always ran into the curtain. At the end of the show, he's about to make a speech; the curtain falls on him.' Engel never heard Welles explaining a characterisation: 'he moulded you. Orson only knew his own way and that was "Now everybody keep quiet and I'll tell you what to do." That was his only way of working. He simply didn't know any other . . . The style of his *Shoemaker's Holiday* depended on the precise machine-like interplay of movement, music, curtains and light. It was the director's expression. The actors were his puppets . . . usually he demonstrated movements of hand and feet in precise detail, speaking the lines in precise time relationship to them. Then he would have the actors imitate him.' The results were brilliantly funny and effective, delighting most of the actors, but not, curiously enough, the comic star of the production, Chubby Sherman. 'Welles was a choreographer. You'd turn here and go around there. This is where he and I fall out. I don't believe you can choreograph a comic routine and make it comic in terms of movement alone – especially if there is nothing funny about it to begin with. We had a lot of "You go around in back of Norman. Norman goes back of you." Being spaced around. Having to hold a position endlessly. You get cramps that way, not laughs.'

Welles was also ruthless about the delivery of the text and the sharpness of the cues: 'it was going lickety-spit all the time,' according to Arthur Anderson. Around and beyond the drilling was horseplay. Welles, unencumbered by the need to participate in the action, installed himself at his table in the stalls with a constant running buffet from Longchamps in front of him, roaring out instructions and mock abuse as he chomped his steaks and muffins and swilled brandy. The particular target of his comic rage was the stately Marian Warring-Manley, known to Welles as

Marian Whoring Boring Manley. Her appetite for food was as large as Welles's and he delighted to torment her, gorging demonstratively as she watched him. 'We thought she would die as she watched him. "Orson, just one strawberry!" she'd beg. "Get away from me you whore! Whore!" he'd cry, as he wolfed another mouthful. It was' recalled Norman Lloyd, 'fun, *wild* fun.'

You can't, of course, please all of the people all of the time, and the atmosphere of bawdy hysteria, awash with anecdote and jest, was not to some people's taste. Whitford Kane, in particular, was enraged by the waste of time and the avoidance of proper rehearsal as opposed to mechanical drilling. Vincent Price was angered above all by Welles's capriciousness over rehearsal schedules. After waiting on one occasion two hours for him to show up, Price walked off and had lunch. But his anger was tempered by Welles's charm – 'he was an enormously likeable oaf' – and by his talent. 'He was the best director I ever had – I still say that. He gave you wonderful things to do.' Chubby, too, despite his reservations about Welles's approach to comedy knew that he was being wonderfully served: 'The way our script was arranged I seemed to be the catalyst . . . it was all very flattering to me.'

Unlike *Julius Caesar*, the production offered no transposition, no concept. It was fairly straightforwardly Elizabethan in period, a simple setting of wooden towers to create the various locations; three curtains divided up the stage to make interiors. Sam Leve maintains that the design was a reworking of his setting for *The Song of the Dnieper* (1936) at the Yiddish Art Theatre which Welles had seen and liked, admiring its use of untreated surfaces. 'Our settings are simple – what I call "factual",' Welles told Helen Ormsbee. 'That is, everything you see is exactly what it purports to be. We don't paint a piece of canvas to look like wood – we use wood itself. No paint or artificial colouring appears in the sets. There is no deep, occult reason for that; it is just that we want to keep the homespun feel of the piece.' Brecht hovers again; his great designer Caspar Neher, with his passion for the textures of lived life, would have approved. Welles was clearly in no mood to acknowledge any input of Leve's; in the Ormsbee interview from which the above comment is taken he attributes both costumes and scenery to Millia Davenport. The costumes were particularly successful. Welles gave her a more or less free hand, only stipulating that codpieces should be prominent, the first time they had been seen on the American stage. This proved a fatal temptation to Francis Carpenter, who couldn't resist rubbing his against fellow actors', causing gasps at matinees.

Chubby Sherman found a more tasteful use for his codpiece: 'he had,' said Davenport, 'the most revolting triangle of shoe leather – absolutely unmanageable – tied on with thongs, which kept coming undone. He spent his entire time onstage keeping himself decent. It was the most adorable thing anyone had seen.' Inventing, in her own words, 'a paraphrase of authentic period dress', she experimented with unconventional materials – ironing board covers, for example, and brightly coloured laces. The women were straightforwardly costumed; men were stratified by class, Lords being 'sober, dark, and dignified', while the shoemakers were clad in varieties of woollens. Andrea Nouryeh reports that Davenport, in order to focus Welles's attention, left the hands and feet off figures on her designs, 'knowing that he'd not be able to resist completing them, and would thus be obliged to look at them'.

His collaborators were getting wise to his foibles. He asked for a boat at the back of the stage, next to the burlap cyclorama; Walter Ash, the stage manager, told him that Maurice Evans – for whom Welles then entertained, and still entertained, even fifty years later, absolute contempt – had used one in his *Hamlet*. There was no more talk of boats. Engel's music (he had to write for exactly the same instrumental combination as Blitzstein had used in *Caesar*: 'an entire score of duets for trumpet and horn with occasional percussive folderol') was planned as carefully as everything else. 'Orson Welles virtually dictated the twiddles I composed for *The Shoemaker's Holiday*. Often he tapped out rhythms for a particular spot and no less often described the quality of the melody and the number of measures needed. The production that resulted from this method was always one very definite idea made up of the scenery he had designed, the play he had revised, the acting he had postulated in great detail, and the accompanying twiddles he had indicated. This was a very stimulating kind of theatre and it achieved exactly what its founder intended it to.' Perhaps partly because he wasn't in it, *The Shoemaker's Holiday* was altogether more achieved than *Caesar*: a unified conception executed with great skill.

The showmanship didn't end with the production, either. Feeling that the cast needed contact with an audience as soon as possible, and perhaps distantly remembering Guthrie McClintic's similar invitation on the tour of *Romeo and Juliet*, Welles invited the spectators of the last performance of *Julius Caesar* before the opening of *Shoemaker's Holiday* to stay behind and watch the set being dismantled and the new one erected, and then to attend a run-through of the show. The press office next thoughtfully alerted the newspapers.

'Getting wind of the event through the Broadway telegraph, this reporter hastened over to the Mercury to see what was in this talk of institution of the double-feature system, and found a group of spectators grimly entrenched in their seats waiting for the promised show . . . the balcony returned first and sat in the orchestra seats, driving the white tie and tails into the balconies. Seven ermine coats watched the Elizabethan comedy from an unaccustomed height and several hundred members of labor unions who had bought seats in blocks relaxed in the divans.'

The curtain was up while the sets were changed, giving the audience a chance 'to assimilate the strange fact that stage hands invariably wear strange hats'. Marc Blitzstein's Hammond organ played while they changed the set; larking about, they accidentally knocked over a large piece of it, narrowly avoiding killing several spectators. Chubby Sherman addressed the audience, telling them that for the purposes of the run they would be using the *Julius Caesar* lighting plot – 'just imagine we're beautifully lit.' The show that night was a riot. A couple of weeks later, the *New York Telegram* threw an interesting light on this episode: 'The audience felt intimately connected with the actors when they heard calls of "Is everybody ready?" "Places please!" and "All right, let her up, boys!" But if only they had known that even these yells had been rehearsed with the cast earlier that evening, line for line. Quite a showman, Mr Welles.'

The very date chosen for the opening of the show was a piece of chutzpah: 'If the Mercury Theatre's courage needed any further proving it would be simply that it has picked New Year's night for the official opening of *The Shoemaker's Holiday* – as bad a theatregoing evening as the season affords. It has also set a flossy (for the Mercury) top of $4.40 for the occasion.' Curiously enough, the show that night played to scarcely a laugh, making something of a mockery of Dekker's dedication which Welles had appended to the play in place of the prologue: 'Take all in good purpose that is well intended for nothing is purposed but mirth. Mirth lengtheneth long life, which with all other blessings I heartily wish you.' As so often on such occasions, even as the actors were wringing their hands and weeping into their gins at the disaster they had just perpetrated, the press was busily reporting unconfined hilarity. The critics had, for the most part, no idea what to expect, no previous experience of the play; their enchanted approval was evidently unfeigned. Welles's audacity with the text seemed to cock a snook at academia, as well as putting Dekker to rights – as if they'd been bored by him once too often. 'To *Julius Caesar*, a terrifying tragedy, now add an uproarious strip of Elizabethan fooling,' said Atkinson of the *Times*. 'If there was any doubt after *Julius Caesar* that the Mercury Theatre is the liveliest drama household in town, *The Shoemaker's Holiday* should dispel it, for the Dekker comedy is the funniest jig of the season and the new year has begun with a burst of theatrical hilarity.' The actors were praised over and over, none more so than Chubby Sherman: 'a masterpiece of low comedy acting, a perfect blend of innocence, mischief and good-natured fooling, poised enough to address the audience without modern self-consciousness, and racy enough to kick Dekker in the pants when necessary' said the *Journal-American*, and it spoke for virtually every review.

The only serious reservations expressed were from the left (John Gassner described the show as 'a series of glittering fragments stuck in a matrix of obvious horseplay', while Clurman thought the show 'much less bawdy than androgynously shrill') and from the visiting English critic Ivor Brown, who was able, a little immodestly, to tell the readers of *The New York Times*: 'Bully boy Dekker is quite familiar to me.' Correctly noting that the play has three elements – 'a kind of lyrical tenderness, a sweet opportunity for song and dance and a lot of rough, rude and roistering fun. In short, it is a three-Dekker sandwich' – he accuses the Mercury of leaving out 'the tender lettuce and give us only the strong meat'. He also abhorred the company's tendency to send Dekker up. 'I protest against the habit of laughing with Dekker and at him simultaneously . . . yes, there is much rude mirth but the players are too obviously having their own fun. This is not the real *Shoemaker's Holiday*. It is a Busker's Night Out.' For all his pedantry, he was perhaps right. The spectacle of actors, as described by Brown, alternately milking and tormenting a defenceless old play is not always an attractive one. There's a great deal more there, which could have been entertainingly and absorbingly revealed. But the bit of the play that Welles had decided to offer, he had done wonderfully well. Ninety minutes non-stop fun is not to be sniffed at.

Among American critics, at any rate, there was no doubt: the show was dazzling, the Mercury was 'still the great comfort of the theatrical season' and Welles – Welles was simply a genius. It was a brilliant calculation on the part of Welles and Houseman to follow *Caesar* so quickly with something utterly different. To do a fascist *Julius Caesar* in 1937 did not require a giant leap of imagination; indeed, Schintzer had got there first. To revive an Elizabethan City Comedy by a more-or-less unknown and almost totally unperformed writer in New York is extraordinary enough; to have played it in more or less Tudor style and still have made everybody notice the modern relevance of it, is a sort of miracle. The production is less remembered because Welles wasn't in it; it contributes nothing to his legend, to the *Guinness Book of Records* dimension of his persona. There was plenty of that to come; but in terms of his work in the theatre, the reviews that he received for *The Shoemaker's Holiday* were the best of his career. All the evidence suggests that it was also his best work.

For the Mercury, too, it was a triumph: a dazzling demonstration of versatility and a peak never recovered. The acting company was acknowledged to be stronger than that of *Julius Caesar*: 'some of his current actors have come to him from the ordinary marts of the commercial theatre – Kane, Price, Barrett, Warring-Manley – and it has done all of them good.' The theatre became fashionable – 'pardon me for shoving, but I'm keeping my seat on this bandwagon before the subway crush, to hail *The Shoemaker's Holiday*, Tom Dekker's jig-and-tale-of-bawdy, that represents another Mercury body blow to an anemic Broadway,' thrilled *The Stage at Eve* – but serious analysis was forthcoming, too.

Atkinson in the *Times* said: 'the general hope in this neighborhood is that the Mercury will become a permanent part of our theatrical life, giving the classics a sturdy hearing and perhaps developing new playwrights in time.' Noting that 'more repertory theatres have been destroyed by a hit than you can shake a stick at', he praises the Mercury's remounting of *Cradle Will Rock*, and subsequent staging of *The Shoemaker's Holiday*, and playing of it in repertory with *Caesar*. 'Although theatregoers have learned to let imposing announcements slip into one ear and out the other, there is every reason to believe that Orson Welles and John Houseman not only mean what they say, but have the ability to do it.' They were being taken terribly seriously; much was expected of them. 'We're all a little skittish now,' Chubby Sherman told the *Times*. 'We know our luck can't hold. We're expecting the deluge any moment, and when it does come we'll quietly withdraw to the country for a while and do some quiet work. All our plays so far have been in the manner of stunts, and some day we'll be producing a real play in which an actor opens a door, a real door, walks in, sits down and begins to talk. And that'll be the end of us!' This was dangerously frank talk; his point about them being found out if they played a realistic play realistically may have had a grain of truth in it. The plays had been trimmed to their talents. 'I don't think I'd better say any more about the Mercury. Orson will rap my knuckles.'

There were now two enormous hits playing in tandem at the Mercury. Discipline was not always of the best: Welles received a report from Dick Wilson and Bill Alland that there was a total breakdown of it on *Shoemaker's Holiday*; he duly went down to the theatre to crack the whip in his own original way. Standing in the wings with a one-fifth of Ballantine's, he simply sprayed Scotch into the offenders' faces. It seems not to have worked; mayhem continued to reign. In fact, the run of *Shoemaker's Holiday* at the Mercury lasted no more than three and a half weeks; it and *Caesar* transferred to the much more capacious (and resonantly named) National Theatre two blocks up. Houseman wanted to exploit the commercial success of the shows by playing in a larger house, while maintaining their much-vaunted repertory policy. The move was fortunate, because he soon needed to find a new theatre for *The Cradle Will Rock*, which had been playing under a commercial management to only moderate business at non-Broadway prices at the Windsor Theatre. The producer, Sam Grisman, begged him to increase the prices. How could he? They were absolutely publicly committed to their cheap-ticket policy; the press were already on the look-out for any attempt to renege on it. 'God keep them from all Broadway entanglements,' wrote Burns Mantle in the *Daily News*. 'My only fear for the Mercury boys . . . is that they might make their productions collectors' items if they kept the cost of them too high or gave with them something less than a fair evening's entertainment . . . happily, the young experimenters have held to their popular-price schedule, despite their success.'

Unimpressed – he was losing money – Grisman broke his contract and pulled out, leaving Houseman with debts and a commitment to complete a thirteen-week run, which he hoped to honour by bringing the show home. He was, in fact, despite the triumphant success of the two shows at the National (nearly twice the size of the Mercury), in some financial difficulty; Welles had wildly overspent on the two classical productions, and the returns from the box office, at the specially low prices, were not sufficient to cover the expenses of what had quickly become a major classical company. A further money-making ploy was a five-month, nationwide tour of *Julius Caesar* from Providence to Toronto (in association with the perhaps unhappily named Alex Yokel). The entirely new company was headed by – as Brutus – Tom Powers (who had created the role of Charles Marsden in *Strange Interlude*) and Edmond O'Brien as Cassius. Welles flew out to Chicago several times to supervise the production, and it opened to great acclaim, though reading the reviews may have given him mixed pleasure. 'Let it be said now and boldly,' wrote the *Pittsburgh Journal*'s Florence Fisher Parry, 'this Pittsburgh *Julius Caesar* far outranks the New York production . . . Orson Welles is the Mercury Theatre Brutus, and a bad one. He is a genius, but not in acting . . . Tom Powers has been vouchsafed the opportunity to reveal, as never before, his innate soundness of spirit.' Her admiration of the production was unstinting, however. 'It shows us in ten minutes the real meaning of rabble-rousing and why men who have that power rule over the world today. It writes the best editorial we have yet been given on WHY Mussolini, WHY Hitler, WHY Lenin and his unearthly post-mortem power.'

Despite the critical enthusiasm, specially arranged lectures, gramophone records of the show (the first in a series of *The Mercury Shakespeare*, with Welles as a plummy Cassius, and the relevant, slightly amended, volume from *Everybody's Shakespeare*), and what Andrea Nouryeh calls 'high-powered selling techniques', business was unexceptional, and the Mercury's half share of the profits never materialised, for the good reason that the show never went into profit. These financial set-backs, whose implications would eventually catch up with them in ways that could scarcely have been predicted, did nothing to daunt their high spirits. As Houseman later wrote: 'during February and March, the Mercury Theatre had one hundred and twenty-four actors performing in four shows in three theatres. Our three New York shows were playing within two blocks of each other on West 41st Street. We renamed it Mercury Street, and without permission from the city, put up temporary signs to that effect on the corners of 6th and 7th Avenues and Broadway.' And they continued with their announced plans: the next show would be *The Duchess of Malfi*, and the one after that *Five Kings*, a two-part, two-evening amalgam of the two parts of *Henry IV*, *Henry V*, *Henry VI*, and *Richard III*: the Royal Shakespeare Company's Wars of the Roses twenty-five years ahead of time.

Welles invited the brilliantly original painter and stage designer Pavel Tchelitchew (his work on the ballet *Ode* had been one of Diaghilev's boldest experiments) to design *The Duchess of Malfi*; work was far advanced when a read-through of the play was announced. At a late-night session, eighty actors were present to read a play which has only eight roles of any length. Welles was late. Finally, when he arrived, 'he'd had his hair just done', according to Norman Lloyd. 'I'll never forget him fingering his gardenia and saying THIS WILL PLEASE A FEW CLOSE FRIENDS AND I.' Sherman, Kane, and Lloyd were designated the roles of madmen; Aline MacMahon read the Duchess; Coulouris, Price, and Welles read the rest. At the end of the read-through, nothing was said. It was never rehearsed again, and immediately thereafter dropped without a word of explanation to either company or press.

It was obvious that there was trouble in the paradise that the Mercury had seemed to be. As they will in any group, half-formed suspicions, anxieties and grievances, invisible while momentum was being maintained, suddenly emerged, confirmed. The complicated manipulations of the repertory had seemed generally fruitful, if not always comprehensible. There had been no consultation; the actors were among those who had to learn, in Welles's phrase, 'to shut up'. An increasing uncertainty as to the future of the group began to be voiced, fuelled by the postponement, hard on the heels of the cancellation of *The Duchess of Malfi*, of *Five Kings*, and the suspension of company night rehearsals to prepare for it. It was decided that *The Shoemaker's Holiday* should be dropped from the repertory at the National; those who were not in *Caesar* or the forthcoming *Heartbreak House* (announced to open in April as the last play of the season at the Mercury after the closure of *The Cradle Will Rock*) were discharged, with neither retainer nor the promise of employment in the second season. A further problem was the overwhelming emphasis placed on Welles himself, both in the press and in the Mercury's own publicity. Few had failed to note the irony of one of the supreme exponents of theatrical caesarism working with such dictatorial fervour on a production subtitled Death of a Dictator:

> Why, man, he doth bestride the narrow world
> Like a Colossus, and we petty men
> Walk under his huge legs, and peep about
> To find ourselves dishonourable graves . . .
> Now in the names of all the gods at once,
> Upon what meat doth this our Caesar feed
> That he is grown so great?

It was scarcely possible to open a newspaper without reading further paeans of praise. The *Time* magazine profile, MARVELOUS BOY, appeared in May of 1938: 'With a voice that booms like Big Ben's but a laugh like a youngster's giggle, Orson Welles plays lead off-stage as well as on. He loves the mounting Welles legend, but wants to keep the record straight. Stories of his recent affluence annoy him . . . as active as a malted-milk mixer, Welles is for all that very heavy-set, his adolescent moon face slowly beginning to resemble an American Emperor's. Told he looks Roman, he asks, interestedly: "Do you mean sensual?" His own description of himself: "I look like the dog-faced boy." Troubled by his asthma, untroubled by his flat feet, Welles gets a little exercise walking and fencing, most by directing and rehearsing. He starts off a Falstaffian meal with a dozen oysters, tops it off with a big black cigar . . . at the Mercury, Houseman runs the business end, Welles is Caesar (not Brutus) where stagecraft is concerned, and in his own opinion "pretty dictatorial." Shadow to Shakespeare, Shoemaker to Shaw – all in one season – might be a whole career for most men, but for Welles it is only Springboard to Success . . . the brightest moon that has risen over Broadway in years, Welles should feel at home in the sky, for the sky is the only limit his ambitions recognize.' The Mercurians were beginning to feel that they were distantly accompanying a spotlit soloist in a concerto of his own composition.

This was not entirely Welles's fault. Like any theatre, the Mercury was always eager to sell itself to the press, and that meant pushing whatever was most newsworthy, and *that* meant Welles. He eagerly embraced this destiny, oblivious of, or at least indifferent to, the disaffection so easily provoked among fellow workers. There was even resentment at the disparity between his income and theirs (his radio career had never faltered for one moment). He defended his standard of living in the *Time* magazine profile, citing 'the Big House at Sneden's Landing, N.Y., the luxurious Lincoln town car and chauffeur'. The Big House, Welles insisted, wasn't such a big house ('eight rooms and four nooks, $115 a month'), the car was second hand, and the chauffeur existed because Welles himself didn't drive. 'I'm one of those fellows so frightened of driving that I go 80 miles an hour,' he says, 'and the more frightened I get, the faster I go.' This has the ring of truth about it. But he was coy about the amount of his earnings, as *Time* reported. 'How much money Welles is making he will not say. He is not even sure he knows . . .' There is no reason to assume that he had fallen significantly below the figure of $1,000 a month, particularly since his assumption of the Shadow's mantle. In modern equivalents, this means that he was earning half a million dollars a year, which might indeed have been a galling thought for his poverty-stricken colleagues, squeezing by on their $28.75 per week. Of course many of them were also doing extensive radio work; and it is absolutely true that he had earned all this money entirely on his own merits. None the less, the him-and-us feeling was hard to counteract; in this same month of April, he received an award for outstanding theatrical achievement from the New York Drama Study Group. Welles, Welles and more Welles. Receiving the award, he seized the opportunity to announce major touring plans; he wanted, he said, to do as many performances on the road as in New York. The Mercury, he said, harking back to Todd and Skipper, was to become an independent film-making company, shooting productions for schools and colleges. There was no end to what he planned: 'Nor does he want the Mercury to pin all its faith in the classics,' continued the *Time* profile. 'He pines to do a real mystery, a real farce, a British pantomime, a fast revue, a Mozart opera.' All of this, which might once have thrilled his fellow Mercurians, may have seemed less enthralling now they realised that they were unlikely to be part of it.

Brooks Atkinson of the *Times*, who was among the Mercury's staunchest and most concerned supporters, noted some of this in a piece entitled GOTHAM HOBGOBLIN: 'He is an intuitive showman. His theatrical ideas are creative and inventive. And his theatrical imagination is so wide in its scope that he can give the theatre enormous fluency and power. Ingenious lighting, stylised grouping, strange sounds and bizarre show effects are the instruments he uses for playing his macabre theatrical tunes. Plays have to give way to his whims, and actors have to subordinate their art when he gets under way, for The Shadow is monarch of all he surveys. It is no secret that his wilfulness and impulsiveness may also wreck the Mercury Theatre, for he is a thorough egotist in the grand manner of the old-style tragedian.' This piece provoked a letter to the editor from 'an ex-Mercury actress': '1) I found Welles less insistent on his own point of view than most directors, more receptive to accepting the actors' alternative interpretation and extraordinarily generous in giving recognition to a good performance. 2) As to "wilfulness and impulsiveness" I encountered nothing of the sort . . . he didn't do the usual shifting from day to day, but simply developed as the play unfolded itself under actual acting.' Tellingly, she adds: 'Welles as a director has faults. For one thing, he's almost always late. For another, he himself wastes time and permits others to waste time in irrelevant discussions. And so on. But he's far too brilliant a force in the theatre to permit an aura of discredit to grow up around him which in the specific respects generally mentioned is quite without basis.' Not many presently employed, about to be ex-Mercury actors, would have felt inclined to append their signatures.

Feeling was so strong in the company that a meeting was called: something which had never before happened. The company expressed their fears and anxieties, particularly concerning the project of preparing a touring version of *Five Kings* as a try-out for its inclusion in the second season. Welles replied: 'Ladies and gentlemen, you may have heard some rumours that the tour is off and it's true. Some of you may have thought that as a part of the Mercury Theatre, the Mercury Theatre owes some obligations. I want to state, here and now, I am the Mercury Theatre.' Hearing this regal pronouncement, Kevin O'Morrison, playing small parts in *Caesar* and *The Shoemaker's Holiday* at the National, told Andrea Nouryeh, 'most of us in our hearts just tore whatever loyalties we had'. Among the defectors was Aline MacMahon, who immediately turned down the role of Hesione Hushabye she had just been offered. It may be argued that the company's success was largely due to Welles; certainly it would have been inconceivable without him, his flair, his courage, his talent, and, to a large measure, his personality, so impressive and intriguing to the press.

The sheer scope of his ambition for the Mercury is exhilarating and inspiring, even though it is inseparable from his ambition for himself: he told a reporter in New Haven at the start of the *Julius Caesar* tour 'I wouldn't be happy if I couldn't convince myself that I will alter at least the cultural course of history in the theatre.' (The 'at least' is a characteristic touch.) What is disturbing is to find him, at the first bright dawn of his career (it is worth remembering that he was just about to celebrate his twenty-third birthday), quite so cavalier in his dealings with his fellow workers. The conclusion is inescapable that he had begun to believe his own publicity: that he had single-handedly and magisterially created the success, instead of forging it minute by minute, effect by effect, with a uniquely dedicated team. He had started to think that because they needed him more than he needed them, he could simply dispense with them and their views. Here are the seeds of self-destruction.

Meanwhile, there was *Heartbreak House* to be rehearsed. The play has a small cast; the company were dismayed to discover that even those few roles were being cast from outside its ranks. Welles, he said, wanted to avoid obvious casting. He himself was slated to play the ninety-year-old Shotover, which was a throwback to his days at Woodstock and in Dublin; Coulouris was Boss Mangan (their two roles in *Caesar* were taken over by Powers and O'Brien from the touring company). Vincent Price played the tiger-wrestling Hector Hushabye, John Hoystradt the flute-playing Utterword. Otherwise the company was entirely new: not at all the nascent American National Theatre that Price and others in the company had hoped they were joining. It was close, in fact, to being a Broadway cast, with a heavy bias towards the English theatre. Erskine Sandford repeated his Mazzini Dunn from the last New York production; Eustace Wyatt, an English actor of episcopal demeanour and a fondness for the bottle, played the burglar; Brenda Forbes, also English, Welles's old and none-too-loving colleague from Cornell days, was Nurse Guinness; Phyllis Joyce, an Australian actress with extensive experience in London, was Lady Utterwood; and the Austrian Mady Christians, one of Reinhardt's stars and already featured in several American films, was Hesione. Ellie Dunn was to be played by Geraldine Fitzgerald, a recent graduate of the Gate Theatre in Dublin and star of two British movies.

Welles may have been nervous of the play, for which he had a respect verging on reverence, and sought to back himself up with seasoned actors, experienced in the demands of modern realistic theatre. Perhaps this was the 'real play' that Chubby Sherman had been so nervous of 'in which an actor opens a door, a real door, walks in, sits down and begins to talk'. Welles knew from his negotiations with the author that he would brook no cuts, no transpositions, and no divergence from the printed stage directions. There was no possibility of a concept here; they must simply perform the play as written, which is essentially what they did, though somewhat unwisely Welles cut up the longer speeches, interspersing them with lines from other actors, thus destroying the musical line on which Shaw placed such stress ('it's Mozart!' the old gentleman would tell his actors).

Rehearsals, it seems, were dominated by the never-ending feud between Coulouris and Welles. To this was added a new one, between Coulouris and Geraldine Fitzgerald, who proved able to give as good as she got, and better: at one point during the run, exasperated beyond endurance, she kicked him on the shins. The ever-crabby Mancunian no doubt resented the special treatment that he felt she was receiving. Welles's charm was extended in its full golden warmth to her; at her audition Fitzgerald had first met Houseman, who had been sober and courteous, then when Welles arrived he said, with an irresistible smile (irresistible to Fitzgerald, that is; less so, perhaps, to Houseman): 'Oh, don't carry on Jack – you know we're going to take her.' She was struck, as so many had been, by his great height (he seemed taller, she said, as a young man), by the round baby face, the amazing eyes, his enormous beauty and charm, his ability to create intense intimacy on first contact. Maintaining it was more of a problem. 'He actually "saw" you: seemed to be very pleased to see you.' In a brilliant phrase, she compared his personality to that of a lighthouse: when you were caught in its beam, you were bathed in its illumination; when it moved on, you were plunged into darkness. Coulouris and Price were well out of the light by now, both exasperated by what they saw as Welles's tricks of personality, and somewhat sceptical about his attitude to his own acting. Rehearsing *Heartbreak House*, he again used William Alland to read in his part; Price said that he never really learned it at any time during the run. A report in the *World Telegram* on 9 April suggested another reason for company frustration: Welles's baby was born on 27 March: 'she timed her entrance into this world so as to create the greatest conceivable commotion, arriving just five minutes before the first reading of our next production, *Heartbreak House*. Needless to say, the reading was called off, and the entire company, which had stayed in town all day for the occasion, felt that their day had been ruined.' Welles was at Virginia's bedside shortly after the delivery of the child, whom they called, for no discernible reason, Christopher. The cavalier approach to naming her proved indicative of Welles's relationship to her in general; the commotion that she allegedly created was not reproduced in Welles's life. Ballerinas continued to be more interesting than either wife or child; Barbara Leaming even reports him flirting with the nurse on the maternity ward because she moved like a dancer. There is an awkward photograph of the young mother, father and child: Virginia looks strongly and almost defiantly at the camera while Welles stares down somewhat theatrically at the bundle of flesh in her mother's arms. There is nothing remotely spontaneous about the pose.

Welles's general distractedness at this period was reflected in his work on *Heartbreak House*. Clearly the atmosphere was very different from that on the two classical plays. Apart from the diversion of the newcomers, he seems not to have fully engaged with the play. Partly this stems from the restrictions imposed by the ever vigilant author and his representatives. Welles's adrenalin was not made to flow at the prospect of interpreting a play on its own terms. It must be his, visually, physically, textually. This is the way of the conceptual director, who regards his relationship to the writer as an equal partnership, in which he has the casting vote; it is also, of course, the way of the film-maker, for whom a script is always only a point of departure. In this *Heartbreak House*, the settings were largely as the author prescribed, executed, to Welles's very specific instructions, by John Koenig ('a window-dresser', the stage manager Walter Ash dismissively called him); the lighting was straightforward, though expert as usual. The only real scope for theatrical effect came with the bomb at the end, a startling moment in this production, created by the deepest notes of the *Julius Caesar* Hammond organ and the thunderdrum being sounded simultaneously. His frustrated creativity was largely channelled into his own make-up, of which several versions can be glimpsed in various production photographs. When he appeared at the dress rehearsal with the first version, Coulouris cried: 'My God, the ceiling's fallen in!' At first, the make-up took Welles three hours to apply; eventually he got it down to an hour and a half. It was a passion with him, which he indulged to the full, even if – to Houseman's chagrin – it meant holding the curtain till he was ready, thus sending the show (at four hours' running time) into overtime.

The reviews were distinctly mixed. The Mercury had taken an extreme gamble in staging a play directly on Broadway's terms, without its own signature stamped on it – a play which was anyway, as it always had been, and still is, highly problematic. Is it, as the author believed, his masterpiece, or an indulgent and misfired attempt at a homage to Chekhov (signalled on the title page, 'A Fantasia in the Russian Manner')? The critics reviewed the play (whose première had been, not in London, but in New York, eighteen years before) almost as much as the production: 'one of Mr Shaw's more interminable plays', as Brooks Atkinson said. 'He steps light but – oh lord! he steps long.' Despite the occasional roar of approval for the production, the general tone was muted (Atkinson even using the dread word 'workmanlike'); there was a feeling of quiet disappointment.

One or two critics rang alarm bells. John Mason Brown, who had been so crucial to the success of *Julius Caesar*, sternly wrote that 'the truth is that the production is not up to the Mercury's high standard. If it were not for the programme, one could swear that Shaw's play were being performed by an over-ambitious stock company.' The acting, with the exception of Coulouris as Boss Mangan, was not greatly admired. Welles's Shotover had its enthusiasts (Lockridge: 'Mr Welles as Shotover plays much better than I have ever seen him') but they were few. Mason Brown continued his mournfully disappointed review: 'Mr Welles behind a great flow of whiskers wins his laughs as Capt Shotover. But, if I may say so, he seems to be winning them in spite of rather than because of himself. The part is almost surefire. Yet in performing it, Mr Welles lacks comic precision and muffs point after point which cries to be made.'

It is hard to see how it could be otherwise. For a twenty-two-year-old, however gifted, to attempt Shotover is an impossibility: an excellent thing to do in repertory, in the course of winning one's spurs, but folly to attempt on Broadway. Of course, the Mercury wasn't (quite) on Broadway, but to all practical intents and purposes it was. It had created an excitement and raised expectations that demanded that its work should be judged by the highest standards. Here it had seemingly set itself up simply to be shot down. The remarkable thing is that only one out of every two critics chose to do so. Their hearts were with the Mercury; the goodwill was enormous, and even the attacking notices came from a position of great affection. One notice, predictably, came from no such position. It is none the less the most penetrating and the most interesting, and it was written, of course, by Mary McCarthy: 'The Mercury Theatre company act out *Heartbreak House* as if it were one of those week-end comedies by Rachel Crothers or Frederick Lonsdale.'

In writing about Welles, she went, again, for the jugular. 'Mr Welles as an actor has always seemed to secrete a kind of viscous holy oil with which he sprays the rough surfaces of his roles. The sentimentality of Mr Welles's acting, the nervelessness of his direction, the bare, mechanical competence of the majority of his supporting cast combine to act as a steam-roller on Shaw's *Heartbreak House* . . . Mr Welles's production can only serve to remind the public that the original still exists in the library.' Despite the gratuitous aggressiveness of the notice, she makes a telling point about Welles's acting: his sentimental side is, as it were, the bank holiday of his rhetorical one. Both modes deny real feeling, seeking rather to impress the spectator than to reveal an inner truth. They are external applications, designed to mask an absence of emotion; they draw attention to the actor rather than to the character. Coulouris, for all his rebarbative and wilful traits, was able, presumably by having access to his own inner life, to create an authentic person: as McCarthy reports 'his Boss Mangan was a genuinely strident, strangled, unhappy self-made man'.

McCarthy's voice was unique in its insistence on Welles's shallowness. The overwhelming view was that, even if they had bitten off more than they could chew with *Heartbreak House*, the Mercury's first season was a dazzling and inspiring one. In a *New York Times* piece in July of 1938 entitled THE SUMMING UP Houseman and Welles (the piece was actually written by Houseman) looked back fairly frankly on their first season at the Mercury: their problems with the repertory system, both in building an audience and in cross-casting, and the need to terminate successes. 'However,' Houseman ended, with a justifiable flourish, 'at the end of the first season we find we have played to over a quarter of a million people at an average price of slightly less than a dollar. Of this: 20 per cent = carriage trade; 40 per cent parties; 40 per cent doors. 120,000 student cards were distributed. 1/3rd of audience comes from educational organisations.' They were already an institution, the white hope of the theatre, both progressive and classical, audacious and serious, innovative and accomplished, polished and affordable, original without being elitist, and they had captured the most vital section of the theatre-going public.

The problems which Houseman had understandably chosen not to air in print – the collapse of company morale and their severe financial straits – now had to be addressed. No one could have imagined that after the exposure and the success they had had they could be in quite such a parlous financial condition. *Heartbreak House* had proved a calamity from that point of view: the solid realistic settings were immensely more expensive than *Caesar's* platforms rescued from a deserted warehouse, or the orange crates and cocoa matting used in *The Shoemaker's Holiday*. The six new cast members had added substantially to the wages bill, too; above all, they had to pay Shaw's royalties. He had offered them terms that were what he called 'not too unreasonable': 15 per cent of the gross when the receipts exceeded $1,500 a performance, 10 per cent when they were between $500 and $1,500, 7.5 per cent when they were between $250 and $500. No doubt, by his stringent standards, the terms were not too unreasonable, but to a theatre that had never paid a penny in royalties by the simple expedient of only working with dead authors, it was a severe blow. None the less, it was a blow they could weather. Their investors remained loyal, despite the somewhat ungenerous attitude of Houseman and Welles: 'Personally, we were grateful to our investors for the generosity that had made the birth of the Mercury Theatre possible. But as business associates, our feelings were as ambivalent towards them as those of adolescents towards their parents.' Their dealings were largely with Houseman, of course, and his formal manner and natural courtesy masked his ambivalence. With Welles, it was another matter. 'While things were going well, he regarded them as parasites and exploiters, fattening on the success wrung from his creative energies. When they began to go badly, this hostility was aggravated by shame and guilt: anticipating their reproaches he developed a loathing for them such as one inevitably feels towards a benefactor whom one has disappointed or betrayed.'

Such was not yet the case with the investors. With the company, betrayal and disappointment was rife. The *Heartbreak House* company was particularly resentful of the unceasing emphasis on Welles: as Price later said, not to be paid a proper salary was one thing; to receive no credit either was intolerable. Uncertainty was rife. The only plans for the second season were vague: a revival of *The Shoemaker's Holiday*, *Five Kings* (which so far existed only in Welles's mind) and *The Importance of Being Earnest*, in which Chubby Sherman was to play Algernon, with Vincent Price as Jack. There were no dates, and no one, apart from those two actors, were allocated roles; the entire company was laid off. Geraldine Fitzgerald was advised to go to Hollywood, since they had nothing to offer her. To all intents and purposes, the acting group ceased to exist. Even the vaguely planned season collapsed completely when Chubby Sherman suddenly withdrew his commitment, effectively making it impossible to revive *The Shoemaker's Holiday*, of which his Firk was the linchpin and making *The Importance of Being Earnest*, specifically planned to find him another starring role, pointless. Having repeatedly failed to get a date for the start of rehearsals, he accepted a part in the Broadway revue *Sing out the News*. His withdrawal from the company was a personal blow for Welles, which he took very badly, repairing to bed for several days. Sherman was as near as Welles came to having a friend. He had been the associate director on *Julius Caesar*, director of the Studio (such as it was), a stalwart colleague, and, as Houseman put it, in some odd way (as revealed in his indiscreet interview in *The New York Times*) 'the conscience of the company'. Thirty years later he told Andrea Nouryeh that it wasn't simply the uncertainty over dates that made him withdraw from the Mercury: it was the life-style. Welles expected him to carouse with him every night after the show, unfortunately neglecting to have any money with him (a regal habit which persisted to the end of his life), leaving Sherman to fork up, which he couldn't afford to do: 'the high-livers were killing me,' he said. His decision was surely encouraged by his partner, the unclubbable Whitford Kane. So he and Welles parted company; they never worked together again. Houseman added a further reflection on Sherman's departure. 'The pace had become so wild, the mood so intense and violent as to be physically and mentally unendurable. Was Chubby, with his low threshold of fatigue and pain, merely the first of those who could not bear to stay around?'

There seems to be little doubt that both Houseman and Welles were out of touch, in their different ways, with the company. It is good and necessary up to a point for the directors of a theatre to be somewhat aloof from the members of the company, who have to have the opportunity to gripe and criticise without it becoming an issue every time. The question is: were Houseman and Welles really thinking about the company's interests? It came back to the fundamental question: what sort of a company was the Mercury to be? Was its objective simply to produce exciting shows as often as possible? If that was the case, the show was the thing, and the group must be reconstituted every time to serve the particular show. But that was not what had brought these particular actors together. The problem was partly one of too many fine words, both Houseman and Welles silver-tonguing their cohorts on a minute-by-minute basis, loosely invoking soul-stirring ideals to negotiate the crisis of the moment. They played with their colleagues' dreams; a dangerous thing to do. Their plans seemed improvised from day to day, as did their views of what they were up to and who they were. They sank no roots. And now, despite their brilliant season and their golden reputation, they had nothing to build on. The very continuance of the Mercury seemed, unthinkably, in doubt. At this moment of peril, once again something quite unforeseen saved them, as it was with quite uncanny frequency to do, until, in the fullness of time, the luck ran out.

CHAPTER FIFTEEN

Theatre of the Air

HOUSEMAN DESCRIBES the moment at which he heard about the Mercury's latest adventure. Having left Welles – still brooding over Chubby Sherman's defection – in a stupor of rage and despair ('limp and huge in a darkened room with his face to the wall'), Houseman sent Augusta Weissberger off on her honeymoon and himself on a brief holiday with his mother. For all he knew, the Mercury's first season would also be its last. No sooner had he set out but 'I saw an oversized black limousine coming up the hill at high speed. As it approached, it began to sound its horn and I became aware of Orson's huge face sticking out of the window with its mouth wide open and of his gigantic voice echoing through the surrounding woods.' His news was that the Columbia Broadcasting System had offered him (and the Mercury) nine weekly programmes to perform adaptations of famous books; the series would be known as *First Person Singular*, and Welles was to be featured as its quadruple-threat creator; 'written, directed, produced and performed by Orson Welles' was to be its epigraph.

This last notion was jointly conceived by Welles's agent Schneider ('you gotta do it all, Orson') and William Lewis of CBS, who was happy to use it as the show's formula. Lewis, the network's chief executive, had acquired considerable respect as someone with an eye for talent and a readiness to back it. 'What can management do to encourage the superb craftsmanship that this business so desperately needs? Mainly it is in the wise and sympathetic handling of the creative people you have developed. Make them feel cherished and important; praise good work or extraordinary effort on the part of creative people – and – above all – see that they get credit for it.' Hence, for example, *Norman Corwin's Words without Music*; hence Welles's billing. The incentive that he fails to mention, of course, is money. He had very little to give. What he offered was freedom to experiment and prestige, which is also what he wanted – not for himself but for his network.

This was no form of philanthropy. Radio listenership was vast, but standards were pitifully low. There had been considerable legal pressure on the networks to counteract the overwhelming amount of mindless (and highly popular) banality being dispensed over the air waves under the sponsorship of commerce, for whom the programmes were the merest peg for their plugs. A coalition of liberals, academics, artists, leaders of labour, agriculture, religion, and, in the words of the historian Eric Barnouw, 'the non-profit world', formed a pressure group in the early days of the New Deal (when no problem seemed unsolvable) to denounce radio's current output with some vehemence as 'a pollution of the air', 'a cultural disaster', 'a huckstering orgy', 'a pawnshop', and, conclusively, 'a sickness in the national culture'. (More moderately, but perhaps even more witheringly, Norman Corwin, later one of the medium's most distinguished practitioners, had written 'There is about as much creative genius in radio today as there is in a convention of plasterers.') The pressure group demanded the revocation of the networks' licences, and a new allocation of frequencies 'with one fourth going to educational, religious, agricultural, labor, co-operative and similar non-profit organisations' (Barnouw). The measure was heard with some sympathy in Congress, galvanising the networks into trying to transform themselves (at least in Congressional eyes) into patrons of art. On the strength of their good intentions, the legal measure was abandoned, but it hovered, a perpetual threat.

The transformation of the networks into Gonzagas and Medicis of the air waves was easily and cheaply accomplished. The pressure groups were offered free slots (of which there were plenty) and there was a move to engender new and serious programmes, unsponsored. This lay the foundation for what is known as The Golden Age of Radio. It was a part of Welles's extraordinary good fortune that he appeared on the radio scene at exactly the moment when it was ready to develop into a major expressive medium. William S. Paley, who had recently bought and revitalised CBS, had 77 per cent of unused air space; this he deployed in the creation of a number of so-called 'sustaining' programmes of which Irving Reis's *Columbia Workshop* was the supreme example: unsponsored, cheap ($400 a programme), but with creative carte blanche. These slots were mostly those impossible to sell to advertisers because the competition – *Edgar Bergen and Charlie McCarthy*, for example – was just too powerful. Absence of advertisers meant that there was no need to pitch the programme at any specific group, which need more than any other factor dictated the nature of the programmes on the mainstream frequencies. Thus Paley accrued great prestige for his network, and created great opportunities for the artists and technicians, and all for a song – to the chagrin of NBC who were loaded with money, but devoid of kudos. Their kudos was acquired later, in the very expensive form of Toscanini.

Lewis offered Welles a total budget of $50,000 for nine programmes, out of which he had to pay for everything but the orchestra. For someone who had been earning as much as $1,000 a week for the previous three years, this was small beer, but a glorious opportunity. Lewis's approach to Welles was characteristically bold, though it was not exactly a reckless gamble.

He was scarcely entrusting the new series to a tyro. *Les Misérables* had placed Welles among the leaders of quality radio; a small group, and not widely known, but a formidable one. The exploration of the medium's possibilities had been recent and remarkably quick, and had already thrown up two or three brilliant producers. Welles was the only actor-director among them; his peers were Reis of the *Columbia Workshop*, the highly original Arch Oboler, master of bizarre suspense stories, William Robson (who had produced a re-creation of the San Quentin prison break as it happened) and Max Wylie. Welles had worked as an actor with most of these men, as well as on *The March of Time*, no mean innovator itself, and was fully aware of the technical possibilities of the moment. He had arrived in radio when it was starting to grow, to develop: the vocabulary was in flux, the scope of expression seemingly limitless.

His show was announced, in *The New York Times*, with predictable flourish: 'Orson Welles, the twenty-three-year-old actor-director who has introduced several innovations in the technique of the legitimate theatre, has been invited with the Mercury Theatre to produce nine one-hour weekly broadcast dramas over WABC's network, beginning July 11, 1938.' Welles was quoted as saying: 'we plan to bring to radio the experimental techniques which have proved so successful in another medium, and to treat radio with the intelligence and respect such a beautiful and powerful medium deserves,' rather cheekily suggesting that no one had thought of this before. He wanted to make it very clear that there was no question of simply transferring the Mercury's repertory to the radio. 'I think it is time that radio came to realise the fact that no matter how wonderful a play may be for the stage, it cannot be as wonderful for the air.' In saying this, he was declaring war on his predecessor in the same slot, Lux Radio Theatre, introduced by Cecil B. de Mille, and, even more directly, on *First Nighter*, billed as being broadcast from 'The Little Theatre off Times Square'. The format of this programme had 'Mr First Nighter' being shown to his seat by an 'usher' just before curtain time. At intermission between acts, the usher would call out, 'Smoking in the downstairs and outer lobby only, please!' After the commercial a buzzer would sound and the usher would call out, 'Curtain going up!' Welles was having none of this. His brief was to innovate; that was his profile: The Innovator. Actually, in this medium, as in others, he was the Fulfiller: absorbing innovations, and applying them at high pressure.

Welles strenuously insisted on the distinction between his theatre work and what he was attempting on radio. In an article for *Radio Annual*, he says 'The less a radio drama resembles a play the better it is likely to be. This is not to indicate for one moment that radio drama is a lesser thing. It must be, however, drastically different. This is because the nature of the radio demands a form impossible to the stage. The images called up by a broadcast must be imagined, not seen. And so we find that radio drama is more akin to the form of the novel, to story telling, than to anything else of which it is convenient to think.' He pursues this theme in his unpublished *Lecture Notes on Acting*: 'There is no place where ideas are as purely expressed as on the radio . . . it is a narrative rather than a dramatic form.' This emphasis on the narrative element was not unique to Welles; Eric Barnouw has identified 'an explosion of interest in radio as a narrative device'. His most distinctive contribution – already evident in *Les Misérables* – was in giving the narrator an identity. He described this rather grandly, but not inappropriately, as 'the revival from desuetude of Chorus, the fellow who used to come out between the acts and explain what was going to happen next and why. Radio's particular amendment is the personalising of Chorus, of making him a character in the play rather instead of an outside character looking in.' In fact, what he describes here, the notion behind the title *First Person Singular*, was a sparingly used device of limited application, even in the series of that name.

A more remarkable innovation was the omnipresent narrator, often playing several roles within the piece. The effect is of direct contact between the narrator and the listener; he becomes not merely a neutral story teller, but the author himself, of whom the characters are simply projections. And this omnipresent, all-knowing figure was, of course, Welles. Reduced to a voice, relieved of the tedium of having to learn the script, get into costume and actually move around the stage, his personality was able to flourish untrammelled. He was able to establish with a numberless audience the gift of immediate intimacy of which he was such a master in life (though less so in the theatre). He acknowledged this, too, in his *Radio Annual* piece: 'radio drama has done another thing. It has continued the process of bringing the actor near the audience, a development which has been detectable for about a hundred years. The actor's problem of projection has ceased to be troublesome and the test of a good performance has come to be its honesty and integrity. The invention of the close-up has had a profound effect upon stage acting. The penetrating effect of radio performing, the last word in bringing the actor and audience face to face, has also had its effect on the stage.' The historical analysis may be faulty (theatres had been getting larger and larger during the hundred years between the mid-nineteenth and the mid-twentieth centuries) but he exactly identifies the genius of radio: it gets inside your head as no other medium can. The narrator has your ear. *Newsweek* told its readers that in the new programme 'avoiding the cut-and-dried dramatic technique that introduces dialogue with routine announcements, Welles will serve as genial host to his radio audience. As narrator, he will build himself directly into the drama, drawing his listeners into the charmed circle. He reasons a radio audience is apt to be bored when it hears someone say "Once upon a time". Not so if you say, "this happened to me." '

The first show – true to his programme outlined above – would not be a play, but a story: *Treasure Island.* He had four weeks in which to prepare it. He had brought Houseman with him to the crucial meeting with Bill Lewis; now, without hesitation or indeed formal invitation, he turned to him to help him in the adaptation. 'He seemed to assume I would be working with him,' wrote Houseman. 'I reminded him that I knew nothing about radio. He said I'd better start learning in the morning.' There is no phrase that better expresses the outrageous charm of Welles, compounded of trust and demand, confidence and challenge. It was, however casually entered into, a huge new development in their relationship, as Houseman saw years later when he wrote his autobiography: 'Throughout my theatrical association with Orson over the past three and a half years, much of the initiative had been mine – strategically and artistically. While I had never hesitated to acknowledge Orson's creative leadership, I had managed, consciously and not without effort, to maintain the balance of power in a partnership which, for all our frequent and violent personal conflicts, had remained emotionally and professionally stable. With the coming of the radio show (though my contribution to its success was substantial) this delicate balance was disturbed and, finally, destroyed. The formula "produced, directed and performed by Orson Welles" was one that I approved and encouraged . . . but its effect on our association and on the future course of the Mercury was deep and irreversible. From being Orson's partner, I had become his employee: the senior member, but still no more than a member of his staff.'

For the time being, Houseman had to produce a script. He started to hack away at *Treasure Island* when, after three weeks, Welles suddenly changed his mind. They would do *Dracula*, one of many pseudo-gothic horror stories he loved, and to which Columbia had just acquired the rights. Now the heat was really on – just the way Welles liked it to be – and he and Houseman set to feverishly. Over several meals and without benefit of sleep, awash with bottles of wine, balloons of brandy and great pots of coffee in cyclical alternation, they gutted the book of its most striking moments, thrashed out a framework onto which they latched dialogue transcribed from the book, cobbled together narrative links (in this case using Stoker's device of multiple narrations) and finally staggered away from the restaurant with a script. Their purpose was maximum effectiveness. They wished to avoid the form and structure of the stage play, and their radio dramaturgy – with its freedom of location, rapid succession of short scenes and liberal use of the narrator – celebrates the medium's unique possibilities. None the less, their approach can only be described as theatrical. There is little here of the multi-layered use of sound that distinguishes the poetic tapestries of Norman Corwin, nor any of the riddling originality of Arch Oboler. 'Welles's specific contribution,' said Barnouw, 'was putting it over in bravura style – he could make anything work.' The Mercury Theatre of the Air was good, old-fashioned barnstorming: Henry Irving (a possible model for Dracula, as it happens) would have warmly approved.

Welles found inspired collaborators. Bernard Herrmann, CBS's head of music, was reluctantly assigned to the show (their *Macbeth* of two years before still smarting in both men's minds), and found himself required to produce ever more music, sometimes, Houseman notes, as much as forty minutes out of a fifty-seven-minute show. Herrmann's unusually catholic taste in music (he had a show of his own devoted to playing arcane and exotic scores; the music of Samuel Pepys was the subject of one) and his uncanny ability to reproduce the musical voice of his fellow composers made him invaluable. Sometimes his instrumentalists were responsible for the sound effects, while sound effects were used to create music – the wind, a whistle, a dog howling. He took advantage of the flexible composition of his orchestra – as he was later to do when writing for films – to introduce unusual instruments, or familiar instruments in unusual numbers. *Dracula* is full of curious orchestral touches, extensive use being made of disturbing harmonics. To his prodigious gifts was added a famously peppery personality, which complemented Welles's in its fanatical perfectionism, allied to deep feeling for language; he knew as much about literature and its byways as he did about music.

The technicians were generally delighted to be challenged by Welles's quest for new and ever more real effects. He created a mood of restlessness and experiment which infected everyone. Paul Stewart recalled the technicians attempting to replicate the sound of leaves with a newspaper. 'Orson in his usual way heard it and said, "That won't do. Leaves don't sound like that. It sounds exactly like a newspaper." Actually, it didn't sound like newspaper at all, but he always had to have his moment of bad behaviour, for his own personal satisfaction. "Go into Central Park," he said, "find me real branches from a real bush." "Orson," said the effects man, "it's February, the bushes have no leaves." "You're right," said Orson. "Use the newspaper." ' (By a nice irony, noted by Houseman, most radio sets were incapable of picking up 'all those wonderful sound effects.' They are now clearly audible on cassette and compact disc.)

Stewart, who had given Welles his first job on the radio, had been called in because he was vastly experienced both as actor and director, having been responsible for some years for *Cavalcade of America*, a pioneering history pageant programme, among many other shows. 'At first Orson tried to produce the Mercury Theatre of the Air on his own, but he was incapable of doing so, being a very poorly organised man,' Stewart told François Thomas, 'and Houseman, at least at the beginning, knew nothing about radio, and was of no use except in matters concerning the script – few people better understood rewriting, reshaping or reworking a script.' Stewart gave structure to the rehearsals, held everything together; he was a crucial figure in getting the shows on. Almost immediately after *Dracula*, Welles established a pattern of work for the Mercury Theatre of the Air in which Stewart was the indispensable linchpin, a pattern which he maintained on all his shows over the next few years. The book, once chosen (generally not till the Monday of the week of transmission), would be turned over to Houseman and whoever else had been roped in to write it. On Wednesday the script would be rehearsed in the studio without Welles; a trial recording on shellac discs was made under Stewart's supervision. Welles would listen to this and make script suggestions, which would then be incorporated. Only on the Sunday, the day of transmission itself, would he be physically involved.

At noon, he arrived in the studio, and all hell broke loose. Richard Barr in his unpublished memoir describes the scene: 'Orson did not direct his shows; he conducted them. Standing on a podium in front of a dynamic microphone (to diminish his sibilant "s") he waved his arms, cued every music, sound and speech cue.' A disc of the dress rehearsal of the *Julius Caesar* broadcast captures him in action, slipping in and out of character, now sonorous Brutus, now screaming and most unstatesman-like autocrat, demanding that the band play louder/faster/with more feeling, that the actors should be more animated or not so rushed, that the wind had to howl more. His impatience is given full voice at this dress rehearsal; the excitement leaps off the acetate. Stewart described to Thomas the aftermath of the final dress rehearsal: 'There was absolute chaos – absolute chaos, every week. Welles is a very destructive man, he has to destroy everything, then put it back together again himself, and there were endless passionate discussions between him, Houseman and me. Then suddenly someone would say "We're on air in two minutes." The ground was strewn with paper. That we got on the air at all was a weekly miracle, because it was always like that.'

The very opening titles of this first programme set the tone: the swaggering first few bars of the Tchaikovsky First Piano Concerto, generating extrovert excitement, as two announcers in alternating phrases tell us that the Columbia Network takes pride in presenting Orson Welles in a unique new summer series. Breathless with excitement, they continue: 'In a single year, the first in the life of the Mercury Theatre, Orson Welles has come to be the most famous name of our time in American drama.' They quote *Time* magazine – 'the brightest moon that has risen over Broadway in years, Welles should feel at home in the sky, for the sky is the only limit which his ambitions recognised' – and finally, the United Press: 'The meteorite rise of Orson Welles's Mercury Theatre continues unabated.' Tremulously noting its four hit shows in a season 'unparalleled in Broadway history', they reveal that 'Mr Welles has long been working on a greater project, the Broadways of the entire United States.' He is about, they promise, to bring to the air 'those same qualities of vitality and imagination that have made him the most talked-of theatre director in America today.' This is the project Columbia is bringing; the first time in its history, they claim, that radio has ever extended such an invitation to an entire theatrical institution. Finally, we get the great man himself: 'Orson Welles – the director of the Mercury Theatre, the star and producer of these programmes: "Good evening," Welles intones. "The Mercury Theatre faces tonight a challenge and an opportunity for which we are grateful." ' They will, he says, present during the next nine weeks many different kinds of stories – 'stories of romance and adventure. Biography, mystery, and human emotion. Stories by authors like: Robert Louis Stevenson, Emile Zoladostoievsky [as he invariably phrases it], Edgar Poe, P.G. Wodehouse.' Then he introduces his cast and tells us what they have played at the Mercury then bids us good-bye 'for a moment. I'll see you in Transylvania.' Finally there is the formal: 'The Mercury Theatre on the air presents Orson Welles as Count Dracula in his own adaptation of Bram Stoker's great novel.' It is interesting to note that within the first three minutes of the programme, Welles's name has been uttered nine times. It is something of a relief when he tells us: 'The next time I speak to you I am Dr Arthur Seward.'

The excitement and intensity of the transmission, as vivid fifty years later as it must have been at the time, is imbued with Welles's personal quality. 'The feeling, the atmosphere, all the Wellesian eccentricity, was there in the show,' as Stewart says. There is, too – surprisingly, perhaps, in view of the circumstances but a vital part of the young Welles – a tremendous sense of fun. There is the odd private joke: in *Dracula*, one of the men overboard is called Balanchine, a jest for the personal amusement of the ballerina Vera Zorina who was at that moment being pursued with equal ardour by both Welles and the distinguished Russian choreographer. 'Balanchine! Balanchine! Is Balanchine below?' the sailors cry. 'Balanchine's gone! – Like the other! – Like all the others!' For those who knew what the joke meant, he was delighted to boast, in this oblique fashion, of his conquest. All in all, radio suited him down to the ground. The immediacy of its impact, the flexibility of its language, above all, perhaps, the circumstances of its creation, were ideal for Welles: a whole world summoned up in a few days' rehearsal, the cycle of theatrical creation speeded up to engender maximum adrenalin (read-through, rehearsal, dress rehearsal, first and last performance). Later he was to find the same cycle in movies, endlessly repeated for each shot. And here, in his first major outing on radio, he was already able to limit his involvement to the day of recording itself, arriving at the dress rehearsal the way Kean might have arrived in Dublin to give his Shylock, suddenly galvanising the unsuspecting local actors. Personality, in these circumstances, becomes everything.

As well as Seward he, of course, plays Dracula. Why, it may be asked, was it necessary for him to play more than one part in the programme? Why, indeed, was it necessary to act in the programme at all, rather than simply narrating? There are obvious reasons, of course (why should the others have all the fun?) and he was the star, after all. But beyond that, it seems to be part of his method – his magician's method, one might say – to draw attention to what he's doing: 'and now, before your very ears, I shall become . . . Dracula!' The transformation demands applause, admiration; but the essential element is that you never forget that it's Welles doing it; you never believe that you're listening to the character himself. His fellow actors – particularly Gabel and Coulouris (who had clearly swallowed his irritation sufficiently to participate in the new venture) – are all highly skilled and effective, all in full command of the microphone and its demands, but they lack the instant identifiability of Welles. That, of course, was their purpose; they create and inhabit their characters to the point that we forget that this actor or that is playing them. Gabel's Viennese Van Helsing is a triumph. For him the accent is a liberation, giving him consistently interesting phrasing. Coulouris's Harker is also strongly and convincingly realised; there are no inverted commas round his performance as there are in Welles's.

No matter what voice Welles assumes, it's always unmistakably him: he doesn't begin to rival Peter Ustinov, for example, in virtuosity of pitch, accent, rhythm, character. He often brilliantly catches a colour, a flavour, but he doesn't submit to its character. He manipulates it, usually to sonorous effect. Above all he creates atmosphere; it is his presence that dominates the entire show. His Dracula voice sounds artificially manufactured, like the controlled belches by which the late Jack Hawkins was able to find a substitute voice when his vocal cords had been destroyed by cancer. Welles's Dracula voice may have been slightly treated – it has an acoustic unlike the others' – but it is really his own special resonance that creates the effect. The camera is said to love certain actors; the microphone positively adored Welles.

The production itself is notable for its continuous web of sound. There is barely a moment unelaborated by some effect or another: doors creak, dogs howl, wolves snarl, horses neigh, carriage wheels turn, women scream, owls hoot, telegraph keys tap, one on top of another. Hitherto, sound effects had politely waited till the speaker was finished; with Welles they rudely break in before the end of the sentence, sweeping you on to the next location, the next emotion, sometimes overwhelming the dialogue: no bad thing in a penny dreadful.

Strictly speaking, *Dracula* is of more literary merit than the average penny dreadful, but Welles wasn't interested in it as literature, as a text. He was interested in it as a pretext, a springboard for his form of radio melodrama. As Eric Barnouw observed, content was of little importance to him: it wasn't what he said, but the way that he said it. He revelled in being able with the simplest means to summon up in the listener's mind dark and crumbling visions beyond the wildest ambition of screen or stage. He launched a passionate assault on radio, thrilled by its techniques, demanding more and more of them: not particularly in order to express anything, simply in order to set the pulse beating faster – his and the audience's. (It is possible, however, to hear, through all the virtuoso texture, the often sounded note of the vampire's pain in his frequent refrain 'Flesh of my flesh, guilt of my guilt!' Pity for monsters is a constant theme of Welles's.)

Dracula was greatly admired, though not hugely listened to: only a fraction of the audience that listened to *The Shadow* tuned in to the Mercury Theatre of the Air. But within the small world of quality radio, there was great excitement. For Welles and Houseman it was a tremendous infusion of confidence, enthusiasm and energy. Their hopelessness of only four weeks before had been turned to boundless optimism, and by some paradox, though they were heavily committed to producing their weekly programme, they were now suddenly able to contemplate a second season of stage work for the Mercury.

Out of their bran-tub of potential projects, they pulled three hopefuls: the William Gillette farce *Too Much Johnson*, Georg Büchner's *Danton's Death*, and the still unwritten *Five Kings*: a stimulating and diverse programme. *Five Kings* would be the Mercury's definitive claim to creating a new American Shakespearean tradition (Welles's gauntlet flung down, both to the McClintics and to the English upstart, Maurice Evans, who had recently had the audacity to tour the country as Richard II *and* Falstaff); *Danton's Death* offered as many parallels to contemporary revolutionary politics as *Caesar* had to the European dictators; and *Too Much Johnson* seemed to have the combined potential of *The Shoemaker's Holiday* and *Horse Eats Hat*, wild comedy built on verbal and physical high jinks. A close observer of Welles, however, might have felt that for all the co-directors' newly surging energy, there was something untoward. At the end of June, Welles had given (to the National Council of Teachers of English) a widely reported speech about the future of the theatre – including the Mercury – in terms of such gloom that the journalists present were reduced to joking uneasily about it. 'Mr Welles's opening criticism, purred quietly into the microphone, issued from the loud-speakers with all the effect of a verbal knockout: The theatre is not worth your attention . . . Broadway provides only the dullest and stodgiest fare. In entertainment value it is vastly inferior to the movies . . . people come to the most incredible things in vast numbers. They come to see revivals of old plays at the Mercury Theatre in much greater numbers than they have any business to.'

Wilella Waldorf in her report (WELLES PEERS THROUGH HIS BEARD AND SEES CHAOS) has him 'tottering up to the microphones and gasping out the news that the theatre is dead, through, finished . . . widely publicised as the outstanding Bright Boy of the American theatre, he is apparently tired out already, gloomy, disillusioned, cracking up . . . Orson Welles has been wearing so many false beards lately that he has grown old before his time. Recently turned twenty-three, he shows distressing signs of wear and tear . . . the director of the Mercury Theatre (which has just completed what is generally agreed to be a hysterically successful first season), he has developed the outlook of an embittered old gaffer suffering from gout, liver trouble and rheumatism.' Her bantering tone is shot through with hostility; the first manifestation of anything other than uncritical admiration that Welles had received as a public figure. 'No wonder Welles is annoyed, for apparently the fool playgoing public simply won't stay away, even from *Heartbreak House* . . . we can see him now staggering around backstage, all ready to shatter into a thousand pieces from the strain of producing plays that people insist upon coming to see even though the theatre is dead.' Saddened by his plight – 'the Makropolous secret behind a twenty-three-year-old face' – she proposes to send him to a spa to recuperate. 'And in the meantime, Mr Welles, cheer up if you can. All is not lost . . . you may yet achieve the Mercury ambition and produce a revival from which the public stays away. The People may turn out to be more discriminating than you think.'

And so it proved. The world-weariness she and others detected in Welles is curious – was it a pose? Or had he really worn himself out, spiritually as much as physically? It's a curious glimpse of him, ageing before one's very eyes – a fast-forward of a life. There is a simpler explanation of his apocalyptic tone, however: at the time that he delivered the speech, the Mercury Theatre was in abeyance. There was no company and no plan for the future. The Mercury Theatre of the Air, on the other hand, was just coming into existence. Welles was becoming excited as only he could by the possibilities of unrestricted access to a new medium; psychologically he may have been preparing to devote himself entirely to radio. In the same speech delivered to the English Teachers, he had attributed the success of the Mercury – 'in an attempt to revive older forms and find newer forms that will impress themselves upon our civilisation' – to having concentrated on delivering lines with as much clarity and authentic inflection as possible. 'Emphasis has been placed on infusing language with as much beauty as the actors can lend through voice and expression. Language never lives until it is spoken aloud. People storm to see our plays because they can really understand what we are talking about.' This was a curious claim from the director of what was surely the most overpoweringly visual theatre in the history of the American stage. It is something of a disappointment, too, if the new form that would 'impress itself on civilisation' turned out to be nothing more than speaking clearly. He may of course have been referring to the relative freedom from interpretation in the delivery of the text – if not in its cutting or in the design of the production. In fact, though, he seems to be staking a claim for the supremacy of words; and what medium depends more on words than radio?

The theatre was also competing for his attention with the movies, which warrant a brief admiring mention in his speech to the conference. He had been approached by Warner Brothers the previous year but the financial offer was unenticing; going to Hollywood would have meant abandoning his freelance radio career. David Selznick made overtures; Welles screen-tested for Metro. None of these offers were sufficiently attractive. It was by no means, as he later liked to maintain, a thought that had never entered his mind. The power, influence and indeed glamour of the movies was very interesting to him. He was biding his time, waiting for the right terms. So, despite the new confidence that their radio work had engendered in them, the Mercury's second season contained the seeds of disaster deep within it: Welles's heart was no longer in it. The successes of the previous season had entirely depended on his unflagging will and energy. It was neither careful preparation, nor technical skill, nor interpretative genius that had created *Caesar* and *The Shoemaker's Holiday*: it was adrenalin and the inspiration of the moment. Subtract these qualities and what was left would scarcely stand up to examination. The dull and routine *Heartbreak House* was a warning; what followed was far, far worse than could have been imagined. The season that looked so lively and challenging on paper turned into a disaster in three chapters: aberration (*Too Much Johnson*); nightmare (*Danton's Death*); and farce (*Five Kings*).

Too Much Johnson at least had the merit of playing out of town. Two of the Mercury's apprentices ran a summer theatre at the pretty little resort of Stony Creek, near New Haven, Connecticut, close to the coast and the spattering of tiny islands called The Thimbles, some seventy-five miles out of New York. They offered the Mercury a slot, free of charge, starting 16 August 1938, even providing the designers. The James Morcom set and Leo van Witsen costumes would be held in reserve for the Mercury. It might have been a rather useful out-of-town try-out; nothing is more valuable for farce than constant repetition: the machine has to work perfectly, and until it does, nothing happens at all. The play itself is unexpectedly delightful, centring on a voyage to Havana, a marital mix-up, and a compulsive liar whose lies keep catching up with him. This central character, Billings, was the part which Gillette wrote for himself, and his dialogue is designed to show off his particular genius for staccato diction. 'All come out of a little affair, you know – come over here – singular, isn't it, how these little – detained in town one night over business dining at French table d'hote – one of the rear ones near Washington Square – she was charming, too – sweetest little – French, you know – and a flirt – great Scott!' It is an unexpected piece from the pen of the definitive American Sherlock Holmes, whose adaptation of the Conan Doyle stories he was still triumphantly playing onstage at the age of seventy-seven, broadcasting the role at the age of eighty. Gillette, a notorious eccentric, living alternately in a houseboat and a castle, surrounded by large numbers of cats and no one else, died the year before the Mercury revival, which is perhaps just as well. Despite Welles's declared affection for the piece and for the American theatre of yesteryear, he decided to subject the play to an experiment. Finding the exposition of the plot boring, he proposed to replace it with a twenty-minute film in the manner of the Keystone Cops; the second and third acts would similarly be prefaced by celluloid interludes.

He had had nothing to do with film since his satirical short, *Hearts of Age*, so to prepare himself he ran a number of Mack Sennett, Chaplin and Harold Lloyd films. Setting aside the question of whether the mixed-media approach is sensible for a play which, like most successful farces, is tightly and economically constructed to deliver its comic goods, it is to be wondered whether the great silent movie comedians provided the right model for a play, like

Feydeau's, set in the world of the wealthy bourgeoisie. Welles was clearly trying to make a certain kind of play become a play of a different sort altogether. Farces generally proceed by means of a steady acceleration from a measured, methodical start. Unless you really experience the set-up, the lunacy has no roots. In the case of *Too Much Johnson* the characters find themselves caught up in socially disastrous situations; it is a bourgeois nightmare. The early slapstick comedians, on the contrary, are heirs to the clowns and fools of another age, persecuted outsiders. Welles's brief was simply to make the show funny; he didn't believe that it could be funny on its own terms.

The shooting of the film was a joyous lark, replete with all the delights of location filming. In addition to the cast (Arlene Francis, Joe Cotten, Edgar Barrier, the ex-vaudevillian Howard Smith – 'would you prefer the slow sit or the fast sit, Mr Welles?' – Ruth Ford, George Duthie and Virginia Welles), Houseman, Herbert Drake the theatre columnist, and Marc Blitzstein were all roped in. Augusta Weissberger generously donated her bosoms to the film, since Arlene Francis's were deemed insufficiently rounded. To achieve the feeling of 'little old New York', Welles shot in those parts of the city which had a nineteenth-century look, the Fulton Fish Market, for example, and other downtown locations. They borrowed an excursion boat normally devoted to day trips to Bear Mountain, and filmed the on-board chase on it. Welles tried to keep shooting even though it had started raining; the rain quickly turned into a hurricane, which of course was grist to his mill. Edgar Barrier and Joe Cotten get caught up in a specially staged suffragette march; they join in, keeping time, and saluting the American flag. Chasing each other, they jump six foot out of windows onto passing wagons. Passers-by thought, pardonably, that Cotten was trying to kill himself. Finally the police moved them on for disturbing the peace. Welles's delight in all this was unconfined. The element of risk was thrilling. He was working like the old-time silent movie directors, Abel Gance firing real pistols over the actors' heads to spur them, or Rex Ingram filming *The Four Horsemen of the Apocalypse*, whip in hand. Trying to catch dangerous exciting life on the wing, he was greatly helped by having a cameraman who was a Pathé News operator and thus used to filming unpredictable events. The second sequence used a model set of a plantation in Cuba, swathed in dry ice, with a miniature boat. The camera, hand-held, panned round to give the impression of travelling up-coast, to give, in Brady's phrase, 'the boat's Point of View'. The third sequence was shot in

Haverstraw, New York, (near Welles's home in Sneden's Landing) on a set in broad daylight; Welles himself described a fourth section to Peter Bogdanovich: 'a sequence in Cuba with a volcano erupting and Joe in a lovely white suit, carrying a big white umbrella and riding a big white horse. The horse had been Valentino's in *The Sheik*, and this was Joe's first experience as an equestrian. It was all quite dream-like . . .'

Rehearsals on the play were fitful. When they did take place, they were spent developing routines, sections of stage business, which Welles typically worked and worked, ignoring character, relationships, or the life of the play. Andrea Nouryeh describes a sequence in which three of the men enter from three different doors singing *Swanee*, exiting and entering with perfect rhythmic and harmonic co-ordination. This was gone over again and again and again, finally attaining the perfection Welles sought. The discipline is essential; but in farce, above all in farce, it's not simply what is done, but *who* does it, and to whom, that creates the comedy. Welles never troubled himself with those considerations.

Apart from the intensive drilling sessions, he was rarely seen at the theatre. He had discovered a new passion, one that lasted to his dying day, never losing its absolute fascination for him: editing. Having repaired to a suite at the St Regis, he had a Moviola installed, and – when not 'on the air or with his paramour', in Houseman's words – he sat surrounded by thousands of feet of film and the young apprentices from the Mercury, 'laughing at his own footage while the slaves hunted in vain for the bits of film that would enable him to put his chases together into some kind of intelligible sequence'. He had discovered the Frankenstein element of film-making. Sitting at the Steenbeck, it is really possible to assemble your own creature, and give life to it. The sense of power is intoxicating: a slow scene can be made fast, a funny one sad, a bad performance can be made good, and actors can be expunged from the film as if they had never been. To shoot is human; to edit, divine.

Both are expensive. Houseman was increasingly disturbed by the outlay for this supposedly cut-price try-out. Not only was the stock and the editing facility expensive; his attempt to pay the actors no more than the ordinary theatre rehearsal money while they were filming failed, Equity demanding the standard rate. At this point, they discovered that Paramount had the film rights: when they did the play on Broadway, they would have to pay the film company. No sooner had they made that discovery, than they realised that they couldn't even show it in Stony Creek: the projection booth in the little theatre wasn't fire-proofed. So that was that. They couldn't show the film; instead the actors had, overnight, to learn and fling together the beginning of Act One of the play – the exposition, always the hardest to learn and the hardest to play. The resident designer's set went up, the most satisfactory element of the production, as it turned out: a surviving photograph shows a ship's deck, square, with a ladder coming down from the poop deck, stage left; the ship's funnels are visible. The impression is slightly cartoonish. Paul Bowles had written a score for small orchestra; this too was cut for economy's sake, and Marc Blitzstein improvised an accompaniment at the piano. The show, inevitably, was chaotic and interminable, studded with occasional brilliantly rehearsed moments, *Swanee* among them.

After the disastrous first performance, there was a rather muted usual celebration. Once the actors had drifted miserably away, Welles, Joe Cotten and Kevin O'Morrison, the stage manager, took a few remaining would-be celebratory bottles of champagne and a copy of the script down to the harbour. After knocking back the champagne, O'Morrison told Andrea Nouryeh, 'Orson opened the script and said, "What do you think of this page?" Joe would look at it and he would say, "Nyah," and he would ask me, and I would say, "Nyah." So he would take it and crumple it up. We went through the script this way, taking pages and throwing them out. Drunk as lords with no idea what we were doing.' This aleatoric method of cutting is one of Welles's less well-known innovations, more Luke Rinehart than Max Reinhardt, but worth a try, perhaps. In the event it didn't work. The audience hurled things at the stage during the remaining few performances. Later, Welles liked to think of the show as pioneering work – 'the play and the film were too surreal for the audience. They couldn't accept it. It was like *Hellzapoppin*, years ahead of its time,' he told Brady; 'one of our best things, I reckon, but aborted' was how he described it to Bogdanovich – but the simple fact is that it was an utter shambles, a flop, and Houseman decided, in the teeth of tremendous opposition from Welles, that it would not go to the Mercury. Welles was later to return to the notion of mixing film with staging, both in *The Green Goddess* of 1941 and the celebrated *Around The World* of six years later. The important thing – for him and for posterity – was that he had found film. He now had the celluloid bug; it would never leave him.

For the present, however, he was shattered by the failure of *Too Much Johnson*: Houseman believes he secretly agreed with his cancellation order but that 'he needed to play out the sabotage scene to salve his pride'. What followed was real: 'he retired into his air-conditioned tent at the St Regis, where he lay in darkness for a week surrounded by 25,000 feet of film . . . convinced that he was going to die, racked by asthma and fear and despair.' Bill Alland was with him during most of that time and reported 'the self-vilifications and the remorse for what he had done to those around him . . . for the cruelty and moral corruption with which he reproached himself.' The failure was unendurable, a confirmation that all his inner voices, the ones spurring him on, and those others telling him that he was fundamentally worthless, were right. At times of crisis, his asthma always asserted itself, forcing him to bed where he would agonise, paralysed, in a state of primordial emotion. His self-accusations were terrifying to those who heard them, utterly negative and destructive. When the fit passed, he would throw himself with redoubled energy into food, drink, sex; he was now, only three months after the birth of Christopher, juggling numerous paramours. But as always, the best antidote for Welles was work. In this instance, the thing nearest to hand was the Mercury Theatre of the Air.

The transmissions had, of course, continued throughout *Too Much Johnson*: *Treasure Island*, *A Tale of Two Cities*, *The Thirty-nine Steps*, a triple bill including *My Little Boy*, *Abraham Lincoln*, Arthur Schnitzler's *Anatol* (actually transmitted the Monday after the disastrous Stony Creek run). There were two more programmes out of the originally contracted nine: *The Count of Monte Cristo*, and *The Man Who Was Thursday*, this last adapted, at his own insistence, by Welles himself. Welles having refused even to give it a dress rehearsal, it transpired during transmission that the show was clearly running at least thirteen minutes short. Houseman thrust various great novels into Welles's hands; he read sections from them as a trailer for future shows, to the great admiration of studio executives, who naturally thought that the whole thing had been carefully planned. Welles never again attempted to adapt the show himself. The second show, a spirited *Treasure Island*, had fallen short too, and to fill in the time he improvised a little speech at the end which gives the sense of his charm and fun and elegance in gorgeous off-the-cuff word-spinning. Houseman said that Welles could make an impromptu speech to fit any occasion; this one is a winner: 'I'd like you to meet Jim Hawkins, Jr. Our leading man is fourteen years old. Last season he made a really startling contribution to the stage history of Shakespeare's plays. This was during the course of some experiments with the Mercury Theatre's sprinkler system. As the consequence of what must certainly have been extensive research in the field, he caused it to rain, actually to rain, and copiously to rain where in more than three hundred years it has never rained in *Julius Caesar* before. It rained on Brutus, it rained all over Brutus in the forum, I was Brutus and I ought to know.' A perfect example of Welles's rhetorical style . . . the rain, the rain, the rain . . . Brutus, Brutus, Brutus . . .

'Now, as dramatic criticism,' he continued, 'I found this telling, and even final. And as a surprise item in the funeral scene I can assure you that the unexpected appearance on the stage of so many gallons of real water created in us all an impression that was almost overwhelming. Our popular leading man says he did it all with a match. I don't dare think what he'll do when he's old enough to run for president, but meanwhile, no matter what happens to the plumbing, he can always work for the Mercury. As you've probably discovered he's something more than a very gifted performer, and as I told you, he's something less than fifteen. His name shall not be withheld. I refer to that fine old actor . . . Arthur Anderson. Mr Anderson is not new to the microphone nor the Mercury.' Welles details Anderson's work for the company, then throws in some comments on the other actors. You can feel his eye on the clock, spinning out his slender material to the point where it almost becomes disc-jockey burble. He starts to advertise the next show. 'Next week we'll offer you the most ominous and authentic click of the world's most famous knitting needles, and Madame herself, Dr Manette, Sydney Carton, and the entire French Revolution, same time, same station. It is a far, far better thing that I do, than I have ever done. Charles Dickens! That is correct, that is absolutely correct! . . . Charles Dickens's *Tale of Two Cities*.' His voice rises to manic levels on 'Charles Dickens! That is absolutely correct!' He's in the home stretch now. 'There is at this moment a disturbance in the sub-control room and if it isn't a tumbril it's Arthur Anderson. It's a good thing the program's over. Good-night everybody. Thanks. Please write me the stories you'd like to hear . . . and good-bye till next week.' The howl of long-suppressed laughter is almost audible.

The show itself follows the pattern, and maintains the standard, of *Dracula*. The narrative form was slightly different, becoming *Moby Dick*-like: the quest for Long John Silver. This form, a very useful one for radio, served him also well as a film-maker – a mystery, the central character only slowly discovered. Welles's Silver is a far cry from Robert Newton's more famous assumption: a sturdy, metal-voiced cockney, harsh and dangerous, but absolutely lacking the English actor's insinuating charm. The much-lauded Anderson is excellent, clear and – thanks to his English mum – credibly British. At one point he stumbles over his script; this is the only fluff heard on any of the programmes, something of a miracle considering not merely that they were broadcast live, the rehearsals taking place in absolute chaos, but that Welles and many of the actors were heavily involved in, first, *Too Much Johnson*, filming and all, and then *Danton's Death*. Neither Welles nor any aspect of the programme bears the slightest trace of the panic and despair which was engulfing the Mercury stage work, nor indeed the frenzied conditions in which the show was made. The show is confident, skilful, good-hearted. *Treasure Island*, as it happens, had been their audition piece for Campbell's Soup, from whom they hoped to get sponsorship. Campbell's didn't like the show, so they carried on under CBS's banner; the contract was renewed for a further ten programmes (no longer under the banner *First Person Singular*, which had never been given great prominence anyway).

It is hard to imagine what more the potential sponsors had wanted: the programmes are direct, accessible, colourful, funny when appropriate and always lapel-grabbingly urgent, with Welles himself an irresistible master of ceremonies. They are neither high-brow nor lowbrow; their appeal is, literally, to all the family. A ten-year-old could enjoy them (and most of the stories, with the exception perhaps of *Anatol*, Schnitzler's study of sexual compulsion, were children's classics) but there is no condescension in the presentation. They exploit the medium fully, but without a trace of self-consciousness. The Mercury Theatre of the Air programmes embody everyone's ideal of radio drama, projecting larger-than-life images onto our mental screens, plundering our own memories to tell the story. The most radical medium devised by man (nothing but disembodied voices and sounds; talking furniture, as the man said), its decline in the latter half of the twentieth century (with the honourable exception of the BBC) into a mere carrier of music and news is a shameful waste. Welles and his collaborators' work in radio (now available on Compact Disc and cassette) is a great memorial to an exceptional art form, one whose influence remained central to his output.

With the radio shows, out of the chaos came something marvellous. Back at the Mercury, where, after a false start with *Too Much Johnson*, rehearsals for *Danton's Death* were underway, chaos simply bred worse chaos. Things started uncertainly then rapidly descended into total confusion. For once, Welles had been unable to find a concept for his production. In *Heartbreak House*, the author had banned him from having one; here, he was simply unable to reach one. There are few unhappier human beings than a conceptual director without a concept. The truth is that he hardly knew why he was doing the play at all. It had been included in the season on the spur of the moment: Martin Gabel had thrown it on his and Houseman's desk during one of the first of the Mercury broadcasts, saying how much he'd like to play Danton. 'It struck us as a brilliant notion,' Houseman reports, 'a contrast to the frivolity of *Too Much Johnson* and something we could sell to our politically minded theatre-party audience.' The play is notoriously difficult to interpret, much less bring off. Dealing with the most stirring period of the French Revolution, it is strangely undramatic: almost an anti-play. A hundred years before Brecht ('there are no great criminals, only great crimes'), the twenty-one-year-old Büchner, on the run from the Prussian police for political subversion, was concerned to de-mythologise the giants of the Revolution. 'The individual just foams on the wave, greatness mere chance, the rule of genius a puppet-play, a laughable struggle with an iron law . . . it no longer occurs to me to bow down before the monuments and big-wigs of history. I cannot make virtuous heroes out of Danton and the bandits of the Revolution!' This is an immensely sophisticated and elusive theme, one which, on the face of things, was a rather unexpected subject for Welles, with his post-romantic sense of fated personality, of good and evil, guilt and nemesis. The drama of the individual was at the heart of Welles's approach; nothing could have been further from Büchner, whose incomplete masterpiece *Woyzeck* gave the drama its first real anti-hero, a man of no qualities, no interest, no personality in any discernible sense.

No doubt Welles was stimulated but also perhaps awed by the reputation of the only previous New York production of the play, Reinhardt's, with his German company. It had created a sensation. 'I doubt,' wrote R. Dana Skinner, 'if any stage in this country has witnessed anything so impressive, so moving or so filled with magnificent vitality as the scene in the Convention.' The production was the supreme example of Reinhardt's animation of the crowd, though this was achieved with consummate theatrical cunning. 'The impression of a tremendous plenitude and variety of life, the impression of passionate movement, was obtained by lighting up only one small part of the stage at a time whilst the rest remained in gloom,' wrote Heinz Herald. 'Only individuals or small groups were picked out in the spotlight whilst the masses always remained in semi-darkness, or even in complete darkness. But they were always there and could be heard murmuring, speaking, shouting. Out of the darkness an upraised arm would catch the light, and in this way thousands would seem to be where hundreds were in fact. The principle of the rapid play of light and darkness was maintained throughout.' It is doubtful whether Welles actually saw the production (he was twelve at the time) but it must have been a constant point of reference for him, especially since he had hired Reinhardt's Robespierre, Vladimir Sokoloff, to repeat his immensely admired performance for the Mercury. Since emigrating to America, the Russian actor had played a couple of routine parts in Hollywood, which was rather good luck, since he could barely speak a word of English.

He was in Hollywood when Houseman heard of his desire to return to the stage. His availability and interest seemed like an answer to prayer, since they were having inordinate difficulty in casting the role of Robespierre. Coulouris had turned it down point blank, finding the play 'turgid' and the part 'monolithic'. Nor was he inspired by the idea of Gabel as Danton. With this, Houseman must have been in sympathy. Whenever the play had been discussed in the past for inclusion in the Mercury programme, it was with the idea of Welles playing Danton. The part of the great, flawed aristocratic friend of the Revolution, finally undone by his appetites, would have been a wonderful opportunity for him. Certainly it requires an actor of the utmost force to play the role; one who will be a counterpoint to Robespierre and St Just, spreading massively where they are tightly reined in. Dapper, incisive Martin Gabel was unsuitable at every level, and Houseman argued passionately against casting him, despite having already offered him the part and him having accepted it. Welles had no desire to act in the show at all; reluctantly, he agreed to play the ice-cold fanatic St Just, another very curious casting stroke. Coldness was a quality hard for Welles to summon – vocally, apart from anything else. Depressingly, he agreed to play the part because it was one 'in which he could be replaced without damage'. None of the casting was easy; actors were drawn from the *Too Much Johnson* company (including Mary Wickes, and the ever faithful Joe Cotten) and from the pool of radio actors who constituted the Mercury Theatre of the Air. It must have been dismaying to Houseman and Welles that the company which had auditioned 1,700 eager actors during their first year, now found it hard to find three actors suitable or willing to play the leading roles in the first production of their second season. Either word was getting around – from Vincent Price and other disaffected actors – or Houseman and Welles weren't trying very hard. It seems that they had rather expected the Mercury to be running itself by now; not that they would have to start all over again, as Houseman laments.

Significantly, Welles had failed by the first day of rehearsal to adapt the long and sprawling play. He had simply and rather arbitrarily cut it to reduce its playing time. The script changed from day to day, as he tried to fashion some sort of coherent vision out of the material. Rehearsals took place in the theatre (now expensively dark, since the cancellation of *Too Much Johnson*) on the very dangerous set that Welles and his designer Stephen Tichacek had devised. Once again, as in *Julius Caesar*, but much earlier – without benefit of rehearsal at all – the technical aspect of the show took over entirely. The central element of the design was an elevator, thirty foot by twenty foot. On either side of the elevator, there were two traps. There was a thirty-foot-wide, two-foot-deep trench between the back wall and the elevator containing a pyramidal staircase on castors, very small at the top. When all of the traps were open and the elevator was dropped, the stage was, in Andrea Nouryeh's words, 'a treacherous system of gaping holes, catwalks, and scaffolding (connecting to the positions of the elevator) – the effect from balcony was of criss-cross pastry on apple pie'. The potential for mishap was terrifyingly high, particularly since the light was highly directional, coming from below or from the side at strange angles, tending to dazzle and even temporarily blind the actors. They must have courted death every time they stood on the stage. Welles explained his intentions in a couple of paragraphs of *The Director in the Theatre Today*: 'My conception of the play was such that the elevator seemed to me to represent, when it was raised, the constant threat. It was made like scaffolding because the republic of France at that time was an impermanent affair, and upon such existed the lives of these people, and it was made to look like a guillotine.'

These defensive intellectualisations, which can have meant nothing to any but an exceptionally alert audience, are unconvincing as an approach to staging the play. The only effect the scenery of *Danton's Death* could have had on the playing was in creating a literal terror within the company – which it did. Had the actors rehearsed on it for six months, and had they become so familiar with it that it became an expressive means for them, then perhaps something extraordinary could have come out of it. But this too presupposes that Welles was able, or willing, to work on their acting itself, to help them to find a style with which to realise the play. There is total absence in Welles's utterances on either acting or directing of any suggestion of the nature of the work the actors need to do: the exploration of the play's style or of themselves. The director will look after all that, he believes. In *The Director in the Theatre*, he says 'If the director is an actor he can think up wonderful pieces of business.' That was his notion of the job.

In *Danton's Death*, he hardly had time for that: he was obsessed by the physical problems of the play, and left the actors to fend for themselves. He and Gabel had fallen out badly, and were, as Houseman put it, at a stand-off. As for Sokoloff, who was deeply anxious about his accent and worked hard but unavailingly on it, Welles 'had that awed and child-like respect which he showed for theatrical figures whom he admired'. He didn't direct him at all. 'Orson let him play his speeches exactly as he had played them for Reinhardt . . . the company used to applaud at each rehearsal.' That was at the beginning, when tempers were even. The applause soon died. Rehearsals went on to two, three or four in the morning, after which everyone was called for ten, when they would work with Marc Blitzstein on his score incorporating *Ça ira*, the Carmagnole and the original version of the Marseillaise which he had discovered in the Lincoln Center. He had written a deal of spinet music and two original songs, an *Ode to Reason* and *Christina*, sung by Mary Wickes and Joe Cotten, with its lyric that must have come very easily to Blitzstein:

Mister Soldier, handsome soldier
Mister handsome, handsome soldier
Play me mild, or play me rough
I just can't get enough

He and Kevin O'Morrison also worked with the actors on the sound score Welles had requested: in effect a live soundtrack. Standing in the wings, they would imitate crickets, the crying of babies, all the sounds of everyday life: an interesting idea, much in evidence in avant-garde work of the sixties, but in the circumstances of this production another bewilderment. The actors, totally exhausted and under-rehearsed, became resentful: there was no overtime, so all their extra work was unrecompensed. Often the work they had done was pointless, since Welles changed the script minute by minute and entire elaborately rehearsed sequences would be cut.

The pressure to change the text was not merely aesthetic; it was political, too. No doubt, as Houseman says, *Danton's Death* had struck them as a promisingly political play; they could do a *Caesar* on it. Unfortunately, as they were soon to discover, the game of political analogy is one that has to be played very carefully, especially in times of ferment. In this case, they only just got away with it. They were political amateurs, and had not thought through the explosive implications of the parallel with the revolutionary power struggle of their own times. Danton, Robespierre, St Just seemed unmistakable emblems of Lenin, Stalin, Trotsky, in one permutation or another. The interesting resonance that this set up (and it is to be remembered that *Danton's Death*, unlike *Julius Caesar*, was being played in period costume, and came with no explanatory subtitle like *Caesar*'s 'Death of a Dictator') was regarded by the left as a slap in the face; and in its present financial circumstances, the Mercury couldn't ignore the solid audience base that the left-wing organisations had provided for it. With Blitzstein as their negotiator, these organisations applied massive pressure on Welles and Houseman to dispel what they described as the 'reactionary implications of the text': a bad press for Revolution.

The Party openly boasted of its success in the *Daily Worker*: 'backstage at the Mercury Theatre . . . a three-cornered discussion is in progress . . . Orson Welles, Marc Blitzstein and John Houseman, all concerned with the production of *Danton's Death*. "If it isn't changed, I'll pull out the music." "If it's that bad politically, I'll pull out the show," replied Welles. Houseman agreed. So it appears that at the very time we were offering our critical suggestions in last Wednesday's paper the need for correcting the reactionary implications of the play also suggested themselves to the producers.' Trying to overcome the apparently insuperable physical problems of the production, not to mention getting the weekly radio show on the air, Welles and Houseman simply gave in to the (to them) obscure demands of the various parties and organisations with axes to grind. At the same time, Henry Senber issued a bullish press release: 'The Welles production will make it clear that it is a characteristic of Danton's own personality and not a characteristic of revolution or revolutionaries which brings him to his decadence and fall . . . Robespierre will not be a snivelling fanatic but take on his true stature of social revolutionary as opposed to the bourgeois reformism of Danton . . . the author does not take sides.' This is scarcely the usual language of press releases. It would be interesting to know who was dictating it. As a compromise, Houseman and Welles agreed to send out 'one of their more philosophical actors' to inform the audience that the play is 'a recital of certain true events, that as in every good historical play certain historical parallels were more or less sure to be drawn, but that the play is not to be construed as sponsoring any political philosophy or theory . . . what Welles and Houseman are up to is producing a show, not operating, as they had occasion to remark before, a cause.' The organisation which had so fearlessly resisted government pressure when it was staging its labour musical, was obliged, in order to keep its financial base, to justify and to some extent censor its work on ideological grounds, something the FTP had never required. Things were getting very sticky indeed.

Finally, Welles acknowledged that the script had been subject to so many changes, for so many different reasons, that it was necessary for him to deliver a definitive version. He cancelled rehearsals, and withdrew for thirty-six hours, finally calling the company together to read the new text, as they waited patiently, there was a howl offstage: he had left it in the taxi. Search parties were despatched to recover it, without success. Rehearsals grimly resumed, using the old text, as the unending labour of hanging and re-hanging lights, rigging and re-rigging the elevator continued, Welles moved a cot into the stalls, lest he lose a single precious minute. In between manoeuvres, he would fall into a deep sleep. ACTORS OFTEN 'LIVE IN THEATRE' – THIS ONE ACTUALLY DOES was the headline of Helen Ormsbee's report: ' "You have to run as hard as this to stay in the same place," the Red Queen told Alice. "If you want to get to the next square, you must go a lot faster." That is about the way Orson Welles regards the preparations for *Danton's Death*. "We're compelled to work under pressure here at the Mercury. That is because we must make up in intensity of effort what we lack in money. We can't afford to take a show out on the road to whip it into shape; if we could, I'd be glad of it . . . for me as the director it means going without sleep and forgetting to eat." ' In the light of the relays of triple steak sandwiches and bottles of brandy coming from Longchamps, the company may have found the last part of that sentence rather funny, though it is to be suspected that their laughter had by now a hollow ring to it.

'Once you start a production the momentum pushes everybody,' he continued. 'An actor can let himself be pushed by that momentum, but the director's case is different. He has got to keep ahead of his routine . . . still, high pressure has its advantages. A play, taken out of script and acted, is a living impulse. It has to reach the audience with all the freshness that is in the minds of the cast and the technicians, and you can't bottle up that freshness too long.' More hollow laughter. 'Compared with pictures, work in the theatre is volatile. Picture directing is an exact science; stage directing is not. You can take two years to make a film and the portions of it that are finished and recorded won't deteriorate while the rest is being done. But the theatre is different; here a play is a living organism . . . that is why rehearsals can't lag along indefinitely. The Moscow Art Theatre spends six or eight months getting ready for a play, but Stanislavsky had to devise his system to sustain that method.' The Mercury actors, stranded on bits of unstable scenery, bleary eyed with sleep when they weren't dazzled by the lights, barely knowing which scene followed which, much less why, may have longed for the continuity and steady discovery of a Moscow Art Theatre rehearsal. The alternative, the path of adrenalin, adrenalin and then more adrenalin, seemed to be leading nowhere. But then Welles didn't seem to have much enthusiasm for his actors' work: 'I haven't great regard for present artistic standards in the theatre. I'm sure our success only goes to show that the public don't expect too much. But I'm convinced there are wonderful opportunities among present actors and one day we shall see really wonderful acting.' How this might come about was never explained.

Meanwhile, back to the inferno. At the dress rehearsal, the young costume designer Leo van Witsen (originally hired for *Too Much Johnson*) was summarily dismissed; somewhat unfairly, it would seem, since he had never been given a line on what he was supposed to be doing. Costumes were being supplied by Brooks Costumes on the cheap, but they had provided the worst tailor on their staff to execute and alter them; as a result, nothing fitted. Millia Davenport took over, simplifying things; the only simplification that occurred on the entire production. There had never been such a complex lighting plot. There were (for the Mercury) an unprecedented number of eighty-five lights, each of which had a number and a name, and which had to be unplugged throughout the show. All the dimmers were operated manually, and separately. The huge task of co-ordinating this was achieved by a system of counts which were quite audible during performances, but which fortuitously abetted Welles's notion of having the auditorium filled with cries, shouts and whispers coming from all parts of the theatre. Howard Teichmann was operating the board from the wings, and was unable to see the effect of what he was doing; Jean Rosenthal had no intercom facility, and could only keep in touch with him by telephone. The greatest difficulty was lighting the huge cyclorama which stretched two hundred foot against the back wall. Inspired by the play's lines 'You have built a system as Bajazet built his pyramids, out of human skulls' and 'You need loaves and they fling you heads' Welles and his designer, Tichacek, had the notion of creating a sort of cranial panorama, a wall of skulls. Bill Alland suggested that they use hallowe'en masks; Dick Barr and other apprentices were sent out to scour the shops: 'We pre-empted all the masks in New York that year. I never did find out what the kids substituted because there were literally no masks left in the shops.' They ended up with 5,000 unpainted, white masks, which had to be bent a quarter of an inch around, then glued on to the cyclorama and finally sprayed with a sort of purplish paint. The colour and angle of the light varied according to dramatic need: for Robespierre's nocturnal meditations it turned 'a steely-gray, vicious, as though the whole pile were about to fall on him and stone him to death . . . at the end of the play, as Danton goes to his execution, the whole wall of skulls split apart to reveal a narrow slit against a blue sky topped by glittering steel' (Richard France). For the final curtain, drums rolled, the guillotine knife flashed down, and there was a sudden blackout.

The difficulty for Jean Rosenthal, designing the light, was to isolate the sections of the cyclorama and avoid spill, which would have ruined the concentrated effect. This feature of the design, which everyone who worked on the production recalls for its originality and boldness, is curiously little alluded to or described in the reviews; the truth is that it was impossible finally to make it work. 'I kept saying, "it's going to look like a lot of pebbles, Orson." Well, I was wrong. It didn't look like pebbles. It just looked like a purple cyke. They didn't see it at all,' said Teichmann. No doubt with time, and a certain amount of calm a solution could have been found; but neither were available any more. Hysteria pitch was approaching. 'Orson yelled out for some lights. Jeannie looked at me and bowed her head and pulled the main switches and went down. "You're asking for lights from *Horse Eats Hat*. We're not doing any more, we're going home." We pulled all the switches, and that was that. We were all so groggy.' The desperate struggle against machinery and time began to look unwinnable. No doubt many of Welles's ideas were excellent, though he seemed to be making them up as he went along. Improvisation within a simple operation can work; to improvise at this level of technology is to put an impossible burden on everyone. Welles obviously began to think that anything could be done, if he shouted hard and long enough. But the human beings rebelled, realising, perhaps, that he was just thrashing around – in the dark, almost literally. The light at the first preview was improvised:

a homicidal procedure on that particular set. Immediately after the preview, at nearly midnight, there was a further lighting rehearsal at which they managed to plot the first act (the entire show lasted no more than ninety minutes). The next preview was cancelled while lamps were hung, rehung and hung again. Miraculously, no serious accidents had occurred, though Kevin O'Morrison, making a rapid exit to the cellar with a large group of extras, reached for a crossbar that had been moved, lost his footing and fell twenty-five foot to a concrete floor below. He got up and walked away, unharmed.

Then calamity struck, as it inevitably must in the presence of so much tension. The elevator (a cheap one, the only one they could afford) always operated fitfully; at a run-through, it juddered and suddenly collapsed. Erskine Sandford, sitting aristocratically at the tea table inside the elevator, was hurled to the floor and broke his leg; he was rushed to hospital, never appearing in the show. He was the lucky one. As the actors stood round, ashen-faced, Jeannie Rosenthal demanded three days to get it working, which she was given. It failed again, this time at a public preview, bringing the show to a halt. Welles and Gabel played scenes from *Julius Caesar* to divert the audience; finally Rosenthal gave up, and the show had to be cancelled, Houseman appearing onstage with a hurriedly snatched-up piece of paper on which he claimed was recorded the audience's majority decision to come back to another performance instead of having their money back. It was at about this moment in the infernal proceedings that Howard Koch, only recently appointed to the writing team of the Mercury Theatre of the Air, was handed a copy of *The War of the Worlds* 'with instructions from Houseman to dramatise it in the form of news bulletins'. Finding the book dull and dated, he tried to persuade them to switch to something else. The only alternative, he was told, was *Lorna Doone*, at which prospect he understandably blanched and agreed to attempt to liven up Wells, H.G.

CHAPTER SIXTEEN

War of the Worlds/ Danton's Death

HOWARD KOCH'S breakthrough with *The War of the Worlds* came when he decided to change the location of the novel from England to America, randomly selecting the New Jersey village of Grover's Mill as the site of the invasion. From then on, realistic imperatives dictated the course of the script. He would use news bulletins, as Houseman had suggested, interrupting a programme to give the reports added urgency and credibility; a broadcast of music from a hotel seemed the most likely. 'Radio was full at that time of remote programs from hotels,' said Eric Barnouw, 'they were always filling in time by going to the Hotel Pennsylvania, and so forth.' The adaptation he produced, though ingenious, reads fairly creakily, and the second half, in which the apparently lone survivor of the invasion, Professor Pierson of Princeton, meets an artilleryman living underground before stumbing towards the light at the end of the Holland Tunnel, is frankly dull, quite unlike the usual brilliant montages and swiftly succeeding scenes so characteristic of the Mercury Theatre of the Air.

There was certainly no jubilation when the script was presented to Houseman and Welles. Snatching a few minutes from the nightmarish activities in the theatre, they picked at it in their usual way, pulling it about structurally and demanding more realism. In this they were stymied by the legal department of CBS, who demanded a number of changes in the names of real organisations, though they were able to retain the place names. As usual a mid-week recording of the material was made; again it met with little favour. Welles dismissed the script as 'corny', urging Koch to break it up more and more. Paul Stewart devised the sound effects and rehearsed them in careful detail; these might be spectacular enough to distract attention from the thinness of the piece. Even the technicians were unenthusiastic about the show; the secretaries denounced it as silly. Finally at noon on Sunday, tearing himself away from another *Danton's Death* lighting rehearsal, Welles arrived at the studio direct from the theatre, and assaulted the unsatisfactory material.

'All during rehearsals,' wrote Dick Barr, 'Orson railed at the text, cursing the writers, and at the whole idea of his presenting so silly a show.' He hardly changed the script. What he did was to play it for all it was worth, and then some more.

Focusing on the device of an interrupted programme, he dared to attempt a verisimilitude that had rarely been essayed before. The apparent breakdowns in transmission, the desperate irruptions of dance music, the sadly tinkling piano were all held longer than would be thought possible. The actors too were galvanised into startlingly real and precisely observed performances. Frank Readick as Carl Phillips, the reporter on the spot who describes the invasion and then collapses dead at his mike, had listened over and over again to a recording of the report of the explosion of the Hindenburg air balloon from a year or two before and exactly imitated the original commentator's graduation from comfortable report through growing disbelief to naked horror. Using skills honed on *The March of Time*, the show became, until about its halfway point, a brilliantly effective transposition of the original novel, sharp enough to make even the most sceptical listener wonder, however idly, how Americans might react to the unprecedented event of an invasion, not from Mars, of course, but from Europe – from Germany or perhaps even from England.

This was a matter much in the minds of Americans, who were daily reminded in the press that they alone of all Western nations had failed to devise a system of civil defence against attack from the air. Only three days before, *Air Raid*, a play by Archibald MacLeish, vividly directed by William Robson, had been broadcast, bringing home the brutal bombing of helpless citizenry, 'awakening many listeners,' in LeRoy Bannerman's words, 'to the swift and violent terror advanced by the warplane.' The sense that war in Europe was daily more likely was not far from anyone's mind, the feeling of defencelessness creating a mood of national jumpiness – compounded that fall by reports of terrifying hurricanes that had ravaged the East Coast. 'You really had the feeling,' said Eric Barnouw in an interview, 'that the world might come to an end at any minute.' The vividness of the dramatisation stems from its imitation of the newscasts whose bulletins so frequently concerned events ominously gathering in Europe. Neither Koch nor Houseman nor Welles intended any serious parallel, of course; they were simply trying to liven up a dull book, using what was all around them, on the air and in the papers.

What no one at all could have predicted was that anyone might have thought that an actual invasion from Mars was being reported. There was no attempt to conceal the fact that the listener was hearing a dramatisation of a novel, from the beginning of the programme, with its standard announcement ('CBS present Orson Welles and the Mercury Theatre on the Air in a radio play by Howard Koch suggested by the H.G. Wells novel *The War of the Worlds*') and the appropriately but conventionally chilling introduction from Welles, taken with only small modifications from the novella: 'We know now that in the early years of the twentieth century this world was being watched closely by intelligences greater than man's but as mortal as his own . . . [who] regarded this earth with envious eyes and slowly and surely drew their plans against us. In the thirty-eighth year of the twentieth century came the great disillusionment.' Only towards the end of this introduction does Koch start the process of relocation. 'It was near the end of October. Business was better. The war was over. More men were back at work. Sales were picking up. On this particular evening, October 30, the Crossley service estimated that 32 million people were listening in on radios . . .' So the programme is clearly framed as a broadcast within a broadcast. Then comes the neatly devised sequence of weather report, musical interlude (from the non-existent Hotel Park Plaza in downtown New York), news flash about peculiar explosions, more music, more announcements, rambling interview with Professor Pierson, head of the Observatory at Princeton (a gruff and bumbling and highly recognisable Welles), followed by the brilliant on-the-spot reporting sequences.

It was at this point (8.12 p.m. according to Houseman) that the crucial event occurred which precipitated the subsequent panic. The programme that had freed up the slot which gave the Mercury access to the air waves at all was the massively popular *Edgar Bergen and Charlie McCarthy Show*, that most improbable of radio successes, featuring a ventriloquist and his anarchic dummy. Just under a quarter of an hour into the programme, the monocled dummy, his operator and the assembled zanies including Mortimer Snerd, Effie Klinker, Ersel Twing, Vera Vague and Professor Lionel Carp, were given a rest while a vocalist trilled. Immediately, and rather depressingly for the vocalist in question, a large proportion of the listeners would reach for their dials and twiddle until they found something more congenial, usually returning to the dummy after a few minutes. On the night of 30 October 1938, 12 per cent of *Bergen and McCarthy*'s audience, twiddling away, suddenly found themselves listening, appalled, to a news report of an invasion, by now well under way, by Martians.

'Ladies and gentlemen, I have just been handed a message that came in from Grover's Mill by telephone. Just a moment. At least forty people, including six state troopers, lie dead in a field east of the village of Grover's Mill, their bodies burned and distorted beyond all recognition.' Music was played; experts were interviewed, then a reporter started to describe the scene. 'Good heavens, something's wriggling out of the shadow like a gray snake. Now it's another one and another. They look like tentacles to me. There, I can see the thing's body. It's large as a bear and it glistens like black leather. But that face . . . it's indescribable. I can hardly force myself to keep looking at it. The eyes are black and gleam like a serpent. The mouth is V-shaped with saliva dripping from its rimless lips that seem to quiver and pulsate . . . this is the most extraordinary experience. I can't find words . . . I'm pulling this microphone with me as I talk . . . hold on, will you please, I'll be back in a minute.' Shortly afterwards, they heard the microphone fall to the ground, then dead silence. There were more announcements, in the excitable, stentorian tones familiar from newsreels. The heads of the armed forces were brought to the microphone, and then finally, the Secretary of the Interior: 'we must continue the performance of our duties each and every one of us, so that we may confront this destructive adversary with a nation united, courageous, and consecrated to the preservation of human supremacy on this earth.'

By now a small but significant proportion of the audience (with a heavy concentration in the New Jersey area) were in a state of high hysteria. The Mercury audience had effectively doubled from its usual 3.6 per cent of the total audience (*Bergen and McCarthy* had a regular listenership of 34.7 per cent) to six million. Before the programme was even halfway through, the CBS switchboard was jammed with demands for verification, as were switchboards all over the country (Koch reports an operator who very properly replied to a question as to whether the world was coming to an end, 'I'm sorry, we don't have that information here'). Other listeners assumed that the broadcast was the unvarnished truth needing no verification. Hadley Cantril writes in the introduction to *The Invasion from Mars*, his masterly sociological account of the incident, that out of the then 32,000,000 families in the United States, 27,500,000 had radios – 'a greater proportion than have telephones, automobiles, plumbing, electricity, newspapers or magazines'. The radio was their principal, in some cases their only, source of information about the wider world. They were accustomed to trusting it; why should they doubt the familiar voices, describing events in their familiar manner? The nature of radio, whose unique appeal to the audience's imagination Welles and his collaborators had so brilliantly exploited in their earlier broadcasts, made the Martian broadcast horribly convincing.

Despite the fact that three times during the course of the rest of the programme an announcement was made to remind listeners that they were tuned in to the Mercury Theatre of the Air who were presenting an adaptation of H.G. Wells's *The War of the Worlds*, the pictures that had been evoked in the minds of those who had accidentally tuned to the on-the-spot reports were entirely real. Some of them just sat down and waited to die; others desperately tried to call relatives, but found all the lines engaged. Some took to the streets, some went to church. The numbers involved were relatively small, but they were scattered across the country, creating tiny pockets of panic. In Harlem, a black congregation fell to its knees; in Indianapolis a woman ran screaming into a church where evening service was being held and shouted 'New York has been destroyed. It's the end of the world. Go home and prepare to die.' A woman gave premature birth, and another fell down a whole flight of stairs (her husband, according to Norman Corwin, called CBS to thank them for the broadcast. 'Geez, it was a wonderful programme!'). In Newark, New Jersey, all the occupants of a block of flats left their homes with wet towels round their heads as improvised gas masks. In Staten Island, Connie Casamassina was just about to get married. Latecomers to the reception took the microphone from the singing waiter and announced the invasion. 'Everyone ran to get their coats. I took the microphone and started to cry – "Please don't spoil my wedding day" – and then my husband started singing hymns, and I decided I was going to dance the Charleston. And I did, for 15 minutes straight. I did every step there is in the Charleston.'

This outburst of mediaeval millennial frenzy was short-lived. The Mienerts of Manasquan Park, New Jersey, leaping into the car – taking the dog and the canary with them – paused in their headlong flight down the motorway to ask the latest news from bewildered passers-by, who, not having heard the broadcast, could tell them nothing. Desperate for information Mr Mienert called his cousin in Freehold, NJ, 'whose farm I knew was in the destructive path'. 'Are the Martians there?' he asked. 'No,' his cousin said, 'but the Tuttles are, and we're about to sit down to dinner.' The Mienerts went back home and started to clean up the paint. Inside the CBS building it was a different matter. The panic reached the control room of the studio. Having uttered the last scripted lines of Professor Pierson, a slightly shaky Welles announced 'out of character', as he said, that the programme had 'no further significance than the holiday offering it was intended to be. The Mercury Theatre's own radio version of dressing up in a sheet and jumping out of a bush and saying Boo! . . . so good-bye, everybody,' he continued, rising to some rather forced jocularity, 'and remember, please, for the next day or so, the terrible lesson you learned tonight. That grinning, glowing, globular invader of your living room is an inhabitant of the pumpkin patch, and if your doorbell rings and there's no one there, that was no Martian . . . it's Hallowe'en.'

The laughter died on Welles's lips the moment the programme was over. Terrified listeners who had called CBS angrily threatened violence against Welles and the company on discovering that they were victims of what seemed to them to be a malicious hoax. 'Someone had called threatening to blow up the CBS building, so we called the police and hid in the ladies' room on the studio floor,' wrote Dick Barr. 'Houseman denies this, but I distinctly remember a group of frightened men squeezed in the ladies' room of the CBS building.' Reporters besieged the building; when they could get through by telephone, they asked Welles or Houseman how they felt about the many deaths the broadcast had caused. Bewildered, frightened and genuinely remorseful, with no means of checking what the reporters were telling them, they could only protest the innocence of their intentions. Columbia were very nervous and steeled themselves for the legal actions which duly followed. They put out hourly disclaimers, affirming the fictional nature of the broadcast. The planned official midnight Hallowe'en broadcast, in which ghosts were to figure prominently, was cancelled.

Meanwhile, Welles had something else on his mind. He had a dress rehearsal to get back to, the only slightly less nightmarish *Danton's Death*. Dick Barr had been sent back to the theatre to tell the impatiently waiting actors what had happened, but they didn't believe his story; to them it was simply the most outrageous of Welles's many outrageous excuses. Finally Barr was reduced to taking them out into Times Square to show them the Moving News sign: ORSON WELLES FRIGHTENS THE NATION. Rehearsals were cancelled, while Welles prepared to face the wrath of America. The press was in seventh heaven. Columns of newsprint in Monday's papers were devoted to descriptions of what had happened and columns more to analysis of the event. It was held to offer on the one hand, doleful evidence of the gullibility of the American people, and on the other, worrying proof of the power of radio. This part of the analysis was not entirely objective, the press having for some time been fighting a losing battle with radio as the chief disseminator of news. The opportunity was seized to berate its manipulative ways. In a piece entitled FRIGHTED WITH FALSE FIRE, quoting Hamlet's scorn at Claudius's reaction to the Mousetrap, a *New York World Telegram* columnist hoped that 'young Mr Welles, a student of Shakespeare, might have remembered Hamlet, and remembering, might have foreseen the effect of too much dramatic realism on an audience already strung to high nervous tension . . . let all chains, all stations, avoid the use of the news broadcasting technique when there is any possibility of any listener mistaking fiction for fact.' In response the broadcasting companies solemnly pledged never to present a programme again in the form of a news broadcast.

Anxiety was expressed as to the reaction of the populace in the event of a real air raid. There were even calls for censorship, fiercely resisted. 'The dictators in Europe use radio to make their people believe falsehoods. We want nothing like that here. Better have American radio remain free to make occasional blunders than start a course that might in time deprive it of freedom to broadcast uncensored truth.' The *New York Tribune* columnist, Dorothy Thompson, in a striking piece, acclaimed the broadcast: 'one of the most fascinating and important events of all time . . . it is the story of the century . . . far from blaming Mr Orson Welles, he ought to be given a congressional medal and a national prize for having made the most amazing and important of contributions to the social sciences . . . he made the scare to end all scares, the menace to end menaces, the unreason to end unreason, the perfect demonstration that the menace is not from Mars but from the theatrical demagogues.'

Welles himself was palpably shaken by the furore he had unleashed. In a newsreel interview with assembled pressmen, he apologises, unshaven and boyish, for the distress unwittingly caused. He has the attitude of a repentant schoolboy, big-eyed, serious-mouthed, frightened and exhilarated at the same time: circumspect, but nervously ready to burst out laughing. He says, his voice nervously high-pitched and slightly adenoidal, that the only anxiety they had before the broadcast was that it might have been boring, his only thought as he came off the air that he hadn't given a very good performance. It was planned simply as a Hallowe'en joke, he says, ('I'd every hope people would be excited, just as they are in a melodrama') and he certainly would never do anything like it again. He is charming, but shifty, not quite sure whether he'd got off without any more serious penalties. (Legal actions were filed against both CBS and the Mercury; all failed.) Later, Welles became more articulate about the incident. 'The most terrifying thing,' he told the *Saturday Evening Post*, 'is suddenly becoming aware that you are not alone. In this case the earth, thinking itself alone, suddenly became aware that another planet was prowling around.' He had another theory, too: 'the last two generations are softened up because they were deprived in their childhoods, through mistaken theories of education, of the tales of blood and horror which used to be part of the routine training of the young. Under the old system the child felt at home among ghosts and goblins, and did not grow up to be a push-over for sensational canards. But the ban on gruesome fairy tales, terrifying nursemaids and other standard sources of horror has left most of the population without any protection against fee-fi-fo-fum stuff.' This second theory seems very personal: the need to embrace demons; the necessity of healthy terror and – presumably – guilt.

The War of the Worlds incident, though giving rise to an extraordinary event, and revealing some remarkable aspects of America in 1938, was one of the most purely fortuitous events of Welles's career. His personal responsibility for it is negligible, beyond having directed it with great flair. Houseman precisely analyses the skill of the production, especially its slow build-up of tension; but most of the people who had been frightened by it had only joined the programme a third of the way through, so they were never subject to that manipulation. Nor was Welles responsible for the adaptation. He later attempted to claim authorship for the script, but there is a great deal of entirely conclusive evidence to the contrary. When in 1940 Hadley Cantril published the script as part of his study of the phenomenon, Welles tried by every means to prevent him from attributing it to Howard Koch; Cantril courteously replied that as Koch had written it, Koch would be credited with it – and so he was, to Welles's inexpressible fury. There is, moreover, no evidence that the programme was planned as the devilishly clever Hallowe'en prank that it seemed to be. Describing the programme as a practical joke was an idea improvised on the spot as a sop to the panic released during the broadcast. Nor was there a conscious attempt to play on fears of a European invasion. The fact is that Welles had barely thought about the programme, being wholly occupied until the very last minute by his losing struggle with *Danton's Death*.

Welles was praised for having his finger on the pulse of his times, and for being the conman of the century, able to make anybody believe anything. The truth is that he was more surprised than anyone at what had happened, and extremely irritated by it: the day after the broadcast, a Mercury employee who wandered into the auditorium eating a Mars bar was sacked on the spot. In years to come, his attitude was first one of vexation that he should be so persistently associated with this accidental event, but then he absorbed it comfortably into his myth, adding, in later life, a final puckish touch: 'Now it's been pointed out,' he said on the Dean Martin show in the early seventies, 'that various flying saucer scares all over the world have taken place since that broadcast . . . everyone doesn't laugh anymore. But most people do. And there's a theory this is my doing. That my job was to soften you up . . . ladies and gentlemen, go on laughing. You'll be happier that way. Stay happy as long as you can. And until the day when our new masters choose to announce that the conquest of the earth is completed, I remain, as always, obediently yours.'

For Welles in October 1938, the immediate result of the broadcast was notoriety. People who had never been to the theatre, who had never so much as read a review and who would never have dreamed of consciously tuning in to the Mercury Theatre of the Air, suddenly knew who he was. And not just in America: the news of the panic flashed round the world, where the incident was held up (particularly in Europe) as proof, if any were needed, of the ingrained idiocy of Americans. 'America today hardly knows whether to laugh or to be angry,' scoffed the London *Times*. 'Here is a nation which, alone of the big nations, has deemed it unnecessary to rehearse for protection against attack from the air by fellow-beings on this earth and suddenly believes itself – and for little enough reason – faced with a more fearful attack from another world.' It was left to the more popular end of the market to report on Welles himself: the *Daily Express* piece was headed HE'S A LAD. Recapitulating favourite yarns it hailed him as 'America's best villainous radio voice', whose 'ha-ha's and hee-hee's are adored by millions'. The *Star* (STORMY WELLES) offered a more sober assessment: 'he has had a career almost as remarkable as his broadcast . . . making history at the Mercury Theatre, New York.' The *Evening News* was also more interested in his theatrical reputation: 'by his energetic direction and ruthless manhandling of the classics, he has made his theatre, the Mercury, the liveliest in New York . . . the broadcast has set the seal on his reputation as the enfant terrible of the New York stage.' It had certainly done that, though its most important effects were to come. It was a sort of time-bomb, whose full force was not felt until a year later. One immediate outcome, however, was that Campbell Soup decided at last to sponsor the Mercury Theatre of the Air; CBS withdrew with some relief. Meanwhile, *Danton's Death* finally opened to the press.

The catastrophes continued to the last moment. After the final preview, as yet more adjustments were being made to the lighting plot, an electrician keeled over, having been at his switchboard for seven hours without relief. By now the postponements had become a matter for keen speculation. Events at the Mercury were being regularly and accurately reported; clearly a mole was at work. Even as the electrician was being put in a taxi, Sam Zolotow of *The New York Times* rang the theatre. 'He said he was sorry to hear about the electrician and hoped it wasn't serious,' reports Houseman. 'I said no. He asked if this meant another postponement. I said no and goodnight.' The informer, it turns out, was one of the extras – an interesting indicator of the lengths to which the press were prepared to go for their Mercury story. It had become hot news again – not because of what was happening onstage, but because imminent disaster seemed in the offing, an irresistibly attractive prospect for an editor. Nor had the left-wing pressure let up. The *Daily Worker* carried a minatory paragraph two weeks before the opening: 'LEFT ON BROADWAY: DANTON'S DEATH SCARES PREVIEW AUDIENCE: Having been a Wellesian admirer so long entitles this column to a plea that the script be changed or the show dropped from the repertoire before the hue and cry raised throughout town begins to echo too harshly in the ears of the wonder boy of American theatre.' In fact the first night (on 2 November, only two days after *The War of the Worlds* broadcast) went reasonably well, despite Welles's inability to remember much of his role. Bill Alland was in the wings, at the prompt desk. 'Welles stumbled and stumbled. I threw a line at him, then another. He couldn't take the prompt. Finally he came into the wings and spat at me saying "You sonofabitch, I didn't ask you to do that." Then he went back onstage.' All this went unnoticed by the press, who were transfixed with anxiety for the other actors, 'living one hour and a little more in fear, expecting the actors to fall down into the cellar and break their necks. The stage gapes for them,' wrote Arthur Pollock in the *Brooklyn Eagle*. There were no broken necks. The evening rather hung fire, but this was no disaster.

So the vultures were baulked of their prey. That did not stop them from conducting something in the nature of a collective post-mortem. The reviews as a whole constitute an extended inquest into Welles, his methods and aims. Whither Welles? was the underlying theme of nearly every notice. *The War of the Worlds* had made him a figure of national importance. Not just *Danton's Death* but the whole Mercury phenomenon was put in the dock; the majority verdict was not altogether favourable. There were enthusiastic notices; Atkinson in the *Times* proclaimed it 'overwhelming and a worthy successor to the *Caesar*, and *Shoemaker's Holiday* of last season.' But this and one or two others were rare exceptions. Even stalwart supporters were troubled by what they saw. Atkinson waggishly concluded his notice 'Ladies and gentlemen, you have just been reading a review of a theatrical performance of *Danton's Death* at the Mercury Theatre last evening. There is no occasion for alarm.' This was not a view shared by all of Atkinson's fellow critics.

While generally speaking they acknowledged Welles's skill and imagination, there was a widespread sense of a machine operating in a void. 'It is too arty,' wrote John Mason Brown, the Mercury's first important champion, 'too self-conscious for comfort. It is empty of everything except tricks. It is all technique and no drama; all switchboard and no soul; all fury and no sound. One tires of its lights, its actors running up and down stairs, and its overworked elevators. Except as a director's holiday, it proves to be a bore.' Again and again, critics expressed distaste at the directorial dominance of the production. 'Its only purpose,' wrote Sidney Whipple, 'was to demonstrate the undeniable talent of one man rather than a group of men – including the original playwright.' The play had been used as the merest excuse for theatrical experiment: 'it may be electrically, mechanically, and scenically inventive,' said George Jean Nathan, 'but someone in the factory somehow neglected to do much about inventing the drama.'

The reviewers naturally assumed – what else could they assume? – that it was all effortless virtuosity, instead of having been achieved on the brink of the total collapse of nearly everyone involved – including Welles. John Mason Brown memorably expressed the overwhelming presence of the director's personality: 'You are forced to feel as if, having sailed on a boat filled with interesting passengers, you found that, in addition to having to sit at the captain's table three times a day, you were permitted to talk to no one else except the captain in between meals.' ORSON WELLES DOES BÜCHNER'S DANTON'S DEATH OVER INTO A LITTLE THING OF HIS OWN, ENJOYING LIFE AS A BOY PRODIGY, ran the aggressive headline in the *Brooklyn Eagle-Examiner* in which Arthur Pollock wrote, eerily prophetic, 'at twenty-three a man's future must appall him if he has begun where others at their peak left off. Is he good enough to get better throughout two-thirds of a lifetime? . . . he is treating the theatre as a plaything, giving himself a good time at his games.'

Who but Welles has received school reports spread across the national press? Only an heir to the throne, perhaps. He was already in early manhood an exemplary case, the Icarus of the age. It was no longer possible simply to write about his productions; they were merely symptoms of his monstrous progress, which the press was keenly monitoring. Later in life Welles plaintively lamented that 'nobody reviews my films; they review me.' By the time he was twenty-three, the pattern was already set. The Welles Problem was definitively established with *Danton's Death*. Despite the danger signals detected by most critics, there was none the less faith in his ability to solve it. Pollock concluded his piece with a reassurance: 'Don't worry. When Master Welles gets to be an old man of twenty-eight or -nine he will have given up the idea that the theatre is his own particular playroom and he'll settle down to work. All this *Danton* business is just animal crackers. Boy prodigies do not always disappear altogether.'

This perception of Welles's failure actually to engage with the play in question dominated the notices to the exclusion of almost anything else. Atkinson pointed out the oddity of approaching a play bursting with 'matters of contemporary pertinence' as an exercise in style. The idiom that Welles was exploring was essentially filmic – soundtrack and all. He protested in *The Director in the Theatre* that 'I have not arbitrarily taken *Danton's Death* as a shooting script for elevators and lights', but it is hard to detect any other motive. Pollock specifically noted the filmic nature of the production: 'There are black holes to the left and to the right and in the middle. Light shoots from all directions, light smartly thought out, cleverly manipulated. Men stand alone on the stage and orate to unseen singing or shouting multitudes. Little groups appear out of the darkness and talk awhile about the French Revolution, what it is doing to them. We get Büchner's play in short takes, a badly connected series of flashes.'

It is interestingly paradoxical that, despite the constant use of the word virtuosity, many notices comment on the slowness of the production. 'Every movement,' wrote Richard Watts, another erstwhile admirer, 'is made as if it were artistically precious, and it manages to achieve not a rhythm that seems appropriate to the French Revolution but rather one that indicates a belief on Mr Welles's part that everything he is doing is pretty significant.' (It is noteworthy how personally vexed so many of the notices sound.)

'It is done with great deliberation,' wrote Burns Mantle, 'in what we probably will come to know as the Orson Welles manner.'

This is odd. Hitherto his productions had been noted for their celerity. *Danton* seems to represent a thickening of Welles's theatrical arteries; an impression confirmed by accounts of his own performance as St Just. 'Mr Welles plays him behind a grave mask and a booming voice with some of the melodramatic solemnity of The Shadow,' wrote Atkinson in the *Times*. 'His eccentric phrasing of the last speech sacrifices meaning to apostolic sound.' His voice and the uses to which he put it – hitherto his glory – now also came under heavy criticism. 'Incoherent and handsomely fatuous,' wrote Stark Young of his delivery of the speech, 'merely stylised exhibitionism, arbitrary and too hard to follow.' In another peculiarly personal rumination, Brooks Atkinson (under the heading GOTHAM HOBGOBLIN) noted the uses to which Welles put his voice: 'that baleful voice has already had a persistent career, ululating dooms for quite a spell . . . Mr Welles likes the roar that words like that can make, and the little Mercury Theatre trembles with his prophetic diapason as the shivering curtain comes down. No wonder innocent radio listeners thought the world was coming to an end a fortnight ago. Mr Welles's voice is the cry of demons.' He was not being taken altogether seriously.

As for the rest of the cast, Vladimir Sokoloff was also gently (and sometimes not so gently) mocked: Robert Benchley reported that 'he had trouble with the English language, being strongly opposed to pipple in welwet gowns.' Gabel was accused of giving a lazy performance as Danton, and several times of having the wrong face for the part ('so genially constructed that sometimes he seemed to utter his most dismal sentiments with a beaming smile') and hardly anyone else was mentioned at all.

Business was not good. *The War of the Worlds*' publicity helped the box office not one whit. The apparent political confusion of the production lost the Mercury its committed audience. Theatre parties cancelled their bookings, while ticket agents ignored the production. *Danton's Death* was a flop – the Mercury's first, and, as it turned out, its last. In an interesting comment on *The War of the Worlds*, Houseman wrote that 'Welles is at heart a magician whose particular talent lies not so much in his creative imagination (which is considerable) as in his proven ability to stretch the familiar elements of theatrical effect far beyond the normal point of tension. For this reason his productions require more elaborate preparation and more perfect execution than most. At that – like all complicated magical tricks –

they remain, until the last minute, in a state of precarious balance. When they come off, they give – by virtue of their unusually high intensity – an impression of great brilliance and power; when they fail – when something in their balance goes wrong or the original structure proves to have been unsound – they provoke among their audience a particularly violent reaction of unease and revulsion. Welles's flops are louder than other men's.'

The crucial factor in the débâcle of *Danton's Death* was the lack of preparation, the absence of forward planning, the failure to think through. Welles began to believe that he could make anything happen as long as the pressure was enough. Buoyed up by alcohol, amphetamines, food, sex, while almost totally deprived of sleep, he drove himself and everyone on to destinations of which he had only the vaguest sense. Improvising and experimenting, he had ceased to explore. Any interesting results of the *Danton's Death* production were accidental, randomly achieved. That he kept going at all was something of a miracle. During the play's run, he was still working on the weekly radio show (*The Pickwick Papers*, of all things, *A Passenger to Bali*, and, fittingly, *Heart of Darkness*) and making public pronouncements of ever darker purport. Continuing the public inquest into the Welles Problem, Brooks Atkinson noted in his 'Gotham Hobgoblin' piece that Welles's Voice had been 'ringing the tocsin lately. It solemnly forecast the death of the theatre before the stunned National Council of Teachers of English last summer . . . "we do not know if we will be alive to go to the World's Fair next year," the voice of The Shadow bellowed, for Mr Welles's voice is an organ that has an independent existence, divorced from mind and purged of sense of humor. When he starts laying tunes on it, dynasties rumble, civilisations start falling apart and radio listeners fly into the streets.' Atkinson had accurately identified the tone which informs most of Welles's public utterances of this period: frustration, weariness, impatience (a crabbiness which would seem more appropriate to a fifty-year-old) and doom. He starts more and more to appear in the role of Cassandra, or the theatre's own Savonarola, seemingly impelled to make general statements of some pomposity about art and life. There is a sense, behind all this rather jejune Spenglerian despair, mixed in with awkward after-dinner humour ('there are a few actors in England, but they're coming') and some ringing if unproven contentions, that he is impatient at having to keep proving himself over and over. He seems to be defending himself, but against what or whom? He has had nothing but praise and admiration.

That was of course in itself a large part of the problem. Expectations were running ridiculously high. 'If *Danton's Death* does not seem very important it is, after all, simply because Orson Welles did it,' wrote Pollock in the *Brooklyn Eagle*. 'He suffers by comparison with himself. Done by anyone else this *Danton's Death* would have looked like an American miracle. Done by anyone else it would not seem quite so precious.' In an astonishingly short space of time and at a startlingly early age, he had placed himself at the centre of the American Theatre. He was no longer a private citizen. His flops were not a personal grief, but a betrayal of the future of the American stage. 'What chiefly worries me is the mannered quality that has got into his production,' wrote John Mason Brown, 'and I think he should be spoken to about it before it is too late, for he is one of the valuable men of the theatre and we need him.' Atkinson had done a little research into The Problem. 'Plays have to give way to his whims, and actors have to subordinate their art when he gets under way, for The Shadow is monarch of all he surveys,' he wrote. 'It is no secret that his wilfulness and impulsiveness may also wreck the Mercury Theatre, for he is a thorough egotist in the grand manner of the old-style tragedian.'

Little did the analysts of the Mercury's malady know that only ten days after delivering their diagnoses, they would be writing its obituary. 'After twenty-one performances,' wrote Houseman, 'we threw in the sponge – not just for *Danton's Death* but for the Mercury Theatre.' They had had enough. 'The truth is – we were no longer interested. In the grandiose and reckless scheme of our lives, the Mercury had fulfilled its purpose. It had brought us success and fame; it had put Welles on the cover of *Time* and our radio show on the front page of every newspaper in the country. Inevitably, any day now, the offers from Hollywood would start arriving. It was too late to turn back and we did not really want to.' Any suggestion that the Mercury Theatre might have been one of the great idealistic theatrical experiments of the century is conclusively dispelled by Houseman's candid if unattractive admission that the purpose of the organisation had been to provide its directors with fame and success, not perhaps an admission that Stanislavsky or Nemirovich-Danchenko would have made, nor Micheál Mac Liammóir or Hilton Edwards, for all of whom the glory was incidental. Their dreams of art demanded a commitment to something bigger than themselves that neither Welles nor Houseman (at this stage of their lives) could pretend to.

Well, why should they? They had created many memorably

gaudy hours on their tiny stage. It had been fun while it lasted. The only real casualties were a few actors who had for a moment thought that they were engaged in the remaking of the American Theatre; a few technicians who had been driven to the point of physical collapse getting Welles's extravagant and heavily impractical visions onto the stage; and a new audience which had become excited by the possibilities of a young and radically imaginative theatre. To none of these groups did Welles and Houseman feel they had any particular loyalty. They had arrived with their box of fireworks and let them off to loud acclaim; then they produced a squib. At the first murmurs of disappointment, they departed, leaving nothing behind but the memory of brilliant cascades and thrilling explosions. What more can one ask? The critic of *The New York Times* had no quarrel with it. Identifying the Mercury as 'Hobohemia in the theatre' and a generous contributor to the gaiety of nations, he accepted its capriciousness as a lively virtue. Others were sterner. Sidney Whipple in the *New York World Telegram* devoted two aggrieved pieces to the Mercury's demise, the result, he claimed, of an absence of a definitive programme and a refusal to accept that a successful venture in the theatre must be 'co-operative in every sense of the word'.

Welles answered him by pretending that the theatre had closed because it had been denied the right to fail. 'The Mercury has many faults, including its inability to produce an unbroken succession of smash hits, which is exactly and with absolutely no exaggeration essential to the maintenance of the permanent repertory company devoted to elaborate experimental productions under present Broadway circumstances.' On the contrary, the Mercury had produced an unbroken succession of hits; with its first flop, it folded. A company that cannot withstand the impact of one failure is clearly built on unstable foundations, psychologically as well as financially. It was as if the Mercury depended for its life on the acclaim of the press. Sustained by that bright sun, it flowered; at the first cloud, it withered and died. Harold Clurman described the Mercury, with justice, as 'an enterprise that the press was sincerely fond of'. The press operation, shrewdly directed by Houseman, skilfully run by Hank Senber and incomparably fronted by Welles was without parallel in the modern American Theatre. A torrent of witty, informative press releases kept things bubbling along; no journalist was ever refused an interview with Welles, who always provided memorable if erratic copy. The critics (with the single uninfluential exception of Mary McCarthy) were on the Mercury's side from the beginning, always ready to play down the minuses and to write up the pluses. This sort of relationship with the press is always – like any dependent relationship – fraught with danger. Who needs whom? The plug can be pulled at any moment; but it wasn't. The critics had certainly turned on *Danton's Death*, but not on the Mercury. And yet they had put up the shutters for good. It was puzzling.

For a moment, it seemed as if Welles was going to attempt to create the theatrical heavenly kingdom on earth. This was not foisted on him: he and Houseman had made such bold declarations when they founded the Mercury that hope for this elusive vision was born again; now it appeared that he hadn't really meant it. Instead, he simply offered a lively alternative to what was on offer elsewhere. Welles later insisted that there had never been a possibility of creating an ensemble because the real talent was never available to him. This is shameful nonsense. He had the pick of the younger profession, and chose well. Certainly in his first season, the company had the makings of a world-beating team. For a multitude of reasons, he failed to keep them together. The *Danton's Death* company was equally promising: with players like Joseph Cotten and Mary Wickes in tiny roles, he had a strength in depth which is the essential requirement of a serious acting company. But he did nothing with them; had no plans for them.

The Mercury was a maverick actor-manager's outfit, existing to support the leading actor's performances and serve his brilliance as a director. 'I think it might almost go without saying,' wrote Sidney Whipple in his aggrieved article, 'that some of the most valuable talent has been lost to the Mercury because, to the actor, the road lying ahead was so uncertain. It is not security alone that actors want. Their great desire is to demonstrate and enlarge their artistic abilities. The question of a program should be determined by joint consideration and the plays that are chosen should have not only the best of direction, which is Mr Welles's forte, but the best of writing and the best of acting.' This was simply not the way Welles functioned. Whipple was dreaming, as so many American theatre people had for so long dreamt, of a National Theatre, an organisation nourished by and nourishing talent; a company with roots, capable of growth; an ensemble, in fact, in the tradition of the great European ensembles, the Comédie Française, the Moscow Art Theatre, the Burgtheater in Vienna and the Schiller in Berlin.

In contrast to all these other groups, the Mercury had neither theory nor vision, neither craft nor continuity. It depended on justifying the moment – providing thrills. Its particular originality was that it did this with classical plays. As such, it may have been a wonderful antidote, but it was incapable of sustained growth. Clurman, defending himself and his theatre against accusations that the Group was rigidly theory-bound and lacked a sense of humour, noted that 'Behind [all this] is the need to be free, to pick up or drop any notion according to convenience, to avoid choice, lest one be caught in the rigidity of a definite position, for in that lies difficulty and even danger.' The Mercury was never dangerous; was, according to Clurman (who cannot of course be described as an objective witness, though his point is well made) 'sensational and not controversial. It had the rebel air of a "hep" and hearty youth that suited the rejuvenated epoch of the late 30s. The Mercury was safe. It treaded on no toes, but rather kicked the seat of plays and traditions for which our reverence is more advertised than real . . . the theatre in our slippery society has become very much like gambling. The reviewers, like the financiers, hate to back a loser.' The Mercury was a speculators' delight; once it was bust, it proved to be perfectly dispensable.

And it had been a beacon: in its verve and fearlessness, it had seemed to revitalise the idea of the theatre, for a while. In their 1938 play *The Fabulous Invalid*, Kaufmann's and Hart's survey of the theatre's indestructibility, an eager little group, led by THE YOUNG MAN, appears at the end of the play, when all seems lost.

> THE YOUNG MAN
> Well, you know why we're here, everybody, and what we're going to do. There's only one thing I want to say today. We've got our own theatre. It's not in a very good neighborhood; it's been closed for years, and it's in pretty bad shape. But it's a theatre, and it's ours. It's got a stage, and it's got seats, and that's all we care about . . . they'll tell you it isn't important, putting make-up on your face and play-acting. I don't believe it. It's important to keep a thing alive that can lift men's spirits above the everyday reality of their lives. Remember, you're going to be kicked around, and a lot of the time you're not going to have enough to eat, but you're going to get one thing in return. The chance to write, and act, say the things you want to say, and do the things you want to do. And I think that's enough.

No Broadway theatre-goer in 1938 had the slightest doubt as to which particular YOUNG MAN was supposed to be doing the talking. He ran the flag up for the theatre, for a while. Time for someone else to take over.

Welles and Houseman were in it for the pleasure and the gain of the moment. It is hard not to think of them (however affectionately) as opportunists and buccaneers. Certainly they shed no tears for their lost theatre, whose lease, the one Welles had insisted would keep them in business for at least five years, was made over to Laurens and Benjamin, for their children's theatre; later it passed to the radical Yiddish group ARTEF. The neon sign which had raised such a cheer when it was installed a mere fifteen months earlier remained incongruously in place till the demolition men moved in four years later to knock the theatre down.

Welles and Houseman had gone rapidly on to the next projects, the first of which, significantly, involved further dismantlement of the Mercury in its other shape: the Theatre of the Air. The radio programmes were about to undergo a change of gear, with the arrival of a sponsor (always referred to by Houseman as The Soup Company) and a change of name. Now the programme was *The Campbell Playhouse*. 'I guess they figured if we could sell the end of the world,' said Houseman, 'we could sell tomato soup, too.'

CHAPTER SEVENTEEN

The Campbell Playhouse/ Five Kings

THE MERCURY Theatre of the Air made its last transmission on 4 December with *The Bridge of San Luis Rey* by Welles's old mentor Thornton Wilder. The broadcasts had, astonishingly, continued their ambitious and sparky course through the débâcles of *Too Much Johnson* and *Danton's Death* and *The War of the Worlds* sensation. Adaptations of Schnitzler (*Anatol*), Chesterton (*The Man Who Was Thursday*), Dumas (a thrilling *Count of Monte Cristo*) and Brontë (*Jane Eyre*) jostled with Jules Verne, Saki and Sherwood Anderson. For *Julius Caesar*, Welles again stressed the contemporary parallel, this time having the relevant chunks of Plutarch read by the foremost political commentator of the day, H.V. Kaltenborn, whose mid-European accent, regularly heard by millions of listeners describing the gathering storm in Europe, must have given a peculiar urgency to the story for contemporary listeners. There were larky versions of *The Pickwick Papers* (featuring Welles's Sergeant Buzzfuzz) and *Sherlock Holmes*, a somewhat sketchy version of *Heart of Darkness* as part of a triple bill, and a genuinely First Person Singular adaptation of *My Little Boy* by Carl Ewald (a shamelessly sentimental but curiously affecting piece which is perhaps the most experimental production they had so far attempted, pioneering an almost stream-of-consciousness approach). In addition, with *Clarence* and *Seventeen* Welles celebrated his affection for the work of the Middle West's great chronicler, Booth Tarkington, an affection that resulted first in his radio adaptation, then his film, of *The Magnificent Ambersons*.

The programming – eclectic, middle-of-the-road, but always stimulating and personal – was as characteristic as the versatile and witty performances by the regular team, a tight-knit group of masterly radio actors – Ray Collins, Agnes Moorehead, Gabel and Coulouris foremost among them. The tone was only occasionally reverential, more often blithe, high-spirited, dashingly dramatic. Not all of that was lost with the reinvention of the programme as *The Campbell Playhouse*, but it was a radically different animal, and it made of Welles a rather different animal, too. The first show,

Rebecca, set the pattern; being the first show, it was launched with fanfares, both musical and verbal, quite unlike anything heard on the Mercury Theatre of the Air. Bernard Herrmann's specially composed Hollywood-style musical call to attention merges into a new treacly allargando version of the opening of the Tchaikovsky First Piano Concerto, over which the announcements are made. If the Mercury Theatre of the Air had seemed to glorify Welles, this was his apotheosis.

'I am here,' the announcer tells us, 'to introduce the white hope of the American stage as the director and star of *The Campbell Playhouse* – he writes his own radio scripts and directs them, and makes them live and breathe with the warmth of his genius.' Having lamented that there is no time to adventure into the story of his life, the announcer feverishly recapitulates the familiar events, culminating with his foundation of the Mercury Theatre and his operation of it 'with magical success'; news of its disbandment had clearly not yet reached Campbell's Soup. 'He had four hits last year on Broadway, which beats Noël Coward's record from here to Kalamazoo. And he's generally recognised today as being the most gifted stage director and actor of our time.' Referring to his radio productions, the announcer tells us that though Orson Welles is 'the master of realism over the air on radio, unique, exciting – he shocked you, he sent the cold shivers racing up your spine – that is not the thing he does best, or best likes to do. He loves,' the announcer consoles us, 'to tell a story, a great human story, welling up from the heart, brimming with deep and sincere emotion and lively with comedy.' Such are the stories, apparently, that he will bring to *The Campbell Playhouse*.

Then, unable to restrain himself any longer, the announcer finally comes off the fence about Welles in a thrilling peroration. 'Because of all his gifts, his genius at playwriting, his ambition, his dynamic direction, his amazing character acting, he has been selected by Campbell's as the ideal man to conduct *The Campbell Playhouse*. And so tonight Orson Welles makes his bow as the outstanding programme director of the air, and I have the very great pleasure of presenting him now. Mr Orson Welles.' Welles, quite unabashed by the preceding hosannas, briskly takes the microphone, telling us that it's a great big chance for him and a great big challenge, pledging himself to tell good stories 'from everywhere, from the stage, from moving pictures and from literature . . . and to try to tell 'em as well as I know how,' finally staking a claim to quality which was, perhaps, a message to his sponsors as much as it was to his audience. 'You know the makers of Campbell Soup don't believe in all this talk about the radio audience having the average mentality of an eight-year-old child. I can only hope that what I do with *The Campbell Playhouse* will prove how much they mean it and how right they are.' He reiterates his familiar commitment to radio radiophonic as opposed to radio theatrical. 'We have no curtain real or imaginary and as you see, no audience. There's the only illusion I'd like to create; the illusion of a story.'

So far, so Mercury. Then the announcer brings up one of the innovations. 'But the star too is important, Mr Welles is that not so?' The massive enhancement of the budget had enabled Welles to employ the biggest names in Hollywood and on Broadway; his usual team continued to work for him, but no longer in leading roles. Welles eagerly agrees about the importance of the stars: 'Yes, indeed. I'd like to say how very fortunate I am in having with me tonight the loveliness and the magic gift of Miss Margaret Sullavan.' This is a new tone, quite different from his Mercury manner: what would later become familiar as the manner of the chat show, but which in 1938 was the unmistakable tone of the sponsored programme. It is about selling, about puffing. The puff here extends to the book being adapted. 'It's this year's contender for the five-foot shelf, your best bet for anything from a weekend to a desert island and it's a book you should read, the ideal Xmas gift to yourself.' Then the double puff: of self and author. 'Miss Du Maurier has flattered me with her confidence in permitting *The Campbell Playhouse* the great privilege of making for radio the first dramatisation of her book.' She will be listening to the programme; at the end they will talk 'by special shortwave communication from London'. He signs off (or rather signs on; the programme proper hasn't started yet) 'so ladies and gentlemen and Miss Du Maurier, *The Campbell Playhouse* is Obediently Yours' – the famous tag has a slightly ironic feel; the multiple genius to whom we have just been so comprehensively introduced makes an unlikely servant.

We are suddenly plunged into *Rebecca* by means of Bernard Herrmann's luscious waltz-laden score, full of sudden intensities created by the Lohengrin instrumentation of trumpet and tremolo strings. Hardly have we begun, though, than we are rudely interrupted. 'Here's an important message from a man who keeps one eye on the dining table and another on the pantry . . .' There follows an apostrophe to chicken and the soup derived from it by Campbell's. 'Why not plan to have Campbell's glorious chicken soup tomorrow?' Innovation number two. The commercial breaks always occur at cliff-hanging moments, a curiously dislocating effect; they are elaborate and emotional, including an extraordinary tribute from the announcer to 'the good hardworking honest men' who make Campbell's Soup. 'I know the Campbell kitchen, the Campbell soup, the Campbell men: their success is due to the human side of this business, its policy.' No doubt, accustomed to sponsored broadcasts of which this was quite typical, listeners' ears simply glazed over during these interludes, but the layers of fiction involved in the broadcast are somewhat bewildering: palpably unreal tributes to soup by paid announcers are seamlessly interwoven with Mrs Danvers's tributes to her dead mistress, overlapping with overwrought accounts of Welles's career and fevered sales pitches for the novel and forthcoming film.

At the end of the adaptation (which barely accounts for two-thirds of the broadcast) Welles, still quite recognisably Maxim de Winter, and Margaret Sullavan, as husky and breathless as she was as the second Mrs de Winter, have a chat. 'Two things I like are good stories and good soup,' says Miss Sullavan, 'and when I tell you my idea of a great soup is Campbell's chicken soup, that, Mr Welles, is no story.' A curiously coy exchange follows. 'Until we met for rehearsals,' says Welles, 'I've never – to put it bluntly – had the pleasure of your acquaintance, and now in six and a half minutes, you'll have gone out of my life. The point is – the point is – I'm the director of a theatre, the . . . the . . .' Sullavan: 'The . . . Mercury Theatre?' Welles: 'The Mercury Theatre, thank you. I'm talking to you as a theatre director. What are you doing next year? I'll bring you a script tomorrow. Forgive me, ladies and gentlemen, for trying to date up one of the nation's most gifted and attractive young actresses. I'm sure you'll sympathise and I hope Miss Sullavan understands.'

Finally, incongruously after all this smooching, comes the conversation with the author, her fastidious vowels singing out loud and clear across the Atlantic, her consonants clipped: 'Thenk you for an ebsolutely splendid broadcast.' She gives Sullavan instructions on how to visit the 'real Manderley'; there is some pleasant banter about the heroine's name, which she playfully cuts short. Welles signs off, Obediently Ours.

For Welles on the air, omnipresence was no innovation. The Welles of *The Campbell Playhouse* however was a significantly different person to the Welles of the Theatre of the Air: master of ceremonies, celebrity, leading actor, salesman, he had become appreciably more a product of the image makers. Sincerity and intellectual urgency are replaced by flannel and a sort of confidential charm. The leader of the avant-garde, the dashing and daring adventurer has become a cosier, less challenging figure, authoritative but unthreatening.

He has, above all, gone commercial, the selling of the sponsor's product and his own indistinguishable from one another; both indistinguishable from the selling of himself. The tone in which he extols the beauty of radio as a medium is the same as the one in which he lauds the makers of Campbell's Soup. It is one more stage in the abolition of the boundaries between Welles's persona and his work, and represented a great increase in his public prominence; the process that Houseman described shortly afterwards, not without bitterness, as 'the situation of Orson becoming a great national figure (a figure only less frequently and vastly projected into the news and the National Consciousness than Franklin D. Roosevelt, Adolf Hitler and maybe N. Chamberlain). This has happened in almost exactly inverse proportion to the success of his artistic and professional endeavours.' He overstates; but there was increasingly in Welles's work a confusion as to whether he was selling it or doing it.

As for *Rebecca*, insofar as one can disentangle it from the surrounding puff and pitch, all of the skills developed for the Mercury Theatre of the Air are as ingeniously deployed as before (with one or two quite startlingly effective new sound effects), Herrmann's score is if anything more powerful and imaginative (he later used large sections of it for the film *Jane Eyre*), and the performances of the staple radio repertory are admirable. Of the guests, Mildred Natwick is disappointingly mild as Mrs Danvers (despite the heart-freezing leitmotiv Herrmann wrote for her); Margaret Sullavan is fresh and true. Welles himself is a gruff and generalised de Winter; powerful, but not haunted. Though not vintage, the programme thrilled its new audience – one of whom was David O. Selznick; describing the show as 'one of the greatest successes the radio has ever known' he sent a transcript of the broadcast to Alfred Hitchcock, with whom he was then struggling over the screenplay for the forthcoming movie. 'A clever showman,' he wrote to a perhaps less than enthralled Hitchcock, 'Welles didn't waste time and effort creating anything new but simply gave them the original. I hope we will be equally astute. If we do in motion pictures as faithful a job as Welles did on the radio, we are likely to have the same success the book had and the same success that Welles had.' At a stroke, *The Campbell Playhouse* had established itself; Welles was now reaching more people than he ever had, and many of those people were highly influential.

Over the two years of the programme's run, a galaxy of stars appeared: Beatrice Lillie, Katharine Hepburn, Burgess Meredith, Helen Hayes in the first couple of months alone. The choice of works was more downmarket, less idiosyncratic, than those of the Mercury of the Air, often featuring bestsellers of the previous decade; though from time to time, Welles remade successes from the Mercury seasons. Some of the zip seemed to have gone out of it. 'The thing became a constant squabble with the soup-maker – a compromise between *Saturday Evening Post* material and material not necessarily highbrow but of some human and aesthetic interest,' wrote Houseman. 'Alas an end of our fun.'

The constant squabble grew in intensity over the two years; shortly after launching the new programme, however, Welles and Houseman became involved in a new theatrical venture compared to which a month in the Gulag Archipelago would have seemed fun. This was the much announced, much postponed Wars of the Roses cycle *Five Kings*, the one remaining Mercury project still to be honoured. In the heady days of May 1938, at the end of their triumphant first season, Houseman had entered into partnership with the Theatre Guild, to co-produce the vast – and as yet unwritten – adaptation of the two parts of *Henry IV*, *Henry V*, *Henry VI* (all three parts), and *Richard III*. The Guild, for nearly twenty years the dominant organisation in the American theatre, was brilliantly administered and run, but currently uninspired; much of its vigour had evaporated when the two factions that became the Group Theatre and the Playwrights' Company had broken away. The Mercury seemed irresistibly vital, and apparently infallibly successful. 'One of our board members, in an objective mood, analysed our situation,' wrote Lawrence Langner in his sly, witty memoir, *The Magic Curtain*, 'and decided that what we needed was more contact with "youth".'

They were willing to pay for their rejuvenation: Houseman struck a brilliant deal by which the Mercury contributed only $10,000 (five in cash, five in services) to the total budget of $40,000, while availing itself of the Guild's organisation and (most attractive of all) its built-in subscription audience in several major cities (Boston, Baltimore, Washington, Philadelphia) to which they would tour before opening in New York. For Houseman, there was also a pleasing personal dimension to the arrangement; only four years before, Langner and his partner had sacked him as director of Maxwell Anderson's *Valley Forge*. The boot was on the other foot – for the moment, at any rate. It seemed at the time another coup for the Mercury, a clever liaison with an older and maturer partner, and a stunningly audacious idea in itself. The plan was to stage the Falstaff-dominated first half (*Two and a Half Kings?*) separately, only rehearsing the second half, with Welles as Richard III, once that was successfully running. Finally the two evenings would play alternately; both would be given in one day on Wednesdays and Saturdays. 'The performance of Shakespeare's historical plays in batches has become a commonplace of festival showmanship,' wrote Houseman. 'In 1939 it was a bold and original notion.'

The idea clearly had its roots in his Todd School *Richard III* adaptation. It was, in Welles's mind, a means of creating a recognisable profile for a number of plays which (with the exception of *Richard*, one of Barrymore's great triumphs) had rarely been seen in America. Announcing the production at a luncheon to celebrate Shakespeare's birthday, Welles said: 'Some of the plays of Shakespeare have been lost to the living theatre. My new production is an effort to return these to theatre audiences. I hope our performance will make these more lucid.' He continued in his neo-Spenglerian vein: 'so much of everything we seek in art is to be found in the great Shakespeare heritage which will be existing in the world when everything we believe in has ceased to exist.' This was his credo: great art, above all the plays of Shakespeare, was the one talisman against the welling evil all around and within us. There were, of course, other, simpler motives. Looking back only a year later, Houseman was inclined to give these prominence. 'I allowed Orson to use the theatre not only as an instrument of personal aggrandisement but as a tilting ground for a particular, senseless and idle competition with an uninteresting and essentially unimportant theatrical competitor by the name of Maurice Evans,' he wrote to Virgil Thomson. '*Five Kings* was never a pure aesthetic conception – it was conditioned in its conception and its execution by a desire to go Evans one better in Shakespearean production.'

Ambition and rivalry have powerfully fuelled many a great performance and production; purity of motive is no prerequisite for great art. Houseman is untypically prim here; though there is no question that Welles's feelings about Evans were somewhat unhinged. Thirty years later, he was still in a lather about him. 'Almost any bum can get a crack at Boris Godunov or Lear,' he told Peter Bogdanovich. 'Sometimes the bums even make it with the public. Look at Maurice Evans.' 'Bad?' enquires Bogdanovich.

'Worse!' Welles roars back. 'He was poor.' The distinction is a good one. In every generation, there are a number of actors whose success mystifies their fellow players. For reasons that are never entirely clear the press and the public appear to elect to the summit of the profession actors of no discernible physical, vocal, intellectual or sexual distinction. They are constantly cast in leading roles, and are invariably well reviewed in them. If there are prizes to be won, they will win them; when they do, they are held up as an example to all: the good little boys and girls of the business. It would appear that Maurice Evans was one of these: teachers' pet for a whole generation of American reviewers. He has left almost no trace behind him, apart from his glowing encomia in the pages of the American press. People who saw his performances can remember nothing about them, though, equally, they can find nothing on which to fault him. He was intelligent, polished, well spoken, pleasant enough to look at, with the small features of a nicely groomed toy dog, an impeccable professional down to his manicured finger-nails.

In short, he was everything that Orson Welles was not. Fifteen years older than Welles, the English actor had arrived in America to replace Basil Rathbone as Katharine Cornell's Romeo. He had been acclaimed for that, and for pretty well everything else he did. His Napoleon in *St Helena*, his *Richard II* and his *Hamlet* (favourably compared to Gielgud's) were lauded to the heavens. It was when he played, to ever riper superlatives, the role of Falstaff ('a part which Orson regarded,' said Houseman, 'as he did every great classical part, as exclusively his own') in repertory with *Richard II*, that Welles was goaded beyond endurance. *Five Kings* was, as Houseman put it, 'a means of dealing a crushing blow to that English upstart'. It would 'by its sheer magnitude . . . reduce Mr Evans once and for all to his true pygmy stature.' It was not to be; Evans's career continued unchecked. There followed a triumphant cockney Malvolio, then *Macbeth* with Judith Anderson; with *Dial M for Murder* he became a boulevard star and a millionaire. His last great role was – a final slap in the face for Welles – a definitive Captain Shotover in *Heartbreak House*. Nothing, Peter Ustinov notes in *Dear Me*, rankles as much as the undeserved success of contemporaries; Evans's career never ceased to bewilder and enrage Welles. For the purposes of *Five Kings*, this excess of contempt had an unfortunate effect on the clarity of his thinking about the vast project.

Meanwhile, the publicity machine swung into action. The first task was to explain the resurrection of the Mercury. Herbert Drake (later Welles's personal publicist) protested in his 'Playbill' column in the *New York Herald Tribune* that reports of the Mercury's death had been greatly exaggerated: 'That subdued muttering you hear these days is made by the disgruntled mourners over the Mercury Theatre's bier who are being set on their ears by the renewed activity in that most stimulating of the current theatres.' *Five Kings*, he reports, 'the much heralded and much disbelieved *Five Kings*' is cast and ready to go into rehearsal. The Mercury is dead; long live the Mercury! Drake reports that the details of the operation of the tour were being worked on; the problem was how to combine it with the radio operation. 'John Houseman, partner and detail arranger for the soaring ideas of Welles,' says Drake, in a phrase that must have delighted Houseman, 'suspects that the company will give three matinees instead.' *Campbell's Playhouse* was transmitted on a weekday; there could be no question of ambulance ferries between onstage appearances. Something much more elaborate was being schemed. 'Welles's participation in the radio broadcasts will be by remote control. He will speed to the nearest large station and will recite his lines in tune with his unseen supporting cast here in New York.' It was not enough that he was attempting to play one of the greatest roles in dramatic literature, at the same time directing a company of forty-two players; not enough that he was attempting to forge seven sprawling plays into two coherent evenings in the theatre. He also had to be involved in lightning dashes to far-flung studios to record radio shows under the most peculiar circumstances. Had Welles attempted to swim the channel, you feel, he would have been performing his conjuring act at the same time; had he played the 'Emperor' Concerto, it would have been while cooking lobster thermidor. It was part of the myth; people expected it. He rather liked it himself.

The press releases continued, stressing the scale of 'the glamorous project'. 'Never before has the entire series [of Histories] been coordinated for presentation in their historic sequence . . . probably one of the most ambitious events ever to be undertaken on the English-speaking stage.' Expected contemporary parallels (which required no pointing as the second European Civil War of the Twentieth Century grew daily more imminent) were avoided except in the most general terms; instead Houseman's press release shrewdly played to the escapist longings of the American public in 1939. 'Picture the interest we should feel today seeing a trilogy giving the history of the House of Windsor, concluding, perhaps, with Edward VIII's farewell address, and we can know why the histories were so popular in their own day.' Aware of a need to prepare audiences for the epic quality of the chronicle plays, he added that 'only by combining them can an audience grasp both their historical significance and the development of their characters as they move from play to play . . . Falstaff, Hal and Hotspur are three great characters, but in *Henry IV, Part 1* they are both incomplete. Only when their scenes in Part 1 are succeeded by the ones in Part 2 do they really work their spell.' This of course is true, and it is also true that there is a considerable amount of both parts of the play which does not directly concern the three central characters. Welles's approach to the text was, as before, that of an actor-manager; his cutting of it served above all to focus on the great roles and eliminate what was not essential to them. Moreover, he would be stealing a march over that fraud Evans, who never played Part 2, though even he had interpolated into Part 1 the Recruiting scene from that play.

The publicity generated considerable excitement, as well as a certain amount of good-natured joshing about the length of time the project had taken to materialise. Welles's prodigiousness was now the subject of wry humour. A cartoon in *The New Yorker* shows him at his desk, a pair of scissors in his hand, a pot of glue at his side, hacking up the Complete Works while Shakespeare looks sternly on through the window against a Manhattan skyline. The expression on his face is of a sort of childish intensity, his tongue slightly protruding from his mouth. The cast he had assembled was starrier than usual for the Mercury: his Hotspur was John Emery, Laertes to Gielgud's Broadway Hamlet and, famously and disastrously, Antony to his wife Tallulah Bankhead's Cleopatra. Hal was Burgess Meredith, hot from triumphs in Maxwell Anderson, accustomed, therefore, to verse, but not to Shakespeare in which this would be his debut. Welles's Falstaff would complete the central trio of characters identified by Houseman; but there was a fourth crucial piece of casting to be accomplished: Chorus.

Welles extended the function of the Chorus – who figures so prominently in *Henry V*, but not elsewhere – so that he became, in effect, the historian Holinshed from whom Shakespeare had drawn so much of the detail of the play. The additional text was taken directly from the *Chronicles*. Welles's first choice for the part was Thornton Wilder, who had recently scored something of a success as the Stage Manager in his own play *Our Town*; when Wilder demurred, Welles asked Robert Speaight, the English actor who had created the role of Becket in *Murder in the Cathedral*, which he had toured in America. Morris Ankrum, an experienced Shakespearean director and actor, was to play Henry IV. There was thus great strength at the top of the company. The rest of the actors were drawn from the usual pool: people from earlier Mercury shows like Edgar Barrier, Eustace Wyatt and George Duthie plus a handful of trainees and stage managers (Dick Baer, Bill Alland, Dick Wilson); Lawrence Fletcher who had played the title role in *Julius Caesar* on the road; radio actors (Erskine Sandford, John Adair, Frank Readick); a number of rather vapid actresses, following the pattern Houseman had discerned at the time of *Caesar*; the vaudeville artist Gus Schilling as Bardolph; and Francis Carpenter, still screaming, still fiercely loyal, still apparently indispensable to Welles. A more unusual piece of casting was that of James Morcom as Shadow. Morcom was the designer of *Five Kings*. In name only, of course. Welles's adaptation was specifically intended to play on a set of which the essential element was a turntable. Morcom's task was to make this scenic idea actually work. It defeated him; but then, *Five Kings* defeated everyone.

Lawrence Langner claimed to have foreseen the tragedy at the first demonstration of the model. 'I was introduced to a young lady who showed me a large model consisting of a rotating stage carrying miscellaneous-looking structures made out of pieces of cigar boxes connecting into something that resembled a mediaeval city made of banana crates and painted dark brown. I remarked that it would be quite impossible to tour the play, as it would take at least two days to set up this cumbersome scenery in a theatre, in travelling from one town to the next.' This insight was swept away in the general enthusiasm inspired by the notion. Jean Rosenthal (the 'young lady' referred to by Langner) wrote later that 'once again, Orson was startlingly lucid about what he wanted and how it should look'. Two very attractive woodcuts by James Morcom give an excellent sense of the rough-hewn London that Welles wanted to put on stage: with its towering street scenes constructed out of bare wood (beech, birch and maple, cut into narrow slats), it was *The Shoemaker's Holiday* on wheels.

The settings were contained on a twenty-eight-foot revolve, and were constantly to be replaced or reversed during the action to create new locations. There were two sorts of scenes: those set in London (with the royal castle and the Boar's Head tavern, a street running through centre) and those set on the battlefield, where mounds and hillocks were created by wooden ramps. There was in addition a small flight of stairs to give a second level in the tavern scenes, a wooden curtain and gothic screen for playing scenes on the apron while the setting was being changed from behind, plus, more informally, a traveller curtain, in front of which Speaight as Chorus/Holinshed would stand. And finally – crucially – there was the turntable, designed not merely to facilitate changes from one scene to the next but to create the effect, as Andrea Nouryeh describes it, of a travelling shot, the actors seeming to pass through a moving landscape.

It is easy to see why not only Rosenthal and the technical staff but the actors too were excited by the concept. It offered an eventful fluidity far away both from the measured progress of set-bound productions and from the scenic anonymity of those which depend entirely on light to change the location. Moreover, the cinematic concept of travelling sequences on the turntable (pioneered by Piscator and Brecht in Berlin) offered the possibility of something quite new – or perhaps something quite old, a reversion, as so often with Welles, to the Victorian theatre and its travelling painted-canvas panoramas which Wagner put to such extraordinary use in *Parsifal*. The difficulty with productions that are inextricably linked to machinery is, first, that the machinery must work; and secondly, that the action must be rehearsed on it. Neither condition obtained on *Five Kings*. Rehearsals took place in a room in the Claridge Hotel which was much too small for the large company, even without the turntable. In the absence of that item, Welles found that there was little he could do in terms of staging, so he simply stayed away for a great deal of the allocated five weeks. Richard Barr stood in for him – 'much to the annoyance of Burgess Meredith. He was monumentally impatient with my twenty-one-year-old interpretation, but' – unlike his boss – 'I *did* know the lines.' Denied the experience of Welles's twenty-three-year-old interpretation, Meredith took to staying away as well (after one spree he telegraphed Welles, 'Dear Orson, Where am I? Buzz'); in fact, he and Welles frequently stayed away together. They had become soul-mates before rehearsals started, both in love with the idea of the actor as outsider, roaring their way through the night in various dives and various arms, both extravagantly moved by Great Art (Meredith took to his bed – whether alone or accompanied, history does not relate – on hearing of the death of Yeats). 'I was fascinated by the talents of Orson Welles,' he said many years later in an interview, 'and I joined him in *Five Kings*. We thought we'd combine our immortal talents, but we shared colossal disaster instead.'

The absence of both leading men from rehearsals (there was no question but that they were the stars of the show; the contract with the Theatre Guild bound both of them to do two more shows for the Guild) was a serious limitation; when one of them was also the director, it became crippling. When Welles did show up, he was never on time, and filled most of what was left of the rehearsal period with elaborate explanations for his lateness. Houseman noted his use of anecdote, no longer as a rehearsal technique, à la Guthrie McClintic, but as a work evasion tactic. There were cycles of stories: 'those vaguely based on truth . . . including encounters with Isadora Duncan in Paris . . . bullfighting . . . and the Glaoui. There was also an Oriental cycle . . . then there were fantasies that were invented on the spot out of sheer exuberance or to cover up some particularly outrageous piece of behaviour.' The anecdotal filibustering technique had another use, too: avoiding surveillance by the Theatre Guild, representatives of whom would drop by from time to time to see how things were coming along. All pretence of rehearsal would be suspended, Welles would call for a bottle of whiskey, and the actors would sit round while he entertained. Eventually the Theatre Guild people would depart, none the wiser. Richard France notes that the Guild, among the shrewdest, most experienced and effective operators in the American theatre was 'inordinately willing to suspend their disbelief and abandon their usual procedures in the hopes of cashing in on the Mercury Theatre's mysterious aura of success'. This was unlike anything they had ever seen before; it might just work.

Welles's one interest in *Five Kings* was staging it; without the turntable, he had no motive to work. Indeed, one of the problems Welles had increasingly to face in the theatre was that, denied the enormous resources of the Federal Theatre Project, his method of working without any plan, without even any tentative moves, of depending on the inspiration of the moment and what the other actors and the setting could offer him, was totally impractical. Only a fully subsidised European State Theatre could have provided him with what he wanted: the full set in the rehearsal room from the first day. So he stayed away, until the technical period, when he could really work on the set. Meanwhile the other actors struggled on as best they could. This was not very well at all. They were in the dark, despite all the preparatory work that had been done when the show was going to be part of the Mercury's New York seasons: all the research into the historical background, previous productions and past performances; all the company fencing lessons and martial technique classes (including special classes in cross-bow work). All this good work continued. But not only were the leading actors and the director rarely in attendance, there was no script. There had been no read-through; no one had seen the complete adaptation, for the good reason that there wasn't one. Chubby Sherman's joke to *The New York Times* that 'one actor asked another actor in our bunch when we'd start rehearsing *Henry IV*. The second answered: "Oh, when Orson's finished writing it" ' no longer seemed so funny.

After reciting a couple of the speeches of Chorus from *Henry V* to immense approval, Robert Speaight was told not to bother to come to rehearsals at all; he needn't come back till the technical period in Boston. He was the linkman; as there was nothing to link yet, what would be the point of hanging around? It may be suspected that Welles was happy not to have the punctilious, slightly pretentious actor around; it might have made him feel nervous. There is a strong sense, through all the whiskey fumes and raconteurial bonhomie, of a growing terror about the reality of getting the monster on the stage; but also of a growing resentment at the pressure. All work and no play was making Orson a very grumpy boy. He wanted to have *fun*; instead he had to work. Why had it all become so difficult? His relationship with Meredith gave him a sort of encouragement; the two naughty boys who had to be broken up. They played truant together. The Director As Truant would make an interesting, if brief, study, Welles being pretty well the only instance in recorded history. The director, if he does nothing else, simply has to be there, and he has to be there on time. Punctuality is not merely the politeness of directors; it is their raison d'être. They create the rhythm, the attitudes, the energy of the enterprise. On *Five Kings*, Welles was abdicating from that crucial responsibility.

Houseman adds an interesting gloss: he believed Welles to be involved in competitive debauchery with his own dead father: 'having demonstrated his superiority as an artist and a public figure, he must now defeat his rival on his own grounds – that of Champagne Charley, the man about town . . . it was as though he was determined to bury the ghost of Richard Welles, once and for all, under the mass of his own excesses.' If there was a ghost spurring him on, it is much more likely to have been that of his mother, demanding more and better work from him, refusing to allow him to derive satisfaction from his achievements; the excess was an attempt to escape from that nagging inner voice. Houseman's description of the scale of his indulgence details the meals, each one a feast; the nightly consumption of one and two bottles of whiskey or brandy; the sexual prowess 'which was reported in statistical detail . . . also, apparently, immense'. A final detail of Houseman's is striking: Welles had bought himself a huge new apartment on East

57th Street, replete with stained glass windows, balcony and monumental fireplace, filled, Houseman says, with enormous furniture: an odd preview of Charles Foster Kane's 'Xanadu'. The whole catalogue suggests someone who on the one hand needed to lose himself, on the other to make himself feel bigger. In fact all he succeeded in was becoming bigger – not feeling it.

Eventually (a week later than planned; Baltimore had been dropped) the technical period in Boston arrived: now everything would fall into place. But of course, the precise opposite happened. Jean Rosenthal and her team were as well prepared as they could be; her lighting plot was as thorough as she could make it without Welles's input. The set was up, and it seemed to be more or less as conceived. However, due to one of a thousand failures of communication, its basic colour had been changed from burgundy to silvery-grey without Millia Davenport, the costume designer, having been notified. She had based the costumes on silver and peach – disastrous against the new colour scheme; virtually every costume had to be remade, dyed or altered in some way. But this was as nothing compared to the gradual realisation that the show, which had never been run from beginning to end, would last about five and a half hours. Panic cutting was immediately undertaken. The forty-six scenes of the three-act show were reduced to thirty-two; entire characters and sub-plots were axed. These cuts, designed to maintain the narrative line, failed however to take into account the turntable, whose moves had been plotted in some detail, linked to particular lines in the dialogue, and now flicked restlessly back and forward, sometimes changing position every thirty seconds. On stage the chaos was complete. The stage management attempted to try out the innumerable mortars required for the show's many explosions while actors ran through battle scenes, putting their crossbow classes to the test; arrows flew everywhere, mostly landing in the auditorium into which smoke from the mortars was now belching, while the turntable proved to be totally out of control, either creeping round with infuriating slowness or suddenly whizzing manically off in the opposite direction.

Lighting rehearsals, scheduled for ten in the morning, started at midnight. Welles hurled himself at his task with manic energy. Joseph Hardy, then a Boston drama student, slipped away from his job at the Hide-A-Way Restaurant, hoping to catch a glimpse of him in person. 'Welles, looking like a large moon-faced boy about six foot two inches was bellowing orders. He shouted *Stop that hammering!* in such a roar that everyone cringed. When a girl assistant entered from the wings with a problem he embraced her passionately looking aloft and shocking a New England boy of twenty. Welles then stepped into the orchestra and took a belt from a whiskey bottle, barking commands.' He demanded a further postponement of the opening; Houseman, under severe financial pressure from the Theatre Guild (who had set an absolute ceiling of $10,000 on expenditure before opening), refused; Welles threw a telephone at him. He was, understandably, on the edge of complete hysteria. When one of the actors complained because he kept the company waiting forty minutes while he talked to Meredith, he threw a stool at him. But it was Houseman who bore the brunt of the worst tantrums. Not knowing that Welles had expressly forbidden it, he ordered the prop department to put dry ice in Falstaff's tankard to simulate mulled wine. Finding it, and finding that Houseman had ordered it, Welles fell to the floor accusing Houseman of having finally succeeded in poisoning him. He then screamed for milk, swigged large quantities of it, spat it up all over the floor, and was finally driven back to the Ritz-Carlton 'having achieved,' Houseman drily notes, 'his real objective, which was, once again, to avoid rehearsing the second act.'

In these situations, the nightmare eventually gives way to mere disaster. Somehow, the show opens; and then – sometimes, but not always – the disaster can be worked on. Very occasionally, it is turned into a triumph. This was not the pattern of *Five Kings*. The opening night at the Colonial Theatre in Boston was a semi-disaster; it never got very much better, despite a great deal of work by Welles and the company. The show in Boston started as badly as it could have done from a technical point of view. Lawrence Langner wrote an account of it in *The Magic Curtain* which takes more delight in the misfortune than he may have felt at the time. He describes the unhappy Robert Speaight making his first entrance – the first moment of the show – in total darkness. A spotlight eventually appeared, but never on him. He spent the whole of the Prologue running around the forestage, in pursuit of the light. In the midst of this, a brilliant light suddenly went on behind the silk curtain, revealing the silhouette of a dozen extras strapping on their codpieces. The light went out as suddenly as it had gone on, leaving the Boston audience rubbing its eyes. At this point, according to Dick Barr, an old lady in the front row urgently beckoned the actor. Thoroughly confused, he leaned towards her. 'Please,' she said, 'would you hand this note to Mr Meredith?' Langner continues: 'his prologue ultimately over, he tried to get back onto the revolving stage again, which transported him to the wings in imminent peril of his life. The traveller curtains were then drawn open, disclosing a large group of stage hands running off the stage, after which the play proper began.'

This first scene, over the corpse of Richard II, and the first Boar's Head scene leading into the robbery went smoothly and effectively enough. At Speaight's next entrance, he found the light but lost his page in the book from which he was reading; having found it and completed his narration, he avoided the turntable, walking instead along the forestage, from which there was, alas, no exit. 'By the time he tried to struggle through, the curtains were flung back and covered him in his corner. The next time the curtains were drawn together, Speaight was revealed crouching in the corner.' Trying to escape, he broke through the curtains, but by now the turntable was revolving, so, to avoid being struck again by scenery, the desperate actor leaped off the forestage into the orchestra pit, to the delighted applause of the audience, who from that point on broke into merry smiles at his every appearance, in anticipation of further catastrophe. The smile would soon be on the other side of their faces. People in the front rows fled as the turntable whizzed round at increasingly alarming speed, hurling pieces of wooden scenery and flaming arrows into their laps; at one point, it moved so swiftly that extras were thrown off it and into the wings. Reversing Karl Marx's axiom about great events always recurring, the first time as tragedy, the second time as farce, *Five Kings* was like a tragic re-run of *Horse Eats Hat.* All the carefully rehearsed calamities of that show returned, but for real. Small wonder that by the time the traveller curtain had travelled its last – 12.20 a.m., four and a quarter hours after the show had begun – the auditorium was less full than at the beginning. The curtain call, however, was effusive – partly orchestrated by Gertrude Lawrence and her *Skylark* company who were in the audience. 'Not until Mr Welles, still wearing the flesh of Falstaff, expressed appreciation and voiced apology,' reported *The New York Times*, 'were his admirers content to depart. By all tokens, they would have remained if his *Five Kings* had been raised to ten or a dozen.' It was one of those evenings, characteristic of the preview period and the out-of-town tour, where the audience, though aware of problems and shortcomings, feels that it has been on a long journey with the performers; that it has climbed Everest with them.

The reviews were on the whole generous in overlooking the running problems ('when practice oils up the mechanics of the revolving stage, those thirty-two scenes will be gone with the wind before you can say *Five Kings*') and by no means unanimously unenthusiastic. 'FIVE KINGS EXCITING FOR WORLD PREMIER AUDIENCE' said the *Boston Evening American*'s Peggy Doyle: 'If they don't stop him, the fat boy of Broadway is going to make Shakespeare competition for *Hellzapoppin*. He is a director-producer to reckon with and his motion-picture technique in the handling of this fast-paced production with the chorus or interlocutor in place of subtitles, an inspiration.' The cinematic quality of the production was lost on no one. The chief fascination for most reviewers was Welles's Falstaff: Miss Doyle was transported. 'We wouldn't change an eyelash shading his rheumy eye. He is magnificently lusty and splendidly vulgar, and when he is practising his inveterate habit of playing on words, robustly comic. The wonder of it is that this voluminous old bag of wind and wit is actually a handsome, 23-year-old youth under his blowsy gray wig and filthy ragtag garments.' There was more wonder from Miss Doyle's colleague, L.A. Sloper, despite reservations: 'There are moments when mannerisms intrude. Mr Welles has an odd habit of dividing his sentences abruptly in the middle, without reference to meaning or to dramatic effect.' He was particularly enthusiastic about 'something human and something pathetic that endears him to us. This human quality and this pathos were deftly caught by Mr Welles.' He describes a moment that throws us twenty-five years ahead to the film *Chimes at Midnight*. 'There was a touching dignity in the quiet way in which Sir John turns to speak with Shallow of the money he owes him, and then leaves the stage, his vast bulk accompanied only by the tiny figure of his page. This was the high point,' says Mr Sloper, in a gentle allusion to the length of the show, 'of as much of the presentation as I was able to see last night.'

That, as they say, was the end of the good news. John K. Hutchens, the formidable critic of the *Boston Evening Transcript*, weighed in, pulling no punches: 'To this courier, just back from Agincourt, it seems a ponderous marathon without style or particular point of view and utterly lacking in the magic with which this same Mercury Theatre once finely honored the bard in *Caesar*. Circus is no casual word for it.' Nor was he impressed by Welles: 'Mr Welles is simply not funny here. His humor, such as it is, does not bubble up out of the great Falstaffian heart. It is laconic and mechanical.' Even Hutchens, though, was struck by the pathos he brought to the renunciation scene. Praising Meredith and Speaight (but not John Emery: 'having shouted himself hoarse, he was not at his best') he concluded 'when it is all over, you find yourself wishing that they had done one play instead of three, and had done it three times as well'.

Or had six months to rehearse it, perhaps. From now until the show was finally closed down, Welles never ceased trying to pull *Five Kings* together. This was, after all, only the first leg of an out-of-town tour. The New York press was hovering. *Variety*, in its brass tacks way, had already passed judgement: 'Orson Welles has bitten off a big hunk in his production of *Five Kings*, and he will have to do a lot of chewing during the tryout here.' Its prescription for success was to cut more. The *Times* was troubled by the turntable: 'Like Ol' Man River, it threatens to engulf the show as it still keeps rollin' along.' *Time* was witty, too, but more sceptical: 'What might have been a tour de force jumps so fast from one thing to another as to be a non-sequitur de force. *Five Kings* covers Shakespeare as a two-day Cook's tour covers England: 8.45 visit Mistress Quickly's Inn. See Falstaff, Prince Hal, Bardolph, Poins. 9.31: Good view from the train (no time to get off) of the Justice Shallow country. 9.58: Trip to Shrewsbury. See Hotspur killed.'

The verdict was unanimous: the show was too long and too incident-packed. The inherent difficulty for Welles in working on the show was that if he addressed the first problem – the length – he compounded the second: the relentlessly episodic text. Each scene was already passing too quickly to be savoured. Shorten a scene, and it would be over before it had begun. By the end of the Boston run he had managed to cut the show down to two acts, to be played in three and a half hours. This was still too long, both for audiences and in terms of overtime payments to stage-hands (who earned, in a figure quoted in the press, an enormous $5,700 for the sixth week of onstage rehearsals), and there was no marked gain in focus or narrative coherence. The show moved to Washington, where the headlines were more affirmative (FIVE KINGS IS VITAL, LIVING DRAMA; FIVE KINGS IS DRAMA OF UNIQUE DESIGN). But the financial position was desperate. The revised tour schedule (Pittsburgh, Detroit, Chicago) had been abandoned; only Philadelphia remained. His relationship with the Guild hung by a thread. The costs of the show were increasing by leaps and bounds, having already exceeded the original $40,000 budget by $25,000, and the returns at the box office were unremarkable. Welles himself (having taken a cut in salary to $150) had poured thousands of his own dollars into the show in Boston and was now desperately trying to raise money by any means he could. (The one person who offered to invest in the show was his friend Toots Shor; Welles refused to let him risk his New York restaurant. A show is just a show, after all, but a *restaurant* . . .) Unsuccessful in his efforts, he attempted to release what was left of his father's legacy, not due until May 1940; Dr Bernstein was adamantly opposed, nor would the bank contemplate it.

The *Five Kings* company now began rumbling ominously. Press interest in the crisis was keen, provoking a Welles Problem piece in the *Washington Daily News*. Under the headline THEATRE GUILD AND WELLES MAY PHFFT, IT'S REPORTED, Katherine Hillyer wrote: 'Not only are certain members of the *Five Kings* company growing more allergic to 23-year-old director Orson Welles every day, according to reliable report, but the puff-faced prodigy is also in hot water with the Theatre Guild, sponsors of the production . . . backstage ruffs are constantly being raised when Welles turns what the actors call prima donna, and they growl that while insisting on long rehearsals he offers little constructive advice.' Her report doesn't stop at reporting company discontent, however. The whole world was obviously fed up with Welles. 'Meanwhile outsiders speculate on how long the beetle-browed youngster can keep delivering the goods in public. Some, while admitting it is wishful thinking, believe he will burn out by the time he is thirty, if not before. Others looking carefully at his exciting arrangements in the theatre listlessly predict a succession of rose-beds for baby to grow old in.' Hillyer had no doubt that he'd be around for 'a long, long time. And legendary stories will flourish until as many odd activities are attributed to him and as many amusing anecdotes piled up around his English bull-doggish head as there are about Alexander Woollcott and Dorothy Parker combined.'

She understated. Meanwhile, the show moved to Philadelphia. If Boston had been a nightmare, Philadelphia was the apocalypse. The Chestnut Theatre was in every way unsuited to the production. With company morale at its lowest, the actors were told that the theatre, never intended for large shows, had no dressing rooms for them. They had to use an adjacent theatre, taking a bridge to get them back into the Chestnut. The technical staff, equally exhausted after working all day and all night, found on arrival that the stage had a rake, which meant that they had to construct an anti-raked floor on which to put the turntable. Moreover the fire curtain was far upstage, which meant that the turntable had to be moved deeper, too; which was not only bad for sight-lines, it was a huge undertaking. Finally, when the turntable had been placed on its anti-raked floor and pushed twenty foot further upstage, it was plugged in; nothing happened. The theatre's electric current, it transpired, was not compatible with that required for the turntable, which duly had to be hand-cranked by a crew of two dozen audibly grunting and cursing stage-hands. It was of course very slow, with consequences the opposite of those in Boston: instead of falling off the stage into the audience's laps, the actors were left stranded in the middle of the stage, having run out of text. Eventually a converter was found; too late, too late.

A number of these problems – the rake, the current – should have been anticipated. The responsibility for this was, strictly speaking, neither Welles's nor Houseman's, but the technical director's: Jean Rosenthal's. In the prevailing madness, with the levels of exhaustion that she was having to cope with, it's hardly surprising that she slipped up. Langner had told her at the very outset that touring the set of *Five Kings* was impossible; simply making it work in each venue was an enormous task. To have to start all over again with each move must have been pulverising. Philadelphia's critics were less indulgent than those of Boston. 'The occasion consisted of a lot of Shakespeare, a lot of actors, a lot of revolutions of the merry-go-round stage,' wrote J.H. Keen in the *Philadelphia Daily News*. 'But for all of that, the presence of Franchot Tone, the sin-ema actor, in the audience caused more of a stir on the shady side of the footlights than most of the goings on on the sunny side . . . as a stage colossus, it is something to gape at as one might at a prehistoric creature brought back to life. But as an entertainment, it has something to be desired.'

More sober critics were even less encouraging. Sensenderfer of the *Bulletin* felt that the production was at best 'only a gigantic Shakespeare vaudeville . . . the company assembled performs earnestly though without particular inspiration. Welles himself is a fat and repulsive Falstaff with a greasy make-up and a voice like thick brown gravy. His humour is heavyhanded and his wit slow.' For Schloss in the *Record* 'its weakness appears to be in the blood – a condition indicated by a lack of stride and eloquence in its higher-pitched scenes and a certain juiciness in its comedy.' The problem, Schloss thought, lay with Meredith and Welles himself, both fatally miscast. 'Orson Welles's Falstaff hits nearer the mark than Meredith Prince. But it suffers from understatement. Mr Welles's great success with last year's modernised *Caesar* perhaps led him to essay Falstaff in a more realistic and casual mood than, say, Maurice Evans did last year.'

If Welles read his own notices this is perhaps the point at which he might have thrown the paper across the room. Schloss embarked on a detailed and for Welles excruciating comparison of the two actors. The Evans Falstaff laughed, to a degree, with his audience. 'Welles's Sir John, however, seldom came across the footlights to dig anyone in the ribs with his picturesque bawdiness. The lines were deliberately speeded-up and underplayed, in the interest, we suppose, of "modernising" the part. In Fat Jack's famous mock-heroic speech about honour, for example, a speech of broadest humors, Welles rattled the lines off as if he were mumbling a shamefaced catechism. The result was a sodden and witless Sir John. It is a little painful to report thus on one of the most brilliant young men in our theatre, especially since his performance had its moments . . . it appears that Mr Welles either understudied or mis-studied his part.' Schloss allowed Welles the touch of pathos that others had discerned: 'on the credit side, however, was the note of tragicomic pathos, a nice touch and . . . a new one of considerable plausibility and merit.' The *Inquirer* didn't mess around: 'To compare Orson Welles's Falstaff to Mr Evans's Falstaff, John Emery's Hotspur to Wesley Addy's Hotspur, Burgess Meredith's Prince Hal to Winston O'Keeffe's Prince of Wales or Mr Welles's coarse-keyed direction to the electrifying direction of Margaret Webster would be as unconscionable as it would be unkind.'

Better reviews might have given the show a chance, however slight, of surviving. As it was, it was on the most unreliable of life-support machines. Closure of the show on the Saturday after the notices had appeared instead of completing its allotted two weeks was narrowly but embarrassingly averted only by a passionate plea from the astonishingly named Mrs Favorite, Philadelphia representative of the Guild, who feared letting down her subscribers. The paper reports her public statement: 'with her distress of last week turning to a deep and bitter burn, Mrs Favorite said the Guild would consider another Orson Welles effort only "if he comes forth with something worthy of the Theatre Guild." ' There was a flicker of hope that Martin Beck might transfer the production as a World's Fair – 'summer show, that is' – attraction, then Lee Shubert was mentioned. 'According to latest reports, the Guild doesn't care what happens to Mr Welles, Mr Meredith and the *Five Kings*, as long as nobody wants any more money from the Guild.' Their last formal communication with the Mercury was being presented with a bill from the Ritz-Carlton Hotel covering repairs to chandeliers, venetian blinds and other items 'which our confreres, in the exuberance of their youth, had demolished'. Langner seemed as drily amused by this episode as by the entire experience, though determined – needless to say – not to repeat it ('After you and Orson Welles, no more geniuses,' he told Robert Lewis as he sacked him from *The Time of Your Life*). 'In spite of all the drawbacks, this contact with youth provided a refreshing interlude, and if any of us were complacent before the episode, we were shaken out of it by the time *Five Kings* was packed up and sent to the storehouse to await that day, yet to come, when Orson Welles will revive it.'

Houseman had long ago accepted the inevitable: the show would never reach New York. But Welles was possessed of a sort of frenzied determination to get it there, somehow, sometime. Herbert Drake was encouraged to go to Philadelphia to keep the embers of interest alive. 'The reports from the road,' he said, 'have evoked the usual drama column reports of mutiny, sabotage and more earnestness in the battle scenes than required by the script, so this department went down to see what was brewing in what sounded like an exciting production.' His report was independent enough to describe the production as it stood in somewhat unflattering terms: 'the play ambles its way through its schedule each night, like its notorious character, fat Jack Falstaff, stewing and fretting, heaving its ponderous way over the mechanical hurdles that the very momentum of the tour perpetuates.' Quite reasonably he continues 'You cannot adequately rehearse such a large-scale enterprise when you have to move from town to town and when the platform is one of those enormous revolving affairs which cover the whole stage floor and when the totalitarian chief in charge is further burdened with the incubus of a radio programme. What the problem boils down to is to find the time for those rehearsals.' After stating roundly that 'Orson Welles himself has developed 80 per cent of a truly great Falstaff', his parting flourish insists that *Five Kings* has 'all the earmarks of his directorial genius. The boy wonder can still pull the rabbit-hearted Falstaff out of the hat if the theatre will accommodate itself to his unusual operating methods.'

The staging might possibly have worked, given time. What certainly did work (as in the film) were the battle scenes. Martin Gabel attended the show after Welles had done a substantial amount of re-rehearsal, and he described what he saw in an interview in 1985. It was evidently as fresh in his mind as when he'd first seen it: 'Orson had a kind of No Man's Land onstage, a painted canvas looking like churned earth over mounds, and in the centre he had a single, leafless tree . . . as they began fighting, the stage started to revolve, and the music came in to support the fight. They fought on this stage as the knights of old must have fought – up hill and down dale, fighting it out. As the battle became more intense, the revolving stage went faster, the music approached a climax. And then finally when Hal stabbed Hotspur behind a huge mound, you heard the death cry of Hotspur, saw the flashing blade. The minute he was hit, the music stopped, the revolve stopped, everything stopped. And then, slowly, the revolve was brought round and Hotspur gave his death speech, lying prostrate below the mound. It was an absolutely perfect piece of work.' Drake, too, was thrilled by the fighting: 'the battle scenes are the best I ever saw on any stage . . . the scenes in which the Welles flair for spectacle is most adequately exhibited are the battles of Shrewsbury and Agincourt. He has exploding bombards, the usual banners and highly effective, if somewhat terrifying flights of arrows which fly across the stage and plink into the side drapes. Welles has ordered up the correct broadswords and bucklers, no pink-tea fencing for his princes and kings. They lay on with roundhouse swings and highly satisfactory clanging of claymores. The actor mortality will doubtless be high. The property room already had replaced more than a dozen broken swords, but it is worth the expenditure.'

Welles had concentrated on these physical scenes, as he always had, to the exclusion of psychological complexities. They could be made perfect; the complexities depended on the actor's discovery for himself of some inner meaning. This was more elusive. Moreover, he was still uncertain of the whole; dwelling on manageable parts like the battle sequences was an outlet for his energy. In a passionate analysis of what had gone wrong – with the Mercury, with their relationship, with *Five Kings* – Houseman wrote to Virgil Thomson: 'It fell on its face not through any difficulties of time or inadequate rehearsal, but because it was a half-baked, impure idea, in which size and "notions" took the place of love and thinking.' Jean Rosenthal wrote, more dispassionately but to equally devastating effect: 'all of us on the production staff had a fine time working on it, but no excitement ever reached the audience, even through the stars who supplemented the company, like Burgess Meredith. That really marvelous production was boring – catastrophic from an audience point of view, appalling, really – in spite of extraordinary moments.'

His passion for the show was intense and stayed with him, manifesting itself first in a stage show some twenty years later, then in a movie, both called *Chimes at Midnight*, and both (as the change of title suggests) concentrating more on the figure of Falstaff than on the political history in which he is a minor player. What was it about Falstaff that drew Welles to him? Not what attracted most actors of his period. The description of Maurice Evans's approach is fairly typical of most actors' conception of the character at the time: an aristocratic rogue, a lordly buffoon, over-fed, over-sexed, over the top – a comic figure, above all. Schloss, in his Philadelphia review, gave the standard line: Falstaff, to be Falstaff, needed 'a belch, a wink, and a soupçon of ham'.

Welles explicitly dissociated himself from that view: in an interview in the *Christian Science Monitor* before the Boston opening he said 'I will play him as a tragic figure. I hope, of course, he will be funny to the audience, just as he was funny to those around him. But his humor and wit were aroused merely by the fact that he wanted to please the prince. Falstaff, however, had the potential of greatness in him.' And the notices again and again comment on the pathos which he brings to the role. Thirty years later, he told Peter Bogdanovich, speaking of *Chimes at Midnight*, 'the closer I thought I was getting to Falstaff, the less funny he seemed to me. When I'd played him before, in the theatre, he seemed more witty than comical. And in bringing him to the screen, I found him only occasionally, and then only *deliberately*, a clown.' Certainly, no one found him very funny in *Five Kings* – and Welles liked to be funny, as the joshing about on his radio programmes testifies. Though scarcely endowed with natural comic flair, he could certainly have made his Falstaff funny: there is every opportunity in the text. But he chose not to. Usually, with Welles, it doesn't do to go too deeply into his performances; he brings his personality to them, adding superficial touches of colour: a nose here, an accent there, neither of which generally adhere too well. But Falstaff seems to have engaged him deeply, and the quality in the character that he instinctively relates to is his sadness.

Without delving too deeply into that inexhaustible character's lineage and symbolism, from Silenus and Ganesha, through Bes of Egypt and Ilya of the Slavs to the Japanese Ondeko-Za, nor following Auden's suggestion that he is both Lord of Misrule and 'comic symbol for the supernatural order of Charity', it is possible to say a couple of simple things about him: he is a drunkard, a trickster, a braggart, a womaniser, a gentleman and a charmer – and he is rejected by the person he loves most. It takes no trained psychologist to recognise the figure of Richard Head Welles in this description. There is a striking quotation from Niccolo Tucci quoted by Auden in his Falstaff essay, 'The Prince's Dog', which is full of resonance for Welles and his father: 'the death song of the drunkard

– it may go on for thirty years – goes more or less like this. "I was born a god, with the whole world in reach of my hands, lie now defeated in the gutter. Come and listen: hear what the world has done to me" . . . he may be unable to distinguish a person from a chair, but never an unprofitable lie from a profitable one. How could he see himself as a very insignificant entity in a huge world of others, when he sees nothing but himself spread over the whole universe.' Equally, it takes no great leap of imagination to understand why Welles engaged so intensely with the scene in which Falstaff is rejected by his surrogate son and former drinking companion: 'I know thee not, old man.'

Welles must have been aware, too, that he himself was going, far faster and more furiously, down the same path that had ended in his father's death at the age of fifty-five. Auden, in his essay, continues: 'the drunkard is unlovely to look at, intolerable to listen to, and his self-pity is contemptible. Nevertheless, as not merely a worldly failure but also a wilful failure, he is a disturbing image for the sober citizen. His refusal to accept the realities of this world, babyish as it may be, compels us to take another look at this world and reflect upon our motives for accepting it. The drunkard's suffering may be self-inflicted, but it is real suffering and reminds us of all the suffering in this world which we prefer not to think about because, from the moment we accept this world, we acquired our share of responsibility for everything that happens in it.' Welles was all too acutely aware of suffering in the world; he did 'prefer not to think about it'. Small wonder that he saw the character as tragic. Despite applying a mountain of padding made for him by the Firestone Rubber and Latex Company to his body and more mountains of make-up to his face, there is every reason to believe that this Falstaff and both the subsequent ones (in Belfast in 1960 and in Spain, on film, in 1965) are among the most personal performances he ever gave. In 1939, everything in the reviews suggests that he had not found how to integrate what he felt about the character with the text itself, his own or that of the play. When he started shaping the text entirely round Falstaff, his vision of the character began to fall into place.

But it was a long way from 1939 to 1965. Houseman was somehow prevailed upon to announce, somewhat querulously, that *as always intended* the show would definitely be revived in the fall, with some cast changes. The reporter was unable to contain his scepticism. 'Still, Welles would not accept defeat,' wrote Houseman. 'The scenery – all seventeen tons of it – was shipped to New York, where it was held in demurrage for several days at great expense while Orson made his last desperate bids for backing. Finally, he was forced to have it unloaded in a theatrical warehouse, where it lay, with the rest of the Mercury scenery, piling up storage charges for the next twenty years. As a final token of defiance, Orson announced that he was retaining his beard and would not shave it off until he had appeared as Falstaff on a New York stage.' (This was the beard that became notorious when he went to Hollywood.)

If Welles was kept going by his determination to get *Five Kings* to New York, Houseman had no such passion, nor any appetite to continue the turbulent partnership with Welles. 'Fatigue, humiliation, mutual reproaches and, through it all, our growing inability to communicate except in anger – all these were having their cumulative and corrosive effect on an association from which all affection seemed to have been drained and only self-interest (expressed at the moment by our weekly radio show) remained to bind us together.' Houseman, as always when he writes of Welles, is using the language of a love affair. This is not to impute homosexuality (though there is undoubtedly a complexity in that area which Houseman never explicitly acknowledges, while never censoring the words which give it away): collaboration of this sort is intense, personal, emotional, desperate in exactly the same way and to the same degree that a sexual relationship is. In his memoir, he is able to distance himself in stylish prose; at the time he was almost incoherent with loss and rage. 'The *Five Kings* year (since *Five Kings* pre-influenced and pre-distorted, or post-influenced and post-distorted every single thought and action of ours that season) found us fertile, successful, happy,' he wrote to Virgil Thomson the following year, 'foolish, perhaps, but in love with ourselves and each other and the theatre and the public . . . it left us tired to the point of sickness, loaded with debts and full of hatred and distrust of each other, of our audience, of our theatre – weary and full of fear and loathing for the whole business of producing plays in the theatre. And it left me, personally, without the excitement and, worst of all, without the faith which was, during its brief, brilliant career, the essential quality of the Mercury and before that 891 and before that *Macbeth*.' And, he might have added, the essential element of his relationship with Welles. He was writing to Thomson, specifically, because it was he who had given him his first taste of what he called 'work-in-the-theatre-by-those-who-have-faith-in-each-other'. Now he began to doubt whether the youth he had plucked from Katharine Cornell's company, for whom and with whom he had foreseen a brilliant and never-ending future, was not going seriously wrong, running out of hand both personally and artistically. 'To tell the story of *Five Kings* is like trying to record the terminal stages of a complicated and fatal disease,' he writes in *Run-Through*. 'The name of our disease was success – accumulating success that had little to do with the quality of our work but seemed to proliferate around the person of Orson Welles with a wild, monstrous growth of its own.' The crucial phrase is 'of its own'. He had planted the seed; but now things were out of his control.

The Mercury, as an idea, was now well and truly dead; as a name, it continued to front Welles's activities for many years. The only remaining formal association between Welles and Houseman was the radio programme (which Houseman had held together for the duration of *Five Kings*) which would shortly go into its summer recess. The repertory was distinctly lowbrow: every Friday night, after the show, Welles would abandon the inscrutable horrors of the turntable and the labyrinthine complexities of the fifteenth century, for the worlds of Dodie Smith, Philip Duffield Stong or P.C. Wren (in this last – an adaptation, of course, of *Beau Geste* – Welles played Beau to Laurence Olivier's John). Light relief indeed. Radio does have the tremendous advantage for an actor that it is possible in that medium to play roles that you could by no stretch of the imagination essay on stage; thus Welles played Elyot in *Private Lives* (opposite Gertrude Lawrence) and Vincent Price's old role of Prince Albert, opposite Helen Hayes as Queen Victoria. He returned to *Les Misérables*, this time as Javert to Walter Huston's Valjean, and played the Stage Manager in his old friend Thornton Wilder's *Our Town*. The level of radiophonic invention was commensurately lower with the literary and imaginative level of the writing; what can you do with *Private Lives* on the radio but do it, very, very well? His input during the run of *Five Kings* was confined to his own performance, which, almost literally, he phoned in. Paul Stewart ran the programmes very efficiently, and Houseman produced them with skill and taste. The former spark was largely missing; this proved no barrier either for the audience or for the sponsors, both of whom were highly satisfied. The programme became one of the most successful on the air. One of the few shows to stretch the medium a little had been the adaptation of William Archer's *The Green Goddess*, with Welles in the role written for George Arliss, a preposterous and rather offensive melodrama which gave the author, who had spent his life fighting the genre of which it is a particularly abject example, an enormous financial success at the end of his career. Its aeroplanes and mountainside temples, the crucial telegraphic equipment, bands of mysteriously appearing soldiers all made for enjoyable radio hokum. When *Five Kings* finally collapsed, Welles impulsively decided to take the play on the road in the most peculiar circumstances.

What exactly it was that made him think *The Green Goddess* suitable for performance on stage as part of a vaudeville act is hard to fathom, nor what drew him, a good liberal, to the part of that Nietzschean nabob, the Rajah of Rukh, with his wicked designs on the body of the hapless white woman stranded in the mountains and the lives of any other whites who might happen to be kicking around. He did, it is true, have a weakness throughout his career for epigrammatic villains, smoothly wicked men whose perfect manners conceal an abyss of wickedness, in which case the Rajah must have suited him to the ground: 'I don't know if I care very much for the millions that you speak of. Life is a weed that grows as fast as death mows it down.' Nor did his love of melodrama ever desert him. *The Green Goddess*, however, a pastiche written in 1920, is really scraping the bottom of the barrel in both departments. This, none the less, is what he chose to do next: a tour of the RKO Orpheum Vaudeville Circuit with Archer's absurd farrago reduced to twenty minutes, of which five minutes – continuing the experiment he was forced to abandon in *Too Much Johnson* – was on film. This footage (assembled from stock on film from libraries) depicted the aeroplane crash with which the play begins; it has disappeared. Four times a day, with a full orchestra underscoring the show, he and a few remaining Mercurians slogged through selected purple passages: 'I knew it! You are playing with me! But the confiding barbarian is not so simple as you imagine. No woman has ever tried to fool me that has not repented it. You think, when you have to pay up, you will fob me off with your dead body. Let me tell you, I have no use for you dead – I want you with all the blood in your veins, with all the pride in that damned sly brain of yours. I want to make my plaything of your beauty, my mockery of your pride' and so on, ad libitum. A handful of people bent on entertainment sat in silent bewilderment in the vast spaces of the Palace Theatre in Chicago and the Stanley in Pittsburgh. In both places, there were technical mishaps (the crucial public address system broke down; the film was run backwards); from time to time, the ailing John Barrymore – already, Welles believed, in the grip of Alzheimer's disease – would drop by and take over one of the roles, able to remember even less of it than he could of the role he was playing at a nearby theatre. Welles himself, amused by the absence of an audience, decided to play the

Rajah as a different actor at each performance, which led to some tart comment in *The New York Times*: 'when and if *Five Kings* actually materialises, Mr Welles is now in a position to add even more novelty to the presentation by doing Falstaff as Raymond Massey might play him, or as Jimmy Durante would do it, or maybe Victor Moore.' They thought he was behaving idiotically, childishly, irresponsibly. He was. He was behaving like a schoolboy playing hooky – he who was supposed to be the Head Boy, the School Captain. The sense of Great Things being expected of him was oppressive.

It is difficult to imagine the state of mind which led Welles to embark on this particular lunacy. Floored by *Five Kings*, he might have been expected to retreat and review his situation. Instead, he leaped off in an altogether unpredictable direction. Obviously, he thought it would make money. Equally obviously, only someone seriously out of touch could possibly think that. Melodrama, whether spoofed or not, was quite dead by 1939. The 1920's sense of liberation from the values of the Victorian and Edwardian past from which they had just emerged made parodied melodrama (as in *The Drunkard*, or the Grand Guignol seasons in Paris, London and New York) naughtily daring: sending up Mummy and Daddy. By the thirties, the thrill had long passed. Vaudeville itself was now in terminal decline. Most of the great houses had been converted into cinemas showing films starring those troupers who had so recently topped the bill live. In its great days, vaudeville had lured the biggest stars of Broadway to perform twenty-minute digests of their hits; but the age of these 'tab' versions (tabs being the curtains in front of which they were played) was over, too. Besides, when Alla Nazimova and other great stars had brought their trimmed-down triumphs to the vaudeville stage, they were exactly that – triumphs that were closely associated with them. Had Welles concocted – as had originally been requested – a twenty-minute version of *The War of the Worlds*, the box office would have been mobbed.

There was another factor, never to be discounted with Welles: sentimentality. He had accompanied his father to the great Chicago vaudeville theatres (including, of course, the Palace) as a child at exactly the moment of its greatest peak in the mid-twenties, when, as he often recalled, Houdini, W.C. Fields and George M. Cohan were topping the bill. He would go backstage with his father, whose intimate relationship with the chorus girls led to introductions to the stars. This was the magic of the theatre for Welles – not Broadway, still less the Mercury. So, as he told Barbara Leaming, he was thrilled to have his own dressing room 'with three rooms and bathrooms and a grand piano'. The interesting phrase that he uses elsewhere recurs in his conversations with Leaming: 'it's *real* stardom in vaudeville.' The sense of having actually arrived – of being *someone* – remained as elusive as ever, this quixotic venture having simply added to the humiliation already inflicted in ample measure by *Five Kings*. Of course, both ventures (despite some marginal reporting in the New York press) had taken place out of town, and concerned a small section of the population: theatre-goers.

The wheels of celebrity grind surprisingly slowly; to the world at large – excluding the theatre-going public of Boston, Philadelphia, Chicago and Pittsburgh, and not many of them – he was the young man made up to look like God Almighty on the cover of *Time* magazine, the triumphantly audacious perpetrator of *The War of the Worlds* and the suave frontman and leading actor of *The Campbell Playhouse*. More distantly, he was the head of something called the Mercury Theatre, which had done *Julius Caesar* in jackboots – still was doing *Julius Caesar* in jackboots, for all they knew. While Welles was crawling round the cities of the East Coast and the Middle West, his theatrical dreams collapsing all around him, on the other side of the country, unbeknown to him, the moguls of Hollywood were trying to figure out how best to deploy his talents.

There was no lack of interest in him. Far from it: from as early as *Julius Caesar* the New York office of RKO had noted that he was 'such a brilliant talent that he cannot be ignored'. The studios' overtures suggest that they were uncertain of how to use him. In 1937, David O. Selznick, having seen *Doctor Faustus*, invited him to head his story department, a bold and imaginative notion which Welles naturally, and rightly, turned down because, he wrote to Selznick, it would not 'represent a step toward my ultimate aim: my profession of actor-director'. Warner Bros were equally uncertain as to what kind of an actor he was: that same year of 1937, they approached him about playing a role in *The Adventures of Robin Hood*: either Friar Tuck or King Richard – which is like wondering if an actor would be better as Hamlet or Polonius. The offer was turned down on financial grounds, but Welles had no intention of joining the ranks of young hopefuls in Hollywood; above all, he was not going to mortgage his soul to a studio. The contract system was now at its height; those few actors who had attempted to defy it had been cast out of the celluloid Garden of Eden. Hollywood represented in his eyes an abject deal; you surrendered your freedom – as an artist, as an individual – for gold, whether you were an actor, a director or a writer, and he was all three. As far as he could see, in 1937 the only place where he could exercise his 'profession of actor-director' was the theatre. Nothing less would satisfy him. In motion pictures, the only practising member of that profession was Charles Chaplin, who was a case apart. Erich von Stroheim, the only other serious contender, had been effectively debarred from directing since the débâcle of *Queen Kelly* ten years earlier, his career an awful example of the punishment meted out to those who refuse to compromise artistically – or financially. Small encouragement there. Above all, Welles was nervous of the figure of the producer, controlling, authorising, permitting, refusing. This was merely Houseman writ large. He was all for father-figures, until they told him what to do. Then he was off. So he held the moguls at arm's length, while graciously allowing himself to be, from time to time, screen-tested.

Not that he was uninterested in the movies. Despite his avowed commitment to the theatre, his statements on the subject were becoming gloomier and gloomier, while he began to speak more and more warmly about film. 'The theatre has lost its narrative style,' he jotted down in his *Lecture Notes on Acting* of 1938. 'The novel took over,' he somewhat questionably continued. 'The novel exhausted itself and the movie took over from there. The movies can do narrative, character, ideas, mood – unquestionably the most flexible form imaginable.' He was coming round to it, no question. At one of the early peaks of the Mercury's success, he had announced the filming of all the productions, and of course *Too Much Johnson* had given him a practical taste of the excitement that filming can bring. He simply wanted it on his terms. His continuing resistance to all blandishments made the Hollywood headlines. ORSON WELLES GIVING METRO THE PIX CHILL, reported *Variety* at the end of 1937. Successful tests had caused MGM to tender him 'a juicy offer' drooled *Variety*, with 'company toppers seeing strong possibilities. Player, however, prefers the legit and nixed offers that would bring him permanently to Hollywood.' Welles, the report continued, had even held out against an offer of a contract which would release him for a few months every year for stage work. He said he 'preferred it the other way round, a few months for pictures and the remainder of his time on the stage'.

The studio that pursued him with the greatest ardour was RKO, fittingly enough, since its existence – its very name – was the outcome of a liaison between the interests of radio and celluloid, which Welles, in turn, was ideally placed to embody. Radio-Keith-Orpheum was the brainchild of David Sarnoff, head of the Radio Corporation of America. It was Sarnoff who created the slogan 'A Radio Picture' which appeared under the logo of a radio transmitter prefacing every RKO film. Eager to link up his sound technology with movies as they rushed headling into talkies, he had bought into the Robertson-Cole Film Company, at the same time acquiring the Keith-Albee-Orpheum circuit of vaudeville theatres for conversion into cinemas – a brilliant manoeuvre, linking technology with production and production with distribution. A TITAN IS BORN, said the headlines. However, as Richard Jewell observes in *The RKO Story*, the new company failed to develop either a guiding philosophy or continuity of management for any length of time. 'As a result, RKO's films tended to reflect the personality of the individual in charge of the studio at any given time – and since this time was always short, a dizzying number of diverse individuals became involved in RKO's creative affairs over the years, and the pictures never evolved an overall style unique to the studio.' In the late thirties, RKO's latest 'individual in charge of the studio', George J. Schaefer, had instituted radical and ambitious changes in policy, seeking to turn it into a 'prestige' studio. Welles, in one form or another, was a catch he was determined to net.

Schaefer enters Welles's life in around 1938; as one of the most important instruments of his destiny, he is worth a little consideration. Fifty years old when he took over RKO, he had been in the business for twenty-five years, almost as long as it had existed. Starting as Louis J. Selznick's secretary, he was, said his obituary in *Variety*, 'the last of the old line of top-flier industry chieftains who were the architects of the distribution system'. Sales were his sphere, and he was as successful in building them as anyone in Hollywood; as general manager and vice-president of United Artists, his work in selling their output in 1938 ensured that he alone of the senior management survived Sam Goldwyn's putsch of that year. Wisely, he took his leave of the organisation to take over from Leo Spitz – once Capone's lawyer – as Corporate President (business head) of RKO. 'A bulldog of a man,' as *Variety* said, 'who was often referred to in fear and admiration as The Tiger', Schaefer made it clear that he wanted total control, soon ousting Pandro S. Berman, one of the master producers of the age, and taking over as production chief himself. He proved to be no crass front-office man. If anything his plans erred on the side of art: embarking on a huge spending spree, he bought up as many literary properties, stars and directors as he could, often in one-sided deals which disadvantaged the studio. Similarly (since he had no artistic ambitions himself) he encouraged the development of unit production, engaging independent producers like Sam Goldwyn and Erich Pommer to work under RKO's banner. It was a dazzling burst of confidence from a studio which – only just about to emerge from receivership – had had a rocky, if intermittently glorious, history. It was as part of that surge of expansion that Schaefer courted Welles.

He was at first reluctant to consider Welles's directorial ambitions, seeking to win him with ever-better acting roles. First he offered him the part of Quasimodo in the forthcoming *Hunchback of Notre Dame* to be directed by Dieterle; like Robert Morley before him, he turned it down, as he turned down *Dr Jekyll and Mr Hyde*. The stakes were rising substantially, but Welles stuck to his guns. Actor-director or nothing. He was very careful, too, about the choice of parts. He would presumably have relished playing either Quasimodo or Jekyll/Hyde on stage; on screen he knew that character acting was only rarely compatible with stardom. He had thought a great deal about the archetypal quality possessed by stars; he was not going to be the next Laughton or Muni, dependent on their vehicles. Schaefer's board would have been only too delighted for Welles to fight *The War of the Worlds* all over again, but he wisely steered clear of that, too. Schaefer was sympathetic; Welles, he told the board, 'does not want to be the horror man'. MGM, also slightly nervous of offering him an assignment as a director, instead talked to him about being script consultant and leading actor in a film version of the FTP's great success, *It Can't Happen Here*; once war was engaged in Europe, the project folded because of nervousness about offence to Germany and Italy.

Back to RKO, where Welles's recently-appointed agent, Albert Schneider of Columbia Management, was playing a brilliant game of brinkmanship. He was able to do so, since his client (though certainly in the long run determined to make films) was in mid-1939 frantically trying to get *Five Kings* into town; this was both more real and more pressing to him than dealing with Hollywood. A glimmer of possible backing for *Five Kings* enabled Schneider to cable Schaefer: 'new developments regarding welles make it impossible for him to consider films at this time'. Like any suitor, Schaefer became more ardent with every rejection, until finally, backed by Arnold Weissberger's legal brilliance, the masterly Schneider secured a contract for his client (in the form of Mercury Productions) the like of which no one in Hollywood has ever had before or since – not financially (the $150,000 he was to earn for each film was not an uncommon fee, and somewhat less than the highest fliers,

Hitchcock or Wyler, might expect) but in terms of control. 'I didn't want money; I wanted authority,' said Welles, years later. He was to act in, write, direct and produce a film a year. To his 'profession of actor-director' he had added not only writing but producing. This was another sensational development. There was some controversy during this period about what was called 'the one-man show' film: the movies of Capra and Preston Sturges were supreme examples; Walt Disney's, of course, even more so. Chaplin and now Welles were the only actors to be included in this category; the crucial element in their one-man showmanship being that they produced their own films. In other words, they were responsible for every aspect of the picture, from beginning to end; they were, to translate a later phrase of film theory, the 'authors' of them, not merely supervisors of the actual shooting. This has now become the standard definition of the director's role: he will involve himself at every level; it is *his* film, even though he is not nominally the producer.

Directors in Hollywood in 1939 had a much less exalted function, and were expected to fulfil the requirements of the front office in terms of casting, design, even the manner in which the film was lit and shot. Studios had a 'look', a set of values which the director was expected to reproduce. David O. Selznick – an independent producer who nevertheless exerted total control over his own pictures – and Alfred Hitchcock, for example, had a classic producer–director relationship in their work on *Rebecca*: scarcely a page of the screenplay goes uncommented on by Selznick. He is particularly fierce about what he calls 'movie-ization' of the original. This sort of relationship is what Welles wanted above all to avoid. Pathologically resistant to authority imposed from above, he was intent on creating (in whatever medium) the equivalent of a Wagnerian gesamtkunstwerk: something using all the means of expression at his disposal which he would then personally unify into a piece of work bearing the unmistakable imprint of his own personality. It may be no good, he was often to say, in one form or another, of his work, but at least it's mine. More than anything else, more than any idea or concept, more than any human feeling or interpretation of experience, this is what Welles stood for: the insistence on imprinting his own personality on his work. It had been true in the theatre; it was true on the radio; it would most certainly be true in movies. And he had the contract to make it possible.

The all-important feature of that famous contract was the sensational phrase 'The distributor shall be entitled to confer with the producer on the final cutting and editing of each of the pictures prior to the delivery thereof, *but the control of such cutting shall vest in the producer.*' Everything in the history of Hollywood during the previous twenty years had been directed towards devolving power into the hands of the studio bosses. This centralisation was not to last for even so much as another decade, but in 1939 it seemed as if the moguls' success in consolidating power was unassailable, and the approval of the final cut was the symbolic embodiment of that power. Schaefer surrendered it to Welles, a stranger in Hollywood who had never directed a movie in his life before. The moguls must have heard the tumbrils rolling.

Part Three

QUADRUPLE THREAT

CHAPTER EIGHTEEN

Hollywood/ *Heart of Darkness*

'JUST SIGNED!' screamed RKO's ad in the trade press. 'Orson Welles . . . – brilliant actor and director, to make one picture a year . . . and WHAT a picture is planned for his first!' Hollywood failed to be set alight; was, in fact, highly sceptical, not to say resentful, from the beginning, not only at the presumptuousness of this outsider from the theatre being given the run of the coop, but at the bombardment of publicity which accompanied him. Hollywood's feelings about him are brilliantly embodied in the Pat Hobby story, 'Pat Hobby and Orson Welles', which Scott Fitzgerald wrote for *Esquire* magazine shortly after Welles's arrival. Hobby is a washed-up screenwriter. ' "Who's this Welles?" Pat asked of Louie, the studio bookie. "Every time I pick up a paper, they go on about this Welles." "You know, he's that beard," explained Louis. "Sure, I know he's that beard, you couldn't miss that, but what credit's he got? What's he done to draw one hundred and fifty grand a picture?" ' Unable even to get onto the studio lot to scrounge some lunch, Hobby broods darkly about Welles. 'Welles was in; Hobby was out. Never before had the studio been barred to Pat and though Welles was on another lot it seemed as if his large body, pushing in brashly from nowhere, had edged Pat out the gate . . . Orson Welles had no business edging him out of this. Orson Welles belonged with the rest of the snobs back in New York.' Hobby finally gets a lift from Mr Marcus, a mogul, and begs him for a pass to the studio lot. Marcus is on his way to meet 'this new Orson Welles that's in Hollywood'. 'Pat's heart winced. There it was again – that name, sinister and remorseless, spreading like a dark cloud over all his skies. "Mr Marcus," he said so sincerely that his voice trembled, "I wouldn't be surprised if this Orson Welles is the biggest menace that's come to Hollywood for years. He gets a hundred and fifty grand for a picture and I wouldn't be surprised if he was so radical that you would have to have all new equipment and start all over again like you did with sound in 1928." ' He had entered Hollywood's collective subconscious, a real bogeyman.

Who needed him? was the widespread reaction. Hollywood

was, in 1939, at its dazzling zenith. The system had perfected itself under those thugs the moguls, who somehow, despite their artistic intellectual, moral and social inadequacies, had got something very right. The most remarkable actors, writers, designers, technicians and craftsmen in the world had been lured into their gilded prisons in Hollywood and given the wherewithal to practise their skills in almost ideal circumstances. For this privilege, their loss of artistic and personal freedom seemed a small price to pay. Both the industry and its leaders were, with rare brave exceptions, happy with the status quo; it was working – why fix it? Then along comes Welles: Mr Fix-It in person. Welles later stated that established directors like Ford and Wyler had been pleasant to him; it was the producers who caused all the trouble 'because if I could do all those things, then what is the need for a producer? It exploded the Thalberg myth, who is in my view the biggest villain in the history of Hollywood. Because he erected the myth of the producer and everybody believed it.' This belief confirmed Welles's loathing of authority, but the truth is that initially, at any rate, the industry felt threatened at every level, and insulted. Why should someone – a twenty-three-year-old someone – with no experience of film-making whatever be extended conditions that were denied to the cream of the movie community? CAN IT BE THE BEARD? one periodical satirically enquired, while Gene Lockhart, jester laureate of the Hollywood Masquers' Club, wrote a savagely funny ditty which encapsulated the scorn and dislike that Welles provoked, providing him with a nickname which stuck like a limpet.

LITTLE ORSON ANNIE

Little Orson Annie's come to our house to play
An' josh the motion pitchurs up and skeer the stars away
An' shoo the Laughtons off the lot an' build the sets
  an' sweep
An' wind the film an' write the talk an' earn her
  board-an'-keep;
An' all of us other actors, when our pitchur work is done,
We set around the Brown Derby bar an' has the
  mostest fun,
A-listenin' to the me-tales 'at Annie tells about,
An' the Gobblewelles'll git YOU
Ef you DON'T WATCH OUT!

This is concentrated malice, and it was not the only instance.

It might have destroyed a less determined man. Welles's uncommon gift of fearlessness – his sheer courage – was sorely strained throughout his time in Hollywood; whatever black moods he may have endured privately, he never gave any public impression of being in the least daunted, which is the more remarkable since he had, up to this point, very little experience of being publicly disliked or disapproved of. Now his every action, public or private, was scrutinised in a far from friendly spirit. Hollywood noted immediately that he came unaccompanied by his wife. Fooling no one, Welles airily claimed that Virginia was allergic to Californian life. In fact, their marriage had irretrievably collapsed under the weight of his compulsive fornication, to the extent that they had secretly filed a separation suit. Hollywood knew that it was over, but what, Hollywood wanted to know, had taken its place? Hollywood abhors a sexual vacuum.

It was not just his wife from whom he was estranged. His relations with Houseman had cooled to freezing point; none the less, always ready to give the thing one last try, when Welles asked him to Hollywood, Houseman followed. RKO's contract, after all, was with Mercury Productions, and in letter, if not in spirit, that still meant him. Renting an expensive house in the university area of Brentwood, Welles installed them in some style. His curious ménage (which did nothing to allay prurient speculation) consisted of a tiny Irish chauffeur whom he nicknamed Alfalfa, Charles, a supercilious and indolent French butler, and a maid; Houseman, Bill Alland and Dick Baer formed the Mercury contingent. There were also, says Houseman, 'a full contingent of slaves, from whose presence Orson seemed to derive security and comfort in a strange and hostile town'. This was an expensive set-up, and Welles had very little income: the RKO money was due in instalments, most of it on completion. Naturally spendthrift, he now became reckless, as if to demonstrate his status. Made to feel small by Hollywood, he spent like a big shot, behaving as if he were already a great success. His reputation as an inordinate personality preceded him; instead of downpedalling this reputation, he defiantly played up to it, to the despair of Arnold Weissberger, who had now taken on the thankless task of being his financial adviser. He and Richard Baer, the Harvard graduate who had been stage managing and playing bit parts at the Mercury and was now Welles's personal assistant, tried to keep the spending under control. Left to himself, Welles was perfectly capable of buying a plane to get back to New York, believing that this represented a saving.

Weissberger wrote to Baer, 'Orson does not think of his income in concrete terms in relationship to his expenditures. He does not ask how much he can spend in the light of his income but spends without regard to his income and then has payments arranged for as best can be done.' There was throughout the Hollywood period, an army of minders in Los Angeles and New York trying to contain his excess. Now, at the beginning of his sojourn, the expenditure was focused on riotous living at Brentwood. 'Rumours,' wrote Houseman, 'began to circulate about the strange all-male population of the house in Brentwood.' It was because of those rumours, rather than simple professional hostility, that Welles was accosted as he sat one evening in the Brown Derby restaurant. The interestingly named cowboy actor Big Boy Williams (later one of the 'Bad Men of Tombstone') came up to his table, and accused him of being a 'queer': at the climax of their altercation, the cowboy picked up a knife and sliced off Welles's tie.

Big Boy and Welles had it out, according to Welles, in the car park (curiously, in later tellings of the story, he names Ward Bond, the rather more distinguished actor, later hero of *Wagon Trail*, as his symbolic castrator); but the suspicion and hostility were not going to go away easily or quickly. He attempted some clumsy gestures at reconciliation with the film community, but these were not successful: when he threw a party, no one, it is said, came. He was photographed with Shirley Temple, but this was regarded as patronising. Wisely, he hired a personal press representative, the shrewd and witty Herbert Drake, until then Drama Correspondent of the *New York Herald Tribune*, a seasoned newspaperman with sterling contacts. Drake could not make Welles liked or even respected, but he could at least ensure that he was heard on his own terms. This he did; there was an unparalleled outpouring of articles and items over the next couple of years which matched every snide report with another startling fragment of the hagiography that Drake was busily recycling, not shaming to add colourful details of his own. Referring privately to him as 'the Christ Child', he nosed out and fleshed out a great deal of what became the standard Welles legend. This was not simply promotion; it was a necessary antidote to the dominant anti-Welles outpouring of the Hollywood press. And it was not difficult: liked or loathed, Welles was always news.

He was not helped in his attempts to become part of the motion picture community by his weekly journey to New York to transmit his *Campbell's Playhouse* offering. These absences stressed his involvement with 'the rest of the snobs back in New York'.

Welles had no desire to keep returning to the East Coast; on the contrary, he was eager to persuade the agency, Ward Wheelock, to transfer the broadcasts to Los Angeles, particularly since he planned to use his regular *Campbell's* actors in his films – whatever they turned out to be. The company was adamantly opposed to this ('Wheelock says absolutely not,' wrote the programme co-ordinator, Diana Bourbon. 'Not being obstructive – he says sponsor wouldn't hear of it. They're 101 per cent sold on the idea of establishing the *Playhouse* as the glamour market for Broadway, just as Hollywood Hotel in its day was the glamour market for Hollywood'). In fact, Wheelock was far from pleased with the RKO contract altogether, despite its extraordinary provision – yet another unique feature of that remarkable document – that 'the actor may be absent from the studio . . . during one working day each week in order that he may render services in connection with radio broadcasting.' For a while it seemed as if they might take legal action: they had signed the RKO contract without consulting Wheelock; Welles desperately wired him that it was 'irrevocable' and absolutely within the terms of his original contract with the agency. In the event, no action was taken, but they remained suspicious that Welles's radio work would become marginal to his involvement in film. They were not altogether wrong.

Houseman sent a defensive telegram to Wheelock which is revealing in a number of ways, not least in giving an indication of how Welles intended to approach film-making: 'practical considerations suggest enormous advantages to campbells of present picture tie-up stop orson's function as actor director master of ceremonies and narrator in this picture identical to his function on radio show so that picture will be in itself unprecedented and highly effective plug for campbell playhouse stop many radio stars have made appearances in pictures but no recognisable and complete radio show with its formula intact has ever before been made into a motion picture'. This is precisely how Welles approached his first screenplay. Houseman continues: 'we were completely dissatisfied with last season's publicity work on campbell playhouse stop orson has assumed expense of special public relations man [Drake] to make tremendous rko investment serve best interests of radio program'. Welles liked to suggest that he had strolled into Hollywood, wide-eyed and a stranger to the ways of a wicked world, but, as this shows, he was acutely aware of the importance of publicity and image. Houseman insists that they will continue to stress the Broadway character of the radio show. If Wheelock will agree to move it to Los Angeles, they will ship out at their own expense anyone needed for the show who was not in the film 'during these few weeks when we are shooting picture'. This telling last remark gives a clear indication of Welles's innocence of the process of film-making. He believed that he could have it all: the radio programme, the film, and, of course, the theatre. He had already planned his return to the boards after the 'few weeks' of filming; it was a typically ambitious programme: *The Playboy of the Western World*, *Peer Gynt* and, he told Barbara Leaming, 'something by John Ford'. He reckoned without the complexity of the work of film-making, and, more importantly, without the fascination it would exercise on him.

His involvement with the radio programme continued hectic and combative: Diana Bourbon, as imperious as her name suggests, proved a formidable sparring partner, one of the few people who treated him as an equal ('Now listen dear' a typical letter starts). She took no nonsense from him: 'Why did you two lice can *Mr Chips*?' she wrote to Welles and Houseman. 'You were all agog to do it last year when it didn't mean much. Now that it's real box office you turn it down.' Complaining about the sloppiness, incomprehensibility and expensiveness of one broadcast (*Algiers*), she wrote to the Campbell's front-man Ernest Chappell, in a letter also sent to Welles, 'They tell me you had 9 native musicians and a girl singer. Is Orson paying for these or did you get an okay direct from Ward? Look Chappie, dear – one thing I want to warn you about. Orson is a very fascinating personality. He sings a siren song to anybody who listens to him. Keep your feet on the ground, a firm grasp on your common sense and DON'T LET HIM HYPNOTISE YOU!' Welles liked Bourbon personally, even enjoyed their jousts, but her interventions were exactly what he most detested: she was telling him what to do. The sooner he could get out of it the better, to enjoy his new freedom in Hollywood as his own master, choosing his own scripts, making his own experiments, choosing his own actors.

'Now listen dear,' she wrote, in an effort to get him to face the realities of his situation. 'We are not advocating a star-spangled month of January just for the sake of spending money or making agents happy. We are doing it in a desperate attempt to save you and to save your show . . . who will you take? Who – of comparable box-office stature? I don't give a god-damn whether they're great actresses. We're past the point where we can consider that. ARE THEY BOX OFFICE? Will the public – a large and sizeable proportion of the illiterate, tasteless proletariat that is the radio audience of America tune out Charlie McCarthy simply and solely because they NEVER miss ANYTHING their darling does? I don't care who you choose. But tell me SOMEBODY. Don't just waste time by telling me who you WON'T have. Tell me who you WILL. Who you WANT to HAVE?' 'Welles was famous, terribly famous and highly regarded,' Paul Stewart told François Thomas. 'So much so that the guests, and they were great stars, were more terrified of broadcasting than of anything else. They had no experience of it. One week, a great star came on the show, and he sacked her. It was unbelievable: we had to call the sponsor and they gave her an enormous sum for the period, $5,000, unheard of. He rehearsed her, and then sacked her. It was terrible. He did it decently, apologising, privately first and then in front of other people, saying that it was entirely his fault, that he'd made a mess of the casting, and had been misled by others. It was not funny at all.' Compromised by celebrity casting and the increasingly recycled nature of the material (*It Happened One Night*, *Broome Stages*, *Only Angels Have Wings*, *The Citadel* and *June Moon* being typical fare), the programmes had fallen into an unremarkable routine level, half drama, half chat-show, reflecting Welles's waning enthusiasm for the medium. Still, Welles wrote a defiant telegram to Diana Bourbon, stating his credo: 'please remember that whatever gives our format individuality beyond regular interest attaching itself to our guest is my own extremely personal rather particular style which must needs express authentically my own enthusiasm and tastes'. Welles's Playhouse ended in March of 1940, after prolonged squabbles throughout his first year in Hollywood; but that was the credo which alone kept him going through the dark months ahead.

His most pressing concern, of course, was to decide on a subject for his first film. He had been contracted to make two films, the first to be delivered 'no later than January 1st, 1940'. One of RKO's few remaining contractual rights was that of story approval; intensive consultations with Schaefer had produced a list of potential titles of which the favourites for Welles were *Heart of Darkness* (which he had included in a recent triple bill for the Mercury Theatre of the Air) and that old ignis fatuus of stage actors, *Cyrano de Bergerac*. Like Charles Laughton, Welles was convinced that the adventures in rhyming couplets of the nasally challenged Gascon would make a successful English-language film; Schaefer and his advisers were less convinced. Out of deference to Welles, to show very clearly that they were not interested in simply imposing their will on him, they decided to put it to the test. The Gallup organisation was commissioned to poll the relative popularity of various projects. Their results were unequivocal: to the question 'Which would make best movie?' *Northwest Passage* was chosen by 44 per cent, *Rebecca* 28 per cent, *Grapes of Wrath* 25 per cent; both *Heart of Darkness* and *Cyrano* were chosen by 3 per cent. (The services of Dr Gallup were further employed to discover what the public thought about Welles himself, and the results were gratifying: only 36 per cent of those questioned liked him; but – a sensational figure – 91 per cent knew who he was; and only 2 per cent, reassuringly, were against his beard.) Perhaps encouraged by these findings Schaefer backed Welles to do *Heart of Darkness*, despite the unequivocal verdict of the market researchers, because Welles had convinced him that it would be cinematically experimental and could be made political and controversial. Although Schaefer had no intention of losing money from whatever Welles finally came up with, he saw clearly that there was no point in trying to get a merely well-made film out of him. He needed something that would trade in on his notoriety – that would be distinctively Wellesian: flamboyant, ambitious, and controversial, without being too nakedly theatrical (as *Cyrano* could certainly have seemed). The RKO board, meanwhile, had other ideas: they were still pressing Welles to film *The War of the Worlds*, but Schaefer saw that as merely réchauffé. If, as Welles promised, *Heart of Darkness* would be innovative and provocative, as well as being Prestige Work, then he would back it. It would define the new RKO as nothing else could.

So Welles set to work on making a screenplay out of Conrad's dense, mysterious, endlessly resonant story of Charlie Marlow's search up river in quest of Mr Kurtz, the trader turned God. It was a challenge that few experienced writers would have dreamt of taking on. Welles asked Houseman to do a treatment for him, but he gave up almost immediately, finding the undertaking both impossible and pointless. 'Orson, who was beginning to have his own doubts about the project,' wrote Houseman, 'had the satisfaction of feeling that he had, once again, been betrayed.' Houseman returned, sulkily, to New York to run the radio show; their only contact was when Welles made his weekly journey east. In his work on the screenplay, Welles proceeded slowly and methodically, pasting the pages of the novel into large scrapbooks, making drawings and notes on every phase of the story. He had Richard Baer conduct a study of tribal anthropology which ran to 3,000 pages, meanwhile conducting a self-education in film-making wherever he could get it. Amalia

QUADRUPLE THREAT

Hirschfeld on the contrasts in the 1937 Broadway theatre – the medieval with Welles as Faustus and Paula Lawrence as Helen of Troy in *Doctor Faustus*, the modern with Norman Lloyd in *Power*

Opposite above Welles casts a cold eye on his modern dress production of *Julius Caesar* in a *New York Times* cartoon by Hirschfeld

Below A galaxy of stars in Welles productions

Preceding page Cartoonist Al Hirschfeld's view of Welles at work

© Al Hirschfeld. Drawing reproduced by special arrangement with Hirschfeld's exclusive representative, The Margo Feiden Galleries, New York.

Welles arrives on the West Coast, 1939

Opposite above Dinner with journalist Fred Smith in Hollywood. The inscription reads: 'We look as though we'd already made that million.'

Below Maurice Abraham (Dadda) Bernstein, Welles's guardian, who moved to California to be his personal physician

Welles working on his never-produced screenplay for Joseph Conrad's *Heart of Darkness* in 1939

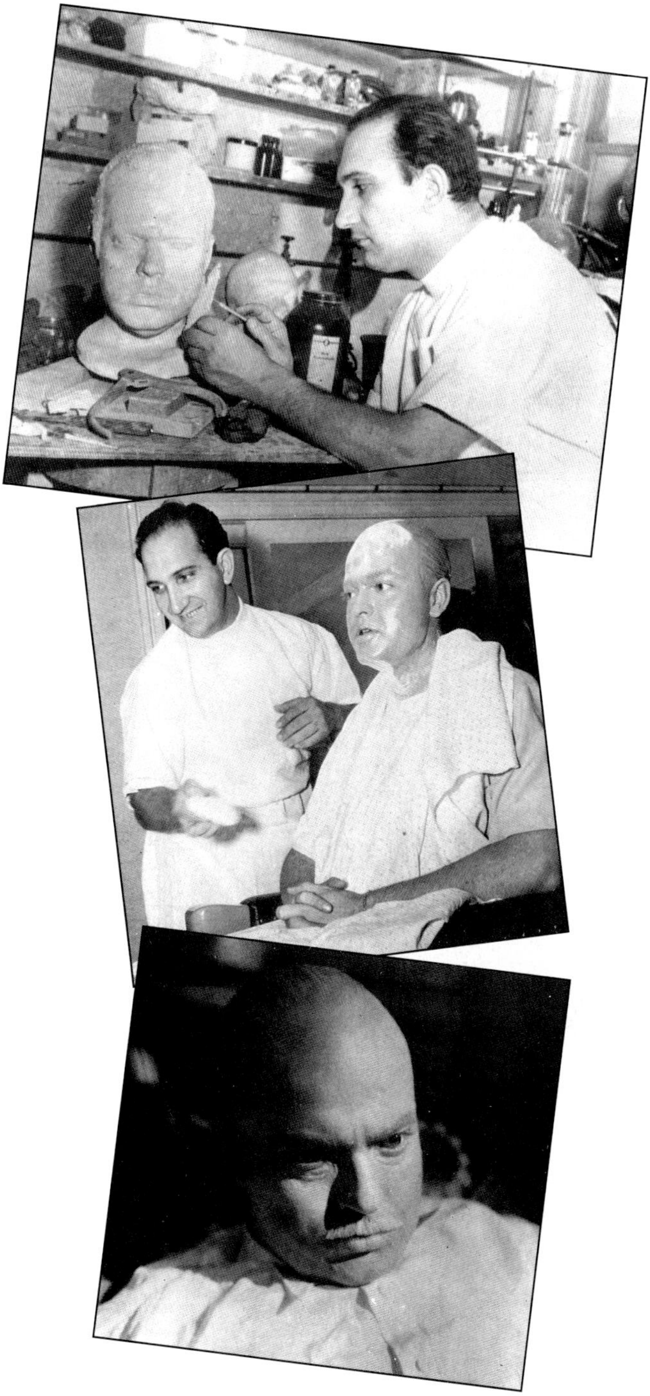

The transformation of Orson Welles into Kane
Above Make-up man Maurice Seiderman with his cast of Welles's head *Centre* Halfway done
Below The finished product

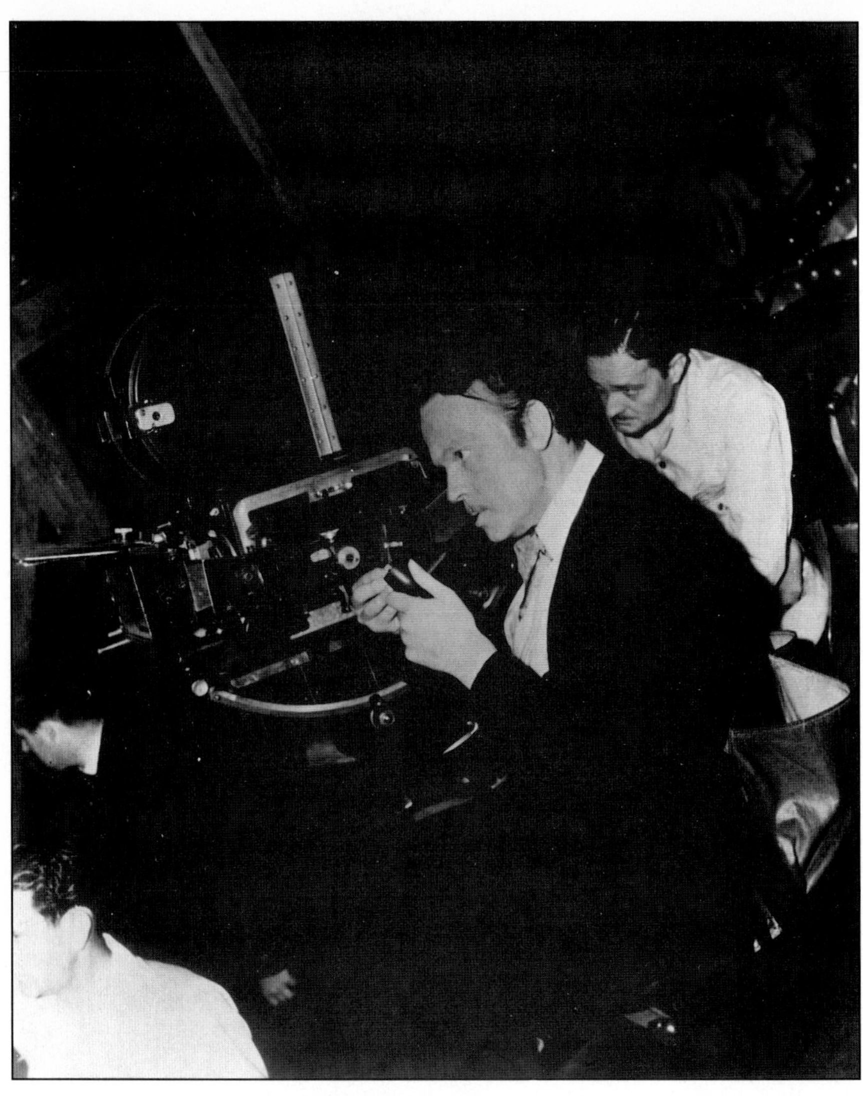

Orson Welles, made-up as the young Kane, frames a shot during the filming of *Citizen Kane*

Kent, an experienced and quick-witted continuity supervisor, was seconded to brief him on screenplay form, while Miriam Geiger taught him the essential grammar of film-making; her hand-made lexicon of lenses and shots is, even today, a model of simplicity and clarity. Thus instructed by these two ladies, he put their lessons into practical effect in his script, as well as everything that he learned from the RKO technical departments. Wide-eyed, he toured the mediaeval manor that was a Hollywood studio in 1939 – like Todd School writ large – meeting the craftsmen, taking note of the capacity of the workshops, examining the contents of the wardrobe and property departments. It was now that he made his justly famous remark about a studio being the best electric train set a boy ever had: he was powerfully struck by the comparison with the bloody-minded willpower and dogged ingenuity that he, Houseman and Jeannie Rosenthal had needed to make anything happen in the theatre at all. His passionate technical curiosity was answered to his total satisfaction; he had films run for him night after night, returning again and again to the recently completed *Stagecoach* to study its narrative mastery. He would ask a different technician each time to watch it with him, asking 'How was this done? And why?' It was, he said, like going to school. No one could have been a better student. For once, he prepared everything as thoroughly as could be.

He intended, it is almost superfluous to say, to seize both Conrad and the cinema by the scruffs of their respective necks, and to leave both transformed out of recognition. As far as Conrad is concerned, the initial pull of the story on Welles is clear to see. It had great personal resonance for him; many of its themes continued to fascinate him for the rest of his life. His work on the story, moreover, fed in various subtle and subliminal ways into his first complete film. The central figure of Kurtz is an epitome of the ambiguity of greatness, or, more precisely, of greatness gone wrong; this was an obsession of Welles's from the first, starting with the brilliantly wicked hero of his teenage play *Bright Lucifer* and the charismatically inspired but wrong-headed John Brown of *Marching Song*. It is, in essence, the figure of Faust, the over-reaching genius, willing to trade for passing pleasure – mere material gratification – what it is that truly makes him great. 'Both the diabolic love,' says Marlow of Kurtz, 'and the unearthly hate of the mysteries it had penetrated fought for the possession of that soul satiated with primitive emotions, avid of lying fame, of sham distinction, of all the appearances of success and power.' And again 'I saw the inconceivable mystery of a soul that knew no restraint, no faith and no fear, yet struggling blindly with itself.' It is above all his emptiness that defines Kurtz: 'there was something wanting in him – some small matter which, when the pressing need arose, could not be found under his magnificent eloquence. Whether he knew of this deficiency, I can't say.' He is a hollow man (the announcement of his death being the celebrated epigraph, of course, of T.S. Eliot's poem, *The Hollow Men*): 'the wilderness echoed loud with him because he was hollow at the core.' This hollowness, this absent centre, is common to many American heroes (Gatsby a noted instance); it seems to have rung a bell with Welles himself, as, of course, did the 'magnificent eloquence' of Kurtz.

'Of all his gifts, the one that stood out pre-eminently, that carried with it a sense of real presence, was his ability to talk, his words – the gift of expression, the bewildering, the illuminating, the most exalted and the most contemptible, the pulsating stream of light, or the deceitful flow from the heart of an impenetrable darkness.' The uncanny power of the voice, the diabolical seduction of words, was a magical attribute with which Welles was entirely familiar. Formally speaking, too, there are aspects of Conrad's tale which intrigued Welles: Marlow is an 'unreliable narrator' – we are never entirely sure whether what he tells us is absolutely true. One of the many reflections that *Heart of Darkness* provokes is on the nature of story telling: an enormous story within a story, it casts a peculiar and bewitching spell. Story telling, its power and its dangerous seduction, profoundly fascinated Welles. And one of the most compelling aspects of the story Marlow tells is that its hero dies with a mysterious phrase on his lips.

So much for Conrad. Welles determined to make explicit what he found buried in the story. He would bring it up to date, relocate it (to South America) and identify Kurtz for what so obviously he was: a fascist. Possessed by perverted eloquence, fathomlessly corrupt yet worshipped as a god, threatening with his primitive emotionalism the very basis of civilisation, what else could he be? Conrad offers a hint of Kurtz's political activity ('He had been writing for the papers and he meant to do so again "for the furthering of my ideas. It's a duty" '); Welles made the hint a fact. 'The picture is, frankly,' he wrote in a memo to Herb Drake, 'an attack on the Nazi system.' He felt a need to give Marlow a character, lacking, he believed, in the book: 'He is willing to tell you how he murdered his wife but seldom volunteers his name. Being lonely, he protects himself from the spirit of loneliness, by candour. You are immediately in his confidence but he never gives you intimacy.' Further, he decided that

Kurtz and his fiancée (whom he named Elsa; she is known only as the Intended in Conrad's text) should be gripped by overwhelming lust for each other. At a certain point during the evolution of the script, Herb Drake issued a synopsis of Welles's treatment to the publicity department of RKO. It gives some indication of Welles's eagerness to be all things to all men.

'The story,' says the memo, 'is of a man and a girl in love. They are separated by his career at the moment and the girl is coming to find him. The man is exploiting the river as a trader and as an explorer and is the head man of a whole company that is doing this in the name of a non-named foreign government. Girl goes to help rescue him, since he has gone beyond the point reached by any of his assistants and has been missing for some months. There is a hell of an adventure going up the river. The action takes place largely on board a rusty steamwheel paddle steamer and at the stations of the trading Co. along the shore. There is an unhappy ending which we won't need to mention, man dies and the girl goes away unfulfilled. There are cannibals, shootings, petty bickering among the bureaucrats, native dances, fascinating light-colored native girl who has some connection with our hero. There is a jungle in flames and heavy storms of a spectacular nature . . . it all builds to a terrific climax . . .' Worried, perhaps, that someone at the publicity department may actually have read the original story, he adds: 'While he is changing the locale . . . and adding characters and moving the girl from Europe to the river, Welles is in no way violating Conrad. His feeling is that his treatment of *Heart of Darkness* is completely in the Conrad spirit and represents what the author would desire done in a film if he were alive today,' which is what they all say.

Having allayed the anxieties of students of English literature, he next addresses those concerned with the box office: 'Story appeal: Welles and the girl . . . Mr Welles is a handsome young man as you know, and we feel that it is important in advertising that he is a broad, muscular, tanned, and handsome leading man . . . we feel once we get them in the theatre they will go away completely thrilled and satisfied by the film even though it is not exactly in the boy-meets-girl tradition.' In a description that would certainly have surprised Conrad, Drake avers that the 'Theory of the story is two moderns who have a hell of an adventure in the dark places of the earth. The idea is more or less that this is the God-damnedest relation between a man and a woman ever put on the screen. It is definitely not "Love in the Tropics". Everyone and everything is just a little bit off normal, just a little bit oblique – all this being the result of the strange nature of their work – that is, operating as exploiters in surroundings not healthy for a white man.'

They were feeling their way; the script as finally realised abandoned a great deal of this, and added sequences of great visual audacity. The one thing that didn't change was the thing Drake held to the last – and even then he hesitated to come right out with it. 'An important selling angle – not only the stars and the story but the *audience* play a part in this film . . . it will be a definite experience, a completely unprecedented experience for the audience since it will see a story told in an entirely different way . . . as Welles develops his method, we will be able to talk about it, but it is still somewhat in the experimental stage so he doesn't wish to mention it until we can find a convenient formula to express its meaning.' The secret innovation was that much discussed, almost never deployed technique of the Subjective Camera: the camera is an I. Welles became deeply intrigued by its possibilities, convinced that it was an essentially cinematic notion. This would show them! His final script is perhaps the most thorough-going attempt to realise the technique ever made.

What it is, in fact, is a literal translation of the First Person Singular technique of the radio programmes; so Houseman's assertion to Ward Wheelock that they would be translating the formula intact into film terms ('Orson's function as actor, director, master of ceremonies and narrator in this picture identical to his function on radio show') was nothing but the truth. 'Ladies and gentlemen, this is Orson Welles' is the first line of the script, over a black screen. 'Don't worry, there's just nothing to look at for a while. You can close your eyes if you want to, but – please open them when I tell you to.' This magician's patter leads the audience, their eyes now open, into the notion of the subjective camera: they become a canary in a cage. On the screen is Welles's mouth, enormously magnified, seen through the bars of the cage. An enormous gun appears, is pointed directly at the camera and is fired; the screen goes to black again. 'Everything you see on the screen is going to be seen through your eyes and you're somebody else,' Welles's voice explains. The first somebody else is a prisoner being taken to the electric chair and executed. The screen goes into a blinding red stain; the camera blurs, there is a fade to black. 'Ladies and Gentlemen, there is no cause for alarm. This is only a motion picture. Of course you haven't committed murder and believe me, I wouldn't electrocute you for the world. Give yourself your right name, please. It might help. All right, now, I think you see what I mean. You're not going to see this picture – this picture is going to see you.' Frank Brady describes the rest of this introductory section: 'a human eye, Magritte-like, with clouds reflected in it, filling the entire scene and then transposing into the view of a golfer who hits a ball; an interior of a motion picture theatre seen from Welles's perspective on the screen, so that all the members of the audience are cameras.' Welles says: 'I hope you get the idea.' A human eye appears on the left of the screen, an equals sign appears next to it, followed by a capital I. 'Finally, the eye winks and we . . . Dissolve.' Then, and only then, does *Heart of Darkness* itself actually take to the screen.

The subjective eye is Marlow's, and a dozen amusing tricks are played as he lights cigarettes, gets down onto the floor, and is even, at a certain crucial point, glimpsed in a mirror. Marlow, was, of course, to be played by Welles, as was Kurtz; add to that the whimsically didactic introduction, and you are never out of Welles's presence, whether vocal or physical. 'One-man picture' indeed. Welles was simultaneously trying to reinvent the camera, do justice to a great story, make a film that was highly entertaining and politically provocative, and provide himself with several very interesting roles. So much artistic ambition is astonishing. Certainly no one else in Hollywood was capable of a tenth as much. His ability to fulfil all these ambitions is in some question: the screenplay itself, while full of extraordinarily stimulating directions, has newly written dialogue of numbing dreadfulness, replacing Conrad's mystery with melodrama. Kurtz finally confronts Marlow in these words: 'Understand this much – Everything I've done up here has been done according to the method of my government – Everything. There's a man now in Europe trying to do what I've done in the jungle. He will fail. In his madness he thinks he can't fail – but he will. A brute can only rule brutes. Remember the meek. I'm a great man, Marlow, really great – greater than great men before me – I know the strength of the enemy its terrible weakness – ' and so on, for some pages. This could come from the weaker passages of *The Green Goddess*. The introduction to the subjective camera, though absolutely charming in itself, is a curious way in which to start a film as complex and sombre as *Heart of Darkness*. It is almost impossible to see how that story could follow that wink of Welles's. As for the subjective camera technique in general, though it is developed, as Jonathan Rosenbaum points out, with some complexity and carefully planned not to draw attention to itself (though the introduction of course does just that), it is anyone's guess as to whether it could have actually been made to work. None the less, the screenplay was a fearless, provocative and immensely talented achievement. It was also, of course, very expensive, which proved to be its undoing.

At first, however, he got a go-ahead, Schaefer and the RKO board approved the project. He started casting immediately. There was difficulty in finding the right actress for the part of Elsa. His ideal, Dita Parlo, the incandescent star of *L'Atalante*, was in Europe and hard to get hold of; Ingrid Bergman, newly arrived in Hollywood, demanded too much money; Carole Lombard turned the part down. They continued to search. This was the only casting problem, however: all the other roles had been specifically conceived for 'his' company, that informal troupe who had been with him on and off on his three-year meteoric journey, in triumph and in disaster, on stage and in the studio, loosely called the Mercury Company. Not one of them had ever stood in front of a camera. He made a big feature of bringing a group of fresh new faces to the screen, calculating at the same time, of course, that directing experienced movie actors when he had never stood in front of a camera himself might have been a challenge even to *his* confidence. The roles were distributed to actors from various areas of his working life: Edgar Barrier, John Emery, Erskine Sandford, Gus Schilling, Frank Readick from the recently disbanded *Five Kings* company; Everett Sloane and Ray Collins from radio work, Norman Lloyd and George Coulouris from the Mercury, and Chubby Sherman (having forgiven him, presumably, and been forgiven) from boyhood days. Another cooled friendship was restored in his concept of the Steersman (the African who falls overboard, whose life Marlow in the original story calls a greater loss than that of Kurtz); he wrote the role for Jack Carter, his Macbeth and Mephostophilis, companion of those steamy Harlem nights. The character is written up into a sort of Charon figure – as he had written all the roles with the specific actors' qualities in mind, quirky characters encountered along the way, as Marlow chugs steadily closer to the nameless horror.

All the actors were duly contracted, while Welles worked closely with his art director, the story-board artists and the make-up department. Locations in Louisiana were scouted, and found wanting; tests to explore the subjective camera went ahead (none too successfully); more conventional screen-tests for make-up were undertaken, revealing Welles's wild-eyed, scarred and bearded Kurtz; the casting department wrestled with Welles's request for 3,000 black extras. There were, they reckoned, no more than a thousand black extras in the whole of Los Angeles, and the cost of convincingly making up white people was considered prohibitive. RKO threw itself into preparing to realise the extraordinary and complex document that was the screenplay for *Heart of Darkness* with its usual thoroughness, despite alarm bells from the accounts department, which foresaw costs of over a million dollars. Suddenly, in the midst of all these preparations, Welles had a telegram from Schaefer, then in Europe: the date was 1 September 1939. The German army had just marched into Poland; France and England were about to declare war. Schaefer, like the good businessman that he was, was worried about business. Blackouts, curfews: it could only spell bad news for sales.

'All this severe blow as you of course know,' wired Schaefer, 'and puts us in position where I must make personal plea to you to eliminate every dollar and nickel possible from heart of darkness script and yet do everything to save entertainment value stop never in my twentyfive years in industry have we been so confronted with need using our ingenuity and eliminating all material not necessary for story value stop of course this is not encouraging to your good self but believe there is nothing else I can do . . . we must be prepared for the worst sincere regards'. Welles rallied to this heartfelt request with equal charm (but a fortnight later): 'dear mr schaefer: you have my word because of conditions as you explained every cent will be counted twice in heart of darkness stop no single luxury will be indulged only absolutely essentials to effectiveness and potency of story stop because you have entrusted me with full authority in this i will be the more vigilant and painstaking about costs have already cut two production sequences from script and am working on innumerable changes in production method and approach stop please believe every possible effort will be made to justify confidence expressed in times when confidence is expensive stop am trying very hard to be worth it regards orson' which is Welles at his most boyishly ingratiating; it must have sealed their friendship. It is interesting to note the form of address: Orson/Mr Schaefer – the correct way for a nicely brought-up young man to address an older man. 'Thanks so much for your wire of the 19th,' wrote back Schaefer. 'It heartens us very much and comes at a time when we appreciate such assurances of co-operation . . . wishing you the best of success in your undertaking . . . I am sincerely yours, G.J. Schaefer.' They would return to the original budget ceiling of $500,000.

Their perfect understanding was not enough to prevent rumbles from the outside world. The European crisis was a threat to all the Hollywood studios. The general tightening of belts and trimming of programmes caused widespread anxiety, which inevitably led to renewed focus on the fledgling outsider, the smart-ass who hadn't even managed to announce the subject of his first offering. Wilkerson, editor of the influential industry paper, *The Hollywood Reporter*, wrote in his column 'Trade Views': 'If Mr George Schaefer had come out with an announcement . . . that the Orson Welles picture was too much of a gamble to take during these critical times . . . the RKO president would have been a big guy in town yesterday. But Mr Schaefer evidently does not think that an investment of $750,000 or more with an untried producer, writer, director, with a questionable story and a rumored cast of players who, for the most part, have never seen a camera, is a necessary cut in these critical times.' The sniping continued. Herb Drake wrote sharply to a columnist who had implied that Welles was twiddling his thumbs by the poolside, describing how he had gone about producing *Heart of Darkness* screenplay: pasting the pages in the book, the discussions of shooting and character, the sketches for the art director; and the final shooting script. 'I would say Welles has produced between 700 and 800 pages of double-spaced typing on 8 × 10 paper and another book of sketches. When I saw him on Sunday he said he had only four hours' work left on the script.' Drake was a pro, not a man to waste his time; he wrote at such length in such detail because it was crucial to counteract the growing rumours that the script was either unfilmable or – even more widespread – that it did not exist at all.

Welles still had no relationship with the movie community as such. Whispers about his private life had been stilled by his new relationship with Dolores del Rio, the first in a succession of iconically beautiful consorts who were always to be found at his side for the rest of his life. They met at a party thrown by Jack Warner; he had, he told her, been in love with her since the age of eleven, and knew that one day they would be lovers (this pattern was repeated with his second wife, Rita Hayworth, whom he had determined to marry after seeing her photograph on the cover of *Life* magazine, making him some sort of serial fetishist). Del Rio's image had exerted such a powerful hold on him that, spotting her in a New York night-club, he had followed her out of the club and some way down the street. She was married to the famous art director Cedric Gibbons, some years older than her; finding herself violently drawn to the twenty-four-year-old Welles, her junior by ten years, she determined immediately to divorce her husband. Her friend Fay Wray notes that 'she apparently didn't consider having an affair with Orson, but thought she must leave Cedric, get a divorce. She seemed herself a lady of purity.' She did, of course, start an affair with Welles, but only after informing her husband that it was all over between them; divorce followed in the fullness of time. Sexual attraction, though undoubtedly strong, does not seem to have been the essential ingredient in the relationship between her and Welles; she seemed to have had all too much of that with Gibbons. 'He wants only to talk about sex,' she told the judge when filing her application for divorce. Welles reported to Barbara Leaming that del Rio was as perfectly composed in bed as out of it. What was inspiring for Welles was to be associated with her glamour and beauty. 'He was goggle-eyed that she would even hang around,' said James Morcom, Welles's set designer on *Five Kings*. But equally, 'she was so in awe of him and his genius, and he *loved* that, lapped it up.' She gave him two things Virginia could no longer provide: glamour plus adulation; Virginia knew him too well, had known him too long. She did not sufficiently confirm the image of him in which he needed so deeply to believe.

At first, to protect Gibbons, their relationship was conducted clandestinely; always a bonus for Welles. When not alone with her he fraternised with the Hollywood outsiders, attending (Frank Brady tells us) a 'forbidden' book launch, that of Aldous Huxley's *After Many a Summer*, unmistakably based on the life of the key host and hostess of Los Angeles high society, the newspaper baron William Randolph Hearst and his mistress, the comedienne Marion Davies. Only those who did not wish to dine, or who were no longer invited to dine, at Hearst's Spanish gothic folly San Simeon on the coast near Santa Barbara appeared at the Huxley launch; Welles fell in with this crowd.

None the less, Welles was keenly aware of the need, not merely to fight back, but actively to improve his image. Under Drake's brilliant tutelage, he now started to cultivate the Hollywood media. In practice, this meant those arch-rivals, Hedda Hopper and Louella Parsons, queens of poolside gossip, both of whom he now courted assiduously and with due care not to favour one above the other. To be caught in the crossfire between them could be fatal, as he was later to discover. His fabled charm worked its familiar magic on them. 'Too bad Orson Welles isn't an Englishman,' wrote Hopper (by far the sharper of these two weird sisters) in September of 1939. 'If he had been, Hollywood would never have given him such a run-around. We reserve that for our own citizens. Mr Welles doesn't scare easily and I'm thinking he'll make

Hollywood sit up and beg for mercy.' A month later, Parsons was writing: 'If Mr Welles makes a great picture, I'll be the first to say so . . . we cannot deny that Mr Welles is a brilliant young man.' Drake's counter-campaign was beginning to take. He identified an insatiable interest in the legends surrounding 'the Christ Child', and, having issued a summary of the salient miraculous events for the attention of editors, he applied to Dr Bernstein for more.

Even that arch-idolator had become aware of the absurdity of some of what was written. 'As for the chronological story of Orson the thing which is definitely known is the fact that he arrived in Kenosha on the 6th of May 1915. On the 7th May, 1915, he spoke his first words, and unlike other children who say commonplace things like "mamma" and "pappa", he said "I am a genius." On May 8th, 9th and 10th, 1915, little was heard about him in THE PRESS, but on May 15th he seduced his first woman. After that date, things happened fast since the Rajah of Geck came through Kenosha in the guise of a Fuller Brush man and gave Orson a brush which he uses as a beard and set out on his theatrical career playing, as you and the whole world knows, Peter Rabbit.'

Welles continued to be in close contact with Bernstein (still, after all, his legal guardian for another two years) and the Hills. Roger and he were still business partners in the Mercury Shakespeare on discs; their plan to bring out a fourth (*Macbeth*) to add to the already available *Caesar*, *Twelfth Night* and *Merchant of Venice* was to engender correspondence throughout the next eighteen months. Hill had, in his own sphere, been passionately promoting Welles: in a circular for *Everybody's Shakespeare* (now, seemingly, called *Orson Welles's Shakespeare*) he writes under the headline THE FOREMOST NAME IN AMERICAN AESTHETIC LIFE TODAY: 'I have seen no movement appear upon the education horizon comparable in immediate importance and in future hope to the instantaneous success and worldwide acclaim of Orson Welles and his Elizabethan offerings. Hailed throughout the press as the white hope of the American theatre, Orson Welles's destiny is, to my mind, of even greater magnitude than this. He is also the white hope of the American classroom. The contagious enthusiasm for great literature which should be part of every student's heritage is today woefully lacking.' The Mercury can be persuaded out on the road, he says, if only there are enough postcard requests to him to do so. 'I have told Orson that he owes it to himself and that he owes it to America to found a truly National Theatre – to spend at least six months out of each year carrying his stimulating offerings to aesthetically undernourished students and adults throughout the length and breadth of our country.' Welles had, apparently, promised that the 1938 tour would last till the following winter. Hill's final sentence explains the momentary coolness between them since Welles had taken up residence in Hollywood. 'The young man who finds no temptation in fabulous movie offers can be persuaded I hope not to confine his performances to the few large cities that can offer long and completely underwritten performances.'

It is one of the many uncommon aspects of Welles's life that he, a grown and famous man, should remain in constant contact with these two openly adoring and demanding older men, neither of whom was either his father or his lover. He remained highly responsive to both of them, affectionate and considerate, even through the more tedious of Dr Bernstein's demands, and even at times of greatest pressure. Bernstein was invited by Welles to California; he came ('I have never been happier in my life') for a stay at the Château Marmont, then, returning to Chicago, he decided that he should settle in Los Angeles for good, partly to be close to 'Pookles'. In order to do so, he asked Welles for a year-long loan to establish him; the letter is couched in Bernstein's usual terms of emotional blackmail: 'I never stood in your way and never imposed on you and will not start now. But I know that you are in a position to help me without a great sacrifice on your part . . . you can imagine how unhappy this writing makes me and what a battle it was to decide to do this. But I am driven to distraction and have no alternative . . . lovingly and distractedly, Dadda P.S. Whatever you decide will make no difference in my feelings for you.' Then, handwritten, he adds: 'you have helped many stranded actors who meant nothing to you. I hope that I mean more than they did to you.'

It worked, of course; he moved to California, where Welles, in addition to helping him financially, attempted to get him employed as RKO's medical consultant. Failing in that, he used him as his personal physician; accident prone as Welles was, this kept Bernstein busy until he was accepted by the California Medical Board as a regular practitioner. He was, at any rate, (and despite the occasional whimsy) an excellent source for Herb Drake, who had secured a major coup for Welles: a three-part series on him to be written by *Saturday Evening Post*'s star reporters Fred Smith and Alva Johnston, who needed all the colourful detail they could get. Drake wrote to Bernstein asking for childhood pictures of Welles, especially those relating to 'the fabulous Dick Welles' about whom, he says, Alva Johnston wanted to do a separate article, shamelessly adding that the doctor would be the next subject.

Welles, meanwhile, had submitted his 19 November Final Shooting Script to the Hays Office for their comments. 'We are happy to report,' wrote the secretary, Joseph H. Breen, 'that the basic story seems to meet the requirements of the Production Code.' There were minor cavils: in the introductory prologue 'some censor boards may delete scene of gun being fired . . . many censor boards will delete scene in death chamber.' Racial issues seemed to concern them above all: 'care will be needed with the costumes of all natives . . . there must be no suggestion of nudity, of course, and the breasts of the women must be covered at all times . . . the same care should apply to heads on poles, etc . . . please take care to avoid any inference of miscegenation.' Blasphemy was, of course, out of the question ('the expression "Thank God" must be changed') and, interestingly, they warn that the British Board of Censors will not like the portrayal of Kurtz as being partially insane, nor the burial service. With these few reservations, Welles had the go-ahead from that troublesome quarter. There now seemed no further obstacle; shooting could at last begin, silencing the still virulent scepticism. The war in Europe, however, began to loom larger with every passing day. Schaefer became more and more nervous about the film, urging Welles to drop the overt political parallels (the very possibility which had at first recommended the project to him); Welles immediately agreed. Too late; the final blow, in December, was the costing estimate for the Final Shooting Script: $1,057,761, more than double the agreed figure.

A great deal of the expense was due to the particular requirements of the subjective camera: in order to preserve the continuity crucial to the notion, Welles wanted to maintain enormously long takes over considerable distances. The only solution to this problem was the elaborate technique of feather wiping: the camera is locked off at the end of a shot; the next shot resumes at the same place, and the camera moves off again. As Robert Carringer describes it: 'if Marlow was standing on the deck of a boat that had just docked, his eyes would pan to the side of a building on the shore. The pan would continue in the new shot and come to rest as Marlow engaged in conversation.' A concomitant of this method was that the special effects would have to be created before principal photography began; Vernon Walker's department estimated twelve or fourteen weeks for this work. This meant, as Carringer points out, delaying the start of shooting till March at the earliest; the actors would have to be laid off till then. Schaefer and a desperate Welles met in New York to discuss the situation. Welles brought with him a script he had been working on alongside *Heart of Darkness*: *The Smiler with a Knife*, from a thriller by the Anglo-Irish poet C. Day Lewis under his nom-de-plume Nicholas Blake. Based squarely on the English fascist Sir Oswald Mosley and his plans for a coup, it was witty, topical – and cheap. He could make it, Welles assured Schaefer, while the Special Effects for *Heart of Darkness* were being prepared, for as little as $400,000. He would take no salary, just a cut of the profits; this was agreed.

With the new deal in place, he returned to Hollywood in mid-December of 1939. Houseman describes a party in the Brentwood house at which Welles announced his good news and his bad news: the postponement of *Heart of Darkness*, and – as a consolation prize – the imminence of *The Smiler with a Knife*. The urgent question of the payment of the actors during the inevitable delay while the new project was set up was broached a couple of weeks later over a supper at Chasen's; Richard Baer, Bill Alland, Herbert Drake, Albert Schneider (now his personal manager) and Houseman were present along with Welles. The description of what he calls a 'staff meeting' provides a memorable set-piece in Houseman's book. Waiting until the end of the meal before addressing the matter in hand, Welles – by now having consumed a great deal of wine, washed down with a comparable quantity of brandy – airily proposed that the actors should be taken off RKO's payroll and put onto that of the Mercury. Being told that there was no money for this, he accused Albert Schneider of 'pissing it away'. Houseman, weary of sorting out Welles's impasses, demanded to know what he was going to do. Welles wanted to know what *he* would do. 'Tell them the truth for once,' said Houseman. At which Welles roared like a gored bull. 'I never lie to actors!' he howled, and then started to throw the contents of the table, including two dishes of flaming methylated spirits, at him. Houseman prudently withdrew, not just from the room, but from Los Angeles, and, he supposed, Welles's life. Avoiding Welles's calls and not responding to his telegrams, Houseman drove stolidly to New Mexico, where he wrote him a letter terminating their working relationship – at least, on its present basis. 'In the past year my position with you and the Mercury has become something between that of a hired, not too effective manager, a writer under contract and an aging, not so benevolent relative,' he wrote, in words subtly different from those he printed in his memoir. 'There seems to be some emotional thing between us, lately, which instead of being helpful and fruitful merely succeeds in embarrassing and paralysing us both.' Even though he had started the letter by saying that 'nothing that has happened recently affects the very deep affection I have for you and the very real delight I have found in association with such a talent as yours', and ended by saying 'nothing would make me happier than, one day, again to produce plays together', his every word attests to the severance of the bond that had united them, their mutual dependence. 'We have gone through too much together in the theatre and had too much joy of it for me to be willing to let our partnership follow the descending curve of misunderstandings along which I see it so clearly moving.' They no longer complemented each other; indeed, the other's very existence was a sort of indictment. For Welles, Houseman was the living evidence of an earlier self, a self he had left behind, the boy he was; for Houseman, Welles had grown to a monstrous independence which made him feel dowdy, small, insignificant – and petty. 'I have found myself accepting this new position of mine not always with good grace, and I have found myself far too frequently buttressing my position with a kind of cynical, destructive passivity which I do not like any better than you.'

Once happy with the role of witty, deep-revolving Buckingham to Welles's Gloucester, Houseman too might have cried: 'And is it thus? Repays he my deep service/With such contempt? Made I him King for this?' Not only had he ceased to be important in Welles's life, Welles had now become so public a figure that Houseman was no longer able to see the artist in him, and his association with Welles's artistry was the elixir that made life worth living. In a letter to Virgil Thomson (also, interestingly, rewritten for publication in his memoir) he announces the break-up of their partnership, saying: 'If an artist finds that public response can be stimulated by monkeyshines (social and mechanical), then the necessity for, even the interest in, creative work inevitably dwindles. That is the main reason why, for seven months now, a picture (under the most magnificent contract ever granted an artist in Hollywood) has been "about to be made," talked of, speculated over, defended, attacked, announced, postponed, reannounced to the tune of millions of words in thousands of publications without the picture itself (either on paper or even in Orson's own mind) having got beyond the most superficially and vaguely conceived first draft.' He was wrong about the amount of work Welles had done; the reasons for the delay on the film are none the less interesting: 'the moment it gets made it enters the world of tangible-work-to-be-appraised instead of potential-work-of-a-genius-which-can-be-talked-conjectured-about-written-about . . .'

It is evident that Houseman had been looking for an occasion to precipitate their rift, and the meal at Chasen's had served well for the purpose. He said as much in his letter to Welles: 'what happened the other night has, of course, nothing to do with all this. It merely brought to a head a situation which I have seen existing and growing worse for some time' and there is no reason to doubt it. As always, he analysed himself better and more harshly than anyone else could. 'It is my great virtue that I can impart terrific initial acceleration to any project to which I am a part,' he wrote to Thomson. 'It is my great weakness that I am incapable (and not always desirous) of controlling or moderating its speed once it is under way.' A day arrives when he suddenly finds himself 'disliking the direction in which we are moving and sick of that very inertia which I have helped impose'. That day had assuredly arrived with Welles. 'Being,' as he says, 'an adventurous amateur rather than a creator, an operator rather than an artist', he hurriedly abandons ship 'having first made quite sure that there is a safety-door open and working'. His instinct for survival was infinitely better developed than Welles's; eventually, it led him to a life of fulfilment and satisfaction. As well as an abandonment of ship, however, that supper at Chasen's was also, classically, a demonstration of the need to provoke a feeling, *any* feeling, from the estranged partner. Such was his involvement with Welles that he was not able simply to walk away from it. Not yet.

Curiously, Welles told Barbara Leaming that *he* had contrived the whole incident – in order to get Houseman off salary. 'I couldn't say to him "you're not working for me anymore" after all our time together and all. So that's why I turned over the table. It was cold-hearted. It wasn't a BIG end of it; I just got him off salary for a while, which was all I wanted to do.' This sounds unconvincing by the side of Houseman's account of Welles's bloodshot eyes and damp, white face, his cries of 'Crook!' and 'Thief!'. Houseman's final leave-taking proved not to be so final; but the association, that inspired partnership, that match made in heaven (as far as Houseman was concerned) had been dying for some time, and was now, in any deep sense, over. And yet Houseman was unable to resist leaving the door a little way open.

Though he had written to Virgil Thomson of 'the uprooting of a three years' artistic marriage', his letter to Welles had specifically disavowed any such thing: 'I do not consider this a divorce from the Mercury.' Furthermore, 'at the risk of being wearisome,' he insisted that 'at this moment I love and admire you no less than ever.' Earlier, he says that 'nothing would make me happier than again to produce plays with you . . . I don't think that the theatre will ever be as wonderful for me again as it was for two years with you.' Nor will he cause any trouble; no one need know. In his final paragraph he assures Welles that he could rely on him to make his going to New York 'a very natural thing', that he would be happy to stay for a week or two to help with *The Smiler with a Knife*, or indeed, the radio show. He ends with the standard civilised sign-off in all would-be amicable terminations of intense relationships: 'and now let's have dinner together.'

They didn't have dinner together; not yet. Welles, to whom all the foregoing was simply a tedious irrelevance, did what he always did in situations of emotional complication: he threw himself into work, in this case preparations for *The Smiler with a Knife*. He had managed to persuade Schaefer that it could be turned into a popular hit along the lines of *The Thin Man*. The flip from *Heart of Darkness* to *The Thin Man* is rather abrupt, though it is not unknown for desperate commercialism to be the bank holiday of high art. Day Lewis's Nigel and Georgina Strangeways could certainly have matched Nick and Nora Charles as married sleuths, and the book has considerable entertainment potential, as Georgina stumbles upon The English Banner, a proto-fascist movement under the leadership of Lord Chilton Canteloe. Welles had changed the setting to America, North and South (with a scene set in Todd School), but it is easy to see why he was drawn to the character of Day Lewis's charismatic fascist. Even physically he was not unlike Welles: 'his magnetic, brown, gold-flecked eyes could turn so easily from playfulness to an almost tigerish fury of concentration . . . his gait lacked the incomparable grace of his head and shoulders: he walked a little clumsily, leaning forward, his arms swinging stiffly in front of him, rather like a bear.' And 'Chillie', like Kurtz, like Welles, is a verbal wizard. 'His belief in himself was so implicit that he could never doubt, at the moment, the truth of his own words. He was a self-deceiver on the heroic scale, and of that stuff dictators are made.'

The studio was sufficiently enthused to allow the script to be sent to Carole Lombard; she turned it down. Welles was very keen for the young and still untried Lucille Ball to play his girl sleuth, but RKO, one of whose few other contractual rights was that of employee refusal, insisted that she wouldn't be able to carry the picture. Now Schaefer started to get anxious about the political thread in this picture too, and tried to push Welles towards other pictures which would be both less controversial and more substantial. They realised that *The Smiler with a Knife*, whatever its charms, was not the right first film for the 'spectacular genius of the show world'; while *Heart of Darkness*, though still officially slated, seemed a more and more distant prospect. An air of desperation came over their deliberations as public humiliation loomed for both of them: Schaefer suggested *The Man Who Came to Dinner* (which Woollcott had wanted Welles to play on stage from the beginning, according to Brady); they considered great novels (*Jane Eyre* and *The Pickwick Papers*), history (Machiavelli, *The Borgias*, Cortez's invasion of America), biography (*The Life of Dumas*), all and any of which could possibly have made splendid films. But to start from scratch at this late stage with no clear concept and time running out rapidly, was a hopeless prospect.

Welles had been in Hollywood for nearly six months and was no nearer making a film than when he arrived. Meanwhile, the tricoteuses mocked with gleeful anticipation. 'Orson Welles confers with himself in a three-way mirror, as actor, director, and producer. The actor wants something, producer says budget won't stand it, director sees it another way. So it goes, with Little Orson Annie fighting himself . . . Orson Welles was chic in a silver fox beard trimmed with old RKO scripts.' He was in a desperate corner.

CHAPTER NINETEEN

Mank

As it so often had, but for very nearly the last time, benevolent destiny intervened at the moment that Welles most needed it, introducing him to exactly the right person at the right time. Drawn as always to old-timers, particularly if they were also reprobates, he had been delighted to make the acquaintance in New York of the screenwriter Herman J. Mankiewicz, only in his mid-forties but after fifteen years in Hollywood and twenty-five years on the bottle, a veteran of an industry he viewed with trenchant contempt. Author or co-author of over ninety screenplays, producer of several movies (including the Marx Brothers' *Duck Soup*) he was the archetypal East Coast wit, ex-foreign correspondent, sometime publicist for Isadora Duncan, former drama editor of first *The New York Times* then *The New Yorker*. He was bought up and shipped over to Hollywood at the start of the talkies boom and thrown unceremoniously into the writing factory where his gift for witty one-liners was the salvation of many another man's script. The downside was that his own scripts were subject to amendment by yet other hands, which fed his already deep reserves of bitterness and cynicism. He could almost have been the prototype of Fitzgerald's Pat Hobby (with his 'credits that would knock your eye out, extending up to – well, up to five years ago when Pat's credits had begun to be few and far between') except for his rebarbative wit and forceful opinions, freely expressed without regard to the sensibilities of his listeners, whose own opinions were dismissed with contempt. 'Idiocy is all right in its own way,' he would roar at them, 'but you can't make it the foundation of a career!'

His contempt (which was real enough) was always transmuted into laughter; few took offence, his worst behaviour invariably redeemed by a wonderful joke. Throwing up at dinner, as he often did, he managed, just before passing out, to reassure his notoriously snobbish host: 'It's all right. I brought up the white wine with the fish.' He was, until his perverse political stances (pro-German, anti-Semitic) became insupportable in time of war, one of the most prized dinner guests in Hollywood, not only funny but intellectually brilliant. Welles was drawn to all that, of course, but especially to the danger: 'you felt this fondness, though you knew that if he had a chance, he would cut you off at the knees.' Here was Jack Carter all over again in the form of a middle-aged, stout Jewish Voltaire. 'Mankiewicz was some sort of tremendous performer in a Hieronymous Bosch landscape of his own. There was always the feeling that you were in the presence of thwarted violence,' Welles told Richard Meryman. 'It was this thrashing of some great creature, some beached creature. Some magnificent creature. You didn't know what it was because you had never seen one of those before. It was Mank.' Occasionally, the comments of the later Welles on Mankiewicz have an eerily premonitory autobiographical feel to them. 'He liked the attention he got as a great, monumental, self-destructing machine . . . it was the vulnerability that brought the warmth out from his friends. And people loved him. *Loved* him. That terrible vulnerability. That terrible wreck.' Mankiewicz for his part was drawn to Welles in an equally complicated manner. 'It is a real genius that he has and not any particular talent or combination of talents that have become fortified or outstanding through training. He is no Meglin Kid or premature Quiz Kid. And he provokes a hero worship that makes it possible to react to his bad behaviour as if somebody else were guilty of it. God knows why. When he has walked among men, they loathe his guts. But they miss him more than they would somebody they loved.' Mankiewicz recognised the divine spark in Welles; Welles loved Mankiewicz's lack of compromise, his incorruptible subversiveness. This was not Falstaff, but Thersites.

'Both came away,' wrote Houseman of their first New York meeting in that tone of naked envy and exclusion so peculiarly his own, 'enchanted and convinced that between them they were the two most dashing and gallantly intelligent gentlemen in the Western world. And they were not far wrong.' They were also both in trouble, financially and professionally; Welles less visibly so, perhaps, than Mankiewicz, who was not only nearly unemployable as a result of his unfettered tongue and chronic unreliability, but also now bed-bound, after a car crash in which his leg had been broken in three places. Welles was in a position to help him: he engaged him to write scripts for *Campbell's Playhouse*. The first of these, *The Murder of Roger Ackroyd*, was not an unqualified success (he omitted one of the crucial clues), but the scripts got better, partly as a result of being 'harshly' edited by Houseman. Welles would visit Mankiewicz at his bedside; they would mainly speak, as people in the same business will, of projects. Welles spoke of Dumas, Machiavelli and the Borgias, but also of an unformed idea for a film about some larger-than-life American figure – who, he wasn't quite sure. So much of his work had been to do with the idea of greatness and its limitations: right back to his childhood performances, Francis Lightfoot in *Wings over Europe* and Richard III, on through Duke Karl Alexander in Dublin, Claudius in Woodstock, McGafferty in *Panic*, Doctor Faustus and Brutus, above all his still unfilmed Kurtz. He had dealt again and again with the flaws that stop extraordinary men, men of potential genius, from fulfilling their promise; it was his great subject. Now he wanted to look at his own times, to find a figure of Shakespearean, or maybe rather, Marlovian, scope, to address.

Mankiewicz, a keen student of power and its abuses (which is a slightly different thing from what Welles was interested in), had, for his part, long dreamed of a screenplay about a public figure – a gangster, perhaps – whose story would be told from the many different points of those who had known him. This had already been attempted by Preston Sturges in his screenplay for *The Power and the Glory* (1935); and the 1930 Claude Houghton novel *I Am Jonathan Scrivener* presented an investigation into a man's life from many angles. The idea was very much in the air. Mankiewicz himself had written an unperformed play (*The Tree Will Grow*, about the gangster John Dillinger) to this prescription: in Act One, as described by Mankiewicz's biographer Richard Meryman, news of Dillinger's death is brought to his family. The play is a complex and contradictory portrait gradually accumulated from the recollections of mother, father, friends, and minister. Immediately enthused by the idea of the multiple viewpoints, Welles was less excited by the idea of playing Dillinger (hardly a part for him). Instead he and Mankiewicz began to think in terms of someone nearer at hand about whom they had also chatted a great deal: William Randolph Hearst, at whose parties Mankiewicz had been a welcome guest till his alcoholism had had him barred; Hearst did everything he could to keep Marion Davies away from anyone who might encourage her fondness for the bottle. Mankiewicz, nursing his resentment, had subsequently become obsessed by both Hearst and Davies, collecting stories about them the way small boys collect stamps.

Immediately they hit on the idea of using Hearst as their central character, all Welles's separate needs fell into place: a great theme, one which, because of Hearst's extraordinary career, encompassed a substantial amount of recent American history; a great role for him; and an original cinematically exciting method, barely explored as yet, of telling a story. It is hard to exaggerate the relief and excitement that he felt once the idea had crystallised. As 1939 drew to an end, he had again – in the nick of time – been saved by the bell. Still expecting to shoot *The Smiler with a Knife*, with which Mankiewicz had been unenthusiastically tinkering, Welles was desperate to get cracking on the new idea.

The pressure on him mounted. Herb Drake's great publicity coup, the lavishly illustrated three-part series in *Saturday Evening Post* (HOW TO RAISE A CHILD) had just appeared. What would normally have been a triumph was, in the circumstances of Welles's continuing non-productivity, something of an embarrassment. The tone of the articles verges on the satirical, as the authors solemnly catalogue their subject's legendary doings. 'He talked like a college professor at two. At three, he looked like Dr Fu Manchu and spouted Shakespeare like a veteran. At eight he started making his own highballs. He was leading man for Katharine Cornell at eighteen. Today, at twenty-four, he has the most amazing contract ever signed in Hollywood.' And nothing to show for it, the subtext loudly whispered. He must start work immediately, and when he did, it had better be good. Mankiewicz had expressed willingness to work on the idea, but (perhaps mischievously; he knew all about the recent supper at Chasen's) specifically requested Houseman to join him as collaborator on the initial stages. Without hesitation, Welles took a plane to New York to have lunch with the man at whom he had only ten days earlier hurled several flaming dish-warmers. Equally unhesitatingly, the target of those dish-warmers, only a week after severing their working relationship, agreed, over that lunch, to come and work on the new screenplay. Things couldn't move fast enough for Welles. He knew he was on to the most tremendous subject anyone could hope to find, and they had hit on a brilliant and original way of telling it.

A bald summary of Hearst's life reads in itself like the treatment for a movie. Heir to a mining fortune, after a profligate youth he had sought elected office without ever once coming close; abandoning the ballot box, he had used his fortune to buy up a chain of newspapers, through whose pages he then promoted his political beliefs. Like Oswald Mosley in England (the model for *The Smiler with a Knife*) he had rapidly developed from a progressive to a fascist, consorting with Hitler and Mussolini; as a man, he had developed from a high-spirited anti-authoritarian prankster (he had been business manager of the Harvard *Lampoon*) into a crusty and pompous reactionary, using the American League of Decency to disseminate his anti-communist, pro-family views in twenty-eight newspapers, thirteen magazines and on two radio stations. In rather naked contrast to this, he lived, very publicly but unreported, with his mistress Marion Davies. Just as he attempted to control American public opinion by sheer will-power and money, he attempted to turn Davies from a delightful and accomplished comedienne into the biggest star in Hollywood. Buying a studio in which to make starring vehicles for her, orchestrating frenzies of excitement at their premières, and then having them reviewed in apocalyptic terms, he succeeded only in making the films, Miss Davies, and himself ridiculous. His Spanish-gothic folly, San Simeon, built as temple to his love, was a bizarre aberration of the otherwise impeccably tasteful Beaux-Arts architect Julia Morgan, an extraordinary operatic creation, crammed with art works cheaply bought from impoverished European noblemen arranged in a sequence of enormous rooms without regard to period or style. An art lover's Disneyland, it is impressive only as a monument to its creator's will. In San Simeon, he arranged a succession of fêtes galantes, fancy dress balls and banquets to divert his beautiful captive, now middle-aged and drinking heavily. The photographs of these sumptuous events reveal the vast sums spent on them. Marion cavorts charmingly as Marie-Antoinette or Columbine, while Hearst, small-eyed and large-bodied, peers anaemically out of his pachydermatous frame, ludicrous in lederhosen.

All this was going on on Hollywood's doorstep, a couple of hours' drive up the coast. It was an irresistible subject; why had nobody attempted it before? The reason was simple: they had not dared to. Though financially weaker than he had been, Hearst was still not an enemy anyone in Hollywood wanted to take on. Mankiewicz dared; he was aching to bring all his bile to bear on this embodiment of everything he despised: 'a great WASP institution', as Welles later characterised Mankiewicz's delineation of Kane. Curiously enough, Mankiewicz's own politics were not very far from those of Hearst: starting as a radical (in the early thirties he had written an anti-Hitler screenplay, *Mad Dog of Europe*, which the largely Jewish Hollywood establishment suppressed), he became increasingly anti-communist and isolationist, believing that *they* (the Establishment: the Pentagon and the armaments industry) were lined up behind war for their own purposes. He started declaring that the Nazis were right about the over-dominance of Jews, though at the same time, with entirely characteristic perversity, sponsoring many Jewish émigrés as they arrived in America. Mankiewicz's grouse against Hearst was not political; it was personal. He loathed tycoons of any persuasion; his screenplay of two years before, *John Meade's Woman*, had been a savage assault on one. Entirely lacking power himself, he detested those who had it. *American*, as he and Welles decided to call their screenplay (the very title an allusion to Hearst's newspapers), was to be his revenge on the pack of them.

He, Welles and Houseman had many discussions in Hollywood, poring over the almost-too-rich material, establishing a structure which included a summary of the leading character's life in the form of a newsreel; an idea which Welles had earlier planned to use in *The Smiler with a Knife*. That project, in the mounting excitement over the new screenplay, was quietly abandoned due to 'casting difficulties'; *Heart of Darkness* was shelved, too. Neither these nor any other that Welles had contemplated could begin to compare in cinematic potential to Mankiewicz's idea, and none of them could give him the opportunities he was ideally equipped to take advantage of. He knew it. A contract was drawn up with Mercury Productions by which Mankiewicz was to be paid $1,000 a week. As often, he was to have no credit for his work, a small matter to him, screenplay doctor extraordinaire, but a large one to Welles, 'actor-director-producer-writer'. The publicity surrounding the prodigality of Welles's talents, and the subsequent and ever-increasing sniping about it, meant, he felt, that for him to acknowledge co-authorship would be a public humiliation; his contract with RKO precisely stipulated that the screenplay would be written by him.

So Arnold Weissberger took particular care to insert a clause in Mankiewicz's contract stating that 'All material composed, submitted, added or interpolated by you under this employment agreement, and all results and proceeds of all services rendered or to be rendered by you under this employment agreement, are now and shall forever be the property of Mercury Productions Inc who, for this purpose, shall be deemed the author and creator thereof, you having acted entirely as its employee.' A similar clause was to be found in the contracts of writers on *Campbell's Playhouse*; it was an understanding that Welles was known as the author, just as politicians' speeches, though rarely written by them, are deemed to be theirs. Welles had, in fact, he said, created a rudimentary script, three hundred pages of dialogue with occasional stage directions under the title of *John Citizen, USA* (which continued for a while to be the RKO project title). This he handed to Mankiewicz before he started work. Mankiewicz may or may not have read it; certainly no one else has ever seen it.

Mankiewicz's contract contained a further stipulation: that he would keep dry. It was partly to guarantee this that Houseman accompanied him to the little village of Victorville. But Mankiewicz also needed a collaborator of some sort. It was not in his nature to write alone. Without peer as a screenplay doctor, he had more difficulty initiating work. Carefully avoiding any suggestion that he actually wrote any of the screenplay (although he says that the NEWS ON THE MARCH section was his special responsibility), Houseman describes his work with Mankiewicz: that of any editor, responding, disagreeing, arguing, suggesting. When they had had their daily editorial session, he would withdraw. While Mankiewicz wrote, still in his plaster cast stretching from his navel to his toes, Houseman rode in the surrounding hills; their relationship was one of the utmost cordiality. Houseman glowingly describes their routine, the spartan living, the visits to the Green Spot for the permitted one drink a day. Houseman was drawn to Mankiewicz, as he was always drawn to self-assured but somehow incomplete people. He describes their friendship, which lasted over thirteen years till Mankiewicz's death, in almost identical terms to those in which, three years earlier, he had described his relationship with Welles: 'he was, variously, my collaborator, my father, my wayward son, my counsellor and a source of inexhaustible stimulation, exasperation and pleasure.'

Here in the desert, with Houseman as a catalyst, Mankiewicz found his form again. As they worked, they developed a sort of schoolboyish attitude to their employer, Welles. 'Sadly,' Welles wrote to Bogdanovich, 'the closer Jack got to Mank, the further Mank moved away from me.' He became 'Maestro, the Dog-Faced Boy' and they took naughty pleasure in slipping elements from his life and his character into the screenplay. (It is above all this, Pauline Kael maintained, that deprived Mankiewicz of his proper acknowledgement for his work. 'As a result of Mankiewicz's wicked sense of humour in drawing upon Welles's character for Kane's, his own authorship was obscured. Sensing the unity in Kane and Welles, audiences assume that Kane is Welles's creation, that Welles is playing "the role he was born to play", while scholars, seeing the material from Welles's own life in the movie, interpret the film as Welles working out autobiographical themes.') Welles believed that Houseman used his time in Victorville to poison Mankiewicz against him. 'When Mank left for Victorville, we were friends. When he came back, we were enemies. Mank always needed a villain.' It is not to be doubted that Houseman was perfectly capable of trying to suspend the mutual admiration society which Welles and Mankiewicz had established; it is none the less equally true that Welles was again speaking autobiographically when he speaks of Mank's 'need for a villain'. For him Houseman filled this role. 'I have only one real enemy in my life that I know about,' Welles told Meryman, 'and that is John Houseman. Everything begins and ends with the hostility behind the mandarin benevolence.' This is palpably untrue, since Houseman withdrew from Welles's life just at the moment that he became hugely successful; Welles engineered his subsequent downfall all on his own.

Now running *Campbell's Playhouse* without Houseman – who had resigned from it after their bust-up in Chasen's – Welles was heavily involved in the radio programmes and left his collaborators to get on with producing the first draft. He would pay the occasional visit to Victorville; pages would be sent to him in Hollywood. The script was constantly amended according to his input; Houseman describes their struggles integrating his latest thoughts into the structure, which none the less remained firmly in place: the death of the central figure, followed by the newsreel of his life and the investigation of his final word, Rosebud. Cheering though the work on the script was, Welles was now in serious trouble financially. In addition to his own extravagant life, he had to pay alimony to Virginia, their divorce (on the grounds of his mental cruelty) having gone painlessly through – in Reno – in February of 1940. 'He's a genius and sometimes works around the clock without sleep,' she gallantly explained. 'He has no time for marriage and a family.' The settlement, as well as providing for maintenance for Virginia and Christopher, additionally determined that he must take out $100,000 life insurance cover, half to benefit Virginia, half Christopher. It was all adding up; and there was no income to meet it. *Campbell's Playhouse* had now finally come to an end, for good, Ward Wheelock having decided that the battle to get Welles to keep the sponsor sweet was too troublesome; that had been his only regular salary. *Jane Eyre*, starring Madeleine Carroll with Welles as Rochester, was the last programme. He was due no more money from RKO until the commencement of shooting, so he gladly embraced the notion that Albert Schneider (still at Columbia Management) came up with: a tour on the burgeoning lecture circuit. Since at this moment Welles's celebrity was the only area of expansion in his life, Schneider sought to exploit it. A LECTURE RECITAL BY ORSON WELLES the posters said. DIRECTOR-STAR OF THE MERCURY THEATRE, PRODUCER, WRITER, ACTOR – FOR RADIO, THEATRE, MOTION PICTURES.

As if in mockery of this boast, he became involved, just as he was about to set out on his travels, in an unseemly exchange with the sociologist Hadley Cantril over that perennially sensitive matter in his life, authorship. Cantril, having completed his survey of *The War of the Worlds* panic, wanted to publish Howard Koch's script alongside it in a single volume, and asked Welles to endorse the book. Welles's impassioned reply took Cantril by surprise. Welles complained of 'an error so grave, and in my opinion so detrimental to my own reputation that I cannot in all fairness speak well of it until some reparation is made'. This was the attribution of the script to Koch. He does not regret, he says, the exclusion of himself as dramatist, so much as he regrets the absence of any mention of the other people who 'as it happened in this particular broadcast were of much greater service'; these include, he says, John Houseman, 'my partner in all Mercury Theatre enterprises and my chief collaborator', as well as the other members under him in the writers' department. This was a new slant: collective authorship; his acknowledgement of Houseman's input is remarkable and unlikely to have been made under any other circumstances. He expands: the idea for *The War of the Worlds* broadcast was his; Koch was 'very helpful' in the second portion of the script and did some work on the first, most of which, he says, it was necessary to revise. His advice, he says, 'both legal and in the fields of publicity and personal relations', is unanimously to the effect that the reference to the broadcast script as the 'Howard Koch dramatisation' is 'something worse than merely untrue'. Every one of his collaborators, including the actors, brought more to the programme than Koch. Finally he comes out into the open: 'I do strongly feel that you have unwittingly implied a slur on my position as the creator and responsible artist of my broadcasts.' It had by now become essential to him (in his own mind, at any rate) to maintain his position as Renaissance Man. Under constant pressure from a carping, mocking press, he dreaded being found out as less than what he claimed to be. This is not vanity; it is terror.

Cantril, wiser than Solomon, suggested an ingenious formula: 'Script ideas and development by Orson Welles assisted by John Houseman and Mercury Theatre staff and written by Howard Koch under the direction of Mr Welles.' Welles blasted back with a telegram by return of wire: 'your suggested revision for the second printing is far too elaborate and incorrect a statement stop i repeat war of the worlds was not written by howard koch'. In his earlier letter he had suggested an erratum slip, an idea to which Cantril had not warmed. 'Think how much more unfavourable an impression your book will make as it now stands and try to conceive the effect on my professional prestige and position in the theatre world. Can see no conceivable reason for your steadfast refusal to believe *The War of the Worlds* was not only my conception but also, properly and exactly speaking, my creation. Once again, finally, and I promise for the last time, Howard Koch did not write *The War of the Worlds*. Any statement to this effect is untrue and immeasurably detrimental to me.'

Cantril replies citing affidavits and a telegram from Houseman's secretary at the time saying that Koch dictated the script to her from a manuscript in his own handwriting, and that Houseman and Paul Stewart made only minor corrections in it. 'In view of all the evidence we have from him,' Cantril ends, 'I find no other alternative than to acknowledge him as writer but not as creator.' Welles blasts back with the magnificently seigneurial statement that 'I should most certainly think that the word of the producer-director-star and star of the broadcast which is the subject of your book would hold more weight with you than the word of one of the authors employed by him at the time.' Cantril has resorted to underlings, Welles continues. 'I cannot understand why you have so steadfastly refused to believe me. *Mr Howard K. did not do the actual writing of The War of the Worlds script.* He only did some of it.' He adds 'my interest in this matter is not to receive credit. My only interest, like yours, is accuracy,' rather spoiling his objective stand by adding 'I'm sure you can appreciate the untold damage done to my professional reputation that the publication of this book in its present form will create. I know that you will understand that I cannot permit this to occur.'

The note of desperation is explained by his public standing at that moment. *Citizen Kane* was not even at first draft stage yet, and like all such things, a tremendous gamble. It could have gone either way. He was surfing on a tidal wave of publicity which threatened to engulf him, since there was nothing visible to justify it; his most recent work in the theatre had passed either unnoticed or unloved, his radio programme, though commanding solid audience figures, generated little excitement. None of his Hollywood projects had materialised. *The War of the Worlds* was, in effect, his only real claim to widespread fame: it was the reason that he was in Hollywood at all, the real reason that he had been able to negotiate the famous contract, the only living proof of his multi-faceted genius. The revelation that he had not actually written it would deprive his image of one of its crucial dimensions, making him look a fraud; the discovery that the whole thing had been an accident would have finished him off for good. Or so it seemed from his pardonably paranoid position. He lost this battle; the book (*The Invasion from Mars*) duly appeared with Koch credited as author of the script. In the event, no one except Welles even noticed; the legend was undented. The level of his anxiety about all this, however, is a good index of quite how vulnerable he felt in April of 1940.

Meanwhile,, there was money to be earned. Newly shaven (*Five Kings* was clearly now abandoned), he set out on his travels: Pasadena, Kansas City, Portland, Seattle, Tacoma, Wenatchee. These engagements, though they may have helped his overdraft, did little to improve his position in Hollywood. Herb Drake described the event in press briefing-ese: 'Lecture is informal. Invites hecklers from outset. Is obliged. Welles approves films; also stage. Points out errors both mediums. Besides talking, reads speeches *Hamlet, Richard III*, Congreve etc. Believe me audience shocked and amused. Welles opens and closes with jokes. All this done without benefit of beard.' This was a rather different event from Charles Laughton's famous lecture programme, designed to communicate some of his almost carnal passion for the arts, theatrical, literary, visual. Welles was in the business of punditry. He was out to opine, to provoke and to instruct, and of course it got him into trouble. The United Press Association reported from Kansas City – only his second date – that he had said 'I'll speak only in terms of contempt. Hollywood is just like any other small town. Movie actors have ceased to think of themselves as servants. As a matter of fact, they are really in the same class as those who wait on tables. The average person goes to the movies because it is better than drink.' This provoked a flurry of much publicised resentment from leading Hollywood actors and industry spokesmen, the last thing he needed at this delicate moment. 'As you can imagine,' he wrote in an open letter to his host in Kansas City, 'these misrepresentations of my sentiments place me in an acutely embarrassing position as regards my work in Hollywood.' What he actually said, he claims, was that movies were a better bargain than the theatre and aesthetically more valid; that 90 per cent of the theatre talent was in Hollywood; that he personally preferred the movies of today to the theatre of today; and that actors should always remember that they are the servants of the public. It seems that Welles could embrace something only by renouncing something else. His Kansas City host, confirming his account of the lecture, adds 'Let me know when you are ready to come to Kansas City again. Next time you will have an audience of ten thousand instead of five thousand, though five thousand is nothing to sneeze at. There are not half a dozen people in the country who could draw this number.' The paradox continued. His fame, even in relatively out-of-the-way places, was growing daily, while his achievements remained invisible. The lectures were so successful that, Drake told the press, though there were no definite Broadway plans for Welles's talk-in he intended to play New York with it for at least six weeks in the coming season. Depending on how *American* turned out, that might be all he had to look forward to.

The script, all 350 pages of it, was waiting for him on his return. It was, according to Robert Carringer, whose brilliant researches on the making of *Citizen Kane* have finally put paid to speculation about the genesis of the screenplay, a literal reworking by and large of specific incidents and details from Hearst's life, most of it first-hand observation on Mankiewicz's part, but some evidently derived from a current biography, Ferdinand Lundberg's *Imperial Hearst*. Comprehensive and over-literal though it might be, it was not lacking in cinematic boldness: much of the story was told in montage form. Among many striking scenes, there was a particularly audacious one in Rome where the young Kane has taken up residence, surrounding himself with ambi-sexual decadents and works of art of dubious propriety. A sub-plot involved Kane's father, a rip-roaring, globe-trotting old party determined to marry the young tart (Miss Henrietta La Salle) with whom he is travelling; he runs across his son, who, finding out about the marriage, attempts to throttle him. It is hard not to see some sort of sly allusion by Mankiewicz and Houseman to Welles's own father in the figure of Kane, Senior.

The screenplay as presented was a rich pudding; Welles immediately went to work as editor. He slashed through Mankiewicz's text just as he had slashed through Shakespeare's and Dekker's. As with those writers, he added none of his own words, preferring to isolate or rearrange someone else's. His skill, and, equally important, his courage in this department was unparalleled. Sometimes (as in his Mercury scripts) he would slash whole pages of writing, ending up only with one line, or none. He had now been thinking about and working on films for nine months; he had begun to have pretty clear ideas about how a scene is constructed and how best to tell his story. His first task was not an aesthetic one, however. It was legally impossible to shoot this script: Hearst was absolutely, unmistakably and actionably the central character. A great deal of Welles's initial work consisted simply in smudging that clear profile. There was, too, something of a hole at the centre. Welles maintained later to Richard Meryman (in one of his more analytical, less defensive interviews on the subject of *Citizen Kane*) that Mankiewicz, for all the brilliance of his writing, and the excellence of his structure – which remained basically the same throughout the many versions of the script – had not found the essential character of the man. 'In his hatred of Hearst, or whoever Kane was, Mank didn't have a clear enough idea of who the man was . . . I felt his knowledge was journalistic, not very close, the point of view of a newspaperman writing about a newspaper boss he despised.' Welles, both as director and as actor, was eager to create a distinctive character: one, moreover, that was not entirely unsympathetic.

This was to be a continuing source of negotiation between Welles and Mankiewicz. A classic instance of their different views of Kane (and also of the nature of Welles's contribution) is the scene in the *Inquirer*'s offices, where Leland falls asleep drunk over his bad review of Susan Alexander Kane's operatic debut. This incident, drawn from Mankiewicz's own experience, ended, in Mankiewicz's draft, with Leland being fired by Kane. It was Welles who insisted on the ending eventually filmed, with Kane personally finishing and then publishing the bad review. 'I always wanted Kane to have that sort of almost self-destructive elegance of attitude which, even when it was self-regarding and vain, was peculiarly chic. Mank fought me terribly about that scene: "Why should he finish the notice? He wouldn't. He just wouldn't print it." Which would have been true of Hearst.' In one of the most pertinent of all observations about *Citizen Kane*, Welles remarked to Meryman that their disagreement over the character of Kane 'probably gave the picture a certain tension: that one of the authors hated Kane and one of them loved him'. He added something which exactly describes what we see on the screen: 'There is a quality to the film – that was Mank and that I treasured . . . it was a kind of controlled cheerful virulence.'

Welles returned the script with his many suggestions to Mankiewicz, who, working in his continuing bed-bound isolation at Victorville, completed the second draft, duly delivering it on 9 May. Now off the payroll, Mankiewicz went to work on *Madam X*, for which, as Carringer points out with nice irony, he was uncredited. Houseman departed for New York, and Welles settled down to read the new version with the yelping of the press pack echoing in his ears. His twenty-fifth birthday had fallen a few days before, and the hacks rushed to offer their own acid greetings. 'Orson Welles is 25 years old tomorrow and comes into an inheritance. Uncle Sam gets most of it for taxes. Well, the boy wonder needn't worry too much since he almost inherited RKO in salary checks without making a single picture there.' 'Orson Welles, celebrating his 25 birthday,' said another, 'made a resolution to produce that picture if it takes him another 25 years.' Never mind; the latest draft of *American* was highly encouraging, and Welles, in a somewhat theatrical procedure, read it out loud to Schaefer and RKO's corporate lawyer, Edington.

Schaefer was understandably pleased with the reading: a film of this magnitude, scope, daring and originality was precisely what he had brought Welles to Hollywood for. Edington was happy to note a general moving away from the facts of Hearst's life. He was relieved to discover that an earlier sequence in which Kane has Raymond, the butler, murder a suspected lover of his wife had gone; it was modelled all too directly on a widely rumoured scandal involving the death of the director, Thomas Ince, on board Hearst's yacht. (Typically, Mankiewicz had insisted that keeping the sequence in the movie would deter Hearst from suing: how could he admit then that the character was him?) In order to move the movie still further away from Hearst, Schaefer (whose contract with Welles gave him title approval) suggested that they drop the provocative *American* in favour of – his idea – *Citizen Kane*. Welles enthusiastically accepted the new title; apart from anything else, no one had been able to think of a suitable one (his secretary's proposal of *A Sea of Upturned Faces* being only the least satisfactory). Adopting Schaefer's title had another advantage: psychologically, he would feel that it was his project. The film got the go-ahead, with an authorisation to proceed to third draft.

Welles followed up the reading with a memo describing the film's structure – the four interviews and the quest for Rosebud – adding revealing comments on the different aspects of the character of Kane as revealed by the various interviewees. It is interesting to note his view of the screenplay before he had even shot a frame. Leland, says Welles, shows Kane's dual personality: 'the tremendous vitality, gaiety and joie de vivre combined with the idealism which expresses itself in such a document as the Manifesto'. In the Boss Gettys scene 'Kane's monomania finally exerts itself: his enraged conviction that no one exists but himself, his refusal to admit the existence of other people with whom one must compromise, whose feelings one must take into account.' There is some sense here of an overlap between Kane and Welles. Like a first novel, a first movie is more than likely to be autobiographical; in this instance the elements that had gone into the brew were many: Mankiewicz, Welles, even Houseman, working from a central perception, were adding more and more personal ingredients, partly in order to cover up the resemblance to Hearst's life, partly because the narrative thread they had established offered innumerable opportunities for personal detail. The screenplay is a tapestry of private references.

Names were culled from whoever was around: Susan Alexander got hers from Mankiewicz's secretary Rita Alexander, Boss Jim Gettys from Hortense Hill's maiden name, Mr Bernstein, of course, from Dadda. The central character was renamed. Mankiewicz had favoured Craig; Welles felt it was weak, and he was right: *Citizen Craig* has the air of a minor sit-com. Kane was Welles's choice, after his old colleague and sparring partner, Whitford Kane, also perhaps subconsciously recalling Kane County in the state of Illinois; he overrode Mankiewicz's concern that it would suggest the biblical Cain. It amused Houseman enormously to model the butler Raymond after Welles's creepily indolent butler, Charles. In the same random way, things were absorbed whenever they seemed appropriate: Mankiewicz's wife Sara had given him a snow-scene in a glass globe; as he worked on the new draft at home, he would idly pick it up and shake it about. Into the screenplay it went. Perhaps, too, as Carringer and others have suggested, he was vaguely remembering a sequence in *Kitty Foyle*, 1939's Ginger Rogers vehicle, which makes much of just such a snow scene in a crystal globe; perhaps not. As for Rosebud, various prurient suggestions have been offered (Hearst allegedly referred to Marion Davies's pudenda by that name); in fact Mankiewicz had had in boyhood a bicycle named Rosebud. The sled, embodying the normal life from which Kane was ripped, comes, as we have seen, from the Todd School, which represented as near to a childhood idyll as Welles knew. Thus the ingredients were assembled. What is important is that all these things were put together by controlling intelligences who were very aware of what they were aiming for. What came from where hardly matters; the question is why?

Some years later, Welles was required to make a deposition on the subject of *Citizen Kane* before a court set up to establish, ironically enough, whether its authors had plagiarised Lundberg's biography, *Imperial Hearst*. He outlined the story they were telling in terms which make it perfectly clear that they had a very strong conception of the meaning of the film. 'We postulated a fairly classic psychological set-up,' testified Welles, 'involving the loss of a mother, the failure to make what psychoanalysts speak of as a "transference" to any other woman and the need to wield power as an expression of ego. Kane was a spoiled child, but spoiled without benefit of human affection. In other words, we wished to show a man with an urge to assume a position of responsibility in public affairs but having himself no sense of responsibility, only a series of good intentions, fuzzy sentiments and numb, undefined yearnings . . . his failure in public life and the transference of his efforts from his own broken political career to those of an untalented woman, a singer at whom audiences laughed, all this grew out of the initial character set up. Kane's retreat to one of those enormous imitation feudal kingdoms, which his type of public man tends to construct for himself, was another natural result of the character as conceived. If the world did not behave the way he wanted it to behave, then he would build a world of his own where all the citizens were his subjects and on his payroll. Such men as Kane always tend toward the newspaper and entertainment world. They combine a morbid preoccupation with the public with a devastatingly low opinion of the public mentality and moral character.' The notion of a man who rebuilds the unsatisfactory real world in a parallel world of invention and propaganda was at the heart of the script as they had evolved it; this too was something Welles understood deeply.

Once the picture had been given the go-ahead, the collaborators, whatever tensions or distrust underlay their work, were in high spirits, so much so that the *New York Herald Tribune* of 19 May 1940 reported that 'John Houseman, Herman J. Mankiewicz and Orson Welles announce the formation of United Productions. UP will present for Pacific Coast runs 5 new productions a year originating in Hollywood . . . the Mercury Theatre will operate in partnership with the new producing firm, furnishing it with 2 productions a season, directed and produced by Mr Welles.' This expansion was a sure sign of Welles's confidence; whenever things were going well, he announced a five-year plan. These were not to be taken seriously: an ambitious press release was for him the equivalent of a shot of vitamin B12. Of this particular plan, like most of them, no more was heard, though Houseman began to sound out properties. Houseman continued to be involved in the three-way collaboration on the script of *Kane*: a telegram of 16 June 1940 shows both how basic to the project was Houseman's participation, and how active was Welles's work on the script: 'dear mank received your cut version also several new scenes of orsons stop approve all cuts stop still don't like rome scene and will try to work on it my humble self stop after much careful reading i like all orsons scene including new montages and chicago opera scenes with exception of kane emily sequence stop don't like scene on boat stop query any first meeting scene between them before oil scandal comes to shatter it stop simply don't understand sequence or sense of orsons telescoped kane leland emily assassination scenes stop there again will try and make up my own version stop please keep me posted'. Meanwhile, the accounts department had got their hands on the second draft. Their assessment was $1,082,798: twice the agreed budget. The third draft, which had been Welles's exclusive responsibility, and which was further extensively trimmed, was received gloomily by accounts: Welles's cuts had made no substantial difference to the cost. It was, they pointed out, fifty to sixty pages longer than any film ever previously shot by RKO. Frustrated but still forging eagerly ahead, Welles was happy to put Mankiewicz back on payroll to work on further condensation and elimination, leaving him to work on it alone while he started to work on the physical aspect of the filming: the art work and, above all, the cinematography.

The art director assigned to him by Van Nest Polglase, overall head of design at RKO, was Perry Ferguson, a man known, Carringer reveals, for his even temper, his diplomatic skills, his speed and his versatility. From *Gunga Din* to *Bringing up Baby*, from *The Story of Vernon and Irene Castle* to *The Swiss Family Robinson* he had easily moved from one period to another, from screwball comedy to romance, desert island drama to military epic. This admirable man worked happily with Welles, story-boarding every scene, suggesting, modifying, advising. Welles was supremely confident visually; design in the cinema is essentially the same as design in the theatre if you believe, as Welles passionately did, in the expressive importance of it. He had a very clear concept of what he wanted from the settings: they should help to trace the rise and fall of the central character. Making the story-board immediately brought Welles to the fundamental question: the framing of the shots. What would the film look like? He needed the input of his cameraman. The story-board process, which requires crucial decisions, is a severe test of a tyro director. Technically speaking, of course, Welles the superb illustrator naturally thought in terms of groupings, tableaux. The difficulty is that the enormous number of successive images that is a film requires some sort of organic logic, like images in a poem. It is a language, and it has a grammar, but scarcely one that can be taught, except by experience. It is a different way of communicating, and no matter how heightened your visual awareness, a grasp of the language is essential. It may even be said that the more visually sophisticated the aspiring director, the firmer his grasp must be. Proliferating astonishing images is the easiest thing in the world; telling a story through them is another matter. A wonderful vocabulary will get you precisely nowhere if you can't frame a sentence. The tyro director desperately depends on his cameraman for guidance.

The director of photography is the technician who records the images, but, in the nature of things, he or she is often the person who engenders them. It is perfectly possible as a director to concern yourself with the dialogue, the characterisation, the hair-cuts or the extras and leave the pictures to the cinematographer. Many famous directors have done just that. Welles was not going to be among them. The appointment of his director of photography was the crucial decision now the screenplay existed. In this instance, he needed someone who was open to suggestion, who had initiative and was good-humoured, who was also aware that his director, however imaginative and intelligent, was not going to have all the answers, nor would he resent him for that. Praying for such a paragon, Welles's prayers were answered beyond his wildest expectations. Improbably, the most famous cameraman in Hollywood, who was also its boldest experimenter, as well as being the most agreeable of men, approached Welles out of the blue and offered him his services. This was Gregg Toland, fresh from *The Grapes of Wrath*, *The Long Voyage Home* and *Wuthering Heights*, for his work on which he had just won an Oscar, and he was the last of the instruments of Welles's destiny.

'I know nothing about film-making,' said Welles when they met. 'That's why I want to work with you,' said Toland. 'That's the only way to learn anything – from somebody who doesn't know anything.' The first thought that struck anyone who met Toland, according to his friend George Turner, was that he appeared frail, even ill. 'He had a sallow complexion, was under-weight and walked with a stoop that made him appear older than he was. He seemed to be carrying the weight of the world on his shoulders. When he spoke of the thing that dominated his life – cinematography – the melancholy look vanished. No one could speak more eloquently or knowledgeably or with greater enthusiasm. When he was at work, an even greater change took place: he was a dynamo of energy to whom long hours and difficult working conditions meant nothing.' Temperamentally opposite, Welles and he were perfectly matched in their passion for work, and each realised that the other would be an ideal collaborator. In fact, Toland knew Welles's theatre work, having been especially struck by *Julius Caesar*, with its boldly sculpted light and swift transitions. He knew that Welles was no slavish adherent of naturalism and had a hunch that Welles would allow him to pursue certain developments further than any of the distinguished directors for whom he had most recently been working – Wyler, Ratoff and Ford – even though Ford had allowed him an extraordinary degree of freedom in the highly composed *Long Voyage Home*. Toland was a man with a mission; in his own sphere, he was as determined a self-publicist as Welles, writing passionately polemical articles in the specialist press. He had already created something of a division in the ranks of cinematography.

After early experience with the ceaselessly experimental Arthur Edeson, he had frequently worked with the highly original director/designer of *The Shape of Things to Come*, William Cameron Menzies. Famous for his speed and adaptability, Toland quickly worked his way through the system, avoiding being attached to a studio, which would have curbed his independence and required him to do routine work. Eventually he signed a contract with Goldwyn which provided him with two unique opportunities: the virtually unheard-of right to work with the director and designer six weeks before the start of shooting and free access to Goldwyn's experimental laboratory. He made tough demands of himself. 'Not only should the cameraman know all about the science and mechanics of photography but he should be a student of the drama,' he wrote. 'I found it to my advantage to take a course in playwriting. Also a course in hair-dressing and another in screen make-up. I continually observe and study new styles in women's clothes, from the viewpoint of their values in enhancing certain dramatic methods.' Along with this thorough practical preparation, he had a slightly mystical, slightly subversive view of his profession. 'Of all the people who make up a movie production unit, the cameraman is the only one who can call himself a free soul' – because, he says, you don't see the results of the cameraman's work till the rushes are viewed, twenty-four hours later. 'No, the cameraman is perfectly at liberty to carry out his own ideas, even to introduce an occasional revolutionary departure – within the bounds of reason, of course.' These were the bounds he sought to test with Welles.

'A great deal has been written and said about the new technical and artistic possibilities offered by such developments as coated lenses, super-fast films and the use of lower-proportioned and partially ceilinged sets,' he wrote. 'We (cinematographers who have experimented with them) wished that instead of using them conservatively for a scene here or a sequence there, they could experiment free-handedly with them throughout an entire production.' Because of the special character of *Citizen Kane*'s screenplay, 'as both Welles and I saw it, we were forced to make radical departures from conventional practice.' Of course Welles was delighted to facilitate Toland's experiment. It was in his nature to innovate; besides, it was what was required of him.

Toland swiftly converted him to the principle tenets of his celluloid faith, all of which were designed to honour its greatest gospel: Realism. As in every age, in every art, the innovators claim that their development breaks the mould of convention to restore the fresh impact of truth. 'Both Welles and I felt that if it was possible, the picture should be brought to the screen in such a way that the audience would feel it was looking at reality, rather than merely at a movie.' For Toland, and therefore for Welles, that meant, self-evidently, sharp-focus, great depth-of-field and ceilings on rooms. The finished result seems to us, now, the opposite of real. It seems stylised in the extreme. Paradoxically, though, it meant that Welles could stage the film almost as if it were a play. He had to make no concession to the camera; it would follow him wherever he wanted it to go. Another crucial principle that Toland gave to Welles was that of continuous action. 'I was constantly encouraged by Toland, who said, under the influence of Ford, "carry everything in one shot – don't do anything else." In other words, play scenes through without cutting, and don't do alternate versions. That was Toland in my ear,' Welles told Peter Bogdanovich. 'And secondly, I didn't know to have all kinds of choices. All I could think of to do was what was going to be on the screen in the final version.' The single biggest difficulty for someone directing a film for the first time is that (with rare exceptions) he or she will never have edited one. It is extraordinarily difficult to judge what shots will be needed when the picture is edited, to imagine in advance the sequence of shots within a single scene, or the breakdown of the scene into different cuts (close-up, two-shot, three-shot and so on). This problem of 'coverage' is one Welles never had to face. According to Toland 'we tried to plan the action so that the camera could pan or dolly from one angle to another whenever this type of treatment was desirable.'

Another concomitant of Toland's belief in realism was the notion of seamlessness, something on which Welles had placed considerable stress in his screenplay of *Heart of Darkness*. Welles, said

Toland admiringly, 'instinctively grasped a point which many other far more experienced directors and producers never comprehend; that the scenes and sequences should flow together so smoothly that the audience should not be conscious of the mechanics of picture-making.' This, too, seems very nearly the opposite of what was achieved, though technically it is true that *Citizen Kane* is a film of a thousand transitions, all of them carefully worked out and then shot in the camera, with lights on individual dimmers to facilitate the smoothness that Toland so desired. Toland knew that everything they were attempting must be planned to the last detail. He and Welles, co-conspirators, set to with evangelical determination. 'To put things with brutal frankness, these things simply cannot be done by conventional means. But they were a basic part of *Citizen Kane* and they *had* to be done.' In order to achieve the sharp focus that he believed was the essence of realism, he experimented with high-powered arc lights, coated lenses, super-speed (XX) film and low f= stops. He describes the shot of a man and a loving-cup which would, he said, normally be cut 'between close-up and cup. Yet we were able to keep the man's face fully defined, while at the same time the loving-cup was in such sharp focus that the audience was able to read the inscription from it,' he writes. 'Also beyond this foreground were a group of men from 12 to 18 foot focal distance. These men were equally sharp.' His excitement is palpable even now; it must have knocked Welles sideways.

He was preparing to demonstrate nothing less than the future of film in *Citizen Kane*. There was no universal agreement that his developments constituted progress. Within the cinematographic profession, there was a large body of practitioners who regarded the principles of 'good photography' as hard won and not to be easily traded for flashy sharpness: 'that illusion of roundness which – fully as important as depth of definition – is a necessity in conveying the illusion of three-dimensional reality in our two-dimensional pictures.' There was concern, too, that so-called universal focus, whereby the whole screen was equally sharp in focus (the Holy Grail of Toland and like-minded cameramen), would confuse the eye, which would scarcely know where to look. These debates recall those that raged around the introduction of stereophonic sound and, later, compact discs: warmth, naturalness, mellowness would all be banished. These, of course, were the very last things that Welles or Toland were interested in: sharpness, fluidity and contrast were their ideals. They gloried in their Brave New World. It was pan-focus this, and pan-focus that – a phrase which, Welles delightedly confessed to

Bogdanovich, didn't mean anything at all. 'We called it pan-focus in some idiot interview – just for the fun of it.'

Perry Ferguson was party to all Toland's experimentation; they were of pressing concern to his department, as floors were cut up, sets built on parallels, muslin ceilings (to allow both light and sound to pass through them) installed. His particular problem was one of budget. The scale conceived by Welles was one which the film could not afford; it became necessary to cheat many of the settings, particularly those at Xanadu, as Mankiewicz and Welles had named Kane's castle (having first toyed with calling it Alhambra). This he proposed to do by borrowing many of the crucial architectural elements of the set from the RKO stores; other settings would simply have to be filmed from cunning angles to conceal the fact that they were only partly there, the larger part of them shrouded in darkness created by velvet drapes. Ferguson, too, seems to have got into the swing of all this with great enthusiasm. Imagination and technical cunning were taking the place of sheer expenditure.

As the three collaborators thrilled each other with their daring, work on the script continued, Welles constantly feeding back developments in pre-production to Mankiewicz, who did his best to absorb them. Welles had by now cast all the leading roles, as much as possible from his usual pool, but slightly differently in composition to the *Heart of Darkness* cast: the *Five Kings* contingent had thinned out (Emery, Readick and Barrier had no parts in *Citizen Kane*), the old pals, Sherman and Carter had gone. Joe Cotten, who had been triumphantly playing in *Philadelphia Story* with Katharine Hepburn in New York (she had seen him in *Too Much Johnson* and obviously not held it against him) was cast in the crucial role of Jedediah Leland. Welles remained desperately eager that the actors should be unknown faces in Hollywood. Only Coulouris, somehow typically, had let his celluloid virginity go, but in heavy disguise. Agnes Moorehead came to Hollywood to play Kane's mother after having worked with Welles for some years on radio: she had been Margot Lane to his Lamont Cranston, the Shadow's shadow. The two newcomers to the group were Ruth Warrick and Dorothy Comingore as Kane's two wives. Warrick, a radio singer and off-Broadway actress (and former Miss Jubilesta) was to play Kane's first wife, Emily: 'I'm not looking for an actress who can play a lady,' he said to her. 'I want an actress who *is* a lady.' Comingore he cast as Susan Alexander Kane ('probably the most important character in the picture', he told her, alarmingly). He was looking for someone who could convincingly be 'frightened, whining, pathetic'. Stepping outside his regular troupe, he obviously sought to cast to type.

With Comingore, particularly, he detected something within her own personality that he knew would be invaluable to Susan Alexander. An old girlfriend of Chaplin's, her career had failed to take off despite his attempts to advance it. She had even changed her name; Welles insisted that she change it back. To an extent he reproduced in his behaviour to her Kane's behaviour to Susan; but to a large degree he sought to root all of the characters in the specific actors he had cast, just as he had meant to in *Heart of Darkness*. In the case of his old team, the parts had been precisely tailored to them: to some aspects of them that Welles perceived. Now, in mid-June, he held unofficial rehearsals at Mankiewicz's house (to avoid paying full salaries as required by Equity) with any of the actors who were available; more modifications took place. The Revised Final Draft was delivered on 24 June. By 7 July, the accounts department gave their verdict: the script as it stood would cost $737,740, fully 50 per cent over the agreed figure. Schaefer none the less gave the film the go-ahead. His anxieties of the previous year had given way to a much more bullish mood; thanks to 1939's royal flush of successes, RKO finally freed itself from official receivership in January 1940. 'The new RKO' was much publicised under Schaefer's headline: 'Quality Pictures at a Premium Price'. To confirm the new mood, he spent $390,000 in seven days. *Citizen Kane* would be the living proof of RKO's new-found status.

The script had further evolutions to undergo, each resulting in greater concision. The Second Revised Final Draft dropped an attempted assassination sequence. In this draft the celebrated breakfast scene between Kane and Emily, covering in one brief montage the whole history of their marriage, was introduced. This was Welles's idea, stolen, as he was always delighted to admit, from Thornton Wilder's then famous experimental one-act play *The Long Christmas Dinner* written seven years earlier, in which ninety years of a family's life, over several generations, are played around the same unchanging seasonal table. Under financial pressure, the scene in which Susan plays with a jigsaw puzzle had to be moved from a dining-room set, which could not be afforded, to the Great Hall, which was already being used for several other scenes; it is the location which, as Carringer says, makes the scene. In the Third (and Final) Revised Final script the newspaper party and opera review scenes which had both been broken up by other scenes, were, for financial reasons, both played straight through. This is the script that was filmed; even then, of course, changes were made. Robert Carringer's detailed exposition of the development of the screenplay is an entirely convincing account of the nature of creation in a collaborative art: there was no master script, neither Welles's nor Mankiewicz's nor indeed Toland's – no pure concept, unswervingly followed and masterfully realised. Under legal and financial and creative pressure it had changed and changed and changed. All was compromise: adaptation, alteration, condensation; trimming, sharpening, honing. In this, as in all of the lively arts, the readiness is all: the ability to accommodate new inspiration and to shed what no longer works, to recognise solutions wherever they come from, to be willing shamelessly to beg, borrow or steal whatever is useful to you. At this stage of his life, Welles was supremely responsive to all this, a creative opportunist without peer.

Now, approaching countdown, he was about to put the script (and his own abilities) to the proof. Toland was not available to shoot the tests; instead another distinguished cameraman, Russell Metty (later to shoot *A Touch of Evil*), was responsible for them. Make-up was a crucial consideration. Welles had come across Maurice Seiderman literally sweeping the cut hair off the floor of RKO's make-up department. The twenty-five-year-old Russian immigrant, who had worked on *Gunga Din* and *Swiss Family Robinson*, had no official job in the department; he was not a union member, never became one and is thus uncredited on the film. Welles noticed him experimenting with latex and, passionately interested as he was and always had been in make-up, discussed its possibilities. He became convinced that Seiderman was the man for the job. Once again, he added someone to his team who was bursting with ideas and theories and would go to any lengths to explore them; someone, too, who would respond to *his* ideas and theories, rather than fob him off with routine applications. Welles was convinced, for example, that film stars represented types rather than detailed individuals; it would therefore be necessary for his actors to learn to concentrate and simplify their personas – particularly, their appearances. Accordingly, he had Seiderman sculpt make-up portraits for them that, in Frank Brady's phrase, 'followed Hollywood genre types'.

His own make-up was based on photographs of Samuel Insull, the Chicago magnate, and, inevitably, Hearst. (Seiderman made a cast of Welles's head: looking like a young pharaoh, large-eyed, large-eared, bald and boyishly imperious, it is an essence of his young self.) Ageing from twenty-five to seventy on camera presents huge challenges; in this case, the actor was as heavily made up young as he was old. He was certain that Kane should be beautiful as a young man, and equally certain that he would need a great deal of help in order to fool anyone into believing that he was. He had, for a start, a false nose. Like Laurence Olivier, he had always found the organ with which he was born disappointing, and rarely appeared in character without augmenting it in one way or another. For Kane, it was nobly aquiline. Then, conscious of his jowls despite the fierce diet (supplemented by Benzedrine) that he had been following, he had Seidermann apply fish skin behind his ears to pull back his facial flesh. The effect is of cheeks being permanently sucked in, but it achieves the desired result: he looks very dashing. 'Norman Mailer wrote that when I was young, I was the most beautiful young man anyone had ever seen,' he told Bogdanovich. 'Yes! Made up for *Citizen Kane*! And only for five days!' The ageing process called for skull caps upon skull caps, a network of rubber bands to create the flexibility of flesh, artificial jowls on top of the natural ones, contact lenses (just invented) on contact lenses. Technically, Seiderman, like Toland, was passionately for realism; given the materials available to him, he succeeds to a striking degree. But his real concern was to create a bridge between the actor and his character.

To this end, he had William Alland read aloud from Ben Hecht's curious, uncharacteristic *The Kingdom of Evil – A Continuation of the Journal of Fantasius Mallare*, so that Welles might imaginatively connect with what his face was becoming. Pauline Kael strongly suggests that the high bald dome of the later Kane, one of the most memorable of the film's images, may have been fashioned after Peter Lorre's in Karl Freund's film, *Mad Love*, on which the second cameraman was Gregg Toland; more to the point, as with all the ingredients of *Citizen Kane*, is the expressive purpose. The egg-head of Kane's lonely old age renders him strangely frustrated, an unexploded bomb of a man, endowed with an archaic quality, out of time and out of place. He seems (as he roams the vast echoing halls of his palace) a Fairy Tale King inconsolably mourning. The spirit of Fantasius Mallare lives.

Of great value in refining the make-ups were the screen tests. Ruth Warrick's was played opposite Welles: his debut on film. He could neither remember the lines nor play the scene. It was all right, though; he had the part.

CHAPTER TWENTY

Shooting *Kane*

THE OFFICIAL starting date for the movie was August 1st. Perry Ferguson shrewdly suggested that since they were attempting so many new things, it might be a good idea to shoot the first few scenes under the guise of screen tests. Welles can only have been relieved by the suggestion; RKO were planning to make a great to-do about the first day of shooting. So, three days earlier, the crew and Welles, with a couple of actors piled into a screening room on the RKO lot, and attempted to shoot the scene immediately following the NEWS ON THE MARCH newsreel: the crucial scene in which the editor sends Thompson out to discover the meaning of Rosebud. (Welles was always rather sniffy about Rosebud, attributing it and everything to do with it to Mankiewicz; it is, in fact, an almost perfect McGuffin in the classic definition of Hitchcock: something which greatly exercises the characters but is not crucial to the plot.)

It was an ideal scene for their purposes: it tested Toland's experiment with both very low and very high light, it enabled Welles (who was not in it, another advantage) to stage a group scene of no psychological complexity but some physical difficulty, it challenged the sound department to deal with the for the most part overlapping dialogue. It worked brilliantly; even the drawback to doing the scene – the absence of the newsreel itself, which had not yet, of course, been shot – turned out to be a boon: the image of the vacant screen, with light streaming out of it, is in itself highly arresting. Welles and Toland had set, in this very first clandestine day of shooting, the style for the film: they were speaking a language, with remarkable fluency. The same scene, as written, could have been shot very staidly. The newsreel would have come to an end; the lights would have come up in the projection booth, and the set-up: Who Or What Was Rosebud? spelt out *very clearly*. Instead, at the risk of confusion, the audience is hurled from the familiar but stylised world of the newsreel into the centre of a scene of urgency and mystery. This atmosphere was the achievement of all the collaborators. The second revised final shooting script (the published script) dated

15 July 1940, two weeks before the scene was shot, says: 'During this scene, nobody's face is really seen. Sections of their bodies are picked out by a table light, a silhouette is thrown onto the screen and their faces and their bodies are themselves thrown into silhouette against the brilliant slanting rays of light from the projection booth.' It is impossible and fruitless to determine who wrote these words, Welles or Mankiewicz. The fact is that what was shot on that first, bootleg day, was what they intended to shoot. It had been imagined and planned; and it worked.

Still claiming that what they were shooting were tests, in rapid succession they filmed three particularly challenging sequences. The first was the scene with Susan Alexander in the nightclub, backgrounds for which were appropriated from a Western set on the lot. (Welles's ploy of 'testing' turned back on him when the casting department sent the actor Gino Corrado for the part of the waiter: 'he's the waiter in every movie ever made! And I couldn't possibly send him away on the basis that he was too well-known a face because I was claiming to be testing.') Technically, Toland was faced in this sequence with the challenge of an extreme pan down into the club, and a track to behind the telephone booth, revealing the whole of the club with figures in the middle and the full depth of the set. Depth of focus was again the challenge in the suicide scene, keeping the foreground pill bottle, the middle ground Susan and the background Kane and servants all equally sharp. With those three days under their belts, the team was ready to go public. 'Silence! Genius At Work!' cried the *Motion Picture Herald*, not without mockery, unaware that the genius had pulled a fast one, and was now fully in his stride.

Early on, there came, as there inevitably must, a crisis of inexperience. Welles charmingly suggests that he had not realised that in a film, the cameraman is responsible for lighting, and had gone round setting the lights, while Toland quietly followed behind, readjusting them. In the theatre, Welles claims, he had always been responsible for this. Setting aside the slight to Jean Rosenthal, it is inconceivable that Welles should have thought that the lights were his responsibility. The gaffers, who are directly answerable to the cinematographer, would never have taken instruction from anyone else, and it is quite impossible on a film set to arrange the lighting apparatus without the gaffers. What does have the ring of truth is Welles's assertion that Toland always covered up for his ignorance, taking him to one side and murmuring advice, away from the other technicians or the actors. A film crew is a daunting organisation for a first-time director: a team of experts any one of whom must, in the nature of things, have been involved in many more films than the tyro director. They've seen it all.

Welles shrewdly treated them with respect, and formed a healthy relationship with them, but Toland's attitude was the crucial one. Film crews are pack animals: if the leader extends his approval, then they follow suit. Toland, thrilled to be working with someone who trusted him absolutely and was prepared to listen to him at any time, repaid that trust with the same willingness to try anything Welles suggested. He was particularly grateful to Welles for giving him time. 'He was willing,' he wrote admiringly, 'and this is very rare in Hollywood, that I take weeks to achieve a desired photographic effect.' Soon, however, Welles stumbled. It was the question of screen direction, a vexed and undying controversy: which way do you look when what you're looking at is off-camera? Having, he told Leslie Megahey in his BBC interviews, watched *Stagecoach* forty-five times, in which all the directions are wrong, he didn't see why it was important. Failing to understand the explanation proffered, he very wisely closed down shooting for the day; Toland took him home, and quietly made it clear. 'I said, well, God, there's a lot of stuff here I don't understand and he said there's nothing I can't teach you here in three hours. It was his remark.' Lucky, lucky Welles to have a collaborator who was prepared to spend the time explaining, instead of using his ignorance as a way of dominating him. And brave Welles, for not simply soldiering on in ignorance, but getting on top of it. These things can only be learned on the floor. No amount of preparation could have taught him.

Welles made the startling claim to Peter Bogdanovich that he knew from the first day of this, his first film, where he wanted the camera: in other words, what the frame was, and how to achieve it. 'I think I share with Hitchcock the ability to say what lens goes in the camera and where it stands without consulting a finder or looking in the camera,' he said. 'I just walk over and say "There it is." I may be dead wrong, but I'm so certain that nothing can shake it. It's the only thing I'm certain of. But to me it seems there's only one place the camera can be . . . it's not creative, because it IS an instinctive thing . . . the one thing I'm rock-like about is where it's seen from, by what lens and so on. That doesn't seem to me to be open to discussion.' These are heart-stopping words. This ability of Welles has been attested by many of Welles's later collaborators; if it is true that he knew it already on *Citizen Kane*, then his understanding of film was indeed in his bones, in his blood. There is no evidence, one way or the other, but is indeed remarkable for someone who a bare year earlier had diligently swotted up Miriam Geiger's kindergarten film primer. He was a very quick learner, without question, and film was clearly a medium for which he had both appetite and flair. The instinctive placement of the camera and choice of lens (something to which cameramen with years of experience would hesitate to lay claim) is in the realm of the mystical, and is not, perhaps, susceptible to further investigation.

His rapport with actors, however, and his ability to vitalise them were not in question. Surrounded by old friends, and a few new ones, he spurred them on to a freshness and verve which fifty years has done nothing to diminish. Their delight in the new medium is as infectious as Welles's. Given the decision to avoid cutting from one actor to another as much as possible, he was able to stage scenes with great theatrical vitality. Most of the scenes in *Citizen Kane* are what would simply be the starting point for another film: the master shot, encompassing all the action, into which all manner of details – reactions and close-ups – would be interpolated. In some films, the master shot is a mere formality, establishing the scene's essential choreography and scarcely if at all appearing in the film; this approach calls for very different skills from both the actors and the director. In shooting *Citizen Kane* Welles behaved much as he would have done in the theatre: he staged the scene, then ran it a couple of times, then Toland shot it. Their technique of the endlessly dollying camera required the utmost precision from the actors in the matter of hitting marks. Welles was ruthless, as he had been in the theatre, in drilling the scenes to the point of perfection; he was equally ruthless in establishing the right mood or feeling, however long it took. In the theatre, where the actors, the stage managers and the director are alone during rehearsals, this is quite normal; in film, where nearly a hundred people are present for even the smallest shot, it is another matter. There is, too, the question of the schedule; artists are employed for restricted periods, after which they become unavailable; the same is true of technicians.

Welles was unmoved by any of these considerations. The single most remarkable thing about Welles's approach on his first film – beyond even his talent and imagination and leadership – is his refusal to accept anything that was unsatisfactory to him. Nor did he ever seem not to know what to do next. He always had an idea, however much he might modify it. Brady unconvincingly reports that Welles disappeared for a few days at a time during the shoot 'always returning refreshed'. This is inconceivable; RKO would have closed the picture down, and they would have been right. The notion of the Director as Truant, odd in the theatre, is simply out of the question in movies, particularly one in which the director is also the leading actor. Just once, he was stumped, and said so. 'I walked away, early in the morning – just quit for the day and went home,' he told Bogdanovich. 'Made a big scandal. I just had no idea what to do. Came back the next day.' This is confirmed by Mark Robson, the assistant editor. 'He had a huge set of Xanadu built on Stage 9 at RKO and then he didn't know what to do with it. He feigned sickness and stayed home until he figured out how to use the set. What he finally decided was brilliant. Meanwhile the entire cast and crew remained idle.' This is staggeringly brave.

It is a measure of his almost inhuman confidence that he was prepared to shoot a scene, as Paul Stewart reports, as often as it took to get it right. 'He shot more film than anyone in the history of the cinema. One day he shot more than three thousand metres of film. He got up to the hundredth take, then started again at five, so the studio wouldn't know. He printed nothing from that day's work, then the next day he got the shot in two takes.' In the case of Joseph Cotten, when Welles simply had to release him so that he could start his tour of *The Philadelphia Story*, he worked him (and the crew, and himself) for twenty-four hours without sleep. This had the advantage of making Cotten's drunkenness uncommonly convincing; when he stumbled over his lines, saying crimitism instead of criticism, it is a spontaneous mistake, one with which Welles was delighted, and which he incorporated into the scene. Stewart made some interesting observations to François Thomas about Welles's approach: 'My first line in *Citizen Kane* is "Rosebud? I'll tell you about Rosebud. How much is it worth to you?" We rehearsed that for two and a half hours: just that line. And he'd say, Again, again.'

Often it was to make the actor relax, to forget that he was acting, to get from him something only he knew was there. So much so that the result was something which in its final form belonged entirely to the actor. His character note to Stewart is typical: 'You've made more money running Xanadu than Kane ever did . . . you've been stealing for years. You've ordered tomatoes and stolen half of them. You've ordered hundreds of crates of champagne and sold them. That's your character; that's all you need to know. No one has the slightest idea how you do what you do.' Welles always referred to his old radio colleague, a sophisticated, elegant man, as the Godfather, or the Mafioso, and he cast him in this film and others, quite openly, for a sinister quality he saw in him.

He carried this life-into-art approach painfully far with Dorothy Comingore. Having cast her as Susan Alexander, he cultivated her socially, building up her confidence and self-esteem. The moment the film started shooting he changed his entire attitude, harassing and abusing her. Ruth Warrick, appalled at what she took to be his schizophrenic behaviour, drew him aside and reproached him. 'Oh,' he said, airily, 'it's good for the character.' The terrible fact is, he may have been right. Certainly her performance in the film is outstanding; equally certainly, she never did anything to match it. Welles's method (one common to many film directors) was to secure the result that satisfied him – and he was never sure in advance what that might be – by any means that seemed appropriate. He was not interested in psychology. His notes to actors, as to Paul Stewart as Raymond, were based on a notion of character which expressed itself in paradoxical types (the butler who steals). This approach can best be described as anecdotal; its impact is cerebral, not visceral. The audience feels that they've got the point of the character, not that they've experienced him in all his richness. Welles's real concern was not with the essence of the character but his tempo, pitch and rhythm: his texture. This is as true of his own performance as those of his fellow actors. It is a curious fact that whenever Welles spoke of films that he admired, he cited the great neo-realists: Rossellini, de Sica and so on. Their warmth, richness, and sense of life lived transcended, he said, any technical limitations. *Stagecoach* itself is suffused with humanity, and this was his textbook. And yet in his own films, his own performances and those of his actors rarely touch a human core. The shining exception, in *Citizen Kane* and even more strikingly in *The Magnificent Ambersons*, is Agnes Moorehead, whom Welles, interestingly, described as 'the best actor I've ever known'. He was drawn to her work, but he could neither touch his own centre in the way she touched hers, nor bring it out in the other actors. What he gave them was fun, energy, intelligence, and, as Vincent Price had said of him at the Mercury, 'wonderful things to do'.

As far as his own performance is concerned, he takes his keynote from Hearst's life: a high-spirited young radical becomes an angry old reactionary. He plays straight down that line, finding the appropriate texture at every point. The performance amounts to a series of statements about each of the phases of Kane's life. Even in the scenes of Kane's young manhood, there is about the performance a stiffness (partly the result of the corsets and the fish-skin, the arch supports for deportment and the steel brace for a flat stomach), a lack of spontaneity which is undoubtedly highly appropriate for Charles Foster Kane: the performance, like Kane's life, is a triumph of will. It is a triumph of another sort, of course: simply logistically, it is staggering to have undertaken the leading part in your first film as a director which is also your first performance in front of the cameras, especially in a role like that of Kane, where you age over fifty years. The disadvantage is that, however intelligent and sympathetic your colleagues, and no matter what excellent advice they may give you, there can never be a moment in which you are alone, able simply to dwell in the character, to let it flow mysteriously through the underground chambers of your own personality. The character will never have an independent existence, will simply be a creature of the film itself. You will never, however egotistical and imposing a personality you may be, have the opportunity of being properly selfish as an actor must be, demanding time for yourself, giving yourself over wholly to your intuition and letting your mind rest. Unless you have a defined star persona (such as Welles only acquired during his later, fatter years) you are condemned to linearity. There is no more linear performance in the history of film than that of Welles in *Citizen Kane*. And what is wrong with that? Nothing; except that what comes only from the mind, reaches only to the mind. Nothing more is stirred.

Naturally, Welles worked with a double. He would walk through his scenes, then the double would run them for him again and again; finally, he would take over. Always at his side was Bill Alland; when, that is, he wasn't playing Thompson, the shadowy reporter who takes us through the story. This casting too was some sort of half joke, half calculation: Alland was Welles's whipping boy, the butt of his unceasing abuse and rage, taunted by him as a cipher, a nobody. 'Alland was treated almost as a personal slave,' wrote Dick Barr in his memoir. 'Bill seemed to enjoy the abuse.' Vladimir Sokoloff had told Alland that he resembled the great Russian director, Vakhtangov; Welles never let him forget this preposterous idea: Vakhtangov! Vakhtangov! he would roar whenever he wanted anything. Alland was also the dialogue director, which meant above all that he had to run over Welles's text with him; like all texts, he had the greatest difficulty in memorising it. He was equally unable to remember moves, and almost totally unable to reproduce what he'd done before; these were all critical elements in such a tightly controlled mise-en-scène. Part of the reason for this, Alland maintains, was that he was always terrified of letting go: 'if he ever let himself go in a part he'd lose control.' Alland has often recounted the story (always denied by Welles) that the only time he did let go as an actor – significantly in a scene without dialogue, but with tightly plotted moves – was in the scene in which Kane destroys Susan Alexander's apartment. A storm of pent-up violence was released in him as he staggered about the set, not entirely executing the right moves, smashing the furniture. As he came off the set, clutching the hand he had accidentally cut in the course of the carnage, he was trembling. 'I really felt it,' he said. 'I really felt it.' The scene, though not, Alland reports, as extraordinary as it was in the flesh, remains uncommonly disturbing, both frightening and feeble, a big man's impotent rage against things.

Among other injuries, Welles sustained a sprained ankle as he chased Ray Collins (Boss Jim Gettys) down the stairs in their great confrontation scene at Kane's love nest; Dadda Bernstein was flown in from Chicago to treat him, but shooting itself scarcely broke its stride. Joe Cotten's scenes in the old people's home were rushed forward, Welles directing from a wheelchair, as Cotten's eyes streamed from his ill-fitting contact lenses and his head smarted from his ill-fitting wig (fortunately concealed by his eye-shade). Other scenes were played by Welles in a plaster cast, framed out of the shot. The energy and high spirits never flagged; for most of the participants in the movie, this was as good as it would ever get. The secrecy surrounding the filming enhanced the sense of community among the film-makers. Few people had ever seen a complete script; the actors were given their scenes the night before they shot them. Welles's personal dislike of being watched combined with anxiety about the Hearst connection becoming public made *Citizen Kane* virtually a closed set. If Schaefer visited, Welles would divert him with conjuring tricks and anecdotes, which Mr Schaefer, his assistant recalls, 'did not appreciate'. For other visitors, the actors and crew would break and play softball. Some people were welcome, however. When John Ford arrived on the set, he imparted a useful piece of information: the first assistant director, Eddie Donahue, was an RKO spy. 'Ford's greeting to him was the first hint we had of his real status,' Welles told Bogdanovich. ' "Well, well," he said, "how's old snake in the grass Eddie?" ' Whatever Donahue told his bosses, they were powerless to interfere. Welles was protected by his cast-iron contract.

About a month into shooting, he showed a forty-minute rough-cut to John Houseman, who was passing through. 'It was clearly going to be an extraordinary piece of work. Once again I was astounded at his instinctive mastery, the sureness with which he moved into a new medium and shaped it to his own personal and original use.' Earlier, his nose as ever pressed against the window of the sweet shop, Houseman had seen Welles at work during the pre-production period: 'Orson,' he wrote yearningly, 'was working again with a concentrated, single-minded intensity that I had not seen since the first years of the Mercury.' Mankiewicz, the third of the Victorville collaborators, after demonstrating violent opposition to the casting of Dorothy Comingore and losing, was hardly present on the set, though he occasionally attended rushes. Herb Drake reported to Welles a telephone conversation with him after one of these visitations. The headline on Drake's memorandum gives a strong flavour of how he was seen by the Mercury team: 'RE FURTHER TELEPHONE CONVERSATION WITH HERMAN J. MANGEL-WURZEL RE CUT STUFF HE SAW.' The memo also gives the flavour of that idiosyncratic man. '1. Everett Sloane is unsympathetic-looking man, and anyway you shouldn't have two Jews in one scene. (Bernstein's office with Bill.) 2. Dorothy Comingore looks much better now so Mr M. suggests you re-shoot Atlantic City cabaret scene.' The third of his observations is the most striking. 'There are not enough standard movie conventions being observed including too few close-ups. It is too much like a play.' This thread of comment runs through a number of early reactions to *Citizen Kane*. Like the cinematographers who opposed Toland for abandoning the painstakingly evolved aesthetic of 'good photography', whose essence was that it did not draw attention to its own techniques, a number of observers felt that Welles had abandoned a truly cinematic language in favour of a bravura technique which had more to do with the theatre, and maybe even the circus, than film. They found it difficult to understand why Welles didn't take advantage of what is obviously the essence of the freedom the camera gives – the ability to go close, and the ability to cut within a scene. 'Mark you,' continues Drake's memorandum, 'he thinks the stuff is "magnificent." If he says it is "magnificent" I'm beginning to worry. Please understand that he made it a point that he approves very much of what you are doing from the aesthetic point of view, but wonders if the public will understand it.' Mankiewicz's doubts were well placed.

There were no doubts, however, on the floor: 'picture sensational!' Dick Baer telegrammed to Houseman, and Welles was sufficiently happy with the work to give himself over, during whatever spare moments he was able to claw from the film, to completing the designs for Roger Hill's *Macbeth* (they are as fluid and assured and straightforward as all the series, nearer in feeling to Welles's 1947 film than the *Caesar* designs were to the stage production). Sensing something wonderful on his hands, he also became very interested in the question of publicising *Kane*. Towards the end of the first stage of filming, Drake wrote him a mock-aggrieved memo in response to an anxious enquiry: 'As of Sep 30, there have been eighteen major wire service FEATURE stories on you in CITIZEN KANE. According to the best advice I can get from my competitors this is roughly 6 times more than any other star or production ever had in a two-month period . . . According to Hedda Hopper you have been mentioned in her column since June 27 at least twice as much as any other performer. Since lunch with L. Parsons, you have had better representation there than any other Hollywood performer.' Welles had been handling both ladies with great skill: over dinner he even invited Hopper to play the *Inquirer*'s Society Editor. She had been a great supporter of his from the beginning, even giving over her radio programme (*Hedda Hopper's Hollywood*) to a six-part series on his life, complete with full cast, in February 1940.

There were no offers of a part for the rather lumpy Parsons, though he made a great deal of fuss over the fact that she came from Dixon, Illinois, just up the road from Grand Detour: somehow (one of his greatest acting performances) he managed to convince her that he was 'just a hometown boy making good'. Over lunch he told her that the film dealt with 'a dead man . . . I have everyone voice his own side and no two descriptions are alike'; later, by phone, in response to an anxious enquiry, he categorically assured her that the film was not about Hearst. This was wise: her loyalty to both Hearst and Marion Davies was extreme; she owed everything to them, having been snatched from obscurity by Hearst to publicise Davies. She was, in fact, more than a little in love with Hearst, whose blessing had been the sine qua non of her marriage; in addition to the blessing, he gave her a $25,000 ring as a wedding present. His loyalty to her was as great as hers to him: 'a quarrel with Louella was a quarrel with the entire Hearst Empire,' in Richard Meryman's words. Ignorant and unstable, there is something pathetic about the woman that is somehow summed up by the title of her autobiography: *The Gay Illiterate*. It is extraordinary that Welles thought he could softsoap her into believing that *Citizen Kane* had no connection with Hearst – or softsoap anyone into believing it, for that matter. The rumour was definitely abroad that something out of the ordinary was going on on the RKO lot: for all that the press (supplied by the ever-industrious Drake) was full of statistics (93 sets! 796 extras!)

and tittle-tattle (the Chicago *Sunday Tribune* revealed that Welles's nicknames on the set were Mr Moneybags, Pappy, and Monstro, the whale from *Pinocchio*), no one could discover what the film was actually about.

The general mood of buoyancy was threatened by something unexpected. A casual phrase dropped by Welles in an interview with Louella Parsons – 'and so I wrote *Citizen Kane*' – provoked a response of surprising vehemence from Mankiewicz. Drake wrote to warn Welles that 'Mr M. is in the biggest fever yet over Louella's Sunday column.' Mankiewicz was threatening, Drake told him, 'to *come down on you* because you are a "juvenile delinquent credit stealer beginning with the Mars broadcast and carrying on with tremendous consistency." Specifically, he says he has you by the ——s, and that unless you "behave" he will . . .

1. Take a full-page ad in the trade newspapers.
2. Send a story out on every leased wire in the country.
3. Permit Ben Hecht to write a story for the *Saturday Evening Post*.

'Mr Hecht allegedly is in such a state of moral fervour about your delinquent behaviour that he will write it for nothing.' Shortly after, in early September, Drake wrote more reassuringly to Welles: 'Mankiewicz says that the last thing he wants is for us to write any stories indicating he is the author of *Citizen Kane*, co-author or had any connection with it. He says he realises completely that we can't stop the result of a year's four-ply publicity. He will take no action when such things appear. What he wants is simply this . . . he asks that you don't in a personal interview say that you wrote *Citizen Kane*.' By a curious irony, this plaintive (and not unreasonable) request is exactly the one that Welles himself made of Cantril and Koch in the matter of *The War of the Worlds* script: he didn't want credit himself, but he didn't want Koch credited. Arnold Weissberger swiftly dealt with Welles's anxiety, citing the clause in the contract which stated that all material composed, submitted, added or interpolated by Mankiewicz was the property of Mercury Productions who were 'deemed the author and creator of this product'. 'It would seem to me,' wrote Weissberger, 'that the construction of this clause would not entitle Mankiewicz to any credit whatever. If a man chooses to sell his right to be known as the author of a work, he ought not thereafter to be able to come forward and claim that right, especially in view of the fact that this particular provision in the contract was put in for the very purpose of eliminating that right.'

After sounding Mankiewicz out, however, Weissberger found him in militant mood: he was claiming that 'he wrote the entire script, and he will probably take the position that Orson did not contribute even 10 per cent to it, and is, therefore, not entitled to credit.' The boot was suddenly on the other foot. Weissberger advised Welles 'It would be unwise to deny Mankiewicz credit on the screen and have him get credit therefore through the press by publicising his complaint,' which suggests that Welles, who always insisted that he intended Mankiewicz to have a credit, did want to deny him one. In the light of these documents, it is impossible to accept Welles's pretence that 'as soon as he started behaving like a real writer' Mankiewicz was offered equal credit. Clearly he thought that the situation was identical to his relationship with the radio writers: they proposed, he disposed, and the end result was his. The ugly dispute rumbled on. It was Welles's misfortune that it came at a critical moment for writers in Hollywood: after years of being trampled on they were just beginning to feel their muscle. Hence Hecht's passion. Only recently, a Producers–Writers agreement had been signed which said:

> No production executive will be entitled to share in the screenplay authorship screen credit unless he does the screenplay writing entirely without the collaboration of any other writer

Here again, Welles was saved by the bell: his contract with Mankiewicz had preceded the agreement by three months; it had no force.

It is quite true, as Weissberger and Brady, echoing him, say, that Mankiewicz clearly, in the presence of advisers and witnesses, signed away his rights to a credit. He was paid quite handsomely for doing so. None the less, there is something murky about Welles even contemplating taking the whole credit for the screenplay. Certainly, there were pressures on him to do so: contractual (his deal specifically required him to write the screenplay) and professional (the tremendous and menacing build-up of publicity positively defying him not to be an all-round genius). The inner pressure, however, was even greater. Writing was something at which he felt he should be good; he never was. A pervasive feeling of déjà lu hangs over everything he wrote. In the light of all his other gifts, this lack seems unimportant: but not to him. In Houseman's acute words 'his ability to push a dramatic situation far beyond its normal level of tension made him a great director but an inferior dramatist. His story sense was erratic and disorganised; whenever he strayed outside the solid structure of someone else's work, he ended in formless confusion.' He was, however, an inspired editor. Most directors, whether in the theatre or on film, fulfil this function for the writers with whom they work; most directors submit ideas, propose substantial restructuring, suggest phrases, even whole speeches – as, frequently, do the actors. In his Lundberg deposition, Welles describes the rewriting of one of *Citizen Kane*'s scenes: 'we closed the picture for a day in order to rewrite this scene. This rewriting was done by myself and the actors involved in the scene.'

The actors did not expect, and did not get, a credit, nor any additional payments. This is all part of the job; this is what they get paid for. It doesn't warrant a credit. The directors' credit is: 'Directed by', which means that the film, in the last resort, is theirs; the finished film is what they have made of all the ingredients. There was in Welles a sort of confusion in this area, as if anything less than total authorship would expose him as a fraud. Later, he maintained that he had wanted to credit Houseman, too: 'I tried to persuade Houseman to put his name on, since he'd been working all this time,' he told Meryman. 'But Houseman was more interested in mischief than glory.' Houseman, for his part, sat down and wrote Welles a letter: 'I informed him that if anyone but Mank was to get credit for the script of *Kane* it would be me, and that I was prepared to enforce my claim through the Screenwriters' Guild on the basis of my writer's contract with Mercury Productions.' The next morning he tore the letter up. For Welles, the real dread now was not that he would have to share a credit for the screenplay, but that he would not get one at all. The dispute was not finally resolved until January of the following year, when Welles and Mankiewicz signed a joint declaration that they wished to confirm the screen credit:

ORIGINAL SCREENPLAY

Herman J. Mankiewicz
Orson Welles

which is how it stands in the film. The order of the names was by Welles's personal decision. It is of course simply alphabetical; the other way round would have been a further provocation, and by now Welles was weary of the whole thing.

Meanwhile, principal photography was complete: 'we close the picture today stop isnt that wonderful query' Dick Baer telegrammed Arnold Weissberger on 23 October, a week later than scheduled. It was not a moment too soon, since both Ruth Warrick and Dorothy Comingore were pregnant. On the last day of shooting, Welles threw a party in Culver City, converting the studio into a Wild West bar; at the climax of the party, a stage-coach appeared, whether in homage to John Ford is not clear. Welles left town the next day: 'which will give us all a little bit of rest,' wrote Baer. Welles's chronic financial instability was responsible for this surprising departure. There was at least another six weeks' shooting to be done, mostly special effects, for which the camera crew (minus Toland, whom Goldwyn had reclaimed) was kept on, but no further instalments from RKO being due till delivery of the completed picture, he had to raise some money immediately. He took to the lecture circuit again for a fortnight while preparations for intensive post-production took place without him. After his tour de force, Welles, in the old theatre joke, was forced to tour. Omaha, Cleveland, Toledo, Fort Worth, San Antonio, Dallas, Houston, Oklahoma, Tulsa, Detroit, Des Moines were the dates.

He found himself in San Antonio, Texas, on the 28th at the same time as a fellow lecturer, H.G. Wells. Someone had the wit to bring them together in a studio. Whatever animosity the author of *The War of the Worlds* may have harboured against Welles – and he had at the time of the notorious broadcast threatened to sue for unauthorised changes – it had disappeared. The old boy couldn't have been more agreeable, chirping away in his London accent, saying that of all the very pleasant things that have happened to him since he arrived in America, quite the best so far has been meeting 'my little namesake'. He dismisses the panic over *The War of the Worlds* as Hallowe'en humour – on both sides ('that's the nicest thing a man from England could possibly say about the Men From Mars,' purred Welles, 'that not only I didn't mean it, but the American people didn't mean it'). The younger man betrays a rather nasal, distinctly Mid-Western voice in this chat, quite different from his Narrator voice, or his poetry voice. He seems a little nervous, but is naturally delighted when Wells brings up the subject of *Citizen Kane*. 'Mr Wells is doing the nicest kindest thing,' says Welles. 'He is making it possible for me to do what here in America is spoken of as a plug.'

> HG: This new picture of yours – you're the producer, the art director, you're EVERYTHING.

> OW: It's a new sort of a motion picture with a new method of presentation and a few new technical experiments and a few new methods of telling a picture.
> HG: If I don't misunderstand you completely there'll be a lot of jolly good new noises in it.
> OW: I hope there will be a lot of jolly good noises in it . . . it's just what the motion pictures need these days. They could well afford these days, some jolly good new noises . . . I can think of nothing more desirable. I'm all for it.

It was to implement those jolly new noises that Welles returned to Hollywood (somewhat richer, though large amounts of his earnings had already been disbursed in advances). The shoot had been hugely successful, but it was only the beginning.

It is easy for an inexperienced director to use up all his energy on the dramatic activity of actually shooting the film; not Welles. He instinctively knew the importance of sound and music, and had planned both carefully in advance. He may not, on the other hand, have immediately realised what he could do with optical technology, but when he did, there was no holding him back. RKO had one of the most advanced special effects departments in the industry, headed by Vernon Walker (whose speciality was back projection) but effectively dominated by the brilliant innovator Linwood Dunn, pioneer of optical printing. The methods he developed lent themselves to many more purposes than would normally be understood by the phrase 'special effects'. They did not necessarily concern themselves with the extraordinary or the extra-terrestrial. Their essence was their invisibility to the naked eye. Almost everything concerning the leopard in Hawks's *Bringing up Baby*, shot for RKO in 1938, for example, was achieved by superimposing the scenes containing the stars onto previously shot footage containing the leopard and its handler who had been blotted out; all this was Dunn's work. Welles and he applied their combined brilliance to the footage of *Citizen Kane*, transforming it to a quite unheard of degree.

A great deal of celluloid wizardry had already been achieved in the camera, things that would normally be achieved optically. Toland was an inventive man, and he was proud of what his camera could do. Many of the remarkable compositions in *Citizen Kane* had been shot by means of double exposures: a foreground figure would be shot, the film would be threaded through the camera again, and then the background figures would be shot on the same film. Many of the fade-ins and fade-outs were actually created on the set, using controlled dimmers. Observing Toland at work, Dunn, a forthright man, told Toland that a lot of the effects he was labouring to achieve could much more easily be accomplished by optical printing. Toland loathed the technique because of the deterioration of the image, and said so. By a strange irony, however, thanks partly to Welles's passionate embrace of the optical printer, a large number of the scenes Toland shot (up to 50 per cent of the entire film; in some reels 80 to 90 per cent) were modified by Dunn. Some of the elements most espoused by Toland were in fact created optically. 'Many of *Citizen Kane*'s deep-focus effects had been created by [Vernon] Walker's unit,' writes David Bordwell in a remarkable account of Toland's achievements in the cinema of the thirties and forties. 'Several of the Xanadu shots, ceilings included, were mattes. The shot of Kane firing Leland was done in back-projection . . . many normally looking scenes were optical composites of units photographed separately.'

'Telling Orson about the optical printer was the kiss of death,' said Dunn. He might have said 'kiss of life'. Welles had discovered a means of introducing almost limitless improvements to what he had shot. Dunn told him that he could do 'anything at all' with optical printing; the only obstacles were time and money. The processes involved are slow and complex. Robert Carringer cites a memo from Vernon Walker to the front office, explaining that the delays in completing its share of work are due to Welles's intransigence and his habit of coming up with new ideas after the fact. One of the most extraordinary of these is in the sequence at the Thatcher Memorial Library. The camera pans down a monumental statue of Thatcher onto the female guard. Both the statue and the pan are entirely the work of Dunn. As Toland shot it, the scene started on the guard. Dunn made a miniature model of Thatcher (George Colouris, who was paid for sitting for it) and perfectly matched the base of the statue with what had been shot. This is breathtaking, and it accounts for scene after scene: the famous crane shot over the roof and into Susan Alexander's night-club is two separate shots linked by an apparent flash of lightning; the pan up into the wings during the opera sequence is another.

Welles the conjuror delighted in the informal name of optical effects: 'trick shots'. Dunn was a sorcerer, to be sure, (if a slightly grumpy one) and Welles, enchanted by the process, wanted to join in. Dunn acknowledged his apprentice's talent, revealed in 'flashes of inspiration': when confronted with the blurred effect of shooting closer and closer, optically, on the glass globe containing the snow scene, Welles suggested superimposing more snow onto it. The result was a triumph. As his own producer, of course, Welles was able to authorise all the extra work. Again, what is striking is his insistence on his complete satisfaction with the results. This is the 'intransigence' noted by Vernon Walker. 'I was months and months and months turning down versions of them, day after day, until they got good enough,' Welles told Bogdanovich. 'Trick work *can* be good enough, but you must be brutal about it. Just refuse it, refuse it till it gets better.' For a tyro to deal so surely and uncompromisingly with a seasoned pro like Dunn is remarkable; he, and many of his colleagues, while neither specially liking nor admiring Welles, acknowledged that they had learned a great deal from him. He pushed them further than they knew they could go. Not that he knew where he was going; he just knew it could be better. As far as Dunn's and Walker's department is concerned, their contribution to the film is immeasurable. It also explains, as David Bordwell points out, why Toland's other films (in which he didn't use optical effects) lack such extreme depth of focus. A lot of the film as it stands is a kind of trompe-l'oeil, a visual conjuring trick. Even more than most films, *Citizen Kane* is not quite all it seems to be.

Special effects thus proved more important to the film than editing in the formal sense. Welles started filming with a senior editor, George Crone, at his side, but it soon became apparent that he was too slow for Welles, and was replaced by whizz kid Robert Wise, only a year older than Welles, hotfoot from working on *The Hunchback of Notre-Dame*, RKO's blockbuster of the previous year, where he had equal editing credit with Robert Hamilton. He brought with him his assistant, Mark Robson. Both men became directors in their own right within a couple of years of their work on *Citizen Kane*. Though, as Welles said, there was, because of the way he shot it, 'nothing to cut in *Citizen Kane*' by comparison with many movies, the all-important question of rhythm exercised the department for many weeks under Welles's ruthless if erratic guidance. One frame more or less can transform a sequence; Welles would not rest until he was perfectly satisfied with the results.

The flashiest piece of editing in the film, the pastiche *News on the March* newsreel was, by another brilliant directorial decision, farmed out to actual newsreel editors with their idiosyncratic cutting style; the music came from RKO's stock library. In further pursuit of authenticity, he had tried to hire Van Vorhees, the actual voice of *The March of Time*, but his fee was prohibitive, so the cry of Vakhtangov! was heard again. Bill Alland did a creditable impersonation, aided by

Houseman's wickedly parodistic text (which is not far from Wolcott Gibbs's celebrated send-up of *Time*-ese: 'Backward ran sentences until reeled the mind!'). Mankiewicz, Pauline Kael reports, had wanted to use the *News on the March* sequence as a summary of the transformation of popular journalism: pre-Hearst, Hearst, and then Luce; Hearst's own Hearst-Metrodome news film, *News of the Day* is mocked in the title, as much as Luce's *March of Time*. Formally speaking, it is interesting to note that the newsreel within the film offers a synopsis of the story in advance, in the Greek manner; this was scarcely in the authors' minds at the time. As Houseman says: 'if you're going to do a chronicle picture about a great man, you almost inevitably were going to use *The March of Time*.' The crucial thing, private parodistic jokes apart, was to make it convincing. Toland's Realism was the criterion. It was Wise and Robson, in pursuit of that realism, who shocked their colleagues by dragging the completed sequence across the studio floor and trampling on it, in order to create the authentically grainy and battered effect. The result of all this was the single most impressive, most spoken-of element in the movie.

The integration of the optical elements was another crucial and painstaking task, but Wise was most struck by Welles's approach to sound. 'He overwhelmed me with his radio background and his masterful use of sound, stretching the boundaries of how I thought sound could be used.' *Citizen Kane* represents a real leap forward in the use of sound in motion pictures. It really was a 'radio picture', the first RKO film that could be so described since Sarnoff had invented his slogan. The function of sound in a movie is surprising, contributing enormously but generally subliminally. Ambient sound and sound effects can transform a sequence with the simplest of means: a clock ticking, a distant dog barking, the wind, the laughter of children. Any or all of these radically alter the sense of time or place in what is perceived by the eye; most of them are only subconsciously registered. For Welles with his acute awareness of selection and manipulation of sounds, this was only a beginning. His greatest innovation on radio had been the creation of a melos in which he dared to mingle voices (often overlapping) with effects and music; equally striking was his strong sense of the value of silence – not something of which a lot was heard in movies of the thirties. Applying all of this experience to his new medium, he used sound to lead the eye.

Hitherto, in film, what you heard was what you saw. In *Citizen Kane*, for the first time, you heard something – a line, a sound –

and then saw where it was coming from. The audience's mind is thus kept in a state of continuous curiosity and alertness. There is, further, no pretence that you are not watching a film (pace Toland). What's the next shot? Where is the next scene? the audience wants to know. It is one step further away from the beau idéal of film-makers of the thirties, the illusion of reality. The implications for the editors were considerable, as, of course, for the sound engineers. Welles's slavish attention to the precise quality of the sound effects, often requiring them to be made and remade, was exactly the same as that with which he had tormented his radio engineers. James G. Stewart, dubbing mixer on *Kane*, later an Oscar winner, and an old radio hand, told Carringer that much of what he knows aesthetically about sound came from Welles. Again, he felt little personal warmth for the man: 'I'd work all day. He'd make an appointment for 8 o'clock to run rushes,' Stewart told Richard Meryman. 'He'd show up at midnight. No apologies. Just "let's get going now." And we'd work to 3 or 4 a.m. He'd have a jug of whiskey, but no offering it to anybody else in the room. Just for Orson. I don't remember asking him a favor. And I don't think it would have occurred to anyone else.' None the less, he described his work with Welles (he later worked on *The Magnificent Ambersons*) as one of the most significant experiences of his working life.

The film's musical score was crucial for the editors, too. Bernard Herrmann, Welles's musical director on most of his radio shows, composed a substantial amount of the music before editing began so that scenes could be cut to its rhythms. 'I was given twelve weeks to do my job. I worked on the film reel by reel, as it was being shot and cut. In this way I had a sense of the picture being built and of my own music being part of that building.' The breakfast sequence for which Herrmann wrote a cunning Theme and Variations in which the Waldteufel-like waltz becomes increasingly fragmented and sourer as the marriage falls apart is a famous instance; another the arrival of Kane at the newspaper office for the first time done to 1890's dance forms. Calling it the *Chronicle Scherzo*, Herrmann says 'this whole section in itself contains a kind of a ballet suite in miniature.' Though Welles was no musician himself – 'his ear was not for music,' said Virgil Thomson – he was uniquely aware of the value of music. His entire approach to film (and to the theatre, for that matter) could be described as musical. He knew from the outset that the composer's contribution to *Citizen Kane* would be enormous. Long before shooting began, Welles sent Herrmann a telegram which must have made his mouth water: 'in second scene we cut to kane in audience during which time full act or scene is supposed to have been sung since curtain comes down following susies aria which opens act never mind logic please stop camera and composer must make this seem logical by ingenuity . . . here is chance for you to do something witty and amusing dash and now is the time for you to do it stop I love you dearly stop orson'.

Herrmann made brilliant use of his 'chance', creating something that is indeed witty and amusing, but something else, too. A parody but also a homage, the aria he wrote for Susan Alexander Kane is almost superior to its models, the French romantic operas with which Welles was so familiar from his nights at Ravinia: *Hérodiade*, *Thaïs* and the rest. Using a massive orchestra, he adds a Straussian dimension to the palette of Massenet, horns whooping, trumpets braying, flutes skirling, over which the soprano hurls herself, surfing over the cascades of glissandi, finally leaping up to a lurid top D. That, at any rate, is what Herrmann wrote, and what has subsequently been performed by Eileen Farrell in the concert hall and the young Kiri Te Kanawa on disc. For the film, Herrmann found the sixteen-year-old Jean Forward, her voice true but tiny, and set her adrift in a sea of instrumental activity; like Susan Alexander Kane, she sinks. The *Salambo* aria is one of the few occasions in the film where Herrmann deploys a regular (if augmented) symphonic band; as in his radio work, he took the opportunity of being able to employ as many musicians as he wanted to create 'unorthodox instrumental combinations . . . sound effects blended with music, music used in place of soundtrack'.

Radio had been his training ground as much as Welles's: he found that in films 'cues of a few seconds were often overlooked: on radio every scene must be bridged by some sort of sound device . . . I felt that in this film, where the photographic contrasts were often so sharp and sudden, a brief cue – even two or three chords – might heighten the effect immeasurably.' Many of the most striking effects in the film are perfectly complemented by just such brief musical accompaniments: Kane's light being switched out as he dies, for example, where Herrmann's sudden brass sforzando gives the moment a chilling finality. This is a fundamentally different approach to writing film music from the prevailing ethos, represented by Steiner and Korngold, both of whom, Viennese in background, were intent on creating operas without words, symphonic tapestries under, over and around the film itself. In *Citizen Kane*, Herrmann does use leitmotivs (their essential method) though it was not something he was generally to employ in his film music.

It helps to integrate the film still further: the *Rheingold*-like four-note descending Power theme, heard right at the beginning on low brass and strings with bassoon overtones, undergoes extraordinary transformations, becoming now a ragtime, now a hornpipe, finally a massive maestoso statement for full orchestra. That final statement is for the last sequence of the film; the music was pre-recorded and played on the set, Toland moving his camera to it.

Herrmann had unprecedented involvement in every stage of the work on the film. He was closely involved in the dubbing: in a radical departure from normal practice, all his music for the film was actually recorded at the level at which it was to be used in picture, not artificially made louder or softer. It was often re-recorded six or seven times before the proper dynamic level was achieved. Welles supported him at every turn in his quest for perfection. In the Souvenir Booklet for *Citizen Kane*, it is excitedly reported that 'Welles even supervised the score.' While it is unlikely that he ever prised the baton out of Herrmann's hand, or altered the instrumentation, it is true that he expected, as a theatre director, to be more involved at every level than a regular Hollywood director would, and that included the music. He had, naturally and properly, an opinion about everything, which is one definition of being a director. He and Herrmann had a notoriously fractious relationship, Herrmann sensitive and explosive, Welles insensitive and explosive, but their respect for each other's work was deeply grounded. James Stewart, the sound recordist, tells a story of Herrmann inveighing bitterly against Welles's methods and manners for close on half an hour, finally stalking out of the room and slamming the door behind him. Immediately afterwards, he returned saying: 'I want to make it absolutely clear that everything that I have just said refers to Orson the man, not Orson the Artist.'

The music was the last element of the film to be completed; it wasn't finally added until January of 1941. Welles, in rising high spirits, had been planning his cinematic future: the top of his list for development was a *Life of Christ* to be set in New Mexico, at the turn of the last century 'as a kind of primitive Western'. He carefully explained to the dozens of heads of churches whom he approached for advice and endorsement that he meant no impiety: he was simply following the precedent of painters through the ages who had painted biblical scenes 'in their own epoch'. He gained a surprising amount of support for the project; the following year he, Toland and Ferguson scouted locations. He was also eager to find a film in which he could direct Dolores del Rio, with whom he was still closely and passionately involved. A project that he had first discussed in 1939 was reconsidered (*Mexican Melodrama*, loosely based on Arthur Calder-Marshall's *The Way to Santiago*); more immediately engaging was a screenplay that del Rio had been sent by the Mexican director Chano Uruta, an adaptation of the already twice-filmed classic of Mexican realist literature, Frederico Gambao's *Santa*. Welles became fascinated by its story of the corruption and destruction of a young girl, and wrote a treatment of his own, in consultation with Toland. It shows the beginnings of a highly personal style, an advance in this regard on *Citizen Kane*. Welles restructured the novel, starting with Santa's funeral, to which the film returns at the end; it is, in effect, an enormous flashback, introduced by the dead woman as narrator. 'Don't think me a saint because Santa was my name. I was a number – a thing to be rented. When I laughed, I was scolded. When I cried, no one believed in my tears. I died miserably and left nothing. I will tell you my story, and although I was guilty, you will pardon me I am sure – as sure as I am that God has pardoned me.' Silence. Darkness. 'As the picture opens, we fade in to the door of the brothel.' Santa, new to the brothel, watches her first client fall asleep, having failed to make love. In another flashback, her past floats into her consciousness.

Welles's description of this flashback reveals a strikingly independent concept: 'SANTA'S PAST: This is, properly speaking, of course a flashback – but a flashback implies a sustained narrative and the effect of continuity within its own framework which I think should be carefully avoided . . . the first consideration here is a painstaking avoidance of the pat regulation Hollywood flashback – a perfect little movie within a movie. Memories are like the uncut rushes of a movie. They make their own patterns, unlike the patterns of drama. The emphasis is never the emphasis of a script writer – so that a loaf of bread, or a cup of cocoa – a lithograph on a wall – a shrine – any inconsequential blade of grass may find itself a star performer in one's memories of things past. The unities find no special observances in Memory.' The rest of the film is told in relatively straightforward, realistic terms, detailing the rise, downfall and death of The Queen of Courtesans. The treatment is filled with notes about the nature of sexual contracts – between lovers as well as prostitutes and their clients. This is an unusual area for Welles. There is also an unexpected degree of compassion for the oppressed and their oppressors. The screenplay was never shot, though Norman Foster, shortly to collaborate with Welles on *Journey into Fear*, later made a film from the same material, incorporating elements of Welles's treatment. The treatment is in its way a remarkable document, suggesting a new departure for Welles, into a genuinely realistic world: the opportunities for virtuosity are limited despite set-piece scenes in the brothel and at the bullfight. It shows him starting to think cinematically as second nature. Above all, it represents his feelings for del Rio, now at their height. Her calm strength and wide experience of Hollywood had obviously sustained him through his work on *Citizen Kane*; the treatment of *Santa* (completed in November 1940) was his acknowledgement of that, and embodies his growing sense of mastery.

His expansiveness is evident in a telegram he sent around this time to Houseman (which suggests that both of them retrospectively exaggerate the degree of hostility that existed between them). Houseman had wired Welles's secretary: 'please give orson all my dearest love i am terribly busy but i have lots of ideas for us and either when he comes here for the opening or by letter before that i will communicate them to him also to you puss my love you will be glad to hear that i am doing two radio shows a week and directing phillip barrys new musical extravaganza i love you all john'. Earlier, on 7 October, he had signed a short affectionate note to Welles: 'Lots and lots and lots of love.' Welles's reply was equally exuberant: 'my beamish jack citizen kane all done with only scoring and trick sequences yet to come stop i am enormously anxious for you to see it and excessively interested in your statement quote i have lots of ideas for us unquote was beginning to fear you were permanently including me out and that will never never do stop hope to come east for a christmas week or so and see much of you stop how about a job on your campbell playhouse query every means of income as you possibly know has been cut off and i have no prospects whatever stop my very dearest love to you'. What Houseman did not know was that Arnold Weissberger was already involved in protracted plans to get Houseman off the board of Mercury Productions, as he wrote to Dick Baer at the beginning of November. Perhaps Welles didn't know, either. His high spirits continued in a telegram to Roger Hill, proposing publicity for the *Macbeth* discs: 'give your friends a night at the theatre exclamation no waiting for seats walk do not run to the nearest exit see a show with your shoes off how would you like a little murder in your home query all the glamour and glitter of the theatre in one succulent christmas package'. His Christmas present list for 1940 is interesting: 'Marc Blitzstein ($6), Jo & Lenore Cotten ($15), Chubby Sherman ($2–5), Francis Carpenter (book), John Houseman ($10).' Houseman and he had one more date together with destiny; then it really was all over.

The Stage reported the completion of filming on *Citizen Kane* under the somewhat passé headline BOGEYMAN MAKES A MOVIE. The piece says that the story is based on the Faust legend (which is accurate as far as it goes); there is of course no mention of Hearst. It was almost the last time that would happen. RKO had become increasingly jumpy about the connection and Welles had ordered, in November 1940, the names of Northcliffe, Beaverbrook, Patterson, McCormick, Hearst, Stalin, Roosevelt, Churchill, Rockefeller and Ford to be removed from the film. It was as if he suddenly wanted to take the movie out of the real world. There were rumours that Hearst knew that the movie was about him, and was simply biding his time. In an almost incomprehensible action, Mankiewicz had shown a copy of the script while the film was being shot to his chum Charles Lederer now, by extraordinary coincidence, Virginia Welles's new husband. Lederer just happened to be Marion Davies's nephew; he and Virginia were, accordingly, married at San Simeon, guests of Marion Davies. And this was the man to whom Mankiewicz, always irresistibly drawn to danger, showed his screenplay. Lederer returned it, according to Mankiewicz, covered with pencil marks made by Hearst's lawyers. Lederer denies this; certainly nothing was heard from Hearst.

The exigencies of magazine publication made it necessary to show the more important editors some version of the film, even an incomplete one, and this was duly arranged. Inevitably, either Parsons or Hopper would get wind of this showing. It was Hopper. 'Dearest Hedda,' wrote Welles, 'I owe you the biggest apology of my life and here it comes.' He says that Herb Drake insists on showing the magazine people the movie in incomplete form. 'I fully realise I have broken a solemn promise that you'd be the first to see *Kane*. Please understand and forgive. Come tonight if you must but it still stinks. Many shots are missing or only tests are cut in and we need music like Britain needs planes. Love Orson.' She came, and what she saw did not please her. 'Not only a vicious and irresponsible attack on a great man,' she said, 'but the photography is old-fashioned and the writing very corny.' Thus armed with a magnificent weapon against her rival, she called Hearst. 'As the story was reported to me,' Louella Parsons recalled, 'Hopper said "Mr Hearst, I don't know why Louella hasn't told you this picture is about you." Mr

Hearst thanked her.' Parsons now had some ground to make up, particularly since the newspapers' silence was suddenly broken by the maverick magazine *Friday*. Seeking to attack Hearst, it ran a preview piece on *Citizen Kane*, describing it as a straightforward portrait of him. The piece culminated in a supposed quote from Welles saying that Louella Parsons was a great fan of his and the film: 'This is something I cannot understand. Wait until the woman finds out the picture's about her boss.' Shown a preview copy of the magazine, Welles tried to stop publication. Failing that, he demanded and was given a right of reply, meanwhile dashing off a letter to Parsons: 'It has been assumed that *Citizen Kane* is about Mr Hearst. People seem to have forgotten Bennett, Munsey, Pulitzer and McCormick, to mention only a few you could name. Not that it matters; *Kane* isn't any of them. Of course if there hadn't been great publishers, I couldn't have created a fictitious one, and some similarities to these men. I do hope you can help me to make this distinction clear. May we have lunch sometime next week, and when may I show you *Citizen Kane*? My sincerest gratitude for all the wonderful things you have done for me and my very best to you. As always, Orson.' Too late: Hearst (or his lieutenants) read the magazine as soon as it appeared; that day (8 January) a directive was issued to all his titles to ban mention of any RKO picture.

Now they were in serious trouble. Hollywood and the press had a symbiotic relationship; they needed each other deeply. At the height of its glamour, Hollywood and its doings took up half of all the pages in the popular papers. Hearst, though less financially powerful than he had been, was prepared in this matter to cut off his nose to spite his face; for RKO it was much more serious. Welles went into action immediately, taking the agreed line that *Citizen Kane* had no connection with Hearst apart from the coincidence of the central character's profession. To do so, he described in detail the plot of the unseen film. '*Citizen Kane* is the story of a search by a man named Thompson, the editor of a news digest (similar to *The March of Time*) for the meaning of Kane's dying words . . . the truth about Kane, like the truth about any man, can only be calculated by the sum of everything that has been said about him . . . he is never judged with the objectivity of an author, and the point of the picture is not so much the solution of the problem as its presentation . . . *Friday*'s constant reference to the career of William Randolph Hearst . . . is unfair to Hearst and to Kane.' Welles was not being entirely disingenuous. Kane had travelled a long way from Hearst, and the film is no crude denunciation of its central character, anyway. It is also true that the finished film, far from being an anatomisation of a press lord, suggests that Kane is essentially unknowable. The mysteriousness of personality was a profound conviction of Welles's; he believed it of himself. None the less, he was obliged, more and more stridently, to deny any relationship whatever between Charles Foster Kane and William Randolph Hearst.

These were the first shots fired in what became a verbal war of unrelenting intensity, during which the film, its plot, characters, themes, techniques and meaning were described, discussed, analysed, applauded and denounced for the benefit of a reading public who had never seen it, but who must soon have felt that they had. Never can a film have held less surprises for its public when they were eventually allowed to see it. Being a cause célèbre is a mixed blessing at many levels. Earlier in his article, Welles wrote, with some urgency '*Friday* says my "antic voyages ate into the night with a hundred technicians hooraying for the fun." This means I haven't been doing my job at RKO, and if it were true, I should be fired. I can't help it if *Friday* doesn't take me seriously. I don't take myself seriously but I'm very serious about my work. Maybe it stinks, but I don't joke with other people's money.' Even more important, perhaps, than rebutting charges that Kane was Hearst, was the need to establish that he didn't go over budget or schedule. Lèse-majesté Hollywood could take; over-spending, never. The awful example of Stroheim loomed again.

Meanwhile, Louella Parsons, goaded by her rival and betrayed by the 'hometown boy made good' whom she had praised and encouraged, sprang into action, demanding an instant screening. Schaefer immediately acceded. Attending with lawyers (and her chauffeur, who, famously, thought it 'a fine picture'), she reported back to Hearst that it was worse than anyone feared. Hearst telegrammed her: 'stop citizen kane'. Using every ugly tactic she could think up, Parsons did her best. 'If you boys want private lives, I'll give you private lives,' she told Schaefer, threatening to print fictional versions of the lives of RKO board members in Hearst papers. Her next calls were to Schaefer's fellow producers. Mankiewicz described the strategy in a characteristically dry letter to Alexander Woollcott: 'Mr Hearst casually gave them a hundred examples of unfavourable news – rape by executives, drunkenness, miscegenation and allied sports – which on direct appeal from Hollywood he had kept out of his papers in the last fifteen years. General observations were made – not by Mr Hearst but by high-placed Hearst subordinates – that the proportion of Jews in the industry was a bit high and it might not always be possible to conceal this fact from the American public.' Live by the press, die by the press. Hearst, this episode makes clear, operated a sort of journalistic cosa nostra, a protection racket in print.

There is no clear evidence as to whether Hearst himself ever saw the movie. Bill Hearst Junior denies it. Virginia Welles, on the other hand, told Brady that she had been present when Hearst ran the film at San Simeon for her, her husband, and Marion Davies. At the end of the film, he simply grinned and took Davies upstairs. It is certainly true that Schaefer sent a copy of the film to Hearst, to prove how innocent it was. It was sent back to him without comment – whether seen or not. Other versions have him sneaking into a cinema in San Francisco; yet others insist that he never saw it. Welles liked to say that he travelled with Hearst in a lift on the day of the premières, and offered him a ticket. Hearst refused to acknowledge him. If he had seen it, it might well have given him something of a turn. The first ten minutes of the film are so unmistakably based on his life, and feature so prominently what is obviously his house, that it must have been a nasty shock to witness his own premature obituary. 'Then last week, as it must to all men, death came to Charles Foster Kane,' says the newsreel narrator, in startlingly life-like fashion. On the screen, in case he'd missed it, he would have seen CHARLES FOSTER KANE – DEAD spelt on a moving electric screen atop a newspaper building. For anyone, this might be somewhat disturbing; for a seventy-eight-year-old man, preoccupied by and terrified of death, it must surely have been very upsetting. After these opening scenes, Kane's life (as Welles was always keen to point out, right up to the end of his own life) diverges somewhat from Hearst's. The central relationship, with Susan Alexander, is clearly a parallel to his relationship with Marion Davies – a very inexact parallel, and all the more wounding for that. Susan Alexander is a no-talent whom Kane pushes into trying to be an opera star, finally building an opera house for her; Marion Davies was a very successful and talented comedienne for whom Hearst built a studio and whom he over-promoted to preposterous levels. Kane's love for Susan dies; she leaves him. Hearst, on the other hand, worshipped Davies, despite the alcoholism which so dismayed him.

There was something about the use that he and Mankiewicz made of Hearst's story which disturbed Welles; he alluded to it in terms which suggested that he felt himself guilty of a lack of chivalry. The most comprehensive righting of wrongs was done in his introduction to Marion Davies's posthumously published memoirs, *The Times We Had*: 'William Randolph Hearst was born rich. He was the pampered son of an adoring mother. That is the decisive fact about him. Charles Foster Kane was born poor and raised by a bank . . . and what of Susan Alexander? What indeed. It was a real man who built an opera house for the soprano of his choice, and much in the movie is borrowed from that story . . . as one who shares much of the blame for casting another shadow – the shadow of Susan Alexander Kane – I rejoice in the opportunity to record something which today is all but forgotten except for those lucky enough to have seen a few of her pictures: Marion Davies was one of the most delightfully accomplished comediennes in the entire history of the screen.' However unattractive a man's policies and conduct, there is something that gives one pause about displaying his life for public ridicule and examination without him having the right to reply. For all the abomination of the attempt to suppress *Citizen Kane*, there is an injustice embedded in the film. The reimagining of the basic material could have gone further. But of course the real facts, so colourful and bizarre, were irresistible to the co-authors, particularly, perhaps, to that Lord of Misrule, Herman J. Mankiewicz.

Whether personally directed, or whether merely the knee-jerk reaction of his lieutenants, Hearst's camp swung into action. RKO were duly terrorised; the lawyers counselled straightforward denial. Herb Drake was tormented by his impotence: 'I am going slowly mad because my hands are tied. I want to lead a crusade, I want to get the whole independent and liberal Hollywood element behind us, but the big battle, apparently, is being fought among the money boys. Hopeful indication is the sniffing of Schaefer and his growing annoyance at the pressure.' Two days later, Arnold Weissberger wrote to Welles in more strategic terms, suggesting that RKO could dig up the Mexican birth certificate of Marion Davies's two twins; there was, he said, no point in creating a crusade of public opinion until there had been an actual move on Hearst's part. Hearst now had the initiative; he hardly needed to do anything. The threat of action was enough. Floyd Odlum and David Sarnoff, the major shareholders in RKO, began to express their concern. Schaefer gritted his teeth, announcing *Citizen Kane* for February 1941, to open at RKO's flagship house, Radio City Music Hall. Parsons immediately called the manager, Van Shmus, threatening him with a total press blackout if he showed the movie. He gave in, and the première was cancelled. Next, Hearst's people appealed to the film industry's internal watchdog, Will Hays, to suppress the film, in line with the ban on films about living persons; surprisingly, Joseph Breen, Hays's deputy, declared that *Citizen Kane* was not about Hearst; for this he was rewarded, a year later, by being made Schaefer's head of production at RKO. (Welles amusingly suggested to Peter Bogdanovich that he had contrived to drop a rosary in Breen's presence, thus melting the ardent Catholic's heart.)

The story, having been neutrally reported in *The New York Times*, became public debate with a long piece in the widely read Marxist paper, *New Masses*: 'Until quite recently,' wrote Emil Pritt, 'a lot of people in Hollywood thought that Orson Welles was just a great big beautiful publicity stunt. They knew that a young boy, five or six years old, had come from planet Mars to Vine Street in the summer of 1939 and was given a contract by RKO studios to make three pictures. They heard vaguely that he was about to make his first picture, and then something happened to it. He grew a beard and shaved it off and broke his ankle and had a radio program sponsored by soup. It was all rather fantastic and other-worldly. And then, early this year, Mr Orson Welles and Mr William Randolph Hearst collided head-on and everybody suddenly discovered that it was all very real . . . through an intricate process (referred to by the wise boys as two parts blackmail and one part doddering frenzy) Hearst is in effect trying to prove that *Citizen Kane* is a disruptive force trying to destroy national unity, imperil the defence program and outrage relations between this country and South America.'

Fearing capitulation, Pritt points a finger at Hollywood: 'as far as the producers are concerned, a grave mistake has been made and must be corrected. The mistake was bringing Orson Welles to Hollywood. It was known that Orson Welles had too many ideas of his own; it was known that his sympathies were with the opponents of either alien or native fascism. To bring such a man into a studio and give him an open hand was to court disaster. And if the result has been a picture that displeases Mr Hearst, it's only what might have been expected. Throw him to the MGM lions. So say the Hearst stooges. But what of the others . . . the case of Orson Welles and *Citizen Kane* must not be judged by a frightened or conniving Hollywood autocracy but by the people who pay the admissions: not by the Jew-baiting, Red-baiting studio vigilantes but by those who carry the weight of the little golden calf labelled Box Office: not by a bellowing old tyrant but by those ultimately responsible for having made the movies a *mass* entertainment. Theirs, as always, will be the final verdict.' Pritt's last words proved prophetic; the immediate effect of his article, however, was further to polarise the situation, establishing Welles as a threat not merely to Hearst, but to Hollywood and those who ran it, the producers. Whether this was a great help in getting *Citizen Kane* released is to be doubted, but it can hardly be said that the role of producers' scourge was thrust upon Welles. In this same month of February he published in *Stage* an article of such direct provocativeness to the Hollywood establishment at the very moment when he most needed it that it can only be concluded that his judgement was severely distorted by the anxiety and pressure under which he was labouring.

'This article,' Welles wrote, 'will probably make me no friends in Hollywood, but I haven't been making friends there at a rapid rate, and since my recent lectures on the motion pictures, it would be hard to say how I could make any new enemies. This is because I have proposed and contracted to do more work on a movie than anyone on the regular assembly line of the industry is allowed to do, and as though this weren't enough, for some time I didn't make the movie.' Clearly having decided that nothing was any longer to be gained by defence, he opts to attack, starting with an easy target – the critics – then moving on to a taboo one: his fellow artists in Hollywood. 'Its inhabitants, deeply tanned but unresigned to the sunshine and the flowers, all confidently expect to take the next boat home – to write a novel, play another part on Broadway, resign, or commit suicide. But if nobody lives here, nobody leaves.' Why? he wants to know. The movies offer limitless opportunities: 'the actor is just now in possession of the means to act without the need to project. The close-up is the first new thing he's had to play with since he took off his mask three thousand years ago and added his face to his voice.' (He seems to have forgotten radio; moreover, didn't he announce before shooting *Citizen Kane* that he was going to eschew close-ups – as he largely does?) Writers, too, should rejoice: the dramatist 'mostly impotent,' he says, 'since the invention of the novelist' – poor Chekhov, Ibsen, Shaw, O'Neill and Büchner! – 'has a new dimension now, a new thing to write besides words – he is again capable of poetry.' Composers are fortunate, too: 'a public is drafted for serious music, whose composer . . . now finds himself unbelievably with a paying job and availed of a fresh and flexible narrative form.' Finally he comes to directing. In movies, it becomes 'a major art'. A new art in the theatre, its importance was exaggerated, 'and still is'. 'But if an actor can do without a director, a camera can't. Call directing a job if you're tired of the word "art." It's the biggest job in Hollywood (it should be anyway, and it would be, if it weren't for something called the producer). If you don't like artists, call a movie director a craftsman. He won't mind. He's the world's happiest man, and if he isn't, it's because there are producers in the world.'

He seems to be coming to the heart of his tirade. But no, he has a few more targets in his sights: agents, for example. 'It's always Christmas morning for the percentage boys . . . the majority of ankles into which these artists' representatives have clenched their parasitic teeth belong to people who need agents as much as a street-car needs an attendant stationed on its step to announce that for a fare the street-car will carry passengers along the track . . . your agent needs the goodwill of the studios more than you do, so he can't afford to fight for you as hard as you could.' This leads directly to the main target: 'He's either afraid of getting in bad with a producer, which makes him useless to you, or he's useless to you because he's in bad with a producer . . . only a little less superfluous than the agent and almost as successful, unlike certain others among Hollywood's middle-men (the publicity man and the columnist, for example) the producer is not a necessary evil. He's unnecessary and he's evil . . . in England, a producer is a man who stages a play; on Broadway, he's a man who finances a play; in Hollywood he's a man who interferes with a movie. I say nothing against the executive head of any studio. I wouldn't if I dared.' He then dares; he can't resist. 'Several studio executives are seriously ignorant and some are absolutely foul. A lot of them are just old-fashioned smalltime showmen who got in cheap on a new thing that turned out to be a sure thing and were shrewd enough to hang on . . . let them die rich. They found more gold than they earned, but it's all theirs. None will outlive the boom, and nobody wants them to.'

Hollywood had made Welles feel small: this is his revenge. 'Like the writer – the actor and the designer of sets, and the composer of music, the cameraman, the wardrobe man, the make-up man – all are subjects of his undeniable highness, the Hollywood producer.' All his rage against Houseman was now transferred to more general authority figures. Did he think that he would get the rest of Hollywood on his side by abusing producers? Was he waging a democratic crusade? Far from it. 'Please understand, I think a movie needs a boss.' The argument shifts. 'There has never been a motion picture of consequence that has not been, broadly speaking, the product of one man. This man has been the producer, could be the writer, has been and usually should be the director. Certain pictures are rightly dominated by their stars or even their cameraman. The dominant personality is the essential of style in the motion picture art. When it is absent, a motion picture is a mere fabrication of the products of various studio departments from the set-builder to the manufacturer of dialogue, as meaningless as any other merchandise achieved by mass production.' It is as if he were terrified that someone might say that *Citizen Kane* wasn't his doing. 'Let's have more dominant personalities in the picture business and let them dominate all they want to, but let them be the personalities of those who really make the pictures. What we can do without is the dominating personality of a high-salaried official with nothing to do but dominate, and no other talent.'

The puzzle of this sustained outburst is that Welles was one of the few people in the history of Hollywood never to have had to submit to a producer in any way. Schaefer had been heroically supportive from the beginning of their association, only hesitating when it seemed the budget might be out of control; even then he was exceptionally flexible. He never imposed himself for one moment in the sphere of artistic decision-making. Part of Welles's attack may be an anticipation of submission on the part of individual producers to Hearst's tactics, though Hearst's target was not them so much as the studio heads. Whatever his purpose, it can scarcely have been served by this rant. He leaves 'this sketchy discussion of the motion picture producers' feeling it essential 'to point out that being a motion picture producer myself, I am utterly without bias on the subject. I must further admit that producers, agents and other personal grudges are merely contributors like myself to what's wrong with Hollywood which is, finally, absolutely and simply the scarcity of good movies. There have been, I anticipate the answer, four or five pictures recently of truly adult excellence, but Hollywood makes almost six hundred feature pictures a year, and every year for almost twenty years has presented a public with at least a couple of pictures good enough to make it look as though Hollywood had come of age.'

This was clearly a good moment at which to leave Hollywood for a little while. Supper at Chasen's was likely to be somewhat strained should he bump into a fellow producer – or an agent, for that matter, or indeed anyone not connected with those four or five pictures of truly adult excellence. Welles's attack on producers found vocal support in the crusading press: in his piece HEARST OVER HOLLYWOOD in *The New Republic*, Michael Sage bluntly asked

'Will Hollywood stand up to William Randolph Hearst over the matter of Orson Welles's film *Citizen Kane*? . . . many people find it hard to believe the producers really intend to defy the lord of San Simeon.' Scorning the neutral position of the Hays Office, 'which is supposed to defend the interests of RKO as well as the other companies' Sage was reminded of 'the sterling fortitude displayed by the late Neville Chamberlain when Hitler trampled Czecho-slovakia'. Dangerously shifting the dispute from Hearst versus Welles into Welles versus Hollywood (dangerously for Welles, that is), Sage observed that 'Hollywood is oozing with synthetic geniuses; an authentic one would be a menace. Welles did no boot-licking. He defied the Hollywood caste system, ate with his aides and was even seen publicly with people who made less than $1,000 a week. Instead of casting shopworn stars he brought his Mercury Players from New York for the picture. Now, in certain quarters,' continued Sage, 'he is the greatest villain in Hollywood. Instead of praising him for his forthright determination to make an interesting character study, even if it did offend Hearst, instead of condemning the effrontery of anyone who tries to suppress a creative work, some leaders of the industry say privately that Orson Welles must be stopped. Whether they will join hands with William Randolph Hearst remains to be seen.' Hearst, meanwhile, continued to focus the attack on Schaefer, blowing up a little local dispute over rights into front page news (RKO BROKE CONTRACT!).

Welles showed a complete print of the film to Houseman, who was passing through. Over supper, Houseman handed him a play, the outcome of his first purchase for United Productions, that company set up with such flourish the previous May. With the première of *Citizen Kane* still in abeyance, and feeling daily less comfortable in Hollywood, Welles leaped at it. Back, then, to Broadway; the sooner the better.

CHAPTER TWENTY-ONE

Waiting/*Native Son*

THE PLAY was *Native Son*, adapted by Paul Green and Richard Wright from the latter's novel, published with sensational success at the beginning of 1940. Wright records in a narrative of Zola-like realism the journey of a frustrated young black man in Chicago's South Side to the electric chair. Finding work as a chauffeur, he kills first, accidentally, the daughter of the philanthropist for whom he works, then his girlfriend. In his cell, waiting to die, he realises that he has achieved a sort of freedom for the only time in his life. 'I didn't want to kill! But what I killed for, I *am*! It must have been pretty deep to make me kill! I must have felt it awful hard to murder . . . I didn't know I was really alive in this world until I felt things hard enough to kill for 'em.' Houseman and Mankiewicz had read the novel while they were working on *Citizen Kane* in Victorville, later giving it to Welles; like most of the novel's first readers in spring of 1940, they were overwhelmed not only by its unrelenting power but by the urgency for all Americans of what Wright was saying. 'A blow at the white man,' as Irving Howe wrote, 'the novel forced him to recognise himself as an oppressor. A blow at the black man, the novel forced him to recognise the cost of his submission . . . the day *Native Son* appeared, American culture was changed for ever.'

Wright had created in his central character, Bigger Thomas, a complex emblem of a life stunted and finally wrecked by social conditions, but he had done so without crude determinism and with no vestige of sentimentality. Bigger, like Büchner's Woyzeck, embodies the uncomprehending destruction of the potential of a whole section of humankind; as Wright put it to Houseman in a letter, 'Bigger Thomas is not presented in *Native Son* as a victim of American conditions of environment; neither is he presented as a boy destined to a bad end by fate . . . here is a human being trying to express some of the deepest impulses in all of us through the cramped limits of his life. The emphasis was upon the impulse, upon the boy's feelings.' Understandably eager though Welles, Houseman and Mankiewicz were to do something with this extraordinary material, and despite Wright's own description of his novel as 'a special première given (for the reader) in his own private theatre', it is to be doubted whether *Native Son*, depending to a considerable degree on the thought-by-thought reconstruction of Bigger's mental processes, was really susceptible to dramatisation. Houseman was convinced that it was, however, and found Wright equally enthusiastic.

Their correspondence reveals the seriousness and passion with which Houseman had returned to the stage, his frustration and humiliation in Hollywood way behind him. He had skilfully persuaded Wright that his novel had a place in the theatre, then set about allaying his doubts. 'I realise the limitations of the stage and screen in America,' wrote Wright, anxious that any play from his material should be done 'in a light that presents Bigger Thomas as a *human being*?' The idea of purveying more negro stereotypes was abhorrent to him: 'To stage or screen *Native Son* in the old way means nothing to me.' Houseman wrote back: 'Please believe that both Welles and I understand fully the way you feel about your book.' He and Welles, he continued, 'were convinced that the material was capable of extension and development in the dramatic form', an extension, he claimed that 'would not merely illustrate and narrate your story, but give it that particular heightening and tension that make the drama with all its current sluggishness and inertia, still the greatest medium in the world'. The theatre was the only place for it. 'The chances of it being shown on the screen in a final form that would give you as an author any pleasure at all are virtually nil. The theatre, however, in the hands of a few people, is still a free medium in which a serious artist can express himself directly and courageously to his audiences.'

He was clearly happy to be in harness again, and exhilarated to be able to speak of Welles and himself as 'we'. 'In producing, we have always had one other basic rule,' he went on, ' – that our only reason for doing a show is that we were crazy about it, and that we have felt that in its particular field it was the best work we could produce with all our excitement, enthusiasm and resources, regardless of expediency, prudence or any other considerations. It is in this way that we have thought of *Native Son*.' Of course Wright was persuaded. 'Knowing what you and Welles have done in the past, I do believe you both could do a courageous job.' In June of 1940 Houseman was able to telegram Welles that the deal was closed; a $1,000 advance had secured the play for a year: 'please inform our crippled and choleric partner stop'. ('Eagerly await latest scenes and inspirations,' he added; he was then still part of the writing team for *Citizen Kane*.) To Houseman's regret, Wright had already agreed to collaborate with the playwright Paul Green should he ever choose to dramatise *Native Son*. Green was a somewhat anomalous figure, a white writer from the South who had, with his first, highly successful play *In Abraham's Bosom*, presented a sympathetic account of black aspirations; soft-edged though it was, it was considered something of a breakthrough in 1927. It was not this play, however, which had recommended him to Wright. In 1936, as a writer attached to Chicago's Federal Negro Theatre, Wright had arranged a staged reading of Green's tough assault on the chain gangs, *A Hymn to the Rising Sun*; he had been impressed by its grim, poetic power, and its avoidance of stereotypes – more impressed than the black actors in Negro Theatre, who had refused to perform it. ('This play is indecent. We don't want to act in a play like this before the American public,' one of the actors said. 'I lived in the South and I never saw any chain gangs. We want a play that will make the American public love us.') In approaching *Native Son*, however, Green was determined to lighten up Wright's terrible vision of black life; he wanted to add humour and charm. Above all, he wanted to explain Bigger Thomas, to render him sympathetic. In his introduction to the novel, Wright had fiercely rejected the white sympathy that his first book had provoked: 'When the reviews of *Uncle Tom's Cabin* began to appear, I realised that I had made an awfully naive mistake. I found that I had written a book which even bankers' daughters could read and weep over and feel good about.' He had not repeated the mistake in *Native Son*.

Green, the senior partner of the playwriting team, managed to push him a surprisingly long way in that direction as they worked on the adaptation. Wright went to stay with Green in North Carolina; the deep rift in their attitudes to the material was immediately revealed. Wright (the inventor of the phrase Black Power) saw Bigger Thomas's act as positive; Green attempted, in Houseman's words, 'till the day of the play's opening – through madness, reprieve, suicide, regeneration and other "purging" and sublimating devices – to evade and dilute the dramatic conclusion with which Wright had consciously and deliberately ended a book in which he wanted his readers to face the horrible truth "without the consolation of tears." ' Wright was strangely quiescent during the collaboration; the rough working draft they produced was too long, stuffed with unnecessary scenes; the second version was shorter, but with a sentimentalised, hysterical ending. Houseman at first refused to produce it as it stood; then decided (with Wright's collusion) to do it, simply changing the ending back to Wright's original text 'on my authority as producer' without telling Green. Wright (living in the legendary Brooklyn rooming house where W.H. Auden, Benjamin Britten, Carson McCullers and Gipsy Rose Lee also lodged) worked on the script for three weeks with Houseman; most of what they did was concerned with restoring as far as possible Wright's words. Green's structure (in which the action is framed by Bigger Thomas's trial) was sound and theatrically effective; this they did not touch. This version of the play is what Houseman handed to Welles in Los Angeles.

'I had set my heart on directing this one,' writes Houseman in *Run-Through*. 'But I was anxious to end my theatrical association with Welles on a note of triumph and I felt that with the strong text of Wright's book to support him, his direction of *Native Son* would be more dramatic than mine.' Both of these latter points may have been true, but there was never, as Houseman's letters to Wright make clear, any question of anyone but Welles directing it. With no opening scheduled, *Citizen Kane* was still in limbo as Schaefer and RKO continued to consult lawyers; Welles was in a state of impotent desperation. *Native Son* was the safety valve he needed. He hurled himself at it with ferocious intensity. The entire production, from supper in Los Angeles to opening night on Broadway, took seven weeks to achieve. The money was immediately raised from – in Houseman's phrase – Welles's Hollywood friends; a small group, but evidently well-heeled. Casting was rapidly accomplished: bringing Ray Collins, Paul Stewart and Everett Sloane with him from Hollywood, auditioning the younger white actors, he recruited most of the black actors in the company from the old Negro Project team, including in the make-or-break role of Bigger Thomas, his Harlem Banquo, Canada Lee. James Morcom (presumably recovered from the nightmare of *Five Kings*) was enlisted to interpret Welles's ideas about design, Jean Rosenthal to execute them and create the lighting plot. Vakhtangov! was put in charge of sound; as always, Welles's aim was to integrate the work of all these departments into an overwhelming statement. Taking his cue from the novel, he sought to create a swift-moving vision of urban hell.

Chicago is the location, 'the fabulous city in which Bigger lived, an indescribable city, huge, roaring, dirty, noisy, raw, stark, brutal; a city of extremes: torrid summers and sub-zero winters, white people and black people, scabby poverty and gaudy luxury, high idealism and hard cynicism! . . . a city whose black smoke clouds shut out the sunshine for seven months of the year; a city in which, on a fine balmy May morning one can sniff the stench of the stockyards; a city where people have grown so used to gangs and murders and graft that they have honestly forgotten that government can have a pretence of decency!' It was Welles's city, too. 'I want this show to be surrounded by brick,' he told Jean Rosenthal. 'Yellow brick.' Morcom gave him a proscenium of brick. Inside it, the set was made up of seven little wagon stages with brick facings and brick returns which would open out to join the brick of the frame, thus varying its width. A movable header (also, of course, brick) would be raised or lowered to alter the height of the opening. The width varied from twenty-five foot to fourteen foot; the height from seven and a half foot to twenty foot. The side walls were raked sharply to counter the serious sight-line problems created by this arrangement. Ceilings, writes Rosenthal, were 'faked down in extreme perspective'. The depth of the stage was limited to a very shallow ten foot.

'From the tiny, poverty-stricken interior of Bigger Thomas's room, through the elevated "murder" bedroom, set four foot above the stage level on a raked platform and back-lit through chiffon curtains, to the low brick prison wall,' in Rosenthal's words, 'the Mercury scenery plays its sinister part.' The varying aperture is as nakedly cinematic a device as can be imagined. The sets themselves (three of which were flown: the cellar, the warehouse and the prison) were filled with realistic detail; a new approach for Welles in the theatre. He was baulked in his desire for a practical furnace onstage by the New York Fire Department, but at least he was able to have real cornflakes and canned peaches with milk for the breakfast consumed by the cast every night. The lighting, clean and sculpted, was none the less used to serve realistic purposes: Andrea Nouryeh describes the crack of morning sunlight in the first scene; the street lights (shone through grillework in the theatre's flies) to create the narrow back alleys of Chicago; eerie moonlight in Mary's bedroom as she is smothered by Bigger.

Sound, in Welles's conception, was as important as any of the scenic elements. His purpose was to unify the ten scenes of the play with an almost continuous sound plot; more than in any of his previous theatre productions, he used in *Native Son* what he had learned from radio. Applying a musical technique of transformation, he would establish a sound at the end of a scene which, by the beginning of the next scene, had become something else. Nouryeh cites the chiming of the clock at the end of the first courtroom sequence: during the brief blackout and scene change it transforms into the ringing of an alarm clock; as the lights come up on the new scene, Bigger's mother comes in and switches the alarm off. Here, as in many places, Welles takes his cue directly from the novel, whose very first word is BRRRRRIIIIIIIIIINNG! He also experimented (not altogether successfully, in the view of some critics) with the use of recurring sounds at moments of intensity, sonic leitmotivs, as it were. The sound of the furnace in which Bigger burns the body of Mary Dalton reappeared frequently. Welles's ambitions for the use of sound were often somewhat in advance of the equipment at his disposal. In *Julius Caesar*, he had had to abandon his efforts completely; in *Native Son*, with the inspired collaboration of Bill Alland, he came close to what he had wanted. This was not achieved without intense work, as was the fluidity of the production, vital to his sense of the play. Like *Caesar* and *The Shoemaker's Holiday* it was to be played without interval; unlike them, it was unremittingly sombre, and lasted nearly two hours. The speed of scene changes was crucial, achieved with the aid of no less than thirty-seven highly drilled stage-hands. The technical rehearsals continued, on one celebrated occasion, over thirty-six unbroken hours. Time was desperately short, Welles did not have the facilities or crew of a major studio at his disposal, and many of his company, including his leading actor, were relatively inexperienced. He drove them all, actors and technicians, to the very brink; but the results justified the suffering. Welles was able to go further and quicker than usual because he was not acting in the show himself.

Andrea Nouryeh has reconstructed elements of the physical production to give a vivid sense of its overall feel. The scene in which Bigger desperately pulls a gun on the young Marxist, Jan Erlone, ends with a blackout; the sound of the furnace suddenly stops. The outline of the Prosecutor from the first courtroom scene is darkly visible for a second, lit from above. During the ensuing blackout, the audience hear a collage of sounds of wind, trains idling, pulling out and then stopping, finally a piece of tin banging on a roof. The lights come up on the abandoned warehouse where Bigger and his girlfriend Clara are hiding from the police. A neon sign blinks. Through a skylight, snow is seen to be falling. Sirens are heard. The neon light switches off; a beacon flashes through the skylight. The skylight suddenly crashes down. Shots are fired, in which Clara is killed. Policemen advance; Bigger scurries across a ramp over the orchestra pit, and fires into the audience. He screams his defiance, which is drowned by the sirens; the lights snap out. The lights come up again, and we're in the courtroom. Like the Prologue (also set in the courtroom) this scene is played against a yellow brick front cloth 'in one' on the apron of the stage; stairs lead down into orchestra pit. The witnesses sit with their backs to the audience, who become the jury, and are addressed directly by the lawyers. In the final scene, after judgement has been delivered, Bigger is left alone with his lawyer. In the production's final, somewhat controversial, image, he hurls himself at his cage, arms stretched out, as if crucified. The lighting, outlining his body, heightens the image. 'I want the play to end,' Welles had written to Paul Green, 'with Bigger Thomas behind the bars standing there with his arms reaching out and out, his hands clinging to the bars – yes, yes, the crucified one, crucified by the Jim Crow world in which he lived.' Again, Welles takes a cue from Wright's words in the novel: 'He ran to the steel door and caught the bars in his hands and shook them, as though trying to tear the steel from its concrete moorings,' though the martyr imagery of Welles's stage picture is arguably alien to the more humanistic purport of Wright's philosophical outlook; it is an eerie reminiscence of John Brown in Welles's boyish *Marching Song*: 'with a shock we realise that the attitude is no longer that of triumph but of crucifixion!' In working on the play, Welles's habitual energy had a demonic quality to it, fuelled both by his deep and life-long loathing of racism and his impotent rage about what increasingly seemed to him to be the suppression of *Citizen Kane*.

Houseman describes him during this period as 'overbearing but exciting to work with'. They had occasional spats, but these were between manager and director, not between partners; there was no longer anything behind the rows, no struggle for power, no dream of mutual involvement. Houseman now knew better than to attempt to create a closeness that Welles refused. It was the last time he would say 'we' of the Mercury Theatre. Bill Alland describes Houseman and Welles, in yet another word that more usually belongs to marital relations, as 'estranged' – adding that in his memoir 'Houseman doesn't quite reveal how shat on he was.' It was an end of being shat on, and a return of dignity. Quietly, Houseman was becoming his own man. Before embarking on *Native Son*, he had directed a show for the Theatre Guild. It was a flop – a flop d'estime, but a flop none the less, more noticeably so since it was Phillip Barry's first show since *Philadelphia Story*, the theatre hit of the decade. The show (*Liberty Jones*) folded during the first weeks of rehearsals for *Native Son* after twelve performances on Broadway. It was still a major production of some class and style; the fault was universally acknowledged to be in the play itself, not the production. Houseman held his head high, undaunted, as he would previously have been, by witnessing the white heat of Welles's creativity in action so soon after a personal failure.

Richard Wright was drawn by that white heat. More Houseman's man than Welles's, he nevertheless acknowledged his 'profound admiration' for him. 'He is beyond doubt the most courageous, gallant, and talented director on the modern stage in the world today. He presents here something never before seen on the stage in America. The stamp of his hallmark has been vital in advancing the production of *Native Son* to this stage.' He noted, with approval, that 'running through all of Welles's directing is a high spirit of play and fun.' Wright rather fell in love with the company, too. 'Never in my life have I been associated with a more serious, young, spirited and talented theatrical group than that which comprises the Mercury Theatre.' Initially Wright had been bemused by the process. 'My first reaction naturally was one of confusion. Welles and Houseman . . . warned me to keep away from the theatre till some coherence and continuity had been reached through rehearsals.' But his 'old love of witnessing something new' overcame him. 'I ignored their advice and hung around anyway . . . that was precisely what I wanted to see: – the process whereby the repetition of single lines and passages were welded into a coherent dramatic pattern.' His somewhat unloving biographer Margaret Walker believes that Wright, as co-author, felt that 'he had a constant privilege and duty to interrupt and give advice on how he wanted to produce *Native Son* on the stage. Knowing Wright, there is no way he would have kept his hands off and let Houseman, Welles, Paul Green and Canada Lee take care of what he considered his business.' For this, there is no evidence whatever.

His co-author, Paul Green, on the other hand, might have liked very much to interfere, but he had wisely been kept away from the theatre until the last moment. Turning up for a run-through, he stayed to the end of the play – which of course bore no resemblance to what he had written – then left without a word, returning the next day with his lawyer. Houseman calmly refused to restore to the play a single line of his text, while Green and his attorney unconvincingly threatened lawsuits; they scarcely had a leg to stand on here since only Wright's words from the novel had been used. At a strategic moment, Houseman had Welles summoned from rehearsals. 'Orson began to howl at him, Green got up and left, and I have never seen him again.' Work proceeded more or less according to plan, though the traditional Mercury postponements were observed (Houseman, in *Run-Through*, claims otherwise, but the delays were sufficient to be reported in *The New York Times*: 'TWO POSTPONEMENTS IN A ROW'). Welles was unable to resist an ironic reference to his still imprisoned film; he placed a sled inscribed (invisibly to the audience, of course) ROSEBUD on a corner of the set, to the complete satisfaction of Richard Wright. 'I had the honor recently of seeing a preview of *Citizen Kane*,' Wright said in a contemporary interview. 'Running through this great film is a rather poignant and symbolic sub-theme of a boy's sled, called Rosebud. You can imagine my surprise and delight when I discovered that Orson Welles had taken the beautifully varnished sled of the white boy in *Citizen Kane* and thrown it into the first scene of *Native Son*.'

Kane beat incessantly on Welles's brain throughout the period of work on *Native Son*. Most terrifying was the silence from RKO. On 7 March – a third of the way into rehearsals – in some understandable distress, Welles sent a wild and impassioned telegram to Schaefer: 'think about the impossible strain you have put in my faith in you stop i see a good many important people in the ordinary course of things in new york and a great many more now make a point of seeing me stop they all tell me what i refuse to believe and i tell everybody what i have no reason to believe beyond my belief in you stop as a matter of fact as regards kane im the only person i know who has any faith in you at all'. Turning rather swiftly from this dangerous tack, he darkly suggests that strings in Washington may be about to be pulled. Then he turns to his personal feelings. Principal among these, obviously, is humiliation: 'my mail is one long accusation from the american public which truly believes i have sold out and the sympathy and good advice of my friends make their society intolerable stop my nights are sleepless and my days are a torture stop this is no exaggeration . . . dont tell me to get a good nights rest and keep my chin up stop dont bother to communicate if thats all you have to say stop theres no more rest for me until i know i have something concrete, and as for my chin ive been leading with it for more than a year and a half . . . i must know if i overrate our friendship . . . as ever, my fondest regards orson'.

RKO's silence was finally broken on 11 March – *Native Son* was in its final week of rehearsal – by an unexpectedly impassioned statement from the strictly non-political George Schaefer in *Variety*: 'A free speech, a free press, and a screen free for expression tell the story of American democracy. They merit no criticism. They need no defence.' This was encouraging. Schaefer (a notoriously obstinate man) was digging his heels in. Then, just days before the opening of *Native Son*, Welles gained an important ally. Henry Luce, sometime investor in the Mercury Theatre, owner of *Time* and *Life* magazines, rival and opponent of Hearst, took up the cause of *Kane*. 'He has ordered his staff to unleash their guns to get the film released,' reported *Variety*. The first fruit of Luce's commitment to Welles appeared in an article in *Time* on 17 March, a week before the opening of *Native Son*. 'As in some grotesque fable, it appeared last week that Hollywood was about to turn on and destroy its greatest creation,' said *Time*. 'The objection of Mr Hearst who founded a publishing empire on sensationalism is ironic. For to most of the several hundred people who have seen the film at private showings, *Citizen Kane* is the most sensational product of the US movie industry . . . it is as psychiatrically sound as a fine novel, but projected with far greater scope for instance than Aldous Huxley was inspired to bring to his novel on the same theme. It is a work of art created by grown people for grown people.' The danger that Welles was now caught in the crosslines of a new war, that of the newspaper barons, was nothing to the exhilaration the public support brought. *Newsweek*, the same day, carried an even more complete encomium, from John O'Hara, already the sensational author of the novel *Butterfield 8* and the musical show *Pal Joey*, currently running on Broadway: 'It is with exceeding regret that your faithful bystander reports that he has just seen a picture which he thinks must be the best picture he ever saw. With no less regret he reports that he has just seen the best actor in the history of acting . . . reason for regret: you, my dear, may never see the picture.' He offers a pleasing side swipe at the Hopper–Parsons axis: 'a few obsequious and/or bulbous middle-aged ladies think the picture ought not to be shown,' then launches into his blazing finale: '*Citizen Kane* is Late 1941. It lacks nothing . . . there never has been a better actor than Orson Welles. I just got finished saying there never has been a better actor than Orson Welles, and I don't want any of your lip. Do yourself a favor. Go to your neighborhood exhibitor and ask him why he isn't showing *Citizen Kane*. Then sue me.' The still unshown *Citizen Kane* was rapidly becoming the *Look Back in Anger* of its day, polarising the progressives and the conservatives, the young and the old – except that no one ever tried to stop *Look Back in Anger* being seen. *Kane* was still on ice. Encouraged by the support, Welles took time out from the rehearsals for *Native Son* to call a press conference.

He threatened to sue, first RKO, then Hearst, if the film was not released. 'How can you copyright an enterprise, a profession? I must be free to film a story of a newspaper publisher. If I am restrained, it will force us all to go back and take our characters, say, from Greek mythology. And even then I suppose somebody would contend he was Zeus . . . I believe that the public is entitled to see *Citizen Kane*. For me to stand by while this picture was being suppressed would constitute a breach of faith with the public on my part as a producer.' He had, he said, sufficient financial backing to buy *Kane* from RKO and to release it himself, and the legal right both to demand that the picture be released and to bring legal action to force its release. 'RKO must release *Citizen Kane*. If it does not do so immediately, I have instructed my attorney to commence proceedings.' Roy Alexander Fowler, Welles's first biographer, suggests that this threat of legal proceedings was a ruse agreed by Welles and Schaefer. It seems likely. RKO certainly had no intention of writing off the $800,000 it had cost, and Schaefer's entire 'new Prestige RKO' depended on its release. His regime could scarcely have a worse start than the non-appearance of the most publicised film in the history of Hollywood. Herb Drake signed off the press conference in characteristically hard-boiled manner: 'Welles will show the picture and show it in tents, if necessary. He will probably open it at Soldiers' Field and saw Dolores in half at each intermission.'

Meanwhile, *Native Son* opened to the press. The Broadway first night audience (the show was playing at the St James's Theatre, slap in the heart of mainstream Broadway) was taken aback by the lack of an intermission, even more so by the decision not to issue programmes until the end of the show; Welles refused to allow the tight grip he had exercised over the play to be diffused by an audience rustling programmes and lighting matches to scan the cast list. The performance was remarkably successful; among many telegrams of congratulations was one from a man Welles knew had little regard for him personally or artistically, the ever-brittle Joe Losey: 'saw your show tonight stop its the first theatre job since little foxes for which i have complete respect and admiration stop would like to have done it stop that may not mean much to you but it means plenty to me stop i envy you profoundly stop wish you the long run which it deserves my sincere congratulations joe losey'. Richard Wright, too, was delighted, even if his telegram was to both Houseman and Welles: 'let me thank both of you for the energy talent speed and courage which both of you brought to the staging producing and directing of native son stop i have said time and again and i say now that i feel that native son has been in the hands of the two most gallant men in the theatrical world stop good luck always to both of you stop richard wright'. Canada Lee's telegram promised nothing that it didn't deliver: 'thanks for my big chance orson stop i shall live up to your confidence in me stop i will be there punching till the curtain comes down canada lee'.

The reviews the following day were full of stentorian acclaim for Welles, even if the venture as a whole provoked reservations. These came principally from two quarters: those who felt the book had not been well served, and those who felt that it had been too well served. Most critics, however, before entering reservations, took time to welcome back the prodigal son. It was his return, rather than the play itself, that was the news item. Sidney Whipple, an old scourge of Welles's, led the huzzahs: 'STARK DRAMA STAMPED WITH GENIUS: *Native Son* proves that Orson Welles, whether you like to admit it or not, is not a boy wonder but actually the greatest theatrical director of the modern stage.' Stark Young, who had also not been uncritical of Welles as both actor and director, was almost equally enthusiastic, observing that 'it may at times be quite ham, but this is not too dreadful a fault in these soft days.'

Brooks Atkinson of the *Times*, staunch supporter from the beginning, was just as glad to see him back: 'It is as if the theatre had been shaken up and recharged with life.' Then came the reservation: 'Mr Welles's wide pulsating style of direction is not the only possible approach to *Native Son*. In fact, it may not be the best.' This note was sounded elsewhere: 'there is no way of telling how far this rushing and plentiful use of the theatre medium *per se* that he is capable of and practices here cuts down the pathos, or the tragic element, that might have been possible to *Native Son* and its performance,' wrote Stark Young, who admitted to being 'excited rather than moved' by the play. No one denied the theatrical excitement engendered; the widely expressed doubt was whether it served the material. 'Beyond a bit of theatre commotion, publicity, sitting in our seats through ten scenes without intermission, and running into waves of intermittent emotion, there is very little remaining with us when the evening is over, though the subject matter of the play concerned one of the most pressing issues in America.' It was, of course, melodrama, Welles's essential technique; but was that appropriate to his searing, epic subject?

The *Daily Worker* (by no means predictably, since Wright, as an ex-member of the Communist Party, had fallen foul of the Marxist establishment) had no doubts: 'in comparison, all the productions of the current season seem dim and ancient chromos.' This included *The Grapes of Wrath* and *Watch on the Rhine*, so this was no idle praise. 'The theatre, that slumbering giant, tears off its chains in this production. From the theatrical point of view it is a technical masterpiece. As a political document it lives with the fire of an angry message.' The Catholic *Commonweal*, coming from the other end of the political spectrum, was outraged that a murderer should be glorified; and the *Journal-American*, not entirely surprisingly, since it was the flagship title of William Randolph Hearst, found that the play had more to do with Moscow than Harlem. This was the first hint of Hearst's new tactic in the *Kane* war of attrition: vilifying Welles's politics.

For Canada Lee, the praise was unanimous: 'Mr Lee's performance is, in fact, the best I have ever seen in New York from a Negro player,' in Stark Young's words; particularly so, he says, in view of the weakness in the writing. Rosamond Gilder made an important point in her review for *Theatre Arts Monthly* which transcends these stylistic cavills: 'Canada Lee has added a figure of heroic dimensions and tremendous implications to the theatre's gallery of great portraits.' How often had that happened in the history of black theatre? Atkinson called Lee 'superb' adding that 'not all of the acting measures up to the play or the performance. Perhaps Mr Welles is not sufficiently interested in the minor parts.' The truth may be that Welles lavished an enormous amount of time, patience and energy on working with Lee who, for the rest of his short life, was thereafter regarded as the finest black actor of his generation. Lee, ex-boxer, ex-violinist, ex-jockey and currently proprietor of the Chicken Coop Club on West 136th Street, had worked steadily as an actor since *Macbeth* in 1936, to mixed critical response; *Big White Fog*, his previous show (for the Negro Playwrights' Company), had not gained him many plaudits. Despite this, and his universally noted sweetness of demeanour (an unlikely qualification for playing the unexploded bomb that is Bigger Thomas), Welles had had no hesitation in casting him in the role; his confidence was rewarded with one of the most celebrated performances of the American theatre of the period.

The production in general marked an enormous breakthrough in the depiction of a black person's life and death; whatever its compromises in the interest of dramatic form, it was as unyielding as the novel itself in its confrontation of the baffled rage of Bigger Thomas. There is no concession. 'To most people, as to this department, the hero is inhuman,' wrote a chilled Atkinson. 'Although the drama flames with violence, the authors give a cold, unyielding conclusion to the most biting drama ever written about a Negro in America . . . after more than two years in Hollywood, Mr Welles has dropped by to stage a hard-hitting play.' He had not sold out. 'The simple fact is that Mr Welles has come back to the theatre with all the originality and imagination he had when he was setting off fire-crackers in the Mercury two or three seasons ago,' said Atkinson in the *Times*. 'Mr Welles is a young man with a lot of flaring ideals and when he is standing on the director's podium, he renews the youth of the theatre.'

Native Son represented two important things, not necessarily serving each other: Wright's vision, and Welles's talent. It was impossible to consider the piece itself, or its meaning, or the individual elements within it, except in terms of Welles himself. He was inescapable. Not for nothing did the marquee outside the theatre say simply

ORSON WELLES
NATIVE SON

Business was, to begin with, brisk. That was no mean achievement in a season as crammed with attractive delights as that of spring 1941 (*Arsenic and Old Lace*, *Lady in the Dark*, *Johnny Belinda*, *Pal Joey*, *Panama Hattie*, *The Corn Is Green*, and *The Man Who Came to Dinner*). The run was not untroubled, however. The theatre was picketed by both the Urban League, who thought its tragic ending, in Ethan Mordden's words, 'counterproductive to progressivism' and the Communist Party, waging war on the apostate author, Wright. By the end of the run, business had slacked off sufficiently to provoke an unsigned document produced for the Mercury press office under the headline BLUEPRINT FOR AN EMERGENCY. It is a striking indication of the continuing difficulty in persuading black people into theatres in Central Manhattan (the Negro Playwrights' Company had foundered on that rock), but also of the importance of the production.

> 1. Get support of Negro press. ANGLES: What *Native Son* means to the negro people. They must see that the success or failure of the show will influence the type of Negro production on Broadway for many years to come. If the show fails, producers will be reluctant to present Negroes in anything but the old and highly undesirable formulas; as clowns, rapists or creatures just a little bit better than the apes . . . *Native Son* voices their aspirations, problems etc with

> clarity and conviction and now is the time to throw their complaint right back on their laps.

For the second time in his short career Welles had spearheaded the hopes of the Negro profession. The author of the anonymous document (who might conceivably be Wright) suggests a *Native Son* rally to be held in Colonial Park in Harlem which should feature a broadcast from Hollywood by Welles and any famous people who have seen the show. 'Orson is well thought of in Harlem and I can't stress too highly the effect of such a personal touch on his part.' They finally clocked up a highly respectable (though not especially profitable) 114 performances at the St James's Theatre; the show was then toured, in simplified form, and brought back to New York, where it was again acclaimed. It was, by common consent, the most completely achieved of all Welles's productions to date. As it happens, it was the last success he was ever to have in the theatre, though he continued to work there, intermittently and eccentrically, for another twenty years. He had returned from Hollywood with a new sense of purpose and concentration; his relationship with Houseman, though by now lacking in personal warmth, was one of complete professional trust. He would never again in the theatre have the framework that Houseman had provided. His schemes became wilder and wilder, and less and less considered. Houseman's influence, in the case of *Native Son*, was crucial. Wright sent him a letter after the opening saying that 'it was a little shameful that you could not have gotten public credit for your help.' Stabilising, grounding and rooting Welles was only half of Houseman's contribution: he was a master of the forethought and manipulation (as his handling of Green amply demonstrates) upon which any collective enterprise must depend; Ulysses to Welles's Achilles. Welles despised him for the very thing that was his greatest contribution. There was no reason why he should endure that; instead he forged a career for himself which, though it would never know the explosive excitement that accompanied everything Welles ever did, had at least as great an influence on his life and times, both artistically and politically, as Welles ever did.

A few months after the closure of *Native Son*, Houseman was appointed to a job that called on every talent he possessed, and for which all his varied experiences had uniquely prepared him. He was made head of what became *The Voice of America*, and thus, by an extraordinary irony, this English-educated, Rumanian-born, half Alsatian, half Welshman became responsible for the audible presence in the world of his adopted country. Now, at last, he was free of Welles, and the need of a Welles-figure. It is noteworthy that there is no mention in his memoir of his last meeting with Welles; they had simply died to each other. In March 1941, Welles was at the pinnacle of his career in the theatre, still the uncontested great white hope of the American theatre who came to nothing in the end. The disappointment of all those hopes, though not attributable to, is discernible in, the breakdown of his relations with Houseman.

For the meantime, *Citizen Kane* had to be released from its Bastille. Despite Schaefer's impassioned words, RKO were once again wavering; the lawyers had delivered another verdict: Hearst could after all sue, and he could win. The phony war continued. Schaefer's tactic was to show the film to as many influential people as he possibly could to build on the groundswell of informed opinion in favour of the film. Welles himself had shown it to studio executives in New York in February, at the beginning of rehearsals for *Native Son*; he made a speech about freedom and the threat of fascism which had been greeted with polite applause. Schaefer had had a showing in Los Angeles for Hollywood's great and good. Reactions were almost universally favourable; an exception was Louis B. Mayer who claimed to have been so upset on behalf of Hearst that he wept. Weeping was something that came quite easily to the flint-hearted Mayer, but in this case, he backed up his tears by deputing Nick Schenck of MGM to extend an invitation to Schaefer to have the master of the film and all copies burnt: $805,000 was the figure proffered, which thoughtfully included a consideration for the wasted publicity budget. Schaefer heroically refused, wisely refraining from conveying the offer to his board. By April, the uneasy silence which was most unendurable of all to Welles had fallen again; had RKO done a deal behind his back? Suddenly the silence was rudely broken by Hearst. This time he miscalculated; and the shackles fell from *Citizen Kane*.

The occasion was *His Honor the Mayor*, an innocuous radio play by Welles, who had some months before joined a loose federation of authors, actors and directors calling themselves The Free Company. Of a broadly liberal persuasion (the group included Sherwood Anderson, William Saroyan, Stephen Vincent Benét, Paul Green, George M. Cohan and Burgess Meredith), their purpose in coming together was to affirm, in a time of impending war, the basic beliefs of democracy. James Boyd, convenor of the group, commissioned from each of the author-members of the company a short piece for radio; the idea was 'to illustrate by a series of plays the *meaning of freedom* and particularly those basic civil rights which make that freedom possible'. The authors were, they proudly stated, 'unpaid, uncensored and uncontrolled'. Each episode was prefaced with the lines:

> For what avail, the plow or sail
> Or land or life, if freedom fail?

The Columbia Broadcasting System, demonstrating its own commitment to democracy, broadcast the plays in the spring of 1941. *His Honor the Mayor* was transmitted on 6 April. The story is straightforward: Bill Knaggs, Mayor of Benton, has to decide whether to allow Colonel Egenhorn's anti-labour, anti-Hispanic, anti-Semitic White Crusaders to hold a meeting in the town. Without a single supporter in the town – even the old communist, the Catholic priest and the local garage owner strongly advise him against it – he allows the meeting to be held.

> Don't start forbiddin' anybody the right to assemble. Democracy's a rare precious thing and once you start that – you've finished democracy! Democracy guarantees freedom of assembly unconditionally to the worst lice that wants it. If they don't get it, they'll go underground so we can't see 'em. Let 'em thumb their noses at the Stars and Stripes, just so long as they don't touch it. Let 'em jeer at everything we're willing to die for. That's anybody's right – the right to be what's called nowadays 'un-American.'

In insisting on the right of a right-wing group to assemble, Welles slyly makes his point about the freedom of left-wingers. The manner is homespun; Thornton Wilder seems to be the influence ('Mrs Knaggs looks a little older than she ought to, because her life hasn't been easy. But she wears the smartest clothes she can afford, which isn't true of most of the other ladies in town; doesn't especially enhance her popularity' says Welles as narrator) though there is something of Marc Blitzstein's deliberately unvarnished quality about it, too. And there is a charming autobiographical touch: throughout *His Honor the Mayor*, Knaggs eats. 'Take my word for it, when responsibilities get to be almost unendurable, a man on a diet takes to his sugar and starches as an addict retreats to his opium pipe, or a drunkard to his bottle.' The piece is mild in tone, but all the more telling for its absence of tub-thumping; Welles as narrator insists that 'you can draw your own conclusions; I hope you do.' He quietly and cunningly builds the dramatic tension (his special gift, as Houseman rightly observed) by maintaining the evenness of tone. 'Thanks everybody,' says Knaggs, having won the day. 'If you don't like what I've done, please wait till Election Day.' Boyd, serving as announcer for all of the plays, underlines the message: 'Like his honor the mayor, then, let us stand fast by the right of lawful assembly.' Finally Welles signs off his gentle little lehrstück by introducing his cast: 'of course, they're Mercury people, all featured in *Citizen Kane* and *Native Son* . . . this is the cast which remains, with your producer – as always – obediently yours.'

No sooner had the play been transmitted than it was immediately and vehemently denounced as communist propaganda in the Hearst press. The American Legion (Hearst's moral arm) took up cudgels against it, and held meetings to denounce it. The *Herald Express* offered as a headline on 17 April: 'Thrasher Asserts Welles's broadcasts Are Spearhead for Red Propaganda', while the *New York Journal and American* in its turn asserted: 'We must rid the country of every type of subversive propaganda. For years such elements have been edging towards key positions elsewhere, and now they are cropping up in radio.' But the attacks backfired; *Variety* reported the following month that audiences for the programmes had doubled since the Hearst press attacks. They ceased. Other papers came to his rescue; yet again he was a cause célèbre: 'If Orson Welles is a communist for preaching free speech, free radio, freedom of worship,' wrote *The New York Times*, 'then Paul Muni is a communist for being one of his associates; then too, is George M. Cohan, a leader in The Free Company, a communist.' The *Chicago Sunday Times* said 'if it weren't sad, it would be silly. William Randolph Hearst is piqued with Orson Welles. The rest is camouflage.' The Hearst attacks had one notable side effect: the Federal Bureau of Investigation opened a file on Welles that they were not to close until the end of the fifties. Oblivious of this, Welles sued a Los Angeles gossip columnist who had accused him of being a Marxist; he won, and that particular untruth ceased to figure in press reports. He was moved to make a lengthy press statement, in which he stated 'the Hearst papers have repeatedly described me as a communist. I am not a communist. I am grateful for our constitutional form of government, and I rejoice in our great American tradition of democracy. Needless to say, it is not necessarily unpatriotic to disagree with Mr Hearst. On the contrary, it is a privilege guaranteed me as an American citizen by the Bill of Rights . . . I want to say that I am proud of my American citizenship. As a citizen I cherish my rights, and I'm not fearful of uncertainty. I only ask,' he concluded with a scarcely veiled reference to the still unseen product of his last two years, 'that I am judged by what I am and what I do.'

Hearst and his men had gone too far, finally. He had succeeded only in arousing public interest in Welles and *Citizen Kane* by methods of vilification transparent even to his natural supporters. Schaefer was finally able to convince his board that they must take advantage of the overwhelming amounts of increasingly positive publicity; Rosamond Gilder later observed that 'William Randolph Hearst served as voluntary press agent in the largest unsought publicity build-up since *Gone with the Wind*.' Inspired by a four-page spread in *Life* magazine detailing the technical innovations of *Citizen Kane*, Schaefer announced the release of the picture for the beginning of May 1941, the week, as it happens, of Welles's 26th birthday. There would be four premières, New York, Los Angeles, San Francisco and Chicago. The advertising campaign was immediately mounted, underlining in extravagance everything that had gone before. This is publicity about publicity: 'America's most talked-about man presents long-awaited film debut marked by unique story, clever technique, brilliant acting.' Even balder: 'THE MOST TALKED ABOUT PICTURE IN YEARS! Nothing deleted! Nothing changed! So different it's best to see it from the beginning. I HATE HIM! I LOVE HIM! HE'S A DIRTY DOG! HE'S A SAINT! HE'S CRAZY! HE'S A GENIUS!' It was Kane they were describing; but it might as well have been Welles. The posters stress his fine manly posture and noble – if false – profile.

The trailer, however, has great playful charm. Welles never appears, but is omnipresent as the narrator: a joke – a rather knowing one – in itself. Shot by Toland at the same time as the film, it is a miniature documentary, almost an introduction to the cinema, in the manner of the opening section of the unfilmed *Heart of Darkness*. The scene is an empty, moodily lit sound stage. A voice – guess whose? – calls for lights. Lights are snapped on. 'Get me a mike.' It swings in on its boom. 'Thank you,' says the director-as-God. 'How do you do, ladies and gentlemen,' God continues, unseen. 'This is Orson Welles. I'd like you to meet the actors.' Cut to the chorus girls from the *Inquirer* part scene. 'I'm just showing you the chorus girls for ballyhoo. Still, what lovely chorus girls they are.' Cut back to the darkly lit soundstage. Joe Cotten is standing in the shadows. 'Light!' cries God. There is light, by which Joe is dazzled. 'Smile,' says God. And he does. One by one the cast, in their street clothes, are introduced – 'you don't know Dorothy Comingore, but you soon will; we've caught Ruth with her hair up: smile for the camera, Ruth!'– and each is disposed of with a rapid wipe, which introduces the next: Erskine Sandford with a parrot on each shoulder, Agnes Moorehead ('the best actress in the world') and finally, Everett Sloane, who appears at the other side of the studio at a canter, running straight into his own reflection. 'You see, ladies and gentlemen, it's all done with mirrors.'

'What's the film all about?' asks God. 'It's a modern American story about a man called Charles Foster Kane.' A montage of the characters in extreme close-up talking about Kane – spluttering, smiling, grimly denouncing – is rounded off by Welles (still unseen) saying: 'Ladies and Gentlemen, I can't imagine what you'll think about him, but you'll have a chance to find out when *Citizen Kane* comes to this theatre.' Teasing, charming, completely original, it is a sort of conjuring trick: without his face appearing once on the screen, Welles entirely dominates its five minutes' duration. The approach is entirely characteristic; Welles seeks to fascinate the audience with the process. Now they're actors, now they're the characters: magic! Sloane seems to be running towards us: he's actually running into a mirror, as you see when I move the camera. The film appears to be taking place in real life: actually, it's shot in a studio. The voices are transmitted by microphones, the faces lit by lamps. To describe what Welles is up to here as Brechtian is too stuffy. Nor is it Pirandellian; there is no metaphysical dimension to it. It is, to be precise, a trick.

If anything, it is a bit of Chinese opera. The dragon thrillingly devours the stage; a switch is thrown and you see twenty men dressed in black holding aloft a lot of colourful fabric and ribbon and painted papier-mâché; another switch is thrown and there the dragon is again, ten times as terrible and beautiful as life. The charm of Welles's trailer is that he, the magician, like many youthful conjurors, is keen to demonstrate how the trick works; otherwise how will you know how clever he was? The poster campaign was more traditional; the focus was directly on Welles. The central image was of him as the twenty-five-year-old Kane, arms outstretched (Welles had protested when the image of the older Kane was used: 'a pretty serious mistake by way of exploitation'). The key slogan blazed everwhere answered the question supposedly on everyone's lips: IT'S TERRIFIC!

CHAPTER TWENTY-TWO

Release

MEANWHILE, HAVING at last achieved a release date for his film, Welles collapsed. Dr Dudley Bumpus's medical exam of 24 April reports his chief complaint: 'Attacks of knife-like pain behind the sternal notch with sensations of smothering.' The physical examination (which records his height as 72 inches, three and a half inches shorter than his usual reported height, and his weight as 218 lbs: 15½ stones) further reveals scoliosis of the spine, and spina bifida occulta. 'These congenital anomalies of the spine give rise to backache resulting from trauma.' In addition he has 'a very marked degree of pes planus [flat foot: everted] which accounts for the great amount of foot and ankle trouble which you experience.' Dr Bumpus discovers tenderness over the duodenum. 'There is nothing very serious with the heart action but you cannot afford to abuse that organ because of a tendency to be susceptible to damage.' It must have been a relief to discover that, despite a vast alcoholic intake, coupled with regular infusions of benzedrine and amphetamines, the sorely abused organ in question was holding up so well. The report was doubly reassuring to Welles; not only did it explain the great physical discomfort that he had experienced in his corsets, and the continuing weakness in his ankles, it also offered perfect grounds for him to avoid being drafted. The Roosevelt government had slowly, and by means of an elaborate lottery system, been conscripting able-bodied men into the armed forces in anticipation of America's entry into the war. Since the inception of this drive, Welles and Arnold Weissberger had anxiously tried to find ways by which Welles could avoid being recruited. Weissberger sent him a letter of congratulation in October of 1940 on being 5,283rd in the draw. By April of 1941, however, the prospect was not so distant: despite his later claims that he was deeply disappointed not to have fought in the war, he, Dick Baer and Arnold Weissberger were frantically looking for ways to get him out of it. Bumpus's diagnosis of pes planus ensured that Welles need never get into uniform. For the present the good doctor proposed that 'you get away from Hollywood for at least 60 days and follow a strict diet'. With the New York première of *Citizen Kane* fixed for May 1st, the advice was only partially effected, though he did manage to get away for a fortnight; he was scarcely going to be absent from one of the longest-awaited events in the history of film.

In newsreel footage of the various gala openings, Welles appears in glowing good health and, as well he might, triumphant, surrounded by his Hollywood stalwarts, actors, mostly, and a few directors, as well as the usual group of gala folk. John Barrymore was his guest in New York; they had become a sort of unofficial double act on the *Rudy Vallee Show* in which they were billed as THE TWO GREATEST SHAKESPEAREAN ACTORS IN THE WORLD TODAY (Barrymore: 'Orson Welles?! He's an exhibitionist, a publicity seeker, a headline hunter, a cheap sensationalist . . . why, he's another John Barrymore!') At the New York première, Welles told Bogdanovich, Barrymore, to Welles's immeasurable delight, informed a reporter who had asked him why he was there 'you might say I'm a relative,' continuing with perfect dead-pan, 'I think it's time the public heard the truth – Orson is, in fact, the bastard son of Ethel and the Pope.' Over Barrymore, as he spoke, and over the milling crowds and the limousines and the police escorts, loomed the marquee of the Palace Theatre on Broadway, with Welles, legs akimbo, arms outstretched, reproduced ten times over, each representation larger than the one in front of it, till Kane seems to stretch backwards to the crack of doom. IT'S TERRIFIC, the slogan cried, above the last and largest Kane, and above that, written with electric bulbs in letters six foot high

ORSON
WELLES

The whole carnival was repeated in Los Angeles, where he appeared, finally fully public, with Dolores del Rio (her divorce now through) at his side. According to Welles himself, the only one of the premières that was not triumphant was the one in Chicago, where 'no one came'. He had wanted to bring del Rio to what he still regarded as his hometown, but it proved a damp squib. He had outgrown the Mid-West, and the Mid-West wanted none of him. Roger Hill did his best, mustering a chorus of Todd-ites headed by his own fifteen-year-old son, singing

Happy Birthday to you
Felicitations we strew
On our dear friend Orson
From the boys old and new
Let the Hearst face turn blue
Shouting red bunk at you
Those who know you Orson
Know you're white through and through.

Of course, by then Welles knew that he had the thing in the bag. The reviews, written days, in some cases weeks before, appeared after the New York opening, and they could scarcely have been more satisfactory; the whole thing was a publicist's dream come true. There was surprisingly little resentment of the hype; many of the critics even managed to top it.

'Last Wednesday afternoon, I went to see a picture that had the most terrific critical build-up of any picture ever made,' wrote Sidney Skolsky in the *New York Post*. 'After seeing the picture, I felt that everything that had been said was an understatement.' The *Hollywood Reporter*, which had so publicly urged Schaefer to ditch Welles altogether, made a complete recantation on its front page: 'Mr Genius comes through; *Kane* astonishing picture.' Bosley Crowther in *The New York Times* also cried vindication: 'Now that the wrappers are off, it can be safely stated that the suppression of this film would have been a crime . . . *Citizen Kane* is far and away the most surprising and cinematically exciting motion picture to be seen here in many a moon. As a matter of fact, it comes close to being the most sensational film ever made in Hollywood . . . he has made a picture of tremendous and overpowering scope.' Other reviewers spoke of *Citizen Kane* as being the culmination of movie history, the summation of all that had gone before – and, at the same time, as a revolutionary work. 'Welles has built new thresholds for the films,' said Schallert in the *Los Angeles Times*. 'He dares to see that things are done with the camera which most picture-makers would shun as bad technique and these lend a fascination unparalleled to many of the scenes.' '*Citizen Kane* is a great motion picture,' cried the dramatically repentant *Hollywood Reporter*.

A certain uneasiness began to spread among reviewers even among those who had cheered loudest first, as the waves of hyperbole became tidal. After all, to call *Citizen Kane* the greatest film ever made is like saying that *Love's Labour's Lost* or maybe *Titus Andronicus* is the greatest play ever written. 'Perhaps,' said the

Nation, hedging its bets, 'when the uproar has died down, it will be discovered that the film is not quite as good as it is considered now, but nevertheless, Hollywood will for a long time be in debt to Mr Welles.' There are two contradictory myths about the reception of *Kane*: that it was ecstatically acclaimed, and that it was a critical flop. The response, taking in both extremes, was more complex, and it evolved by stages. Bosley Crowther returned to the fray two days after his initial notice in *The New York Times*: 'Now that the returns are in from most of the local journalistic precincts and Orson Welles's *Citizen Kane* has been overwhelmingly selected as one of the great (if not the greatest) motion pictures of all time' he finds himself asking 'is it a great picture – saying "great" with awe in one's voice? And does it promise much for the future of its amazing young producer? We, a minority feline, are not altogether certain.' Acknowledging the film's technical brilliance ('he has made use of all the best devices of pure cinema which have been brought out through the years. And he has invented a few of his own') Crowther was 'inclined to suspect that the enthusiasm with which Mr Welles made the film – the natural bent of a first-class showman toward eloquent and dramatic effects – rather worked against the logic of the story . . . unquestionably, Mr Welles is the most dynamic newcomer in films and his talents are infinite. But the showman will have to acquire a good bit more discipline before he is thoroughly dependable. When he does – and let's hope it will be soon – his fame should extend to Mars.' It was not simply that the film was too clever by half (though this opinion began increasingly to be expressed); there was something wrong at the heart of it.

Even in his first notice, Crowther had observed that the film fails 'to provide a clear picture of the character and motives behind the man about whom the whole thing revolves . . . at the end, Kubla Kane is still an enigma – a very confusing one.' If this was a flaw, he felt first time round, it was an unimportant one. 'It is cynical, ironic, sometimes oppressive, and as realistic as a slap. But it has more vitality than 15 other films we could name.' In the face of the subsequent hosannahs and halleluias, he came back to it with more concern. 'Most people who have seen the picture so far have come away with the solid conviction that they have beheld the image of an unscrupulous tycoon. Yet at no point in the picture is a black mark actually checked against Kane . . . we are bound to conclude that this picture is not truly great, for its theme is basically vague and its significance depends on circumstances.'

This emptiness at the centre – the undefined nature of Kane, despite his being, in Atkinson's phrase, 'a theatrical character presented with consummate theatricality' – was felt by a number of critics. Rosamond Gilder wrote that 'it is . . . when all has been told, the picture of a man who is not really worth depicting, and here is the film's weakness. *Citizen Kane* depends for its importance on implications which are external to the movie itself . . . in the picture his sway over the multitude is hinted at but never demonstrated; and yet it is only this power that lends the man stature enough.' The English critic, James Agate, expressed the same feeling with characteristic directness: 'Miss Powell talked of Charles Foster Kane as a "colossus." I could see nothing of Miss Powell's colossus . . . my colleagues will agree that to be the owner of a chain of drug stores ten thousand links long, with each link represented by a city and the whole stretching from Hollywood to San Francisco, does not make a man a colossus. I see no difference when the drug stores are newspapers having the greatest circulation in the solar system. It depends what he does with them, and Kane did nothing with his newspapers except increase the vulgarity of an already vulgar world.' From the other end of the political spectrum, the same complaint was lodged. 'Not one glimpse of the actual content of his newspapers is afforded us,' wrote Joy Davidson in *New Masses*. 'One or two advertised scenes of political relevance, indeed, appear to have been cut out of the picture. As a result the audience is left with a vast confusion as to what Kane stands for. This grotesque inadequacy in the midst of plenty keeps *Citizen Kane* from fulfilling its promises . . . the picture resorts to the trick of giving Kane a mysterious dying speech, supposed to be the "real clue to Kane," the sentimental explanation of which is coyly delayed until the fade-out.' Davidson, a feminist avant la lettre, interestingly criticises the film from another political standpoint: 'Welles has not escaped one Hollywood convention, the smirking thesis that the important thing about a Hollywood figure is not how he treats his country but how he treats his women.' Now, in the mid-nineties, it might be argued on the contrary that we see clearly from the way Kane treats his women, how he treats his country.

It is interesting to note how early (this is the first week of its release) critics detected this hollowness in the film, the void at its centre. Twenty years later Welles made a revealing admission to Richard Meryman: '*Citizen Kane* was made in the most wildly fun-and-games kind of way. But from the very beginning I felt it had a curious iciness at its heart. It has moments when the whole picture seems to me to echo a bit. I was always conscious of the sound of footsteps echoing in some funny way – a certain effect made by the proportions of certain chemicals.' The question, of course, is whether the coldness is thematic. 'He couldn't give love,' says Leland. 'He hadn't got any to give.' Or is it simply that such feeling as there might have been is submerged in technical rodomontade? Welles evidently felt so: 'There are more conscious shots – for the sake of shots – in *Kane* than anything I've done since,' he told Bogdanovich. 'I've tried to avoid that sort of thing since then.' Joy Davidson (an enthusiastic supporter of the film, on the whole, for its essential progressiveness) was of the contemporary too-clever-by-half school: 'far too many trick-camera angles, too many fantastic combinations of light and shadows indicating an incomplete translation of Welles's famous stage technique into screen terms. Frequently he lets his showmanship run away with him, preferring to astound than to convince.'

Public resistance to so much innovation was widely predicted: 'Orson Welles never once makes concessions to ordinary film-goers. His film is so intelligently adult that half its audience will miss its point. This very subtlety may be Welles's downfall (from a box office, not an artistic, point of view),' wrote Philip Hartung in *Commonweal*. 'The excellent acting . . . will confuse fans looking for romance, glamor and heroes. Although these fans might overlook Gregg Toland's photography, even they cannot miss its beauty. To Toland's expert work *Citizen Kane* owes much of its success. Already Hollywood is abuzz over the technique. But just how much of it will be copied depends on box office. And who should get credit for what is hard to say,' Hartung adds, anticipating the debates that have haunted the film's subsequent fifty years of existence. 'Welles deserves applause for hiring Toland, for giving him time and money to experiment. In any case, the finished result is yours.' Belfrage in *The Clipper* was alone in identifying the exceptional use of sound in the film: 'It is as profoundly moving an experience as only this extraordinary and hitherto unexplored medium of sound-cinema can afford in 2 hours . . . perhaps of all the delectable flavors that linger on the palate after seeing *Citizen Kane*, the use of sound is the strongest.' Kenneth Tynan's observation that if you close your eyes during *Kane* the experience is almost as rich remains one of the most acute remarks made about the film. Belfrage is equally enthusiastic about the multiple flashbacks, the same action described from different angles: 'Here we are really in the cinema medium, in that and nothing else.'

It is notable how anxious all the reviewers are to assert the distinctive nature of film, versus any other medium: the glut of new media in such a tiny timespan had led to fierce arguments on the essential elements of each. 'What other medium,' cried Belfrage, 'could show so forcefully that truth is not merely objective, but subjective also and at the same time?' Tangye Lean advanced another version of the same conviction: one of the few who accepted 'Rosebud' as entirely successful, he notes 'If you accept the discovery of "Rosebud" as something more significant than an O. Henry ending, a vast pattern of interrelated human themes becomes clear – as a different one does in the last volume of *À la Recherche du Temps Perdu.*' Technically, he rates the precise focus and the overlapping dialogue as crucial innovations. 'We are forced by these devices to lay our own emphasis on the data, to make our own selection' – an anticipation of André Bazin's claim for *Citizen Kane*, nearly ten years later. 'Orson Welles likes this confusion. He extends it beyond the technical management of light and sound. He will give us, partly because he is a first-class showman, five or ten superb minutes of chorus girls dancing as a background to a serious conversation, five minutes of a political speech by Kane, but only thirty seconds of a vital conversation in which his mother sends him into exile. But Welles would certainly answer that life itself treats the important things in this arbitrary fashion.' Quoting Mr Bernstein's undeniably Proustian speech about the girl on the ferry, (Welles's favourite writing in the film, he always claimed, and pure Mankiewicz, as he freely acknowledged) Lean continues: 'Orson Welles believes that the significant things that happen to us are the ones that get condensed, overlooked, forgotten. He does something to point the significance of the muddle, more than is done for us by life itself, but less than by a medical case history or a political novel.'

This is decidedly highbrow criticism. A magisterial rebuke from the populist but highly informed Otis Ferguson came in *The New Republic.* Offering the most sustained and perhaps most perceptive contemporary analysis, it is worth looking at in some detail. 'It is the boldest freehand stroke in major screen production since Griffith and Bitzer were running wild to unshackle the camera; it has the excitement of all surprises without stirring emotions much more enduring; and in the line of narrative film, as developed in all countries but most highly on the West Coast of America, it holds no great place.' Ferguson's aesthetic was predicated on what might be called humanist realism. 'The picture,' he muses, sarcastically. 'The new art. The camera unbound. The picture is very exciting to anyone who gets excited about how things can be done in the movies; and the many places where it takes off like the Wright Brothers should be credited to Mr Welles and his cameraman second . . . the whole idea of a man in these attitudes must be credited to Welles himself. And in these things there is no doubt the picture is dramatic. But what goes on between the dramatic high points, the story? No. What goes on is talk and more talk. And while the stage may stand for this, the movies don't. And where a cameraman like Gregg Toland can be every sort of a help to a director, in showing him what he will pick up, in getting this effect or that, in achieving some lifting trick the guy has thought up, the cameraman can't teach him how to shoot and cut a picture, even if he knows himself. It is a thing that takes years and practice to learn. And its main problem always is story, story, story – or, How can we do it to them so they don't know beforehand that it's being done? Low key-photography won't help, except in the case of critics . . . the real art of movies concentrates on getting the right story and the right actors, the right kind of production and then smoothing everything out. And after that, in figuring how each idea can be made true, how each action can be made to happen, how you cut and reverse-camera and remake each minute of action, and run it into a line afterwards, like the motion in the ocean.'

It is extraordinary how widespread the unease was, once the initial rush had passed. In this, criticism of *Kane* mirrored the criticism of his work in the theatre. The gap between form and content seemed unbridgeable for him, in any medium. *Citizen Kane* was by far the greatest of all Welles's firework displays, simply dazzling. And then? Even at the time, many people saw this, and felt it. Ferguson returned remorselessly to his theme, the following week. 'Orson Welles was naturally entranced by all the things the moving camera could do for him; and while much has resulted from this preoccupation, I think his neglect of what the camera could do *to* him is the main reason why the picture leaves you cold even while your mouth is still open to its excitements. There may have been the heart and belief to put into it, but there wasn't the time to learn how this might be done, or much regard for any such humdrum skill.' Ferguson sternly insists on his gospel of true cinema. 'This stuff is fine theatre, technically or any other way, and along with them the film is exciting for the recklessness of its independence, even if it seems to have little to be free *for*. There is surely nothing against it as a dramatic venture that it is no advance in screen technique at all, but a retrogression. The movies could use Orson Welles. But so could Orson Welles use the movies, that is, if he wants to make pictures. Hollywood is a great field for fanfare, but it is also a field in which every Genius has to do it the hard way; and *Citizen Kane* makes me rather doubt whether Orson Welles wants to make pictures.' In this, Ferguson strangely echoes Mankiewicz's anxiety in the cutting room: is it really film? Or simply celluloid put to theatrical uses? – an extension of the filmed sections of *Too Much Johnson*. Truffaut makes the telling observation that Welles favoured low angles so much because they create the equivalent of the spectator's position in the theatre.

Perhaps the deepest of all Ferguson's points is his crucial observation that you need time to acquire simplicity. Thrown in at the deep end, under gala conditions, Welles could never simply learn how to swim: he had to compete in all the most demanding categories, and win all the prizes. This he had certainly done, whatever the reservations. It was a curious grounding in his art, however. Welles was, of course, given time and his concept of movie-making matured. 'I am so bored with the aesthetics of the cinema,' he told Huw Wheldon in 1960, oddly echoing Ferguson ('story, story, story') with every word of whose aesthetic he could eventually find himself in whole-hearted agreement. 'The story teller's first duty is always to the story.' But nothing he made subsequently was given anything like the exposure or the attention of *Citizen Kane*. His reputation as a stylistic virtuoso was established for all time, and he was forever judged as such – either a brilliant stylistic virtuoso or a failed stylistic virtuoso. His artistic personality, at least as far as the average critic was concerned, was fixed. Just as he felt himself to be in perpetual competition with the fifteen-year-old prodigy he had been, so his films were forever in competition with this first freakish triumph. Kane's line: 'If I hadn't been born rich, I might have been a really great man' was another personal resonance for Welles: not financially rich, of course: rich in talent, rich in opportunity. So much for his directing. As for his acting performance, that, too, was a source of controversy and confusion. For the most part, he and the Mercury Players were wildly applauded (which may have come as a surprise to the cast themselves who, as Augusta Weissberger reports, left the first screening dejected, convinced, like all actors from the dawn of film, that their best work had been maliciously excised). Bosley Crowther's review in *The New York Times* is typical: 'Mr Welles has directed with the sureness and distinction of a seasoned master and the entire cast . . . perform it in a manner which puts to shame the surface posturings of some of our more popular stars.' There were, inevitably, rumbles of dissension even in this area. 'Of the actors you can say that there are good jobs done and also still better ones to be done,' wrote Ferguson. 'Dorothy Comingore . . . is too ham as the opera singer (subtlety never hurt anyone, and those of us who aren't gaping yokels are not alone, Mr Citizen Orson). Joseph Cotten had a part that was possibly short on savor because when he was with the great man he had to be something of a chump and when he was talking to him afterwards he had to be something of a Mr Chips, with a twinkle and lip-smacking . . . the man to remember was Everett Sloane, who seemed to understand and seemed to represent it, the little man with the big mind, the projection without the face motion and flapping of arms. You may be surprised, when you take the film apart, that his relations to any analysis of Kane were as much as anything the things that made him real.'

The flashback technique of the film ensures that we think of the actors as actors at all times, monitoring their make-ups and noting the angle of their stoops as they proceed towards and away from the grave. Only Agnes Moorehead is exempt from this consideration, and her performance, with the sturdy gravity of an American primitive artist, has an actuality that gives Kane's mother an intensified feel quite different from any of the other characters. Perhaps this was Moorehead's instinct; perhaps the character lends itself to such an approach. Moorehead always spoke of Welles's abilities as a director of actors with immense warmth, so no doubt Welles had encouraged and helped her. These scenes are filled with a degree of emotion rarely encountered elsewhere in the film. It may be, too, that he had a special understanding of the severely loving mother who believes that success in the world is more important than the provision of maternal warmth. He allows himself a moment of sentimental pause in the scene of Kane's wooing of Susan Alexander: 'you know what mothers are,' she says, and he hesitates before his 'yes'. That we are able instantly to recall Kane's mother, halfway through the film, only having met her for a few minutes, is high tribute to Moorehead.

Ferguson is interesting about Welles's own performance: 'it is as though Welles, as the man who conceived and produced this film story, had little enough grasp of the issues involved; but Welles as the actor somehow managed, by the genius that is in actors when they have it, to be more of the thing than he could realise. His presence in the picture is always a vital thing, an object of fascination to the beholder . . . without him the picture would have fallen all into its various component pieces of effect, allusion and display. He is the big part, and no one will say he is not worth it.' Pauline Kael in her sloppily researched, entertainingly written introduction to the printed script, reveals greater delight in Welles's performance than she had originally taken, finding his youthfulness and vulnerability touching now, where before it simply seemed bombastic. Another point she makes with great force echoes Ferguson: 'Welles . . . has an almost total empathy with the audience. It's the same kind of empathy we're likely to feel for smart kids who grin at us when they're showing off in the school play . . . without Orson Welles's physical presence – the pudgy, big prodigy who incarnates egotism – *Citizen Kane* might . . . have disintegrated into vignettes. We feel that he's making it all happen. Like the actor-managers of the old school, he's the man onstage running the show, pulling it all together.'

Citizen Kane is palpably an effort of Orson Welles's will, as Xanadu, the success of the *Inquirer* and Susan Alexander's career are efforts of Kane's. Rosamond Gilder, in *Theatre Arts Quarterly*, was unconvinced: 'Just as Orson Welles, producer and director, deserves credit for the excellence of *Citizen Kane*, Orson Welles, co-author (with Herman J. Mankiewicz) and Orson Welles, actor, must be held responsible for the fact that it falls short of greatness . . . Orson Welles would be even more successful if he were willing to build his emotional scenes through the actor's power to develop feeling from within himself. Instead he resorts frequently to the trick of bursting in with his lines without allowing another actor to finish.' (So much for over-lapping dialogue!) It is hard to disagree with Gilder that Welles fails to create the inner emotional life of the character. Again, however, it is at least possible that this is the very point that Welles wants to make.

The questions What does the film mean? and What did Welles mean? clung to *Citizen Kane* from the beginning. Borges's terrible verdict that it is a labyrinth without a centre is another way of saying that it is endlessly enigmatic. Otis Ferguson was unaware of any complexity in the film's content: 'His troubles are personal, and his death is that of a domineering and lonely man, known to all for his money, loved by none. The only possible moral of the picture is, don't be that way or you'll be sorry.' For the FBI, to quote their report, '*Citizen Kane* was inspired by Welles's close associations with communists over a period of years. The evidence before us leads inevitably to the conclusion that the film *Citizen Kane* is nothing more than an extension of the Communist Party's campaign to smear one of its most effective and consistent opponents in the United States.' David Bordwell, in an elegant summary holds that '*Citizen Kane* is a tragedy on Marlovian lines, the story of the rise and fall of an overreacher. Like Tamburlaine and Faustus, Kane dares to test the limits of mortal power; like them, he fabricates endless personae which he takes as identical with his true self; and like them, he is a victim of the egotism of his own imagination,' an account of the film that would surely appeal to Welles. For Peter Bogdanovich, 'it is not his best film, but its aura is the most romantic: the initial courtship of an artist with his art.' (Courtship scarcely seems the word: the ravishment of his art, the twenty-four-hour copulation with his art, more likely.) For Pauline Kael, *Citizen Kane* is a magic show; for the present writer it is about size and the doomed quest for significance. The little boy versus the big man, getting more and feeling less; getting bigger and seeming smaller, projecting the image bigger and bigger, so the centre seems further and further from the surface. It is curious that it did not occur to Welles to make Kane grow fat.

Citizen Kane may be any or all of these things and many more besides. Part of its seeming multifariousness is due to the circumstances of its creation. It is the work of many people influencing Welles, principally Toland and Mankiewicz. Contrary to reputation (the reputation Welles and RKO between them sought to give it) it is emphatically not the work of one man. A great deal of what is on the screen is there not because it grew out of his vision but because it was what his collaborators wanted. Only in the area of sound is it uniquely his. His own presence in the film of course lends it tremendous brio and colour, and an ineffable flavour. Truffaut's observation that it is the only first film directed by a famous man has a deep relevance; public as he was, he had little time for private reflection. In his later career, he had all too much time for that; alas, the means to put his reflections into practice were no longer available to him. That he was able – in cahoots with RKO's special effects division – to accommodate the influences and weld them into something that seems coherent and organic is another brilliant trick of the great conjuror. The truth is that after *Citizen Kane* he needed to start all over again. It was an end, as much as a beginning for him. Well, why not? He was young, hugely acclaimed and with a splendid contract. He was only at the beginning. 'Orson Welles is 26,' wrote Tangye Lean at the end of his review in *Horizon*, 'with say 40 years work ahead of him.' Welles became a symbolic figure for some in the struggle for film-makers' independence, of the press, and of the system, a dangerous thing for his future: 'There has never been a more exciting press show,' averred Cedric Belfrage in the little magazine, *The Clipper*. 'For on that screen the slaves, the houris, and the camp-followers of the press lords saw some of the truth told about what enslaves, degrades, and makes prostitutes of them. And at the same time, they saw the whole spangled pyramid of Hollywood movie conventions, which they had had to support with their bodies in their advertisement-controlled "criticism", toppled over by the heroic Orson Welles and his Mercury Theatre nobodies.'

Rampaging in all directions, Belfrage reports that 'there are in Hollywood a score of cameramen, a score of writers, a score of sound experts, a score of make-up artists – all equal to Orson's men in their own field – is probably to underestimate. For years they have been hoping and trying for a chance to show their skill and originality, but always the film salesman, speaking through the producer, has the last word; and the film salesman is one trained in not seeing the wood for the trees.' Belfrage's peroration elects Welles to supreme status among film-makers. '*Citizen Kane* is correctly described as being "by Orson Welles" – not "produced" or "directed" or "from a story" by Welles, but *by* him. And because it is all *by* him, because of his conception and coordination of the work, his collaborators on camera and art direction and sound and all the rest shine more brightly. He is the biggest man in Hollywood today. And he is the Prince Charming whose bold smacking kiss on the brow of a bewitched art puts us all in his debt.' Once again, Welles and Welles's film become causes célèbres: once again, it is almost impossible to separate his real merits, personally and as an artist, from the circumambient hyperbole.

Now the task was to sell the movie. Whatever criticisms or cavils there may have been, there was no shortage of selling angles; the press pack bulged with ecstatic quotes, including many in the exhibitors' press: 'A super effort!' hollered Chick Lewis in the *Showmen's Trade Review*. 'To showmen we say, see this picture! To those who play it there is the plain duty to themselves to give it every ounce of showmanship they possess in exploiting its extraordinary box-office potentialities.' Schaefer set about doing what he did best: selling. He launched into a positive orgy of salesmanship. The RKO Publicity Department turned out an interesting booklet for distribution to exhibitors: it starts with a picture of Welles/Kane, in his legs akimbo, arms outstretched poster position, now standing astride the globe: AMERICA, LAND OF OPPORTUNITY: EVERYWHERE NEWSPAPER, MAGAZINE AND RADIO VOICES SAID: GO WEST ORSON WELLES TO HOLLYWOOD. There is a picture of a cactus, then a palm tree, then the gates of Xanadu. BUT THE GATES WERE CLOSED: there is a padlock on this last word, and a huge hand held up minatorily. The page is studded with unfavourable quotes from Welles's first year in Hollywood. Then: CAME THE PREVIEW, CAME THE VERDICT. Ecstatic quotes now vie with each other on the page. The climax of the booklet is a personal message from George J. Schaefer: 'THANK YOU ORSON WELLES! CITIZEN KANE IS A VERY FINE PRODUCTION, THE RESULT OF GREAT INITIATIVE AND COURAGE, ESPECIALLY UNDER THE MOST TRYING OF CIRCUMSTANCES. The essence of show business is to present the new, the novel and the unusual to the public. You were not given the chance to present your ideas, but you were severely criticised for even daring to have an idea! You were condemned before being tried! Your triumph is one of the great accomplishments in motion picture history, and proof that America is still the land of opportunity, where there will always be room for those with dreams and the courage to bring them to reality. RKO PICTURES INC – GEORGE J. SCHAEFER, PRESIDENT.' This personal endorsement is surely unprecedented in the history of film publicity.

It was backed by a souvenir booklet which might have been entitled *He's Terrific!* The frontispiece shows a pipe-sucking, deep-thinking Orson. Page one tells us about THE AMAZING MR WELLES, accompanied by photographs of him on the radio, as Faustus, as Brutus, as himself, hatted and bearded looking merrily into the mirror: the text tells us that after a couple of false starts 'finally he went to work producing *Citizen Kane* from his own story of an American colossus striding across sixty years of living history. He directed it, starred in it, learned to dance for it, put all his recently acquired knowledge to work, picked up more as he went along. When it was finished, he supervised the scoring, too.' This was news, perhaps, to Bernard Herrmann. Page two, optimistically entitled MAN OF ENDLESS SURPRISES tells 'the story of Orson Welles, or the case history of one of America's most amazing young geniuses . . . he showed a surprising proclivity for painting. He was so good, as a matter of fact, that his instructor predicted he would become America's greatest painter.' That *is* new. Page three brings HIGHLIGHTS IN THE LIFE OF CITIZEN KANE, page four the credits for *Kane*. Pages five and six break into capital letters again: NOW IT'S ORSON WELLES OF HOLLYWOOD: QUICK-STEPPING THROUGH A FEW OF THE OUTSTANDING SCENES OF CITIZEN KANE WITH THAT UNPREDICTABLE PERSONALITY, ORSON WELLES, WHO BRINGS TO THE SCREEN IN HIS FIRST PRODUCTION AN UNUSUAL,

COMPELLING, DRAMATIC ENTERTAINMENT – AND A DISTINCT NEW MOTION PICTURE TECHNIQUE THAT IS YEARS AHEAD OF ITS TIME. Pages seven and eight celebrate THE 'FOUR-MOST' PERSONALITY OF MOTION PICTURES! in four photographs of Welles as author, director, producer, star. Page nine introduces us to those shadowy figures, THE MERCURY ACTORS. Their photographs are dominated by a much larger one of Welles, his arms outstretched. Pages ten and eleven give us THE MASTER OF MAKE-UP. (EVEN THE FIGURES PROVE THAT ORSON WELLES DOES THINGS IN A BIG WAY.) Pages twelve and thirteen describe how Welles reinvented the cinema. STAR ORSON WELLES MAKES FLUID CAMERA THE STAR OF CITIZEN KANE: 'It's a revolution: Welles blandly said a room wasn't a room without ceilings, and he wanted ceilings.' The final page is the celebrated shot of Kane standing on the piles of newspapers, which, in this context, looks like an image of Welles's own destiny: a man made into a giant by standing on top of a mountain of newsprint.

Under a particularly noble head of Welles as the middle-aged Kane, drawn by von Hentschel, the text further tells us that 'Orson Welles comes to the film industry with more salvos of advance and current publicity than have ever been given to any showman. His career, past and present, makes national and international news. Every publication in the country reports his spectacular activities. He has become the best-known showman of his generation.' An interesting phrase, and indubitably true. Early on, the campaign shifted its emphasis from the controversial many-sidedness of Kane to the love interest. 'THE FILM THAT HIT FRONT PAGES FROM COAST TO COAST. The love story that "dared not be made." WIFE NO 1: society belle. He gave her everything but the one thing she wanted. WIFE NO 2: shop girl. She scoffed at his $60,000,000 – broke his heart. What was the fatal weakness of the world's richest man?' IT'S TERRIFIC! SEE WHY AMERICA IS ONE BIG GOSSIP COLUMN ABOUT ORSON WELLES/CITIZEN KANE. So she walked out on $60,000,000! Would you? THE LOVE STORY HOLLYWOOD DARED US TO FILM! WHISPERED AND RAVED ABOUT FOR ONE SOLID YEAR . . . AND AT LAST IT'S HERE.' This press release (designed for exhibitors) emphasised Welles's marketability. '91% of the population know of and are curious about Welles. *Citizen Kane* . . . was a sensation even before it was released . . . into *Citizen Kane* Welles has put all the fascinating vitality which distinguished him from the ordinary showman. The result is simply TERRIFIC. The phrase' confides the press release, 'has great shock value to the reader. Standing alone, it permits no argument, no choice. A solid use of the campaign cannot fail to excite tremendous audience attention.'

Alas, the prophecy was not accurate. Schaefer was to some extent still baulked by the continuing efforts of the Hearst organisation. Spyros Skouras of 20th Century Fox had refused to take the movie for his theatres; many other theatres submitted to RKO's muscle and accepted it but never showed it. In the cities business was good initially, but quickly slid even in New York, where it closed after fifteen weeks. In the regional theatres, despite a special low-price launch, things were much worse. Among exhibitors, the picture became a byword for disaster. Charles Higham quotes the report of the manager of the Iris Theatre of Velva, North Dakota: 'Stay away from this. A nightmare. Will drive 'em out of your theatre. It may be a classic, but its plum "nuts" to your show-going public.' By the end of the year it had closed everywhere, not to be seen widely again in America till RKO sold its library to television; the renewal of interest in the film caused by this persuaded RKO to revive it in movie theatres, where it consolidated its influence but still failed to make money. Even its fiftieth anniversary comeback was disappointing; but its influence – or more precisely, its inspiration – had by now grown to stupendous dimensions. In Europe, it became a virtual textbook for the new criticism; in England, famously, the movie magazine *Sight and Sound* polled its readers to discover that *Citizen Kane* was the most popular of all films, a position it has never lost. Among the cognoscenti, that is; seeming prohibitively avant-garde to ordinary film-goers in 1941, it now seems dreadfully old-fashioned to them. Virtually every film maker to whose work the public flocks, however, has been in some way affected by its example. It is the supreme expression of the legend of Orson Welles; no one has ever been able to see the film without thinking about him, frame by frame, whether to curse him or to bless him. His young self has been trapped in it, like a fly in amber.

Citizen Kane, as well as being the first, is also the last fully achieved, uncompromised work of Welles's career – except, perhaps, for *Moby Dick*, which ran to rather poor business for three weeks in London, in 1955. Welles had done *Kane* exactly the way he wanted to, under ideal conditions; it failed commercially, despite the biggest brouhaha in the history of the cinema. In the wake of that failure, the nightmare that he had striven so hard and, he thought, so successfully to avoid became his fate for the rest of his career: interference, containment, manipulation, limitation. It is a melancholy truth that he had, by May of 1941, at the age of twenty-six created a body of work in several media that he would never surpass: in the theatre, in radio, in book illustration, in film. In each of these spheres, he had made his mark as an innovator, although it is closer to the truth to say that he was an inspired consolidator; his work was an end, rather than a beginning. Certainly it proved so for him. Denied by temperament and circumstances the opportunity to develop his work, every new venture was conceived, produced and finally delivered in such a constant glare of publicity that it was never possible for him quietly to cultivate his talent. Driven from within to achieve ever more, his work in all the areas in which he was employed had been amazingly accomplished for one so young; it did not, however, contain the seeds for future development. The same may be said of his personality, equally completely formed at an uncommonly early age. In fact, the work is the personality, the personality the work to an alarming degree. His creations have no autonomy; they are but his creatures. The first person singular, whether frankly and formally, as in much of his output, or simply in applause-seeking virtuosity of execution, is unavoidable. It was not a question of early maturity, either in his work or his being, as of forced growth. Thus he and his work of this period are brilliant but somehow lacking in illumination; full of flavour, but unnourishing. This was exceptionally stimulating both for his collaborators and his audiences; but only briefly. There is about both man and work a drive and a barely controlled feverish energy that suggests that the centre cannot hold, that things will fall apart.

The remaining forty-five years of Welles's life are a sort of sustained falling apart in which, Lear-like, as his world crumbled further and further around him, and as his own behaviour became more and more extravagant, he was vouchsafed extraordinary insights. Mocked by a world in which he was famous for fish-fingers and sherry, fatness and a cameo role in a film directed by somebody else, denied access to the means of production, he began to explore his medium further and further, no longer exclusively – or at all – interested as he had been in his earlier years, in results. Still reluctant to go within, to examine himself, he produced, in more and more original forms, a body of wildly uneven work that could never have been predicted from his early efforts. His engagement with his own personality led to the complete abolition of the dividing wall between himself and his creations; but he came increasingly, as he and his legend, the legend of the self-destroyed artist, grew to monumental dimensions, to display himself as a phenomenon. He became a figure of pity and terror. He had no castle, no baronial mansion: the world was his Xanadu; he roamed its corridors, looking for money with which to make films, but also, beyond that, for the chances which he had lost. Eventually, he found an extraordinary benevolence towards life, coming finally to smile even on his younger self, that self preserved for ever in *Citizen Kane.*

Welles was not unduly daunted by the commercial failure of *Citizen Kane*. He had projects by the dozen: not one but three South American films in a sort of compendium form under the title *It's All True*, an adaptation of an Eric Ambler novel, *Journey into Fear*, and Booth Tarkington's Mid-Western family saga, *The Magnificent Ambersons*, all three of which he started shooting in the fall. He started a new radio programme, *Orson Welles's Almanac*, consisting of adaptations of short stories, skits and poems. *The Magnificent Ambersons* and *Journey into Fear* completed principal photography, and Welles left the United States to begin shooting *It's All True*, now under the aegis of Nelson Rockefeller's Office of Inter-American Affairs. This meant that he was out of the country for the Oscars ceremony. He received nominations in four categories: as producer, as director, as actor and as co-writer, along with Mankiewicz, who had decided to stay at home. *Citizen Kane* itself was nominated in nine categories.

Each announcement of the film's name was greeted with hostility: boos, hisses, jeers. John Ford's *How Green was My Valley* swept the board. *Citizen Kane* won in one category alone: screenplay. When the award was announced, Mankiewicz was cheered to the echo, drowning out Welles's name. 'Mank, where's Mank,' the cry went up. It has been computed that if the voting rules were the same then as they are now, *Citizen Kane* would have won the award for best film; for obscure reasons, the extras' union voted conclusively against Welles (why? He had hired 796 of them on *Kane*). Notwithstanding, the mood at the ceremony was strongly against Welles. They had had enough of him, Welles the boy wonder, Welles the genius, Welles with an opinion about everything, Welles the cause célèbre, Welles the scourge of Hollywood, Welles the pundit, and now finally, Welles, director of the greatest film ever to come out of Hollywood.

Welles telegrammed Mankiewicz a high-spirited message from Rio: 'heres what i wanted to wire you after the academy dinner colon you can kiss my half stop i dare to send it through the mails only now that i find it possible to enclose a readymade retort stop i don't presume to write your jokes for you but you ought to like this colon dear orson colon you dont know your half from a whole in the ground stop affectionately orson'. Mankiewicz, indulging in a little esprit de l'escalier, had a joke of his own, the acceptance speech he never made: 'i am very happy to accept this award in mr welles absence because the script was written in mr welles absence'.

THE STAGE PRODUCTIONS

Macbeth
by William Shakespeare, adapted by O.W.
14 April 1936
Lafayette Theatre, New York

Horse Eats Hat
by Eugene Labiche and Marc-Michel (*An Italian Straw Hat*), adapted by Edwin Denby and O.W.
26 September 1936
Maxine Elliott Theatre, New York

Doctor Faustus
by Christopher Marlowe, adapted by O.W.
8 January 1937
Maxine Elliott Theatre, New York

The Second Hurricane
by Aaron Copland (musical score) and Edwin Denby (libretto).
21 April 1937
Henry Street Playhouse, New York

The Cradle Will Rock
by Marc Blitzstein.
16 June 1937
Venice Theatre, New York

Caesar
by William Shakespeare (*Julius Caesar*), adapted by O.W.
11 November 1937
Mercury Theatre, New York

The Shoemaker's Holiday
by Thomas Dekker, adapted by O.W.
1 January 1938
Mercury Theatre, New York

Heartbreak House
by George Bernard Shaw.
29 April 1938
Mercury Theatre, New York

Too Much Johnson
by William Gillette, adapted by O.W.
16 August 1938 Stony Creek Summer Theatre, Connecticut

Danton's Death
by Georg Büchner, translated by Geoffrey Dunlop, adapted by O.W.
5 November 1938
Mercury Theatre, New York

Five Kings
by William Shakespeare (*Richard II, Henry IV*, Parts I and II, *Henry V* and *The Merry Wives of Windsor*), adapted by O.W.
27 February 1939
Colonial Theatre, Boston

The Green Goddess
by William Archer, adapted by O.W.
June 1939 Palace Theatre, Chicago

Native Son
by Richard Wright, adapted by the author and Paul Green.
24 March 1941
St James's Theatre, New York

THE RADIO BROADCASTS

Hamlet
by William Shakespeare, adapted by O.W.
Fall 1936 *Columbia Workshop* CBS

Fall of the City
by Archibald MacLeish.
11 April 1937
Columbia Workshop CBS

Les Misérables
by Victor Hugo, adapted by O.W. in seven parts: *The Bishop, Javert, The Trial, Cosette, The Grave, The Barricade, Finale.*
23 July, 30 July, 6 August, 13 August, 20 August, 27 August, 3 September 1937
Mutual Broadcasting System

The Escape
by John Galsworthy (two parts).
15 and 22 August 1937
Columbia Workshop CBS

Twelfth Night
by William Shakespeare.
30 August 1937
Shakespearean Cycle CBS

The March of Time
A weekly dramatisation of news events, in which O.W. first took part on 22 March 1935 and continued to appear during the following four years. National Broadcasting Corporation

The Shadow series
based on the comic-book stories of Walter B. Gibson.

The Temple Bells of Neban
24 October 1937 CBS
The Three Ghosts
31 October 1937 CBS
The League of Terror
9 January 1938 CBS
Sabotage
16 January 1938 CBS
Society of the Living Dead
23 January 1938 CBS
The Poison Death
30 January 1938 CBS
The Phantom Voice
6 February 1938 CBS
The Bride of Death
6 March 1938 CBS
The Silent Avenger
13 March 1938 CBS
The White Legion
20 March 1938 CBS
and fourteen other undated episodes

First Person Singular series/ *The Mercury Theatre on the Air*
adaptations by O.W.

Dracula
by Bram Stoker
11 July 1938 CBS

Treasure Island
by Robert Louis Stevenson
18 July 1938 CBS

A Tale of Two Cities
by Charles Dickens
25 July 1938 CBS

The Thirty-Nine Steps
by John Buchan
1 August 1938 CBS

My Little Boy/The Open Window/I'm a Fool
by Carl Ewald, Saki and Sherwood Anderson
8 August 1938 CBS

Abraham Lincoln
by John Drinkwater
15 August 1938 CBS

The Affairs of Anatol
by Arthur Schnitzler
22 August 1938 CBS

The Count of Monte Cristo
by Alexandre Dumas
29 August 1938 CBS

The Man Who Was Thursday
by G. K. Chesterton
5 September 1938 CBS

The Mercury Theatre on the Air series

Julius Caesar
by William Shakespeare
11 September 1938 CBS

Jane Eyre
by Charlotte Brontë
18 September 1938 CBS

Sherlock Holmes
by Arthur Conan Doyle, dramatised by William Gillette
25 September 1938 CBS

Oliver Twist
by Charles Dickens
2 October 1938 CBS

Hell on Ice
by Edward Ellsberg
9 October 1938 CBS

Seventeen
by Booth Tarkington
16 October 1938 CBS

Around the World in Eighty Days
by Jules Verne
23 October 1938 CBS

The War of the Worlds
by H. G. Wells
30 October 1938 CBS

Heart of Darkness/Life with Father/The Gift of the Magi
by Joseph Conrad, Clarence Day and O. Henry
6 November 1938 CBS

A Passenger to Bali
by Ellis St Joseph
13 November 1938 CBS

The Pickwick Papers
by Charles Dickens
20 November 1938 CBS

Clarence
by Booth Tarkington
27 November 1938 CBS

The Bridge of San Luis Rey
by Thornton Wilder
2 December 1938 CBS

The Campbell Playhouse series

Rebecca
by Daphne du Maurier
9 December 1938 CBS

Call it a Day
by Dodie Smith
16 December 1938 CBS

A Christmas Carol
by Charles Dickens
23 December 1938 CBS

A Farewell to Arms
by Ernest Hemingway
30 December 1938 CBS

Counsellor-at-Law
by Elmer Rice
6 January 1939 CBS

Mutiny on the Bounty
by Charles Nordhoff and James Norman Hall
13 January 1938 CBS

Chicken Wagon Family
by Barry Benefield
20 January 1939 CBS

I Lost My Girlish Laughter
by Jane Allen
27 January 1939 CBS

Arrowsmith
by Sinclair Lewis
3 February 1939 CBS

The Green Goddess
by William Archer
10 February 1939 CBS

Burlesque
by Arthur Hopkins and James Manker Watters
17 February 1939 CBS

State Fair
by Philip Duffield Stong
24 February 1939 CBS

Royal Regiment
by Gilbert Frankau
3 March 1939 CBS

The Glass Key
by Dashiel Hammett
10 March 1939 CBS

Beau Geste
by P. C. Wren
17 March 1939 CBS

Twentieth Century
by Charles MacArthur and Ben Hecht
24 March 1939 CBS

Show Boat
by Edna Ferber
31 March 1939 CBS

Les Misérables
by Victor Hugo
7 April 1939 CBS

The Patriot
by Pearl Buck
14 April 1939 CBS

Private Lives
by Noel Coward
21 April 1939 CBS

Black Daniel
by Honoré Morrow
28 April 1939 CBS

Wickford Point
by John P. Marquand
5 May 1939 CBS

Our Town
by Thornton Wilder
12 May 1939 CBS

The Bad Man
by Porter Emerson Browne
19 May 1939 CBS

American Cavalcade
by Orson Welles
26 May 1939 CBS

Victoria Regina
by Laurence Housman
2 June 1939 CBS

Peter Ibbetson
by George du Maurier
10 September 1939 CBS

Ah, Wilderness!
by Eugene O'Neill
17 September 1939 CBS

What Every Woman Knows
by J. M. Barrie
24 September 1939 CBS

The Count of Monte Cristo
by Alexandre Dumas
1 October 1939 CBS

Algiers
by John Howard Lawson and James Cain
8 October 1939 CBS

The Escape
by John Galsworthy
15 October 1939 CBS

Liliom
by Ferenc Molnár
22 October 1939 CBS

The Magnificent Ambersons
by Booth Tarkington
29 October 1939 CBS

The Hurricane
by Charles Nordhoff and James Norman Hall
5 November 1939 CBS

The Murder of Roger Ackroyd
by Agatha Christie
12 November 1939 CBS

The Garden of Allah
by Roger Hichens
19 November 1939 CBS

Dodsworth
by Sinclair Lewis
26 November 1939 CBS

Lost Horizon
by James Hilton
3 December 1939 CBS

Vanessa
by Hugh Walpole
10 December 1939 CBS

There's Always a Woman
by Gladys Lehman
17 December 1939 CBS

A Christmas Carol
by Charles Dickens
24 December 1939 CBS

Come and Get It
by Edna Ferber
31 December 1939 CBS

Vanity Fair
by W. M. Thackeray
7 January 1940 CBS

Theodora Goes Wild
by Mary McCarthy
14 January 1940 CBS

The Citadel
by A. J. Cronin
21 January 1940 CBS

It Happened One Night
by Samuel Hopkins Adams
28 January 1940 CBS

Broome Stages
by Clemence Dane
4 February 1940 CBS

Mr Deedes Goes to Town
by Clarence Budington Kelland
11 February 1940 CBS

Dinner at Eight
by Edna Ferber and George S. Kaufman
18 February 1940 CBS

Only Angels Have Wings
by Howard Hawks and Jules Furthman
25 February 1940 CBS

Rabble at Arms
by Kenneth Roberts
3 March 1940 CBS

Craig's Wife
by George Kelly
10 March 1940 CBS

Huckleberry Finn
by Mark Twain
17 March 1940 CBS

June Moon
by Ring Lardner and George S. Kaufman
24 March 1940 CBS

Jane Eyre
by Charlotte Brontë
31 March 1940 CBS

The Free Company

His Honor the Mayor
by O.W.
5 April 1941 CBS

THE FILMS

Hearts of Age
Produced by William Vance, co-directed by O.W.
1934 Woodstock
Summer Theatre Festival

Too Much Johnson
Sequences for insertion in stage play, never used.
Produced by O.W. and John Houseman
1938 Stony Creek
Summer Theatre, Connecticut

The Green Goddess
Introduction to stage play.
Produced by O.W.
1939 Orpheum Circuit

Citizen Kane
Written by O.W. and Herman J. Mankiewicz
Produced by O.W.
1941 RKO
(Radio Keith Orpheum)

REFERENCES

CHAPTER ONE
Kenosha

p.4: 'Welles's father was in trade.' Leaflet about Badger Brass Company.

p.5: 'The big city.' Chicago at the turn of the century: *Chicago's Left Bank* by Alston J. Smith; *Insight Guide*; various Chicago books.

pp.5–7: Information on Welles's family background largely culled from *Orson Welles: The Rise and Fall of an American Genius* by Charles Higham, whose work in this area is unrivalled.

p.7: 'Orson Welles', Christmas edition of French *Vogue*, December 1982.

p.7: 'They were both charmers.' *Orson Welles* by Barbara Leaming.

p.8: '. . . a microcosm of industrial America.' Charles Higham, op. cit.

p.9: '. . . she was a very handsome woman.' From *My Life* by Mary D. Bradford.

p.10: '. . . among the best-known pianists in Kenosha.' From *Music in Kenosha* by Mrs Brown, an unpublished study.

p.11: 'Over and over again . . .' Russell Maloney, 'This Ageless Soul': *The New Yorker* 8 October 1938.

p.12: 'It is the spirit of Loyalty . . .' Quoted in *The Todd School*, an unpublished thesis by John Hoke.

p.13: '. . . the desire to take medicine.' Quoted in *The Fabulous Orson Welles* by Peter Noble.

CHAPTER TWO
Chicago

p.17: 'Out in Chicago . . .' H. L. Mencken quoted in *Chicago's Left Bank* by Alston J. Smith.

p.17: 'Chicago the jazz-baby . . .' Smith, op. cit.

p.17: '. . . a paradise he'd lost.' Quoted in *Orson Welles* by Barbara Leaming.

p.18: 'A crazy thing happened . . .' Quoted in *Insight Guide to Chicago*.

p.19: '. . . with the blood and sweat . . .' Quoted in Smith, op. cit.

p.20: '. . . the creaking of leather . . .' Orson Welles in *Vogue*, December 1982.

p.21: 'I'd see my father . . .' ibid.

p.21: 'I was surprised . . .' ibid.

p.22: 'She was not the musical version . . .' ibid.

p.22: ' "Well," says Beatrice . . .' ibid.

p.22: 'There never was anything . . .' Quoted in Smith, op. cit.

p.23: Grand Detour background: from *John Deere & the Billion Dollar Plow Gamble* by David Shiaras.

p.25: 'Mark Twain . . .' Orson Welles in *Vogue*, December 1982.

p.26: 'Do you want to see the stars?' Quoted in Shiaras, op. cit.

p.26: '. . . a prison . . . a pestilential handicap'. Orson Welles quoted in *Hortense Hill Memorial Service*, a pamphlet.

p.26: 'There was a country store . . .' Quoted in *This is Orson Welles* by Peter Bogdanovich.

p.27: 'I was marinated . . .' Orson Welles in *Vogue*, December 1982.

p.28: 'I knew very well . . .' ibid.

p.28: 'How much like her . . .' ibid.

p.30: 'Mothers of heroes . . .' From *Absent Fathers, Lost Sons* by Guy Corneau.

p.30: '. . . a perceptive American director . . .' *Playboy*, March 1967.

p.31: 'It wasn't that I didn't love my mother . . .' Quoted in *Orson Welles* by Barbara Leaming.

p. 31: '. . . er, no, didn't touch Lear till later . . .' Quoted by Kenneth Tynan, *Playboy*, March 1967.

p.33: 'From my earliest years, I was the Lily Langtry . . .' Quoted by Barbara Leaming, op. cit.

p.34: 'The school did to him . . .' Quoted in *The Fabulous Orson Welles* by Peter Noble.

CHAPTER THREE: Todd

p.35: '. . . responsibility is the great educator . . .' Quoted in *The Todd School*, an unpublished thesis by John Hoke.

p.35: 'When, by accident of birth . . .' From *One Man's Time and Chance* by Roger Hill.

p.36: 'Boyhood is not a preparation for life.' Roger Hill, op. cit.

p.36: 'I wonder what new hobby . . .' ibid.

p.37: 'The adolescent's adolescent.' Hascy Tarbox in an interview with S.C.

p.37: 'Other students stuck their heads . . .' From a letter from John C. Dexter to S.C.

p.37: 'But Orson . . .' Quoted in *The Fabulous Orson Welles* by Peter Noble.

p.37: '. . . a semi-orphan with a surplus . . .' Orson Welles. Quoted in *Hortense Hill Memorial Service*, a pamphlet.

p.37: 'I'm the boy you could have had.' Quoted in *Orson Welles* by Barbara Leaming.

p.38: 'We all recognised almost immediately . . .' From a letter from John C. Dexter to S.C.

p.38: 'He was not one of us . . .' Hascy Tarbox in an interview with S.C.

p.38: 'When I first saw him . . .' Quoted by Peter Noble, op. cit.

p.38: 'He had a kind of youth that I never had . . .' Quoted by Barbara Leaming, op. cit.

p.38: 'Of everyone I've known . . .' Orson Welles. Quoted in *Hortense Hill Memorial Service*, a pamphlet.

p.39: 'It's that Christian marriage . . .' Quoted by Barbara Leaming, op. cit.

p.39: 'What's the formula?' Roger Hill, op. cit.

p.39: 'Orson could talk a good talk . . .' Joanne Tarbox in an interview with S.C.

p.39: 'He didn't look or feel like a twelve-year-old.' Hascy Tarbox in an interview with S.C.

p.39: 'I knew he was going to be a great man . . .' Quoted in *Crain's Chicago Business*, 21 October 1985.

p.39: 'It was either the best thing . . .' Hascy Tarbox in an interview with S.C.

p.40: 'I attacked the textbooks . . .' Quoted by Barbara Leaming, op. cit.

p.40: 'If he even so much as dangled . . .' From a letter from John C. Dexter to S.C.

p.40: 'He was a good kid . . .' Tony Roskie in an interview with S.C.

p.41: 'Orson really looked up to other children . . .' Quoted by Peter Noble, op. cit.

p.41: '. . . the second genius in Todd's class of 1931 . . .' Roger Hill, op. cit.

p.41: 'I became a man of importance . . .' From a letter from Paul Guggenheim to S.C.

p.41: 'Orson was distressed . . .' ibid.

p.42: 'Welles does not want to explain himself . . .' Interview in *Réalités* (Paris) no. 201, 1962.

p.42: 'Our philosophic discussion . . .' From a letter from Paul Guggenheim to S.C.

p.42: 'I always had a feeling . . .' ibid.

p.43: 'He told me that his dream . . .' ibid.

p.43: 'I have had this recurring dream since I was 12 . . .' Quoted in *This is Orson Welles* by Peter Bogdanovich.

p.43: 'Todd is the most complete laboratory . . .' Quoted by Roger Hill, op. cit.

p.44: 'The theatre was totally Orson's . . .' Hascy Tarbox in an interview with S.C.

p.44: 'Our activities are genuine . . .' Roger Hill, op. cit.

p.44: 'Soon a whole country was finding . . .' ibid.

p.44: 'The chubby 11-year old was just the size and shape . . .' ibid.

p.44: 'When he finished with me he kissed me . . .' From a letter from John C. Dexter to S.C.

p.44: 'Yes. They're Boys . . .' Roger Hill, op. cit.

p.45: 'Mystic, Ibsenic, Maeterlinckian . . .' *New York American*, 3 May 1921.

p.45: 'It was Simon Legree . . .' Hascy Tarbox in an interview with S.C.

p.46: 'I can remember a number of times . . .' From a letter from John C. Dexter to S.C.

p.46: 'The Theatre blends in a common art the talents . . .' Orson Welles in the Todd catalogue, 1931.

p.47: 'The whole piece was rather loosely put together . . .' Orson Welles in *Red and White*.

p.49: 'I rollicked around my whole childhood . . .' From the BBC TV interview with Huw Wheldon, 1960.

p.49: 'What places do you remember most vividly . . .' *Playboy*, March 1967.

p.50: 'All the great ones . . .' Quoted by Peter Bogdanovich, op. cit.

p.50: 'How you'd love it here . . .' Quoted in *Orson Welles: The Rise and Fall of an American Genius* by Charles Higham.

p.51: 'America's most exclusive hotel . . .' French *Vogue*, 1982.

p.51: '. . . wonderful Chicago-built toys . . .' Quoted in *John Deere & The Billion Dollar Plow Gamble* by David Shiaras.

p.51: 'You'd wake up in the morning . . .' Quoted by Peter Bogdanovich, op. cit.

p.51: '. . . never got to know Orson well . . .' Shiaras, op. cit.

p.52: 'We'd just returned from China . . .' French *Vogue*, 1982.

p.52: 'He didn't want to admit he was interested . . .' Quoted by Barbara Leaming, op. cit.

p.58: 'I felt that the ordinary audience . . .' Roger Hill, op. cit.

p.54: '. . . even though you did not get the first prize . . .' Letter from Maurice Bernstein in the Lilly Library Welles Collection.

p.58: 'I discovered the magic of money . . .' Quoted in an interview with David Lewin, London *Daily Mail.*

p.59: 'He hoped to be mistaken for one of those . . .' French *Vogue*, 1982.

p.59: 'They guess at what normal behaviour is . . .' From *Adult Children of Alcoholics* by Janet Woititz.

p.60: 'I was, in my childhood, determined to cure myself . . .' Orson Welles quoted in *Hortense Hill Memorial Service*, a pamphlet.

p.62: 'I'll try to write about that later . . .' French *Vogue*, 1982.

p.63: 'I didn't think I was doing the right thing . . .' Quoted by Barbara Leaming, op. cit.

p.63: 'Orson once tried to scare Grandma . . .' Quoted in Bate, 'Debunking the Orson Welles myth': *Kenosha Evening News* June 1941.

p.63: 'I was in no position to interfere . . .' French *Vogue*, 1982.

p.63: 'The ballroom on the top floor of the old woman's house . . .' ibid.

p.65: 'You see, the Italians believe . . .'

Quoted by Barbara Leaming, op. cit.

CHAPTER FOUR
Ireland/*Jew Süss*

p.72: 'I was never any good . . .' Hascy Tarbox in an interview with S.C.

p.73: 'The irresponsibility of said Richard I. Welles . . .' Quoted in *Orson Welles: The Rise and Fall of an American Genius* by Charles Higham.

p.74: 'He feared his ward . . .' Alva Johnston and Fred Smith, *Saturday Evening Post*, 27 January 1940.

p.84: '. . . was gracious and candid . . .' From a letter to Hortense Hill.

p.86: ' "Terrible, wasn't it?" ' Quoted in *The Fabulous Orson Welles* by Peter Noble.

p.87: 'I said I was a star already . . .' From *This is Orson Welles* by Peter Bogdanovich.

p.92: 'We wanted a first-hand knowledge of the new methods of presentation . . .' From tenth anniversary booklet of the Gate.

p.92: '. . . when the theatre once again makes its audience . . .' ibid.

p.92: 'The theatre has lost the individuality it once had . . .' ibid.

p.92: 'They gave me an education . . .' From RTE radio documentary *The Hilton and Micheál Show*.

p.93: '. . . behaving – their behaviour was Irish . . .' From Micheál Mac Liammóir's address to the Abbey Society.

p.93: 'The actor works with himself as surely as . . .' From *All For Hecuba* by Micheál Mac Liammóir.

p.93: 'There were moments . . .' From Micheál Mac Liammóir, op. cit.

p.93: 'It runs the gauntlet . . .' From a letter to Roger Hill.

p.94: 'He had indeed that unwavering energy . . .' From Micheál Mac Liammóir, op. cit.

p.94:'In all the striving years since my debut . . .' From RTE's *The Hilton and Micheál Show*.

p.95: '. . . in the bliss of ignorance . . .' ibid.

p.95: '. . . a full-blooded, soldierly figure . . .' Stage direction to *Jew Süss* by Ashley Dukes from the novel by Lion Feuchtwanger.

p.96: 'When Orson came padding onto the stage . . .' From Micheál Mac Liammóir, op. cit.

p.96: 'His extraordinarily mature acting . . .' Quoted by Peter Noble, op. cit.

p.96: 'Dubliners, besides being very keen critics . . .' From *The Hilton and Micheál Show*.

p.98: 'the friendship of two men with no sexual overtones . . .' From *Orson Welles* by Barbara Leaming.

p.98: '. . . or even in playing a part that called for a romantic side . . .' Quoted by Peter Noble, op. cit.

p.98: 'Micheál would have seen through it . . .' Orson Welles in an interview with Leslie Megahey for the BBC.

p.99: 'I am like Hilton; I believe anything anyone tells me . . .' ibid.

p.99: '. . . a touch of humanity . . .' *Irish Independent* 14 October 1931.

p.99: '. . . looked the uncouth, hard-drinking . . .' From *Joseph Holloway's Irish Theatre Vol. One, 1926–1931*.

p.99: 'It will be necessary to see . . .' *Irish Times* 14 October 1931.

p.99: '. . . the Duke is played by a young American . . .' *New York Times* November 1931.

p.100: 'People began to talk about Orson . . .' From Micheál Mac Liammóir, op. cit.

p.100: '. . . his favourite words were virile . . .' From Peter Noble, op. cit.

p.100: '. . . the new American boy Orson Welles playing what he calls . . .' From the unpublished diaries of Denis Johnston, Trinity College Dublin library.

p. 100: 'The extraordinary thing about Orson . . .' Quoted by Peter Noble, op. cit.

p. 101: '. . . a time of balls and parties . . .' From the unpublished diaries of Denis Johnston, Trinity College Dublin library.

p. 101: '. . . people had tea parties . . .' From *Dublin* by V. S. Pritchett.

p. 101: 'British or Irish Free State . . .' From the unpublished diaries of Joseph Holloway, National Library, Dublin.

p. 101: 'It is astonishing . . .' From V. S. Pritchett, op. cit.

p. 102: 'When the demon of showmanship . . .' From Micheál Mac Liammóir, op. cit.

p. 102: 'With theatre people he was at his best . . .' From Micheál Mac Liammóir, op. cit.

p. 102: 'The whole show gave one the idea . . .' From the unpublished diaries of Joseph Holloway.

p. 102: 'The settings, designed and decorated . . .' *Irish Independent* 28 December 1931.

p. 103: '. . . while on the subject of the Gate . . .' *Daily Express* 11 November 1931.

p. 104: '. . . he must not be given . . .' *Irish Independent* 4 November 1931.

p. 104: 'I didn't like Orson Welles . . .' From the unpublished diaries of Joseph Holloway.

p. 104: '. . . qualities of subtlety sufficient . . .' *New York Times* 22 November 1931.

p. 104: '. . . at the première, the young American actor . . .' *New York Times* 8 December 1931.

p. 105: 'He had put most of the contents of his make-up box . . .' Quoted by Peter Noble, op. cit.

p. 105: '. . . with a pantomime head . . .' From the unpublished diaries of Joseph Holloway.

p. 105: 'My greatest success was at the Abbey . . .' In an interview with Leslie Megahey for the BBC.

p. 105: 'At the Gate, I got less and less good parts . . .' ibid.

p. 106: '. . . several pounds of nose putty . . .' From Micheál Mac Liammóir, op. cit.

p. 106: 'His performance is good enough . . .' *Irish Times* 28 December 1931.

p. 106: 'Mr Orson Welles did much to satisfy . . .' *Irish Times* 13 January 1932.

p. 106: '. . . hints at Cézanne . . .' *Irish Independent* January 1932.

p. 106: '. . . can the Ghost have been more movingly . . .' *Irish Press* 3 February 1932.

p. 106: 'Orson Welles made the speech . . .' From *Joseph Holloway's Irish Theatre*.

p. 107: 'Of course it was said . . .' From Micheál Mac Liammóir, op. cit.

p. 108: 'In Dublin, when he started in the theatre . . .' From *The Cradle Will' Rock*, a screenplay by Orson Welles.

p. 109: '. . . in reaction against the conditions it found at its birth . . .' From *The Mantle of Harlequin* by Hilton Edwards.

p. 109: 'It was Berlin with its Russian influences . . .' From Micheál Mac Liammóir, op. cit.

p. 109: 'Anew McMaster is an unashamed exponent . . .' Quoted in *The Story of the Abbey Theatre* by Sean McCann.

p. 110: 'Anew McMaster convinces us that he knows more . . .' ibid.

p. 110: '. . . who drifted into Dublin a few months ago . . .' From the unpublished diaries of Joseph Holloway, National Library, Dublin.

p. 111: '. . . when Kernoff tried to see the stage behind . . .' From *Joseph Holloway's Irish Theatre*.

p. 111: '. . . who could be thirty though he was only sixteen . . .' Geraldine Fitzgerald in an interview with S.C.

CHAPTER FIVE:
Hiatus/*Everybody's Shakespeare*

p. 113: '. . . enthusiasm and perseverance . . .' From *Citizen Welles* by Frank Brady.

p. 113: 'I recall the way in which he received me . . .' From *The Fabulous Orson Welles* by Peter Noble.

p. 114: 'After being a celebrity at sixteen in Dublin . . .' Johnston and Smith in *Saturday Evening Post* January 1940.

p. 115: '. . . to get him out of my hair . . .' From *Time and Chance* by Roger Hill.

p. 117: 'Stick with this boy! . . .' Quoted by Roger Hill, op. cit.

p. 117: 'complete with its chauffeur-cook . . .' ibid.

p. 118: 'It's a swell show . . .' Quoted in a letter to Roger Hill.

p. 118: 'I do hope you won't continue . . .' Quoted in *Orson Welles* by Barbara Leaming.

p. 119: 'An idiot, with a loose, wet mouth . . .' Stage direction from the unpublished play *Marching Song* by Orson Welles and Roger Hill.

p. 122: '. . . haven't had fish like that in four years . . .' From the unpublished play *Bright Lucifer* by Orson Welles.

p. 126: '*Bright Lucifer* is a likely sounding piece . . .' Russell Maloney, 'This Ageless Soul': *The New Yorker* 8 October 1938.

p. 126: '. . . a great deal of Welles's work can be explained . . .' From *The Magic World of Orson Welles* by James Naremore.

p. 127: 'I needed a new project . . .' From Roger Hill, op. cit.

p. 127: 'Write a Shakespeare book . . .' ibid.

p. 130: 'If I said that Tangiers struck me as a dream city . . .' Paul Bowles quoted in *An Invisible Spectator* by Christopher Sawyer-Laucanno.

p. 130: 'A noble-looking old man . . .' From *Cities of Spain* by Edward Hutton.

p. 131: 'It was the year 1346 of the Mahometan calendar . . .' From *In the Lap of Atlas* by Richard Hughes.

p. 131: 'Much as Europeans visualise the Baghdad . . .' From *The Lords of Atlas* by Gavin Maxwell.

p. 132: 'In the 1920s T'hami became . . .' ibid.

p. 133: 'Vast banquets . . .' ibid.

p. 133: 'The curious droop of his mouth . . .' Quoted by Richard Hughes, op. cit.

p. 135: 'There are some tiny cottages with clean patios . . .' From *Letters from Spain* by Karel Capek.

p. 135: 'They are employed . . .' From Edward Hutton, op. cit.

p. 136: '. . . expressly based on what Orson imagined . . .' From Barbara Leaming, op. cit.

p. 136: '. . . wearing white pants and waving a red cape . . .' From *Hemingway* by Carlos Baker.

p. 137: 'Still, even with all that untold Yankee wealth . . .' From *This is Orson Welles* by Peter Bogdanovich.

p. 137: 'All that hot summer . . .' From Roger Hill, op. cit.

p. 139: 'A mixture of poet, prophet . . .' Quoted in *The Enthusiast* by Gilbert A. Harrison.

p. 139: 'By some curious jump of association . . .' Quoted by Peter Noble, op. cit.

p. 139: 'The reviews were so astounding . . .' Quoted in *Smart Aleck* by Teichmann.

p. 140: 'You have given me a whole ring of keys to this city . . .' Quoted by Gilbert A. Harrison, op. cit.

p. 140: 'I remember shortly after Orson . . .' Quoted by Teichmann, op. cit.

CHAPTER SIX:
Wonder Boy of Acting/*Romeo and Juliet*

p. 143: 'It is an old story that the balcony and the gallery . . .' Quoted in *Me and Kit* by Guthrie McClintic.
p. 144: 'It was obvious to me . . .' Quoted in *The Fabulous Orson Welles* by Peter Noble.
p. 144: 'We were all struck by . . .' ibid.
p. 145: 'He began by having his cast sit round a table . . .' From *The American Theatre* by Mary Henderson.
p. 145: 'Talkative, nervous, very witty . . .' From *The Player* by Lilian Ross and Helen Ross.
p. 145: 'Orson at that time always played to the top row . . .' Quoted in *The Theatre of Orson Welles* by Richard France.
p. 146: 'She has agreed to the selection . . .' *New York Times* October 1933.
p. 147: 'In the 1930's Broadway . . .' Quoted in *The Magic of Light* by Jean Rosenthal.
p. 147: 'All the rest was just dead wire . . .' From *The American Theatre* by Ethan Mordden.
p. 147: '[Miss Cornell] was so beautiful . . .' From *In and Out of Character* by Basil Rathbone.
p. 148: 'His Marchbanks to my way of thinking . . .' Quoted by Peter Noble, op. cit.
p. 148: 'He could play *Jew Süss* . . .' From *Time and Chance* by Roger Hill.
p. 148: 'He was flamboyant, exciting, hammy . . .' Quoted by Richard France, op. cit.
p. 148: 'He appealed to the general run . . .' ibid.
p. 148: 'That he got by was by no means enough.' From Guthrie McClintic, op. cit.
p. 148: 'By the crescendo of her playing . . .' *New York Times* 10 February 1931.
p. 148: 'He was just adequate . . .' Quoted by Richard France, op. cit.
p. 148: 'I personally believe . . .' ibid.
p. 149: '. . . his performance begins to confirm the suspicion . . .' *New York American* 26 February 1935.
p. 149: '. . . his entrance was so strange . . .' Tom Triffely in an interview with S.C.
p. 149: '. . . it is admirable Shakespeare . . .' *Chicago Tribune* December 1933.
p. 150: '. . . which seemed to meet with McClintic's . . .' From Basil Rathbone, op. cit.
p. 150: 'Orson Welles, who has scored a hit . . .' *Chicago Tribune* December 1933.
p. 151: '. . . well-disciplined, strictly ordered family . . .' Gertrude Macy quoted by Richard France, op. cit.
p. 151: 'He was at all times . . .' Quoted by Peter Noble, op. cit.
p. 152: 'About twice a year I wake up and find myself . . .' Quoted by Richard France, op. cit.
p. 153: 'I found myself wondering . . .' Quoted by Peter Noble, op. cit.
p. 153: 'He was gauche and tiresome . . .' Quoted by Richard France, op. cit.
p. 154: '. . . on "Big Time" so to speak . . .' From Guthrie McClintic, op. cit.

CHAPTER SEVEN:
Woodstock/*Romeo and Juliet* Again

p. 158: 'Hail to thee, blithe spirit! . . .' From *All For Hecuba* by Micheál Mac Liammóir.
p. 160: 'My God, Roger, do you realise what you're up against . . .' From Roger Hill, op. cit.
p. 161: 'The party had cost a fortune . . .' ibid.
p. 161: 'Orson Welles says that the festival . . .' *Chicago Herald and Examiner* 28 June 1934.
p. 162: 'Anyone who had 500 big de-

pression-time dollars . . .' ibid.

p. 162: 'The work of Mac Liammóir and Edwards . . .' *Chicago Tribune* 1 July 1934.

p. 162: 'Orson began to swell again . . .' From Micheál Mac Liammóir, op. cit.

p. 163: 'Michael Mac Liammóir talked the least . . .' *Chicago Tribune* 1 July 1934.

p. 163: 'A great grandson of Gideon Welles . . .' Margot Jr, *Chicago Daily News* 13 July 1934.

p. 164: 'Young Mr Welles . . .' *Chicago Herald and Examiner* July 1934.

p. 165: 'It was a real vendetta . . .' Quoted in *Orson Welles* by Barbara Leaming.

p. 165: 'They were really, I think, rather mean to Orson . . .' ibid.

p. 165: 'To us it looked like . . .' From Micheál Mac Liammóir, op. cit.

p. 166: 'It represents, chiefly . . .' *Chicago Tribune* July 1934.

p. 166: 'It is a gala occasion . . .' *Chicago Tribune* 13 July 1934.

p. 166: '. . . the natives sat . . .' *Chicago Daily News* 13 July 1934.

p. 167: 'A man of impeccable social standing . . .' From Roger Hill, op. cit.

p. 167: 'I could only quail and shiver . . .' *Chicago Daily News* 13 July 1934.

p. 167: '. . . he played the villain last night . . .' *Chicago Herald and Examiner* 13 July 1934.

p. 167: 'Wunderschon! . . .' and ff. from *Trilby* by Paul Potter after George du Maurier.

p. 168: 'Even his fakes . . .' From Micheál Mac Liammóir, op.cit.

p. 168: '. . . due obviously to the youth's . . .' Lloyd Lewis: *Chicago Daily News* 22 July 1934.

p. 168: '. . . the production was disappointingly vague . . .' From Micheál Mac Liammóir, op. cit.

p. 168: '. . . said to be one of the few . . .' *Chicago Tribune* 22 July 1934.

p. 169: 'I fancied at times to have penetrated . . .' ibid.

p. 169: 'A Hamlet of metropolitan stature . . .' and ff. *Chicago Tribune* 27 July 1934.

p. 171: 'Orson Welles departed from the orthodox king . . .' *Chicago Herald and Examiner* 27 July 1934.

p. 172: 'An unhorrific old ghost . . .' *Chicago Daily News* 27 July 1934.

p. 172: 'Hilton Edwards, Orson Welles and Micheál Mac Liammóir . . .' Lloyd Lewis, *Chicago Daily News* 11 August 1934.

p. 173: 'His Count Pahlen kept all the essentials of the part . . .' From Micheál Mac Liammóir, op. cit.

p. 173: 'His variety and range are amazing . . .' *Chicago Tribune Magazine* article.

p. 174: 'Oh, it was wild because . . .' Quoted by Barbara Leaming, op. cit.

p. 175: '. . . vigorous, non-homosexual types . . .' ibid.

p. 175: 'Our Woodstock season ended for us all . . .' From Micheál Mac Liammóir, op. cit.

p. 177: 'Plug at that book . . .' Quoted by Roger Hill, op. cit.

p. 177: '. . . to make the Elizabethan popular in the classroom . . .' ibid.

p. 177: 'I found that actors were plainly frightened . . .' From an article in *Theatre Quarterly*.

p. 185: 'Orson's extreme and obvious youth . . .' Quoted in *The Fabulous Orson Welles* by Peter Noble.

p. 186: 'I told him of my newly-conceived decor . . .' From *Me and Kit* by Guthrie McClintic.

p. 186: '. . . with their high colour and total lack of sophistication . . .' From *The Theatre of Joe Mielziner*.

p. 186: '. . . ending with a marvellous dark . . .' From Guthrie McClintic, op. cit.

p. 187: '. . . how fine the play was

when left intact . . .' ibid.

p. 187: '. . . all during the rehearsals of *Romeo* . . .' ibid.

p. 187: 'The actors must be made to forget . . .' and ff. ibid.

p. 188: 'Orson seemed friendly and good-natured . . .' From *A Proper Job* by Brian Aherne.

p. 188: 'Audience warm in its commendation . . .' *New York Times* 4 December 1934.

p. 188: 'It was a performance at once . . .' Grenville Vernon, *Commonweal* 21 December 1934.

p. 188: 'Guthrie McClintic has somehow managed to persuade all the members of the cast . . .' Richard Lockridge, *New York Sun* 21 December 1934.

p. 189: 'Miss Cornell has kept faith with her audiences by giving . . .' Brooks Atkinson, *New York Times* 21 December 1934.

p. 189: '. . . the smooth, veinless look of a young girl's . . .' From *Leading Lady* by Tad Mosel.

p. 189: '. . . instances of minor parts played with . . .' *New York Times* 21 December 1934.

p. 189: '. . a performance to watch and applaud . . .' John Anderson, *New York American* 21 December 1934.

p. 189: 'Before our beautiful green sage curtains . . .' Guthrie McClintic, op. cit.

CHAPTER EIGHT: Houseman/*Panic*

p. 193: '. . . that glossy and successful evening . . .' and ff. From *Run-Through* by John Houseman.

p. 196: 'Let's not talk about Houseman . . .' From *This is Orson Welles* by Peter Bogdanovich.

p. 196: '. . . meeting Welles was the most important event of my life . . .' Houseman in an interview with S.C.

p. 196: 'Orson Welles's initial impact . . .' and ff. From John Houseman, op. cit.

p. 198: 'At first he fell in love with me . . .' Quoted in *Orson Welles* by Barbara Leaming.

p. 200: '. . . slim and graceful of movement . . .' From *The New Theatre*, ed. Herbert W. Kline.

p. 200: 'Hearing that voice . . .' and ff. From John Houseman, op. cit.

p. 200: '. . . the voice of the hopeless individual . . .' From *The Oxford Companion to American Literature* by James D. Hart.

p. 200: '. . . it had become necessary to me . . .' From John Houseman, op. cit.

p. 201: '. . . to his own part . . . he brought us . . .' ibid.

p. 201: '. . . for such a young actor as Welles to play . . .' Gabriel, *New York American* 16 March 1935.

p. 201: 'The Revolution!' From *Panic* by Archibald MacLeish.

p. 202: '. . . the work of our protean poet . . .' Brooks Atkinson, *New York Times* 16 March 1935.

p. 202: 'A pretentious bore . . .' John Anderson, *New York Evening Journal* 16 March 1935.

p. 202: 'The words of the play . . .' *Theatre Arts Monthly* April 1935.

p. 203: '. . . swept by one of those groundswells . . .' and ff. From John Houseman, op. cit.

p. 204: 'I saw this very strange guy dressed . . .' and ff. Dwight Weist in an interview with NYU.

p. 205: '. . . a select group of anonymous radio artists . . .' Alva Johnston and Fred Smith, *Saturday Evening Post* 27 January 1940.

p. 206: '. . . a curious one-room residence . . .' and ff. From John Houseman, op. cit.

p. 208: 'He would, by voice and presence . . .' Peg Lloyd in an interview with S.C.

p. 208: '. . . of whose talent he was so fanatically convinced . . .' From

John Houseman, op. cit.
p.208: 'We parted friends . . .' and ff. ibid.
p.210: 'He admires radio as a medium . . .' From an interview with John Hutchens, *New York Times* 26 November 1937.
p.210: 'We saw Reinhardt's productions . . .' From *The Fervent Years* by Harold Clurman.
p.212: '. . . there was excitement because . . .' From *The American Theatre* by Ethan Mordden.
p.212: '. . . attached to anything critical of war . . .' From Introduction by John Gassner to *Drama Was a Weapon*.
p.213: '. . . the overriding dramatic topic of the decade . . .' From *The Political stage* by Malcolm Goldstein.
p.213: 'We expected to bring the actor . . .' From Harold Clurman, op. cit.
p.214: 'I say that Group productions lack music . . .' From *Slings and Arrows* by Robert Lewis.
p.214: '. . . the painstaking love of detail . . .' From *Upstage: Types of American Direction* by John Mason Brown.

CHAPTER NINE: FTP/*Macbeth*

p.216: '. . . the arts projects were being set up . . .' and ff. From *Arena* by Hallie Flanagan.
p.217: '. . . the theatre must become conscious . . .' and ff. ibid.
p.218: 'Mother Goose is no longer a rhymed escapist . . .' Brooks Atkinson, *New York Times* 21 May 1937.
p.218: 'Imagine an organisation producing in a season . . .' Quoted in *Free, Adult and Uncensored* by O'Connor and Brown.
p.219: '. . . a white man was needed . . .' From *Run-Through* by John Houseman.
p.219: 'like a colonial governor . . .' Quoted by John Houseman, op.cit.
p.219: '. . . bitter, but brilliantly clear . . .' ibid.
p.221: '. . . a dozen and one vivid . . .' *American Mercury* 21 February 1929.
p.221: 'My set has discovered something . . .' Quoted in *When Harlem was in Vogue* by David Levening Lewis.
p.223: 'Mr Welles has the idea that an Elizabethan play . . .' Reproduced in *Sights and Spectacles* by Mary McCarthy.
p.223: 'I rehearsed them on a count of one . . .' From an interview at the Federal Theatre Research Project.
p.223: '. . . a round-faced prodigy . . .' Brooks Atkinson, *Broadway* 1970.
p.224: 'Orson, don't do that . . .' and 'So get back to work!' Quoted by O'Connor and Brown, op. cit.
p.224: 'I don't know what this guy's up to . . .' From an interview at the Federal Theatre Research Project.
p.225: 'I always seduce actors . . .' Quoted in *Orson Welles* by Barbara Leaming.
p.225: 'Jack's turn before . . .' Notes on the production preserved at the Federal Theatre Research Project.
p.226: 'For several days running . . .' Alva Johnston and Fred Smith, *Saturday Evening Post* 27 January 1940.
p.228: 'Our most original and imaginative mind . . .' From Hallie Flanagan, op. cit.
p.229: 'What would the negro interpretation . . .' and ff. Federal Theatre Research Project.
p.231: '*Steps in Lighting* . . .' and ff. From *Putting on the Play* ed. John Gassner.
p.232: 'Orson Welles? It was just like . . .' and ff. Abe Feder in an interview with S.C.
p.232: 'My other close director friend . . .' and ff. From *Virgil Thomson* by Virgil Thomson.

p.233: '*Macbeth* was staged by a romantic tragedy . . .' and ff. Interview with NYU for their Welles project.

p.233: 'Orson Welles knew nothing about musical ideas . . .' ibid.

p.233: '. . . instead of telling you in musical terms . . .' ibid.

p.234: 'When you do that play . . .' From *This is Orson Welles* by Peter Bogdanovich.

p.234: 'Why had they mustered the audacity . . .' and ff. *New York Times* 5 April 1936.

p.236: 'Flash of ten thousand people . . .' From Hallie Flanagan, op. cit.

p.236: 'Negroes have taken Shakespeare to themselves . . .' Quoted by Hallie Flanagan, op. cit.

p.236: 'African drums beat . . .' From Hallie Flanagan, op. cit.

p.237: 'The floor became a moving forest . . .' From John Houseman, op. cit.

p.237: 'At the conclusion of the performance . . .' *New York Times* 15 April 1936.

p.237: 'They have always worried the life out of . . .' ibid.

p.238: 'This is not the speech of negroes . . .' *Sunday News* 26 April 1936.

p.238: 'Extremely vivid, though a bit bizarre . . .' *New York Sun* 15 April 1936.

p.238: 'The production is only as interesting . . .' *New York Herald Tribune* 16 April 1936.

p.239: 'In *Macbeth*, the negro has been given . . .' *Amsterdam News* 18 April 1936.

p.239: 'Hallie Flanagan and Phillip Barber . . .' *New York Age* 20 April 1936.

p.239: 'It turns out to be a colorful and rousing . . .' *New York Times* 18 April 1936.

p.240: 'A FURTHER CONSIDERATION . . .' *New York Post* 18 April 1936.

p.241: 'No event in the art galleries . . .' Edward Alden Jewell, *New York Times* 24 April 1936.

p.241: '. . . a tragedy of black ambition . . .' From Hallie Flanagan, op. cit.

p.241: 'Cocteau did not understand . . .' From Virgil Thomson, op. cit.

p.241: 'When Macbeth and Lady Macbeth . . .' From *My Life, My Stage* by Ernst Stern.

p.242: 'The Harlem *Macbeth* . . .' From *Sights and Spectacles* by Mary McCarthy.

p.242: 'I like *Macbeth* and I like negroes . . .' From *My Journey Round the World* by Jean Cocteau.

p.242: 'It is significant that our white culture . . .' From Mary McCarthy, op. cit.

p.243: 'Welles has all the gall . . .' Phillip Barber in an interview with the Federal Theatre Research Project.

p.244: 'It was here that my first male relationship was formed . . .' From John Houseman, op. cit.

p.244: 'I was really the King of Harlem! . . .' From Barbara Leaming, op. cit.

p.245: 'You have to take into account . . .' Quoted in *The Theatre of Orson Welles* by Richard France.

CHAPTER TEN:
Horse Eats Hat/Doctor Faustus

p.246: 'I must leave the project . . .' and ff. From *Run-Through* by John Houseman.

p.247: '. . . the Federal theatre . . .' From *Arena* by Hallie Flanagan.

p.250: 'For eight years I have cherished . . .' Quoted in *Lost Theatres of Broadway* by Nicholas van Hoogstraten.

p.250: 'Ageing character actors . . .' From John Houseman, op. cit.

p.251: 'Working with him in his youth

. . .' From *Virgil Thomson* by Virgil Thomson.

p.253: 'He fed them every line . . .' Quoted in *Free, Adult and Uncensored* by O'Connor and Brown.

p.253: 'Everyone had their own aria . . .' Paula Laurence, interviewed at NYU.

p.254: 'Hiram said he wouldn't do it . . .' From O'Connor and Brown, op.cit.

p.255: '. . . most talented . . .' Quoted in *Copland 1900-1942* by Aaron Copland and Vivian Perlis.

p.255: 'Within ten minutes of our meeting . . .' From *Without Stopping* by Paul Bowles.

p.255: '. . . in that way . . .' From Virgil Thomson, op. cit.

p.256: 'If *Macbeth* had in Orson's hands . . .' ibid.

p.256: 'The last scene . . .' From *Voices Offstage* by Marc Connelly.

p.258: '. . . imaginative, vigorous . . .' Quoted in *Conversations with Losey* by Michel Ciment.

p.258: '. . . dozens of young men and women . . .' *New York American* 28 September 1936.

p.258: 'It looked as though somebody from . . .' John Mason Brown, *New York Post* 28 September 1936.

p.258: '. . . this sort of calculated nonsense . . .' *Brooklyn Eagle* 28 September 1936.

p.258: '. . . that dismal embarrassment . . .' Richard Watts, *New York Herald Tribune* 28 September 1936.

p.258: 'It is as though Gertrude Stein . . .' and ff. *New York Times* 28 September 1936.

p.260: 'I'm afraid you'll never make it as an actor . . .' Quoted in *Vanity Will Get You Somewhere* by Joseph Cotten.

p.261: 'A prototypical American businessman . . .' Quoted in *The Theatre of Orson Welles* by Richard France.

p.261: 'His versatility and enthusiasm . . .' Richard Watts, *New York Herald Tribune* 28 September 1936.

p.261: 'It is a government-subsidised . . .' John Chapman: HORSE EATS HAT IS MAD, BUT NOT MAD ENOUGH: *New York Daily News* 28 September 1936.

p.261: 'Mr Welles, the triple threat of the evening . . .' Lewis Nichols, *New York Times* 28 September 1936.

p.261: 'Mr Welles (wonder-product) . . .' B.I. n.d.

p.261: 'Mr Welles, an unusually gifted young man . . .' John Mason Brown, *New York Post* 28 September 1936.

p.262: 'Welles, as an actor, for all his fine bass voice . . .' From Virgil Thomson, op. cit.

p.263: 'What I do have in common with Jack . . .' From *This is Orson Welles* by Peter Bogdanovich.

p.263: '. . . the moment rehearsals were over . . .' Charles Bowden in an interview with NYU.

p.263: '. . . a flashing screen of headlines . . .' From *The Encyclopaedia of the New York Stage 1930-1940* by Sam Leiter.

p.264: '*Ten Million Ghosts* is not the sort of play . . .' *New York Times* 25 October 1936.

p.264: 'Nor can I say . . .' *New York Herald Tribune* 25 October 1936.

p.264: 'That is one of the biggest pieces of schweinerei . . .' From Peter Bogdanovich, op. cit.

p.266: '. . . since the mention of any . . .' and ff. From John Houseman, op. cit.

p.269: '. . . the performance was run continuously . . .' From *Putting on the Play* ed. John Gassner.

p.269: 'He had miles . . .' Quoted by O'Connor and Brown, op. cit.

p.270: 'The stage manager of that show . . .' ibid.

p.270: '. . . can often float you into the

scenes' Elysium . . .' *New Republic* 10 January 1937.

p.270: 'Going into the Maxine Elliott . . .' From Hallie Flanagan, op. cit.

p.270: 'Go across the street . . .' Quoted by O'Connor and Brown, op. cit.

p.271: 'She liked a drink . . .' Paula Laurence in an interview with NYU.

p.271: 'Orson designed everything . . .' ibid.

p.271: 'Here was one of the goddam biggest . . .' Quoted by O'Connor and Brown, op. cit.

p.272: 'The apron causes . . .' Quoted by Richard France, op. cit.

p.273: '. . . because we couldn't see any more . . .' and ff. From John Houseman, op. cit.

p.275: '. . . nothing but a curio . . .' *New York Daily News* 9 January 1937.

p.275: '. . . including that of Mr Welles . . .' *Theatre Arts Monthly* February 1937.

p.275: 'The prologue is spoken . . .' Wyatt, *Catholic World* February 1937.

p.275: '. . . boldly thrust an apron stage . . .' and ff. *New York Times* 9 January 1937.

p.275: '. . . whose name . . .' *New Republic* 10 January 1937.

p.277: 'There were so many dark sides . . .' Paula Laurence in an interview with NYU.

p.277: 'Their presence on stage together . . .' From John Houseman, op. cit.

p.277: '. . . pride and despair . . .' From Roma Gill's introduction to her edition of *Doctor Faustus*.

p.278: 'The old Marlowe opus . . .' Robert Benchley, *New Yorker* 12 January 1937.

p.278: 'I suppose they wanted Lenin's blood . . .' Quoted in *Hallie Flanagan* by Joanne Flanagan Bentley.

p.282: '*Doctor Faustus* is the definitive . . .' Paula Laurence in an interview with NYU.

p.282: '*Doctor Faustus* was truly successful . . .' From *Sights and Spectacles* by Mary McCarthy.

p.282: '. . . the audience was fresh . . .' Quoted by O'Connor and Brown, op. cit.

p.282: '*Faustus* played to just people, you know . . .' Paula Laurence in an interview with NYU.

p.282: 'We should have had a national theatre . . .' Quoted by O'Connor and Brown, op. cit.

p.284: 'Orson was very well aware . . .' Norman Lloyd in an interview with S.C.

p.285: 'I see myself in those old stills . . .' From *Orson Welles* by Barbara Leaming.

p.287: 'When I played *The Cradle Will Rock* . . .' Quoted by O'Connor and Brown, op cit.

CHAPTER ELEVEN: *The Cradle Will Rock*

p.289: '. . . that most resistant of all . . .' Quoted in *Mark the Music* by Eric A. Gordon.

p.289: 'He was nervous . . .' From *This Bright day* by Lehman Engel.

p.289: '. . . he was the first American composer . . .' Quoted by Eric A. Gordon, op. cit.

p.290: 'Orson was excited by this . . .' and ff. From *Run-Through* by John Houseman.

p.290: 'Marc Blitzstein sat down . . .' From *Arena* by Hallie Flanagan.

p.290: 'Hallie Flanagan . . . is crazy for it . . .' Quoted by Eric A. Gordon, op. cit.

p.291: '. . . to Bert Brecht . . .' From the published text of *The Cradle Will Rock*.

p.293: 'Even during those early years . . .' From Lehman Engel, op. cit.

p.293: 'Orson was in a regular fever heat . . .' Interview from Federal Theatre Research Project.

p.294: '. . . as actors, it diminished . . .' ibid.

p.294: 'Federal Theatre Workers were striking . . .' From Hallie Flanagan, op. cit.

p.295: 'Before this date, the WPA chiefs . . .' Alva Johnston and Fred Smith, *Saturday Evening Post* 27 January 1940.

p.296: 'The theatre was sealed . . .' Interview from Federal Theatre Research Project.

p.297: 'Like partners in a vaudeville team . . .' From John Houseman, op. cit.

p.297: '. . . made a too-long speech . . .' From Lehman Engel, op. cit.

p.298: 'STEEL STRIKE OPERA . . .' *New York Times* 17 June 1937.

p.299: 'I cannot get out . . .' Quoted in *Backstage at 'The Cradle Will Rock'* by Barry B. Witham.

p.300: 'Important as the issue raised . . .' Quoted by Eric A. Gordon, op. cit.

p.300: '. . . if you go ahead . . .' Quoted in Witham, op. cit.

p.300: 'There is good contemptuous laughter . . .' *Time* 28 June 1937.

p.301: 'The formerly audacious left-wingers . . .' *Saturday Evening Post* 3 February 1940.

p.302: 'Denby and I . . .' From Aaron Copland and Vivian Perlis, op. cit.

p.303: 'The fact that the orchestra sat in every-day dress . . .' *New York Times* 22 April 1937.

p.303: '. . . there is here the suggestion . . .' *World Telegram* 22 April 1937.

p.303: 'Gradually the real reasons began to come out . . .' From Hallie Flanagan, op. cit.

p.303: '. . . we had little to say . . .' From John Houseman, op. cit.

CHAPTER TWELVE: Mercury

p.309: 'AGAIN – A PEOPLE'S THEATRE . . .' *Daily Worker* 18 September 1937.

p.310: 'It is the duty of all . . .' Grenville Vernon, *Commonweal* 27 August 1937.

p.310: '. . . has already given . . .' *New York Times* 1 September 1937.

p.311: '. . . inveigled some wonderful night watchman . . .' From *Run-Through* by John Houseman.

p.313: 'Emphasis has been placed . . .' Quoted in 'Welles Peers Through his Beard and sees Chaos', Wilella Waldorf, *New York Times* 1 July 1938.

p.316: '. . . everything in the theatre depends on a great personality . . .' From Notes in the Lilly Library Welles Collection.

p.320: '. . . the role he'd been given . . .' From *This is Orson Welles* by Peter Bogdanovich.

CHAPTER THIRTEEN: *Caesar*

p.323: 'As those familiar with the play . . .' *The Mercury* September 1937.

p.324: 'Here we have true fan psychology . . .' An interview with Michael Mok, *New York Times* 24 November 1937.

p.324: 'In drastically cutting the last twenty minutes of the play . . .' and ff. *The Mercury* September 1937.

p.325: 'Welles dictated very clearly . . .' From *The Magic of Light* by Jean Rosenthal.

p.325: 'At the Mercury nobody else had any identity for him at all . . .' and ff. ibid.

p.326: 'When he felt like rehearsing . . .' and ff. From an interview with Federal Theatre Research Project.

p.327: 'He seemed a prep school boy

. . .' Peg Lloyd in an interview with S.C.

p.327: 'Every scene had to have a production idea . . .' Norman Lloyd in an interview with S.C.

p.327: 'Be a singer, be a singer!' Quoted in an interview by Elliot Reid with S.C.

p.328: 'I thought you could say . . .' Norman Lloyd in an interview with S.C.

p.329: '. . . that they're thinking about what they're saying . . .' From *This is Orson Welles* by Peter Bogdanovich.

p.330: 'His own performances happened suddenly . . .' From *This Bright Day* by Lehman Engel.

p.330: 'The idea, the actor and a pool of light . . .' From Jean Rosenthal, op. cit.

p.331: 'Jeannie considered the most important lighting . . .' ibid.

p.331: 'Every elaborate effect had to be created by hand . . .' From *The Mercury Theatre* by Andrea Nouryeh.

p.331: 'One effect, spoken of as stunning and innovative . . .' From Jean Rosenthal, op. cit.

p.333: 'The way they came up the ramp . . .' Norman Lloyd in an interview with S.C.

p.334: 'In those days we never took him very seriously . . .' ibid.

p.334: '. . . in anguish, fear and righteous indignation . . .' An interview with Federal Theatre Research Project.

p.334: 'He was the most insecure . . .' Augusta Weissberger in an interview with S.C.

p.335: 'Orson would argue with you as he ate . . .' Norman Lloyd in an interview with S.C.

p.335: 'Its great success . . .' ibid.

p.336: 'When he started acting out . . .' ibid.

p.337: 'Of all the many new plays and productions . . .' and ff. *New York Post* 12 November 1937.

p.338: '. . . modern variations on the theme . . .' and ff. *New York Times* 11 November 1937.

p.338: '. . . a wavering liberal . . .' Eric Englander, *Daily Worker* 12 November 1937.

p.338: 'It is as if a great poet had risen in our midst . . .' *New York Journal American* 12 November 1937.

p.339: 'It is when the play . . .' *New York Sun* 12 November 1937.

p.339: 'With most of Antony excised . . .' *Theatre Arts Monthly* January 1938.

p.339: '. . . on the whole pretty much disappointed . . .' *New Republic* 1 December 1937.

p.339: 'The production of *Caesar* . . .' From *Sights and Spectacles* by Mary McCarthy.

p.340: '. . . playing *Julius Caesar* in modern dress . . .' *Newsweek* 22 November 1937.

p.340: '. . . the hysterical critical endorsement . . .' *Scribner's Magazine* February 1938.

p.340: '*Julius Caesar* opened with tremendous éclat . . .' From Jean Rosenthal, op. cit.

p.341: 'After a succession of muffled death-rattles . . .' From 'Marvelous Boy: Shadow to Shakespeare, Shoemaker to Shaw,' *Time Magazine* 9 May 1938.

p.341: 'If they are still complaining around the Lamb's club . . .' *New York Times* 26 November 1937.

p.341: 'Mr Welles looks the way musicians used to look . . .' Michael Mok, *New York Post* 24 November 1937.

p.342: 'Welles was so masterful . . .' Quoted in *Citizen Welles* by Frank Brady.

p.342: 'I believe in the factual theatre . . .' *New York Post,* 24 November 1937.

p.342: 'Strange things are happening

. . .' *New Yorker* 18 December 1937.

p.343: 'He also admires films . . .' *New York Times* 28 September 1937.

CHAPTER FOURTEEN:
Shoemaker's Holiday/Heartbreak House

p.344: 'George Zorn (the box office manager) grew resigned . . .' From *Run-Through* by John Houseman.

p.345: 'It is the best thing militant labor . . .' *New York Times* 6 December 1937.

p.345: 'A savagely humorous social cartoon . . .' *New York Herald Tribune*, 6 December 1937.

p.345: 'I only wish that the present production . . .' Alistair Cooke on NBC Red Network.

p.346: 'His acrid personality is, in fact . . .' From *Sights and Spectacles* by Mary McCarthy.

p.346: 'It's lucky I'm playing tragedy tonight . . .' Quoted in *Virgil Thomson* by Virgil Thomson.

p.346: 'Why do you have everybody dress up like chauffeurs?' Quoted in *This is Orson Welles* by Peter Bogdanovich.

p.347: 'I say this in all seriousness . . .' Reported in *New York World Telegram* 5 February 1938.

p.348: 'We were all very serious actors . . .' Vincent Price in an interview with S.C.

p.349: 'How do you like that for a title?' and ff. From Helen Ormsbee, 'The Welles Theater Philosophy: Everything Old Once Was New.' *New York Herald Tribune* 2 February 1938.

p.349: 'The play is laden with sentiments . . .' *New Masses* 18 January 1938.

p.351: 'All the groupings and firkings . . .' Quoted in *The Theatre of Orson Welles* by Richard France.

p.351: 'He rehearsed with military discipline . . .' From *This Bright Day* by Lehman Engel.

p.351: 'One day accidentally Hiram ran into the curtain . . .' Arthur Anderson in an interview with S.C.

p.351: '. . . he moulded you . . .' From Lehman Engel, op. cit.

p.351: 'Welles the choreographer . . .' Quoted by Richard France, op. cit.

p.352: 'We thought she would die as she watched him . . .' Norman Lloyd in an interview with S.C.

p.352: 'He was the best director I ever had . . .' Vincent Price in an interview with S.C.

p.352: 'The way our script was arranged . . .' Quoted by Richard France, op. cit.

p.352: 'Our settings are simple – what I call factual . . .' Quoted by Helen Ormsbee, op. cit.

p.353: 'he had the most revolting triangle of shoe leather . . .' Quoted in *The Mercury Theatre*, unpublished thesis by Andrea Nouryeh.

p.353: 'An entire score . . .' and ff. From Lehman Engel, op. cit.

p.353: 'Getting wind of the event through the Broadway telegraph . . .' Herbert Drake, *New York Herald Tribune* 2 January 1938.

p.354: 'The audience felt intimately connected with the actors . . .' *New York World Telegram* 11 January 1938.

p.355: 'To *Julius Caesar*, a terrifying tragedy . . .' *New York Times* 3 January 1938.

p.355: '. . . a masterpiece of low comedy acting . . .' John Anderson, *New York Journal-American* 1 January 1938.

p.355: '. . . a series of glittering fragments . . .' John Gassner, *One-Act Play Magazine* January 1938.

p.355: 'Bully boy Dekker is quite familiar to me . . .' 'Shuffling Through the Winners: in which a Visiting Critic tells what he likes and what he does not like, about the Times Square Shows' *New York*

Times 23 January 1938.

p.355: '. . . still the great comfort . . .' Richard Watts, 'Elizabethan Romp' *New York Herald Tribune* 3 January 1938.

p.356: '. . . some of his current actors have come to him . . .' Brooks Atkinson, *New York Times* 3 January 1938.

p.356: 'We're all a little skittish now . . .' Quoted in a profile, *New York Times* 20 February 1938.

p.357: 'God keep them from all Broadway entanglements . . .' *New York Daily News* 9 January 1938.

p.358: '. . . during February and March, the Mercury Theatre . . .' From John Houseman, op. cit.

p.358: 'He'd had his hair just done . . .' Norman Lloyd in an interview with S.C.

p.359: 'With a voice that booms like Big Ben's . . .' 'Marvelous Boy', *Time Magazine* 9 May 1938.

p.361: 'He is an intuitive showman . . .' *New York Times* 7 November 1938.

p.361: '1) I found Welles . . .' from letters page, *New York Times* 20 November 1938.

p.362: 'Ladies and gentlemen, you may have heard some rumours . . .' Quoted by Andrea Nouryeh, op. cit.

p.362: 'Most of us in our hearts . . .' ibid.

p.362: 'I wouldn't be happy if I couldn't . . .' Quoted in an interview with Harold Stagg, *New Haven Ledger* 21 January 1938.

p.364: 'She timed her entrance . . .' *New York World Telegram* 9 April 1938.

p.365: 'My god the ceiling's fallen in . . .' Quoted by Vincent Price in an interview with S.C.

p.365: 'One of Mr Shaw's more interminable . . .' *New York Times* 30 April 1938.

p.365: 'the truth is that the production . . .' *New York Post* 30 April 1938.

p.365: 'Mr Welles as Shotover plays much better . . .' *New York Sun* 30 April 1938.

p.366: 'The Mercury Company act out *Heartbreak House* . . .' and ff. From *Sights and Spectacles* by Mary McCarthy.

p.366: 'THE SUMMING UP . . .' *New York Times* July 1938.

p.367: 'Personally we were grateful to our investors . . .' and ff. From John Houseman, op. cit.

p.368: 'the high-livers were killing me . . .' Hiram Sherman quoted by Andrea Nouryeh, op. cit.

p.368: 'The pace had become so wild . . .' From John Houseman, op. cit.

CHAPTER FIFTEEN:
Theatre of the Air

p.370: '. . . limp and huge in a darkened room . . .' and ff. From *Run-Through* by John Houseman.

p.370: 'What can management do to encourage . . .' Quoted in *On a Note of Triumph* by R. LeRoy Bannerman.

p.372: 'Orson Welles, the twenty-three-year-old actor-director . . .' *New York Times* 12 June 1938.

p.373: 'The less a radio drama resembles a play . . .' *Radio Annual 1939*.

p.373: 'There is no place where ideas are as purely expressed as on the radio . . .' *Lecture Notes on Acting* at the Lilly Library Welles Collection.

p.374: '. . . avoiding the cut-and-dried dramatic technique . . .' *Newsweek* 11 July 1938.

p.374: 'He seemed to assume I would be working with him . . .' and ff. From John Houseman, op. cit.

p.375: 'Welles' specific contribution was putting it over . . .' An interview at NYU.

p.376: 'Orson in his usual way heard it

and said . . .' Paul Stewart quoted in *Positif*, edited by François Thomas, translated by S.C.

p.376: 'At first Orson tried to produce the Mercury . . .' ibid.

p.376: 'There was absolute chaos . . .' ibid.

p.381: 'Tottering to the microphone . . .' *New York Times* 1 July 1938.

p.383: 'All come out of a little affair . . .' From *Too Much Johnson* by William Gillette.

p.384: 'Would you prefer the slow sit or the fast sit, Mr Welles?' Quoted in *Citizen Welles* by Frank Brady.

p.385: 'A sequence in Cuba . . .' From *This is Orson Welles* by Peter Bogdanovich.

p.385: '. . . laughing at his own footage . . .' From John Houseman, op. cit.

p.386: 'Orson opened the script and said . . ' Quoted in *The Mercury Theatre*, unpublished thesis by Andrea Nouryeh.

p.386: '. . . the play and the film were too surreal for the audience . . .' Quoted by Frank Brady, op. cit.

p.386: '. . . one of our best things, but aborted . . .' From Peter Bogdanovich, op. cit.

p.387: '. . . he retired into his air-conditioned tent at the St Regis . . .' and ff. From John Houseman, op. cit.

p.387: 'I'd like you to meet Jim Hawkins . . .' Transcribed from the *Mercury Theatre on the Air* broadcast of *Treasure Island*.

p.390: 'It struck us as a brilliant notion . . .' From John Houseman, op. cit.

p.390: 'I doubt if any stage . . .' *Commonweal* 4 January 1928.

p.390: 'The impression of a tremendous plenitude and variety of life . . .' From *Reinhardt and his Stage* by Heinz Herald, translated by J. L. Styan.

p.392: '. . . a treacherous system of gaping holes . . .' From Andrea Nouryeh, op. cit.

p.393: '. . . had that awed and childlike respect . . .' From John Houseman, op. cit.

p.393: 'Mister Soldier, handsome soldier . . .' Quoted in *Mark the Music* by Eric A. Gordon.

p.394: '. . . backstage at the Mercury . . .' Quoted in *Drama was a Weapon* by Morgan Himelstein.

p.395: 'ACTORS OFTEN "LIVE" IN THE THEATRE . . .' *New York Herald Tribune* 23 October 1938.

p.397: 'We pre-empted all the masks in New York that year . . .' Richard Barr in his unpublished memoirs.

p.397: '. . . a steely-gray, vicious, as though . . .' From *The Theatre of Orson Welles* by Richard France.

p.307: 'I kept saying, "it's going to look like a lot of pebbles . . ." ' Howard Teichmann in an interview with NYU.

p.397: 'Orson yelled out for some lights . . .' Quoted by Andrea Nouryeh, op. cit.

p.398: '. . . with instructions from Houseman . . .' From Howard Koch's introduction to *The Panic Broadcast*.

CHAPTER SIXTEEN:
War of the Worlds/Danton's Death

p.399: 'Radio was full at that time of remote programs . . .' Eric Barnouw in an interview with NYU.

p.400: 'All during rehearsals Orson railed at the text . . .' Richard Barr in his unpublished memoirs.

p.400: 'Awakening many listeners to the swift . . .' From *On a Note of Triumph* by LeRoy Bannerman.

p.400: 'You really had the feeling that the world . . .' Eric Barnouw in an interview with NYU.

p.401: 'We know now that in the early years . . .' and ff. From the script of

The War of the Worlds by Howard Koch from the novel by H. G. Wells.

p.402: 'I'm sorry, we don't have that information here . . .' Quoted in the introduction by Howard Koch to *The Panic Broadcast.*

p.403: 'Everyone ran to get their coats . . .' Letter to *New York Daily News* magazine 30 October 1938.

p.403: 'Whose farm I knew was in the destruction path . . .' ibid.

p.404: '. . . no further significance than the holiday . . .' Transcribed from the *Mercury Theatre on the Air* broadcast of *The War of the Worlds.*

p.404: 'Someone had called threatening to blow up the CBS building . . .' Richard Barr in his unpublished memoirs.

p.405: '. . . young Mr Welles, a student of Shakespeare . . .' *New York World Telegram* 1 November 1938.

p.405: '. . . one of the most fascinating and important events . . .' *New York Herald Tribune* 2 November 1938.

p.406: 'The most terrifying thing . . .' and ff. Alva Johnston and Fred Smith, 'How to Raise a Child', *Saturday Evening Post* 3 February 1940.

p.407: 'America today hardly knows . . .' London *Times* 1 November 1938.

p.407: 'HE'S A LAD . . .' London *Daily Express* 1 November 1938.

p.407: 'He has had a career . . .' London *Star* 1 November 1938.

p.407: '. . . by his energetic direction . . .' London *Evening News* 1 November 1938.

p.408: 'He said he was sorry . . .' From John Houseman, op. cit.

p.408: 'LEFT ON BROADWAY . . .' *Daily Worker* 20 October 1938.

p.408: 'Welles stumbled and stumbled . . .' William Alland in an interview with S.C.

p.408: '. . . living one hour and a little more . . .' *Brooklyn Eagle* 6 November 1938.

p.409: '. . . overwhelming and a worthy successor . . .' *New York Times* 3 November 1938.

p.409: 'It is too arty, too self-conscious . . .' *New York Post* 5 November 1938.

p.409: 'Its only purpose . . .' *New York World Telegram* 3 November 1938.

p.409: '. . . it may be electrically . . .' George Jean Nathan: *Newsweek* 14 November 1938.

p.409: 'ORSON WELLES DOES BÜCHNER'S DANTON'S DEATH . . .' Arthur Pollock: *Brooklyn Eagle-Examiner* 6 November 1938.

p.410: 'Every movement is made as if it were artistically precious . . .' *New York Herald Tribune* 3 November 1938.

p.411: 'It is done with great deliberation . . .' *New York Daily News* 3 November 1938.

p.411: 'Incoherent and handsomely fatuous . . .' *New Republic* 30 November 1938.

p.411: '. . . that baleful voice . . .' *New York Times* 7 November 1938.

p.411: '. . . he had trouble with the English language . . .' and ff. *New Yorker* 12 November 1938.

p.411: 'Welles is at heart a magician . . .' From John Houseman, op. cit.

p.413: 'After twenty-one performances we threw in the sponge . . .' ibid.

p.414: '. . . co-operative in every sense of the word . . .' *New York World Telegram* 29 April 1939.

p.414: '. . . an enterprise the Press was sincerely fond of . . .' From *The Fervent Years* by Harold Clurman.

p.417: 'I guess they figured if we could sell . . .' From John Houseman, op. cit.

CHAPTER SEVENTEEN:
The Campbell Playhouse/Five Kings

p.419: 'I am here to introduce the white hope of the American stage . . .' and ff. Transcribed from *Campbell Playhouse*'s broadcast of *Rebecca*.

p.422: 'The situation of Orson becoming a great national figure . . .' From *Run-Through* by John Houseman.

p.424: 'The performance of Shakespeare's historical plays . . .' ibid.

p.424: 'Some of the plays of Shakespeare have been lost to the living theatre . . .' *New York Times* 24 April 1939.

p.424: 'I allowed Orson to use the theatre not only as an instrument . . .' Letter quoted in *Virgil Thomson* by Virgil Thomson.

p.424: 'Any bum can get a crack at . . .' From *This is Orson Welles* by Peter Bogdanovich.

p.425: '. . . a part which Orson regarded . . .' From John Houseman, op. cit.

p.426: 'That subdued muttering you hear . . .' *New York Herald Tribune* 26 March 1939.

p.428: 'I was introduced to a young lady . . .' From *The Magic Curtain* by Lawrence Langner.

p.429: '. . . much to the annoyance of Burgess Meredith . . .' From Richard Barr's unpublished memoirs.

p.430: 'Those vaguely based on truth . . .' From John Houseman, op. cit.

p.430: 'inordinately willing to suspend their disbelief . . .' From *Orson Welles on Shakespeare* by Richard France.

p.431: 'Having demonstrated his superiority as an artist . . .' and ff. From John Houseman, op. cit.

p.432: 'Welles, looking like a large moon-faced boy . . .' Joseph Hardy in a letter to S.C.

p.433: '. . . having achieved his real objective . . .' From John Houseman, op. cit.

p.433: '. . . his prologue ultimately over . . .' and ff. From Lawrence Langner, op. cit.

p.434: 'Not until Mr Welles, still wearing the flesh of Falstaff . . .' *New York Times* 5 March 1939.

p.435: 'FIVE KINGS EXCITING . . .' Peggy Doyle: *Boston Evening American* 28 February 1939.

p.435: 'There are moments when mannerisms intrude . . .' *Christian Science Monitor* 28 February 1939.

p.435: 'To this courier, just back from Agincourt . . .' John K. Hutchens: *Boston Evening Transcript* 28 February 1939.

p.436: 'Orson Welles has bitten off a big hunk . . .' *Variety* 22 March 1939.

p.436: 'Like Ol' Man River . . .' *New York Times* 5 March 1939.

p.436: 'What might have been a tour de force . . .' *Time* 13 March 1939.

p.437: 'Not only are certain members of the *Five Kings* company . . .' *Washington Daily News* 14 March 1939.

p.438: 'The occasion consisted of a lot of . . .' *Philadelphia Daily News* 21 March 1939.

p.438: '. . . only a gigantic Shakespeare vaudeville . . .' *Philadelphia Evening Bulletin* 21 March 1939.

p.438: '. . . its weakness appears to be . . .' *Philadelphia Record* 21 March 1939.

p.439: 'To compare Orson Welles' Falstaff to Mr Evans's . . .' Linton Martin, *Philadelphia Inquirer* 21 March 1939.

p.440: 'The reports from the road . . .' *New York Herald Tribune* 26 March 1939.

p.440: 'Orson had a kind of No Man's Land . . .' Martin Gabel in an interview with NYU, 1985.

p.441: 'It fell on its face not through any difficulties . . .' Quoted in Virgil Thomson, op. cit.

p.441: '. . . all of us on the production staff . . .' From *The Magic of Light* by Jean Rosenthal.

p.442: 'I will play him as a tragic figure . . .' Quoted in an interview with *Christian Science Monitor* 17 February 1939.

p.442: 'The closer I thought I was getting to Falstaff . . .' From Peter Bogdanovich, op. cit.

p.442: '. . . comic symbol for the supernatural order of Charity . . .' From 'The Prince's Dog' in *The Dyer's Hand* by W. H. Auden.

p.442: '. . . the death song of the drunkard . . .' ibid.

p.443: '. . . the drunkard is unlovely to look at . . .' ibid.

p.443: 'Still, Welles would not accept defeat . . .' From John Houseman, op. cit.

p.444: 'Fatigue, humiliation, mutual reproaches . . .' and ff. Quoted in Virgil Thomson, op. cit.

p.446: 'I don't know if I care very much . . .' and ff. From *The Green Goddess* by William Archer.

p.447: '. . . with three rooms and bathrooms . . .' From *Orson Welles* by Barbara Leaming.

p.449: 'The theatre has lost its narrative style . . .' From *Lecture Notes on Acting*, Lilly Library Welles Collection.

p.449: 'ORSON WELLES GIVING METRO THE PIX CHILL' *Variety* 29 December 1939.

CHAPTER EIGHTEEN: *Hollywood/Heart of Darkness*

p.457: 'Who's this Welles?' and ff. From 'Pat Hobby and Orson Welles', *Esquire* May 1940.

p.458: 'LITTLE ORSON ANNIE' Gene Lockhart. Quoted in *Orson Welles* by Roy Alexander Fowler.

p.459: 'a full contingent . . .' From *Run-Through* by John Houseman.

p.460: 'Orson does not think of his income . . .' Letter in the Lilly Library Welles Collection.

p.460: 'Rumours began to circulate . . .' From John Houseman, op. cit.

p.461: 'Wheelock says absolutely not . . .' Letter to John Houseman in the Lilly Library Welles Collection.

p.461: 'Practical considerations suggest enormous advantages . . .' Telegram in the Lilly Library Welles Collection.

p.462: 'Why did you two lice can Chips . . .' and ff. Letters in the Lilly Library Welles Collection.

p.463: 'Please remember that whatever gives our format individuality . . .' Telegram in the Lilly Library Welles Collection.

p.464: 'Orson, who was beginning to have his own doubts . . .' From John Houseman, op. cit.

p.465: 'Both the diabolic love and the unearthly hate . . .' and ff. From *Heart of Darkness* by Joseph Conrad.

p.466: 'The picture is, frankly, an attack on the Nazi system . . .' Quoted in *Citizen Welles* by Frank Brady.

p.467: 'The story is of a man and a girl in love . . .' and ff. Undated memo to the RKO publicity department, in the Lilly Library Welles Collection.

p.468: 'Ladies and gentlemen, this is Orson Welles . . .' and ff. From the screenplay to *Heart of Darkness* printed in *Film Comment* November/December 1972 with article by Jonathan Rosenbaum.

p.471: 'All this severe blow . . .' Telegram in the RKO archives.

p.471: '. . . dear mr schaefer: you have my word . . .' Telegram in the Lilly Library Welles Collection.

p.471: 'Thanks so much for your wire

. . .' Letter in the Lilly Library Welles Collection.

p.472: 'If Mr George Schaefer . . .' *Hollywood Reporter* 26 September 1939.

p.472: '. . . she apparently didn't consider having an affair . . .' From *On the Other Hand* by Fay Wray.

p.473: 'He was goggle-eyed . . .' Quoted in *Orson Welles* by Barbara Leaming.

p.474: 'As for the chronological story . . .' Letter in the Lilly Library Welles Collection.

p.475: 'I never stood in your way . . .' Letter in the Lilly Library Welles Collection.

p.476: 'If Marlow was standing on the deck of a boat . . .' From *The Making of Citizen Kane* by Robert L. Carringer.

p.477: '. . . pissing it away . . .' and ff. From John Houseman, op. cit.

p.477: 'In the past year my position with you and the Mercury . . .' Letter in the Lilly Library Welles Collection.

p.478: 'If an artist finds that public response . . .' and ff. Quoted in *Virgil Thomson* by Virgil Thomson.

p.479: 'I couldn't say to him . . .' Quoted by Barbara Leaming, op. cit.

p.480: '. . . his magnetic, brown, gold-flecked eyes . . .' and ff. From *The Smiler with the Knife* by Nicholas Blake (C. Day Lewis).

CHAPTER NINETEEN: Mank

p.482: '. . . credits that would knock your eye out . . .' From 'Pat Hobby and Orson Welles' by F. Scott Fitzgerald, *Esquire* May 1940.

p.482: 'Idiocy is all right in its own way . . .' and ff. Quoted in *Mank* by Richard Meryman.

p.483: '. . . you felt this fondness . . .' and ff. ibid.

p.483: 'Both came away enchanted and convinced . . .' Letter to Richard Meryman quoted in *Mank*.

p.488: 'He was, variously, my collaborator . . .' From *Run-Through* by John Houseman.

p.488: 'Sadly, the closer Jack got to Mank . . .' Quoted in 'Is it true what they say about Orson?' *New York Times* August 1971.

p.488: 'As a result of Mankiewicz's wicked sense of humour . . .' From 'Raising Kane' by Pauline Kael, introduction to *The Citizen Kane Book*.

p.488: 'When Mank left for Victorville . . .' Quoted in *This is Orson Welles* by Peter Bogdanovich.

p.489: 'I have only one real enemy in my life . . .' Quoted by Richard Meryman, op. cit.

p.490: '. . . an error so grave . . .' Telegram in the Lilly Library Welles Collection.

p.490: 'Script ideas and development . . .' Letter in the Lilly Library Welles Collection.

p.490: 'Your suggested revision . . .' Telegram in the Lilly Library Welles Collection.

p.494: 'In his hatred of Hearst . . .' and ff. Quoted by Richard Meryman, op. cit.

p.495: '. . . the tremendous vitality, gaiety and joie de vivre . . .' and ff. Quoted in *Citizen Welles* by Frank Brady.

p.497: 'dear mank received your cut version . . .' Telegram in Houseman collection, UCLA.

p.499: 'He had a sallow complexion . . .' From 'Gregg Toland ASC' by George E. Turner, *American Cinematographer* November 1982.

p.500: 'Not only should the cameraman know all about . . .' and ff. From 'The Motion Picture Cameraman' by Gregg Toland, *Theatre Arts Monthly* September 1941.

p.500: 'A great deal has been written and said about the new . . .' and ff. Gregg Toland in 'How I Broke the Rules in *Citizen Kane'. Popular Photography* June 1941.

p.501: 'I was constantly encouraged by Toland . . .' Quoted by Peter Bogdanovich, op. cit.

p.501: 'We tried to plan the action . . .' and ff. From 'How I Broke the Rules . . .' op.cit.

p.502: '. . . that illusion of roundness . . .' Quoted in *The Classical Hollywood Cinema* by David Bordwell.

p.503: 'We called it pan-focus . . .' Quoted by Peter Bogdanovich, op. cit.

p.506: 'Norman Mailer wrote that when I was young . . .' Quoted by Peter Bogdanovich, op. cit.

CHAPTER TWENTY:
Shooting *Kane*

p.508: 'During this scene, nobody's face is really seen . . .' From the screenplay to *Citizen Kane*.

p.508: 'He's the waiter in every movie ever made!' From *This is Orson Welles* by Peter Bogdanovich.

p.509: 'He was willing, and this is very rare in Hollywood . . .' Gregg Toland in 'How I Broke the Rules in *Citizen Kane', Popular Photography* June 1941.

p.509: 'I said, well, God, there's a lot of stuff . . .' and ff. From Peter Bogdanovich, op. cit.

p.511: 'He had a huge set of Xanadu . . .' Quoted in 50th Anniversary souvenir booklet.

p.511: 'He shot more film than anyone in the history of the cinema . . .' and ff. Quoted in *Positif* October 1988.

p.513: 'Alland was treated almost as a personal slave . . .' From Richard Barr's unpublished memoirs.

p.514: 'Ford's greeting to him was the first hint . . .' From Peter Bogdanovich, op. cit.

p.514: 'It was clearly going to be an extraordinary . . .' and ff. From *Run-Through* by John Houseman.

p.515: 'RE FURTHER TELEPHONE CONVERSATION . . .' Memo in the Lilly Library Welles Collection.

p.516: 'As of Sep 30 . . .' Memo in the Lilly Library Welles Collection.

p.517: 'Mr M. is in the biggest fever . . .' Memo in the Lilly Library Welles Collection.

p.517: 'It would seem to me . . .' Letter in the Lilly Library Welles Collection.

p.518: '. . . he wrote the entire script . . .' ibid.

p.518: No production executive . . . Quoted in *The Making of Citizen Kane* by Robert L. Carringer.

p.518: '. . . his ability to push a dramatic situation . . .' From John Houseman, op. cit.

p.519: 'I tried to persuade Houseman . . .' Quoted in *Mank* by Richard Meryman.

p.519: 'I informed him that if anyone . . .' From John Houseman, op. cit.

p.520: '. . . which will give us all a little bit of rest . . .' Letter to Arnold Weissberger in the Lilly Library Welles Collection.

p.520: '. . . that's the nicest thing a man from England . . .' and ff. Transcribed from KTSA broadcast, 28 October 1940.

p.522: 'Many of *Citizen Kane*'s deep-focus effects had been created . . .' From 'Film Style and Technology' by David Bordwell in *The Classical Hollywood Cinema*.

p.522: 'Telling Orson about the optical printer . . .' Quoted in Robert Carringer's laser-disc documentary about *Citizen Kane*.

p.523: 'I was months and months and months . . .' From Peter Bogdanovich, op. cit.

p.524: 'Backward ran sentences . . .'

Quoted in *Raising Kane* by Pauline Kael.

p.524: 'He overwhelmed me with his radio background . . .' Quoted in 50th Anniversary souvenir booklet.

p.525: 'I'd work all day. He'd make an appointment . . .' Quoted by Richard Meryman, op. cit.

p.525: 'I was given twelve weeks to do my job . . .' 'Score for a Film.' *New York Times* 25 May 1941.

p.525: 'in second scene, we cut to kane . . .' Telegram in the Lilly Library Welles Collection.

p.526: '. . . cues of a few seconds were often overlooked . . .' and ff. 'Score for a Film,' op. cit.

p.527: 'I want to make it absolutely clear . . .' Quoted by Richard Meryman, op. cit.

p.528: 'Don't think me a saint . . .' and ff. From Orson Welles' screenplay *Santa*.

p.529: 'please give orson all my love . . .' Telegram in the Lilly Library Welles Collection.

p.529: 'my beamish jack . . .' Telegram in the Lilly Library Welles Collection.

p.529: 'give your friends a night . . .' Telegram in the Lilly Library Welles Collection.

p.530: 'Dearest Hedda, I owe you . . .' Letter in the Lilly Library Welles Collection.

p.530: 'As the story was reported to me . . .' Quoted in *Marion Davies* by Fred Guiles.

p.531: 'It has been assumed that *Citizen Kane* . . .' Letter in the Lilly Library Welles Collection.

p.531: '*Citizen Kane* is the story . . .' Article in *Friday* magazine reprinted in *Focus on Citizen Kane* ed. Ronald Gottesman.

p.532: 'Mr Hearst casually gave them a hundred . . .' Quoted by Richard Meryman, op.cit.

p.534: 'I am going slowly mad because my hands are tied . . .' Letter to Arnold Weissberger in the Lilly Library Welles Collection.

p.535: 'Until quite recently, a lot of people . . .' *New Masses* 4 February 1941.

p.536: 'This article will probably make me no friends . . .' and ff. 'Orson Welles Writing About Orson Welles', *Stage* February 1941, reprinted in *Hollywood Directors* ed. Richard Koszarski.

p.538: 'Will Hollywood stand up . . .' *New Republic* 24 February 1941.

CHAPTER TWENTY-ONE:
Waiting/*Native Son*

p.540: 'A blow at the white man . . .' Irving Howe. Quoted in *Richard Wright, Daemonic Genius* by Margaret Walker.

p.540: 'Bigger Thomas is not presented in *Native Son* . . .' and ff. Letter in the Lilly Library Welles Collection.

p.541: 'Please believe that both Welles and I . . .' and ff. Letter in the Lilly Library Welles Collection.

p.541: 'Knowing what you and Welles have done in the past . . .' Letter in the Lilly Library Welles Collection.

p.541: 'please inform our crippled . . .' Telegram in the Lilly Library Welles Collection.

p.542: 'This play is indecent . . .' Quoted by Richard Wright in *The God That Failed*.

p.542: '. . . till the day of the play's opening . . .' and ff. From *Run-Through* by John Houseman.

p.543: '. . . the fabulous city in which Bigger lived . . .' From *Native Son* by Richard Wright.

p.544: 'I want this show to be surrounded by brick . . .' Quoted in '*Native Son* Backstage' by Jean Rosenthal, *Theatre Arts Monthly* June 1941.

p.544: 'From the tiny, poverty-stricken . . .' ibid.

p.546: 'I want the play to end . . .' Letter quoted by Margaret Walker, op.cit.

p.546: 'Houseman doesn't reveal quite how shat on he was . . .' William Alland in an interview with S.C.

p.547: 'He is beyond doubt the most courageous, gallant and talented . . .' Richard Wright in an interview; copy in the Lilly Library Welles Collection.

p.547: 'he had a constant privilege to interrupt . . .' From Margaret Walker, op. cit.

p.547: 'Orson began to howl at him . . .' From John Houseman, op. cit.

p.548: 'Think about the impossible strain you have put . . .' Telegram in the Lilly Library Welles Collection.

p.548: 'A free speech, a free press . . .' *Variety* 11 March 1941.

p.549: 'As in some grotesque fable . . .' *Time* 17 March 1941.

p.549: 'It is with exceeding regret . . .' *Newsweek* 17 March 1941.

p.550: 'How can you copyright an enterprise, a profession . . .' Quoted in *Citizen Welles* by Frank Brady.

p.550: 'Welles will show the picture . . .' ibid.

p.550: 'saw your show tonight . . .' Telegram in the Lilly Library Welles Collection.

p.550: 'let me thank you both . . .' Telegram in the Lilly Library Welles Collection.

p.551: 'thanks for my big chance, orson . . .' Telegram in the Lilly Library Welles Collection.

p.551: 'STARK DRAMA STAMPED WITH GENIUS . . .' *New York World Telegram* 25 March 1941.

p.551: '. . . it may at times be quite ham . . .' *New Republic* 25 March 1941.

p.551: 'It is as if the theatre had been shaken . . .' Brooks Atkinson: *New York Times* 25 March 1941.

p.552: 'Canada Lee has added a figure of heroic dimensions . . .' *Theatre Arts Monthly* October 1942.

p.553: '1. Get support of Negro press . . .' Mercury Productions memo in the Lilly Library Welles Collection.

p.554: '. . . it was a little shameful . . .' Quoted by John Houseman, op. cit.

p.555: '. . . to illustrate by a series of plays . . .' From James Boyd's introduction to *The Free Company Presents*.

p.556: 'Don't start forbiddin' anybody . . .' and ff. From *His Honor the Mayor* by Orson Welles.

p.557: '. . . the Hearst papers have repeatedly described me . . .' Quoted by Frank Brady, op. cit.

CHAPTER TWENTY-TWO: Release

p.560: 'Attacks of knife-like pain . . .' Medical report in the Lilly Library Welles Collection.

p.561: 'Orson Welles?! He's an exhibitionist . . .' Quoted in *Citizen Kane* by Frank Brady.

p.561: 'You might say I'm a relative . . .' Quoted in *This is Orson Welles* by Peter Bogdanovich.

p.562: 'Happy Birthday to you . . .' Quoted in *Orson Welles* by Barbara Leaming.

p.562: 'Mr Genius comes through . . .' *Hollywood Reporter* 12 March 1941.

p.562: 'Now that the wrappers are off . . .' *New York Times* 2 May 1941.

p.562: 'Perhaps when the uproar has died down . . .' *Nation* 26 April 1941.

p.563: 'Now that the returns are in . . .' *New York Times* 4 May 1941.

p.564: 'it is . . . when all has been told . . .' *Theatre Arts* 2 June 1941.

p.564: 'Miss Powell talked of Charles Foster Kane . . .' London *Sunday Times* 5 November 1941.

p.564: 'Not one glimpse . . .' *New Masses* 13 May 1941.

p.564: '*Citizen Kane* was made in the most wildly . . .' and ff. Quoted in *Mank* by Richard Meryman.

p.565: 'There are more conscious shots . . .' From Peter Bogdanovich, op. cit.

p.565: 'Orson Welles never once makes concessions . . .' *Commonweal* 9 May 1941.

p.568: 'I am so bored with the aesthetics . . .' BBC interview on *Monitor*.

p.570: 'Welles . . . has an almost total empathy with the audience . . .' From *Raising Kane* by Pauline Kael.

p.570: '*Citizen Kane* was inspired by . . .' Quoted in *The Magic World of Orson Welles* by James Naremore.

p.571: '*Citizen Kane* is a tragedy on Marlovian lines . . .' *Film Comment* Summer 1971, reprinted in *Movies and Methods* ed. Bill Nichols.

p.571: 'It is not his best film . . .' From *The Cinema of Orson Welles* by Peter Bogdanovich.

p.571: 'Orson Welles is 26 . . .' *Horizon* November 1941.

p.571: 'There has never been a more exciting press show . . .' *The Clipper* May 1941.

p.573: 'Finally he went on to produce . . .' and ff. From the souvenir booklet for *Citizen Kane*'s first release.

p.575: 'Stay away from this . . .' Quoted in *Orson Welles* by Charles Higham.

p.577: 'here's what i wanted to wire you . . .' Quoted by Richard Meryman, op. cit

p.578: 'i am very happy to accept . . .' ibid.

BIBLIOGRAPHY

Aherne, Brian, *A Proper Job*. Houghton Mifflin, 1969.
Auden, W.H. *The Dyer's Hand*. Faber & Faber, 1963.
Baker, Carlos, *Ernest Hemingway: A Life Story*. Scribner's, 1969.
Bannerman, R. LeRoy, *Norman Corwin and Radio: The Golden Years*. Lyle Stuart, 1986. *On a Note of Triumph*. Lyle Stuart, 1986.
Barr, Richard, *Memoirs*. Unpublished.
Blake, Nicholas (C. Day Lewis), *The Smiler with the Knife*. Collins, 1939.
Bogdanovich, Peter & Orson Welles, ed. Jonathan Rosenbaum, *This is Orson Welles*. HarperCollins, 1992.
Bordwell, David, Janet Staiger & Kristin Thompson, *The Classical Hollywood Cinema*. Routledge, 1985.
Bowles, Paul, *Without Stopping*. Putnam, 1972.
Brady, Frank, *Citizen Welles*. Scribner's, 1989.
Buxton, Frank & Bill Owen, *The Big Broadcast 1920–1950*. Viking, 1972.
Cantril, Hadley, *The Invasion from Mars: A Study in the Psychology of Panic*. With the complete script of 'The War of the Worlds'. Princeton University Press, 1940.
Carringer, Robert L., *The Making of 'Citizen Kane'*. University of California Press, 1985.
Clurman, Harold, *The Fervent Years*. Harcourt Brace, 1975.
Cocteau, Jean, *My Journey Round the World*. Peter Owen, 1958.
Connelly, Marc, *Voices Offstage*. Henry Holt, 1968.
Copland, Aaron & Vivian Perlis, *Copland 1900–1942*. St Martin's Press, 1984.
Corneau, Guy, *Absent Fathers, Lost Sons*. Shambhala, 1991.
Cotten, Joseph, *Vanity Will Get You Somewhere*. Mercury House, 1987.
Davies, Marion, *The Times We Had: Life with William Randolph Hearst*. Foreword by Orson Welles. Bobbs-Merrill, 1975.
Edwards, Hilton, *The Mantle of Harlequin*. Progress House, 1958.
Engel, Lehman, *This Bright Day*. Macmillan Publishing, 1974.
Fitzgerald, F. Scott, 'Pat Hobby and Orson Welles'. *Esquire* magazine, May 1940.
Flanagan, Hallie, *Arena*. Duell, Sloan & Pearce, 1940.
Fowler, Roy Alexander, *Orson Welles: A First Biography*. Pendulum Publications, 1946.
France, Richard, ed., *Orson Welles on Shakespeare: The W.P.A. and Mercury Theatre Playscripts*. Greenwood Press, 1990.
France, Richard, *The Theatre of Orson Welles*. Bucknell University Press, 1977.
Gassner, John, *Producing the Play*. Dryden Press, 1941.
Goldstein, Malcolm, *The Political Stage*. Oxford University Press, 1974.
Gordon, Eric A., *Mark the Music: The Life and Work of Marc Blitzstein*. St Martin's Press, 1989.
Guiles, Fred Laurence, *Marion Davies*. McGraw-Hill, 1972.

Higham, Charles, *Orson Welles: The Rise and Fall of an American Genius*. St Martin's Press, 1985.
Hill, Roger, *One Man's Time and Chance: A Memoir of Eighty Years 1895–1975*. Privately printed, 1977.
Hill, Roger & Orson Welles, *Marching Song*. Unpublished play. *Everybody's Shakespeare: Three Plays (The Merchant of Venice, Julius Caesar* and *Twelfth Night). Edited for Reading and Arranged for Staging*. Todd Press, 1934. Reprinted as *Mercury Shakespeare*. Harper, 1939.
Himelstein, Morgan Y., *Drama was a Weapon: The Left-Wing Theatre in New York 1929–1941*. Rutgers University Press, 1973.
Hoke, John, *Todd School*. Unpublished thesis, 1934.
Holloway, Joseph ed. Robert Hogan & Michael O'Neill, *Joseph Holloway's Irish Theatre*. Proscenium Press, 1968.
Hoogstraten, Nicholas van, *Lost Theatres of Broadway*. Princeton Architectural Press, 1991.
Houseman, John, *Run-Through*. Simon & Schuster, 1972.
Hughes, Richard, *In the Lap of Atlas*. Chatto & Windus, 1979.
Hutton, Edward, *Cities of Spain*. Methuen, 1927.
Jewell, Richard B. & Vernon Harbin, *The RKO Story*. Arlington House, 1982.
Kael, Pauline, 'Raising Kane', the introduction to *The Citizen Kane Book*. Little Brown, 1971.
Kaufman, George S. & Moss Hart, *The Fabulous Invalid*. Random House, 1938.
Kazin, Alfred, *Starting Out in the Thirties*. Little Brown, 1965.
Koch, Howard, *The Panic Broadcast*. Avon Books, 1971.
Langner, Lawrence, *The Magic Curtain*. Dutton, 1951.
Leaming, Barbara, *Orson Welles: A Biography*. Viking, 1985.
Leiter, Sam, *The Encyclopaedia of the New York Stage 1930–1940*. Greenwood Press, 1989.
Lewis, Robert, *Slings and Arrows: Theater in my Life*. Stein & Day, 1984.
McCann, Sean, *The Story of the Abbey Theatre*. New English Library, 1967.
McCarthy, Mary, *Sights and Spectacles*. Farrar Straus, 1956.
McClintic, Guthrie, *Me and Kit*. Atlantic, Little Brown, 1955.
Mac Liammóir, Micheál, *All for Hecuba*. Methuen, 1946.
Maxwell, Gavin, *The Lords of Atlas*. Century, 1983.
Meryman, Richard, *Mank: The Wit, World and Life of Herman Mankiewicz*. William Morrow, 1978.
Mitchell, *Blood Sport*. University of Pennsylvania Press, 1991.
Mordden, Ethan, *The American Theatre*. Oxford University Press, 1981.
Mosel, Tad, *Leading Lady*. Atlantic, Little Brown, 1978.
Naremore, James, *The Magic World of Orson Welles*. Oxford University Press, 1978.
Noble, Peter, *The Fabulous Orson Welles*. Hutchinson, 1956.
Nouryeh, Andrea, *The Mercury Theatre: A history*. Unpublished thesis, 1987. *Native Son*. Unpublished thesis.
O Conaire, Pádraic translated by Cormack Dreathnach, *Field and Fair: Travels with a Donkey in Ireland*. Talbot Press, 1928.
O'Connor, John & Lorraine Brown, *Free, Adult, and Uncensored*. New Republic Books, 1978.
O'Flaherty, Liam, *A Tourist's Guide to Ireland*. Mandrake, 1930.
Pritchett, V.S., *Dublin: A Portrait*. Bodley Head, 1967.

Rathbone, Basil, *In and Out of Character*. Ianmead, 1989.
Rosenthal, Jean & Lael Wertenbaker, *The Magic of Light: The Craft and Career of Jean Rosenthal, Pioneer in Lighting for the Modern Stage*. Little Brown, 1972.
Sawyer-Laucanno, Christopher, *An Invisible Spectator*. Weidenfeld, 1989.
Shiaras, David, *John Deere & the Billion Dollar Plow Gamble*. Privately printed, 1983.
Smith, Alston J., *Chicago's Left Bank*. Henry Regnery, 1953.
Stern, Ernst, translated Fitzgerald, *My Life, My Stage*. Gollancz, 1951.
Taubmann, Howard, *The Making of the American Theatre*. Longman, 1967.
Teichmann, Howard, *Smart Aleck: The Wit, World, and Life of Alexander Woollcott*. Morrow, 1976.
Thomas, François, *'Dossier: La Radio d'Orson Welles.' Positif* magazine, October 1988.
Thomson, Virgil, *Virgil Thomson*. Knopf, 1966.
Tynan, Kenneth, *'Playboy* Interview: Orson Welles'. *Playboy* magazine, March 1967.
Walker, Margaret, *Richard Wright: Daemonic Genius*. Amistad Press, 1988.
Welles, Orson. *Bright Lucifer*. Unpublished play. *The Cradle Will Rock*. Screenplay. Santa Teresa Press, 1992. *The Director in the Theatre Today*. Theatre Education League, 1939. *'His Honor, the Mayor'* (text of radio broadcast) in *The Free Company Presents* . . . Dodd Mead, 1941. ed. David Ramon. *Santa*. Screenplay. Universidad Nacional Autonoma de Mexico, 1991.
Welles, Orson, ed., *Vogue*. December, 1982.
Witham, Barry B., *Backstage at 'The Cradle Will Rock'*. Theatre History Studies, vol. xii, 1992.
Woititz, Janet, *Adult Children of Alcoholics*. Health Communications, 1983.
Wood, Bret, *Orson Welles: A Bio-Bibliography*. Greenwood Press, 1990.
Wray, Fay, *On the Other Hand: A Life Story*. St Martin's Press, 1989.
Wright, Richard, *Native Son*. Harper, 1940.

ACKNOWLEDGMENTS

More than most, biographers depend on the kindness of strangers. In the six years of researching and writing, I have been grateful for the openness and willingness to give up their time of the many people whom I have interviewed for the book; I have been touched by the thoughtfulness of the smaller but still considerable number who have written to me, sometimes out of the blue, with their memories and mementoes; and I have been frankly astonished by the generosity of fellow workers in the field, Welles scholars – some published and some not – all gleefully sharing with me their research and their insights. These latter I must thank first, since the book has benefited immensely from their selfless generosity; there could be no motive for their willingness to show me the hard-won fruits of their work but devotion to the truth about Welles (and an extraordinary trust in my ability to make good use of the material). Among these scholars were Richard France, author of *The Theatre of Orson Welles* and *Welles' Shakespeare,* both pioneering texts, which make brilliant use of materials available nowhere else; Andrea Nouryeh, whose uniquely comprehensive *Mercury Theatre* (an unpublished thesis still obtainable from UMI) deserves much wider circulation; Peter Noble, author of the first full-length biography, *The Fabulous Orson Welles*; Professor James Naremore, whose *The Magic World of Orson Welles* remains without question the best sustained piece of critical writing about Welles; M. François Thomas, the leading authority on the radio work (his *Positif* special edition on the subject is the most comprehensive account of those years); and Peter Bogdanovich, in various early writings a perceptive and elegant champion of Welles, who, in the more recent *This is Orson Welles,* provides a direct and entirely lifelike impression of one of the essential Welleses: the conversationalist. Each of these writers, making themselves freely accessible to my unending enquiries, has introduced me to materials and also thoughts that have influenced the book; the work of each remains, despite the extensive use I have made of it, indispensable in its own right, crammed with fascinating information and analysis. Though not strictly a Welles scholar, Sam Leiter, author of the several volumes of the compendious *Encyclopaedia of the New York Stage,* has been unstintingly forthcoming in his detailed information of the theatre of the years covered by the present volumes, helping to reveal the context in which Welles functioned.

As for my correspondents, these have most notably included Welles's school friends John C. Dexter and Paul Guggenheim, both of whom have recounted in vivid detail their experiences of the young Welles, and both of whom gave me rare documents relating to the early theatre work at Todd; and the late Hascy Tarbox, who offered a radically different perspective, and several indispensable documents including his father-in-law Roger Hill's autobiography and a copy of *Marching Song*. Interviewees include Coach Tony Roskie from Todd School, Joanne and Hascy Tarbox from the same period, Tom Triffely, who knew Welles at the time of the *Romeo and Juliet* tour, Peg and Norman ('total recall') Lloyd, Arlene Francis, Paula Laurence and Chuck Bowden, Arthur Anderson, Elliot Reid, Sam Leve, Abe Feder, Frank Goodman, Henry Senber, the late Vincent Price, Geraldine Fitzgerald, Stefan Schnabel, and William Alland from the FTP and/or Mercury days, and Ruth Warrick from *Citizen Kane*. Many of them provided me with materials as well as memories. The late Richard Wilson, custodian of the Mercury Archives and close collaborator of Welles, was exceptionally helpful in providing material, contacts and leads. He was a key figure in the early research; without him my task would have been twice as hard. Henry Senber, the Mercury's matchless press officer, has been in regular contact with me over the six years. Quite unintentionally, I made Augusta Weissberger, Welles's and Houseman's secretary for several years, cry, and for that I am sorry. Finally, I received the warmest support and an extraordinary final interview from the late John Houseman, who was encouraging to the last. I hope I have made his place in Welles's history, and that of the theatre of the thirties, as clear as possible.

Other help has come from many sources: the academic institutions have furnished fascinating material. Among those I must thank are: William G. Simon, of the department of Film Studies, New York University, who put at my disposal the materials which he assembled from his Welles theatre retrospective of 1988; Ruth Kerns, then head of the Federal Theatre Archive, then at George Mason University, Washington (it has since been removed from easy public access), who made available to me the wonderful Project 891 materials; the Theatre Department at Northwestern University, Evanston Illinois, which marvellously tends the archive of the Dublin Gate Theatre, was especially helpful; the Chicago Historical Society was also exceptionally kind. The Billy Rose Collection at the Lincoln Center is another treasure-trove of theatrical material; the New York Public Library is unrivalled as a newspaper archive, and I made considerable use of it. Finally, and with deep gratitude, I must, like all Welles scholars, offer humble thanks to Sondra Taylor and Rebecca Cape of the Lilly Library, at the University of Indiana, curators of the largest Welles collection in the world, who discharge their onerous tasks with incomparable efficiency and good humour. No book of the slightest value on Welles could be written without their collaboration; they have made the researching of this one a positive pleasure.

Then there are my own assistants, James Rodgers and Matthew Wooton kicking things off in London, Ted Schillinger in Chicago (taking time off from his day job as an inspired documentary filmmaker) and Dorothy Hanrahan, dedicated and shrewd, in New York, slogging on through personal tragedy and professional upheaval. I have been through an alarming number of secretaries during the six years, but Janet Macklam was there for the first few, keeping the whole enterprise together with humour and resource; she was succeeded by Pamela Brooke and Sue Slater, who took on the mantle with great spirit. To all of these, thanks for their efficiency and patience.

In addition, Rosemary Wilton, with her unrivalled knowledge of RKO in the thirties, gave me a head start in writing about *Citizen Kane* which I can hardly adequately acknowledge; Leslie Megahey, who conducted the BBC's revelatory 1982 interviews with Welles, was similarly full of direct insights which have much enriched the text. He was one of the dauntless handful of people who read the vast manuscript of the first draft, and who offered sharp and precise criticisms of it; the others were Simon Gray (who was unerringly right about a dangerous tendency in the writing); Angus Mackay, who read it with a theatre scholar's eye and an invaluable sense of period; and Jim Naremore, who made me think hard again about a number of important matters. Nick Hern commissioned the book, David Godwin picked it up, Dan Franklin saw it through to publication and Chuck Elliott subjected it to his fine toothcomb, always and rightly urging concision, if not excision. Peter Ward was responsible for making the final book look so attractive, Margaret Clark read the proofs with tact and wit and assembled the play, radio and film lists, and Helen Baz completed the huge task of compiling the index. Maggie Hanbury, my agent, fought the book's corner with everything at her disposal when all seemed nearly lost.

Lastly, friends: or rather firstly, since it was Nick Hern who urged me to write a book about Orson Welles's theatre, and Kathleen Tynan and Leo Lerman, both untimely deceased, both dreadfully missed, who persuaded me to go the whole hog and take on *le tout Orson*. So it's all their fault. Edward Johnson, musicologist, cinephile and passionate fan, supplied me with all sorts of curious information, as well as tape transfers of *The Mercury Shakespeare* series of records. I would further like to thank two men, Richard Holmes and Robin Lane Fox, for their influence on my approach to biography; one I know (Holmes), the other I do not; both have been beacons in my attempt to make the past live in a credible fashion. My last thought is of two women; first my friend Ann Rogers, for many years Orson Welles's secretary (and before that, Charles Laughton's), whose subtle and shrewd support has kept me in touch with my purposes in writing this book, and secondly, the late Peggy Ramsay. This is the first book I have written without subjecting it to her sharp eye and full heart, and I miss both more than I can say.

Oh, and thank you, Christopher, for putting up with five years of Orson in the morning, Orson in the evening and Orson at suppertime. This book is for you.

S.C.
London
January, 1995

Grateful acknowledgment is made for permission to reprint excerpts from the following copyrighted works: *Virgil Thomson* by Virgil Thomson, Copyright © 1966 by Virgil Thomson, reprinted by permission of Alfred A. Knopf, Inc.; *Run-Through* by John Houseman, Copyright © 1972 by John Houseman, published by Simon & Schuster, reprinted by permission of the Estate of John Houseman; *This Is Orson Welles*, edited by Jonathan Rosenbaum, Copyright © 1992 by Oja Kodar, Jonathan Rosenbaum, and Peter Bogdanovich, reprinted by permission of HarperCollins Publishers, Inc.; an article by Orson Welles from French *Vogue*, December 1982, by permission of French *Vogue*. Excerpts are reprinted from *Orson Welles: A Biography* by Barbara Leaming, Copyright © Barbara Leaming, 1983, 1985.

PICTURE CREDITS

Inset 1: p. 2 *above left* courtesy Chris Brooks; p. 2 *below right*, p. 3 *above left*, p. 3 *below* Kenosha County Historical Society; p. 5 *below left* Hascy Tarbox; p. 6 *all* Highland Park Public Library; p. 7 *both* Gate Theatre Archive, Special Collections Department, Northwestern University, Evanston, Illinois; p. 8 *below* Chadwyck-Healey Ltd and the Consortium for Drama and Media in Higher Education.

Inset 2: p. 1, p. 2 *right*, p. 3 *both*, pp. 4–5 *all*, p. 6 *below*, p. 7 Federal Theater Archive, George Mason University, Washington D.C.

Inset 3: p. 1, pp. 2–3 *all* © Al Hirschfeld. Drawings reproduced by special arrangement with Hirschfeld's exclusive representative, The Margo Feiden Galleries Ltd, New York; p. 4 Culver Pictures; p. 6 Welles Mss. Hohenberger Collection; p. 7 *all* Academy of Motion Picture Arts and Sciences, Margaret Herrick Library; p. 8 Personality Photo, Inc.

All other photographs courtesy of the estate of Orson Welles.

Index